Conscious Experience

Conscious Experience

edited by

Thomas Metzinger

Imprint Academic
Schöningh
1995

Cover photograph: Sense of Sight/Superimposed brain image by Bassem Mora and George
Carman, ©Joseph McNally Photography/National Geographic

British Library Cataloguing in Publication Data:
A catalogue record for this book is available from the British Library.

© 1995 Ferdinand Schöningh, Paderborn

English language edition published in association with Imprint Academic

Orders/enquiries: Imprint Academic, PO Box 1, Thorverton, EX5 5YX, UK
Tel: +44 (0)1392 841600, Fax: 841478, Email: sandra@imprint.co.uk

Printed in the USA by Allen Press, Lawrence, Kansas

ISBN 0 907845 05 3 (paperback)
ISBN 0 907845 10 X (hardback)

This volume is dedicated
to the memory of

NORTON NELKIN

who did not live to see its appearance

Contents

Part 3. Consciousness and the Physical World

Part 4. The Knowledge Argument

Part 5. Qualia

Part 6. Consciousness and Higher-Order States

Part 7. Information-Processing and Neurobiological Approaches

Part 8. Artificial Consciousness

Appendix I.   Selected Bibliography 1970–1995

Appendix II. List of Contributors

Acknowledgements

This book has relied on the active support of many people, to whom I am deeply indebted. My greatest thanks go to David Chalmers: we shared the enjoyment of compiling the bibliography as virtual pen pals, without ever having met in the real world. Dave has also helped greatly with the English versions of my own contributions, struggling to mitigate my Grand Germanic Style at least a little. His unflagging enthusiasm for the topic of consciousness has supported my project in too many ways to enumerate. On the other side of the Atlantic the same is true of Ingrid Weil, who has dealt painstakingly with much of the tedious detailed work.

Michael Kienecker, of SCHÖNINGH-Verlag, has both secured the enterprise financially and accompanied it through various difficult periods. His ready and practical help has again shown the commitment of SCHÖNINGH-Verlag to supporting innovative ventures in a generally conservative climate. I also want to thank Anthony Freeman and Keith Sutherland of Imprint Academic for their part in producing the English version of this book. They have calmly taken many burdens off my shoulders in the second phase of this project.

As this book has been a bilingual enterprise from the outset, I wish especially to thank the translators. They had to solve many particularly difficult problems, and without exception they applied themselves to their work with a great devotion to detail. These must therefore take much of the credit for simultaneously making the material available to German and English speaking audiences: Antonia Barke, Birger Brinkmeier, Andreas Ernst, Christine Gross, Gerhard Helm, Eva-Maria Hesse-Jesch, Martin Kurthen, Thomas Marschner, Markus Reuber, Achim Stephan, Henrik Walter and Frank Pollock. Antonia Barke at Corpus Christi College, Oxford, deserves special mention, because she has translated both ways and invested more work than anyone else. I am very grateful to her for translating the small introductions to the thematic subsections, for help with original sources not available to me in German libraries and for many helpful comments.

I also wish to thank Robert Kirk, for his help with my own translation of his chapter, and Edward Johnson, Petra Stoerig and Dana Nelkin for the great care and continuing effort they put into editing my German translation of Norton Nelkin's paper, as well as for their help in editing the English proofs of his contribution. Andreas Bartels, Andreas Engel and Stephan Hartmann have helped me in solving a number of seemingly intractable terminological problems. I am also deeply indebted for many helpful comments and important suggestions regarding the bibliography: especially I must thank Ned Block, William Lycan, David Rosenthal, Eva Ruhnau, Klaus Sachs-Hombach and again Andreas Engel for their efforts.

Above all, my chief mainstay has been Anja Krug. She is my permanent source of inspiration and has had to forgo much of my attention for this book to come into being.

Gießen, October 1995   *Thomas Metzinger*

Editor's Introduction

Thomas Metzinger

The Problem of Consciousness

I. Do we need a new science of consciousness?

How can consciousness arise in a physical universe? Is it at all imaginable that something like *conscious experience* could emerge from a purely physical basis? Is it *conceivable* that subjective sensations and the emergence of an inner perspective are part of the natural order — or are we now confronted with an ultimate mystery, a grey area on the scientific map of the world that may *in principle* have to remain grey?

Today, the problem of consciousness — perhaps together with the question of the origin of the universe — marks the very limit of human striving for understanding. It appears to many to be the last great puzzle and the greatest theoretical challenge of our time. A solution of this puzzle through empirical research would bring about a scientific revolution of the first order. However, in this case meeting the challenge may require a completely new *type* of intellectual revolution, for a number of reasons. To begin with, when we look closely, it is not at all clear what the puzzle of consciousness actually is, and what we would accept as a convincing solution. Second, the problem in a strong sense concerns *ourselves*: it is always our *own* consciousness, among others, that we want to understand. Therefore the problem of consciousness is also a problem of self-knowledge. It affects all of us, not just philosophers or scientists. Third, such a revolution — if it actually took place — might for this reason have greater social and cultural ramifications than any previous theoretical upheaval. This could be due to the consequences of a radically changed picture of ourselves, or to the impact of new technologies that might result, for instance, from progress in the neurosciences or in artificial intelligence research. These three reasons have recently led to an increasing restlessness in the sciences as well as to a growing interest among the general public in questions concerning the connection between consciousness and the brain.

It has become obvious that, for quite some time, we have been reaching for a new theory of mind. Such a new theory will, among other things, be a

3

theory about the nature of *conscious experience*. It also has the potential to
be the first such theory in the history of mankind to rest on a solid empirical
basis. There seems to be a theoretical revolution in the air, which can be
expected to affect the way in which we see ourselves in a hitherto unknown
fashion. Although empirical research has given only a few indications of
this so far, the puzzle of consciousness has already advanced to become the
'secret research frontier' in a number of scientific disciplines. This development in turn has met with great interest among philosophers.

For the last ten or fifteen years philosophers have shown a rapidly
increasing interest in the problem of consciousness. A number of new
journals and academic organisations have been founded, and large meetings
on the subject are taking place with increasing frequency. Interest has been
further stimulated by the emergence of serious claims about consciousness
in disciplines ranging from quantum physics through neurobiology to cognitive science. In the philosophy of mind many of these proposals have been
watched closely. At the same time, more and more empirical researchers are
beginning to realize that philosophers have been dealing with this theoretical problem for many centuries, and that philosophical analysis has a central
role to play in its resolution. In its origins the concept of consciousness is a
philosophical concept. As a consequence, there is now increasing interest in
a serious and empirically-informed philosophy of mind in the general public
and in the neuro- and cognitive sciences. This is also revealed by the simple
fact that a number of prominent scientists researching the brain have
published popular books with philosophical content.[1]

This rising interest is also shown in the increasingly firm connections
between philosophy and the adjoining areas of research in neuroscience,
cognitive science and computer science. Many hold that the necessary
revolution can only occur when our understanding of the subject transcends
disciplinary boundaries and links between the relevant areas of research are
drastically increased. However, it has also become obvious that a systematic integration of research activities is necessary as well. This situation has
led to a call for a new science, the *science of consciousness*,[2] both from
empirical and theoretical researchers. In considering this fascinating idea,
one must bear in mind two caveats. First, the idea of a 'science of consciousness' is anything but a new idea, especially from the viewpont of the
philosopher. For example, the whole phenomenological movement (and its
demise) can be understood in these terms. In a more general sense, philosophy
— as the love of wisdom and queen of the sciences — has always been the
science of consciousness. The ideal of self-knowledge is a classic ideal of

[1] A selection of these can be found in section 1.3 of the bibliography in Appendix I of this book.

[2] Cf. Penrose 1994: 7 ff. Further important contributions to the debate concerning an independent
science of consciousness are Baars 1988, Chalmers 1996, Flanagan 1992: 213 ff., Revonsuo
1994: 249 ff., the collection of texts by Hameroff *et al.* 1996 and the ongoing discussion
subsequent to Chalmers 1995. See also Greenfield 1995, Scott 1995 and Velmans in press.

philosophy. So professional philosophers may well regard the current euphoria over consciousness with a degree of scepticism, seeing it as merely the latest intellectual fashion. Secondly, the success of such an undertaking is by no means assured. One has to ask: does the concept 'consciousness' really define an independent and coherent domain, a subject area that could correspond to an autonomous *area of research*?[3]

What would be the subject, methodology and aim of such a research area? This brings us back to our starting point: what is the real problem of consciousness? Can it be approached by means of the natural sciences at all? What exactly do we want to *know*? These questions — especially the last one, the setting of the epistemic goal — are typical philosophical questions. As philosophers we also want to know how it is *possible* that a phenomenon as complex as consciousness could arise in a physical universe: we are looking for a conceptually convincing analysis of the phenomenon and its relationship to the objective world. The first aim, therefore, is conceptual clarity and freedom from contradiction. As empirical researchers, on the other hand, we want to know how all this *actually* happened: we are interested in the history of the phenomenon in our own world. Is there a neural correlate of consciousness? Which forms of information processing in the brain lead to those states which we call conscious experiences? Such questions are central to the second goal on our way to a better understanding of the phenomenon of conscious experience. This goal is the achievement of an empirically meaningful and informative theory of consciousness.

How can the emergence of conscious experience be reconciled with the laws of nature that dominate this world? As far as we know, consciousness is a very recent phenomenon in the physical history of the universe. Once again we can say, in a certain sense, that we ourselves are the phenomenon in question. The emergence of organisms with highly organized nervous systems, and soon afterwards of human beings, are events that from a cosmological viewpoint have only just occurred. The idea that, in a strong sense, we ourselves are the phenomenon in question, leads to a third provisional answer to the question what we actually expect from a satisfactory theory of consciousness. To be convincing, such a theory must not only be conceptually coherent and empirically plausible: we must also be able to accept this theory as a theory about our *own* inner experiences. It must account for the subtlety and phenomenological wealth of this experience and take seriously the inner perspective of the experiencing subject. Above all, it must explain the connection between one's own first-person perspective and the third-person perspective of science operating from the outside. If it turns out that our intuitions about consciousness and the interpretation of these intuitions by folk psychology prove radically wrong, then such a

[3] Concerning *sceptical* considerations of this point, cf. the papers by Kathy Wilkes, Martin Kurthen and David Papineau in Part 2 of this book.

theory must offer a detailed explanation of why we are so wrong about the matter. Fortunately, there is a wide consensus that a serious theory of consciousness must account for the phenomenological wealth, colourfulness and variety of our inner life. In the philosophy of mind at least, there are only a few examples of naive and ideological forms of reductionism: it has long been clear that a primitive scientism, attempting to bulldoze the subtlety and depth of our conscious experience simply by introducing new materialistic jargon, would be evading the real problems.

The problems on the path to a convincing theory of consciousness differ fundamentally from other unsolved problems in the natural sciences. Although physics, chemistry and biology have solved many of the fundamental puzzles in their respective domains, a considerable number of grey areas on the map have remained. These sciences are far from being able to describe exhaustively the parts of reality which form their own subjects of research. However, where there are lingering mysteries in physics, chemistry and biology, it is at least clear what would be accepted as a *solution* of the problems. This is not so for the problem of consciousness, for a number of reasons.

To be able to speak seriously about a *science of consciousness*, a number of fundamental questions would have to be answered. It is interesting to note that with the emergence of consciousness, private worlds — spaces of inner experience — are opened up. These spaces, however, are *individual* spaces: ego-centres of experience that suddenly appear in a centreless universe.[4] Each such centre of consciousness constitutes its own perspective on the world. This perspective is what philosophers sometimes like to call the 'first-person perspective'. A phenomenal world of its own is tied to each of these perspectives. These individual worlds of experience also possess a historical dimension: almost always a psychological biography emerges together with them — what we call our 'inner life'. This too can be seen as the history of the genesis of a world, or a *phenomenal* cosmology: within each of us a cosmos of consciousness unfolds temporarily, a *subjective* universe develops. The first part of the problem is to understand how such a variety of subjective universes can constantly form and disappear in our objective universe. Empirical research on the evolution and neurobiological genesis of consciousness is relevant here, but there is also a philosophical aspect to the problem. This consists in understanding how we our selves can *be* such subjective universes, and above all in understanding the meaning of it all. Do we really understand what we are saying when we describe ourselves as dynamic *subjective* universes, that have something like a centre and temporarily light up in an *objective* universe? I do not think we do.

Before our general ideas and epistemic goals can be turned into concrete research projects, we need a careful conceptual analysis of the problem.

[4] In the more recent discussion no one has highlighted this point as clearly as Thomas Nagel. Cf. Nagel 1974, 1979, 1980, 1986.

Empirical practice and philosophical meta-theory must go hand in hand, allowing the various disciplines to work together systematically and productively. This is the context of Owen Flanagan's call for a 'Unified Theory of Consciousness',[5] and it ties in with the fact that from a number of very different fields calls for the establishment of an independent academic discipline of consciousness research have been heard. Such a desire for cooperation, existing alongside suspicion and wrangling both within and between disciplines, is typical of situations in which great theoretical advances are on the horizon. It also leads into the second feature which makes the problem of consciousness a *special* problem, because it raises questions of methodology: what are the appropriate methods with which to approach the problem of consciousness? What relationship have these methods to one another? Again, a typical philosophical objection could be as follows: if we wish to take seriously our own consciousness as a phenomenon bound to individual perspectives of experience, we cannot — as a matter of *principle* — approach it through objective methods, since the essence and the strength of *these* methods consists precisely in moving as far away as possible from any purely individual perspectives.[6] But if we then ask what it would mean to treat conscious experience seriously as a subjective phenomenon, we will be led back to our original question: what exactly is it that we want to know?

The final aspect of the question is that in the present state of interdisciplinary research on consciousness the *explananda* still remain undefined: it is not at all clear *what* it is that has to be explained. Conscious experience is not a single problem, but a whole cluster of problems. One may ask: What are the components of this cluster? How, if at all, are they related? Is it really even a *single* cluster at all? As long as there are no convincing answers to these three aspects of our original question, there is a danger that the present enthusiasm for the subject will degenerate into a euphoria that ultimately fails to produce a tangible advance. One has to admit that consciousness research is still in its infancy. It has not yet left its pre-paradigmatic phase: so far there is no uniform theoretical background against which a *science of consciousness* could develop. To create such a background, we must address not only general questions like the ones concerning the epistemic goal, the methodological canon and the catalogue of explananda discussed above, but also a whole range of detailed problems. This is essential if we are to show that the notion of a unified science of consciousness is not only a fascinating but also a *coherent* idea. I will discuss some of these detailed

---

[5] See Flanagan 1992: chapter 11.

[6] Once again, thanks are due to Thomas Nagel for raising this point very clearly in an unfavourable climate, first in Nagel 1974. See also some of the texts listed in section 3.7 of the bibliography. For criticisms of the assumption of perspectival 'first-person facts' see Lycan 1987: chapter 2, Malcolm 1988, Metzinger 1993: chapters 4 & 5, Metzinger 1995b.

problems in the remainder of this introduction, which is an attempt to approach the problem of consciousness in three steps.

The first step deals with the most important phenomenological characteristics of consciousness. This aims at presenting an initial description of three concrete and global properties of conscious experience, which shows why this phenomenon is indeed a *special* problem. The second step moves from the phenomenological plane to an analytical one, producing a list of the conceptual problems that result from the global description. I will present a short account of these problems, as they appear from the perspective of the philosophy of mind. The third and final step is to engage with the current debate, which will lead us directly into the present collection of texts.

II. Transparency, Perspectivalness and Presence: Concrete Properties of Conscious Experience

1. Pure experience: phenomenal content, phenomenal properties, phenomenal states

Nothing is simultaneously so close and yet so distant as our own consciousness. To start with, nothing in the world seems to be more intimate to us than the contents of our own consciousness: our sensations, our feelings and our thoughts are all given to us in a very direct and self-evident way. True, we can sometimes be deceived about the true causes of our sensory perceptions, and our conscious thoughts and feeling can also mislead us when we have views of the world that cannot be justified. But nevertheless there is nothing in our subjective experience that could be more obvious and natural than the simple facts of experience itself: the fact that I *now* sense the cover of this book to be blue; the fact that I am *now* of the opinion that a fundamentally new image of man is emerging; or the fact that just *now* I am led on by curiosity. One cannot, apparently, doubt pure experience itself.

In the philosophy of mind this pure experience is termed the *phenomenal content* of our mental states. Consciousness in this sense is therefore frequently termed 'phenomenal consciousness' by philosophers. States of consciousness, according to this understanding, are always phenomenal states, because they are those states in virtue of which the world *appears* to us in a certain way, they determine how we experience the world and ourselves. We are thus dealing with a special meaning of the word 'consciousness' that is not immediately related to common phrases such as 'feminist consciousness', 'ecological consciousness', or 'awareness' in the spiritual or psycho-therapeutic sense. When one speaks of phenomenal consciousness, one is always referring to pure subjective experience. It is precisely this aspect which is considered in this book.

The philosophical core of the following discussions is formed by the simple fact that some mental states have more than information content: they also have a certain *feel*. The most popular recent formulation of this point was given by Thomas Nagel: there is something *it is like* to be in these states (cf. Nagel 1974). This property of *what-it-is-like* is the subjective character of experience. But what exactly is meant by saying that many of our sensory or mental states possess a subjective, experiential character? Let me illustrate this experiential character with a simple example. Take a moment to sit back and contemplate the background colour which we have chosen for the cover of this book. The name of this colour is *Pantone Blue 72*. If you allow the colour to make an impression on you, you can experience directly the meaning of 'phenomenal content': in the visual experience of the colour of the cover this phenomenal content is the subjectively felt property of *blueness*, that is, the quality of *Pantone Blue 72* now appearing in the flow of your conscious experience. You perceive a certain object and in the very process of perception the subjective sensation of blueness is formed: the book *appears* to be blue. Because *Pantone Blue 72* is a property of appearance, one also speaks of 'phenomenal properties'. Such isolated phenomenal properties are the simplest examples of the subjective, experiential character of consciousness. Of course, there are higher forms of phenomenal content: *Gestalt*-awareness, object formation, self-consciousness, or the conscious experience of situations and contexts. More about this later. Let us for the moment keep to simple properties.

Among English-speaking philosophers, the mental states associated with such simple phenomenal properties are sometimes identified with the concept of *raw feeling*.[7] Here again, the aspect of pure sensation, the aspect of pure experience, is decisive. One can easily find a variety of examples of such qualities: the painfulness of pain, the scent of sandalwood, the taste of Bourbon-Vanilla or the extraordinary sound quality in the tone of a cello. But the sense of weight that you are just experiencing in your body, or the feeling of 'smoothness' that you have when you run your hand over the cover of this book, are equally examples of such qualia. The subjectively sensed heaviness of one's own body (the 'heaviness-quale') and the subjectively experienced smoothness of the book-cover (the 'smoothness-quale') are phenomena that only exist when there is also consciousness. This subjective aspect of conscious experience, it seems, is something which cannot be measured: phenomenal content is *qualitative* content.

Qualitative content is frequently described as a phenomenal property. However, if one speaks of *properties* in this way, one is immediately faced with the first serious philosophical problem. What is the *thing* of which the phenomenal properties are features? What are the logical subjects to which we assign such properties? Or, rephrasing the question: is *Pantone Blue 72* a property of a non-physical entity, a phenomenal individual, that only exists in the field of conscious experience? This is an unattractive option,

---

[7] Other frequently used expressions are *qualia, secondary qualities, sensory qualities, subjective qualities of experience, experiential properties* and *the subjective character of experience*. See e.g. Kirk 1994 and Clark 1992.

because it confronts us with the classic mind–body problem: the well-accepted principle of the *causal closure* of the physical world is not compatible with the assumption that conscious experience — understood here to imply the occurence of one or more non-physical entities — has an effect on our behaviour and our actions. How should one conceive of the interaction of such non-physical agents with our brain? If conscious experience is interpreted as the mental act in which we grasp a mysterious kind of non-physical entity, then the meaning of such a description becomes notoriously unclear: what exactly is meant by the term 'to grasp'?

Perhaps there is a way to avoid this classic dilemma. Is the subjectively experienced blueness perhaps a feature of a *process* rather than a thing, in this case the process of visual perception? The scientific investigation of human colour vision is now yielding detailed descriptions of such perceptual processes.[8] Unfortunately, nothing figuring in such objective descriptions ever possesses a concrete property such as *blueness* in the sense required here: nothing in the eye or in the brain is *blue* in this sense. Might one therefore suggest that it is really the book 'out there' that is blue? 'Out there', however, there are only electro-magnetic oscillations that are reflected from the surface of the book in a certain mixture of different wave-lengths. In any case, one can have blue-colour experiences even in a dream, when no rays of light fall on the retina. (Perhaps you will be dreaming tonight of *Pantone Blue 72* . . .) Many other examples contradict the idea of phenomenal properties actually being concrete, first-order properties of objects in the environment. When we look into a green light-flash and then close our eyes, we see a *red* after-image. But *what* is it that has the property of redness? Such common observations already suggest that phenomenal properties may not be objective properties. Whatever they are, they do not seem to be 'out there'.

The problem emerges again when we look at *sets* of phenomenal properties — 'phenomenal states' or states of consciousness. When one or more of the properties in such a set change, then we are dealing with subjective events; and when chains of such events link successive phenomenal states together, then we are dealing with phenomenal processes: processes of consciousness. All this appears to be clear and simple. But the question still remains: *what* is it that changes here? What are 'phenomenal states' states *of*? Are they states of the 'soul' or states of an 'ego'? Are phenomenal states simply states of the brain? Or are they something intermediate — information-processing states in the central nervous system, perhaps, states of a large data structure which in the waking and dreaming state is episodically being activated by our brain?

All these attempts to impute possible answers in advance, by the way in which the question is posed, are more than problematical. One might try to

---

[8] Hardin 1988 offers an excellent introduction, tailor-made for the discussion of the underlying philosophical problems.

interpret them as research programmes for the future, as open questions, to which empirical answers potentially exist. However, such research pro-grammes would only be conceptually plausible if it were made clear that our traditional, formal ontology could be projected on the phenomenal ontology of conscious experience. This would require that everything which *exists* in conscious experience, as seen from the perspective of the first person, can be adequately described with the linguistic and conceptual means at our disposal. Only then could there be an abstract analysis of phenomenal states and properties that could, at least in principle, be com-plete. But it is precisely this point which has been frequently doubted by philosophers. I shall therefore return to this later.

For the moment we should take the first step, and, slowly and carefully approaching the problem of consciousness, turn to *concrete* features of phenomenal states. Having clarified the concepts of phenomenal content, phenomenal properties and phenomenal states, we can now ask what the interesting features of these states actually comprise. We are now ready to take an initial look at the phenomenology of consciousness. This first step will once again demonstrate that the problem of consciousness is indeed a *special* problem. Phenomenal states are quite different from physical, chemical, biological or neurobiological states: they are transparent, they are perspectival and they are present.

2. The transparency of phenomenal states

Phenomenal states are infinitely close to us. Before the formation of any philosophical concept takes place, conscious experience is already immedi-ately given to us: nothing could be more natural or more familiar than this. I have already pointed out that, in a certain sense, we *ourselves* are this experience — what would human beings be without phenomenal conscious-ness? Human beings without phenomenal consciousness would not be persons, but 'zombies', roaming dead. Such zombies would probably not have a problem regarding consciousness, either at a scientific or at a philosophical level. For us, on the other hand, the simple facts of conscious-ness have been fixed even before we can start to think about the problem of consciousness. To put this insight another way: from the perspective of the experiencing self the field of phenomenal consciousness is *transparent*.[9] This simply means that we do not experience phenomenal states *as* phe-nomenal states, but that we, as it were, *look through them*. They seem to bring us into direct contact with the world, because we perceive the content of these states in the mode of immediate givenness. We do not have the feeling of living in a three-dimensional film or in an inner representational space: in standard situations our conscious life always takes place *in the world*. We do not experience our conscious field as a cyberspace generated by our brain, but simply as reality itself, with which we are in contact in a

[9] Regarding the concept of 'semantic transparency' see Metzinger 1993, Van Gulick 1988 a,b.

natural and unproblematic way. In standard situations the contents of pure experience are subjectively given in a direct and seemingly immediate manner. It is precisely in this sense that we can say: they are infinitely close to us. This infinite closeness is the first major phenomenological characteristic of consciousness.

How could one explain this fact scientifically? Can one take the transparency of consciousness *seriously* by making it the subject of an empirical theory? If — as the majority of emprical researchers assume today — conscious experience is indeed a phenomenon based on information processing and mental representation in the brain, then one could perhaps suggest that the data structures active at a given time are not recognized *as such* by the system. They do not convey the information *that* they are indeed such data-structures. They contain no variables and are almost always 'fully interpreted'. Therefore we simply feel ourselves to be directly in contact with the content of our conscious states, because our functional design forces us into a naive realism. And this naive realism may, in turn, have its roots in our biological history: we are naturally formed information-processing systems, that have been configured and optimized over millions of years of evolution, and optimal solutions often are simple solutions. Such considerations are fascinating because they not only point towards an explanatory outline of how consciousness 'works', they also illuminate that central paradox: how our own consciousness can so quickly be transformed from something infinitely close into something strange and far distant, when we try to understand it empirically. For what could be more alien to my own experience than 'active data structures in the brain'? What could be more likely to divide me from my own consciousness than the dubious attempts of scientists to explain its transparency by information-processing properties in my central nervous system?

So no wonder, if we strive for a conceptually convincing philosophical understanding of a global phenomenological property like 'transparency', that consciousness easily turns from something infinitely close to something infinitely distant. The Latin tag *esse est experiri* can be applied here and interpreted: 'the reality of phenomenal qualities lies in their being experienced'; meaning among other things that we fully grasp the essential character of phenomenal states just by experiencing them.[10] But if this is really true, then phenomenal states are not only transparent, they are incorrigible: they can never deceive us. Here a series of simple but momentous questions arises again. Is something which could not deceive us therefore also something that we *know*? Is phenomenal transparency really the same as certainty? Is there any guarantee that conscious experience is a form of *cognition*? Or, to put it another way: how do we know that the simple facts of consciousness are really *facts* at all?

[10] See e.g. Bieri 1981: 206.

3. The perspectivalness of phenomenal states

A second important feature — if one wishes to understand what phenomenal consciousness actually is — is that experiences always appear to be experiences for an experiencing ego. It is I *myself* who experiences these feelings and sensory perceptions in a certain way. It is I *myself* who discovers in my sensory perceptions certain subjective qualities — say the 'blueness' in a colour or the characteristic scent of sandalwood. Pure sensory perceptions of these simple qualities are thus always tied to a subjective perspective of experience. It is always true, at least for the normal states of consciousness, that subjective sensory perceptions always are *my* sensory perceptions, they possess their specific character of experience *for me*. Nobody knows what it is like for *me* to hear the tone of a cello or to look at the special blue of the book cover. And I don't know what it is like for a bat to hear the tone of a cello or what it is like for one of my readers to look at the *Pantone Blue 72* of the book cover. One can call this characteristic of phenomenological consciousness its *perspectivalness*: in standard situations phenomenal content is always accompanied by a phenomenal point of view, by an experiencing ego. This experiencing ego turns conscious experiences into *its* experiences. It is also true of this ego that it is infinitely close to itself. Before reflecting about the theoretical problem of self-consciousness in philosophical terms, it is essential to understand an interesting and conceptually puzzling feature to which every convincing theory of consciousness must do justice: a very simple being, that can only feel and not think, might also possess this characteristic. Philosophers sometimes call it 'prereflexive self-intimacy' (cf. Frank 1991). This quality arises from the fact that states of phenomenal *self*consciousness are also transparent in the previously explained sense.

Our consciousness is a *centred* consciousness, since it almost always has a centre. We ourselves are the centre, the focus of consciousness. We 'possess' ourselves prior to all intellectual operations, we have always been intimate to ourselves. It is not just that phenomenal states are tied to an individual perspective; this individuality is also apparent at the level of conscious experience itself. We are infinitely close to ourselves, because a large part of the content of self-consciousness is experienced as being immediately given. Now, it is particularly interesting that in this way our experiental space as a whole not only gains a central focal point of consciousness, but a perspectival structure as well. It is thus at the level of conscious experience that we find the origin of what philosophers call the 'first-person perspective'. There is also a further mental phenomenon, originating together with this structural feature of the perspectivalness, which any reputable theory of consciousness must take seriously. This phenomenon is called *inwardness*.

Let us briefly return to the simple phenomenal properties already mentioned *en passant*. The qualitative content of mental states — the blueness of blue or the painfulness of pain — is not only experientially 'transparent', it also seems to be the *defining* characteristic of such states: a pain that is not painful is inconceivable; a blue experience without the subjective quality of colour is simply *not* a blue experience. It is, however, questionable whether such 'private' properties of mental states could ever be tied in conceptually with public and objective properties of the underlying physical states. Could the subjective taxonomy of these states be projected in principle on an objective categorization such as could be supplied by the cognitive- and neuro-sciences — for example in terms of information-processing states in the brain? Their existence lies precisely in their being experienced, in the way in which they appear to us: an experience of pain that is not painful is just *not* an experience of pain — and a theory about pain from which this qualitative characteristic were missing would not be a theory about pain at all. Such a theory would be utterly remote from us, it would omit precisely what concerns us. This is one of the reasons why a number of philosophers consider the phenomenal content of qualia as an irreducible property of such states.

Some philosophers have a similar attitude to our second feature of consciousness — *perspectivalness*. This is also widely held to be an essential characteristic of conscious states: that they are always tied to a subjective perspective. Seen from the inner perspective, this structural feature of conscious experience is again transparent: what is more natural and self-evident than the fact that only I *myself* know how it feels — at this very moment — to have exactly those conscious experiences that I am just passing through? And what could be simpler to appreciate than the fact that I *myself* am the irreplaceable centre of my conscious field; that although I can always try to *empathize* with the subjective states of another being — say a bat — using the resources of my consciousness, I shall never know what it is like to *be* a bat?

The prereflexive self-intimacy of the phenomenal ego is perhaps the best illustration of the fact that our own consciousness is infinitely close and at the same time infinitely distant. Yet although we speak as if we were infinitely near to ourselves in experience, and as if there were indeed something like the perspective of the first person, no one actually knows what all this is really supposed to mean. 'Closeness' is a spatial metaphor, that alludes to a relationship between spatial objects. (Although it is not clear what it would mean to claim that, say, a chair was infinitely close to itself.) The 'perspective of the first person', by contrast, is the combination of a spatial-visual metaphor with a *grammatical* one. It may just be acceptable to call our experiential space 'perspectival', since this relates to sight, which is our dominant sense. Our visual experience of the world has indeed been constructed around a centre, because as seeing people we experience the world apparently from one viewpoint, and this viewpoint seems to lie behind our eyes and is the centre point of our visual experiential space. We even speak of 'the world around us'. But who then is 'the first person' supposed to be — a little man in our head, looking out into the world through the windows of our eyes? Here again, numerous questions and difficult theoretical problems follow on quickly and obviously.

For the final step, let us again consider first the simple phenomenal properties. If it is correct, that the special phenomenal property of 'blueness' of *Pantone Blue 72* is an intrinsic and essential characteristic of certain conscious colour experiences, then the question arises whether there can ever be a scientific theory about conscious colour experience at all. We have said that in the physical outside world there are only electro-magnetic oscillations of certain wavelengths, and nowhere a property called 'blue'. A variety of physical processes can trigger in *us* a sensation of blue, but there does not seem to be anything to connect all these processes in the physical outside world with each other. On the retina also we search in vain for the property called 'blue': the firing of the optic nerve is not blue, any more than the firing of neurons in those regions of our brain which are responsible for the sensation of pain is painful. All we find are myriads of subtle electrical impulses. Again, the patterns of excitation that build up from those impulses are spatially and temporally very complicated in just those areas of our visual cortex of which brain-researchers say that they are absolutely necessary for our colour-perception: but they are not *blue*. The concreteness of consciously experienced 'blueness' — let us say of *Pantone Blue 72* — cannot be retrieved from the mathematically abstract theories with which scientists will soon be offering a precise description of the relevant patterns of neural activity. Many, therefore, ask themselves privately whether the phenomenal property of 'blueness' really exists in this world: is there a point of contact between the inner world of consciousness and the outer world of physics? We all want scientific psychology to take our consciousness seriously. But *can* it really do this? If already simple phenomenal properties like the consciously experienced blue of the book cover appear to elude the objective grasp of science, what would a theory of phenomenal consciousness be like, which took this really seriously and offered convincing explanations for what we have declared to be the defining characteristic of subjective states — their qualitative character?

Such questions become sharper still when we take account of perspectivalness, the second concrete characteristic of phenomenal consciousness. Given the generally accepted view, that the association of conscious experience with a subjective inner perspective is an essential property of the phenomenon, a satisfactory explanation of what it actually means to ascribe an inner perspective to a system is indispensible. When I confront a completely alien being, and ask myself whether this being is really *conscious*, I do not only want to know, in the sense of Thomas Nagel, *what it is like* to possess the mental states of this being. I want to know whether this being has a genuine inner world, whether in its experiencing it enjoys the immediate self-intimacy described above, whether it really takes on a subjective perspective in relation to its mental states. This inwardness of phenomenal consciousness, resulting from the emergence of an ego-centre, would have to find a place in any scientifically convincing theory of consciousness. However, the principle of objectivity, on which the empirical sciences are based, means avoiding all subjective perspectives and distancing oneself as far as possible from all individual points of view. This gives rise to a fundamental problem: can a means of investigation, whose leading characteristic is the elimination of all subjective perspectives, help us to approach our own consciousness? If we are serious about the project of a *science of consciousness*, then we must build bridges from the outside world to the inner world, that is, to where we already *are*. On closer inspection, however, this proves to be an incoherent idea.

Thomas Nagel devoted himself to this problem as few other philosophers in the last few decades have done. He illustrated the point like this: even if some future physics achieved a complete description of the spatio-temporal world, it would still not explain which time was *now* and which place was *here*. Moreover, this would still be true even if we included an all-embracing description of the inner states of all conscious beings at all times and in all places. The most important of all facts to each of us — at least according to Nagel — would still be missing from such an objective picture of all subjective experiences and states of consciousness: namely, the fact that *I* am identical with one of the persons contained in this picture and that the inner experiences of this person are *my* experiences. In the objective picture of the world I would only be what Nagel aptly calls 'one person among countless others in oceans of space and time' and 'a momentary blip on the cosmic screen' (Nagel 1986: 61). A fundamental question arises from this: can the centreless conception of the world developed by science account *at all* for the phenomenal content that is tied to many individual perspectives of consciousness? Does not consciousness from a scientific viewpoint inevitably change from something very close to something quite distant, from something indisputably real to an illusion? One can quite reasonably doubt whether Thomas Nagel correctly formulated this aspect of the problem. So far no one has demonstrated that the inwardness of phenomenal consciousness is a mystery in the face of which the ideal of scientific investigation has *in principle* to fail. On the other hand, Nagel is quite correct in stating that it is never merely a matter of how we should express ourselves in philosophy, of what we shall say (cf. Nagel 1986: 56). The question is persistent, it constantly appears in new forms: could we ever really accept a new scientific theory — however plausible — about the emergence of a phenomenally conscious ego-perspective as a theory *about ourselves*?

4. The presence of phenomenological states

The first major phenomenal characteristic of consciousness was transparency. The second is its perspectivalness. Let us now turn to the third characteristic: the *presence* of phenomenal content. I said at the outset, that, according to experience, there was nothing more obvious than the simple facts of consciousness itself: for instance the fact that I *now* experience the cover of this book as being blue. It is this subjectively experienced 'Now' which represents the third important characteristic of phenomenal consciousness. This means that the characteristics of transparency and immediate givenness also possess a *temporal* aspect. It is interesting to note that, just as the transparency and closeness are accompanied by an equally obvious aspect of ineffability and cognitive impenetrability, so also our consciousness of time is simultaneously both infinitely close and infinitely distant. In a famous passage in chapter 14 of the eleventh book of his *Confessions* (written c. 400 AD), St. Augustine wrote: *'What then is time? If no one asks me, I know; if I wish to explain to one who asks, I know not.'* That still rings true. The relationship between subjective and objective time is even today one of the most intractable variants of the mind–body problem.[11]

This comes about because however diverse and varied our subjective feelings may be, they are always given to us in the unity of an experienced *moment*. That is how we talk and think. But when we look at the matter more closely — particularly in the light of recent empirical material — we have to ask whether we actually understand *what* we are saying. It seems that my feelings and ideas, my bodily sensations and all other qualities of my sensory consciousness, including the ineffable wealth of subjective nuances and minutest distinctions, are always connected by the fact that they are components of an experienced present. One might simply express this observation as follows: phenomenal content is *present*. In saying this one does not want to imply that phenomenal consciousness is some rigid structure, in which there is no flow and no change. This could not be true, since, in a strong sense, it is precisely the flux of subjective experience (in the sense of the German word *Erleben*) that makes us alive. Rather, one is wanting to spell out, as an essential feature of consciousness, that its contents are always presented to us within a concretely experienced present. *Pantone Blue 72* always is *Pantone Blue 72* — *now*. According to subjective experience, the taste of Bourbon-Vanilla, the scent of sandalwood or the feeling of curiosity are *now* immediately given to us. We do not ourselves construct these subjective qualities of experience: they are without doubt *real* facts of consciousness. Of course, we can *re*-present conscious contents — for instance, when remembering the scent of sandalwood or looking forward to the taste of Bourbon-Vanilla. But then what is present in our consciousness is simply the *memory* of a certain joss-stick or the pleasure in *anticipating* custard. The conscious experience of these higher cognitive processes, like memory or future planning, still always takes place within a

---

[11] See the paper by Eva Ruhnau in the third part of this volume and the references given in the introduction to this part. A good introduction to the empirical aspect of this problem can be found in Pöppel 1988, see also Pöppel 1978.

phenomenal present. Thirdly then, phenomenal content always possesses an aspect of being present. Moreover, this aspect of phenomenal presence also refers to the self, the centre of the experiential field: the experiencing ego is also present, because, in a maximally natural and self-evident sense which precedes all philosophical reasoning, it is a *present* ego. There would be no first-person perspective without the concretely experienced presence of the ego.

The contents of consciousness only become real facts through this general experience of presence. When we wake up in the morning, reality presents itself to us: with the activation of phenomenal consciousness a phenomenal reality is always formed. This phenomenal reality is my world, the world in which I live. I, along with the world around me, am phenomenally present in every single moment, that is, the phenomenal content of self and world is experientially represented as *real right now*. At first, nothing could be more unproblematic and more obvious than this presence of my reality, because from the perspective of the first person it, too, is transparent. The conscious present is infinitely close to us.

We have known for a long time, however, that the presence of a conscious reality can be created artificially. Episodes of conscious experiences that are absolutely real and present from the first-person perspective can, for instance, be created in subjects by directly stimulating the brain with the help of electrodes (although it is in these situations mostly possible to keep up a critical 'meta-perspective'; cf. Penfield 1975). States following the ingestion of certain psychoactive substances, or severe mental illnesses, are further examples of situations in which 'alternative realities' can arise within us through outside intervention. In a dream, a very natural and recurrent state of consciousness, reality appears to us as present and real. Despite the dreamworld's being full of contradictions and bizarre changes, we do not *know*, that we are dreaming.[12] In a number of psychiatric disorders, complex hallucinations occur that make it impossible for the patients to realize *that* they are actually hallucinating. Again, something like an 'alternative present' arises. There are also various disorders in which the experience of time and present itself is distorted or even destroyed. Even in the healthy state, we all know situations in which the phenomenal presence of conscious reality can diminish temporarily, perhaps after a

[12] This need not be so. The importance for consciousness research of so-called 'lucid dreams', in which we develop a critical relationship to phenomenal reality, may have been underestimated in the past. For further references see the introduction to Part 7 of the expanded German version of this book and Metzinger 1993. See also Flanagan 1995 and Revonsuo 1995a. In researching conscious experience, dreams are of great interest for at least two more reasons. First, it may be possible to approach empirically the question of phenomenal coherence and integra- tion of content (see my contribution to this volume) by measuring the *bizarreness* of dream content; cf. Mamelak & Hobson 1989, Revonsuo & Salmivalli 1995. Second, it might be of great importance to delineate the common neurobiological and functional substrate of both waking and dreaming, as both are the paradigmatic types of phenomenality in our own case. As it turns out, waking consciousness may be looked upon as a special form of *online*-dreaming. See Hobson & Stickgold 1993, 1994, Llinás & Paré 1991, Llinás & Ribary 1994, Revonsuo 1995a.

moment of shock and panic or in a situation of danger. Here, the world attains a dreamlike and 'unreal' quality. This shows that the experience of presence can be subject to various fluctuations. As neuropsychological research has clearly demonstrated, these fluctuations are determined by factors that lie outside consciousness, such as complex processes in the affected person's brain.

This understanding consequently concerns the *actuality* of the simple facts of consciousness: from the outside, there is mounting evidence that our conscious experience of reality *as* reality is a construct. But if this is true, then it calls into question the transparency of phenomenal consciousness. That is, empirical research concerning the subjective experience of presence strongly suggests that the traditional assumption that the contents of consciousness are given to us directly and immediately must be wrong. Let us look at an example. Patients suffering from a certain type of disorder known as 'anosognosia' have a deficit in their consciousness, but cannot consciously experience it as such. They lack the higher-order insight into the fact of illness, because of an injury to the brain — that is, because of purely *physical* damage. A particularly impressive example is *Anton's syndrome* (cf. Anton 1899, Benson & Greenberg 1969). Patients who suddenly lose their sight through a lesion in the visual cortex in some cases stubbornly insist that they can still see. They collide with furniture and other obstacles, and show all symptoms of functional blindness, yet behave as if they are not *consciously aware* of the subjective *disappearance* of the visual world. Thus they produce false, but consistent, confabulations in response to questions about their surroundings: they seem to believe the tales which they tell about nonexistent phenomenal worlds, and they deny any functional deficit in their faculty of seeing. These and many other empirical results have given rise to strong doubts at the philosophical level as to whether our subjective field of consciousness, experienced as transparent, really *is* transparent.

Once more it becomes clear why I said at the outset: nothing is simultaneously so close and yet so distant as our own consciousness. The more closely we look into our own consciousness, the more puzzling and mysterious it becomes. Nowadays, the inner perspective increasingly comes into conflict with the outer perspective. Scientific advance, brought about by methods operating strictly from the third-person perspective, now invades our sphere of 'mental privacy', since it casts doubt upon the transparency of our conscious space, and thus questions the authority of the first-person perspective *altogether*. Is Anton's syndrome, the lack of insight into one's own blindness, a neuropsychological metaphor for the cultural situation in which we find ourselves? Are we systems that produce consistent confabulations, that stubbornly play certain traditional language-games and cling to our folk-psychological image of ourselves, although we increasingly collide with obstacles resulting from new empirical material? The irrevocable loss of the (illusory) confidence in the certainty of introspection[13] is making

[13] Concerning the decline of introspective research programmes see Lyons 1986.

us all unsure of our own subjective experience — our own consciousness, apparently so close to us, becomes remote, shadowy and puzzling. It is interesting to note that Descartes' basic assumption of the self-transparency of consciousness which, through Brentano's notion of the 'evidence of inner perception', has exerted a strong influence right into our own century, has become untenable precisely because psychology, from an empirical standpoint, became an autonomous discipline.

If one now, finally, retransfers the theoretical loss of transparency and presence to the second major phenomenological feature of consciousness — the *perspectivalness* of our experiential field — a dramatic consequence results. On closer inspection we no longer know what it means that we *ourselves* experience ourselves as being present. For if the presence of the contents of our experience is a construct, then so are the contents of conscious self-experience, including the experience of what in philosophy of mind is called the 'phenomenal self'. Further, if introspection is not a reliable means of understanding — since looking into one's own consciousness can lead to unnoticed deceptions — then the inner space of self-consciousness also darkens, since the experienced transparency of *this* space too could at any time turn out to be an illusion. But *whose* illusion would that be? Nor is it any longer clear how to understand the the notion of our grasping the 'simple facts of consciousness' from the perspective of the first person. In any case, who is this first person? What do we refer to when speaking of the ego and its perspective? We speak of our conscious experiences, as if we ourselves *had* these experiences and as if we were *present* subjects of experience in an unproblematic sense. But our initial stock-taking of some very general and concrete properties of phenomenal states already showed that we do not really know exactly what we are talking about here. Now, at the end of our first careful exploration of these global phenomenological features, there is already a danger that not only consciousness but also we *ourselves* will be transformed from something infinitely close into something infinitely distant.

The headlong development of the empirical side of research has consequences for the philosophical treatment of our theme. Today it goes without saying that a philosophical theory of phenomenal consciousness must not conflict with empirical knowledge. The problem of consciousness has become an *interdisciplinary* problem. This is an advance in many ways, but it has also blurred the concept of consciousness. By straying into the most diverse disciplines, consciousness has become divorced from its philosophical origins. A semantic inflation has been the unavoidable consequence. This in turn has led to a state of uncertainty at the theoretical level. I have already identified the core of this insecurity: we are frequently not clear about the epistemic goal of our efforts, about what we actually want to know when we investigate consciousness. As the concept of consciousness has become more firmly embedded in empirical theory formation, the diverse facets of the problem have become particularly evident. There is no such thing as *the* problem of consciousness. 'Consciousness' is really only the summary title for a whole cluster of problems and possible research programmes. In such a situation it is urgently necessary, as a first step, to create a solid communications base. Each of the disciplines potentially participating in the project of a unified *science of consciousness* must therefore develop a systematic catalogue of its own questions. Each discipline has to determine its own set of explananda, the accepted methods of approaching these explananda, the respective explanatory basis and what — from the perspective of this discipline — *counts* as an explanation.[14] This also applies to the philosophy of the mind. Of course, this introduction is not the place for establishing such a catalogue, but in the following section I will offer a brief selection of the most important questions constituting the problem landscape today. I hope it can help the readers of this book in their first attempts at an orientation in this landscape.

III. The Problem Landscape: A Catalogue of Questions

1. Consciousness as a conceptual problem

A convincing theory of consciousness must be conceptually coherent. This part of the project unambiguously falls in the area of philosophy of mind. There, the concept of 'consciousness' is only rarely interpreted today in the sense of a non-corporeal substance or a non-physical individual. It is no longer a question of 'the consciousness', but of consciousness in the sense of a *property*. What is, however, the correct analysis of consciousness as a property?

(a) 'Conscious' as a one-place or two-place predicate

If the word 'conscious' is interpreted as a one-place predicate, then it appears as a primitive property of some mental states, which resists further analysis. There is no non-circular definition for this concept of phenomenal consciousness. Consciousness in this sense appears to be an *intrinsic* property of mental states that cannot be resolved into a set of relations between entities on a lower level of description. Consciousness, as a primitive property of mental states, would be irreducible. But it is this interpretation of 'conscious' that is central to the debate on *phenomenal* consciousness.

If 'conscious' is analysed as a two-place predicate, then one confronts the problem of the intentionality of the mental. In this form, consciousness is always 'consciousness *of something*'. Franz Brentano in 1874 described the basic feature of consciousness as the directedness of mental acts towards an object (cf. Brentano 1973 [1874]: 124 f. This notion of a relation between

---

[14] See Robert Van Gulick's contribution in Part 1 of this volume.

intentional acts and their objects led to a conception of consciousness as a psychological act that determined many theories of the late 19th and early 20th centuries. Edmund Husserl abandoned interpretations of this directedness in terms of operation or activity. He introduced the term 'intentional experience' [*intentionales Erlebnis*] in the *Logical Investigations* in order to avoid the concept of a 'psychic phenomenon', but retained the concept of act, in order to accommodate a use of language which was already deeply rooted. The distinction between act and object is still found in current discussion: for example, when it is asked whether the consciousness of a state is explained by its becoming the object of a higher-order thought (for instance in David Rosenthal's theory of *Higher-Order Thoughts*),[15] or by the fact that it is an act (in the sense of a teleofunctionalistic theory of mind) with the help of which an organism attains knowledge about its surroundings (see Dretske submitted). It also plays an important part in the discussion of higher-order forms of self-consciousness.[16]

(b) State consciousness and system consciousness

It can be said of certain states of an agent that they are conscious, using a one-place predicate. Such states are *phenomenal* states. The logical subject to which properties are attributed here are states of a system, for instance *mental* states, that may or may not need to possess the property of consciousness. David Rosenthal calls this kind of consciousness *state consciousness* or *intransitive consciousness*.

A difficulty arises, when one wishes to apply 'conscious' in the second sense (that is, 'consciousness *of something*' or *transitive consciousness*) to mental states. One can well say that mental states often possess an intentional content and with it help a person relate to objects in the outside world. What cannot be said is that these states *themselves* possess a consciousness 'of something': the states themselves are not epistemic subjects; they do not *know* anything and they do not possess an awareness of the relation of intentionality. Rather, these states are more like aids *with the help of which* persons or systems regarded as a whole attain a 'consciousness of something'; instruments with which they can *realize* the relation to intentionality (again, see Dretske submitted). One must therefore ask what are the semantical rules which govern the application of these two interpretations of the predicate 'conscious' to persons or systems as a whole.

---

[15] See Rosenthal 1986, 1993 and especially Rosenthal 1996 as well as his contribution in Part 6 of this volume.

[16] This is for instance true for those forms of an act–object equivocation dubbed the *banana-peel*-fallacy by William Lycan, which he diagnoses in his criticism of Nagel's concept of an 'objective self' and also in Kripke's essentialist argument against the identity theory.

We also wish to know in which sense one can describe a person, an animal or perhaps even an artificial system, as conscious (*creature consciousness*). The interesting sense of the word, once again, is that of conscious experience rather than of unproblematic concepts like alertness, perceptual awareness or the presence of an orienting reaction. A system possesses phenomenal consciousness if and only if one can ascribe to it conscious states in the first sense. This does not mean, however, that these states will necessarily help in relating to the world in the sense of a realization of the relation of intentionality. A person or system has *intentional* consciousness if and only if it possesses phenomenal states with intentional content. These states are states of the second type, they support the person in building up and maintaining epistemic relations with the world. A simple and natural solution for this case seems to exist in the statement: conscious states are states *through which* we become conscious persons. On the other hand, this analysis does not cover such phenomenal states as do not possess an intentional object or a biological function. For this reason, the four interpretations of 'conscious' sketched here also require a careful analysis of the relationship between intentional and phenomenal content.

(c) The strength of the modal relation between consciousness and its explanatory basis

The task of *empirical* consciousnesss research is to set limits to the explanatory basis for phenomenal consciousness. This may relate to consciousness in general or the basis for instantiating particular phenomenal properties. Besides, such research projects will always be related to a certain class of systems. Such classes of systems may be people, animals or artificial systems. Within such classes it is possible to differentiate even further: human beings, for instance, can be investigated in a dream-state or awake, in different life-phases, or as members of differing cultures. Human beings in altered states of consciousness may be investigated: perhaps those who are afflicted with schizophrenia, 'Multiple Personality Disorder' or certain brain lesions; but also human beings in the state of deep meditation or madly in love. Let us assume, that consciousness — in the sense of a minimal materialism — is supervenient on a certain set of physical properties.[17] It is then possible to ask a multiplicity of questions: are the properties that give rise to phenomenal properties under the conditions of the natural physical laws, only intra- or also extra-organic properties? Are they quantum physical, neurobiological or neurocomputational properties? Are they functional, teleo-functional or representational properties? It is always a matter of describing as accurately as possible the *minimal supervenience basis* of the supervenience relation in question.

[17] For the concept of 'supervenience' see Kim 1993.

The *philosophical* project, in this context, is the closer investigation of the analytical strength of this relation. There is a strong modal intuition (a wide-spread assumption about what would be logically possible), that implies an unconscious *Doppelgänger* for each system (whether described as physical, functional, or representational), which indeed has the same physical, functional or representational properties, but no phenomenal consciousness. Whichever cognitive phenomenon of consciousness is chosen for a closer investigation, the inevitable question always arises whether all this would not also be possible *without* consciousness.[18] Causal explanations and functional analyses of cognitive processes seem to be immune to the property of 'consciousness'. In other words: there does not appear to be a *necessary* connection between phenomenal content and certain forms of its physical realization. In recent discussion, three important arguments have crystallized the philosophical debate surrounding this type of issue:

i. The Modal Argument

For any given system with physical, functional and phenomenal properties, there is always a conceivable *Zombie Twin*, a double without consciousness.[19] One recent formulation of this view states: phenomenal properties, even though they are in our world *naturally* supervenient on physical or functional properties, are by this fact alone not *logically* supervenient on them (cf. Chalmers 1996).

ii. The Absent-Qualia Argument

For any conscious system one can imagine a functionally isomorphic twin-system that does not possess qualia, or is realized in such a bizarre way that the assumption of qualia becomes strongly counter-intuitive. If this is correct, it suggests that functionalism in the philosophy of the mind — which after all still forms the meta-theoretical background of the information-processing approach in cognitive science and in cognitive neuroscience — is systematically blind to the phenomenon of conscious experience.[20]

iii. The Inverted-Qualia Argument

It is also possible to develop a weaker version of this argument. This denies only the necessity of tying certain *kinds* of qualitative content to certain functional states. Thus, one can perhaps assume that one of the readers of this book possesses a systematically inverted colour spectrum in her subjective space, that is, she will always experience yellow, when we experience blue, and green where we experience red, etc. Of course, the person with the

[18] See the opening essay by Peter Bieri in Part 1 of this volume.

[19] See Campbell 1970, Kirk 1974 as well as some of the texts listed in sections 3.2 and 3.8 of the bibliography at the end of this volume.

[20] See Shoemaker 1975, Block & Fodor 1972, Block 1980a, b, the contribution by David Chalmers in Part 5 of this volume and the references listed in section 3.8 of the bibliography.

inverted colour qualia will always *say* that she has an experience of blue, whenever we have an experience of blue. In reality, however, a yellow-quale appears in her conscious space. It is unclear how we could determine the existence of such a situation, but the crucial question is whether it is possible in principle.[21]

2. The epistemic asymmetry

This is the modern name for the most fundamental *epistemological* problem associated with consciousness. There are two fundamentally different methodological approaches that enable us to gather knowledge about consciousness: we can approach it from within and from without; from the first-person perspective and from the third-person perspective. Consciousness seems to distinguish itself by the privileged access that its bearer has to it. This poses the question of who actually possesses the epistemological authority over the facts of consciousness: the experiencing subject, or science that takes hold of the phenomenon from outside?

This epistemic asymmetry has found its expression in the history of ideas in two fundamentally different ways of approaching consciousness. The classic example of a philosophical investigation purely operating from the first-person perspective is René Descartes' approach in the *Meditations* (see also Williams 1978). Toward the end of the last century, this strategy turned into what we now call the *phenomenological* approach. Outside of philosophy it turned into what is often called the *introspectionist* phase of scientific psychology. The phenomenological movement was the first comprehensive attempt to establish the conceptual and epistemological basis for a systematic, autonomous *science of consciousness*. That is its merit. Its failure was mainly due to its reliance on the evidence of inner perception. This proved to be an untenable approach of data collection because it lacks a reliable procedure for eliminating false observations and statistical inconsistencies, especially in the case of conflicting statements.

The alternative strategy is that of a naturalistic objectivism, the attempt to approach the problem of consciousness from without. Here, data collection is exclusively limited to information that is objective and accessible from the outside perspective, for instance, human behaviour. The facts deployed in any explanation of consciousness are thus exclusively *public* facts. The *analytical* behaviourism of Gilbert Ryle (cf. Ryle 1949) corresponded to the psychological behaviourism on the philosophical plane. Ryle had analysed statements concerning mental states as statements concerning possible behaviour. One of the reasons for the failure of this strategy lay in the fact of dispositional analyses not being able to explain the 'processuality' of phenomenal states: when I have conscious

---

[21] See Lycan 1973, Shoemaker 1982, Block 1990, Horgan 1984, Hardin 1996, Nida-Rümelin 1995, the text by David Chalmers in Part 5 and the references listed in section 3.8 of the bibliography.

experiences, then *something happens* in me. Functionalism preserved important insights of this phase by extending its explanatory strategy to the investigation of internal states of systems as a form of 'microbehaviour'.

Both kinds of research programme have become ideologies leading to irrationalism and methodological radicalism, to fear of contact and bouts of silence. With the advent of cognitive psychology and the 'computer model of the mind', the situation changed in an encouraging way. One of the reasons why the current debate is so attractive is that the old front lines between phenomenology and analytical philosophy of mind have disappeared, and the subject of consciousness has been accepted even by the best analytical thinkers as a serious and promising area of theory formation. Even advocates of strictly reductionist approaches admit that a theory of consciousness must be characterized by a maximum of phenomenological plausibility. On the other hand, many authors with a background in phenomenology have now started to discover cognitive science. This gives rise to hope. For what we need are answers to the fundamental epistemological problems that take the first-person perspective seriously and that at the same time integrate our new empirical knowledge in a conceptually plausible way.

In spite of this, for many the first reaction to the epistemic asymmetry will be one of scepticism.[22] Does the essential 'inwardness' of consciousness mean that all attempts to study and understand it in the 'public' arena are bound to fail? Does it entail a class of facts that must a priori remain closed to the methods of the natural sciences? When I have a visual experience of *Pantone Blue 72* for the first time, do I then know something about the world that cannot be known in any other way?

i. The Knowledge Argument

The *Knowledge Argument* is an important focal point of the discussion about phenomenal consciousness from the viewpoint of epistemology.[23] The core of this idea, as developed by Frank Jackson, is the intuition that no knowledge about the neurophysiological or physical facts concerning a person is sufficient to derive the conscious experience of the person. The argument also has an ontological version, suggesting that this implies there are non-physical facts and that, therefore, physicalism must be false. Another way of interpreting our obvious epistemic limitation concerning the consciousness of *other* beings is to see it as an explanatory gap in our general scientific picture of the world.

---

[22] See McGinn 1989 and, from other perspectives, the contributions in Part 2 of this volume.

[23] See Jackson 1982, Nagel 1974, the contributions by Martine Nida-Rümelin, William Lycan and David Papineau published in this volume, as well as the references given in the introduction to Part 4 as well as in section 3.7 of the bibliography.

ii. The Explanatory-Gap Argument

In 1983 Joseph Levine transformed a well-known modal argument against the identity theory by Saul Kripke[24] into an epistemological version. Since nothing in the physical or functional correlates of a phenomenal state helps us to understand why this state subjectively *feels* in a certain way, an intelligibility gap opens up.[25] This is the root of Cartesian intuitions which the modal arguments by Kripke and others attempt to explain at a formal level. Reductive strategies to explain qualia seem to leave a gap in the explanation, in that, strictly speaking, such explanations cannot really be *understood*. They do not seem to tell us, in principle, what we want to know.

3. Demarcation of explananda

All this underlines the fact that consciousness is a *special* problem. In spite of the fundamental epistemological problems, an attempt must also be made to characterize the explanatory concepts that are supposed to be the subject of a theory of consciousness. If there is such a list of concepts, then the way is open for differentiated investigations of the methods and targets necessary to approach this explanatory concept.[26] In this area philosophy need not confine itself to a conceptual commentary on the progress of empirical exploration. Philosophers can play a key role in defining the concepts that every convincing empirical theory must explain. Their detailed knowledge of the problem (which is, after all, many centuries old) qualifies them to intervene, actively and critically, in the construction of theories within individual sciences. The dialogue of philosophy with neuroscience has achieved at least one aim in the last two decades: there is hardly a researcher in the neurosciences who has not yet heard of the problem of 'qualia' — and many are now quick to admit that this is indeed a truly deep problem.

4. Qualia

Qualia are the darlings of philosophers of consciousness. In the philosophy of the mind, qualia are mental states that possess a certain elementary kind of phenomenal content. The subjective quality of *Pantone Blue 72* in colour perception, or of 'painfulness' in an experience of pain, are examples.

[24] See Kripke 1972, 1977. Here, Kripke put forward the argument that psychophysical identity-claims, using rigid designators like 'my conscious experience of type P' and 'my brain-state of type X' on both sides of the equation, had to be false, since identity in this sense is a *necessary* identity which holds across all logically possible worlds. Since we all can *imagine* that we have the mental state in question — e.g. the quale of *Pantone Blue 72* — without being in the respective brain state, this applies, at most, to contingent statements of identity and, therefore, in this sense to *false* statements of identity.

[25] The texts by David Papineau and Robert Kirk in this volume are attempts to contribute to closing this gap.

[26] Robert Van Gulick does this in his contribution to this volume.

Subjective qualities of experience create an inner taxonomy of mental states: they appear to be the *essential features* through which we individuate part of our own mental states by introspection. It is, however, debatable whether such 'private' properties of mental states can ever be connected to the public and objective properties of the underlying physical states. Qualia are problematic because they are:

- Difficult to verbalize. We cannot convey the meaning of *redness* to a person born blind.[27]
- Apparently *private* properties. Only public properties can be accessible to a scientific examination. This point concerns the epistemic asymmetry, as well as the ineffability of qualitative content.
- Possibly the *intrinsic* core of a state. That is, we may not be dealing here with properties that are *relational*, and therefore could be accessed by a relational (e.g. functional) analysis. Arguably, non-relational properties cannot be naturalised reductively: they cannot be traced back to relations between elements on more basic levels of description.
- *Homogeneous,* i.e. 'grainless' or 'ultrasmooth' on the level of subjective experience. Simple phenomenal properties *prima introspectione* do not possess an inner structure. They are, therefore, experienced as indivisible, as phenomenal atoms. This problem is closely connected to the *grain problem.*[28]
- *Transparent* and *present.* They appear to be immediately given to the subject of phenomenal states.

5. Higher-order phenomenal properties and structural characteristics of phenomenal space

The field of conscious experience possesses a complex inner structure. Here are a few examples of particularly succinct properties of this structure:

- *Object formation.* Simple phenomenal properties do not appear in isolation, but as components of integral complexes. This creates the problem of binding and integrating phenomenal properties into a whole. It is, however, quite unclear *exactly* what 'holism' means in this context.
- *Relation-types.* This concerns an important part of what is called 'naive physics'. We require a theory of the types of relations between objects and events that our conscious model of reality knows.

---

[27] Regarding the important problem of the ineffability of phenomenal content, I refer readers to Diana Raffman's contribution in this volume. This paper also contains a very striking example of a particular red; the name of this colour is *Pantone Red 032*. See page 298 below.

[28] See Thomas Metzinger's contribution in Part 7 of this volume.

- *Experience of time*. How does subjective time arise from objective events? What is phenomenal 'simultaneity' and how does the experience of 'succession' arise?

- *Experience of space*. How are spatial relationships between phenomenal objects constituted? What are the embedding relations, which enable us to experience consciously one spatial object as part of a larger object? What is the relationship between the part of the human self-model which is phenomenally represented as having *spatial* properties (body image) and that part, which subjectively possesses only *temporal*, and no longer any spatial properties (conscious thought, 'the thinking subject')?

- *Experience of causality*. Under what conditions do we experience an event as the cause of another event? How does this experience influence our higher cognitive operations?

- *Situatedness*. What does it mean that conscious experience is always embedded in situations and contexts? How does implicit knowledge influence the content of our explicit phenomenal states?

- *Embodiment*. What precisely does it mean that our form of consciousness is almost always integrated into a bodily model of the self?

- *Possible phenomenal worlds*. We are beings who can create in our consciousness 'virtual' worlds of experience, e.g. through fantasy, imagination and planning. What are the neurobiological and evolutionary conditions such that we can imagine some things but not others? How do these natural limitations of our mental imaginative space affect our cognitive operations, e.g. in consciously forming concepts of *logical* possibility or in the grounding of certain theoretical intuitions? If the presence of the phenomenal 'Now' can be shown to be an illusion, is it then correct to say that our conscious model of reality *as a whole* is only a virtual world?

6. *Perspectivalness and phenomenal subjectivity*

Here we meet again the perspectivalness of phenomenal states, this time not as a problem of epistemology, but as a concretely experienced structural property of the phenomenal space. To begin with, an important element of every theory of phenomenal consciousness will always be phenomenal *self*consciousness. Therefore, conscious experience of one's own identity is a potential subject for empirical explanation too. The neural and functional correlates of self-consciousness may be central here, but so may be the extent to which its content is determined by social interactions. What is needed is a comprehensive theory of the phenomenal self. We also need to explain its influence on other forms of phenomenal content. What exactly does it mean to say that our consciousness is a centred consciousness?

A convincing theory about the origin of a 'first-person perspective' might also help to resolve some of the epistemological problems I have mentioned.

7. The Unity of Consciousness

If one looks at the history of the concept of consciousness,[29] then two fundamental semantic elements stand out in many of its theoretical precursors: the *concomitant* (i.e. accompanying) and the *synthesizing* functions of consciousness. These still play a major role in the contemporary discussion. The view of consciousness as an activity that *accompanies* mental states by creating higher-order states is reflected for instance in theories of 'meta-cognition' in cognitive science. In the philosophy of mind, it appears in numerous theories of inner perception and higher-order thought.[30] Similarly, the classic problem of the unity of consciousness — in the sense of a synthesis combining the different contents of consciousness into a holistic entity — appears in the contemporary philosophical discussion as the question of the *integration of phenomenal content* and in the empirical sciences as the *binding problem*.[31]

Our field of consciousness has an undeniable holistic quality. The different forms of phenomenal content that are active in it stand in part–whole relationships to this field. This holism is a higher-order property of consciousness, just like its transparency, perspectivalness and presence. The unity of consciousness is a *highest*-order property of the phenomenal model of reality active at a certain time. This global unity of consciousness seems to be the most general phenomenological characteristic of conscious experience, and is therefore difficult to understand on a conceptual level.

8. Consciousness as the core variant of the mind–body problem

In the post-war discussion, the classic mind–body problem has blossomed with many variants. Here are some of them:

- The *nomological incommensurability* of personal and sub-personal levels of description. It is not possible to give detailed descriptions of causal chains across these levels, since the logical subjects of the per-

[29] Many non-trivial misunderstandings in the ongoing discussion arise precisely because the long history of the concept 'consciousness' is both very extensive and full of semantic complexity. The problem of consciousness is the most persistent obstacle in the way of a scientifically complete picture of the world, largely because it stems from a vast and dense network of roots planted in cultural history. Since lack of space would preclude anything more than an inadequate sketch, I am not attempting in this introduction any historical presentation of the development of the modern concept of consciousness. Comprehensive literary references to the conceptual history of 'consciousness' in philosophy and psychology can be found in Diemer 1971, Grauman 1966, Güzeldere 1995a, 1995b.

[30] See the texts in Part 6 of this volume and the references given in the introduction to that section.

[31] See the contribution by Thomas Metzinger in Part 7 of this volume.

sonal and sub-personal level of description differ. There are therefore no law-like generalisations to be refined, as there are no strict (homonomic) psychophysical laws.

- *Mental universals.* A philosophical theory of mind is most interesting when it explains the nature of certain *types* of mental states. The philosophical project consists in the search for a 'universal psychology'. According to a widely accepted view, however, mental states can be physically *realized* in principle by a wide range of physical states, just as the same computer program can run on different machines (cf. Putnam 1967). So *type physicalism* seems to be false, while *token physicalism* gives no access to mental universals.

- The *liberalism–chauvinism dilemma* of classical functionalism: When we individuate mental states according to their causal role, it appears that the resulting criteria for attributing such states are always either too strict or too liberal. Abstract descriptions of mental states, for instance by program listings or by Turing machines, do not capture the subjective concreteness, temporal dynamics and parallelism of phenomenal states.

- *Mental causation.* Non-reductive forms of materialism such as supervenience theory (just like classical interactionist dualism or epiphenomalism) cannot explain 'downward' causation by mental states. The strong variants of supervenience collapse into a reductionist identity statement, the weak forms of *global* supervenience do not conceptually grasp the fact that conscious experience is a phenomenon bound to individual systems or organisms.

- *Brentano's Problem.* Many mental states possess intentional content. They are directed to a part of the world and contain it in a mysterious sense ('mental inexistence'). It is not easy to explain how this *meaningfulness* or *referentiality* of mental states could be grounded in relations in the physical world.

- *The rationality of the mental.* How can reasons be causes? In order to keep on believing in our own rationality as well as in the rationality of our theories, e.g. concerning the relationship between mind and body, insight into reasons must play a causal role in our behaviour. Can one be a *realist* about the rationality of conscious thought? Do attributions of rationality refer to mental processes, or only to a certain coherence in externally observable patterns of behaviour?

- *Personal identity.* Are there firm criteria by which we can delineate the transtemporal identity of persons? Is there an enduring core-property in the temporal development of such systems to which we wish to attribute the property of *personhood*?

- *Parallelism versus seriality*. What is the relationship of serial cognitive processes with symbolic and propositional content to subsymbolic processes on the 'microcognitive' level of neural information processing?
- *Subjective versus objective time*. How can an *inner time order* arise from individual events on the physical level? What is the relationship between physical and psychological time?
- *Theory-neutral inner experience*. What is the epistemological status of introspection? Is there a kind of knowledge about mental states that is independent of all verbal descriptions and not 'theory-laden'? What are the falsification criteria in the introspective attribution of psychological properties? Does the subject possess an epistemicological authority over the content of its own phenomenal states?

This short list of mind–body problems could easily be extended. One might well differentiate these questions in greater detail, and thus even more exactly.[32] They also suggest that the problem of consciousness is the *core variant* of the mind–body problem. Thomas Nagel, in his classic essay of 1974, pronounced this in a sentence that has been widely quoted:

> Without consciousness the mind–body problem would be much less interesting. With consciousness it seems hopeless (Nagel 1974: 261).

Nagel is right in that a solution to the problem of consciousness would lessen most people's interest in the questions listed above. If there were an empirically, conceptually and above all intuitively convincing theory of how phenomenal consciousness in its full content — that is, our *own* conscious experience — can be part of the natural world, then these questions might suddenly be looked upon by many people as merely technical problems for analytical specialists or brain researchers. On the other hand, a complete and detailed answer to all these questions would leave us unsatisfied, if it did not tell us what *conscious experience* actually is. Conscious experience is almost always what we *really* want to understand. It is not only the intuitive root, but also the theoretical core-variant of the mind–body problem.

9. Developing a comprehensive theory of phenomenal content

Approaching the theoretical core of the problem is not only a matter of isolating individual explananda by describing them in as precise and differentiated a way as possible. It is now also necessary to place such analyses into a systematic general context. What has to be worked out is a general *theory of phenomenal content*, a comprehensive theory of conscious experience.

Such a theory would have to yield a 'mark of the phenomenal', by offering demarcation criteria for the domain of conscious experience. (This

[32] See Metzinger 1985, 1990, 1991.

was Brentano's original problem.) This concerns first and foremost the distinction between conscious and unconscious mental states: what exactly is it that makes a mental state the content of conscious experience? In what way do unconscious mental states influence the structure and the explicit content of phenomenal states? Empirical research has shown that the distinction between 'conscious' and 'unconscious' is not simply all-or-nothing.[33] So a theory of phenomenal content must investigate more accurately what the property of 'phenomenality' actually is. A second important point is the development of criteria concering the ascription of phenomenal states: under what conditions can one assume that a given system has conscious experiences?[34] We need to develop empirically plausible and pragmatically satisfactory criteria for the epistemological *Other-Minds Problem*. It may be that descriptions of phenomenal states with the help of concepts such as 'information', 'representation' or 'content' will soon be given up, perhaps in favour of the terminological apparatus that is offered to us by non-linear dynamics. Until this should happen, every theory of phenomenal content must investigate the relationship of this special form of content with other forms of content. This particularly concerns the intentional and the unconscious content of mental states.

Empirical consciousness research approaches the problem of consciousness at many levels of description. This leads to the question of which level is the most interesting for a philosophical theory of consciousness, allowing maximal conceptual precision. What we may need are mathematical models of the phenomenal ontology of the human brain. Which science offers us the best abstract descriptions of the structure of the phenomenal space and of the dynamics of phenomenal states? Can mathematical models of the neural correlate of consciousness be tied to those theoretical entities which are interesting from a philosophical viewpoint? This question remains open. Should it be shown, for instance, that the structure and dynamics of our consciousness can be plausibly described by a connectionist approach supplemented by principles of temporal coding, then one could call the project of an *objective phenomenology* as formulated by Thomas Nagel, a 'neurocomputational theory of phenomenal states'.

The main difficulty lies in linking the often ill-defined mental categories of folk psychology and classical philosophy of mind to the newly-emerging conceptual apparatus of an empirical psychology (such as that modelled on information processing). The *philosophical* project of a universal theory of mind, however, goes much further: it demands that 'consciousness' should be reconstructed as a *mental universal*. The philosophical dream consists not only in a general, but also in a universal theory of conscious experience. This means that, using hardware- and species-independent criteria of ascription, one

---

[33] See e.g. Kihlstrom 1993.

[34] See Dieter Birnbacher's text on this question at the end of this volume.

develops a theory of consciousness that would answer the question of what makes consciousness *consciousness* in *all* possible systems endowed with that property. Yet it could be that this very project has to be given up in the course of a naturalization of the mind, since the 'bottom-up constraints' necessary for the clarification of the concept may be too strong and so entangle us in an anthropocentrism.

IV. This Volume

This collection of articles offers a cross-section of the current debate, carried out at a high level.[35] I have tried to keep a broad perspective, deliberately including a wider range of topics, and to provide readers with the means to go on and pursue their own interests effectively. The articles are for this reason cast at various levels of abstraction and with differing degrees of interdisciplinarity. All these articles are original, and all mark important forward-looking lines of enquiry in the current debate. They are summarized in short introductions to each of the seven main parts of the book. These introductions also include short selections of recommended reading, which I hope the reader will find useful.

References

Anton, G. (1899). Über die Selbstwahrnehmungen der Herderkrankungen des Gehirns durch den Kranken bei Rindenblindheit und Rindentaubheit. *Archiv für Psychiatrie und Nervenkrankheiten*, **32**, 86–127.
Baars, B.J. (1988). *A Cognitive Theory of Consciousness*. Cambridge: Cambridge University Press.
Benson, D.F. & Greenberg, J.P. (1969). Visual Form Agnosia. *Archives of Neurology*, **20**, 82–9.
Bieri, P. (1981). Einleitung: Selbstbewußtsein, Privatheit und Subjektivität. In P. Bieri (1981; 2. Auflage 1993)[Hrsg.], *Analytische Philosophie des Geistes*. Königstein: Hain.
Block, N. & Fodor, J. (1972). What psychological states are not. In Block 1980.
Block, N. (1980a). Are absent qualia impossible? *Philosophical Review*, **89**, 257–74.
Block, N. (1980b). Troubles with functionalism. In Block 1980.
Block, N. (1990). Inverted earth. *Philosophical Perspectives*, **4**, 53–79.
Block, N., Flanagan, O. & Güzeldere, G. (1996)[eds]. *The Nature of Consciousness*. Cambridge, MA: MIT Press.
Brentano, F. (1973)[1874]. *Psychologie vom empirischen Standpunkt*. Erster Band. Hamburg: Meiner. English edition (1973): *Psychology from an Empirical Standpoint*, (edited by Oskar Kraus, translated by Antos C. Rancurello, D.B. Terrell and Linda L. McAlister), London: Routledge & Kegan Paul.

[35] An excellent compilation of articles from the recent Anglo-Saxon debate can be found in Block *et al.* 1996. The anthology published by Sybille Krämer gives an overview of the present state and main lines of the German discussion; see Krämer 1996. Two important interdisciplinary collections are Marcel & Bisiach 1988 and Davies & Humphreys 1993.

Campbell, K.K. (1970). *Body and Mind.* New York: Doubleday Anchor Books

Chalmers, D.J. (1995). Facing up to the problem of consciousness. *Journal of Consciousness Studies,* **2**, 200–19. Also in Hameroff *et al.* 1996.

Chalmers, D.J. (1996). *The Conscious Mind.* New York: Oxford University Press.

Clark, A. (1992). *Sensory Qualities.* Oxford: Oxford University Press.

Davies, M. & Humphreys, G.(1993)[eds]. *Consciousness: Psychological and Philosophical Essays.* Oxford: Basil Blackwell.

Diemer, A. (1971). Bewußtsein. In J. Ritter (Hrsg.), *Historisches Wörterbuch der Philosophie.* Band 1. Basel und Stuttgart: Schwabe & Co. Verlag.

Dretske, F. (submitted). What good is consciousness?

Flanagan, O. (1992). *Consciousness Reconsidered.* Cambridge, MA: MIT Press.

Flanagan, O. (1995). Deconstructing dreams: The spandrels of sleep. *Journal of Philosophy,* **112**, 5–27. Revised German version: Neurowissenschaft und Träume: Geistestätigkeit und Selbstausdruck im Schlaf. In Metzinger 1995a.

Frank, M. (1991). *Selbstbewußtsein und Selbsterkenntnis.* Stuttgart: Reclam.

Graumann, C-F. (1966). Bewußtsein und Bewußtheit. Probleme und Befunde der psychologischen Bewußtseinsforschung. In W. Metzger & H. Erke (Hrsg.), *Handbuch der Psychologie.* Erster Band, erster Halbband: Wahrnehmung und Bewußtsein. Göttingen: Verlag für Psychologie.

Greenfield, S.A. (1995). *Journey to the Centers of the Mind: Toward A Science of Consciousness.* New York: Freeman.

Güzeldere, G. (1995a). Consciousness: What it is, how to study it, what to learn from its history. *Journal of Consciousness Studies,* **2**, 30–52.

Güzeldere, G. (1995b). Problems of consciousness: Contemporary issues, current debates. *Journal of Consciousness Studies,* **2**, 112–43.

Hameroff, S., Kaszniak, A., & Scott, A. (1996)[eds]. *Toward a Science of Consciousness.* Cambridge, MA: MIT Press.

Hardin, C.L. (1988; expanded edition 1993). *Color for Philosophers.* Indianapolis: Hackett Publishing Company.

Hardin, C.L. (1996). Reinverting the spectrum. In Carrier *et al.* 1996.

Hobson, J.A. & Stickgold, R. (1993).The conscious state paradigm: A neurocognitive approach to waking, sleeping and dreaming. In Gazzaniga 1995.

Hobson, J.A. & Stickgold, R. (1994). Dreaming: A neurocognitive approach. *Consciousness and Cognition,* **3**, 1–15.

Horgan, T. (1984). Functionalism, qualia, and the inverted spectrum. *Philosophy and Phenomenological Research,* **44**, 453–69.

Husserl, E. (1993)[1900]. *Logische Untersuchungen. II/1: Untersuchungen zur Phänomenologie und Theorie der Erkenntnis.* Tübingen: Max Niemeyer.

Jackson, F. (1982). Epiphenomenal qualia. *Philosophical Quarterly,* **32**, 127–36. Reprinted in Lycan 1990 and in Block *et al.* 1996.

Kihlstrom, J.F. (1993). The continuum of consciousness. *Cognition and Consciousness,* **2**, 334–54.

Kim, J. (1993). *Supervenience and Mind.* Cambridge: Cambridge University Press.

Kirk, R. (1974). Zombies vs. materialists. *Aristotelian Society Proceedings,* **Supp. 48**, 135–52.

Kirk, R. (1994). *Raw Feeling: A Philosophical Account of the Essence of Consciousness.* Oxford: Oxford University Press.

Krämer, S. (1996)[ed]. *Bewußtsein. Philosophische Positionen.* Frankfurt am Main: Suhrkamp.

Kripke, S. (1972). Naming and necessity. In D. Davidson & G. Harman (eds), *Semantic of Natural Language.* Dordrecht: D. Reidel.

Kripke, S. (1977). Identity and necessity. Reprinted in S. Schwartz (ed), *Naming, Necessity, and Natural Kinds.* Cornell University Press.

Levine, J. (1983). Materialism and qualia: The explanatory gap. *Pacific Philosophical Quarterly*, **64**, 354–61.

Llinás, R.R. & Paré, D. (1991). Of dreaming and of wakefulness. *Neuroscience*, **44**, 521–35.

Llinás, R.R. & Ribary, U. (1994). Perception as an oneiric-like state modulated by the senses. In C. Koch & J.L. Davis (1994)[eds], *Large-Scale Neuronal Theories of the Brain.* Cambridge, MA: MIT Press.

Lycan, W.G. (1973). Inverted spectrum. *Ratio*, **60**, 315–19.

Lycan, W.L. (1987). *Consciousness.* Cambridge, MA: MIT Press.

Lyons, W. (1986). *The Disappearance of Introspection.* Cambridge, MA: MIT Press.

Malcolm, N. (1988). Subjectivity. *Philosophy*, **63**, 147–60.

Marcel, A. & Bisiach, E. (1988)[eds]. *Consciousness in Contemporary Science.* Oxford: Oxford University Press.

McGinn, C. (1989). Can we solve the mind-body problem? *Mind*, **98**, 349–66.

Metzinger, T. (1985). *Neuere Beiträge zur Diskussion des Leib-Seele-Problems.* Frankfurt/Bern/New York: Peter Lang.

Metzinger, T. (1990). Kritierien für eine Theorie zur Lösung des Leib-Seele-Problems. *Erkenntnis*, **32**, 127–45. Reprinted in *Acta Universitatis Lodziensis, Folia Philosophica*, **8**, 151–68.

Metzinger, T. (1991). Das Leib-Seele-Problem in den achtziger Jahren. *Conceptus*, **64**, 99–114.

Metzinger, T. (1993). *Subjekt und Selbstmodell.* Paderborn: Schöningh.

Metzinger, T. (1995a)[ed]. *Bewußtsein – Beiträge aus der Gegenwartsphilosophie.* Paderborn: Schöningh.

Metzinger, T. (1995b). Perspektivische Fakten? Die Naturalisierung des *View from Nowhere.* In G. Meggle & U. Wessels (eds), *Analyomen 2. Proceedings of the 2nd Conference 'Perspectives in Analytical Philosophy'.* Berlin and New York: de Gruyter.

Nagel, (1979). Subjective and objective. In *Mortal Questions.* Cambridge: Cambridge University Press.

Nagel, T. (1974). What is it like to be a bat? *Philosophical Review*, **83**, 435–50.

Nagel, T. (1980). The limits of objectivity. In Sterling M. McMurrin (ed), *The Tanner Lectures on Human Values 1980.* Vol. I. Salt Lake City: University of Utah Press; Cambridge: Cambridge University Press.

Nagel, T. (1986). *The View from Nowhere.* New York and Oxford: Oxford University Press.

Nida-Rümelin, M. (1995). Pseudonormal vision. An actual case of qualia inversion? *Philosophical Studies*, **Supplement**.

Penfield, W. (1975). *The Mystery of the Mind: A Critical Study of Consciousness and the Human Brain.* Princeton: Princeton University Press.

Penrose, R. (1994). *Shadows of the Mind.* Oxford: Oxford University Press.

Pöppel, E. (1978). *Time perception*. In Autrum, H., Jung, R., Loewenstein, W.R., MacKay, D.M. & Teuber, H-L. (eds), *Handbook of Sensory Physiology. Volume VIII: Perception*. Berlin & New York: Springer.

Pöppel, E. (1988). *Mindworks: Time and Conscious Experience*. New York: Hartcourt Brace Jovanovich.

Putnam, H. (1967). The mental life of some machines. First in H. Castañeda (ed), *Intentionality, Minds, and Perception*. Detroit: Wayne State University Press. Also in Putnam, H. (1975), *Mind, Language and Reality. Philosophical Papers, Volume 2*. Cambridge: Cambridge University Press.

Revonsuo, A. & Salmivalli, C. (1995). A content analysis of bizarre elements in dreaming. *Dreaming*, (forthcoming). Also in Revonsuo 1995b.

Revonsuo, A. (1994). In search of the science of consciousness. In A. Revonsuo & M. Kamppinen (1994)[eds], *Consciousness in Philosophy and Cognitive Neuroscience*. Hillsdale, NJ: Lawrence Erlbaum. Reprinted in Revonsuo 1995b.

Revonsuo, A. (1995a). Consciousness, dreams, and virtual realities. *Philosophical Psychology*, **8**, 35–58. Reprinted in Revonsuo 1995b.

Revonsuo, A. (1995b). *On the Nature of Consciousness: Theoretical and Empirical Explorations*. Turku: Turun Yliopisto.

Rosenthal, D.M. (1986). Two concepts of consciousness. *Philosophical Studies*, **49**, 329–59. Reprinted in Rosenthal 1990.

Rosenthal, D.M. (1993). State consciousness and transitive consciousness. *Consciousness and Cognition*, **2**, 355–63.

Rosenthal, D.M. (1996). A theory of consciousness. In Block *et al.* 1996.

Ryle, G. (1949). *The Concept of Mind*. Hammondsworth: Penguin Books.

Scott, A. (1995). *Stairway to the Mind. The Controversial New Science of Consciousness*. New York & Berlin: Springer.

Shoemaker, S. (1975). Functionalism and qualia. *Philosophical Studies*, **27**, 291–315. Reprinted in Shoemaker 1984.

Shoemaker, S. (1982). The inverted spectrum. *Journal of Philosophy*, **79**, 357–81. Reprinted in Shoemaker 1984.

Van Gulick, R. (1988a). Consciousness, intrinsic intentionality, and self-understanding machines. In Marcel & Bisiach 1988.

Van Gulick, R. (1988b). A functionalist plea for self-consciousness. *Philosophical Review*, **97**, 149–188.

Velmans, M. (in press)[ed]. *The Science of Consciousness: Psychological, Neuropsychological, and Clinical Reviews*. London: Routledge.

Williams, B. (1978). *Descartes — The Project of Pure Inquiry*. Harmondsworth: Penguin Books.

Part One
Conceptual Foundations

Introduction to Part One

To come to grips with consciousness, we first have to understand the concept. Within the philosophical tradition, consciousness *(conscientia)* was often regarded as a type of higher-order knowledge of the mind. On this construal, consciousness is a specific form of inner knowledge which can accompany mental processes, and has a concomitant function. Another important aspect of the classical topos of 'consciousness' was the 'unified vision', according a focal point to the unity of conscious experience *(synaesthesia)*. The modern concept of consciousness *(cogitatio)* constitutes itself in Descartes' work, where the modern form of the mind–body problem is also developed. In the contemporary literature, the semantic elements of earlier theories of consciousness appear in many places and in new forms and variants. However, nowadays the focus of philosophical discussion is formed by the concept of 'phenomenal consciousness'. If one speaks about consciousness in this sense, one means the aspect of *experience*: Today we are interested in consciousness as it appears to us in concrete experience from the first person perspective.

This first part of this book offers a preliminary introduction to the philosophical problems linked to the concept of phenomenal consciousness. The three papers included here critically analyse this concept of consciousness from different angles. This process makes it apparent which difficulties arise if we enrich our traditional concept of consciousness, shaped by folk psychology, by endowing it with a more precise content or by attempting to turn it into an explanandum for scientific research.

As a first step, **Peter Bieri** carefully analyses the concept of consciousness. This analysis shows that the *puzzle* of consciousness arises in precisely those instances in which we are interested in their *experienced* aspect: Conscious states do not simply exist, *they feel a certain way* and in this they are part of the inner perspective of an experiencing subject. Now it is notoriously unclear how one could possibly explain this subjective aspect of experience in physical terms. After Bieri has thus localized the puzzle of consciousness, he offers very illustrative step-by-step definitions. In the course of his discussion, an intuition crystallizes which, in philosophical jargon, one may call a 'modal intuition': A persistent intuition about what seems to be *possible*. However precisely we describe the events within a conscious system — be it on the physical, the neurobiological or the functional level — the following seems always to be conceivable: All of this could happen in exactly the same way *without* any conscious experience at all. This is a line of thought which extends from Gottfried Wilhelm Leibniz via Emil du Bois-Reymond up to the most recent discussion in philosophy of mind. In his text, Peter Bieri uses this line of thought in order to encircle the puzzle of consciousness more closely.

41

Robert Van Gulick then turns to the question of what would count as an explanation of consciousness at all. At first he investigates what could function as an *explanandum*, as the target of such an explanation. For this purpose he isolates the six most important explanatory goals: the difference between conscious and non-conscious mental states, the difference between conscious and non-conscious organisms, qualia, the phenomenal structure of experience (e.g. in a Kantian sense or in the line of phenomenological philosophy), subjectivity and the direct givenness or the 'semantic transparency' of the intentional content of conscious states. In the second part of his essay Van Gulick examines candidates for the role of the *explanans* within a potential research programme 'consciousness'. Should the explanatory basis be formed by physical, functional, natural or non-conscious mental states? In the last part, four different relations between the explanandum and the explanatory basis are discussed. Does an explanation of consciousness have to be logically sufficient, nomically sufficient, or merely intuitively sufficient? Does it perhaps suffice to produce a model of the properties of consciousness we are interested in which allows us to predict these properties in a pragmatically satisfactory manner and possibly to influence them? Van Gulick does not intend to answer these questions; rather he offers a systematic logical map of the many possible questions and interpretations currently found in the discussion of consciousness.

The contribution by **Michael Tye** examines many different concepts of consciousness. At the same time it is an example of the interdisciplinary component which is characteristic of much contemporary work on the subject. At the beginning of his essay, Tye describes a remarkable neuropsychological disorder, unilateral visual neglect. He considers a number of experiments by Marshall and Halligan, and demonstrates how new empirical material can force us to continually differentiate the concept of consciousness and perpetually reconsider it. In his paper, Tye distinguishes between four different types of consciousness: introspective or higher-order '*H*-consciousness', discriminatory '*D*-consciousness', reactive '*R*-consciousness' and qualitative or phenomenal '*P*-consciousness'. In his application of these terms in the interpretation of the further cases described, it becomes apparent that, while the first three concepts of consciousness can be related to each other in an unproblematic way, the greatest explanatory and philosophical problems arise through the concept of phenomenal *P*-consciousness.

Further Reading

Allport, A. (1988). What concept of consciousness? In Marcel & Bisiach 1988.

Bieri, P. (1982). Nominalism and inner experience. *The Monist*, **65**, 68–87.

Bieri, P. (1987). Pain: A case study for the mind-body problem. *Acta Neurochirurgica*, **Suppl. 38**, 157–64.

Block, N. (1994). Consciousness. In S. Guttenplan (ed), *A Companion to Philosophy of Mind*. Oxford: Blackwell.

Block, N., Flanagan, O. & Güzeldere, G. (1996)[eds]. *The Nature of Consciousness*. Cambridge, MA: MIT Press.

Chalmers, D.J. (1995). Facing up to the problem of consciousness. *Journal of Consciousness Studies*, **2**, 200–19. Also in Hameroff *et al.* 1996.

Nelkin, N. (1993). What is consciousness? *Philosophy of Science*, **60**, 419–34.

Tye, M. (1986). The subjective qualities of experience. *Mind*, **95**, 1–17.

Tye, M. (1994). Do pains have representational content? In Casati, Smith & White 1994.

Tye, M. (1995). *Ten Problems of Consciousness*. Cambridge, MA: MIT Press.

Tye, M. (1995). What 'what it's like' is really like. *Analysis*, **55**, 125–6.

Van Gulick, R. (1985). Physicalism and the subjectivity of the mental. *Philosophical Topics*, **12**, 51–70.

Van Gulick, R. (1988). A functionalist plea for self-consciousness. *The Philosophical Review*, **97**, 149–81.

Van Gulick, R. (1989). What difference does consciousness make? *Philosophical Topics*, **17**, 211–30.

Van Gulick, R. (1993). Understanding the phenomenal mind: Are we all just armadillos? In Davies & Humphreys 1993. Also in Block *et al.* 1996.

Van Gulick, R. (1994). Deficit studies and the function of phenomenal consciousness. In G. Graham & G.L. Stephens (eds), *Philosophical Psychopathology*. Cambridge, MA: MIT Press.

Further references to the concept of consciousness can be found in the bibliography at the end of this volume. Works which analyse the conceptual foundations of the problem are listed in sections 1.1, 1.2, 2.1, 2.2, 2.3 and especially in section 3.1, as well as in sections 3.3, 3.4 and 3.5.

Peter Bieri

Why is Consciousness Puzzling?

In his famous lecture of 1872 entitled *Über die Grenzen des Naturerkennens (About the limits of natural knowledge)* Emil du Bois-Reymond, one of the founding fathers of experimental physiology, said this:

> . . . at some point in the evolution of life — a point we do not know and need not try to determine — something new appears, something so far unknown, something . . . incomprehensible. The thread of understanding spun in negatively infinite time is disrupted, and our knowledge of nature reaches a gap to be crossed by no bridge, no wing: We face the limits of our wits. This . . . incomprehensible thing is consciousness. I shall now show very conclusively, as I believe, that consciousness cannot be explained from its material conditions, not only — as everyone will admit — at the present state of our knowledge, but according to the very nature of things. (Du Bois-Reymond 1974: 65, my translation)

And he closed the lecture by the declaration which was to become proverbial: 'Ignorabimus'. More than 120 years later, how far have we got with the puzzle of consciousness? Have we succeeded in refuting Du Bois-Reymond's pessimism?

I. Which Sense of 'Consciousness'?

The word 'consciousness' — which in many languages has no equivalent (Wilkes 1988: 16–41) — does not designate a homogeneous phenomenon. The word is ambiguous, its use is plastic; you have to know the context if you want to know what is meant.[1] In this respect the word 'consciousness'

---

[1] The following differentiation of phenomena and concepts is my own. There are other possible ways of organizing the material. Examples are: Wilkes 1984; Natsoulas 1978; Allport 1988.

behaves like other important words, such as 'life', 'intelligence', or 'understanding'. First, then, we must clarify which of the many phenomena referred to by the same word we are talking about.

Behavioural characteristics

Sometimes when we say of people that they are conscious, we mean they are *awake*. What we have in mind here are behavioural characteristics: they move by themselves, by virtue of *internal drives* and *internal control*; their behaviour responds to externally generated information, the behaviour is thus *discriminative*; it is *coordinated* in the sense that the various behavioural elements form a pattern; furthermore, the behaviour is *adequate* to the situation; and finally, it is *coherent* over time. Behaviour of this sort I shall call *integrated* behaviour.

Consciousness in the sense of the capacity for integrated behaviour does not by itself create a puzzle which seems beyond the limits of our epistemic capacities. To be sure, we are miles away from knowing the true and complete story about the integrated behaviour of human beings and animals. Even if it is clear that the crucial things happen in the brain and nervous system, and even if our knowledge about those systems continues to grow — still, sober-minded experts assure us that nobody has as yet a really good idea about how the brain does its job; and once the working principles will be understood, the gigantic complexity of the processes involved will still make us despair. And yet, when the biological clockwork behind integrated behaviour is at issue, we are not under the impression that understanding is in principle beyond reach. Here we know how to separate right from wrong questions, and we know how to seek answers to the right questions.

Cognitive capacities

Next, to have consciousness can mean that we have available a certain range of *cognitive capacities*. That one is conscious of something then means that one *knows* of it by virtue of such capacities. Often the appropriate word here will be 'aware'. First, the topic may be various forms of knowledge about the external world as illustrated by the following sentences. *Collective* knowledge: 'Consciousness concerning the environment has increased.' *Individual* knowledge: 'He was not aware of the consequences.' *Perception*: 'In the dark I wasn't aware of the fence.' *Memory*: 'I am aware of having said this.' *Attention*: 'Only now did I become aware of the noise; I hadn't noticed it earlier.'

Second, the topic may be knowledge of one's own mental states, i.e. *reflexive* knowledge. In distinguishing among such states according to 'conscious'/'unconscious' we may again make reference to different cognitive capacities. We may want to say that conscious states are those of which we know in an *immediate* way whereas unconscious states are states of which we know by *inference*. Or the distinction may be between mental states which are accessible to *memory* and those which are not thus accessible because, for instance, they did not last long enough or are psychodynamically blocked. Furthermore, we may mean that some mental states are within the focus of *attention* and others not. And finally, we may have in mind the distinction between mental states capable of being *verbalized* and others which are not accessible to articulation.[2]

Needless to say, consciousness in the sense of this range of cognitive capacities is even harder to understand than the biological processes behind integrated behaviour. Among cognitive capacities perception has been under closest scrutiny, and there are subtle models of attention. By comparison, the capacity to remember is badly understood, and the explanatory models for the various forms of reflexive knowledge are still very sketchy. Moreover, the gaps in understanding are particularly large where consciousness is determined by language. For neither is it clear how the contextual knowledge required for linguistic understanding can be represented in a system,[3] nor is there a consensus about the question what semantic content really is and how it can be biologically realized. And yet, consciousness in the cognitive sense today no longer appears intellectually impenetrable. A series of empirical disciplines from cognitive neurobiology to artificial intelligence have made many questions tractable, and functionalism in the philosophy of mind has managed to dispel the impression that matter and cognitive content are alien to each other.[4]

Sensing

Neither integrated behaviour nor cognition presents an insoluble problem. A deep puzzle appears only when we turn to yet another reading of 'consciousness', where consciousness refers to *sensing*. Sensing comprises a variety of things: sensory experiences like seeing colours and hearing sounds; bodily sensations like lust and pain; emotions like fear and hatred; moods like melancholy and serenity; and finally, desires, drives and needs, i.e. our experienced will. All these states are not only *there*; rather, *it is like something* to be in them.[5] They determine what it is like to be a human being. As experiences they have some very specific characteristics. To begin with, they only *exist* as long as they are *conscious* in the sense of being sensed. There is no pain and no fear left once the *sensations* of pain and fear are gone. Secondly, experiences *are* just the way they *appear* to us.

[2] Freud's concepts of the conscious and the unconscious comprise, it seems to me, all four facets. Accordingly, they are ambiguous.

[3] It is, of course, the so-called 'frame-problem' which I have in mind here.

[4] I have in mind accounts like Cummins 1983; Fodor 1987; Van Gulick 1980; 1982; Dretske 1981; 1988; Stampe 1984; Stalnaker 1984.

[5] For this phrase see Farrell 1950 and Nagel 1974.

When a state is *sensed* as pain or fear, it *is* pain or fear. And finally, a state's *being sensed* is different from its *being thought of, believed or judged*. The state's being *sensed* in a certain way is different from its being *taken* to be a certain kind of state.[6]

Consciousness in the sense of sensing is crucial when we experience ourselves as *subjects* of our doings. This experience requires more than control of our movements and more than integrated behaviour as they are exhibited even by a sleepwalker. For a piece of behaviour to be an *action* in the full sense of the term, it must be experienced as *performed by myself*. This involves the experience that I, as its subject, am controlling my body, as it were, from the inside; and this means that my movements are issuing from the relevant pattern of my experiences. It is doubtful whether a being which does not perform its behaviour in this way — because it does not possess an inner perspective — is capable of having a genuine will, genuine motives and genuine goals.[7] In any case, both our moral sentiments and the ascription of responsibility tacitly presuppose consciousness in the sense of experiencing.

II. What Does the Puzzle Consist in?

If there is something incomprehensible about consciousness, it is the capacity for sensing and the experience of being a subject. But what does the puzzle actually consist in? What exactly does it *mean* that — as Du Bois-Reymond said — 'consciousness cannot be explained from its material conditions'? And anyway, why *should* we be able to explain it from those conditions?

If there is to be a difference in sensing between you and me, there has to be a physiological difference between us; and if there is to be a change in your sensing, there has to be a physiological change in you.[8] This notion might be called *the principle of minimal materialism*. Innumerable actions prove our belief in it: we turn our head in order to see something else or to

[6] What I am saying here about experiences is not uncontroversial. See e.g. Pitcher 1970a; 1970b and in particular Dennett 1991. For a defence of unconscious experiences, see Rosenthal 1993.

[7] It may seem that I am just dashing off this remark. True, I do not have the space to elaborate on it here. I just want to indicate that the usual discussion of intentional systems, intentional explanations and intentional states seems unsatisfactory to me as long as it does not bring the idea of acting in closer contact with the idea of an inner perspective. The connection between will and motives on one side and sensing on the other is decribed by Charles Taylor (1985: 45–76, esp. 59–65).

[8] In the discussion of the last decade this idea has been captured by the concept of *supervenience*. In this terminology the fact that there is no difference in sensing without physiological difference is expressed by saying that sensing is supervenient on physiological processes. The concept of supervenience was introduced into this discussion by Donald Davidson (1980). The concept was subsequently elaborated above all by Jaegwon Kim (1993).

hear better; we move out of the shadow when freezing and take aspirin against headache; we drink alcohol to raise our spirits and seek action to calm our rage. The leading notion here has different aspects.[9] To begin with, there is a relation of *covariance* between sensing and physiological processes: they invariably go together. Secondly, there is an asymmetrical relation of *dependence*: sensing depends on physiological processes, not the other way round. And thirdly, there is an asymmetrical relation of *determination*: the physiological processes determine the sensing, not the other way round. Given all of this, we can establish a relation of *explanation* and say that a particular sensing or experience occurs *because* a certain physiological process takes place. Of course, we know as yet only very few of the detailed empirical connections to be uncovered. But suppose we knew them all: why should we not say that we had 'explained consciousness from its material conditions'? What could it be that still remained incomprehensible?

Du Bois-Reymond expressed the puzzle as follows:

> What conceivable connection is there between certain movements of certain atoms in my brain on one side, and on the other the original, undefinable, undeniable facts: 'I feel pain, feel lust; I taste sweetness, smell the scent of roses, hear the sound of organ, see redness' . . . It is entirely and forever incomprehensible why it should make a difference how a set of carbon, hydrogen, nitrogen, oxygen etc. atoms are arranged and move, how they were arranged and moved, how they will be arranged and will move. It is in no way intelligible how consciousness might emerge from their coexistence. (Du Bois-Reymond 1974: 71, my translation.)

III. A Guided Tour Through the Brain

It is easy to be captured by this feeling of puzzlement. However, it is very difficult to spell out its precise content. Let us try to triangulate it by following a fantasy of Leibniz (1714: §17). We are to imagine a human brain enlarged true to scale so that we can walk around in it as in a huge factory. We are taking a guided tour, for we would like to know what is responsible for the fact that the human being, which is equally enlarged and owns the brain, is a subject with experiences and an inner perspective or inner world. The guide, a brain scientist on top of present-day knowledge, has time and is eager to show us everything and to answer all questions. To begin with, he demonstrates the structure of single neurons; next, we learn about the dizzy number of their connections and the variety of synapses; our attention is drawn to the difference in the arrangement and density of the material in various areas; the guide explains the various sorts of neurotransmitters and their effects at the synapses; he comments on the pattern of

[9] It was Jaegwon Kim in 'Supervenience as a Philosophical Concept' (in Kim 1993) who made me see how important it is to distinguish these aspects.

spikes; and finally, he tells us that there are patterns of activity between neural assemblies and that things like synchronisation and dissynchronisation apparently play a crucial role in the overall activity.

'Very impressive,' we tell him, 'but where in all of this is consciousness — the sensing, experiencing subject?' He breaks out in laughter. 'Funny question,' he says. 'The conscious subject, as you call it, is nowhere *in* the factory; it is the factory *as a whole* which is responsible for consciousness.'

We understand. A category mistake. But actually, that was not what we were after. What is really worrying us is this: We can easily imagine that everything in here were just as it is now without the human being — in whose head we are — experiencing even the shadow of a sensing. Nothing in what we have been shown seems to make it *necessary* that there is someone experiencing something: not the kind of material, not the architecture of the factory, not the chemical reactions, not the electrical pattern. In a sense it strikes us as *accidental* that there should emerge an experiencing subject;[10] it is as if it had, so to speak, been pasted on later. And we know that this appearance of contingency is just a symptom of the fact that we have not *understood* the intrinsic connection.[11]

'It's a law of nature,' the guide says, 'that when certain processes occur in here, the human being senses certain things. That's necessarily so; we know that.'

He has not understood our problem. We do not doubt that *there are* such laws and necessities. What we do not understand is *why* they exist. We cannot see what it is that *makes* it necessary that the human being senses something. We can understand *why* one chemical reaction results in another one, *why* the chemical processes at the synapses lead to electrical potentials, etc. The situation is entirely different with sensing and experience: *Why* is one substance relevant for pain and the other one for fear? Why not the other way round? *Why* does this pattern of excitation in the visual cortex make me see red, and not green or blue or yellow?

Sometimes, we ponder, connections appear accidental and thus incomprehensible only because there are *intermediate links* which we do not know. But that cannot be the point here. We might analyse the whole machinery in as much detail as we like, down to the molecules, atoms and even further. All our discoveries would remain on the brain's side, none of them would carry us over to sensing and experiencing. The familiar idea of missing links just does not work.

'What exactly do you want to know?' the guide asks. 'Why a certain process in here results in this *particular* sensing, or why there is experience *altogether*?'

[10] This impression of contingency has been described, among others, by Saul Kripke (1980). Kripke derives from it an argument against materialism.

[11] The connection between the appearance of contingency and the felt lack of understanding has been elaborated on by Joseph Levine (1983).

We explain to him that the two questions amount to one and the same problem: If we knew why a particular neural process results in a particular experiential quality — so that the connection would no longer appear accidental but necessary — we would thereby know why it has to be an *experience*.

It is a familiar fact, we tell ourselves, that a system as a whole has properties which are not exhibited by its parts. Think of the hardness and transparency of diamonds. Might this be the key? Are we confused because, by going around in the neural factory, we see only parts and have lost sight of the whole? Wouldn't we have a similar problem if we walked around in a diamond?

No, we tell ouselves resolutely after a while. Precisely not. We would see the lattice of the carbon atoms, we would know the energetic conditions, etc., and we could figure out that the whole system *must* behave in a certain way, given certain conditions of pressure and light. And the same holds with innumerable other examples: a liquid's surface tension or freezing point, a material's inflammability or light absorption, etc. Here the system's property is derivable and thus made intelligible from its elements, their properties and their arrangement.[12] And in principle the situation is not different with living systems such as plants. For this reason the former puzzle of life and the puzzle of consciousness cannot be compared. What makes consciousness intractable is exactly that here this whole appoach fails. If someone were, for the first time, to build a diamond, he would in the end not be surprised by its hardness and transparency. If someone were, for the first time, to build a plant, he would know in advance that it would breathe and turn towards light. If, however, someone were, for the first time, to build a brain, even he, the designer, would be very surprised at learning that he had thereby created a subject of experience like himself. To put it yet another way: if someone knew only the properties of the material world, however complex, it would not be *foreseeable* for him that given a certain configuration of those properties, experiential qualities and sensing will appear; antecedently, this sort of phenomenon was in no way *imaginable* for him, and in this sense it is totally *new*.[13] Or, at least, that is the way it must appear as long as we have not understood the crucial connection.

Our guide still does not understand why we see here a particular puzzle, and you can tell that our insistence strikes him as bizarre. 'At a certain point all explanations come to an end,' he says, 'and all you can do is to acknowledge that the world is the way it is. Why do bodies attract rather than repel each other?'

[12] About this form of explanation and understanding, see Cummins 1983.

[13] In order to express this aspect of the case, experiential properties have been called *emergent* properties. Thus, the notion of emergence has an epistemic aspect which goes beyond the idea of a systemic property. Cf. Beckermann/Flohr/Kim 1992.

We do not like that remark, but it worries us, and we pause for a moment. Consciousness is a systemic property whereas gravitation is a basic and, furthermore, relational property of all components. Systemic properties are both more in need of explanation and more capable of it than others, since it always appears sensible to ask how they emerge from the components' properties. Still, the above comparison might have a point. Even the laws connecting neural processes with sensings and experiences are, however well identified, just laws which might have been *conceived* of as different but which, as a matter of fact, *are* not different. They are, like the law of gravitation, brute facts. Might it be that it is a question of *habituation* whether a fact like this is felt to be puzzling or not?[14] Are there not innumerable contexts where we actually take the connection in question to be familiar and not puzzling at all — as when, for example, we take an aspirin to relieve us from headache? In other words, does the feeling of puzzlement derive from *alienating* the familiar connection? And is this not as fruitless and artificial as alienating gravitation?

At the risk of repetition we must object to this diagnosis. To begin with, the impression of necessity which can be achieved with other systemic properties just does not arise with experiential properties, and this means: the brute fact to be accepted here is of a different kind compared with the case of other systemic properties. Secondly, the covariances to be described between neural processes and experiences are, even if taken as laws, not embedded in the net of other known laws; they form loose ends — a symptom of a systematic lack of understanding in this whole area. And thirdly, whereas all other laws to which we get accustomed relate perfectly *objective* phenomena, we are here talking about the case where something *subjective* emerges from purely objective factors. By using the words 'subjective' and 'objective' we would not want to create a pseudo-problem, and if this danger is pointed out to us, we are willing to withdraw the troubling words. But there is a substantial point we are not willing to give away: sensing or experiencing *is* something different and new relative to all other systemic properties. And that is why we would like to comment on the above suggestion as follows: of course, nobody is obliged to alienate familiar connections, be it with gravitation or with consciousness. But once alienation has occurred, it cannot, in the case of consciousness, simply be switched off. It is there to stay.[15]

The guide now gives us two huge blueprints. On one of them we can make out, although only schematically, the material architecture of the factory, and it is therefore confusing with its maze of circuits. The other blueprint is easier to read, for large complexes of circuits are combined to form units, and some of these units carry the name of capacities as they define

---

[14] I am grateful to Matthias Müller for making me see how strong this point can be made.

[15] Of course, saying this smacks of begging the question. But I do not know how to avoid it.

consciousness in the sense of cognition. 'This is *the purely functional architecture* of the whole thing,' says the guide, 'it might, of course, be realized in an entirely different material.'

This last remark strikes us as doubtful, for a factory made of an entirely different material with entirely different causal properties would be a *very* different factory.[16] Nonetheless, we start asking ourselves whether we have not been looking in the wrong direction. If what counts in the case of cognitive consciousness is functional architecture, might not the same hold for sensing? Might we understand how an experiential perspective emerges from this factory if we managed to read what we see in the right functional terms, by drawing a third blueprint — more abstract than the first one yet somehow more concrete than the second one?

We reject this notion, too. For we would have the very same impression with any functional architecture imaginable: it might be realized in a system which experienced nothing at all. And correspondingly, instead of the experiential qualities being distributed over the functional net in this particular way, they might be distributed in an entirely different way, either systematically shifted or in no order at all.[17] There is no more intrinsic connection between function and experiential quality than there is between material structure and sensing; or so it seems to us.

'What you see here must not be viewed independently of the rest of the body out there,' the guide says, 'and not independently of the wider environment, either.'

We know. This remark would be the key if our question, as in Leibniz, were how the neural factory makes *thought*, i.e. *cognitive* consciousness, possible. 'Certain processes in the factory,' we might say to Leibniz, 'receive cognitive content first by being nomically connected with external events which get thereby represented, and secondly by contributing to adaptive behaviour on the part of the whole human being. Consider, for instance, the whole area over here: the things happening here all derive from excitations of the optical nerve, and they are thus representations with visual content or visual meaning. Or the corner over here: whatever happens here derives from face recognition, and what you see has the corresponding content, the corresponding meaning. But you can't possibly recognize this cognitive content or this meaning by merely walking around *within* the factory.' (Cf. Dretske 1981; 1988 and Van Gulick 1980; 1982.)

Unfortunately, however, our problem is not cognitive content but experiential content, the content of sensing. And here the crucial question is

---

[16] Functionalism — the position I am here alluding to — often pretends to invoke a perfectly clear distinction when it talks of *function* and its multiple *realizations*. I have always found this surprising. In most versions of functionalism 'function' means 'causal role'. But causal roles derive from a material's causal properties. For this reason, the notion of holding a function stable while varying the material arbitrarily strikes me as obviously incoherent.

[17] For this idea, see Shoemaker 1975.

precisely this: why might the factory not be connected with the rest of the body and its environment in exactly the same way as it is now, thereby acquiring the very same cognitive contents and meanings as now, but without producing any sensing? And so we skip the long way through the rest of the body, for we know: the same sort of questions would recur there as well.

'Incidentally,' the guide asks on the way out, 'what is your field of work?' 'Philosophy,' we answer. 'Oh, I see,' he says and closes the door.

IV. Can the Question be Dropped?

It is time to recall that a puzzle is not the sort of thing which sits somewhere waiting to be addressed by someone. A puzzle is not a part of the world. A phenomenon, a state of affairs is puzzling only against the background of certain expectations regarding explanation and understanding. And these expectations can, like others, be justified or unwarranted. Do we simply expect too much when we think we absolutely ought to understand the way in which the material or functional properties of the brain, or both, make the emergence of sensing necessary? Might we perhaps simply break the habit of asking that question which tends, after all, to assume the monotony of a prayer-wheel? Could we content ourselves with what we have already got, at least in principle — covariance, dependence, determination?

The answer is 'no', and the reason is this: unless we achieve the understanding in question, we do not understand how sensing and experience can be causally efficacious in our behaviour, and this would mean that there is something about being a subject which we do not understand — something about which we care more than about most other things in life.

This linkage of topics may be elaborated in two ways. First: the chain of physiological processes controlling our integrated behaviour is *complete*; there is no gap. In the neurobiological clockwork there is no point where episodes of sensing are required for the mechanism to proceed. It follows that in principle there is a complete causal explanation for our entire integrated behaviour which does not mention any sort of experiential subject. As regards causation and control of our behaviour, consciousness thus seems redundant. It might as well be absent — our trajectory through the world would be exactly the same, down to the smallest movement.[18] If that were true, it would be a pervasive *illusion* that we — as I said earlier — control our behaviour from the inside when it is a doing and not a mere happening. We know what it is like when our behaviour is detached from our sensing; it is the experience of *alienated* behaviour. The fact of completeness in the physiological domain suggests the idea that our *entire*

[18] This is the position of epiphenomenalism. It was steadfastly defended by T.H. Huxley (1904: 199–250). Cf. Bieri 1992.

behaviour might be alienated in this way. It would be an alienation unnoticed by us, the victims of the illusion; but that would not make it any less real.

Of course, we refuse to believe a thing like that. We cannot afford to be serene about it: too much of our self-image would be shaken. But refusal is not enough; we want to *show* that we are masters of our doing in the sense that it causally flows from our experience. For this it does not suffice — that is important — to point to the relations of covariance, dependence and determination between sensing and neural processes. For all of these relations would equally hold even if sensing were causally irrelevant. And here, finally, is the connection with Du Bois-Reymond's puzzle: we could prove the causal power of consciousness only if we succeeded in making intelligible its intrinsic connection with the physiological domain. If we could somehow derive experiential qualities from biological properties, we could then derive the causal role of the former from the causal role of the latter. That is how we do it with systemic properties. But this is precisely the model which does not work.

The second point is this: when we start a causal explanation for a piece of behaviour by citing a physiological process, we know in principle how to *continue* this explanation. We know what it is to specify the causal chain and to point out its fine-grained links, thereby elucidating the *modus operandi* of the cause. The situation is different when the explanation starts by citing an experience: how do you specify the *modus operandi* of your pain, your fear or your grief? You have to switch to the physiological level. But then you have changed the topic and might just as well have begun physiologically. It would not be a change of topic only if the experiences and the sensing could be derived from the biochemical processes to the extent that you might say: by talking about those processes we are, in a sense, still talking about sensing.

Well, then: asking Du Bois-Reymond's question is not something we can give up like a bad habit. As long as we do not know the answer, there is something very basic about being a subject which we have not understood. In other words, the question is interwoven with a lot of other things of interest to us. Thus, it is not — as our guide in the factory seemed to think — an idle metaphysical question such as, 'Why is there anything at all rather than nothing?'

V. Where is the Mistake?

The fact that our question appears unanswerable raises the suspicion that we are making a fundamental mistake. If it is not unjustified epistemic expectations which are responsible, it might be the sort of description we have given of sensing and experience. Its decisive feature was the idea that with experiences there is no difference between appearance and reality — that

an experience reveals its nature to us by being sensed or felt in a certain
way. It does then make no sense to suppose that there is, beyond the quality
felt, something more to *discover* about the nature of the experience. But
making intelligible an experience from its material conditions would mean
precisely making further discoveries about its nature. Might it be, then, that
a wrong description of sensing or, rather, a wrong commentary, *a priori*
spoils the understanding we are seeking?

But consider: what could it mean to say that when overcome by panic or
groaning with pain we do not yet know the true nature of the sensations and
have as yet to uncover it? That sounds odd since it cannot possibly mean:
advancing to something which is not an experience. We are familiar with
gradually becoming clearer about the content of an experience such as
jealousy, or disappointment, or rage. But this cannot be what is meant.

Perhaps we have missed the point, and the mistake consists in a different
though related assumption: that experiential qualities are *simple*, having no
internal structure whatsoever. The diagnosis might then go like this:
uncovering the connection between X and Y involves a growth of knowledge about the internal structure of the two phenomena, as in the case of
chemical reactions. Thus, if you believe of one of the relata that it does not
have an internal structure, you must not be surprised that you fail to find an
explanatory relationship between the two.

This diagnosis might be supported by reference to neuropsychological
deficiencies. They can sometimes be understood as showing a hidden
complexity behind a seemingly simple, homogeneous experience, as when,
for example, the body schema is deficient or certain aspects of pain experience are strangely dissociated. The appearance of simplicity is, so to speak,
merely the user surface.[19] But there are two objections which quickly come
to mind. First, there is in the normal case the *experience* of simplicity and
homogeneity, and that experience is, although described as mere appearance, as real as any other user surface, thus raising the old question once
again. Secondly, the components to be discovered in the pathological case
have themselves an experiential content. In other words, hidden experiential complexity does not provide an explanatory path to physiological
complexity and back.

Or might it be that what seems intractable actually are not *experiences* at
all, but just *beliefs*?[20] Might the apparent experiences in the end turn out to
be no more than ideological constructs? This may perhaps be said about
very complex emotions involving a lot of self-image, and you may say it
when talking about the unity of the self or the person which is largely

---

[19] This idea is illustrated by Dennett's analyses in Dennett 1978: 190–220.

[20] Cf. Dennett 1991, passim. In addition, Dennett 1982; 1978: 129–49, 174–89.

fictional. But if someone were to say this about sensory experiences — pain, lust, panic or disappointment — it would make me speechless.[21]

Similar intuitive resistance would be felt against an attempt at resolving our puzzle by dissolving experiential content into cognitive content, thereby removing the entire distinction between cognitive consciousness and sensing. It has been observed that many features of sensing and experiencing have to do with a system's using a *self-model* to keep an update on its overall state.[22] I am not sure about sensory experience, but the suggestion is convincing regarding bodily sensations, emotions and the experienced will. Self-models, it seems, no longer raise deep puzzles. But this fact would help only if we could unconditionally say that sensing just *is* self-modelling and self-representing. And you will not be surprised at hearing me tell the same old story: given that there are innumerable feedback mechanisms in any organism, why could there not be a self-model, or any number of such models, without a trace of sensing and experience?

VI. Should We Blame Our Cognitive Limitation?

Du Bois-Reymond thought that consciousness will forever be incomprehensible for us. This is the hypothesis that, with regard to this phenomenon, we are in principle subject to a *cognitive limitation*. What could such a limitation consist in? We are obviously limited regarding our capacity for sensory discrimination. But that cannot be the point: the problem is not that we do not *see* the things in the neural factory clearly enough. The limitation might, secondly, consists in our incapacity to develop the *concepts* adequate to the topic. And thirdly, the incapability might consist in the fact that we do not find the right conception of *explanation* and *understanding*. For a being without such cognitive limitations there could very well be a solution to our puzzle. Actually, an even better description of the situation would be: for a being of this kind *there never would have been* a puzzle.

The hypothesis might be that the incapacities mentioned prevent us from finding out *what it is about the brain* that is responsible for sensing. We have considered: its material, its material architecture, its functional architecture on different levels of analysis. We have tried both an atomistic and a holistic approach, and finally we have not forgotten the larger causal context in which the brain is embedded. The hypothesis in question would say that it is yet *something entirely different* which is crucial (cf. McGinn 1991). To this our reaction is: there is nothing else *conceivable*. But this, of course, just is the hypothesis: that we cannot conceive of anything else. This

---

[21] A thesis like Dennett's about the essentially narrative character of experiences arises, I think, if the question of how we *know* about our experiences is not distinguished from the question of what they *consists* in. Cf. Block 1993; 1994.

[22] This idea has been sketched by Robert Van Gulick (1983). The point is elaborated in Metzinger 1993.

hypothesis cannot be refuted; that is how it is built. But there is something to discredit it, namely the fact that unless the topic is sensing and experience we are, with respect to the brain, doing pretty well with our explanatory patterns despite all the as yet unsettled questions. We can break down mechanisms, foresee processes, exert influence. Now it would, conversely, be unintelligible that we succeeded in all of this if a whole category of facts about the brain were systematically out of reach for us. For it would sound very odd indeed to claim that the neural facts relevant to sensing have nothing to do with the facts relevant to the rest of neural functioning.

The hypothesis of a cognitive limitation might, secondly, say that the incapacities mentioned earlier prevent us from understanding *why it is sensing and experience* that emerge from the relevant neural processes. In this case the limitation would mainly concern the notions of explaining and understanding available to us. We have considered causal understanding, structural understanding, functional understanding, understanding the whole from its parts. It was invariably a question of understanding the necessity involved in the covariance, dependence and determination in which we as minimal materialists believe. The hypothesis in question would claim that by virtue of being confined to our limited repertoire of understanding we are incapable of asking the right questions and of mobilizing the right sort of reasoning. At times this strikes me as just the right diagnosis; for there is something about the puzzle of consciousness which does not hold for other puzzles: we have no idea about what would *count* as a solution and understanding. When it is television or hereditary transmission or, indeed, neural functioning which strikes us as puzzling, we have an overall idea of what we would *accept* as a satisfactory explanation. In the case of consciousness, it seems, that is not so. And yet I find it hard to hold on to the idea of blaming the puzzle on a cognitive limitation, and for two reasons. First, explaining, probing into things and understanding always involve discovering a particular sort of *relations*. The hypothesis in question would thus amount to the claim that there is in the world a category of relations forever unknown to us. To be sure, this claim, too, cannot positively be refuted. But it would certainly be odd if our topic were to involve a category of hidden relations which are absent everywhere else or which, at least, do not seem to prevent understanding in other areas. One is tempted to say: this thought is incoherent, i.e. it is not a thought at all. The second reason: if there existed a being acquainted with the decisive sort of understanding, it could not *demonstrate* it to us because we could not *recognize* it. That does not make the hypothesis false; but it makes it so totally abstract that it strikes us as perfectly empty — so empty, in fact, that you feel like simply closing the book.

These doubts regarding the idea of blaming the puzzle on cognitive limitations do not prove that Du Bois-Reymond will one day be refuted. But they show that someone who supports the idea ought not to be too sure that he is making a substantial claim. And they provide a reason to continue the search, which should be a search for new concepts, new models and analogies, and above all for new insights into sources of error. I have not solved the puzzle of consciousness. Of course not. But I hope the reader now understands better what it consists in and what role it plays in our thinking about the world and about ourselves. That would be a lot. And more was, after all, not promised by the title.

References

Allport, A. (1988). What concept of consciousness? In Marcel & Bisiach 1988.
Beckermann, A., Flohr, H. & Kim, J. (1992)[eds]. *Emergence or Reduction? Essays on the Prospects of Non-reductive Physicalism*. Berlin: de Gruyter.
Bieri, P. (1992). Trying out epiphenomenalism. *Erkenntnis*, **36**, 283–309.
Block, N. (1993). Review of D. Dennett, Consciousness Explained. *The Journal of Philosophy*, **90**, 181–93.
Block, N. (1995). On a confusion about a function of consciousness. *Behavioral and Brain Sciences*, **18**, 227–47.
Cummins, R. (1983). *The Nature of Psychological Explanation*. Cambridge, MA: MIT Press.
Davidson, D. (1980). *Essays on Actions and Events*. Oxford: Oxford Universtity Press.
Davies, M. & Humphreys, G.W. (1993)[eds]. *Consciousness*. Oxford: Blackwell.
Dennett, D.C. (1978). *Brainstorms*. Hassocks: Harvester Press.
Dennett, D.C. (1991). *Consciousness Explained*. Boston, MA: Little, Brown & Co.
Dretske, F.I. (1981). *Knowledge and the Flow of Information*. Oxford: Blackwell.
Dretske, F.I. (1988). *Explaining Behavior*. Cambridge, MA: MIT Press.
Du Bois-Reymond, E. (1974). *Vorträge über Philosophie und Gesellschaft*. Hamburg: Meiner.
Farrell, B.A. (1950). Experience. *Mind*, **59**, 170–98.
Fodor, J.A. (1987). *Psychosemantics*. Cambridge, MA: MIT Press.
Huxley, T.H. (1904). *Collected Essays, Vol.I*. London:
Kim, J. (1993). *Supervenience and Mind*. Cambridge: Cambridge University Press.
Kripke, S. (1980). *Naming and Necessity*. Oxford: Blackwell.
Leibniz, G.W. (1714). *Monadologie*. Hamburg: Meiner.
Levine, J. (1983) Materialism and qualia: the explanatory gap. *Pacific Philosophical Quarterly*, **64**, 354–61.
Marcel, A. & Bisiach, E. (1988)[eds]. *Consciousness in Contemporary Science*. Oxford: Oxford Universtity Press.
McGinn, C. (1991). *The Problem of Consciousness*. Oxford: Blackwell.
Metzinger, T. (1993). *Subjekt und Selbstmodell*. Paderborn: Schöningh.
Nagel, T. (1974). What is it like to be a bat? *The Philosophical Review*, **83**, 435–50.
Natsoulas, T. (1978) Consciousness. *American Psychologist*, **33**, 906–14.
Pitcher, G. (1970a). The awfulness of pain. *Journal of Philosophy*, **67**, 481–92.
Pitcher, G. (1970b). Pain perception. *Philosophical Review*, **79**, 368–93.
Rosenthal, D. (1993). Thinking that one thinks. In Davies & Humphreys 1993.
Shoemaker, S. (1975). Functionalism and qualia. *Philosophical Studies*, **27**, 291–315.

Stalnaker, R. (1984). *Inquiry*. Cambridge, MA: MIT Press.

Stampe, D. (1984). Towards a causal theory of linguistic representation. *Midwest Studies in Philosophy*, **2**, 42–63.

Taylor, C. (1985). *Human Agency and Language: Philosophical Papers 1.* Cambridge: Cambridge University Press.

Van Gulick, R. (1980). Functionalism, information and content. *Nature and System*, **2**, 139–62.

Van Gulick, R. (1982). Mental representation — a functionalist view. *Pacific Philosophical Quarterly*, **63**, 3–20.

Van Gulick, R. (1983). What difference does consciousness make? *Philosophical Topics*, **17**, 211–30.

Wilkes, K. (1984). Is consciousness important? *British Journal for the Philosophy of Science*, **35**, 223–43.

Wilkes, K. (1988). —, yìshì, duh, um, and consciousness. In Marcel & Bisiach 1988.

Robert Van Gulick

What Would Count as Explaining Consciousness?

Consciousness has again become a hot topic in the philosophy of mind as shown by the recent spate of books about it (Lycan 1987; McGinn 1991; Dennett 1991; Flanagan 1992; Searle 1992). Various theories have been put forward, each of which alleges to fully or at least partially explain what consciousness is and how it fits into our overall picture of the world (Lycan 1987; Rosenthal 1986; Dennett1991; Searle 1992). In contrast, other philosophers have argued that consciousness is systematcally resistant to explanation in one or another important respect (Nagel 1974; Levine 1983; McGinn 1991). Although the dispute between these two competing groups — the optimists and the pessimists — has involved strongly expressed opinions it has also suffered from a fair amount of confusion regarding just what is at issue. Before one can decide how good our prospects are for explaining consciousness we need to be clearer about what would count as doing so. In this paper I propose to do just that; my aim is not to resolve the dispute(s), but just to untangle and clarify the various distinct issues which sometimes get run together in the heat of controversy.

The question of whether we can explain or understand consciousness is systematically ambiguous in three main respects, and to make it more precise we need to be specific about each of the relevant parameters.

A. What is the *explandum*, i.e. what features or aspects of consciousness do we wish to explain or understand?

B. What can go in the *explanans*? That is, in what terms or within what conceptual framework (e.g. physical, functional, naturalistic) must we construct our explanation?

C. What *relation* must hold between the explanadum and the explanans to count as giving a satisfactory expalanation?

Given these parameters we find that the question of understanding consciousness is not just one question but a large family of interrelated questions, which may have quite different prospects for successful resolution. In what follows I will consider some of the main variants, though I will not try to be fully comprehensive nor cover every possible interpretation of the question; there are just too many readings one might give it. Nonetheless if we can clearly state the leading variants, we will have made a lot of progress in clarifying the dispute.

A. The Explananda

Let us begin with the first parameter; what features or properties of consciousness are in need of explanation?

A1

At a minimum we need to explain **the difference between conscious mental states and nonconscious or unconscious mental states or processes**. In so far as it is possible to have unconscious beliefs, desires, and perceptions or engage in the drawing of unconscious inferences, we need to understand how such states or processes differ from others that are of the same type but conscious. Moreover, there may be some mental states that are of types that can never become conscious, e.g. the knowledge or 'cognizing' states postulated by a Chomskyean theory of linguistic competence. Such states are alleged to be genuinely mental (*pace* Searle 1992) though they are in principle inaccessible to consciousness. A common and appealing move is to define the notion of a conscious mental state as a mental state *of which we are conscious*. For example David Rosenthal (1986) analyses a conscious mental state (e.g. a conscious desire) as a first order mental state which is accompanied by a second order thought to the effect that one is in the first order state (i.e. I desire x and have the simultaneous thought that I desire x). There are problems with the proposed analysis, but for present purpose it should suffice to illustrate the relevant explanandum: the need to distinguish between conscious and unconscious mental states.

A2

We must also **explain the distinction between conscious and nonconscious or unconscious creatures**. You are clearly conscious while you are reading this page, and I was surely conscious when I wrote it, but most of us spend a good part of each night being unconscious, and some unfortunate individuals fall into comas from which they never reemerge as conscious. Some nonhuman animals such as mammals and birds strike us as clearly conscious creatures, but about others, such as snails or honey bees, we feel much less certain. But just what are we asking when we ask whether or not fish are ever conscious? Surely not whether they use their sensory organs to perceive the world around them and respond appropriately. There is no doubt that they do that. Perhaps one could explicate creature consciousness in terms of conscious states as follows: a creature is conscious at a particular time only if it has at least some conscious mental states at that time, and a type of creature counts among the conscious types only if it is conscious at least some of the time. But this will be problematic if we accept a higher order thought account of states consciousness: counting fish as non-conscious unless they can have thoughts about their own mental states seems to set too high a standard for qualifying as a conscious creature. Nonetheless the need to find some way to draw the distinction provides another explanandum.

In trying to isolate the deeply problematic nature of consciousness, philosophers often refer to the subjective, qualitative, or phenomenal aspects of conscious experience. All three terms are directed at those features that in Thomas Nagel's phrase make it the case that 'there's something that it's like to be' a conscious thing, i.e. something that it's like 'from the inside' or 'for the creature itself' (Nagel 1974). Although the three terms are sometimes used interchangeably, they in fact refer to distinct though interrelated dimensions of consciousness. Each of the terms is itself ambiguous and open to multiple interpretations, but in each case we can legitimately isolate a central or core use that picks out a specific feature of consciousness in need of explanation, thus providing us with three more explananda.

A3

Qualia and the qualitative nature of conscious experience are often invoked by sceptics about the explanatory value of one or another theory of consciousness, which they charge with failing to provide an adequate account of the raw feels of experience, the redness of experienced red or the experienced taste of a ripe mango; pains do not merely 'signal' or 'represent' the occurrence of bodily harm: they *hurt*, and any theory of consciousness that fails to explain such felt aspects of our mental life will be incomplete. The alleged explanatory lapse may concern only specific qualia, or the general issue of how there can be any such properties at all. 'Inverted qualia' arguments purport to show the former and 'absent qualia' arguments the latter (Block 1978). Thus understanding consciousness requires us to understand its qualitative aspect. If there really are qualia, we will have to understand what sorts of things or properties they are; how something can come to have them; and what makes it the case that a specific mental state involves the specific quale that it does. Even if, following some recent philosophers, we conclude that there are no such things as qualia

(Dennett 1988; 1991), we will still have to explain why it seems that there are, as well as explaining what — if anything — the qualitative aspect of experience does involve and how it fits within our overall understanding of consciousness.

A4

The term 'phenomenal' is sometimes used interchangeably with 'qualitative' in talking about consciousness; 'the problem of phenomenal properties' becomes just another name for the difficulty we encounter in trying to explain raw feels, the hurtfulness of pain or the experienced fragrance of a gardenia. This is a legitimate use of the term, but I prefer to reserve 'phenomenal' for a more comprehensive range of features. Current philosophical debate has focused heavily on raw feels, but they are just one aspect of our experienced inner life and thus only part of what we must deal with if we aim to describe **the phenomenal structure of experience**. In this sense the use of 'phenomenal' accords better with its historical use by Kant and later by the phenomenologists. The order and connectedness that we find within experience, its conceptual organization, its temporal structure, its emotive tones and moods, and the fact that our experience is that of a (more or less) unifed self set over against an objective world are just a few of features other than raw feels that properly fall within the bounds of the phenomenal. All will need to be addressed if we take the phenomenal aspect as our explanandum.

A5

The third member of our triad, the term 'subjectivity', also varies in use with regard to consciousness. Some philosophers use it to mean just that experience has a first person aspect over and above whatever objective or third person properties it many have. In that sense, it involves little or nothing that is not already captured by 'qualitative' and 'phenomenal'. However, there is a distinctively epistemic use of the term that merits separate and special attention. It is in this sense that some (Nagel 1974; Jackson 1982 and McGinn 1991) have argued that facts about the experiential aspect of consciousness can only be known or even understood by agents who themselves are capable of having the relevant sorts of experiences — a view with a long empiricist pedigree. Such facts, Nagel argues, are bound up with a particular (type of) point of view, where (types of) points of view are individuated on the basis of the sorts of qualitative or phenomenal properties that can be experienced by the relevant sort of conscious agent. It is in this empathetic sense that humans supposedly can not fully understand what it would be like to be a bat because we are incapable of having echolocatory experiences like those had by bats. Whether or to what extent this is true is controversial, but 'subjective' used in this way differs enough from both 'qualitative' and 'phenomenal' to provide a distinct explanandum.

A6

A final feature of consciousness that we need to address is the extent to which the intentional or representational content of our conscious mental states is immediately available or accessible to us, a feature that I have elsewhere referred to as the semantic transparency of consciousness (Van Gulick 1988a; 1988b). When we have a conscious thought or experience we typically know on the whole what that thought or experience is about, what state affairs it represents. I believe it is in large part this feature of our conscious mental life that leads John Searle to distinguish between what he calls the intrinsic intentionality of conscious mental states in contrast with the merely metaphoric intentionality he attributes to computers. He treats conscious mental states as intrinsically intentional because they have meaning or content *for* the person or creature whose states they are. In contrast the computer's states have content only from the perspective of some external interpreter of its actions; their meaning is not to any degree transparent to the computer itself — or so at least Searle claims. Though I am not inclined to draw the distinction as Searle does, I do believe that his notion of intrinsic intentionality and what I call semantic transparency are two attempts to get at a real and important property of consciousness that must be explained by a comprehensive theory of consciousness.

B. The Explanans

Although these six clearly do not exhaust the list of possible explananda, they do capture the main features of consciousness that have been at issue in the recent philosophic literature. We can thus turn to the second parameter and consider various restrictions on what can appear in our explanans. We get quite different interpretations of our original question depending on how we limit the range of terms, concepts or processes that can figure in our explanation of consciousness. There are at least five main variants. Although they are not mutually exclusive, and indeed in some cases clearly overlap, it is worth regarding each of the five as delimiting a distinct if not wholly separate explanatory domain.

B1

The first and perhaps most common variant involves limiting the explanans to the **physical or material**. The two are not quite the same since the material concerns only the properties of matter and there is more to physics than matter and its properties, but in philosophic discussion it is common to use the two interchangeably and I will not make much of the difference. Put in these terms the problem of consciousness becomes just a specific if perhaps particularly intractable case of the mind–body problem: 'Can we understand or explain the relevant aspect of consciousness in purely physical or material terms?' As we shall see when we turn to our third parameter this question is itself open to many readings depending on how we unpack the requisite notion of explanation.

Moreover there are unclarities in the very notion of the physical itself. Just what counts as a physical property or relation? One could treat as physical any property that applies to physical things, but doing so would threaten to trivialize the mind–body problem. For example any form of dual aspect theory or even property dualism that allowed brains to have both mental and physical properties would collapse into physicalism; there would be no way to assert that brains could have properties that were not physical properties. One would still be able to distinguish physicalism from substance dualism, but in so far as we wish to do more than that we need a way to delimit the set of physical properties more narrowly than as those that apply to physical or material objects. On the other hand if we turn only to the set of properties that are explicitly referred to or quantified over in current physical theory we face at least two other problems.

First there are many properties that we regard as uncontroversially physical that nonetheless fail to find a place in physical theory proper either because they are higherorder properties of organized physical systems — the properties of being a cornea or a magnitude 7.0 earthquake are physical in this sense but neither is invoked by physicists in their theories Thus we need to extend the range of the physical to cover properties that in some way depend upon or are constituted by underlying physical properties, but just what sort of dependence is required is open to debate.

B2

Rather than restricting our explanans to the physical we might instead restrict it to **functional relations**. Functionalism is the general view that mental states and processes can be characterized and explained in functional terms; what makes something an instance of a given mental state type, such as a belief that interest rates will rise or a desire for a hot cup of freshly brewed coffee is the functional role it plays within the functionally characterized organization of some person, organism or system.

Though functionalism has come under a lot of critical attack it probably still remains the closest thing there is to a mainline view in the contemporary philosophy of mind. Indeed I think many of the alleged refutations of functionalism, e.g. those based on the social nature of mental categories (Baker 1985), are best interpreted as disputes between rival versions of functionalism rather than as attacks on the position *per se*. It's just more exciting to present them as general refutations of functionalism. However, the very fact that functionalism admits of so many interpretations means that it's far from clear just what a commitment to functional explanation involves. It is sometimes said that functional states of a system are to be type-individuated on the basis of their relations to their inputs, their outputs and each other. But then questions immediately arise about what is to count as an input or an output and in what terms are they to be specified or characterized, as well as questions about the nature and range of interstate relations to which one may appeal. In a very simple and restrictive formulation, inputs must consist of externally observable stimuli, outputs are restricted to macroscopic behaviors described in some neutral vocabulary (e.g. as physical movements) and the range of interstate relations includes only basic relations of causation or inhibition among states or groups of states. The fact that many mental states could not be captured within such a narrow framework would not show that they could not be characterized using a more liberal concept of functional role. The same can be said of theories that unpack the notion of functional role in terms of highly abstract computational states, whose realization requires only some form of mapping from the computational states to physical states that preserves formal relations of joint realization and succession. In contrast with such highly abstract forms of functionalism, one could alternatively characterize inputs, outputs and interstates relations in ways that involve significant limits on the range of physical realizations. As numerous authors have noted (Kalke 1969; Lycan 1987), the functional–structural division has no absolute boundaries, and the there is no context-free answer to questions about whether such properties as being a neuron or being a positively selfsustaining neural loop are functional properties or underlying structural properties. They can be classed as either depending upon the particular explanatory project one is engaged in. A similar relativism affects the distinction between *what* role a state plays and *how* it plays that role; it is sometimes said the functional description is concerned with the 'what' while questions about the 'how' are matters about underlying realization or structure. But the what–how distinction collapses as soon as one tries to put any theoretical weight on it.

One further and important issue is whether or not the notion of function is interpreted teleologically. To say that a given state has the teleological role of doing x, is not merely to say that it does x and that by doing so it plays a certain causal role to the operation of the overall system. If one states that the teleological function of the three part bovine stomach is to digest cellulose or that the function of the Dolby circuit on a tape player is to reduce hiss, one is saying more than that they do those things within the operation of their respective systems. The teleological claim implies that in doing so they are doing what they are *supposed* to be doing. However there is no clear consensus about how to unpack that further element. Some take it to concern the structure's origin (Wright 1974) and how its doing x

figured in the selection or design process that lead to its present existence
(it's because the lineage of ancestral bovine stomach structures aided in
digesting cellulose that they were selected for by evolution). Others
interpret it as more a matter of how its doing *x* contributes to the well being
or *proper* operation of the system of which it is a part (Nagel 1976).
Given these many readings of 'functional', claims about which aspects of
consciousness can be explained in functional terms are highly indeterminate. Thus it's surprising that confident claims are made about features of
consciousness not being open to functional explanation. Can one really say
that functional explanations are always vulnerable to inverted or absent
qualia objections given the range of possible ways in which one might read
'functional'? I think not.

B3

A third option would be to restrict our explanans to **naturalistic concepts**.
There has been a lot of recent philosophic controversy about whether and
how one might give a naturalistic account of intentional content — with
covariance theories, causal theories and functional role theories among the
leading contenders. Similar concerns extend as well to consciousness.
However, the conceptual boundaries of the naturalistic are even more
obscure than those of the physical and the functional. In part naturalism
inherits its vagueness from those first two domains. Physical and functional
relations (at least those that don't involve any suspect and unexplained
element of teleology) count as naturalistic, and in so far as their borders
remain unclear the domain of what's naturalstically acceptable in also left
uncertain. However, the naturalistic is generally taken to include more than
the physical and the functional; biological concepts, neurophysiological
properties, historical factors, and more or less any concepts used in any of
the nonmentalistic natural sciences might qualify as naturalistic. Indeed one
might ask, 'What if anything is left out?' The intent seems to be on one hand
to exclude explicitly mental properties such as intentionality and subjectivity, and the other hand to exclude dualistic, supernatural and magical
factors or relations. In the last respect there is a specifc intent to rule out
theories that appeal to unexplained basic corelations between material
properties and mental ones. For example, as McGinn (1991) has noted, any
theory asserting that a given neurophysiological property just causes
conscious episodes without further elaboration would be dismissed as
'magical', on a par with turning water into wine. But this really moves us
into issues better dealt with later in section C.

B4

A fourth and final option concerns a less radical but still substantial
explanatory project: that of trying to explain consciousness in terms of

relations among nonconscious mental states. The project is less radical in that it allows mentalistic notions, such as belief, desire, perception, and intentionality, to appear within its explanans. It is nonetheless nontrivial since it is not obvious that appeals to nonconscious mental states and their interrelations will suffice to explain conscious mentality; if consciousness is what make the mind–body problem (seem) really intractable then showing how consciousness can be explained in terms of less problematic mental states would be great progress. The two most prominent examples of this approach in the recent philosophic literature are Daniel Dennett's (1991) multiple drafts theory of consciousness and the various related versions of the higher order thought theory of consciousness as championed by David Rosenthal (1986). In both cases, the attempt is made to explain consciousness in terms of intentional states (judgements in Dennett's version and thoughts in Rosenthal's) that have other mental states as their intentional objects. Although such theories are less radical than direct attempts to explain consciousness physically or functionally, they have met with lots of spirited criticism (e.g. Shoemaker 1993; Tye 1993). Most critics have questioned whether the alleged theories in fact suffice to explain one or another important aspect of consciousness; for example do they adequately explain the qualitative character of conscious experience? However, our present aim is just to get clear about the nature and scope of the explanatory project not its adequacy. Nonetheless there are some problems even in that regard. In particular it is unclear just which states count as nonconscious. For example does the concept of thought imply consciousness? If so, it could not be used to define consciousness on pain of circularity. Nor are such worries idle. Some philosophers, most notably John Searle (1992), have argued that genuine intentionality presupposes consciousness. Should Searle be right, the order of explanatory dependence proposed by Dennett and HOT supporters would have to be reversed.

C. Relation between Explananda and Explanans

Having completed our survey of possible explananda and explanans, we can turn to the third and perhaps most important paremeter of our basic question: What relation must hold between the two in order to count as an explanation of the relevant feature of consciousness? Here again the options are diverse and which one seems most appropriate depends in part on which pair from our first two parameters we are trying to combine. A relation that might be apt for a physical explanation of qualia might not be right for a functional explanation of subjectivity. There are five main relations to consider.

C1

The first is **logical sufficiency or deductive entailment**. The factors cited
in the explanans would count as adequate only if they provided a logically
sufficient condition from which one could deduce the existence and nature
of the relevant feature of consciousness. A physical explanation of qualia
would have to cite physical conditions that entailed the occurrence of
mental states with specific qualitative characters.

Although the deductive requirement may seem to set a rigorous (perhaps
too rigorous) and precise standard for explanation, it actually shifts most of
the difficult issues elsewhere, onto the question of what additional assumptions are being used to bridge the psychophysical gap. The problem is that
without some bridge principles deducibility is impossible, but with them it
is far too easy unless their range is suitably retricted. If for example one
knew that a particular brain state or even a particular pattern of perceptual
stimulation were invariably correlated as a matter of empircal fact with a
given state of qualitative consciousness, one could add the true conditional
describing that link to one's explanans. One could then deduce the occurrence of the specific conscious state from the occurrence of the brain event
or stimulus condition, but it would not seem that doing so would suffice as
an explanation of the relevant aspect of consciousness. Surely it would not
satisfy the explanatory demands of those who worry about consciousness
and the mind–body problem. The relevant bridge principle provides nothing
more than a brute fact correlation, which even if it is true would not satisfy
our legitimate desire to understand *why* the correlation holds. Thus the
deducibility standard doesn't really do much to clarify the issue of what
would count as an explanation; all the difficult questions are just transfered
to the problem of delimiting the nature and scope of allowable auxilliary
assumptions and bridge principles.

C2

Nomic sufficiency offers a second initially attractive alternative that nonetheless succumbs to the same fate as logical sufficiency. One might require
that an adequate explanans provide a nomically sufficient condition for the
occurrence of a given aspect of consciousness; i.e. the factors cited in the
explanans must necessitate the feature of consciousness as a matter of
natural law, which is all we require in many domains of scientific explanation. The nomic requirement also guarantees that the factors cited in the
explanans are more than just empirically correlated with the relevant
features or consciousness. Despite these advantages, nomic sufficiency is
subject to the same basic objection raised against the logical sufficiency
standard. The laws that bridge the gap from explanans to conscious explanandum might leave too much left unexplained. The unsatisfying element
of brute fact correlation can reoccur at the nomic level. Brute links may be

all we expect at the level of basic laws of nature. For example, it may not make sense to ask why matter gravitationally attracts according to an inverse square law; it just does. But laws linking features of consciousness with complex nonconscious factors such as patterns of neurophysiological activity would not seem appropriate end points of explanation nor candidates for ultimate and basic laws of nature. Thus they would leave our legitimate explanatory expectations unfulfilled. We seem to need explanations that provide some greater degree of intelligibility, ones that perhaps describe some process or mechanism that let us see intuitively why and how the cited factors necessarily produce the relevant aspect of consciousness.

C3

Intuitive sufficiency. Thus a third way of delimiting the required explanatory relation is to demand that the explanans specify a set of processes or mechanisms that can be seen intuitively to produce or realize whatever feature of consciousness we are aiming to understand. Without such a specification our explanatory desires will not be satisfied; too many questions of how and why will be left unanswered. However, once again the details are difficult to spell out; most importantly what is to count as an intuitive process or explanation? One can appeal to examples from other domains that seem to meet that standard, such as explaining the room temperature liquidity of water in terms of its molecular structure or its frozen state below 0 °C in terms of the intramolecular hydrogen bonds that produce ice crystals. But citing examples is not the same as defining intuitiveness, and it is far from clear how are we to generalize from examples like those of liquid water and ice to physical or functional explanations of one or another feature of consciousness. Moreover, the problem is complicated by the fact that what strikes us as intuitive is highly context sensitive and relative. Familiarity for example is clearly a factor; having encountered a form of explanation many times generally enhances its intuitive appeal. Field theoretic explanations might have seemed odd and less than intuitive a hundred and fifty years ago, but today they qualify as paradigms of naturalness. Perhaps all we can say with regard to intuitiveness is what an American Supreme Court Justice famously said about obscenity, 'I don't know how to define, but I know it when I see it.' One would surely like more, but at present that may be the best we can do.

   Those like Colin McGinn (1991) and Joseph Levine (1983) who are sceptical about our ability to explain how consciousness depends on physical processes might argue that no definition of intuitiveness is needed to make their claims. No matter how it is ultimately defined, it seems we do not at present have any intuitively compelling explanations of how to bridge the psychophysical gap, at least not with regard to the phenomenal and qualitative aspects of consciousness. But their claim is not just that we don't have such explanations now but that we will never have any, and that far stronger claim does seem to require something like a definition of intuitiveness. They need to be able to say what it is that brute fact psychophysical corrrelations or laws don't provide, and why we will never be able to meet that further standard.

C4

Predictive models. Though some scientific explanations provide nomic and intuitively sufficient conditions for the features they explain, that is certainly not always the case. We accept as legitimate scientific explanations many theories that provide far less. Some are little more than models that allow us to describe and predict the dynamic characteristics of the features being explained and their dependence on relevant causal factors. A global climate model may predict how temperatures and air circulations will change in response to various levels of greenhouse gases. And an econometric model may describe how housing construction will vary with interest rates or how trade will be affected by tariff reductions. Such models if they are accurate provide a great deal of predictive and explanatory power, but no one would suppose they provide fully sufficient nomic conditions for the phenomena they model. An interest rate/ housing construction model does not specify a complete set of conditions for the existence of a housing industry. Might one not similarly explain various features of consciousness without supplying sufficient conditions for their existence. If so, then we have a fourth way of explicating the relation between explanans and explanandum, namely the factors cited in the explandum must provide us with *a model of the features of consciousness we wish to understand that allows us to predict and perhaps manipulate those features in practically or pragmatically relevant ways*. This sets a considerably lower standard than any of the three prior relations we have considered and it is unlikely to satisfy those who demand a complete and comprehensive explanation of consciousness, but I think it is important to include it among our options since it reflects a notion of explanation that has wide acceptance in other scientific contexts. If some feature of consciousness can be understood in this last sense, then the fact — if it is a fact — that are we unable to provide fully sufficient conditions for it need not mean we are so much worse off with respect to consciousness than we are with respect to many other natural phenomena.

Let us review then the variants we have listed for each of the three parameters of our original question, 'Can we explain consciousness?' With regard to the explanandum we distinguished six different aspects of consciousness in need of explanation: the conscious–unconscious distinction for states and for creatures, qualia, the phenomenal aspect, subjectivity, and the transparency or intrinsic intentionality of conscious mental states. We distinguished four main domains to which our explanans might be restricted: the physical, the functional, the naturalistic, and those features of the mental — if there are any — that do not already entail consciousness, such as the intentional (*pace* Searle 1992). And last we considered four possible standards for the relation that must hold between explanans and explanandum: logical sufficiency, nomic sufficiency, intuitive sufficiency, and providing an accurately predictive and pragmatically useful model. If we list these variants in three columns as in Figure 1, we get a menu of possibilities each one constructed by making a choice from each of the three columns.

A Conscious Explananda (aspect to be explained)	B Domain of Explanans	C Linking Relation
A1 Un / conscious state distinction	B1 Physical	C1 Logical sufficiency
A2 Non / conscious creature distinction	B2 Functional	C2 Nomic sufficiency
A3 Qualitative aspect	B3 Naturalistic	C3 Intuitive sufficiency
A4 Phenomenal aspect	B4 Nonconscious mental states	C4 Predictive and pragmatically useful modelling
A5 Subjectivity		

Figure 1

For example A3, B1, C3 intreprets our basic question as 'Can we provide an intuitively sufficient set of physical conditions for the qualitative aspect of consciousness?' or put in a slightly different form 'Can we provide an intuitively satisfying explanation of how physical processes give rise to qualitative consciousness?' By contrast the triple of A1, B3 and C1 results in the question 'Can we provide logically sufficient conditions for distinguishing between conscious and nonconscious states solely in terms of intentional and other nonconscious mental states and relations?' Given the options along our three parameters our menu generates ninety-six possible interpretations of our original question. Though some of them may not be worth considering, many are.

However, the general strategy of dividing our original question into a number of more specific ones might be challenged on one of two grounds. First someone might object that the various aspects of consciousness that we listed under A are in fact mutually interdependent and should not be

separated nor explained in isolation from one another. Doing so might be
criticized as artificially fragmenting a domain that has a deep and natural
unity. Though some of the aspects we distinguished — e.g. phenomenal
organization and qualitative character — may indeed be intimately interconnected, those links need to be shown and themselves explained rather
than merely assumed. Thus it seems better to begin by distinguishing the
various aspects conceptually; having done so we can then discover what
relations or dependencies hold among them in the course of trying to
explain each. If in fact one aspect is found to depend upon another then
obviously we won't be able to explain the first within a given domain unless
we can also explain the second within that same domain; if subjectivity
depends on qualitative character then we will not be able to explain it in
physical or functional terms unlesswe can do the same for qualia. However,
such connections should emerge from our explanatory efforts rather than be
imposed on them by assumption from the outset.

A second objection to our separation strategy might be that it leaves
something out in so far as its separate explananda fail to capture all that's
included in our original explanatory target. Such an objection might be
unpacked in one of two ways: either by noting some aspect(s) of consciousness not included in our list that require(s) explanation, or by claiming that
consciousness *per se* is something more than just its totality of its aspects
— 'the whole is more than the sum of its parts'. In the first case, the problem
can be easily remedied by adding the allegedly missing aspect to our list of
explananda thereby generating yet further explanatory projects. Indeed I
never claimed the list given under A was comprehensive and there are
surely some plausible candidates for inclusion; if for example consciousness involves some element of freedom or creativity that is incompatible
with determinism or algorithmic specification as Roger Penrose (1994) has
recently claimed then it too would need to be added to our list. The strategy
of articulating our basic question into more specific inquiries would not be
affected. The second form of the objection might present more of a
problem, but it's far from clear what it amounts to; it appeals to a supposed
failure to capture an ill defined and mysterious something which is not itself
an aspect of consciousness , just a something *je ne sais quoi*. I am reluctant
to say that no objection could be raised along such lines, but absent some
better formulation of the problem I think we can safely ignore it.

If we set aside these objections and follow our basic separation strategy,
we will find that our present state of progress and our prospects for future
success vary greatly across the different specific questions that get generated. For example higher order theories such as those offered by Dennett
and Rosenthal seem promising as a means of drawing the logical distinction
between conscious and unconscious mental states in intentional terms
(interpretation A1, B4, C1.) Such theories are not without their problems,
such as the following. First, as noted above, they seem to require us to

attribute sophisticated higher order judgements to nonhuman non-language-using animals and small children. Second defining consciousness in terms of higher order thoughts would be unilluminating if the notion of thought were to turn out to presuppose consciousness. And third there seem to be cases in which the presence of the relevant sort of higher order states fails to confer consciousness on its object. If for example in a Freudian case, a given state — perhaps an illicit desire — is being actively and successfully repressed it seems that we would classify it as an unconscious state even though the intentional activity of keeping it repressed seems to require the existence of a higherorder state whose content is that one has that very desire. Nonetheless these may be just matter of detail that can be handled successfully within the higher-order framework, and such theories do seem to capture at least one important sense of 'conscious' as it is applied to mental states in everday use.

By contrast the project of showing in intuitively obvious terms how qualia depend upon physical properties or relations seems much more daunting if not impossible. It is sometimes claimed that we don't even know what form such an explanation might take; we just find ourselves staring at a blank wall with no real idea of how to begin to construct an explanation. Though the project is a difficult one, I don't believe our situation is quite that bad. As I have argued elsewhere (Van Gulick 1993) the first step in bridging the gap is to articulate structural organization within the qualitative and phenomenal domain. Having done so, it is possible to search for corresponding patterns of structure at lower levels of organization that might underlie what we find at the conscious level.

Part of the reason we get a blank wall feeling when we think about physically explaining qualia is that the problem is posed as trying to find some explanatory relation between a single isolated qualitative property, such as the taste of a mango or the redness of my visual experience when I look at ripe tomato, and some local physical or neurophysiological property. In so far the qualitative component is presented a *sui generis* simple property it is hard to see how any relation it might bear to its neurophysiological basis could be anything other than an intuitively unsatisfying brute fact. However, if we are able to articulate structural organization within the qualitative domain, then more explanatorily satisfying options are possible. For example the qualitative colour space has an inherent internal organization (Hardin 1988) defined in part by relations of similarity and composition; some colours are perceived as unary noncomposite colours (red, green, blue and yellow) while others are experienced as binaries or composites (purple, orange, turquoise, and chartreuse). This purely qualitative organization can be explained in terms of the opponent process organization of the neural processes underlying colour perception. Experiences of red result when the red/green channel is highly active and the yellow/blue channel is near base rate; conversely we experience orange when there is a high level of activation in both channels. Qualitative binariness can be explained in terms of the double activation of the two neurophysiological processing channels. The crucial explantory step is recognizing and describing the qualitative *organization* that needs to be explained; once we have done so the standard scientific practice of explaining organization or structure at one level in terms of corresponding relations at an underlying level can come into play. It is only when we treat the qualitative or phenomenal explanandum as a simple that we confront a blank wall or mere brute fact relations.

A second example is presented by the fact that our normal visual perception involves the phenomenal experience of a meaningful world of familiar objects. We do not normally experience a world of mere shapes and colours; what we see are scenes, events and objects of meaningful types. When I look at my desk, what I see is my computer, my notes, and the afternoon sun dappling the wall behind them. Nor is this a matter of some distinct interpretative element that accompanies our seeing; it is a phenomenal feature of the visual experience itself. However, in some pathological cases, this phenomenal organization is lacking or severly disturbed. Patients suffering from associative visual agnosia have nearly normal perception of the geometrical features of what they see, but they are unable to connect those visual inputs with their knowlege of the world and their scheme for categorizing objects (Farah 1991). Though they know what a stapler is and can name it immediately if allowed to touch it, they cannot recognize it visually despite the fact that they can draw a highly accurate picture of its shape. Given this pattern of deficits we can begin to explain how the phenomenal organization that is present in normal cases might depend on neurophysiological organization. The brain areas damaged in visual agnosia generally involve the cortical regions devoted to the last stages of visually processing (areas V6) and the nearby regions of associative cortex that are concerned with intersensory integration. Thus what was true with respect to the unary/binary distinction in the qualitative here also holds with regard to the phenomenal. Once we have articulated structural organization at the conscious level we can pursue genuinely explanatory links with underlying patterns of neural organization, though admitedly much more needs to be said about the specific case (Van Gulick 1995a).

Nonetheless pessimists or sceptics might object that such appeals to underlying organization can provide at best incomplete accounts of how the phenomenal and qualitative aspects of consciousness depend upon neural structure and activity. They may explain why they have some of the relational structure that they do, but they will not explain the qualitative and phenomenal aspects themselves. But just what is supposedly left out and forever beyond the reach of such explantions? The claim seems to be that we might capture and explain the relations that hold among the phenomenal elements but not those elements themselves; they remain beyond our explanatory reach or so it's claimed. This is an initially plausible claim, but we must be wary not to fall back into the trap of regarding qualia as simples. There is no reason to do so, and good reason not to since it will bring us right back to the blank wall.

Nonetheless there are two genuine worries raised by the pessimists, though neither presents an insurmountable problem. First we do need to explain how there can be phenomenal and qualitative properties at all; relational theories that took their existence for granted would indeed be far from complete. But the correct response is not to look for some non-relational explanation but rather for a relational theory with the right terms as relata. As noted above, we should not try to establish explanatory links between isolated qualitative properties (the taste of a mango) and local brain events; this only provokes objections like the old philosophical standby of asking why C-fibre firings should hurt, feel like pain, or indeed feel like anything at all. We need instead to ask how the overall organized activity of a brain can give rise to a conscious self? If there really are such things as qualia — and I believe there are — they are properties of objects that exist only from the internal perspective of such a conscious self, and such a self can in turn exist only in so far as it is the subject of a stream of experience with the requisite internal phenomenal organization. Both the self and the qualitatively differentiated objects of which it is aware are entities that emerge out of the organized stream of experience rather than independently existing items that precede experience (Van Gulick 1988b; Dennett 1991). Providing a detailed theory of how this entire relational structure might depend upon neural organization is indeed an enormous task, but nonetheless one for which there is a possiblity of success in the long run.

The second genuine worry raised by the pessimists is that there is a form of understanding with respect to specific qualia that no third person expla-nation can provide, namely they cannot give us an empathetic first person understanding of what it's like to have an experience with that quality unless we are capable of such experiences ourselves. Empathetic under-standing can be gained only by undergoing the relevant experience through an act of perception or imagination. This is the familiar empiricist point of Thomas Nagel's (1974) claims about our inability to understand what it's like to be a bat and Frank Jackson's (1982; 1986) example of Mary the super colour scientist who has never herself experienced red. I agree that simply entertaining a complex physical or functional desription of what goes on in someone's brain when he or she experiences red will not provide us with a sympathetic understanding of what it's like to have red experiences, and thus we would be left lacking some understanding about such conscious episodes and qualia.

But there is a sense in which a theory of consciousness might be explana-torily complete even if it is limited in this way. Speaking of a theory that is

both limited but complete may at first sound paradoxical, but there need be
no contradiction as along as the explanatory limits are entailed by the theory
itself. That is, the theory can be complete in so far as it entails the inevitable
existence of certain limits on what we can explain or understand and then
provides all the explanations that are possible within those limits. This is
indeed the position I have argued (Van Gulick 1985) we should take in
response to Nagel's bat example. Although I cannot reproduce the detailed
argument here, it can be shown that the existence of such limits is a direct
consequence of an independently plausible functionalist theory of understanding. Their existence thus provides further support for that theory and
does not in any way impugn its explanatory completeness.

Colin McGinn, though a leading pessimist, has himself recently offered
his own version of completeness within limits (McGinn 1991). He has tried
to show that our human means of forming concepts are incapable of
providing us with concepts able to bridge the psychophysical gap and thus
the the link between consciousness and brain must remain forever cognitively closed to us. He regards his version of naturalistic physicalism as
nonetheless complete in so far as the limits on what it can explain follow
from the theory itself. His account of self-limiting completeness differs
from my own in two major respects. First he is much more pessimistic and
places far greater limits on what we can hope to explain; he places the
psychophysical link in its entirety beyond human understanding while my
own theory only limits us from understanding alien forms of experience in
all the ways that are possible from the first person perspective. There are
many aspects of the psychophysical link that we can hope to understand in
a fully satisfying way. Secondly, his argument relies upon strong assumptions about the limits of human concept formation that are not very plausible whereas the limits in my own model follow from some very general
functionalist principles about the pragmatic nature of understanding. I do
not have adequate space here to present a full defence of my own theory or
a detailed criticism of McGinn's. My present aim is just to make clear how
one might have a theory of consciousness that was both explanatorily
selflimited but complete, as well as to indicate that there are a variety of
ways of formulating such theories. That much I hope to have done.

Indeed my overall intent in this paper has not been to offer or argue for
any given explanation of consciousness. My goal has been more modest:
just to clarify the nature of our initial question and articulate its many
possible interpretations and their interconnections. And again that much I
hope to have done; providing answers to the many specific questions that
get generated will have to wait for another time.

References

Baker, L. (1985). A farewell to functionalism. *Philosophical Studies*, **48**, 1–13.
Block, N. (1978). Troubles with functionalism. In W. Savage (ed), *Perception and Cognition: Issues in the Foundations of Pyschology*, Minnesota Studies in the Philosophy of Science, **IX** (Minneapolis: University of Minnesota Press).
Dennett, D.C. (1988) Quining qualia. In Marcel & Bisiach 1988.
Dennett, D.C. (1991). *Consciousness Explained*. Boston, MA: Little, Brown & Co.
Farah, M. (1991). *Visual Agnosia*. Cambridge, MA: MIT Press.
Flanagan, O. (1992). *Consciousness Reconsidered*. Cambridge, MA: MIT Press.
Hardin, C. (1988). *Color for Philosophers*. Indianapolis: Hackett Publishing.
Jackson, F. (1982). Epiphenomenal qualia. *Philosophical Quarterly*, **32**, 127–95.
Jackson, F. (1986). What Mary didn't know. *Journal of Philosophy*, **83**, 291–5.
Kalke, W. (1969). What's wrong with Putnam and Fodor's functionalism. *Noûs*, **3**, 83–94.
Levine, J. (1983). Materialism and qualia: the explanatory gap. *Pacific Philosophical Quarterly*, **64**, 354–61.
Levine, J. (1991). Absent and inverted qualia revisited. *Mind & Language*, **3**, 271–87.
Lycan, W. (1987). *Consciousness*. Cambridge, MA: MIT Press.
McGinn, C. (1991). *The Problem of Consciousness*. Oxford: Blackwell.
Nagel, T. (1974). What is it like to be a bat? *Philosophical Review*, **83**, 435–50.
Rosenthal, D. (1986). Two concepts of consciousness. *Philosophical Studies*, **49**, 329–59.
Searle, J. (1992). *The Rediscovery of the Mind*. Cambridge, MA: MIT Press.
Shoemaker, S. (1993). Lovely and suspect ideas. *Philosophy and Phenomenological Research*, **53**, 905–10.
Tye, M. (1993). Reflections on Dennett and consciousness. *Philosophy and Phenomenological Research*, **53**, 893–8.
Van Gulick, R. (1985). Physicalism and the subjectivity of the mental. *Philosophical Topics*, **12**, 51–70.
Van Gulick, R. (1988a). Consciousness, intrinsic intentionality, and self-understanding machines. In Marcel & Bisiach 1988.
Van Gulick, R. (1988b). A functionalist plea for selfconsciousness. *The Philosophical Review*, **97**, 149–88.
Van Gulick, R. (1989). What difference does consciousness make? *Philosophical Topics*, **17**, 211–30.
Van Gulick, R. (1993). Understanding the phenomenal mind: are we all just armadillos? In Davies & Humphreys 1993.
Van Gulick, R. (1994). Dennett, drafts and phenomenal realism. *Philosophical Topics*, **22**, 443–56.
Van Gulick, R. (1995a). Deficit studies and the function of phenomenal consciousness. In G. Graham & L. Stephens (eds), *Philosophy and Psychopathology*. Cambridge, MA: MIT Press.
Van Gulick, R. (1995b). Why the connection argument doesn't work. *Philosophy and Phenomenological Research*, **55**, 201–7.
Van Gulick, R. (1995c). Understanding the relation between intentionality and consciousness. In Tomberlin 1995.
Wright, L. (1974). Functions. *The Philosophical Review*, **82**, 741–64.

Michael Tye

The Burning House

There is a striking impairment known as unilateral visual neglect which is typically brought about by brain damage in the parietal lobe. Patients with this deficit typically have great difficulty in noticing, or attending to, stimuli in one half of the visual field. Moreover, the deficit often persists despite free movement of the head and eyes.

One patient, P.S., a 49 year old woman, with unilateral neglect was presented simultaneously with two vertically aligned dark green line drawings of a house. (See Marshall and Halligan 1988.) In one of these drawings, the house had bright red flames emerging from the left side. In other respects, the drawings were matched. P.S. was asked what she saw. She identified each drawing as being of a house. P.S. was then asked whether the two drawings were the same or different. She judged them to be the same. On a number of different trials she never noticed the flames on the left. However, when she was asked which house she would prefer to live in, eighty percent of the time she chose the house without flames. This choice she made only when she was compelled to pick one or the other, since she believed the two houses to be alike and the question 'silly'.

In some subsequent trials, P.S. was shown simultaneously a new pair of vertically aligned drawings, one of a house with flames on the *right* side and the other normal. She immediately noticed the flames and preferred the other house. Then, in five final trials, she was presented with the original pair of drawings again. In the first four cases, she noticed no difference but chose the non-burning house. In the fifth, she finally noticed the flames on the left (remarking 'Oh my God, this is on fire!').

The conclusion drawn by J. Marshall and P. Halligan (the authors of the article from which this case study is taken) is that 'the ''neglected'' stimulus can exert an influence upon cognitive functioning, albeit at some pre-attentional, pre-conscious level' (1988: 767). Now, we can all agree that what the above case clearly illustrates is the absence of what might be called 'discriminatory' or 'attentional' consciousness with respect to the flames or any of their features (e.g. their colour), *prior* to the final trial. P.S. simply does not *notice* the flames. In the last trial, however, given the earlier cue of the house with the flames on the right, she does notice them. Discriminatory consciousness is achieved. So, the 'neglected' stimulus is clearly pre-conscious in the discriminatory sense prior to the final trial.

It is tempting to infer from this that there is *no* difference in the consciousness of P.S., as she views each member of the pair of drawings in the first set of trials. But the temptation should be resisted. The inference is invalid. There is more to consciousness than Marshall and Halligan suppose. I shall now explain why.

I

Let us begin by examining a number of ordinary, everyday cases, in some of which we normally suppose that consciousness is present while in others we deny it.

Case 1: The Distracted Driver

Driving along the road, I find myself lost in thought for several miles. During this time I keep the car on the road, and perhaps change gears, but I am not conscious of the driving. Later on, I 'come to' and realize that I have been driving for some time without any real consciousness of what I have been doing.[1]

Case 2: The Birdwatcher

You and I are both birdwatchers. There is a bird singing in a tree nearby. We both hear it, but only you initially see it. You tell me exactly where to look, and I stare at the right part of the right branch. My retinal image is, let us suppose, just the same as yours when I stand in the spot you are located and look in the same direction. But I report to you that I am not visually conscious of any bird.[2]

Case 3: The Winetaster

Apprentice wine-tasters are much less discriminating than experts. Through training they come to discriminate flavours that initially seemed to them to be the same. They become conscious of subtle differences in wines of which they were not previously conscious.

Case 4: The Brief Encounter

You are looking at a shelf on which there are eighteen books. Your eyes quickly pass over the entire contents of the shelf. You see more than you consciously notice. Indeed, you see all the books (let us suppose). But you are not conscious that you have seen eighteen books.

[1] This case is due to David Armstrong 1968: 93.

[2] Cases 2 and 3 are to be found in Dennett 1991.

Case 5: The Headache That Won't Go Away
You have a bad headache which lasts all afternoon. From time to time during the afternoon, there are distractions. You think of other things, you forget for a few moments. In short, you are not conscious of your headache. When this happens, we do not infer that really you had one headache which ceased at the first distraction, then another quite different headache until the next distraction, so that you were really subject to a sequence of discontinuous headaches. (See Rosenthal 1986.)

Case 6: The Pain in the Night
I am fast asleep. During the night I am awoken by a pain of which, before awakening, I was not conscious.[3]

Case 7: What it is Like
I taste a lemon, smell rotten eggs, feel a sharp pain in my elbow, seem to see red. In each of these cases, I undergo a different feeling or experience. For feelings and perceptual experiences, there is always something it is *like* to undergo them, some felt or phenomenal or subjective aspects to these mental states. They are inherently conscious mental states.

Case 8: The Boring Shade of Blue
I am staring at a wall that has been painted deep blue. My mind wanders for a moment, and I am not conscious that I am undergoing a visual experience of blue. But the wall continues to look blue to me even when my mind is wandering.

Case 9: The Party Animal
I am at a party, and I have been drinking all night. Eventually, not long before dawn, I leave. Upon arriving home, I make my weary way to the kitchen and pass out on the kitchen floor. I lose all consciousness.

Case 10: The Dreamer
I am asleep, dreaming that I am being pursued by a pterodactyl that is swooping down on me with evil intent. Even though I am not awake, I am having conscious experiences. These experiences are real to me, so much so that I wake up in a panic.

Case 11: The Dreaming Dog
My dog is fast asleep. Her eyes are moving rapidly. As they do so, her nose twitches and she growls and shudders. She is having conscious experiences.

Case 12: The 'Haunted' Graveyard
One night I take a short-cut home and cross an old graveyard. I suddenly feel very afraid. I seem to smell a strange sweet odour in the air and to see

[3] John Searle discusses a case of this sort in his 1992: 164–5.

a shape floating over a grave. Although I do not know it, I am hallucinating. I am fully conscious, but the conscious states I am in are delusive.

What are the different concepts of consciousness that these cases illustrate and how are they related? It is to this issue that I turn next.

II

In Case 1, the distracted driver certainly sees the road and other cars, as he drives along, and he reacts accordingly. How else does he keep the car on the road? But he is not aware of his visual sensations. He is not paying any attention to them. In short, he has no thoughts about his perceptions — his thoughts lie elsewhere.

The concept of consciousness this case illustrates is that of introspective awareness. Consciousness, in this sense, is consciousness of one's own mental states. It is plausible to suppose that this sort of consciousness demands only that its subject S have a higher-order thought about another mental state M that S is undergoing. In having the higher-order thought, S is thereby conscious of M. Let us call this 'Higher-order Consciousness' or 'H-Consciousness' for short.

The driver, then, has no H-consciousness of his visual perceptions. In a corresponding sense, we may say that his visual perceptions are unconscious: they are not the objects of higher-order thoughts.

The case of the bird-watcher and the winetaster (Cases 2 and 3) illustrate the concept of discriminatory (or D-) consciousness already mentioned in connection with the case of the burning house. The birdwatcher who is conscious of the bird has successfully picked it out from the branches and foliage in its immediate vicinity. Likewise, the winetaster who becomes conscious of certain differences in wines of which he was, earlier in his training, unconscious, has *noticed* those differences.

The party animal (Case 9) lacks discriminatory consciousness with respect to anything external. He is not processing information about the external world and responding to it in a rational manner. Let us say that the general sort of consciousness lacked by the party animal is 'Responsive Consciousness' or 'R-Consciousness' for short.[4] This sort of consciousness, I might add, can be partial: a person who is limited in his reactions upon opening his eyes in the morning after taking a heavy sleeping draught the night before is not fully R-conscious.

In Case 4 — the Brief Encounter — you are not conscious that you saw eighteen books. Here you lack H-consciousness with respect to this perception. You do not think that you have seen eighteen books. You also lack D-consciousness with respect to some of the books, since there are books you do not *notice*.

[4] Responsive consciousness seems to be similar to what Ned Block calls 'access' consciousness. (See his 1993.)

In Case 5, you have a headache of which you sometimes are not conscious. This again is the absence of both higher-order and discriminatory consciousness, as is the following case of the pain that wakes you in the night. These two cases, however, strongly suggest another kind of consciousness not yet distinguished. If you have a headache then you have a pain. And intuitively to have a pain is to feel pain. As Kripke nicely puts it '[f]or a sensation to be *felt* as pain is for it to *be* pain' (Kripke 1971, p. 163, fn 18.) and conversely that 'for [something] to exist without being *felt as pain* is for it to exist without there *being any pain*.'[5]

So, in Case 5, there is feeling without higher-order or discriminatory consciousness, and in Case 6 (the pain in the night) there is feeling without any of the three sorts of consciousness adumbrated so far (at least prior to wakening up). But if there is feeling, then there must be consciousness, in some sense of the term. To feel a pain is, in some sense, to be conscious of pain. What is this sense?

Well, for a person who feels pain, there is something it is like for him to be in pain. The pain has a definite phenomenal or subjective quality. Call this 'Phenomenal (or *P*-) Consciousness.' This is the sort of consciousness illustrated in Case 7. It goes with talk of 'raw feels', of 'sensational qualities', of 'phenomenal character'. A mental state may be said to be phenomenally conscious if, and only if, there is something it is like for the subject of the state (in being in that state). So, in Cases 5 and 6, the pains are unconscious in the higher-order sense but conscious in the phenomenal one. There is something it is like for me in having each pain, some phenomenal feature that I *would* have been aware of, *had* I been *H*-conscious of the pain.

Exactly the same sort of situation obtains in Case 8. There is nothing incoherent in supposing that something looks blue to me even though, owing to a brief distraction, I do not believe that it looks blue.[6] But if the wall before my eyes looks blue then I must be having a visual experience of blue. And if I am having a visual experience of blue, then I am conscious of blue in the phenomenal sense. There is something it is like for me as I view the blue wall. Of course, if my mind is wandering, I will not be conscious (in the higher-order sense) of what it is like for me at that time in having the visual experience. And if I am of a very sceptical frame of mind, I may even doubt that there is anything it is visually like for me at such moments. But this certainly does not entail that there *really* is nothing it is visually like for me. On the contrary, the wall, by hypothesis, continues to look blue. Had I introspected at the time at which my mind was wandering, I would have

---

[5] Kripke 1980: 151. Cases of subjects who are given morphine after they have begun to experience pain and who report that they no longer mind it, do not undermine Kripke's claims, in my view. The pains of these subjects are still felt as pains, but they are no longer aversive, apparently. So, the subjects continue to experience pain — assuming pain itself continues after the morphine is given — but there is no longer any strong desire that it cease.

[6] For more here, see Tye 1993b.

been aware that I was continuing to have a visual experience of blue. But I did not, in fact, then introspect. There is *P*-consciousness without *H*- or *D*-consciousness.

P-consciousness is integral to experiences and feelings generally. Wherever there is feeling or experience, there must be *P*-consciousness, some intrinsic phenomenology that the relevant state has. By contrast, thoughts, in and of themselves, have no phenomenology. Thinking that water is wet, for example, has no intrinsic phenomenal character, although it may certainly be accompanied by visual images or bodily sensations (e.g. the feeling of thirst). Perhaps it is also the case that upon occasion, particular tokens of the above thought have a felt quality to them. Still, none of these qualitites is essential to the thought itself. Felt qualities can vary without any variation in thought, and even without any variation in conscious thought. Conversely, thoughts (including conscious thoughts) can vary without any variation in phenomenal character. My doppelganger on the famous planet twin earth, who thinks that twin-water (or twater) is wet, rather than that water is wet, does not thereby differ from me at the level of sensory experience or feeling. What he thinks is certainly different from me. His thought has a different content from mine, and if he is conscious of what he is thinking then his thought has a different conscious content. But this is not a difference in *P*-consciousness, at least in any sense that I intend. The difference is rather one of *H*-consciousness.[7]

P-consciousness can be illustrated further by reference to the famous inverted and absent qualia hypotheses, although it does not require that they be true (cf. Block 1993). The former of these hypotheses is standardly illustrated by the example of colour and the idea that you or I might have colour experiences that are phenomenally inverted relative to those of everyone else even though we use colour words and function in colour tests in all the standard ways. The latter hypothesis is the claim that there might be someone who felt or experienced nothing at all, someone who altogether lacked *P*-consciousness, but who functioned in just the same manner as someone who was *P*-conscious.

Returning now to the adumbrated cases, we should note that *P*-consciousness is also present indirectly in Case 4. *Ex hypothesi*, you see all the books. So, each book (briefly) *looks* some way to you as your eyes move along the shelf.[8] In having visual experiences of books that you do not notice, you are

---

[7] Perhaps there is a very broad use of the locution 'what it is like' in ordinary life which concedes a difference in what it is like whenever there is any conscious difference of any sort whatsoever. This is not the usage I intend, however, as my remarks in the text make clear.

[8] This inference might be challenged on the grounds that blindsight subjects see certain items in their blind fields even though they have no visual experiences of those items. In order to sidestep this issue, let us assume that you are a normal perceiver. For a discussion of blindsight, see Tye 1993a. The claim that seeing an object requires that the object visually look some way to the perceiver is given an extended defence in Dretske 1969.

arguably subject to a kind of visual consciousness which is not simply discriminatory. For, to repeat, you have *experiences* of these books — they look some way to you. There is something it is like for you at each moment as your eyes scan the contents of the shelf. What it is like changes, even if you are not introspecting carefully and you are not cognizant of all the changes. Your visual experiences are phenomenally conscious.[9]

In Case 10 (the Dreamer), my experiences are *P*-conscious. There is something it is like for me in dreaming of the pterodactyl. But I am not *R*-conscious. I am not processing information about the external world and responding to it in a rational manner. So, there is nothing external with respect to which I am *D*-conscious. Am I *H*-conscious with respect to my experiences? If I wake up in a panic, to some significant degree I must believe that I am in a situation that is dangerous to me. But I need not have any beliefs with respect to my experiences as such. I need not believe that I am having a visual experience as of a pterodactyl, even if I do believe that I am being pursued by a pterodactyl. So long as the latter belief is present, it will cause in me fright. The former belief, which is higher-order, and hence more complicated content-wise, is not necessary. So, *H*-consciousness need not be present.

This conclusion is reinforced by Case 11. It seems to me plausible to suppose that dogs that growl during REM sleep are subject to *P*-conscious states which cause beliefs about things in the world or people (for example, a coveted bone or a postman). But it seems much less plausible to suppose that in each and every such case, a higher-order belief *must* be present. Surely, one important difference between humans and other animals is that the former are much more reflective than the latter. So, in general with animals there is much less *H*-consciousness. There is certainly *P*-consciousness, however. It would be absurd to suppose that there is nothing it is like for a dog that chews a favourite bone or prefers chopped liver for its dinner over anything else it is offered.

Case 12 is similar to Case 11. Although I am hallucinating, I am still undergoing sensations and perceptual experiences. My experiential states are *P*-conscious: there is something it is like for me as feel afraid, as I seem to smell a strange odour, and as I seem to see a white shape. But in this case I am also *R*-conscious. For I am awake and cognitively processing information from my surroundings.

---

[9] Penfield (1975) describes epileptics who have *petit mal* seizures while driving or walking. According to Penfield, these patients become automata during the epileptic disorders : they continue what they are doing in a purely mechanical, automatic way without any consciousness. This claim is echoed by Searle (in 1992). It seems unreasonably strong, however, to conclude that there is no consciousness at all. Granted, there is no *H*-consciousness, and only limited *D*- and *R*-consciousness, but what reason is there to suppose that the patients have no *P*-consciousness? Interestingly, in his description of the patients, Penfield does not allude to any sensory impairments. See here Block 1995.

Our examples, then, illustrate four different concepts of consciousness (*H-*, *R-*, *D-*, *P*-consciousness). Of these four concepts, the first three are related in straightforward and obvious ways. The list is not intended to be exhaustive, however. There are certainly other senses for the terms 'conscious' and 'consciousness'. But enough has been said to make the point I wish to make about the case of the burning house.

III

Before P.S. notices the flames on the left side of the house, does the house *look* any different to her than the normal house? Clearly, she is not conscious that they look any different. She has no higher-order consciousness of any difference in her phenomenal state. But, not noticing that there is any difference in how things look is consistent with there really being a difference. And if there is *never* any difference in how the two houses look, how is it that insight is achieved, on the basis of viewing, in the final trial? If, immediately prior to her saying 'Oh my God, this is on fire!', the two houses had looked to her to be exactly alike, what was it that triggered the correct identification?

I do not wish to claim here that this question has *no* answer, if the two houses looked exactly alike to P.S. But, the hypothesis of a phenomenal difference does provide *a* plausible explanation. Moreover, as the authors of the study acknowledge, there was no 'sensory loss' for P.S. So, her early visual processing in the post-geniculate region of the brain and the visual areas one and two in the occipital lobe was like that of normally sighted subjects (unlike the case of blindsight, for example). The brain damage occurred in the higher level attentional system located in the parietal lobe.

On this proposal, then, what P.S. failed to do, prior to being presented with the cue of the house with the flames on the right, was to respond consciously, at a conceptual level, to a *phenomenal* difference in her experiences. But the difference was there, in position to trigger such a response, before she actually responded. The two houses did *look* different to her.

So, there was a difference in *P*-consciousness, unaccompanied by any difference in *H-* or *D*-consciousness. I want to stress that the advocate, or defender, of phenomenal consciousness, is not compelled to accept the above view. It could be that there really is no phenomenal difference in the relevant experiences until the moment at which she notices that the house on the left is on fire. Whether the hypothesis I have adopted is correct is ultimately a matter for future empirical investigation. Still, I hope I have shown that from the fact that there is no difference in the discriminatory (or higher-order) consciousness of P.S. in the first set of trials, it does not *follow* that there is no difference in consciousness at all.

All four of the concepts I have distinguished raise interesting questions of one sort or another about the mind, but the one which presents the largest explanatory problems is phenomenal consciousness. These problems are so puzzling that some philosophers have despaired of ever solving them,[10] while others have either denied that there is any phenomenal *consciousness* as such or else held that insofar as it exists, it is identical with consciousness of another sort, for example, higher-order consciousness.[11] Still others have presented theories aimed at explaining consciousness which simply do not make it clear which kind of consciousness they are talking about.[12]

Philosophers, I should add, are not the only ones who have sometimes failed to clarify just what it that their accounts of consciousness are supposed to encompass. Cognitive scientists too sometimes announce that they have a new proposal to make which explains consciousness, only to say nothing about the phenomenal variety. Thereby they ignore the deepest problems, however worthwhile their theories may be for understanding consciousness of one or more of the other varieties. Consider, for example, the following remarks by the cognitive psychologist, Stephen Kosslyn, which are made at the beginning of his discussion of consciousness (co-authored with Oliver Koening):

> . . . people can be conscious of making a decision, being in love, seeing red, having a pain in the lower back, and so forth. And they clearly can distinguish being conscious of these events from not being conscious of them. The fact of consciousness should not be in doubt ; there is something to be explained, not merely explained away. We will address here the everyday sense of the term ; it refers to the phenomenology of experience, the feeling of red, and so forth (Kosslyn & Koenig 1992: 431–2).

In this passage, Kosslyn and Koening appear to equivocate between higher-order and phenomenal consciousness with the result that it simply is not clear what their theory is really intended to explain. However, the specific proposal of Kosslyn's that they subsequently lay out, namely that consciousness is a kind of 'parity check' seems best suited to higher-order consciousness.

So, what exactly is phenomenal consciousness in the larger scheme of things? Is it an ordinary physical phenomenon like life or aging or electricity? Or does it lie outside the physical realm altogether? Is it something magical? I have a story to tell here, but the present paper is not the place to tell it.[13]

---

[10] See, e.g. McGinn 1991; also, to a less marked degree, Nagel, 'What is it like to be a bat?' (in Nagel 1979).

[11] This seems to be the view of Armstrong 1968; also Rosenthal 1986 and, on some readings, Dennett 1991.

[12] This charge has been levelled at Dennett 1991 among others.

[13] For a global theory of phenomenal consciousness, see Tye 1995.

References

Armstrong, D. (1968). *A Materialist Theory of Mind.* London: Routledge and Kegan Paul.

Block, N. (1993). Review of Dennett's Consciousness Explained. *Journal Of Philosophy*, **90**, 181–93.

Block, N. (1995). On a confusion about a function of consciousness. *Behavioral and Brain Sciences*, **18**, 227–47.

Dennett, D. (1991). *Consciousness Explained.* Boston, MA: Little, Brown & Co.

Dretske, F. (1969). *Seeing and Knowing.* Chicago: University of Chicago Press.

Kosslyn, S. & Koening O. (1992). *Wet Mind: The New Cognitive Neuroscience.* New York: Macmillan.

Kripke, S. (1971). Identity and necessity. In M. Munitz (ed), *Identity and Individuation.* New York: New York University Press.

Kripke, S. (1980). *Naming and Necessity.* Cambridge, MA: Harvard University Press.

Marshall, J. & Halligan, P. (1988). Blindsight and insight in visuospatial neglect. *Nature*, **336**, 766–7.

McGinn, C. (1991). *The Problem of Consciousness.* Oxford: Blackwell.

Nagel, T. (1979). *Mortal Questions.* Cambridge: Cambridge University Press.

Penfield, W. (1975). *The Mystery of the Mind: A Critical Study of Consciousness and the Human Brain.* Princeton: Princeton University Press.

Rosenthal, D. (1986). Two concepts of consciousness. *Philosophical Studies*, **49**, 329–59.

Searle, J. (1992). *The Rediscovery of Mind.* Cambridge, MA: MIT Press.

Tye, M. (1993a). Blindsight, the absent qualia hypothesis, and the mystery of consciousness. In Hookway & Peterson 1993.

Tye, M. (1993b) Reflections on Dennett and consciousness. *Philosophy and Phenomenological Research*, **53**, 893–6.

Tye, M. (1995). *Ten Problems of Consciousness.* Cambridge, MA: MIT Press.

Part Two
Sceptical Arguments

Introduction to Part Two

The problem of phenomenal consciousness is one of the most difficult theoretical problems there are. For a long time, it has resisted all attempts at a convincing solution. In a philosophical problem, such intractability can have different causes. It may be the case that we have not *understood* the problem: We ask the wrong kind of questions and allow ourselves to be bewitched by them. It is also possible that the questions are perfectly meaningful, but that we will never find a satisfactory answer because of our epistemic limitations.[1] It might also be that there simply is not, and never was, such a thing as the phenomenon in question — consciousness. In the last case the elimination of the respective theoretical entities is the right strategy.[2]

However, the claim that in reality there is no such thing as conscious experience, would be a thesis which conflicts with our intuitions more strongly than almost any other philosophical thought. Taken by itself, this is of course not a convincing argument against eliminativism. But it draws attention to an important point: There are few other areas of research in which the internal structure of the researcher's own subjective experience and the resulting pre-theoretical intuitions determine equally strongly what he would regard at all as a *relevant* aspect of the problem or as *convincing* solutions. So it may be that the problem of consciousness really arises in ourselves, whether we systematically overestimate the importance of certain questions, or because we cannot imagine certain things, or because we can imagine certain things only *in a very specific way*. Perhaps it is the structure of our own consciousness itself which bewitches us and leads us into certain theoretical *cul-de-sacs* time and time again.

All of these are reasons to take a sceptical position toward the problem of consciousness. In this part, the reader will find three texts in which sceptical positions are developed. The lines of argument in each, which differ widely, then lead to a more or less pessimistic evaluation of our chances of achieving a theory of phenomenal consciousness. At the beginning, **Kathy Wilkes** points to a claim which she has defended in previous publications: The folk-psychological concept of consciousness is philosophically rather uninteresting and is not going to change much in the future. It is unsuitable as basic concept and explanandum of a *scientific* psychology which searches for law-like regularities and systematic explanations. The reason for this is that in reality it does not refer to any natural kind, and it leaves a great number of scientific problems unclassified. Wilkes offers a series of con-

---

[1] Cf. McGinn 1989.

[2] A well known example of this is Dennett 1988. Cf. also Dennett 1991 and the texts listed in section 3.5 of the bibliography.

siderations drawn from the history of ideas and investigates the relationship between folk psychology and scientific psychology. In doing so she redirects our attention in a step-by-step manner to the Greek concept of *psyche*.

Martin Kurthen considers the current prospects for a naturalization of the concept of consciousness. In order to investigate this he examines some central points one by one: The *explanatory gap argument*,[3] Daniel Dennett's strategy to eliminate the concept of qualia, and two attempts to take qualia seriously while still naturalizing them. In the last part of his contribution, Kurthen confronts us with a surprising meta-philosophical twist: In their importance for the philosophy of mind, qualia have been severely overrated — in reality they are rather trivial phenomena. In this sense Martin Kurthen does not only speak as philosopher but as psychiatrist. He offers an amusing diagnosis of the authors of this volume and also of some readers of this book: The psychoanalytical root of our permanent overrating of the epistemological and ontological significance of consciousness is an escalating narcissism. This very narcissism has also lead to an inflation of the subject. In this situation, the appropriate theoretical strategy is not naturalization or elimination, but *deconstruction*.

Georges Rey argues that a number of the problems in the proximity of Levine's *explanatory gap argument* have their root in a systematic and widespread error in the use of mentalist concepts. In a way, Rey's contribution inverts the classical problem of other minds. He maintains that our beliefs about the conscious states of other people are based not on projection of our own conscious states into others, but on projection of a certain property into *both* them and into ourselves. This property is correlated with our characteristic reactions to it as well as with our experience of ourselves. In order to show this he presents recent empirical material demonstrating the fallibility of introspective knowledge and then, on a philosophical level, argues that the property of consciousness in question does not *exist*. The guiding question, apart from the analytical treatment of the problem, is always the following: How do the intuitions emerge in which our current linguistic practice has its roots?

Further Reading

Dennett, D.C. (1988). Quining qualia. In Marcel & Bisiach 1988. Reprinted in Block *et al.* 1996.

Dennett, D.C. (1991). *Consciousness Explained*. Boston, MA: Little, Brown & Co.

Kurthen, M. (1990). *Das Problem des Bewußtseins in der Kognitionswissenschaft – Perspektiven einer Kognitiven Neurowissenschaft*. Stuttgart: Enke.

Kurthen, M. (1993). Kriterien der Bewußtseinszuschreibung bei natürlichen und künstlichen kognitiven Systemen. *Kognitionswissenschaft*, **3**, 161–70.

---

[3] Cf. Levine 1983, 1993, Joseph Levine's article in the fifth part of this volume, David Papineau's contribution in Part 4 and sections 3.2 and 3.7 of the bibliography.

Kurthen, M. (1992). *Neurosemantik. Grundlagen einer Praxiologischen Kognitiven Neurowissenschaft.* Stuttgart: Enke.

Kurthen, M. (1994). *Hermeneutische Kognitionswissenschaft.* Bonn: djre-Verlag.

Kurthen, M. (1996). Das harmlose Faktum des Bewußtseins. In Krämer 1996.

Levine, J. (1983). Materialism and qualia: The explanatory gap. *Pacific Philosophical Quarterly*, **64**, 354–61.

Levine, J. (1993). On leaving out what it's like. In Davies & Humphreys 1993.

McGinn, C. (1989). Can we solve the mind–body problem? *Mind*, **98**, 349–66.

Rey, G. (1992). Sensational sentences switched. *Philosophical Studies*, **67**, 73–103.

Rey, G. (1992). Sensational sentences. In Davies & Humphreys 1992.

Rey, G. (1995). *Recent Philosophy of Mind: A Classical Approach.* Oxford: Basil Blackwell.

Wilkes, K.V. (1984). Is consciousness important? *British Journal for the Philosophy of Science*, **35**, 224–43.

Wilkes, K.V. (1988). —, yìshì, duh, um, and consciousness. In Marcel & Bisiach 1988.

Wilkes, K.V. (1988). *Real People: Personal Identity without Thought Experiments.* Oxford: Oxford University Press.

Further references as regards consciousness can be found in the bibliography at the end of this volume. Works which analyse the conceptual basis of the problem in a critical manner are listed in sections 1.1, 1.2, 2.1, 2.2, 2.3 and especially in section 3.1 as well as in sections 3.3, 3.4 and 3.5.

Kathy Wilkes

Losing Consciousness

'What is meant by consciousness we need not discuss; it is beyond all doubt.'
(Freud 1964: 70)

'Consciousness is like the Trinity; if it is explained so that you understand it, it has not been explained correctly.'
(Joynt 1981: 108)

My ambition here is to explain why I think that both Freud and Joynt are right. The conclusion I want to reach is an essentially simple one; it is getting there that will give difficulty. I shall give the reader the conclusion first, in oversimplified form, so that it will be easier to see how well I succeed or fail *en route* to it.

Here, then, is the conclusion in its crudest form. Common sense psychology (hence: 'CSP') is not the same as scientific psychology (hence: 'SP'), and still less is it like neuroscience or neuropsychology.[1] The question of consciousness in CSP is not, as far as I can see, particularly interesting, though many philosophers have found it so. Consciousness in SP, by contrast, is indeed interesting: a red herring that needs to be nipped in the bud, or at least sharply reined-in.

Now, to get to this conclusion. The first thing to do is to argue (as I have tried to do elsewhere[2]) that CSP and SP are interestingly and importantly different — just as common sense and science in general are different. The best way to show this is by starting at the most inclusive level, looking at the most all-embracing CSP term, 'mind'; and so I shall call this next section, 'Losing your Mind'. Since 'mind' and 'consciousness' need each other, this will not be an irrelevant detour.

---

[1] The only other abbreviation I shall use is 'CS' for common sense: neutral as between CSP, and common sense more generally. I *refuse* to talk of 'folk' wisdom or psychology; however readers should know that what I mean by CSP is what others — belittling, it seems to me, our everyday understanding — call 'folk psychology' (thus implying it is 'folksy' and primitive).

[2] Most thoroughly in Wilkes 1984.

I. Losing your Mind

It is a fact well-known to scholars of ancient Greece that there is no ancient Greek notion that translates adequately as 'mind'. (Nor, by the by, is there a wholly-adequate translation in contemporary Slavonic languages.[3]) The Greeks had the vastly-superior term 'psuche': a term, roughly, that picks out living from non-living things, describing them in terms of the activities characteristic of the sorts-of-things-that-they-are. It is worth describing in rough outline. Imagine a pyramid. At the bottom of the pyramid we find such things as vegetables — grass, nettles, trees — which grow, take nourishment, propagate themselves, and do some other things which we now call photosynthesis (etc.). Thistles do all these things a bit differently from oaks, but the principles remain the same. A little higher, but still presupposing their own forms of the 'vegetable' abilities (nutrition, growth, etc.), are low-level animals, such as amoebae, which can (for example) slowly move to or away from water that is potentially too hot or too cold for safety. Thus: simple locomotion, and fairly primitive sensation, added to nutrition, growth. A bit higher yet — but again, and always, presupposing everything lower — come insects: flies, mosquitoes, or the digger-wasp *Sphex*; perhaps also crabs and shrimps. (I do not consider myself an expert in the evolutionary ladder, but a rough picture is all that is needed.) These have, in various proportions, many of the same capacities, but more: better and more flexible locomotion, sensation of a kind. Then up another rung: the familiar animals — dogs, horses, cattle, cats, rats, bats. Just as before, these have versions of all the lower-level features (perhaps not photosynthesis) but have added flexible ranges of senses and mobile abilities, and they can learn. Then chimpanzees and other primates, and perhaps dolphins, whales, and elephants — non-human animals with some faculty of imagination and reason.

Then we get humans; who of course get in some shape or form most of the abilities lower down the pyramid, but add to them the capacities of practical and theoretical reason. These perhaps or possibly require a developed language-competence.[4]

That then is the *psuche* in crude outline; a notion deriving from observation of, and conjecture about, the living world. The set of *psuche* capacities characteristic of a creature of kind X spells out what it is to be an X (a thistle, a bee, a human). The *psuche* can readily be contrasted with the notion of mind, to the manifest advantage of the former. For 'the mind' is a much less satisfactory notion. It is not surprising that many cultures and languages have no term that translates smoothly as 'mind', for it is not clear

---

[3] I am no linguist, and so have not trawled-through many world languages. I can speak with (relative) confidence only about the major European languages, particularly Croatian, and Chinese; I have had generous advice from those who know Korean and Sanskrit.

[4] At the very tip of Aristotle's pyramid we get the gods, or The God, who needs only perfect rationality. (No digestion, nutrition, locomotion, imagination . . . etc.) I propose here to forget the divinity; my pyramid, for the purposes of this paper, can manage with a flattened top.

that the idea is at all coherent. The twin roots of the modern English term 'mind' sit uneasily together. On the one hand we have the Cartesian-style set of notions that emphasise immediate awareness, privileged access, incorrigibility, privacy. On the other hand there are the Brentano-style set of notions, deriving from the mediaeval scholastics, that take intentionality (roughly, 'aboutness') to be the mark of the mental. For Brentano, intentionality 'sundered' the universe fundamentally: dividing the mental from the physical.

These two strands of the mind, the 'Cartesian' and 'Brentano's', are familiar enough. What I want to emphasise, though, is that there is no particular reason to expect that the Cartesian criteria — mostly *epistemological* — will go along well, or hand in hand with, the primarily *logical* criterion of intentionality. Although a great many mental states can be made to fit both criteria, not all do by any means. ('Being in pain' is not an intentional state, and some would say that 'seeing' is not, either; there are many non-conscious intentional states: consider Freud![5]) In other words, the internal coherence and integrity of the term 'mind' is suspect; there is no particular reason to suppose that we — having the concept 'mind' — have got something *right* which the Greeks, and people in some central and east European countries, have not.

It is therefore somewhat less surprising, inasmuch as the term 'mind' rests in part upon 'consciousness', that in Greek psychology and literature there is no term that translates clearly or well as 'conscious' either. Perhaps they were missing something; but just what were they missing, exactly? It would be rash of anyone to deny the psychological genius of Aristotle and the continuing impact of the psychological dramas of Euripides, even if they had no terms for 'mind' or 'consciousness'. I have discovered that there is no very close equivalent in Chinese or Korean to 'conscious'. 'Yi-shi' is what I have been told is the closest for Chinese; but no non-human animal, as again I have been told, could possibly have *yi-shi*, so it cannot be very close to the English term. Then: in English, French and German the term 'conscious', in its present range of senses, was not found until the mid-seventeenth century (before that it kept the meaning *cumscire*: 'to know together with'). We seem to have managed very well without it for a very long time! In Sanskrit there are at least six different terms which can sometimes (but not always) be translated as 'conscious'. I am not wanting to suggest that such facts about language are conclusive. I do, however, find them *intriguing*.

The notion of a mind became, with and after Descartes, the sum total of *conscious* mental events — at least, this became a powerful strand in philosophy. Indeed, consciousness was for Descartes and the British em-

---

[5] Or Homer, Heraclitus, Euripides, Plotinus, Shakespeare, Dostoievsky, Wordsworth, Coleridge . . . such a list could run on *for pages*. See Whyte 1962: *passim*.

piricists a defining condition for being mental.[6] The combination of these two — 'mind', and 'conscious(ness)' — gave us a picture of mentality which is seen most clearly in Hume's metaphor (which, however, he acknowledged to *be* a metaphor) of the mind as 'a kind of theatre, where several perceptions successively make their appearance; pass, re-pass, glide away and mingle . . .' (Hume 1739, Book I, part iv, sec. vi; 1965, p. 253.), dancing before the little man in the head, picked out by the spotlight of consciousness. This theatre-model of mind, and consciousness, need each other and were made for each other. The metaphor was and remains extremely powerful, even among people who would abjure the implications which it holds. Many have jeered at the theatre model, the ghost in the machine, consciousness as a spotlight; it is more difficult to shake it out of our everyday thinking.

But, perhaps more surprisingly, we do not *need* to shake it out of our thinking. Nor could we, if we tried. The mind and consciousness *are*, now, central concepts for contemporary English-language CSP. I neither want nor need to deny that. These notions and idioms have pervaded our language. Consider: something is in my mind, weighing on it, I can be in two minds, can give you a piece of my mind; he can be out of his mind, she can be making hers up; something can be at the back of my mind (which is roughly the same as saying that it is on the tip of my tongue). He is or is not conscious of something, semi-conscious, unconscious, barely conscious, X is at the centre of my consciousness, the focus of consciousness, the spotlight of consciousness.

I have no quibble with such locutions as these, and it would indeed be stupid to challenge the legitimacy of any term in everyday usage. Wittgenstein argued (or, rather, stated) that philosophy does and must leave everything as it is. If a word or phrase is in everyday usage, what greater legitimacy does it *need*, what greater legitimacy could it have? (In CS, or CSP.) Dozens more examples could be found. For instance: I can do something for your sake, I do not want or need to deny *or* affirm that there are such things as sakes. I can agree that the sky is blue, without committing myself to the existence of 'the sky'; I can observe that the sun has risen without presupposing that the sun moves around the earth. I can cross the Equator, without noticing any line. I can believe things with all my heart, too; and my heart can go out to you with heartfelt feelings, or my heart may be heavy, or be light. Again: 'by the pricking of my thumbs, something wicked this way comes' . . . minds, consciousness, sakes, the sky, travelling suns, the Equator, hearts, prickles in thumbs: I have no quibble with any of them: *in CSP or CS*.

But I would be happy to put them all in the same bag, where CSP (or, indeed, CS) are concerned. Useful; often instrumentalist; such idioms con-

---

[6] See Locke 1690, Bk. II, ch. xxvii, para 11; 1959, vol. I: 448–9. Hume 1739, Bk II, part ii., sec. vi; 1965: 366. Hume 1748, sec. vii, part 1, para. 52; 1963: 66.

tribute to the glory of CS and CSP. And cannot be challenged — because a challenge would be absurd. The vast democracy of native users will fail to notice, or will be immune to, or will be amused by, the suggestions of the 'eliminative materialists' to reject the vocabulary with which we have created, built, rebuilt, and re-charged our cultures; for far longer than we have had the (noble) venture of SP. The main point is that the two, SP and CSP, can coexist. Just as can and do CS and science generally. CSP and SP have no need to fight each other.

By now my strategy may be becoming clearer. CS and CSP and their vocabulary are quite all right, above criticism (because both CS and CSP blithely *ignore* criticism). CSP is very sophisticated and very profound — far more so, by at least some criteria, than is the science of psychology (SP). This is not any criticism of SP. It is a youngster, now only about 120 years old;[7] whereas CSP is of course thousands of years old. Consider what we can do with it. We can say that Susie is wondering whether Davor has realised that if Marija intends to fly to Frankfurt with him, she will have first to persuade her father to assure her mother that Davor's intentions are above-board . . . Thoughts about thoughts, every day. And this, of course, the ancient Greeks could do as readily as any of us — without benefit of Descartes, Brentano, or terms like 'mind' or 'consciousness'. We all do this sort of thing daily, very well, even if we talk about believing with all our hearts, doing it for your sake, being in two minds, and sleeping under the sky.

None of this matters to those working in SP. The sophistication of the explanation imagined above, about Susie's layers of knowledge of thoughts (which, note, is the sort of thing that *anyone* can do: we don't need to be a Euripides, a Dostoievsky, or a Henry James) need not worry those working in SP. This is because explanations such as those offered by the above (stilted) Susie-Davor-Marija scenario are not what SP is trying to provide. That is, the explananda, terminology, methodology, grounds for success, and what counts as verification: all of these are very different in CSP and SP. This last claim has already been foreshadowed, but could do with more defence.

II. CSP and SP

The central task of science (any science) is to describe and explain systematically. By contrast, there are no specific 'tasks' for CSP. It rarely, very rarely, takes-on systematic description and explanation, although it is brilliant at explaining individual actions done in specific circumstances, at a specific time, by just *this* person in relation to just *that* person. Unlike SP, too, the vocabulary of CSP needs to cope with tasks other than systematic description and explanation: joking, jesting, jeering, hinting, hassling, hustling, commending, condemning, consoling, blaming, bullying; threat-

[7] I date the birth of SP (as so many do) to Wilhelm Wundt's reign in Leipzig. It is not irrelevant that he — although trained as a physiologist — held a philosophy chair there.

ening, reassuring, encouraging, sympathising, proselytising, punning, warning . . . and such an Austintatious list could continue long.

The terminology differs in nature as a result of what it is trying to do, too; and this is an important point. The specificity, exactness, accuracy of CSP come largely from *lack* of well-defined precision: from the way shades of nuance in the terms chosen, tone of voice, the context, details of the agent, the particular nature of speaker and audience, and their relationship . . . all contribute to every explanation or assertion. Lack of precision, overlapping partial synonyms, nuances — all this helps CSP. Think how much can be conveyed *in context and to a particular audience, and by overtones* simply by choosing between 'he thinks that p', 'he is of the opinion that p', 'he believes that p', 'he assumes that p', 'he is sure that p', 'he has the prejudice that p', 'he knows that p', 'he takes p for granted', 'he judges that p'; as well as by tone of voice: astonished, admiring, factual, scornful. In SP, clarity and exactness have the very opposite sources: the ambition (even if rarely achieved) is for as clearly demarcated terms as possible, context-independence, the abjuring of partial synonyms, audience- and speaker-independence. Put another way: only in CSP, not in SP, would Russell's famous declension make sense: 'I am firm; you are obstinate; he is pig-headed'.

Again: in CSP generalisations and laws are rarely important; the indubitable generality of common sense stems rather from our command of language. We know how to use terms like 'generous', 'jealous', or 'hopes' without needing explicit laws or generalisations. We get a 'know-how' of the terms in the language, almost never a 'know-that'.

Sciences however seek for, test, and use explicit laws. It is the linguist, not the layman, who seeks *laws* to explain when in English to use 'a', when 'the', and when neither. (I choose that example because I have long been seeking any principle — even a rough one — that works to explain the use of the definite and indefinite articles to foreigners whose native language does not have them.) We don't use laws, but we know how to do it. *There* is your generality. Similarly, although it is a great myth that science cannot manage without (operational or other) 'definitions', it remains true that science aims for a stripped-down vocabulary where ambiguity and overlap are, increasingly, eliminated. In the physical sciences the terms 'field' and 'space-time', were furiously criticised for woolly vagueness when they were first introduced. But they made possible precisely those experiments that sharpened them into concepts on the cutting edge of contemporary physics.

Thus: unlike SP, CSP can cope with descriptions such as 'doing it for your sake', 'I'm in two minds about that', 'he's pig-headed', 'my heart went out to him'. And — for just the same reasons — 'he is / is not conscious of his wife's misery / of the pain in his toe'.

It is important to stress under this heading a point that has been implicit already. Namely: *there is nothing strange about this distinction between CSP and SP*. We get a similar distinction — and accept it — in the physical sciences: between common-sense physics and scientific physics. I mean: we are not in the least surprised when physicists talk about peculiar things like neutral bosons or the (recently discovered) top quark. We are not in the least surprised if the physical sciences do not take seriously as *explananda* doorstops, ashtrays, tables. We should be equally blase if psychology talks about concepts unfamiliar in CSP such as 'hypermnesia' or 'optic aphasia', but do not talk about sakes, souls, or Schadenfreude. In all other sciences we accept a division — albeit a blurred one — between the layman in the street and the scientist in his laboratory and white coat. Laymen's conversations in bars generally deploy few terms that feature in the research-level conversations of physicists; and vice-versa. Why should they?

CSP is thousands of years old, has never been 'a theory', and does not need pompous lectures about its alleged 'stagnation' from its various theoretical offspring. Because of its great age, by and large it does excellently well what it is called-upon to do. (Practice makes perfect). Recently it has found notions like 'mind' and 'consciousness' helpful. Before that it found notions like the 'four humours', 'possession', or 'melancholia' helpful. It has picked up, and will always pick up and discard (magpie fashion) from science and also from elsewhere (mythology, mesmerism, witchcraft, astrology, religion, sport, pop or rock music) any notion that it likes. I am suggesting that 'consciousness' has been one such pick-up, and a relatively recent one. Another example might be the tabloid-press-style-description of someone as 'Oedipal' — usually meaning no more than that someone is a loving son — or 'introvert'. Freud has supplied a lot of terms for the CSP magpie to pick up and adopt and adapt to its own purposes. 'Consciousness' covers more ground than 'sake'; but is not fundamentally different.

I do not see that there is a *problem* here. 'Leave CSP alone!' is my battle-cry; CSP is a great and glorious mixture that can be described as a little bit instrumentalistic, a little bit realist, but primarily a lot of both. It has no greater 'problem of consciousness' than it has a problem with sakes, divided minds, or broken hearts; no greater a problem than that geographers have with the equator, or physicists with ashtrays or doorstops, or botanists with weeds, or astronomers with the sun rising in the morning, or the sky being mottled-blue. And it has no more need systematically to 'identify' beliefs with brain-states than physicists have to 'identify' the type 'ashtray' with physical states, or astronomers to identify anything with 'the sky'. So there is no need to locate, identify, or explain CSP consciousness. The things CS and CSP talk about are, quite often, just *irrelevant* to science. And none the worse for that. Under different descriptions, they all fall under a science, if they exist at all: e.g. every ashtray is made of something — glass, say, or iron — and there is a lot that science can say about glass and iron. So also for the phenomena labelled 'conscious' in CSP; if they are to be taken realistically (unlike sakes, maybe) there will be a description under which they might be amenable to systematic study.

CSP is thus not the same as SP. Just as everyday physics — CS physics — is not what physicists in laboratories are talking about. And, *of course,* the line is blurred. The layman talks about oxygen, gold, water: these are *explananda* that are subject to systematic scrutiny by the sciences too. But we also talk of doorstops, ashtrays, trees, books, the sky, weeds; these are not. So also in CSP — why should it be different? — we are likely to pick on, sometimes, *explananda* that are interesting both to CSP and to SP. Dreaming, for instance, memory, perception, pain. There is no doubt a large overlap (when does a hill become a mountain? There is nothing wrong with overlaps). My point is just that most of the time CSP and SP go their separate terminological and methodological ways (not always); *just as* CS description of the physical world goes its own separate way from science.

III. Recovering the Psuche

SP needs to have or to seek clear and unambiguous *explananda–* phenomena; phenomena such that it makes sense to suppose that we could get laws about them. It is — by comparison to CSP — very straightforward: it is looking for systematic descriptions and explanations of behaviour.

The question is therefore whether 'mind' or 'consciousness' should be *explananda* in *this* game. To clear the ground for consciousness, let us first look once more at 'mind', from the perspective of science.

I have suggested already that the term 'mind' is not shared by all languages, and that its roots — in the Cartesian 'consciousness' and in intentionality — do not make it look promising as a natural *explanandum* for systematic study. The associated adjective, 'mental', of course shares these same unpromising features. The adjective 'psychological' could be more useful (and bland), covering no more and no less than 'term used in a SP theory'.

We have seen that the sciences adopt terms from CS. But they also adapt them: bake them, as it were, in a sort of theoretical oven. 'Energy', for example, in physics is not quite the same as what we get when we eat Weetabix for breakfast. The spin of an electron is unlike the spin of a child's top, and perhaps only a theoretical physicist thinks that a quark has charm. Zoology distinguishes sharply between two kinds of wolf, while CS finds just one kind quite alarming enough. Botany thinks that garlic and lilies belong to the same species, which would seem strange to the cook or the clergyman. So for 'force', 'mass', 'field'. The same holds in SP for 'information', 'memory', 'representation', 'expectancy', 'recognition', 'purpose', and many more. This is neither odd nor deplorable; the sciences often need to put terms to rather different uses than the roles they fulfil in everyday parlance. Psychology, and also neuroscience, use terms we would call 'mental' in contexts we would not consider as mind-like, as when, for instance, Sokolov calls a bit of the rat's brain (the amygdala) an 'expectancy-generator'. Conversely, terms apparently central to CSP may not feature at all in SP, such as 'knowledge', 'willing' 'voluntary', 'sake'. 'Mind' may thus prove to be as inessential to SP as are 'sakes', or 'souls'.

Contemporary SP should not then have a problem over whether rats or robots have minds. It explains their behaviour by using psychological terms; and this is *trivially* true, because 'psychological term' means, exactly, 'term used by SP'. Many but not all of these will also be terms we consider to be 'mental' — perhaps because they are intentional, like 'expectancy' — but even then may be applied across a different extension, as when a rat's amygdala is labelled as an 'expectancy-generator'. Contemporary SP, shading in to neuropsychology and neuroscience, is — I suggest — talking about the psuche.

So, at last, what of consciousness? By now it should be clear that *if* it is to be adopted as a term in a SP theory, we should expect that it must also be adapted and baked in the kiln of a theory. Since — as I suppose all would agree — 'conscious' and its cognates in CSP cover a multitude of sins, we should not be surprised at all if SP, insofar as some SP theories retain the term, uses it in different ways and in different contexts from those of everyday life.

Once we are aware — and who could not be? — of the different distinctions between what are very heterogeneous classes of psychological phenomena called 'conscious'; once we are aware of the difficulties of forcing homogeneity on to the heterogeneity (to say what is in common between a pain in the foot and a thought about Gödel's theorem, between transient visual awareness and forming a plan of action); then we might avoid getting bogged-down in all sorts of unreal difficulties. Dennett (1991) has recently pointed out (as have many others; but he has summarised things excellently) that once we were landed or lumbered with the Cartesian notion of the mind — the theatre picture, the little man in the brain, the spotlight of consciousness — problems surely must abound. The mind as a *res cogitans*, consciousness as infallible, led to the conclusion (or rather, perhaps, presupposed) that consciousness had to be unitary; and given *that* argument, there will inevitably be difficulties when we do not find anything like a 'unitary consciousness'.

There are everyday difficulties, empirically-based ones, philosophical ones and philosophical-scientific ones.

The everyday difficulties with the CSP notion of a unitary consciousness include dreaming; self-deception; weakness of will; how to describe the skilled driver vigorously arguing as he drives — conscious of his gear-changes, or not?[8] Extreme depression. Senile dementia. Slips of tongue, slips of memory. Wishful thinking. Many more, of course.

The empirically based puzzles include the dementias, the agnosias, the alexias, the aphasias. Hemi-neglect; Wernicke's syndrome, Broca's syn-

[8] Professional psychologists and non-psychologists alike tend to divide 50:50 when I have asked them about this. (No scientific survey; just the result of asking colleagues, and hundreds of students, over a twenty year period.)

drome, Anton's syndrome, Alzheimer's disease. Blindsight. Semantic masking. Schizophrenia. Commissurotomy. Multiple personality — if the reader believes there to be such a condition. Many more again: brain disease or damage do not thoughtfully attack *specific* locations, so their effects can be various, and can astonish. The CSP notion of consciousness cannot *begin* to cope with such phenomena; nor could any SP notion which tried to use 'consciousness' as an explanatory term.

Third: philosophers have created problems by asking what it is like to be a bat (Nagel 1974), or a cat, or a rat, or you or me; a question that presupposes that there is some specific essence of this or that creature's consciousness that I can never attain if I have not had it; if, for instance, I cannot echolocate like a bat. Searle[9] worries that nobody — or no *thing* — in his Chinese room understands Chinese. Both Nagel and Searle, albeit for very different reasons, seem to me to want (while rejecting the possibility of) the distilled ambrosia of conscious unity.

Fourth: philosophers and scientists often presuppose that consciousness, if it is to be tracked down at all, must be found *somewhere*. Perhaps in Eccles' 'open neurons'. Perhaps in the frontal lobes. Perhaps in the left hemisphere. Perhaps in the brain stem (the reticular activating system). Perhaps in the pineal gland. Perhaps Aristotle was right: in the heart.

I have not bothered to explain why all the phenomena listed above create problems for 'conscious(ness)' as either an *explanandum*, or an *explanans*, in SP. I hope and assume that it is by now no longer necessary.

Thus: scientists should forget the mind, and consciousness; should return to the *psuche*. CSP, of course, will remain as it was, is, and always will be.

References

Dennett, D.C. (1991). *Consciousness Explained*. Boston, MA: Little, Brown & Co.

Freud, S. (1964). *New Introductory Lectures in Psychoanalysis*. Edited and translated by J. Starchey and A. Freud. New York: W.W. Norton.

Hume, D. (1965)[1739–40]. *A Treatise of Human Nature*. Oxford: Oxford University Press.

Hume, D. (1963)[1748]. *An Enquiry concerning Human Understanding*. Oxford: Oxford University Press.

Joynt, R.J. (1981). Are two heads better than one? *Behavioral and Brain Sciences*, **4**, 108 f.

Locke, J. (1959)[1690]. *An Essay concerning Human Understanding*. London: Constable.

Nagel, T. (1974). What is it like to be a bat? *Philosophical Review*, **83**, 435–50.

Searle, J. (1980). Minds, brains and programs. *Behavioral and Brain Sciences*, **3**, 417–57.

Whyte, L.L. (1962). *The Unconscious before Freud*. London: Tavistock Publications.

Wilkes, K.V. (1984). Pragmatics in science and theory in common sense. *Inquiry*, **27**, 339–61.

[9] First in Searle 1980: 417–57, but repeatedly since.

Martin Kurthen

On the Prospects of a Naturalistic Theory of Phenomenal Consciousness

---

I. Introduction

One of our deeply rooted philosophical attitudes is that *really* to understand something means to have a *theory* of it. This holds especially for those phenomena we — as ordinary, commonsensical people — seem to understand pre-theoretically, e.g. *time, consciousness,* or *love.* Pre-theoretical transparency is philosophically suspect: how could our primordial familiarity with consciousness or time represent a genuine understanding if it leaves questions about the 'nature' or the 'rules' or 'laws' of these domains unanswered? But unfortunately, pre-theoretically familiar phenomena have turned out to be quite resistant to theoretical explication. Consciousness is paradigmatic in this respect: everybody has it, everybody has an immediate grasp of what it is (or appears to be), but there is as yet no convincing *theory* of consciousness, philosophical or empirical. There are lots of possible reasons for that: philosophy and the empirical sciences might just be insufficient instruments; the concept of consciousness might be completely ill-defined; consciousness might 'in fact' be nonexistent, etc. In what follows, I will not try to decide all these issues. Instead, I will pick out and discuss just some points made by contemporary philosophers of consciousness, and as a result of these discussions I will propose that although it has not yet been shown that consciousness *can* be naturalized, (we) naturalists should not be alarmed since it is by no means clear that consciousness *needs* to be naturalized (where to 'naturalize' means to explain without recourse to a mentalistic vocabulary within a theory that can finally become part of the natural sciences). In the following section, the common concept of phenomenal or qualitative consciousness and the notorious 'explanatory gap' will be introduced according to the current literature. In the third section, I will briefly discuss — and dismiss — Dennett's (1991) proposal that qualia don't really exist (although they seem to). In the fourth section, I will review some of the literature concerning the naturalization of qualia. The last section will present some metaphilosophical reflections about the need for a theory of phenomenal consciousness.

II. Phenomenal Consciousness and the Explanatory Gap

Consciousness is not a single entity, but rather a complex of heterogenous phenomena like awareness, self-reflection, wakefulness and others. The concept of consciousness in ordinary language differs from the expressly *designed* concepts used in psychological or physiological theories. Anyway, the concept of phenomenal consciousness as currently used in the philosophy of mind is simply this: a state is phenomenally conscious if it has 'experiential properties' (Block 1995), that is, if there is something 'it is like' to be in that state *for* the respective organism (or, more generally, for the respective subject of consciousness). The property of being conscious is primarily ascribed to total complex beings like men or other higher animals (these are the 'subjects of consciousness'); in a secondary sense, a process in or a state of that being can be ascribed the property of being conscious if it presents itself *to* the subject in the conscious mode, that is, as an experience.

To define phenomenal consciousness as experience does not mean having to postulate a domain of states and processes that are *purely* phenomenally conscious. For if we adopt Block's (1995) distinction between phenomenal consciousness (in the above sense) and access consciousness (consciousness as relevance for reasoning and control of action *qua content* of the respective state), we will find that most, if not all conscious states have both phenomenal and access-aspects: on the one hand it may somehow be *like to* have a certain access-conscious state (e.g. a thought), and, on the other hand, a phenomenally conscious state like a sensing of a coloured object may also have representational relevance in the overall cognitive processing of the respective subject of consciousness. That is, the property of being phenomenally conscious is the experiential aspect of a state that may have one or more additional properties, one of which could be the property of being access-conscious.

This point is of some importance in the discussion about the naturalization of qualia: if qualia were purely phenomenally conscious, then elimination or reduction might be the only strategies worth considering, but if qualia also possessed non-phenomenal properties, then the naturalist could concentrate on these properties (Flanagan 1992: 60 ff.). But what *are* qualia? As Lycan (1987: 83 f.) pointed out, qualia were originally conceived as properties of phenomenal individuals. Lewis (1929: 60) introduced the 'quale' as the repeatable content of the 'given element in a single experience of an object' (this given element Lewis called a 'presentation'). But if the concept of phenomenal individuals is taken seriously, the discussion about qualia will lead back into the realm of out-of-fashion sense-datum theories where Sellars (1981) had indefatigably tried to establish the possibility of a scientific relocation of the 'ultimate homogeneity' of colour (Lycan 1987: 93–111; Kurthen 1990).

Perhaps discouraged by the complexity of these issues, we nowadays employ a less specific concept of qualia as just 'the ways things seem to us' (Dennett 1988: 43) or 'intrinsic mental features of our experience' (Block 1990: 53). This looser notion of qualia is influenced by Nagel's famous definition of the subjective character of experience which says that 'an organism has conscious mental states if and only if there is something it is like to *be* that organism — something it is like *for* the organism' (Nagel 1979: 166). In what follows, I take *phenomenality* as the core notion of 'like-to-be-ness', 'seemingness', 'experiential character' and the like: a quale is a feature of a conscious state, namely its phenomenal quality: the specific way it feels or seems or appears to the subject of that state (Loar 1990: 81). Qualia are the specific guises of phenomenal consciousness.[1]

In the last decades, access-consciousness has mainly been discussed in the context of psychosemantics or intentional causation, that is, the problem of the naturalization of intentionality. This is because access-conscious states have often been taken to be relevant for cognitive processing *owing to* their intentional content (see above). On the other hand, the discussion of phenomenal consciousness seems to be ruled by intuitions rather than arguments, and it is mainly this discussion where the notorious 'explanatory gap' between the mental and the physical (or the mind and the brain) comes into play. The 'explanatory gap intuition' says that the physical story for a sensing of red does not explain why the phenomenally conscious state of sensing 'redly' has *this* specific quality and not an other, e.g. that of a sensing of green (Levine 1983; Block 1992; 1995). Akins introduces this intuition suggestively (before she tries to relativize it):

> The problem of consciousness, simply put, is that we cannot understand how a brain, *qua* gray, granular lump of biological matter, could be the seat of human consciousness, the source or ground of our rich phenomenal lives. How could that 'lump' be conscious — or, conversely, how could I, as conscious being, be that lump? Moreover, because we cannot comprehend how a brain can be conscious at all — *the very fact of physically embodied consciousness* — it makes little intuitive sense to think that any *particular* facts about the brain would prove helpful in this regard . . . Physiological facts and the puzzle of consciousness seem to pass each other by (Akins 1993: 124 f.).

---

[1] See also Flanagan's definition of a quale as 'a mental state or event that has, among its properties, the property that there is something it is like to be in it' (Flanagan 1992: 64).

So, the intuitional qualia freak could claim: 'I can perfectly well imagine a brain physically or functionally identical with mine but yet giving rise to different, perhaps inverted tokens of phenomenal experience (inverted qualia), or even to no such experience at all (absent qualia).' There is an extended discussion of this intuition in the qualia literature, which I do not intend to review here. Just this: two of the main problems of the inverted/absent qualia intuition are (1) whether we can *really 'perfectly well' imagine* the inverted/absent qualia case on the basis of current scientific knowledge and theoretical reasoning, and *if* we can, then (2) whether from this *mere imaginability* anything substantial concerning the possibility of a naturalization of qualia would follow (Horgan 1987; Dennett 1991). But before I enter into the qualia discussion in more detail (sections III and IV), I would like to stress two points which may be evident but deserve being mentioned because of their importance. The first, and probably more evident one, is that the qualia freak's intuition in no way relies on the momentary insufficiency of neuroscience with respect to the total reconstruction of the physical/causal sensory and cerebral story for, e.g. sensing redly. Even if some future neuroscience would have made this story completely transparent, the qualia freak would expect the explanatory gap to persist.

The second point, addressing the above 'two main problems', is that the burden of argument (or the 'burden of intuition') cannot completely be passed over to inverted/absent qualia examples. It is not necessary to imagine identical brains with different qualia or to discuss the relevance of such imaginability. If there is an explanatory gap, it is already notable when we imagine a completely transparent physical story for a factual sensing redly (a story which factually never underlies a sensing greenly) and ask for the sense in which the sensing redly is *explained* by such a story. Reliable correlations between brain states and conscious states would form the explanatory basis.[2] Leaving aside the question of how to determine intersubjectively the occurrence of conscious states in any individual, an explanation of consciousness would proceed from these reliable mind–brain correlations by postulating a certain relation between the two domains — instantiation, supervenience, identity, or whatever. The status of such an explanation is that of an *interpretation of factual correlations between two domains of phenomena that are themselves taken for granted and thus cannot be 'explained' in their internal constitution by this interpretation.* That is: such an explanation may be able to show that conscious states supervene on brain states, but it cannot demonstrate that the supervening states must have *those* phenomenal properties they factually have and not other ones. Compare the explicability of a cerebral state that has (ideally) been identified as the constant correlate of a sensing redly with the explica-

---

[2] It is irrelevant whether the notion of a 'Cartesian theater' (Dennett 1991) is employed here or whether alternative models like Dennett's 'multiple drafts' are preferred. All we require is the notion of conscious events as somehow based on cerebral events.

bility of the phenomenally conscious state of sensing redly itself. The cerebral state can be explained as the final link in a causal chain of physical/physiological events running from the presence of a red object in the subject's visual field via retinal excitation patterns to a centripetal (and also centrifugal) spread of discharge patterns in the cerebral visual system, while these patterns are partly determined by occurrent cerebral excitation patterns before the visual input. On the basis of complete knowledge of the physiological and anatomical characteristics of the brain or at least the visual system (including knowledge of the possible causal chains running through that brain as a result of sensory stimulation), a physiological explanation of the sensing-redly brain state would demonstrate that this state with all the features that individuate it *must* occur under certain ideal or at least definable conditions. This explanation would define a certain structure (the brain or visual system) and an initial functional state of that structure (sensory stimuli 'running along the cerebral causal chain') and could then predict the necessary occurrence of the next functional state (or a bunch of possible functional states, but let them all be correlated to a sensing redly). But there is no analogous procedure for the explanation of the sensing redly itself.

First, it is by no means clear that the sensing redly is a link in the causal chain in the same way as the sensing-redly brain state is, for that would mean that the sensing-redly brain state literally causes the sensing redly. It is much more convenient to interpret the sensing redly as a part of the causal chain in a much looser way — e.g. in the sense that only the brain state is literally a link in the causal chain, while the sensing redly (for example) supervenes on that brain state. Second, in the case of the sensing redly (as opposed to the sensing-redly brain state) there are no total characteristics (structural plus functional) of the preceding or correlating brain states on the basis of which we could specify how to demonstrate that the sensing redly must occur with all the phenomenal features it has (instead of, say, features of a sensing greenly), since to us the characteristics of the brain states are themselves indifferent to *any phenomenal* features. And it is *not* a good reply to say that such a demonstration *consisted* in showing that the sensing-redly brain state necessarily occurs, because we *knew* that this brain state is accompanied by a sensing redly. Why not? Because it remains unclear why the sensing-redly brain state must be accompanied by a sensing redly *in the first place*.

In contrast to the explanation of the sensing-redly brain state, in the case of the sensing redly itself the total physical story cannot explain why the explanandum must have all the features it factually has. The crux is that brain states and conscious states are prima facie completely different kinds of phenomena (neural vs. mental) occurring in prima facie completely different substrates (brains vs. subjects of consciousness), and that theses concerning the *relation between* both kinds of phenomena (e.g. supervenience) cannot account for the *occurrence of* the supervening phenomena in their phenomenal guises. Anyway, thought experiments with inverted or absent qualia are not required to illustrate the 'explanatory gap': all we have to do is imagine a complete physical story for a sensing-redly brain state and ask ourselves if we could establish the necessary occurrence of the qualitative features of the associated phenomenal state on the basis of knowledge of the physical story alone. The answer is negative. Strictly speaking, however, this only shows that *knowledge* of the physical story alone would not enable *us* to infer the necessary occurrence of certain qualia. We would not be able to *decide* about the possibility of inverted or absent qualia on the basis of that knowledge. This leaves space for agnostic theses like this: the complete physical story in fact accounts for the necessary occurrence of the respective qualia, but for some reasons we — as cognitive systems — are unable to grasp this sort of nexus (McGinn 1989). But it is hard to argue for or against such metacognitive theses that are based on a certain judgment of our own cognitive constitution. Hence, at this point I would like to keep with the tradition of qualia philosophy and content myself with the intuition described above. It said: all that can possibly be done is to establish fixed correlations between adequate stimuli, causal sensory/cerebral chains and sensings of red. But even the proof of these correlations leaves open why the correlated sensing must have this specific phenomenal quality (of sensing redly) it has and not a different one. In the following sections, I will discuss just some proposals for how to avoid the acceptance of this intuition.

III. There Seem to be Seemings . . .

One branch of materialist thinking about qualia turns the problem into an ontological one by maintaining that qualia do not 'really' exist. This branch could be dubbed 'eliminativism', although the best-known eliminativist arguments make a linguistic or nominalistic detour to ontology in that they hold that the *concept* of consciousness fails to refer, or fails to designate any actual psychological process, or will be eliminated in a future cognitive science (P.S. Churchland 1983; Rey 1991). I am not going to discuss such arguments for the (scientific) inadequacy of the *concept* of consciousness, but rather take a short view on one actual eliminativist argument to the effect that qualia (themselves, as phenomena) do not exist. I say 'a short view', because I must admit that I feel uneasy in discussions about the 'ontology of the mental'. Ontology is a complicated issue: the ontology you chose partly depends on the philosophy of science you prefer, and your philosophy of science may be backed up by your favorite epistemology, which again may be contaminated by your pet ideas in the philosophy of mind etc.

So, just a short view: Dennett (1991) has proposed to 'disqualify' qualia by denying their existence while admitting their *seeming* existence: there seem to be qualia, but in fact there aren't. I must confess that Dennett's argument against the existence of qualia has not become completely transparent to me, neither through the lecture of *Consciousness Explained* nor through the study of later replies to critics (Dennett 1993). In chapter twelve of *Consciousness Explained*, Dennett's strategy is twofold: on the one hand he criticizes well-known pro-qualia arguments (inverted qualia, knowledge argument), on the other hand he tries to *remove the motivation to believe* in the existence of qualia. Let's focus on the second strategy. Put simply, Dennett holds that colours are in fact properties of objects 'out there' in the world, and that in the likewise 'real world' of brain and behaviour, qualitative colour experience turns out to be the sum of inborn and learned associations and dispositions based on sensory stimuli in the visual mode. That's what colour qualia 'really' are, although they *seem* to have additional properties that determine the way things seem to us. As a result of evolution, we (among other animals) are able to *detect* colours as surface properties of external objects and *react* with the correct colour-discriminative behaviour. There is no reason to postulate additional qualia even if we are not able to actually define the surface properties that make up colours: when someone reports he saw something pink, then he exhibits discriminative behaviour with regard to external surface properties that are in principle within the reach of neuroscience, psychophysics, and biology. So Dennett seems to argue. If this sounds not too convincing, the reason may be that Dennett's adroit and well-presented attempt to remove the motivation to believe in qualia simply loses its magic in my not too sympathetic summary. This loss of magic is not to be understood as a point against Dennett (as an accusation of a lack of rationality or something): the piecemeal removal of deeply rooted, but unwanted intuitions definitely *requires* elements of persuasion, rhetoric and the like. But in my view, this way of treating qualia belongs to the project of questioning the relevance of the whole problem of qualia rather than *explaining consciousness* (Rorty 1993). Dennett's view that there is nothing over and above surface properties, sensory and cerebral detection mechanisms and discriminative behaviour *may* well be correct, but it is hard to see how one could *demonstrate* to someone who experiences a colour quale that what he experiences as a quale is 'in fact' nothing but a complex of dispositions.

What Dennett presents is not a new and compelling argument, but rather a well-presented appeal to the good will of the qualia freak, roughly like this: 'Of course there seem to be qualia, but why insist on their real existence in face of all the problems they cause the Good Naturalistic Project? Why not let the seemings *seem* and complexes of dispositions *be there*?' Perhaps the acceptance of an ontology requires a decision rather than an argument. Then it would also not be a point against Dennett to say that his texts give no conclusive argument for a certain ontological status of qualia. But why, then, did he not just state that he had to decide himself for the denial of the existence of qualia on the basis of other philosophical preferences like verificationism or naturalism? So, the upshot of my all too short view on Dennett's ontological thesis is: either we discuss the philosophical preferences that really motivate an ontology, or we ask ourselves whether we should really take the qualia problem serious. For the latter see section V, the former I don't feel competent to do. But anyway, to me it sounds misleading to say that Dennett had 'explained' phenomenal consciousness.

IV. Qualia and Naturalism

In this section, I am not going to discuss the specific problems of a *functionalistic* theory of qualia, since functionalistic theories are just a small subset of naturalistic theories (as long as functionalism is understood as a naturalistic theory, which in this paper it is), and my general question is whether qualia can be naturalized at all. Just a few words about functionalism. There are two major arguments against a functionalistic theory of qualia:

1.   Qualia are intrinsic, non-relational features of consciousness. Functionalism is restricted to the assessment of relational features. Hence functionalism cannot explain qualia (Nagel 1970).

2.   If qualia could be explained functionally, then differences in qualia should always be associated with functional differences. But inverted-qualia thought experiments show that this does not have to be the case. Hence functionalism cannot explain qualia (Block 1990: 53).

Ad 1: It is controversial whether (and if so, in exactly what sense) intrinsicality and non-relationality are features of qualia.[3] But to me, at least it is not doubtful that *phenomenality* is a feature of qualia. So one might think of the possibility that although qualia are non-intrinsic and relational (in whatever sense), functionalism still cannot account for their phenomenality. One conceivable reason for this would be that no naturalistic theory could explain phenomenality. Instead of giving a 'complete physical story' of a sensing redly as discussed in the previous section, we might just as well give a complete *functional* story without being able to establish the necessary occurrence of a quale *as* a phenomenal state or event.

Ad 2: Inverted qualia thought experiments are even more controversial (Lycan 1987; Harman 1990; Dennett 1991). And there seem to be some ways to escape from argument 2, if not for functionalism, then at least for naturalism. For example, one could grant that qualia are non-functional without giving up the idea of a naturalistic theory of qualia (Horgan 1984; 1987; Block 1990). But as pointed out in the previous section, I hope to get along without inverted qualia examples for the purposes of this paper.

[3]   See Rorty 1993 for a summary of the metaphilosophical aspects of this controversy.

Now what about the prospects of the naturalization of qualia in general? Again, my assessment will not be exhaustive — I will just consider two recently offered strategies to explain qualia in the context of a naturalistic philosophy of mind. The first (Metzinger 1994) is an example of 'going into the details' of science and trying to achieve an understanding of phenomenal consciousness on the basis of our improved knowledge of the mind-brain.[4] The second strategy (Flanagan 1992) focuses on the putative non-phenomenal properties of qualia that should make them 'objectively detectable'. Metzinger (1993; 1994) chooses a cognitive-science-inspired approach to understand why we '*pick out* certain phenomenal states by features, which introspectively appear as *essential* features of those states' (Metzinger 1994: 674). He interprets qualia as input-dependent data-structures, the function of which is to 'signal the actual presence of the stimulus . . . in a very fast and reliable way' (Metzinger 1994: 675). As 'analogue indicators' they possess an intensity parameter in that they are 'able to internally present the intensity or *signal strength* of the presentandum for the organism' (Metzinger 1994: 676). Now the crucial point is that an abstract property of qualia of a certain kind (e.g. sensings of red), namely their 'format', is the common feature that makes them tokens of a quale type. These formats are realized as plastic patterns of activity corresponding to certain partitions of the state-space of modules on the hardware-level — the cortical visual module in the case of sensings of red (*ibid*).

Metzinger (*ibid*) holds that 'it might just be this *format*, which we metarepresentationally grasp when *introspectively categorizing* mental presentata.' For if we transform presentata into other representational media using other formats (e.g. a propositional representation), it is exactly the qualitative aspects which get lost, while the indicator aspect remains. When we experience a concrete quale, the format of the respective data-structure is once more grasped by a metamodelling function of the brain: 'What we experience as a 'quale' are not the neuronal processes themselves, but the *abstract property* of a datastructure generated by these processes depicted by a metarepresentational function . . . ' (Metzinger 1994: 677). In this sense, qualia are representational rather than physical phenomena. Now does this approach promote the naturalization of qualia? Metzinger tries to integrate qualia into a scientific picture of the mind by explaining phenomenal experience as the metarepresented format of mental datastructures. This can be seen as a contribution to a 'closing of the gap' (Hardin 1987) between the phenomenal and the representational (or the brain): if we just confront a quale with a brain state, they seem to be worlds apart; but if we correlate a quale with a cerebrally instantiated metarepresented format in a way that lets the format share some properties with the quale on a certain level of description, then the gap between qualia and the brain is certainly reduced. But can it be closed? This depends on the interpretation of the

[4] See Akins 1993 and Hardin 1987 for similar projects.

relation between qualia and formats. Qualia could be seen as supervening on formats, as being identical with them, etc. — each of these interpretations would again face the well-known problems: how could an identity relation hold between the phenomenal and the non-phenomenal? Does supervenience degenerate into epiphenomenalism? etc. Metzinger remains neutral with respect to this issue when he says that the qualia freak could still find phenomenal aspects of qualia unexplained by a representational account. A theory of mind, he concludes, 'may never be able to eliminate our Cartesian intuitions, but it has to offer a satisfactory explanation for their existence' (Metzinger 1994: 677).

But perhaps an 'explanation of their existence' will weaken the persuasion of the intuitions themselves. If the intuitions themselves become less persuasive by an incomplete reconciliation between the phenomenal and the representational, then our judgment concerning the status of the *phenomena* may also change. Now qualia (as seemings for the subject of consciousness) as phenomena are elements of the total cognitive system that is also the subject of qualia intuitions and judgments about qualia. Then the question arises whether the features of the qualia themselves (as seemings-for-me) at least partially depend on my qualia intuitions and judgments. If qualia intuitions change with social, cultural, historical and evolutionary contexts, then the features of qualia (as seeming *'givens'*) themselves might be overformed by these outward social etc. modifications of how the subject of consciousness *takes* these seemings. Wouldn't this be just another example of how cognitive preconditions influence the further cerebral processing and thus the conscious appearance of sensory or cerebral activation patterns? I am sympathetic with such a view which has also been discussed controversially by Dennett (1991: ch. 7), with arguments in favour, and Block (1995) against; we'll return to this question in the last section. But if for the moment we leave aside this 'cultural transcendentalism' concerning phenomenal consciousness, the strategy of 'going into the scientific details' alone does not provide an explanation of qualia in the sense of a demonstration that tokens of phenomenal consciousness must have the qualitative features they factually have (see section II).

Flanagan holds that qualia in the innocent sense of 'how things seem to us' — as opposed to the problematic sense of ineffable, atomic, non-relational etc. conscious events — (1) 'are for real', (2) are needed in psychological explanations, and (3) can be naturalized since they possess 'other properties than those implicated in their subjectively available aspects' (Flanagan 1992: 61f). Let's focus on (3). What *are* these properties other than those 'available in the first person'? Under the heading 'What qualia are', Flanagan lists five aspects of qualia: they 'help specify the types of subjectivity', they have the well-known property of like-to-be-ness, they have a holistic quality (although they might be decomposed neuroscientifically), some of them are nonsensational, and they have 'nonqualitative aspects'. Only this last point concerns the non-first-person-properties mentioned above. Flanagan says: 'Subjective experiences occur at particular spatial locations in the form of distributed neural activity. The neural properties of qualitative experiences are not revealed in the first-person point of view. They are, however, part of the structure of such experiences.' (Flanagan 1992: 65). A bit further in the same chapter (p. 73), Flanagan adds that qualia not only are 'always realized in the brain', but also 'typically have behavioural effects' (e.g. the link between colours and emotions, p. 71). But even if all this were true, it wouldn't enable us to explain qualia *as seemings*: if a quale has the property of entering into such-and-such actions of the subject of consciousness, then this property might well be independent of the qualitative, phenomenal features of this quale (it might depend on representational features of the quale, which certainly would also have to be *shown* to be properties of the quale *independently*!). Qualia would be explained in their nonphenomenal features alone, and this certainly would not convince the qualia freak. As for the second kind of assumed nonphenomenal properties of qualia, the talk of 'neural properties' of qualia is question-begging: all we can say is that there are neural *correlates* of qualia — to say that qualia themselves have neural properties requires prior knowledge that qualia *are* (perhaps among other things) 'something neural'. But this is just what the intended explanation would have to show. Flanagan's argument was that qualia can be naturalized because they have nonqualitative properties. But the properties he presents would not help to naturalize qualia as seemings, or they are not shown to be properties of qualia in the first place. Hence, Flanagan did not show that qualia can be naturalized. This leaves open the possibility of a naturalization of qualia despite their not having nonqualitative properties. As seen above, the strategy of going into the details of phenomenal structure and cognitive science will not easily convince the qualia freak. Are there any other promising strategies? Since I have discussed just a small part of the relevant literature, I will confine myself to a somewhat vague and intuitive prognosis.

What we can hope to achieve as a 'naturalization' of qualia is an instantiation explanation in the sense of Cummins (1983), that is, an answer to the question 'In virtue of what does an organism possess phenomenal consciousness?' A causal explanation of qualia is much more difficult, since it is completely unclear what it would mean for a state of a cognitive system to be the 'cause' or the 'effect' of a quale. An instantiation explanation that shows how qualia are realized in the brain (or a representational system) could be the final result of the above 'going into the details' of both the phenomenal and the physical (or computational or whatever) realm. The only problem is whether each of us can accept an instantiation explanation of this sort as an explanation of qualia at all. Usually, the explanandum of an instantiation explanation is itself 'objectively detectable' — consider, for example, temperature as instantiated as the average mean kinetic energy of molecules. But in the qualia case, the explanandum is not objectively detectable concerning its purely phenomenal features — and if there is anything that could be interpreted as a nonphenomenal feature of a quale, then this property would presumedly *figure in the explanation itself*, as part of the constitution of an organism *by virtue of which it has qualia*. And the qualia freak is still free to maintain that an instantiation explanation leaves open why a quale must have the phenomenal features it factually has (in the first-person perspective). I do not see how an instantiation explanation could invalidate the pro-qualia intuition I tried to formulate in section II. But do we really have to *expect* from a naturalistic approach of qualia a demonstration of why the subjective, phenomenal features of qualia must be like they factually are? In other words: if a naturalistic approach just shows how an organism factually manages to possess qualia, are the reasons to reject such an approach as insufficient really good and rational ones? Do we really need a theory of qualia that goes beyond an instantiation explanation of the kind described above? These questions lead to the somewhat metaphilosophical aspects of the problem, to which I now finally turn.

V. The (In)significance of a Theory of Phenomenal Consciousness

Do we really need a theory of phenomenal consciousness? There is a sense in which we might need it: qualia might be useful or even indispensable as a basis of hypothesis generation and theory construction in psychology or cognitive science (Flanagan 1992: 64–66).   But this point has also been discussed controversially (Wilkes 1984; P.S. Churchland 1983; Rey 1991), and it is not strictly concerned with a theory of qualia themselves, but rather with a theory of mind employing the notion of qualia. When I question the need for a theory of qualia, I don't want to stress the dispensability of these phenomena in psychological theory. Rather, the above question reads like this: is it really necessary or at least desirable to achieve a naturalistic explanation of qualia *as phenomenal states*? In this final section I would like to argue that it is not.[5]

We have simply taken qualia (as phenomena) too seriously. I would recommend Dennett to draw this conclusion rather than to argue ontologically and claim that qualia don't exist (whatever that means, see section III). Qualia are not to be 'quined' or 'disqualified' or even 'eliminated'. They are to be de- constructed. It is not helpful to view *the ways things seem to us* as stable elements of our inner mental lives and thus as mental sub-entities with a constant constitution at all. There *are* qualia in the sense that *we have* experiences, but these qualia are not awesome mental entities oozing with philosophical significance, but rather ephemeral phenomena dependent on cultural, historical, social, evolutionary, linguistic, etc. — preconditions — and they can change with a modification of any of these

---

[5] If you cannot sleep quietly before everything in the world has been 'naturalized', then my argument is not likely to convince you.

preconditions. This relativity of qualia is also stressed by Dennett (1991, chs. 7; 12) when he interprets consciousness as a huge complex of memes (that is, special sorts of elements of cultural replication) or when he argues that our qualitative experience of a piece of music depends on our cultural background. But, as I said above, Dennett's arguments against qualia are not suited to remove our motivation to believe in the *existence* of qualia — rather, we wouldn't believe in the *significance* of qualia any longer. We will lose interest in qualia, and that is a metaphilosophical shift of attitude as contrasted with the philosophical (in fact, ontological) shift that would take place when we came to believe that qualia did not exist. Dennett himself gives a metaphilosophical characterization of the presumedly unbridgeable gap between Nagel's attitudes and his, where the preference for one of these positions appears as a matter of decision rather than argument:

> I certainly don't think that Nagel is committing some (fatal!) logical gaffe in maintaining his position; there is even something *wonderful* about it . . . If he would rather go on *believing in* intrinsic and ineffable properties, then he will have to forgo the *fun* of being in on the kill when we knock off the mind–body problem . . . (Dennett 1993: 233. Italics by me, M.K.)

In an important paper on this issue, Rorty (1993: 188) also holds that the case between Dennett and the qualia freaks is undecidable on the grounds of internal philosophical arguments. 'This is because it is hardly clear when and whether to change one's mind about what to expect explanatory theories to do — and, in particular, about how paradoxical science has a right to be, how far it can go in substituting explanations of X-talk for explanations of X' (or, in Dennett's case, substituting explanations of believing in qualia for explanations of qualia). With reference to Wittgenstein, Sellars, Ryle and Davidson, Rorty maintains that qualia are relational because they are language-relative: 'to become aware of qualia is the same thing as learning how to make judgments about qualia . . . ' (Rorty 1993: 189). I also think it would be a short-sighted reply to this to say that by making judgments about qualia, we only reach *descriptions* of qualia as opposed to qualia *themselves*, namely their like-to-be-ness. How things seem to us may be a matter of something else, perhaps a matter of 'how you have been accustomed to talk' (Rorty 1993: 186) about these things. But although I also suspect that from a developmental or genetic point of view like-to-be-ness appears as a matter of something else (rather than being atomic, nonrelational, etc. *primordially*), I would not restrict this something to language. And here I see myself in agreement with Dennett's *Consciousness Explained,* a book which seems to come up with quite a heterogenous set of theses about consciousness. Like Dennett, I think that consciousness (and not only the *concept of* consciousness) is, at least to some degree, the result of natural and cultural evolution. If this were true, then a developmental explanation (I would prefer: a developmental reconstruction) of consciousness would be the most prom-

ising strategy. (Phenomenal) consciousness might be the result of developing interactions of an organism with its natural and/or social environment.[6]

Language is but one aspect of the cultural context that determines our
actual constitution of 'how things seem to us'. Sellars (1956) had argued —
convincingly, in my view — that certain aspects of mental states like
privacy or incorrigibility crucially depend on a very special history and a
very special constitution of a linguistic or, more general, social community.
There is no reason to assume that other first-person-aspects of mental states
(like phenomenality) should not possess this dependency and relativity. All
the first-person-aspects of the mental feature this historical or genetical
dimension, so that the way things seem to us *today* is just a snapshot of our
momentary subjectivity without any natural claim to epistemological or
ontological significance (Rorty 1993). And if you want, there is even an
intrasubjective reflection of the intersubjective relativity of phenomenality.
As pointed out in section IV, qualia as phenomena occur in the same total
cognitive system that is also the subject of qualia intuitions and judgments
about qualia, so that features of qualia might well be overformed by
modifications of how the subject of consciousness *takes* these seemings.
The mistake is to view phenomenality as something peculiar and outstanding at all, to take it serious as an aspect of the mind that is in need of
naturalization. And if you are inclined to ask me, 'On the basis of which
argument do you judge this view as mistaken?', I am tempted to reply, 'The
burden of argument lies elsewhere: on the basis of which argument did we
ever see phenomenality as something peculiar and outstanding, as a phenomenon worthy of explanation within a naturalistic theory of mind?'
Phenomenality of consciousness is just part of the way we are: things seem
to us somehow. But this is a trivial fact which simply marks a sort of
experience in which *being* collapses into *seeming*, perhaps without any rest.
The propensity to assign a sort of epistemological or ontological significance to phenomenality is, in my opinion, an expression of our modern
tendency to view our own subjectivity with all its phenomenal *presence* and
immediacy as an epistemologically and/or ontologically exceptional entity
or constitution. In other words: we have taken qualia too serious because
we have taken ourselves *as endowed* — or punished — *with subjectivity* too
seriously. At least as far as the philosophy of mind is concerned, we could
simply *ignore* that things seem to us somehow and concentrate on a cognitive-
science-approach of how things are perceived, thought about, and acted upon.

Why pay further attention to like-to-be-ness? Perhaps the reasons for the
ongoing appeal of phenomenality as part of subjectivity are found in
metaphilosophy or even outside of philosophy. Heidegger (1961) has given
an excellent metaphilosophical analysis of modern philosophy of subjectivity (Kurthen 1994: 163–70) which might at least *explain* our *Subjek-*

---

[6] See a related paper of mine (Kurthen 1996) for the social component; these ideas are not
new, but trace back at least to G.H. Mead, as far as I know.

tivitätsduselei in view of the total absence of an independent *argument* for making subjectivity *that* major philosophical problem. In Heidegger's reconstruction, subjectivity is part of the *Geschick* (destiny?) of *Dasein.* Tracing back to Descartes and even Plato, subjectivity was ultimately established and cemented by Nietzsche in the shape of the *Wille zur Macht.* So subjectivity is not a feature of our mental lives; instead, *we are part of the Geschick of subjectivity in its Selbstermächtigung* (self-empowering?). Heidegger's intricate analysis is not the subject of this paper, but it should at least be mentioned that there are metaphilosophical *reconstructions of our fixation on subjectivity* that might be suited to replace our *attempts to explain or even naturalize the subjective aspects of mind.* Another clue may be found in depth psychology: Freud (1914) described narcicissm as an inadequate libidinization of the ego, and Jung (1951) spoke of an 'inflation of the subject' by an excessive incorporation of the unconscious into an individual consciousness. There certainly is such an aspect of narcicissm and inflation of the subject in our incessant re-flection on subjectivity and the 'genuinely subjective' features of mind.

So, although it may be true that phenomenal consciousness can't be naturalized, the major problem might be our ill-devised attitude towards the subjective aspects of mind in general: we have taken them too serious in epistemological and ontological respects. After a thorough deconstruction, they may appear as ephemeral and ignorable phenomena or even as an expression of a totally degenerate mode of *Dasein* (Heidegger 1976). There are lots of things in the world that are hard to explain or even to 'naturalize' (think of *fashion, playing habits,* and the like). If phenomenal consciousness is one of them, so what?

References

Akins, K. (1993). What is it like to be boring and myopic? In Dahlbohm 1993.

Block, N. (1990). Inverted earth. In Tomberlin 1990.

Block, N. (1992). Begging the question against phenomenal consciousness. *Behavioral and Brain Sciences,* **15**, 205–6.

Block, N. (1995). On a confusion about a function of consciousness. *Behavioral and Brain Sciences,* **18**, 227–47.

Churchland, P.S. (1983). Consciousness: the transmutation of a concept. *Pacific Philosophical Quarterly,* **64**, 80–93.

Cummins, R. (1983). *The Nature of Psychological Explanation.* Cambridge, London: MIT Press.

Dennett, D. (1988). Quining qualia. In Marcel & Bisiach 1988.

Dennett, D. (1991). *Consciousness Explained.* Boston, MA: Little, Brown & Co.

Dennett, D. (1993). Back from the drawing board. In Dahlbohm 1993.

Flanagan, O. (1992). *Consciousness Reconsidered.* Cambridge, London: MIT Press.

Freud, S. (1914). Zur Einführung des Narzißmus. In S. Freud (1960). *Das Ich und das Es und andere metapsychologische Schriften.* Frankfurt a. M.: Fischer.

Hardin, C.L. (1987). Qualia and materialism: closing the explanatory gap. *Philosophy and Phenomenological Research*, **47**, 281–98.

Harman, G. (1990). The intrinsic quality of experience. In Tomberlin 1990.

Heidegger, M. (1961). *Nietzsche* (2 volumes). Pfullingen: Neske.

Heidegger, M. (1976). *Sein und Zeit*. Tübingen: Niemeyer.

Horgan, T. (1984). Functionalism, qualia, and the inverted spectrum. *Philosophy and Phenomenological Research*, **44**, 453–69.

Horgan, T. (1987). Supervenient qualia. *The Philosophical Review*, **96**, 491–520.

Jung, C.G. (1951). Vorwort zu Z. Werblowsky: Lucifer und Prometheus. In C.G. Jung (1971). *Zur Psychologie westlicher und östlicher Religion*. Olten, Freiburg i. Br.: Walter.

Kurthen, M. (1990). Qualia, sensa, and absolute processes. *Journal for General Philosophy of Science*, **21**, 25–46.

Kurthen, M. (1994). *Hermeneutische Kognitionswissenschaft*. Bonn: Djre.

Kurthen, M. (1996). Das harmlose Faktum des Bewußtseins. In Krämer 1996.

Levine, J. (1983). Materialism and qualia: the explanatory gap. *Pacific Philosophical Quarterly*, **64**, 354–61.

Lewis, C.I. (1929). *Mind and the World Order*. New York: Dover.

Loar, B. (1990). Phenomenal states. In Tomberlin 1990.

Lycan, W.G. (1987). *Consciousness*. Cambridge, London: MIT Press.

McGinn, C. (1989). Can we solve the mind–body problem? *Mind*, **98**, 349–66.

Metzinger, T. (1993). *Subjekt und Selbstmodell*. Paderborn, München, Wien, Zürich: Schöningh.

Metzinger, T. (1994). Subjectivity and mental representation. In G. Meggle & U. Wessels (eds), *Analyomen I* (Berlin, New York: de Gruyter).

Nagel, T. (1970). Armstrong on the mind. *Philosophical Review*, **79**, 394–403.

Nagel, T. (1979). What is it like to be a bat? In *Mortal Questions*. Cambridge: Cambridge University Press.

Rey, G. (1991). Reasons for doubting the existence of even epiphenomenal consciousness. *Behavioral and Brain Sciences*, **14**, 691–2.

Rorty, R. (1993). Holism, intrinsicality, and the ambition of transcendence. In Dahlbohm 1993.

Sellars, W. (1956). Empiricism and the philosophy of mind. In H. Feigl & M. Scriven (eds), *Minnesota Studies in the Philosophy of Science, vol. 1*. Minneapolis: University of Minnesota Press.

Sellars, W. (1981). Foundations for a metaphysics of pure process. *The Monist*, **64**, 3–90.

Wilkes, K.V. (1984). Is consciousness important? *British Journal for the Philosophy of Science*, **35**, 224–43.

Georges Rey

Towards a Projectivist Account of Conscious Experience

For Eleanor Saunders

I. Reversing the Problem of Other Minds

The familiar problem of 'other minds' can arise in the following way: every person seems to have immediate knowledge of her own conscious states, and knows about the conscious states of other people only on the basis of an analogy or an inference from behavioural evidence. But the analogy seems shaky at best, and the inference can seem entirely unwarranted, since it's hard to see why positing the kind of conscious states of which we seem directly aware is really necessary to explain anyone else's behaviour. They could equally well be 'mere automata', organized to behave intelligently, etc., but entirely lacking in consciousness. As Joseph Levine (1983; 1988; 1993) puts it, there is an 'explanatory gap' between physical and conscious mental phenomena: no physical/computational facts about our brains seem to necessitate the properties of a conscious being.

In this paper I want to consider a way in which this problem results from a certain systematic error in our deployment of many mental concepts, whereby our beliefs about the conscious states of others are based *not* upon the projection into them of phenomena we directly experience in our own case, but upon projecting into them *and into ourselves* phenomena correlative to both our characteristic reactions to them and our experience of ourselves (where, in a way that I will explain, the having of such reactions and experiences does not presuppose the projected conscious phenomena). This projection becomes so 'automatic' that it seems inseparable from the way we have of thinking about the mental lives of human beings generally, and so we 'see' it in others' behaviour and take it for granted in ourselves when we introspect. However, I will argue we have reason to think no such phenomena exist, and that consequently there is no problem of linking them by analogy, inference or necessity to the physical/computational facts about our brains.

Of course, such an account will seem wildly paradoxical to anyone worried by the traditional problem. How could I be denying the existence of the conscious phenomena of which we all surely have immediate, first-person knowledge? What I want to suggest is that there are a number of different ideas that are conflated in the usual understanding of such knowledge. Doubtless, *some* of it is immediate and unusually reliable, as in the case of knowledge of certain first-person present-tense sensory *states*. But I want to argue that there is no reason to think that it is *that* knowledge that involves knowledge of *phenomena* that give rise to such problems as the above one of other minds.[1] These problems result, I want to suggest, from peculiarities of the aforementioned projection: the robustness of our reactions inclines us to persist in the projection even after we find nothing in the actual facts about our brains that supports it; and so we suppose that there is therefore an explanatory gap to be filled between the projected properties and those details. What I recommend we do instead is to recognize the projection for what it is and not ask that it be grounded in any such details.

In order to begin to make my account plausible, I will present in part II of what follows some reasons for being more cautious about the deliverances of introspection than many people are inclined to be: experiments suggest that much of what we take for introspection may often be less the result of any special epistemic access than the imposition of quite general, popular *theories* of people upon ourselves. Just which cases do and which don't involve such impositions is not yet entirely clear; but the serious possibility of them draws attention to the possibility that, although we may indeed have privileged access to certain features of our mental lives, we still may not have privileged access to *just which features it is to which we have such access*. Ascertaining this latter may require confirming subtler theories of our own minds than are popularly available.

In part III, I will then consider Levine's version of the problem of other minds, his problem of the explanatory gap. Along lines of some earlier arguments of my own, I think this gap invites scepticism not only about other minds, but about the existence of consciousness entirely, both in the case of others *and* oneself. The problem of 'other minds' becomes the problem of the existence of (the relevant properties of) minds generally.

---

[1] As Putnam (1960) pointed out early on, such self-referential states — being in S iff you think you're in S — might be like a Turing Machine state that is specified in part by its disposition to bring about other states, which might include a state of believing it's in the first state.

One can find intimations of this issue entwined in Wittgenstein's (1953: §§243–317) notorious discussion of 'privacy' and 'private language', and I think he has some penetrating insights about it. I will explore some of them briefly in part IV, separating those insights from other features of his treatment of the mind that I find more problematic. As penetrating as I find even his best insights, however, I think they are still not quite adequate as explanations of the explanatory gap. In my concluding part V, I will try to supplement his account with my projectivist proposal.

II. Self-atttribution

In a well-known article, Richard Nisbett and Timothy Wilson (1977) reviewed a wide range of experiments that they claimed showed that people were in fact far less reliable about their mental lives than is ordinarily supposed. Thus, subjects have been shown to be sensitive to, but entirely unaware of, such factors as cognitive dissonance, prior expectation, numbers of bystanders, pupillary dilation, positional and 'halo' effects, and subliminal cues in problem solving and semantic disambiguation. Instead of noticing these factors, subjects frequently 'introspect' material that can be independently shown to be irrelevant to the causation of their behaviour. Indeed, even when explicitly asked about the relevant material, they will deny that it played any role. Thus, for example, the positional effect consists in people tending overwhelmingly (four to one) to choose the *right-most* of a series of, e.g. type-identical socks, without one of them mentioning position as affecting them.[2] Other experiments deal with systematic errors in reasoning and the demonstrably mistaken accounts subjects provide of them (Wason and Evans 1975); and cases of hyponotic suggestion in which subjects respond to whispered commands and even to 'painful sensations', of which they claim to be unaware (Hilgard 1977).

   Perhaps some of the most dramatic, and philosophically interesting phenomena undermining the reliability of introspection concern 'agnosia'. Patients suffering from various sorts of brain damage which demonstrably undermine their normal psychological functioning will sometimes report no awareness whatsoever of their deficiencies. Young (1994), for example, reports the case of a woman painter who was prosopagnosiac (unable to recognize faces) and had laboriously to reason from the apparent age, sex and other cues in her (earlier) paintings, exactly who they were paintings of, all the time denying she suffered from any recognitional deficit at all![3]

---

[2] Indeed 'when asked directly about a possible effect of the position of the article, virtually all subjects denied it, usually with a worried glance at the interviewer suggesting that they felt either that they had misunderstood the question or were dealing with a madman' (1977: 244).

[3] See Young 1994, Damasio 1994, and Block 1995 (from which I drew the above example) for further discussion. Incidentally, Damasio (1994: 62) points out that cases of agnosia

In interpreting their experiments, Nisbett and Wilson raise a possibility that is of considerable significance with regard to the status of introspection generally:

> We propose that when people are asked to report how a particular stimulus influenced a particular response, they do not do so by consulting a memory of the mediating process, but by applying or generating causal theories about the effects of that type of stimulus on that type of response. They simply make judgments . . . about how plausible it is that the stimulus would have influenced the response. (1977: 248)

They speculate that such causal theories may originate not in any special inner knowledge, but rather, in empirical generalizations about their own behaviour, in popular theories about people that they acquire growing up in a particular culture, or simply in theoretical speculations of their own (*ibid*).

Such a hypothesis has received further support in the developmental literature. In a recent article, Gopnik reports experiments with three-year-olds that suggest that

> children make errors about their own immediately past [belief] states that are similar to the errors they make about the states of others . . . even though [they] ought to have direct first-person knowledge of these past states.[4] (Gopnik 1993: 7)

She concludes:

> The important point is that the theoretical constructs [about the mind] themselves, and particularly the idea of intentionality, are not the result of some first-person apprehension that is then applied to others. Rather, they are the result of cognitive construction. (Gopnik 1993: 10)

She goes on to suggest that, as we mature, we may become so knowledgable and reliable about people and ourselves generally, that we become totally unable to notice anything but the grossest inferential steps on which that knowledge nevertheless relies. We are in the position of 'expert' chess-players, medical diagnosticians, or water dousers who often take themselves to be sensing very sophisticated information in their domains 'directly' (Gopnik 1993: 11).

For present purposes, there is no need to endorse either Gopnik's or Nisbett and Wilson's speculations unequivocally. What we obviously need in order to settle questions about introspective reliability are much more

---

cannot be explained as merely due to the repression of unpleasant thoughts, since it occurs in right- but not left-hemispherical strokes.

[4] The experiments involve e.g. asking 3-year-olds who have been recently fooled by some appearances, what others would think when presented with the same appearances, as well as what they themselves previously thought. Up until around 4 years, children claim that they *did*, and that the others *would*, believe the *truth*. Gopnik reports similar results and conclusions in Wimmer and Hartl 1991.

fine-grained theories about the actual information processing details under-lying introspection, theories of the sort Ericsson and Simon (1984/1993), for example, admirably attempt to provide.[5] In providing these details we will have to consider not only the kinds of states to which people have reliable access, but also the kind of case that concerns me here, of *the character of the phenomena, if any, that one can reliably introspect*. I want to suggest that here too there is more than meets the popular introspective eye, and that our understanding of the metaphysics of what we introspect may be as theoretical a matter as any.

Actually, these experimental results on introspection can be taken merely to dramatize what, on reflection, ought to be an unsurprising logical point that has never to my knowledge received adequate discussion: that 'It is introspectively knowable that p' does not necessarily iterate. I might in-trospectively know that p without introspectively knowing *that* I introspec-tively know that p. Claims to know something introspectively may well require empirical support beyond any introspective claims themselves.[6]

Why think, however, there is any particular problem about the character of the phenomena we introspect? Before I set out my own hypothesis about a plausible source of the introspective errors I have in mind, I want to motivate it by considering more fully the philosophical puzzles it is intended to explain.

III. The Explanatory Gap

The 'explanatory gap' that Levine locates between consciousness and standard physical/computational theories about the brain arises from the following consideration: the continuing success of modern science seems to consist in part in presenting satisfying explanations of practically every phenomenon we have reason to believe is real, and it does this by providing a micro-theoretic account that seems to 'upwardly necessitate' the macro-phenomenon in question, i.e. shows how the macro-phenomenon is a *nec-essary consequence* of the truth of the micro-theory. Physics and chemistry, for example, provide an impressive explanation of why water expands when it freezes: given the laws of physics and claims about the bonds between water molecules, it will be ultimately a matter of *mathematical and mere-logical necessity* that the molecules will form a lattice structure that takes

---

[5] They emphasize our greater reliability about states at the very time they are occuring, as opposed to even temporally close memories of them and speculations about their causal role. Ericsson (1993: 42) raises similar issues with regard to Gopnik's discussion.

[6] This issue of iteration of such epistemic operators deserves more discussion generally. In Rey 1994, I argue 'it is *a priori* that p' does not entail 'it is *a priori* that it is *a priori* that p.' Indeed, whether something is *a priori* for someone may itself be a contingent, empirical fact, knowable only by fairly theoretic inference about the structure of the mind. Much of what I say there applies, *mutatis mutandis*, to the case of introspective knowledge that concerns me here.

up more space at temperatures of 32 °F and below.[7] This is in part due to the *nature* of the phenomenon being explained: the *expansion* of freezing water *just is* the fact that the same quantity of water *takes up more space* when it becomes *solid*. Given our ordinary concepts of, e.g. [water], [solidity], [freezing], and of [expansion], it *follows necessarily* from the the truths of physics, merelogy and mathematics, that it will expand when it freezes.

But, now, what physical facts could possibly *necessitate* something's *looking green*, or *red* or being a conscious state at all? It seems that when we reflect upon our concepts of (to use the jargon for 'the ways things feel') 'qualia' and consciousness, no explanation in physical, or even physical/computational terms seems available. Levine writes:

> No matter how rich the information processing or the neurophysiological story gets, it still seems quite coherent to imagine that all that should be going on without there being anything it's like to undergo the states in question. Yet, if the physical or functional story really explained the qualitative character, it would not be so clearly imaginable that the qualia should be missing. (Levine 1993: 129.)

There's something about the properties (and/or concepts) of qualia and consciousness that, unlike the properties (and/or concepts) of water, solidity, etc., does not seem to admit of the same upward necessitation.

One way to appreciate this explanatory gap is to imagine standard psychological accounts of human mental processing being realized on existing computers.[8] In other papers (Rey 1983; 1988; 1993a), I have argued that these stories are much less complicated than their proponents intially suppose, and that it would be a lot easier than they imagine to realize them on existing computers that most people wouldn't for a moment regard as conscious.[9] For example, perceptual states, intentional states, intentional states about intentional states (thoughts about thoughts about thoughts . . .), 'self-consciousness', attention, planning, decision-making, use of a natural language: all these phenomena are, I argue, programmable with relatively little trouble on existing computers.[10] Call the proposed program 'COG'.

---

[7] I've changed Levine's (1993: 129) example of boiling and evaporation to a simpler one of the expansion of ice.

[8] Another way is to read Block's (1980) many purported counterexamples to functionalism, e.g. the nation of China or economy of Bolivia, arranged so as to realize the functional organization of a normal human brain. My example seems to me to avoid possible replies to Block's: e.g. constraints on the mapping of states, unreliability of intuitions about such outré possibilities.

[9] It's important to distinguish in this exercise seriously taking a real machine to be conscious, from accepting a fiction that one is, or treating one so metaphorically (cf. Wittgenstein 1953: §282).

[10] I would actually like to show this in practice, but it turns out that existing AI programs for the different processes of e.g. perception, reasoning, decision making are not written in nearly

Putting aside qualia and consciousness, the only aspect of our psychology that does seem still computationally daunting is *the specific kind of intelligence* we display in commonsense, theoretical and practical reasoning. But while this is of enormous interest in itself, it is not likely to be responsible for *consciousness*, e.g. sensory experience of which someone is aware: animals lacking such intelligence are not counted thereby the less conscious.[11]

I've said that most people wouldn't regard the COG-machine as conscious.[12] The problem, however, is that, even if it turns out that some people *are* entirely comfortable with the suggestion that the COG-computer is conscious, it doesn't seem as though the story of the realization of these processes on the COG-machine *necessitates* ascriptions of consciousness in the way that the story of the molecules clearly necessitates the expansion of ice: precisely along the lines Levine sets out, it seems perfectly *intelligible* to doubt that the COG-machine might be conscious in a way that it doesn't seem intelligible to doubt, given the chemical story, that water expands when it freezes.

What leaves people so unconvinced that the COG-machine is conscious? It could, of course, be due to some lack in the specific program I sketch. But this is seldom what occurs to people in most discussions I have had. What most people claim is that conscious states are not *the kind of states* that will be captured by *any* such computational program. Some claim some as yet unspecified non-physical, 'dualistic' property is required; others, some (equally unspecified) physical property of the medium in which something like the COG program is realized.[13] After Dennett (1991), let us call such people 'qualiaphiles'. I shall not be concerned here with the differences among them, but will simply think of all of them as conceiving conscious phenomena as 'cognitively transcendent' or, for short, 'COG-transcendent'. Such 'strong' notions of consciousness are to be distinguished from a

---

commensurable languages. I hope at a later time to find a way of surmounting this exasperating sociology. [N.B. My 'COG' program discussed here is hypothetical and should not be confused with the 'Cog Project' at MIT described by Daniel Dennett elsewhere in this book.]

[11] This may be an error on our part, but the burden would be on someone to show that it is.

[12] In the many presentations of this issue since I first raised it in Rey 1983, I've encountered only two people who've claimed to have no problem in regarding the COG machine as conscious: David Papineau (in conversation) and William Lycan (forthcoming) — and Lycan actually hedges, claiming merely that *any* self-monitoring device is conscious 'to some degree' (if very small). Everyone else balks. Indeed, notice — as Joseph Levine once put it — that, even in these days of increasingly smart computers, no one thinks of forming a Society for the Prevention of Cruelty to them.

[13] And some of course, e.g. Searle 1980, just claim it is some (again, as yet unspecified) 'biological' property of our brains that has nothing whatsoever to do with any computational program at all; see Rey 1986 for a reply.

'weak' notions — involving mere wakefulness, attention, or introspect-ability — that presumably *could* be satisfied by the COG-computer.

I go on to argue in these earlier papers that the situation in which this leaves us is actually much worse than the traditional problem of other minds, where the problem is merely to find some ground for necessitating the ascription of strong consciousness to *others*. Reflection on the possibility of programming a computer in the ways I have suggested raises the problem of justifying the ascription of such consciousness *in one's own case as well*. For what reason does one have for supposing in one's own case that one *does in fact* have what it takes, i.e. phenomena that are not necessitated by a mere realization of COG? What does one know about oneself that rules out one's self being essentially a COG computer? If being such a computer doesn't necessitate consciousness *generally*, then it doesn't *in one's own case* either. And so we are left with the *possibility* that not only are other people, but each of us ourselves are all 'mere automata'. If we nevertheless think we are conscious and the COG computer isn't, we need to ask what entitles us to our confidence.

Someone might think introspection alone warrants it. But although intro-spection may certainly be reliable about *some* issues, why on earth think it has authority about *this* issue? What are we able to introspect about our-selves that gives us the slightest reason to think that *we've got a property that the COG machine lacks*? There is no doubt that people regularly *think* they are authorities on such matters. But, of course, the COG-computer could be programmed to think it, too, is strongly conscious — even to think that it *knows for certain*, and incorrigibly that it has a COG-transcendent consciousness — while still (for most of us) failing to do so.

Moreover, people regularly express surprisingly strong (often conflict-ing) opinions about the mental lives of many things around them — ants, rats, chimps, infant humans — opinions that bear almost no relation to any serious examination of those things.[14] If the psychological experiments we discussed in part II did not already give us reason for pause about introspec-tion, certainly people's shameless chutzpah about the mental lives of other things ought to raise a worry about what they take themselves to be introspecting that could entitle them to such opinions. In any case, I see no reason to settle the question of the existence of a COG-transcendent consciousness on the basis of introspection alone.

Now, as I've said, the 'qualiaphiles' take the explanatory gap to indicate the existence of something genuinely unexplained *in the world*. Alterna-tively, one could suspect it is not something about the world, but something peculiar about how we think about it. I like to think of this as posing 'the

---

[14] Cf. Wittgenstein's (1980-II:§192) extraordinary pontification, 'The question "Do fishes think?" does not exist among our applications of language, it is not raised' (see also 1953: §25 and his struggle with Köhler's results at 1980-II: §§224-230).

mind/body problem problem': *where do we so much as get the idea* of 'dualism', or that a COG-computer — or other mere material object — couldn't possibly be conscious?[15] There have been a number of suggestions in this regard: some writers (e.g. Lycan 1987: ch 6 and forthcoming)) simply bite the bullet and swallow the claim that the COG-computer *is* conscious (at least 'to some degree'), dismissing the gap as due to confusions about any number of topics. Others (e.g. McGinn 1991: 11–12, 60–1) have pointed to the non-spatial character of introspective concepts, and our lack of concepts that might supply other sources of necessitation. Still others (e.g. Loar 1996) point to the special 'demonstrative recognitional abilities' that underlie our deployment of the 'phenomenal concepts' of consciousness and experience.

Although I think there is some truth in these suggestions, they don't seem to me to be quite adequate. Lycan's bullet-biting seems to me insufficiently motivated and has the consequence that a machine that simply recorded (say, on a hard-disk) every one of its (first-order) states would be more conscious than you or I. And, with regard to McGinn's and Loar's suggestions, there seem to be plenty of examples of non-spatial concepts (e.g. [university], [novel], [political party]), and of concepts with Loar's peculiar epistemics (e.g. demonstrative concepts of artistic or political styles) that don't give rise to anything like the explanatory gap we encounter with consciousness and qualia.

What all these responses have in common, though, is the presumption that *there really are properties* whose peculiarities are responsible for the gap. It is this presumption that I want to question. Indeed, an alternative suggestion that I and others have proposed is that there are no such COG-transcendent phenomena at all that need to be explained: they are a postulation for which there is no non-tendentious — i.e. non-question-begging — evidence. Such phenomena are no more needed to explain anything than are the angels needed to explain the motion of the planets, or God in order to explain people's religious experiences. The need of non-tendentious evidence here is crucial: just as it's not enough in reply to an atheist to beat one's breast and claim that God exists because one has had direct experiences of Her, so is it not a reply to the eliminativist about strong conscious states to claim that one has direct, unquestionable experience of *them*. For that is of course precisely what the atheist and the eliminativist are challenging. What is needed is evidence whose description does not *presuppose* the existence of the phenomena in dispute, but which nevertheless could not be *explained* without those phenomena. It is this sort of evidence

[15] Or, as one might put it less politely, what is it about our thinking about the mind that leads otherwise immensely intelligent people to say many of the extremely bizarre and foolish things that have been claimed about the mind? The psychology of philosophy is of piece with the philosophy of psychology.

that I submit is lacking in the case of strong consciousness, as presumably in the case of God.

It bears stressing that the problem here is not merely that we can't imagine how we could *know* whether we are conscious. Someone who thought that consciousness was a COG-transcendent property could insist on a *reliabilist* theory of knowledge and claim that, as a matter of nomological fact, people *just are* reliable about detecting their own consciousness, whereas mere COG machines are not. And this *might* of course be true. The question is not whether this is (epistemically) *possible*, but what reason we have to believe that it *is true*. What reason do we have to believe that *there really do exist*, either in one's own case or in the case of other people, COG-transcendent phenomena that we're in fact detecting? The explanatory gap does invite an intolerable first-person scepticism, but, more importantly, it raises a worry that there's no fact about which even to be sceptical.[16]

Note that eliminativism about a COG transcendent consciousness need not involve a *general* elminativist claim that there are no mental states at all, as has been proposed by e.g. Churchland (1981). Much less does it involve a constructivism and/or instrumentalism of the sort urged by Dennett (1991).[17] There is plenty of non-tendentious evidence for the existence of genuine propositional attitudes, perceptual states, emotions, moods, intentional action.[18] Indeed, as I said, I see no difficulty in providing such evidence for suitably *weak* notions of conscious states, notions, however, that would be equally satisfiable by the COG-computer. It is only the strong, COG-transcendent phenomena that are being 'eliminated', and the question is where we so much as get *the idea* of such phenomena?

---

[16] I am indebted to Brian Loar and Ray Martin for pressing me on this issue. Notice that I am also not raising the kind of sceptical worry that is often raised about the existence of material objects. It's not that I think that it is the mere *possibility of error* that undermines the possibility of knowledge, much less the existence of the phenomena in question, but rather that I see *no non-question-begging reason* for believing in the postulated phenomena. There *are* non-question-begging reasons to believe in the existence of material objects — they afford the best account of our persistent thoughts that there are — that are lacking in the case of COG-transcendent consciousness.

[17] Although I agree with what Dennett is getting at in such eliminativist proposals as his 'Quining qualia' (1988; see also 1991), I think he wildly overstates the case in rejecting almost *all* internal mental distinctions, as, for example, between the tastes and preferences with regard to beer (1991: 396; see also 392), which might well be distinguished e.g. by counting taste-buds! For discussion of this issue and his instrumentalism about the mental generally, see my (1995).

[18] In Rey 1991: 225–33, I discuss a variety of such data, how in particular they could be elicited by a properly administered standardized test (like the SAT or GRE).

IV. A Wittgensteinian Insight

I think Wittgenstein made a number of insightful suggestions about the sources of our problems here, and I want to explore them in a way divorced from his many other, to my mind unconvincing hypotheses about language and mind (e.g. the thesis of meaning as use, the impossibility of a 'private language', the impossibility of a mentalistic science). Quite apart from his many other theses,[19] there is his suggestion that in thinking about the mind we are often in 'the grip of a picture' whose application we don't fully understand, a picture that inappropriately models our reference to 'inner' phenomena too closely on the model of familiar reference to outer ones. A dualistic realm is posited in order to provide the *referents* of mental terms on the model of the referents of familiar physical terms, like 'table' or 'cat'; but then it is noticed that such referents would have to be peculiarly different — non-spatial, 'private' — from familiar physical objects:

> something that we see and the other does not . . . something that exists within us and which we become aware of by looking into ourselves. And now psychology is the theory of this inner thing. (1980-I: §692.)

Of course, there's no harm in the *ordinary* talk of 'referring' e.g. to sensations (1953: §244). The error, 'the decisive move in the conjuring trick' (§308), is to suppose that referring to a sensation should be understood 'on the model of object and designation' (§293), which is what philosophers presume when they infer the existence of a uniform relation of reference from the use of the word 'refer' in both cases.[20]

Now, if, as I have argued, the COG program *does* capture all the non-tendentiously described evidence that can be adduced for mental states, then the qualiaphile's postulation of some further COG-transcendent property of consciousness would seem to be making just the same error, postulating a superfluous 'inner' property on the model of an ordinary 'outer' one. Indeed, it is at an explanatory point provided by a complete theory of cognition, that one can 'divide through' and say that any such further property 'cancels out whatever it is' (§293)[21]; it is like 'a wheel that can be turned though nothing else moves with it' (§271).

---

[19] Or 'reminders' as he and his followers sometimes insist his nevertheless quite controversial claims be called (1953: §§127–8).

[20] In Rey 1994 and forthcoming, I argue that Wittgenstein (e.g. 1953: §§25, 308, 571; 1980-I: §292, 1980-II: §220) does extravagantly overstate this criticism, including in it not only the peculiarly 'private' mental phenomena that concern us here, but *any* inner mental processes at all! It seems to me we do have good reason to posit processes in our brain corresponding to thinking, reasoning, decision making — in short all the processes well studied by your contemporary cognitive scientist.

[21] As Wittgenstein (1953: §293) prematurely suggested in discussing his 'beetle in the box' example, a suggestion that seems unwarranted given only the behavioural/contextual considerations he cites (see Rey 1994 and forthcoming for discussion).

Unlike Wittgenstein, I doubt it is only philosophers who are captivated by the picture of such 'inner' properties, or only language that is its source (§115). I suspect that it may be simply the best that people ordinarily can do when they try to systematize their everyday mentalistic beliefs: the relation to the brain is so obscure, even in the case of COG-realizable properties, that all one can do is rely on such misleading pictures and analogies.

But nothing in the above explanation explains the peculiar *tenacity* of this wrong analogy, even among those of us who were brought up reading the *Philosophical Investigations*.[22] Why do so many philosophers remain unconvinced? I suspect there is a more interesting explanation than mere obtuseness or lack of theoretical imagination. Moreover, there remains the problem of the explanatory gap, a problem that we saw in the previous section arises with a particular vengeance with regard to the ascription of consciousness to anything at all. What are we to say about our reactions to the COG computer?

Wittgenstein does occasionally address (a version of) this latter problem. In reply to it, he appeals to what would seem to be an uncritical 'biologism':

> But a machine surely could not think! — Is that an empirical statement? No.
> We only say of a human being and what is like one that it thinks . . . only of
> a living human being and what resembles (behaves like) a living human being
> can one say: it sees; is blind; hears; is deaf; is conscious or unconscious.
> (1953: §§359–60, 281; see also §283)

Although these remarks have a force that ought not be lightly dismissed, they do seem indefensible on reflection. Surely we have every reason to suppose that a certain look and behaviour is largely accidental to the possession of a conscious state: as many have remarked, there could be creatures with mental lives who don't look or act like humans (e.g. someone disfigured and paralyzed from an accident;[23] a creature from a remote, perhaps parallel biology), and there could be things that look and act like humans that turn out to be cleverly contrived fakes (marionettes controlled

---

[22] Notice the lack of any such tenacity with regard to other cases in which 'a simile . . . has been absorbed into our . . . language, [which] seemed to repeat it to us inexorably' (1953: §§112–5): e.g. wondering just which 'average American' has 2.3 cars, where a light goes when 'it goes out', or whether a 'train of thought' has a caboose.

[23] Of course, the phrase 'resembles (behaves like)' in this passage could be construed sufficiently broadly to include even the paralyzed and disfigured. Presumably such people *would* be disposed to look and act properly were the paralysis or disfigurement removed. But suppose these misfortunes were due to problems in brain processes controlling motor functions, so that even this disposition were lost? How is this result essentially different from the COG computer I am imagining?

electronically from Mars). In any case, we need an *argument* to restrict mental concepts in this way.[24]

Wittgenstein does make some other remarks that seem to me suggestive of a deeper insight. Anyone concerned with the problem of other minds can't but be struck by what initially seems to be his perverse avoidance of it:

> 'I can only *believe* that someone else is in pain, but I *know* if I am.' — Yes: one can make the decision to say 'I believe he is in pain' instead of 'He is in pain.' But that is all. — What looks like an explanation here, or like a statement about a mental process, is in truth an exchange of one expression for another which, while we are doing philosophy, seems the more appropriate one.

> Just try — in a real case — to doubt someone else's fear or pain. — (1953: §303)

Of course, sometimes it is perfectly easy to doubt someone's pain: they could be acting, exaggerating, maybe mistaking sudden cold for pain. But in these case, as Wittgenstein would emphasize, we usually have some contextual reason for the doubt: something odd about their behaviour, the kind of stimulus to which they were exposed, etc. What I think Wittgenstein is rightly calling attention to is how extremely difficult it is *in a perfectly ordinary case*, say, a child screaming after being hit by a car, actually to doubt that the person is in pain. One would sooner imagine that one is dreaming the whole episode than that the child is seriously 'a mere automaton'. There is something strikingly *compelling* about a perfectly normal case, that the usual statement of the problem of 'other minds' disregards.

A similar point is brought out by a further observation that Wittgenstein makes immediately following one of the previous 'biologistic' passages:

> Look at a stone and imagine it having sensations. — One says to oneself: How could one so much as get the idea of ascribing a *sensation* to a *thing*? One might as well ascribe it to a number! — And now look at a wriggling fly and at once all these difficulties vanish and pain seems to get a foothold here, where before everything was, so to speak, too smooth for it. (1953: §284)

I don't read these passages (as Wittgenstein probably intended them) as anything like an adequate *reply* to the problem of other minds, but I do think that Wittgenstein is drawing attention to an important feature of our mental concepts that has not been sufficiently appreciated, and may help us understand better my 'mind/body problem problem' and Levine's explanatory gap.

---

[24] I fear I don't find that his (1953) talk of 'meaning as use', and his hints at a 'criteriological' account of the meanings of mental terms serve adequately in this regard.

V. A Projectivist Proposal

It is characteristic of many problems in philosophy of mind that issues that elsewhere seem a matter of indifference seem with regard the mind of the profoundest significance. For familiar example, if the issue of *identity* is raised an as issue about 'Theseus' ship', all of whose parts are gradually replaced over the years, it can seem like merely a matter for linguistic decision; but raised as an issue about *my own identity into the future*, it can seem like an issue of the greatest urgency — why, a matter of life and death!

The 'projectivist' approach I want to explore proposes a general diagnosis of such erratic anxieties: they arise in cases where *we expect there to be phenomena in the world correlative to stable psychological states in ourselves, but there turn out not to be any*. Now, the expectation that there are such objective properties is not irrational: when our reactions to things manifest a stability through many local changes it's not unreasonable, by a simple deployment of Mill's methods, to suppose that there *are* corresponding stabilities in the objects themselves: thus stabilities in our perceptions of material objects are a pretty good reason for thinking there are such corresponding objects in the world.[25] But, of course, such suppositions could turn out to be false: we might not have taken sufficient account of the possibility that the stabilities are more in *us* than in the objects themselves.

Of course, given a suitably generous notion of 'phenomenon', there is no doubt *some* phenomenon, however relational and gerrymandered, that is correlative to almost *any* reaction we have. I take it that what bothers people is whether there's a suitably 'natural' phenomenon, a phenomenon that, at any rate, people would be prepared to accept as suitable. Notoriously, in many cases there is not. For starters, there are the naive cases of pathetic fallacy, and many people's reactions to glorious sunsets, the starry heavens, and the sight of the boundless sea, which lead them to project corresponding religious properties into the world itself, as in the case of the 'oceanic feelings' that Freud (1961:11) reports Romain Rolland citing as the source of religious sentiments. Perhaps some are content with merely having the feelings themselves; but most seem disappointed that the world really doesn't really contain any phenomenon appropriately corresponding to the projection.[26]

---

[25] I ignore the predations of quantum mechanics on this innocent supposition.

[26] A cousin idea to this suggestion is T.S. Eliot's (1920) idea of an 'objective correlative':

The only way of expressing emotion in the form of art is by finding an 'objective correlative'; in other words, a set of objects, a situation, a chain of events which shall be the formula of that *particular* emotion; such that when the external facts, which must terminate in sensory experience, are given, the emotion is immediately evoked. (p. 100)

This idea can be traced back to Swedenborg and Baudelaire, and is explored most recently by Wollheim (1993).

Secondary properties provide a perhaps more philosophically interesting example: many of us are deeply disappointed to learn that the redness (that appears to be) in rainbows, grease-spots, tomatoes and roses is no single 'natural' property, but an enormously complex disjunction of such properties, unified only by the fact that they have a certain effect upon (some of) us (cf. Hardin 1988). We are inclined to posit an objective correlate *in* things that standardly look red that corresponds to the apparent simplicity and stability of the experience in us. The wild, relational disjunction just isn't what we expect at all, and the discovery that that's all there is invites the denial that there are such properties as colours at all.

The aforementioned problem of personal identity provides a still more gripping case: we project an enduring object that corresponds (in our own case) to our personal concerns and (in the case of others) to the (more or less) standing effects they have upon us.[27] But, as Hume and Parfit (1984) have argued, there is no 'suitable' thing that corresponds to these projections, nothing that's an appropriate object of our reactions and concerns for them or for ourselves.

What I want to propose then is that a similar sort of projection may be the source of our strong notion of consciousness that gives rise to the explanatory gap. People aren't willing to be just 'good scientists' with respect to consciousness, conceding to psychologists that consciousness is just a COG property in the way that they might concede indifferently to chemists that glass is a liquid. The question of which things have a genuinely conscious life has considerable importance for us outside of scientific explanation. Not only are there (as I stressed in my earlier articles) *moral* issues of chauvinism (e.g. biologism), but there are fairly deep facts about simply how *our nervous systems react* to things that look, move and sound like our conspecifics. There seems, for example, to be dedicated processing for human face recognition (Yin 1969; 1970; Carey 1978; Damasio 1985), human bodily motion (Bernstein 1967), natural language (Liberman *et al.* 1967; Fodor 1983) and emotional expression (Darwin 1872/1965; Ekman 1972) many of which appear to be part of our innate endowment, and give

---

[27] An interesting application of the kind of projectivism I am proposing (an application that suggested the idea to me in the first place) was proposed in conversation by a psychologist, Eleanor Saunders, as an explanation of the otherwise bizarre Capgras syndrome. This is a disorder in which people become convinced that their friends and loved ones have been replaced by duplicates. Saunders suggested that people might in general identify especially emotionally significant objects by the specific emotional effect, a kind of 'emotional fingerprint', that significant others might have upon them; should, for some reason, those emotional reactions no longer be accessible to the person, even in the presence of the usual physical stimuli, the person might well feel as if those other people had been replaced by duplicates, people with the same physical properties, but with 'different souls'. The 'soul', that is, might be regarded as the projection of our stable emotional reactions to others on to them.

rise over time to an immensely rich constellation of reactions in us that regulate our interactions with other people.[28]

An interesting feature of many of these reactions is that, in some cases from the very earliest ages, they exhibit a *first- and third-person indiffer-ence*. This is most evident in our remarkable capacity to imitate one another without observing ourselves in a mirror.[29] In a rudimentary form, this ability is evidently available to humans innately: Meltzoff and Moore (1983) found infants imitating mouth-openings and tongue-protrusions in 40 new-borns (average age 32 hours, the youngest 42 *minutes* old!).[30] But in an increasingly rich form, it seems to be essential to the development of interpersonal understanding: Meltzoff and Gopnik suggest that 'mutual imitation games provide children with a kind of "'primer in common-sense psychology"', a private tutorial in person-related versus thing-related inter-action' (1993: 355) observing that autistic children, who have radically impaired understandings of the mental lives of others, also have severely impaired imitative abilities. (See Meltzoff and Gopnik 1993: 352–4.)

How might this first- and third-person indifference give rise to projec-tion? Consider a 'file' model of concepts:[31] corresponding to each concept in a person's repertoire is a mental file containing various slots for different kinds of information we have about the concept and its extension: for example, in the case of [cat], that it's a biological kind concept; that such and such are typical properties of cats; that such and such are constitutive conditions of being a cat.

Imagine, then, that we have a mental file for [pain], in which is stored information about, e.g. the causes and effects of pain, paradigm cases, remembered instances. But specially marked in that file are two important sorts of representations: representations of what it's like to be in pain in one's own case; and representations of the typical behaviour of others who are in pain. The first-person representations would involve the specially restricted representations alluded to earlier (part II) that would be automat-ically triggered by certain inputs, for example, the stimulation of A- and C-fibres, and which in turn might automatically trigger this file for [pain]. These predications encode various parameters (e.g. apparent location,

---

[28] See the useful review of such capacities particularly as they are relevant to social and emotional interactions in Stern (1985: part I).

[29] Interestingly enough for my present purposes, Wittgenstein (1953: §285) also calls attention to this fact, immediately following the above passage about the wriggling fly.

[30] Meltzoff and Gopnik (1993: 342) report that the result has been replicated in over 20 studies in different cultures, ranging from the US, to western Europe to rural Nepal, and 'fits in with a larger network of perceptual and social-cognitive abilities . . . [e.g.], infant matching of facial movements and speech sounds' (p. 343).

[31] I develop such a model in Rey 1993b.

intensity) of the stimuli, and it is because of their comparatively direct causal accessibility that we are able to report reliably on our own pain states and on those parameters; and a direct effect of the processing of such a representation would be a very high preference not to receive further stimulations of that sort (the 'awfulness of pain').

The other-person case would involve representations of how people in pain typically look and act. These latter representations of others also seem automatically to trigger the file for [pain], rather in the way disproportionately large eyes and forehead (as in Disney cartoons of young animals) trigger the concept [cute]. Thus do we have the difficulty Wittgenstein observed of doubting in a real case, like that of an obviously hurt child, that the person is pain.

Where does the concept of 'strong', COG-transcendent pain arise? I propose that such concepts are deployed at least when we naively *think* about what are in fact the weak states we enter when the above pain concept is triggered in either the first- or third-person fashion, when we reflect upon what 'pain *is*'. Just as we postulate a simple property of redness corresponding to the stability in our experience of red things, so do we postulate strong mental phenomena as the stuff of our immediate experience and as underlying typical behavioural effects in others. The files for these strong mental concepts probably involve a number of the demands about 'qualia' that philosophers have claimed as part of their analysis: 'lack of grain', 'intrinsicality', introspective accessibility of their essences, as well as 'criteriological' connections to typical behaviour. Along the lines of Gopnik's earlier suggestions about the development of expertise, this occurs so 'automatically' that we assume we have the kind of privileged access to the postulated strong phenomena to which we suppose introspection naturally entitles us. That is, *we automatically deploy a concept that happens to involve commitments that exceed anything that introspection alone could possibly establish.*

But, of course, mere COG computers that *don't* act and look appropriately don't trigger those responses, and so seem inappropriate objects for the projection, even were they to turn out to have the (functional) states that from the point of view of psychological *explanation* play the same relevant psychological role. Of course, were a COG computer rigged up to look and act in a sufficiently 'animate' way, it might well trigger the right reactions in us; but note that, in that case, it actually doesn't seem all that difficult to take its 'mental' life seriously; as with Wittgenstein's wriggling fly, the 'difficulties vanish and pain gets a foothold': we begin to be able to project the correlative phenomena.

Such a view begins to account for Levine's explanatory gap. When we think of the projected phenomena we think of phenomena whose relation to behavioural manifestations is largely accidental, and expect to learn about them by an internal theory, in the way, for example, that physiologists develop an internal account, say, of shock.[32] But then when we are con-fronted with a serious psychological account, along the lines of COG, we find, as we find in the case of secondary properties and personal identity, that there is nothing suitable: no physical/computational facts seem to necessitate the projected phenomena; nothing suitable corresponds to the phenomena we had in mind, i.e. to the phenomena we projected from our first/third reactions. We can conclude that there is either a gap between those facts and phenomena, or, more plausibly, as in the case of secondary phenomena and personal identity, there are no such properties to be ex-plained at all.

I do not want to pretend that what I've provided here is anything like an adequate account of the processes by which the projection and the problem of the gap arise. Much more needs to be learned about the development of our understanding of the relevant concepts and their relation to specific (internal and external) stimuli and the curious 'first/third' reactions to which they give rise, as well as about why we count some things and not others 'suitable' correlates to such reactions. But I hope what I have said here suggests a promising approach to the problem of the explanatory gap, and to the broader 'mind/body problem problem' of which it is a piece.[33]

References

Bernstein, N. (1967). *The Coordination and Regulation of Movement*. Oxford: Oxford University Press.

Block, N. (1980). Troubles with functionalism. In Block 1980.

Block, N. (1995). On a confusion about a function of consciousness. *Behavioral and Brain Sciences*, **18**, 227–47.

Carey, S. (1978). A case study: Face recognition. In E. Walker (ed), *Explorations in the Biology of Language*. Cambridge, MA: MIT Press.

Churchland, P. (1981). Eliminative materialism and the propositional attitudes. *Journal of Philosophy*, **78**, 67–90.

Damasio, A. (1985). Prosopagnosia. *Trends in Neuroscience*, **8**, 132–5.

Damasio, A. (1994). *Descartes' Error*. New York: Putnam.

Darwin, C. (1872/1965). *The Expression of Emotions in Man and Animals*. Chicago: University of Chicago Press.

Dennett, D. (1988). Quining qualia. In Marcel & Bisiach 1988.

---

[32] Even Wittgenstein himself seems at one point (uncharacteristically) pulled by such an analogy: 'Psychological words are similar to those which pass over from everyday language into medical language ('Shock').' (1980-II: §21.)

[33] As I mentioned in fn. 27, I am indebted to conversations with Eleanor Saunders for the stimulation to the main idea of this paper, which was originally presented in a lively symposium, 'Showdown at the Explanatory Gap,' with Brian Loar and Corliss Swain in Bled, Slovenia, in June 1993. I am also grateful to Rogers Alberitton and to my colleagues, Ray Martin and Michael Slote, for comments on an earlier draft.

Dennett, D. (1991). *Consciousness Explained.* Boston, MA: Little, Brown & Co.

Ekman, P. (1972). *Emotion in the Human Face.* New York: Pergamon Press.

Eliot, T.S. (1920). Hamlet and his problems. In *The Sacred Wood.* London: Methuen.

Ericsson, K. & Simon, H. (1984/1993). *Protocol Analysis: Verbal Reports as Data.* Cambridge, MA: MIT Press.

Ericsson, K. (1993). Recall or regeneration of past mental states: Toward an account in terms of cognitive processes. *Behavioral and Brain Sciences,* **16**, 41–2.

Fodor, J. (1983). *The Modularity of Mind.* Cambridge, MA: MIT Press.

Freud, S. (1961). *Civilization and its Discontents.* New York: Norton.

Gopnik, A. (1993). How we know our own minds: the illusion of first-person knowledge of intentionality. *Behavioral and Brain Sciences,* **16**, 1–14.

Hardin, C. (1988). *Color for Philosophers: Unweaving the Rainbow.* Indianapolis: Hackett Publishing Company.

Hilgard, E. (1977). *Divided Consciousness: Multiple Controls in Human Thought and Action.* New York: Wiley and Sons.

Levine, J. (1983). Materialism and qualia: the explanatory gap. *Pacific Philosophical Quarterly,* **64**, 354–61.

Levine, J. (1989). Cool red. *Philosophical Psychology,* **4**, 27–40.

Levine, J. (1993). On leaving out what it's like. In Davies & Humphreys 1993.

Liberman, A., Cooper, F., Shankweiler, D. & Studdert-Kennedy, M. (1967). The perception of the speech code. *Psychological Review,* **74**, 431–61.

Loar, B. (1996). Phenomenal states. In Block *et al.* 1966.

Lycan, W. (1987). *Consciousness.* Cambridge, MA: MIT Press.

Lycan, W. (forthcoming). *Consciousness and Experience.* Cambridge, MA: MIT.

McGinn, C. (1991). *The Problem of Consciousness: Essays Towards a Resolution.* Oxford: Blackwell.

Meltzoff, A. & Gopnik, A. (1993). The role of imitation in understanding persons and developing a theory of mind. In S. Baron-Cphen, H. Tager-Flusberg & D. Cohen, *Understanding Other Minds: Perspectives from Autism* (Oxford: Oxford University Press), 335–66.

Meltzoff, A. & Moore, M. (1983). New born infants imitate adult facial gestures. *Child Development,* **54**, 702–9.

Nisbett, R. & Wilson, T. (1977). Telling more than we can know. *Psychological Review,* **84**, 231–59.

Parfit, D. (1984). *Reasons and Persons.* Oxford: Oxford University Press.

Putnam, H. (1960). Minds and machines. In *Mind, Language, and Reality (Philosophical Papers, vol. II).* Cambridge: Cambridge University Press.

Rey, G. (1983). A reason for doubting the existence of consciousness. In R. Davidson, G. Schwartz, & D. Shapiro (eds), *Consciousness and Self-Regulation, vol. III* (New York: Plenum), 1–39.

Rey, G. (1986). What's really going on in Searle's Chinese room. *Philosophical Studies,* **50**, 169–85.

Rey, G. (1988). A question about consciousness. In Otto & Tuedio, 1988.

Rey, G. (1991). An explanatory budget for connectionism and eliminativism. In T. Horgan and J. Tienson (eds), *Connectionism and the Philosophy of Mind.* Dordrecht: Kluwer Academic Publishers.

Rey, G. (1993a). Sensational sentences. In Davies & Humphreys 1993.

Rey, G. (1993b). The unavailability of what we mean. *Grazer Philosophica Studien*

Rey, G. (1994). Wittgenstein, computationalism and qualia. In R. Casati & G. White (eds), *Philosophy and the Cognitive Sciences.* Vienna: Hilder-Pichler-Tempsky.

Rey, G. (1995). Dennett's unrealistic psychology. *Philosophical Topics*, **22**, 259–90.

Rey, G. (forthcoming). Why Wittgenstein should have been a computationalist (and what a computationalist can learn from Wittgenstein). In D. Gottlieb & J. Odell (eds), *Wittgenstein and Cognitive Science*.

Searle, J. (1980). Minds, brains, and programs. *Behavioral and Brain Sciences*, **3**, 417–24.

Stern, D. (1985). *The Interpersonal World of the Infant*. New York: Basic Books.

Wason, P. & Evans, J. (1975). Dual process in reasoning. *Cognition*, **3**, 141–54.

Wimmer, H. & Hartl, M. (1991). The Cartesian view and the theory view of the mind. *British Journal of Developmental Psychology*, **9**, 125–8.

Wittgenstein, L. (1953). *Philosophical Investigations*. Trans. G.E.M. Anscombe. New York: Macmillan.

Wittgenstein, L. (1980). *Remarks on the Philosophy of Psychology*. Two volumes, ed. G.E.M. Anscombe & G.H. von Wright, trans. G.E.M. Anscombe. Oxford: Blackwell.

Wollheim, R. (1993). *The Mind and Its Depths*. Cambridge, MA: Harvard University Press.

Yin, R. (1969). Looking at upside-down faces. *Journal of Experimental Psychology*, **81**, 141–5.

Yin, R. (1970). Face recognition by brain-injured patients: a dissociable ability? *Neuropsychologia*, **8**, 395–402.

Young, A. (1994). Covert recognition. In M. Farah & G. Ratcliff (eds), *The Neuropsychology of Higher Vision: Collected Tutorial Essays*. Hillsdale, NJ: Erlbaum.

Part Three

Consciousness and the Physical World

Introduction to Part 3

Phenomenal consciousness is the crux of the mind–body problem. This concerns not only the relationship between consciousness and the brain, but in a more general sense, the question of how conscious experience can be embedded in the scientific world view at all. How can we conceive of the relation of consciousness to the physical world? What is the relation between the subjective inner world of consciousness and the objective physical cosmos and its governing natural laws? Can physics be of assistance in coming to understand consciousness? Questions of this type are discussed by Colin McGinn, Eva Ruhnau, Rick Grush and Patricia Churchland.

Colin McGinn's article explores the relationship between *space* and consciousness. The non-spatiality of consciousness is a central element of the modern version of the concept of consciousness from Descartes onwards, and it creates a series of well-known theoretical problems; amongst them some of the modern variants of he mind–body problem. McGinn searches for a new path out of the philosophical maze: Is it imaginable that the phenomenon of consciousness is emergent from physical processes, which have spatial properties, and nevertheless has no spatial properties *itself*? This line of thought leads to the conclusion that our picture of the physical universe must be radically incomplete and that we therefore need a conceptual breakthrough in our theory of space in order to solve the mind–body problem.

Eva Ruhnau, on the other hand, investigates the relationship between consciousness and *time*. One of the most difficult aspects of the mind–body problem has always been the problem of developing a convincing conceptual model of the relationship between *internal* and *external* time. The temporal structure of objective events and the emergence of a subjective presence from these events form the thematic centre of Eva Ruhnau's discussion, in which she searches for a philosophical middle course between monistic and dualistic solutions of the problem. At the start she describes the temporal conditions of conscious experience of time and analyses the different levels at which the question of the integration of mental content arises. In the central part, Ruhnau then introduces a new concept, the concept of *Time Gestalt*. With the aid of this conceptual foundation, the complementarity of the discrete and the continuous aspect of consciousness as well as of the constructed and given aspects of consciousness can then be shown. Like a number of authors in this volume, Ruhnau is strongly influenced by empirical results in the neurosciences, but her discussion also displays an extended theoretic strategy. The general principle she searches for in her quest for a theory of phenomenal consciousness can be found not only in neurobiology, but also in physics. In this sense Ruhnau is not only a philosopher of consciousness, but also of physics.

145

This points to a further interesting aspect of the contemporary discussion: Theoretical physicists are joining the debate concerning phenomenal consciousness more and more often. Many philosophers regard this development sceptically, because often it seems unclear *what* theories of this type want to explain in the first place, and often they are uninformed about the philosophical background behind the problems. But the phenomenon can also be interpreted as the onset of a fight among the special sciences for the explanatory basis of consciousness. The disagreement concerns whether consciousness is a fundamental feature of the physical world or whether it is a macrophenomenon which appears only on an extremely high level of organization. If there is to be a reductive explanation of consciousness, on which descriptive level will this reduction be carried out? Is the desired science of consciousness quantum physics, neurobiology or perhaps a new branch of information science?

Among the physicists concerned with the problem of conscious experience, Roger Penrose is perhaps the most prominent. His two books *The Emperor's New Mind* and *Shadows of the Mind* have caused a considerable stir. In their contribution, **Patricia Churchland** & **Rick Grush** offer a thorough criticism of Penrose's theses,[1] including the claim that human consciousness is not based on algorithmic processes or that the microtubules within some brain cells function as 'windows' for effects of quantum gravity. They suggest that there are flaws in Penrose's arguments against the algorithmic basis of consciousness, and they argue that his empirical hypotheses are pure speculation lacking any support by experimental data. In their concluding remarks, Patricia Churchland and Rick Grush offer an interesting suggestion concerning the question of why 'quantum philosophical' theories of consciousness are so very popular with the wider public, although they aim at a much more radical form of reductionism than the neurosciences. Neurobiological theories of consciousness, on the other hand, are often experienced as intimidating and humiliating, perhaps because they are less suitable for a widespread form of emotional obscurantism. Of course, Roger Penrose and his colleague Stuart Hameroff are not examples of this type of attitude. However, Grush and Churchland draw attention to an important point: The attitude in question is not associated with a serious interest in epistemic progress regarding conscious experience, but in emotional profit. This type of obscurantism is the exact opposite of taking phenomenal consciousness *seriously*: It consists in the more or less subtle avoidance of a treatment of the theoretical problems, which is oriented towards clarity and advances in our understanding, by abusing them as a means of satisfying certain emotional needs — e.g. the cultivation of pleasant feelings of the dark, deep and mysterious.

[1] For Penrose's & Hameroff's rebuttal of the criticism printed here, see Penrose & Hameroff 1995, Hameroff & Penrose 1996, Hameroff & Penrose (submitted).

Further Reading

Bitbol, M. & Ruhnau, E. (1994)[Eds]. *The Now, Time, and the Quantum.* Gif-sur-Yvette: Editions Frontières.

Chalmers, D. (1995). Minds, machines, and mathematics. *PSYCHE,* **2,** http://psyche.cs.monash.edu.au/psyche-indexv2.1.html. (Printed version forthcoming with Cambridge, MA: MIT Press.)

Churchland, P.S. (1983). Consciousness: The transmutation of a concept. *Pacific Philosophical Quarterly,* **64,** 80–93.

Churchland, P.S. (1986). *Neurophilosophy: Toward a Unified Science of the Mind-Brain.* Cambridge, MA: MIT Press.

Churchland, P.S. (1988). Reductionism and the neurobiological basis of consciousness. In Marcel & Bisiach 1988.

Churchland, P.S. & Sejnowski, T.J. (1992). *The Computational Brain.* Cambridge, MA: MIT Press.

Görnitz, T. Ruhnau, E. & Weizsäcker, C.F. (1992). Temporal asymmetry as precondition of experience. The foundation of the arrow of time. *International Journal of Theoretical Physics,* **31,** 37-46.

McGinn, C. (1983). *The Subjective View: Secondary Qualities and Indexical Thoughts.* Oxford: Oxford University Press.

McGinn, C. (1989). Can we solve the mind–body problem? *Mind,* **98,** 349–66.

McGinn, C. (1991). *The Problem of Consciousness: Essays toward a Resolution.* Oxford: Basil Blackwell.

McGinn, C. (1993). Consciousness and cosmology: Hyperdualism ventilated. In Davies & Humphreys 1993.

Penrose, R. (1989). *The Emperor's New Mind.* Oxford: Oxford University Press.

Penrose, R. (1994). *Shadows of the Mind.* Oxford: Oxford University Press.

Penrose, R. & Hameroff, S. (1995). What 'gaps'? Reply to Grush and Churchland. *Journal of Consciousness Studies,* **2,** 98–111.

Hameroff, S. & Penrose, R. (1996). Orchestrated reduction of quantum coherence in brain microtubules — a model for consciousness. In Hameroff *et al.* 1996.

Hameroff S. & Penrose, R. (submitted). Orchestrated space-time selections as conscious events. *Journal of Consciousness Studies.*

Ruhnau, E. (1992). Zeit — das verborgene Fenster der Kognition. *Kognitionswissenschaft,* **2,** 171–9.

Ruhnau, E. (1994). The now — a hidden window to dynamics. In A. Atmanspacher & G.J. Dalenoort (eds), *Inside versus Outside. Endo- and Exo-Concepts of Observation and Knowledge in Physics, Philosophy and Cognitive Science.* Berlin, New York: Springer.

Further reading concerning the mind–body problem and the question of the relationship of consciousness to the physical world can be found in the bibliography at the end of this volume. Works which deal with this aspect of the problem are listed in a number of sections, especially however, in sections 3.2 and 3.7.

Colin McGinn

Consciousness and Space

I. The Location of Consciousness

Descartes famously held that, while the essence of body is spatial extension, the essence of mind is thought. Thought is taken to be the defining attribute of incorporeal substance — substance that is non-spatial in nature. He writes: 'For if we . . . examine what we are, we see very clearly that neither extension nor shape nor local motion, nor anything of this kind which is attributable to a body, belongs to our nature, but that thought alone belongs to it.' (Cottingham, Stoothoff, Murdoch 1985: 195.) The mental and the spatial are thus mutually exclusive categories.

It is hard to deny that Descartes was tapping into our ordinary understanding of the nature of mental phenomena when he formulated the distinction between mind and body in this way — our consciousness does indeed present itself as non-spatial in character. Consider a visual experience, E, as of a yellow flash. Associated with E in the cortex is a complex of neural structures and events, N, which does admit of spatial description. N occurs, say, an inch from the back of the head; it extends over some specific area of the cortex; it has some kind of configuration or contour; it is composed of spatial parts that aggregate into a structured whole; it exists in three spatial dimensions; it excludes other neural complexes from its spatial location. N is a regular denizen of space, as much as any other physical entity. But E seems not to have any of these spatial characteristics: it is not located at any specific place; it takes up no particular volume of space; it has no shape; it is not made up of spatially distributed parts; it has no spatial dimensionality; it is not solid. Even to ask for its spatial properties is to commit some sort of category mistake, analogous to asking for the spatial properties of numbers. E seems not to be the *kind of thing* that falls under spatial predicates. It falls under temporal predicates and it can obviously be described in other ways — by specifying its owner, its intentional content, its phenomenal character — but it resists being cast as a regular inhabitant

149

of the space we see around us and within which the material world has its existence. Spatial occupancy is not (at least on the face of it) the mind's preferred mode of being.

No doubt this is connected with the fact that conscious states are not *perceived*. We perceive, by our various sense organs, a variety of material objects laid out in space, taking up certain volumes and separated by certain distances. We thus conceive of these perceptual objects as spatial entities; perception informs us directly of their spatiality. But conscious subjects and their mental states are not in this way perceptual objects. We do not see or hear or smell or touch them, and *a fortiori* do not perceive them as spatially individuated.[1] This holds both for the first- and third-person perspectives. Since we do not *observe* our own states of consciousness, nor those of others, we do not apprehend these states as spatial. So our modes of cognition of mental states do not bring them under the kinds of spatial concepts appropriate to perceptual acquaintance. Perceptual geometry gets no purchase on them. And this is not just a contingent fact about the mind.[2]

Nor do we think of conscious states as occupying an unperceived space, as we think of the unobservable entities of physics. We have no conception of what it would even *be* to perceive them as spatial entities. God may see the elementary particles as arrayed in space, but even He does not perceive our conscious states as spatially defined — no more than He sees numbers as spatially defined. It is not that experiences have location, shape and dimensionality for eyes that are sharper than ours. Since they are non-spatial they are in principle unperceivable.

This is I think what people have in mind when they aver that 'consciousness is not a thing'. The thought expressed here is not the trivial one that to refer to consciousness is to invoke a category of events or states or processes and not a category of objects or continuant particulars. Our intuition that conscious states are not spatial is not the intuition that no *state* is an *object*. For ordinary physical states and events are spatial entities in the intended sense: we apprehend events as occurring *in* space, and states are features *of* spatially constituted objects. So it would be wrong to offer a deflationary interpretation of our non-spatial conception of consciousness by insisting that it comes to nothing more than a recognition that talk of consciousness is talk of events and states — just like talk of explosions and motions and electric charge. The non-spatial nature of consciousness, as we

---

[1] Obviously I am not denying that there is a sense in which we can perceive persons, by perceiving their bodies; my point is that we do not perceive the psychological subject *qua* psychological subject. If you like, we do not perceive the *I* of the Cogito.

[2] We see an echo of this in two doctrines of Wittgenstein's: that self-ascription is not based upon observation; and that the notion of inner ostension (pointing) is ill-defined. In this respect, at least, Wittgenstein and Descartes converge on the same fundamental insights. I think, in fact, that a good deal of Wittgenstein's philosophy of mind is based upon a repudiation of a spatial model of the mind.

conceive it, is much more radical than that diagnosis suggests. Descartes was not committing the simple howler of failing to notice that conscious phenomena are not objects at all and hence not spatial objects. In fact, even when we do speak of something that belongs to the category of continuant object, namely the *subject* of consciousness, we are still insistent upon its non-spatial character.[3] The self is not a 'thing' either, in the intended sense. The realm of the mental is just not bound up in the world of objects in space in the way that ordinary physical events are so bound up. So, at any rate, our pretheoretical view assures us.

That may seem exaggerated, at least under one interpretation of the idea of connectedness to the spatial world. For, it might be said, we do in point of fact locate conscious events in the spatial world — not very precisely perhaps, but at least in a fairly systematic way. Thus we take each subject of consciousness to be somewhere in the vicinity of a distinguished body, and we locate conscious events in the approximate neighbourhood of the physical object we call the brain. We certainly do not suppose that I am in some *other* place than my body, and we locate my thoughts nearer to my head than to my feet. So, it may be said, we do grant spatial characteristics to consciousness, at least of a rudimentary sort.

I think this point should be granted, at least so far as it goes: but it does not go very far in undermining the intrinsic non-spatiality of the mental. How do we actually make the locational judgements about consciousness that we do? Not, clearly, by perceiving that conscious events occupy particular places; rather, by trading upon certain *causal* considerations. Events in particular physical objects are directly causally involved in changes of mental state, and we locate the mental change roughly where those causally proximate physical objects themselves are located. I am where that body is whose physical states bear most directly on my mental state; and my states of consciousness are situated in the vicinity of that brain whose activity is most directly implicated in the causal relations controlling my mental life. For example, my visual states are in the whereabouts of the eyes and brain that produce them, and not somewhere in (say) the Grand Canyon (unless my eyes and brain happen to be there). But this kind of causally based location of the mental should be taken for what it is. First, it is parasitic on a prior location of physical objects; there is no independent route on to mental location, since that is based solely on bearing causal relations to things that *can* be nonderivatively located. If we imagine abrogating these causal relations, by considering a world in which there are no psychophysical causal connexions, but only intra-mental ones, then we see that in such a world no form of spatial location would be available for mental events. They would not be tied down to any location at all, no matter

[3] Again, I am assuming that the conscious subject is not simply identical with the body. But my overall position does not depend upon this, since the point applies equally to conscious states themselves.

how vague. Locating mental events as we do in the actual world is merely
'theoretical', as one might say — a sort of courtesy location. Considered in
themselves, intrinsically, we do not regard mental events as having location. The imprecision of our locational judgements here is a mark of this.
Second, to allow that consciousness can be roughly located is not to grant
it the full panoply of spatial predications. We still do not get predications
of shape, size, dimensionality and so on. And this shows that such spatiality
as we do allow to mental matters is of a second-class and derivative nature.
Descartes himself might readily have allowed this kind of causally based
location of the mental while still insisting that concepts of extension have
no proper application to the mental.

It might now be objected that there are some mental events that do permit
precise location, and that this is based on something *like* immediate perception. Thus I feel a pain to be *in* my hand, and that is indeed exactly where it
is. Isn't this just like seeing the physical injury to my hand that produces the
pain? Well, it is true enough that the pain presents itself as being in my
hand, but there are familiar reasons for not taking this at face value. Without
my brain no such pain would be felt, and the same pain can be produced
simply by stimulating my brain and leaving my hand alone (I might not
even have a hand). Such facts incline us to say, reasonably enough, that the
pain is *really* in my brain, if anywhere, and only appears to be in my hand
(a sort of locational illusion takes place). That is, causal criteria yield a
different location for the pain from phenomenal criteria. And anyway
bodily pain is an unusual case and does not generalise to other mental
phenomena (perhaps this is why in ordinary language we speak of pain as a
bodily state rather than a mental one).

It is instructive to consider the notion of spatial exclusion in relation to
the mind. A well-known metaphysical principle has it that no two material
objects (of the same kind) can occupy the same place at the same time. It is
in the very nature of space and objects that there should be this kind of
necessary exclusion. And analogous principles can be formulated for
material events, states and processes. Now ask whether this principle
applies also to mental items. Can two subjects of awareness occupy the
same place at the same time? Can two thoughts be spatio-temporally
coincident? Can two bodily sensations? The questions seem misconceived,
since the issue does not really *arise* for mental things. We want to say:
'Well, *if* mental things had location and other spatial properties, *then* there
might be such exclusion; but since they don't it is not clear what to say.
Maybe, for all we know, they can be spatio-temporally coincident, since
nothing in their intrinsic nature rules it out.' The fact is that the question is
too much like asking whether two numbers can be at the same place at the
same time. We just do not conceive of these things in ways that bring them
within the scope of the principle of spatial exclusion. This is a way of saying
that the notion of *solidity* has no application to mental phenomena. If the

essential mark of the spatial is competiton for space, as the metaphysical principle records, then the mental lacks that essential feature.

In view of the above considerations there is something highly misleading about the popular suggestion that mental phenomena have the same sort of conceptual status as the posits of physical science: that is, that both are unobservables postulated to make the best sense of the data. Apart from the obvious point that we also know about our mental states 'from the inside', there is a crucial disanalogy here, which underscores the *sui generis* character of the mental case. While we think of the unobservables of physics as existing in space and hence in spatial relation to the things we do observe, we do not think of the mental states that explain behaviour in this way. Explanatory posits they may be, at least from the third-person perspective, but they are not the reassuring spatial entities that other explanatory posits are. It is thus far more puzzling how they relate to behaviour, especially causally, than is the relation of atomic events to the macroscopic behaviour of material bodies. In the physical case, we have notions of contact causation and gravitational force acting across space, but in the mental case it is quite unclear how these causal paradigms are supposed to apply. *How* do conscious events cause physical changes in the body? Not by proximate contact, apparently, on pain of over-spatialising consciousness, and presumably not by action-at-a-distance either. Recent philosophy has become accustomed to the idea of mental causation, but this is actually much more mysterious than is generally appreciated, once the non-spatial character of consciousness is acknowledged. To put it differently, we understand mental causation *only* if we deny the intuition of non-spatiality. The standard analogy with physical unobservables simply dodges these hard questions, lulling us into a false sense of intelligibility.[4]

I conclude, then, from this quick survey of somewhat familiar terrain that consciousness does not, on its face, slot smoothly into the ordinary spatial world. The Cartesian intuition of unextendedness is a firm part of our ordinary conception of the mental. In advance of theoretical reconstruction consciousness is not spatially well-behaved. We shall next look at some consequences of this, inquiring what theoretical response should be made to it.

II. The Origin of Consciousness

If consciousness is not constitutionally spatial, then how could it have had its origin in the spatial world? According to received cosmology, there was a time at which the universe contained no consciousness but only matter in

---

[4] Of course, it is a presupposed materialism that permits the usual insouciance over mental causation. I am simply pointing out that *without* materialism the claim of mental causation, though no doubt correct, is burdened with severe problems of intelligibility. Once materialism is questioned all the old problems about mental causation resurface.

space obeying the laws of physics. Then the evolution of life began and matter started clumping together in novel ways, driven by the mechanism of natural selection. Soon, in cosmic time, neural nuclei appeared, leading to brains of various sizes and structures — and along with that (as we think) came consciousness. Evidently, then, matter fell into ever more complex and ingenious arrangements and as a result consciousness came into the world. The only ingredients in the pot when consciousness was cooking were particles and fields laid out in space, yet something radically non-spatial got produced. On that fine spring morning when consciousness was first laid on nature's table there was nothing around but extended matter in space, yet now a non-spatial stuff simmered and bubbled. We seem compelled to conclude that something essentially non-spatial emerged from something purely spatial — that the non-spatial is somehow a construction out of the spatial. And this looks more like magic than a predictable unfolding of natural law. Let us call the problem of how this is possible the 'space problem' with respect to consciousness.[5]

Notice that this problem has no parallel in the evolution of life forms *per se*. These are indeed cosmic novelties, but they do not essentially transcend the mechanisms of spatial aggregation, and we have a good theory of how the novelty is generated. There is no space problem in explaining the emergence of organisms as such; that problem only begins to bite when conscious states enter the scene. To put it in Descartes' terms: how can something whose essence is to be non-spatial develop from something whose essence is to be spatial? How can you derive the unextended from the extended? Note too that this problem has no parallel in the relation between the abstract and the physical, since, though non-spatial, the abstract is not supposed to have *emerged* from the material. The problem arises from a specific clash between the essence of consciousness and its apparent origin.

We might be reminded at this point of the big bang. That notable occurrence can be regarded as presenting an inverse space problem. For, on received views, it was at the moment of the big bang that space itself came into existence, there being nothing spatial antecedently to that. But how does space come from non-space? What kind of 'explosion' could create space *ab initio*? And this problem offers an even closer structural parallel to the consciousness problem if we assume, as I would argue is plausible, that the big bang was not the beginning (temporally or explanatorily) of all existence.[6] Some prior independent state of things must have led to that

---

[5] There are some suggestive remarks on the spatiality of organisms and the non-combinatorial nature of the mental in Nagel 1986: 49–51.

[6] Here I am raising highly controversial issues. Let me just say that all the arguments I have heard for supposing the big bang to be the beginning of everything take the form of inferring an ontological conclusion from epistemic premises — to the effect that since we can't *know* anything about any earlier state we should suppose there to *be* no such state. But that, I assert,

early cataclysm, and this sequence of events itself must have some intelligible explanation — just as there must be an explanation for the sequence that led from matter-in-space to consciousness. The brain puts into reverse, as it were, what the big bang initiated: it erases spatial dimensions rather than creating them. It undoes the work of creating space, swallowing down matter and spitting out consciousness. So, taking the very long view, the universe has gone through phases of space generation and (local) space annihilation; or at least, with respect to the latter, there have been operations on space that have generated a non-spatial being. This suggests the following heady speculation: that the origin of consciousness somehow draws upon those properties of the universe that antedate and explain the occurrence of the big bang. If we need a pre-spatial level of reality in order to account for the big bang, then it may be this very level that is exploited in the generation of consciousness. That is, assuming that remnants of the pre-big bang universe have persisted, it may be that these features of the universe are somehow involved in engineering the non-spatial phenomenon of consciousness. If so, consciousness turns out to be older than matter in space, at least as to its raw materials.[7]

However that may be, we are still faced with the space problem for consciousness. How might it be dealt with? There are, historically, two main lines of response to the problem, commonly supposed to be exclusive and exhaustive. One response denies a key premise of the problem, namely that mind sprang from matter. Instead, mind has an autonomous existence, as independent of matter as matter is of mind. Perhaps mind has always existed, or maybe came about in some analogue of the origin of matter, or owes its existence to a direct act of God. In any event, mind is no kind of out-growth of matter but an independent ontological category. Thus we

---

is an idealist fallacy. Sometimes it is suggested that time began with the big bang, because of its supposed internal connexion with space. Again, I find such arguments unconvincing. But, actually, my point is consistent with allowing time to start with the big bang, since we could always introduce a notion of explanation that did not require temporal priority. I myself see no good reason to rule out a picture of the universe in which radically new realities come into existence as a result of other realities. Just as it took gravity to convert the gaseous early state of the universe into the clumpy galaxies we now take for granted, so the big bang may have been just one episode in which the universe underwent a radical transformation. In general, I think people are far too ready to suppose that nothing antecedent to the big bang could have existed, usually on shaky philosophical grounds — ultimately of an anthropocentric nature. (No doubt I shall get into trouble for poking my nose into the cosmologists' business here!)

[7] Clearly, there are many large assumptions here: not merely that reality did not begin with the big bang, but also that the prior reality has somehow persisted into the post-big bang state of the universe, presumably by virtue of some sort of conservation principle. These seem to me pretty plausible assumptions, though how to establish them is another question. I should note also that the speculation in the text pertains only to the non-spatiality of consciousness; I am not suggesting that *all* the features of consciousness could be explained by pre-big bang properties. In this paper I am leaving on one side questions about the subjectivity of consciousness, qualia and so on.

have classical dualism, Descartes' own position. In effect, dualism takes the space problem to be a *reductio* of the emergence hypothesis. Mind and matter may causally interact (let us not inquire how!) but it is absurd, for dualism, to suppose that mind could owe its very *being* to matter. That is simply metaphysically impossible, according to dualism. You can no more derive the unextended from the extended than you can derive an ought from an is.[8]

A second response questions what we have been assuming so far, namely that consciousness is inherently non-spatial. We may grant that we ordinarily *conceive* of it in this way, but we should insist that that mode of conception be abandoned. Here we encounter, it may be said, yet another area in which common sense misconceives the true nature of reality. In fact, conscious states are just as spatially constituted as brain states, since they *are* brain states — neural configurations in all their spatial glory. Thus we have classical materialism, the thesis that consciousness is nothing over and above the cellular structures and processes we observe in the brain.[9] Since these admit of straightforward spatial characterization, so, by identity, do conscious states. The case is analogous to the following: to common sense physical objects appear solid, but science tells us that this is an illusion, since they are really made up of widely spaced particles in a lattice that is anything but solid. Somewhat so, the materialist insists that the appearance of non-spatiality that consciousness presents is a kind of illusion, and that in reality it is as spatial (even solid!) as the cell clusters that constitute the brain.[10] It is Descartes' assumption of unextendedness that is mistaken, according to materialism, not the emergence hypothesis.

Now it is not my intention here to rehearse any of the usual criticisms of these two venerable positions, beyond noting that both have deeply unattractive features, which I think we would be reluctant to countenance if it were not for the urgency of the problem. These are positions we feel driven to, rather than ones that save the phenomena in a theoretically satisfying way. My purpose is to identify a third option, and to explore some of its ramifications. The point of this third option is to preserve material

---

[8] In McGinn 1993a I give dualism the best defence I can muster, though it is not a position I subscribe to.

[9] Functionalism and allied doctrines should be included here, since they are broadly materialist. Computationalism is harder to classify because of tricky questions about the ontology of computer programmes. On one natural interpretation computer programmes are constituted by abstract objects, so they are non-spatial. This may or may not be a good way to capture the non-spatiality of consciousness (actually not), but the view is clearly no longer materialist.

[10] This is an unspoken assumption of large tracts of contemporary philosophy of mind. Even those who recognise that consciousness poses problems for materialism in virtue of its phenomenal character seldom acknowledge that its non-spatiality is also a major stumbling-block for materialism — despite the fact that Descartes took it (and not qualia) to be critical.

emergence while not denying the ordinary non-spatial conception of consciousness. The heart of the view, put simply, is this: the brain cannot have merely the spatial properties recognised in current physical science, since these are insufficient to explain what it can achieve, namely the generation of consciousness. The brain must have aspects that are not represented in our current physical world-view, aspects we deeply do not understand, in addition to all those neurons and electro-chemical processes. There is, on this view, a radical incompleteness in our view of reality, including physical reality. In order to provide an explanation of the emergence of consciousness we would need a conceptual revolution, in which fundamentally new properties and principles are identified. This may involve merely supplementing our current theories with new elements, so that we need not abandon what we now believe; or it may be — as I think more likely — that some profound revisions are required, some repudiation of current theory. Consciousness is an anomaly in our present world-view, and like all anomalies it calls for some more or less drastic rectification in that relative to which it is anomalous. Some ideal theory T contains the solution to the space problem, but arriving at T would require some major upheavals in our basic conception of reality.

I am now in a position to state the main thesis of this paper: in order to solve the mind–body problem we need, at a minimum, a new conception of space. We need a conceptual breakthrough in the way we think about the medium in which material objects exist, and hence in our conception of material objects themselves. That is the region in which our ignorance is focused: not in the details of neurophysiological activity but, more fundamentally, in how space is structured or constituted. That which we refer to when we use the word 'space' has a nature that is quite different from how we standardly conceive it to be; so different, indeed, that it is capable of 'containing' the non-spatial (as we now conceive it) phenomenon of consciousness. Things in space can generate consciousness only because those things are not, at some level, just how we conceive them to be; they harbour some hidden aspect or principle.

Before I try to motivate this hypothesis further, let me explain why I think the needed conceptual shift goes deeper than mere brain physiology, down to physics itself. For, if I am right, then it is not just the science of matter in the head that is deficient but the science of matter spread more widely.[11] A bad reason for insisting that the incompleteness reaches down as far as physics is the assumption that physiology *reduces* to physics, so that any incompleteness in the reduced theory must be reflected in the reducing theory. This is a bad reason because it is a mistake to think that the so-called special sciences — geology, biology, information science, psychology, etc. — reduce to physics. I will not rehearse the usual arguments for this, since

[11] cf. Penrose 1989, where consciousness is. also taken to challenge the adequacy of current physics.

they have been well marshalled elsewhere. (See, for instance, Fodor 1974.) If that were the right way to look at the matter, then physics would be *highly* incomplete and defective on many fronts, since all the special sciences have outstanding unsolved problems. But it is surely grotesque to claim that the problem of how (say) the dinosaurs became extinct shows any inadequacy in the basic laws of physics! Rather, the intransitivity of problems down the heirarchy of the sciences is itself a reason to reject any reductionist view of their interrelations. So it is certainly an open question whether the problem of consciousness requires revisions in neurophysiology alone, or whether those revisions will upset broader reaches of physical theory. It depends entirely on what is the correct diagnosis of the essential core of the problem. And what I am suggesting is that the correct diagnosis involves a challenge to our general conception of space. Given the fact of emergence, matter in space has to have features that go beyond the usual conception, in order that something as spatially anomalous as consciousness could have thereby come into existence. Somehow the unextended can issue from matter in space, and this must depend upon properties of the basis that permit such a derivation. It therefore seems hard to avoid the conclusion that the requisite properties are instantiated by matter prior to its organisation into brain structure. The brain must draw upon aspects of nature that were already there. According to our earlier speculation, these aspects may be connected to features of the universe that played a part in the early creation of matter and space itself — those features, themselves pre-spatial, that characterized the universe before the big bang. Consciousness is so singular, ontologically, and such an affront to our standard spatial notions, that some pretty remarkable properties of matter are going to be needed in order to sustain the assumption that consciousness can *come from* matter. It is not likely that we need merely a *local* conceptual revolution.

III. The Nature of Space

Let us perform an induction over the history of science. There is what might be called a 'folk theory of space', a set of beliefs about the general nature of space that comes naturally to human beings in advance of doing any systematic science. It probably develops, in part, out of our perceptual systems and it serves to guide our behaviour; we might think of it as a visuo-motor space. No doubt it would be difficult to describe this mental representation of space in full detail, but I think it is fair to report that it encodes a broadly Euclidian geometry and that it regards motion as relative to the position of the earth. It also has some firm ideas about what it is for something to *be* somewhere. Now it is a platitude of the history of science that this folk theory has come under successive challenges, which have substantially undermined and reformed it. Indeed, most of the big advances in physics and astronomy have involved revising our folk theory of space.

Let me mention, sketchily, a few of these, to give flavour to what I am building up to. First, of course, there was the replacement of the geocentric view of the universe with the heliocentric one, and then the replacement of that with an a-centric view. The Newtonian scheme takes the earth to be just one body in space among others, subject to the same laws of motion; our earthly position does not define some privileged coordinate with respect to which everything else must be measured. We must also recognise the existence of a new force, gravity, which acts across space without benefit of a mechanical medium. Thus space has a hitherto unsuspected power — which Newton himself regarded as dubiously 'occult'. Later, and just as famously, the developments surrounding relativity theory called for the abandonment of a Euclidian conception of physical space, to be replaced by geometries that are counter-intuitive to the folk theory of space. Curved space-time was the upshot, among other exotica. Quantum theory also prompts serious questions about the nature of space: particles have no unique location, and various 'nonlocality effects' upset our usual ideas about physical things and their causal dependence. What it is to be *in* space becomes obscure. Then we have such speculations as string theory and twistor theory and the many-worlds hypothesis, in which further 'hidden' dimensions are introduced. Our folk theory of space has been regularly hung out to dry. From the point of view of the divine physicist, space must look to be a very different creature from that presented to the visuo-motor system of human beings.

All this is suggestive of a certain diagnosis of the problem with respect to consciousness. For here too we have a phenomenon that puts pressure on our ordinary conception of space. Conscious phenomena are not located and extended in the usual way; but then again they are surely not somehow 'outside' of space, adjacent perhaps to the abstract realm. Rather, they bear an opaque and anomalous relation to space, as space is currently conceived. They seem neither quite 'in' it nor quite 'out' of it. Presumably, however, this is merely an epistemological fact, not an ontological one. It is just that we lack the theory with which to make sense of the relation in question. In themselves consciousness and space must be related in some intelligible naturalistic fashion, though they may have to be conceived very differently from the way they now are for this to become apparent. My conjecture is that it is in this nexus that the solution to the space problem lies. Consciousness is the next big anomaly to call for a revision in how we conceive space — just as other revisions were called for by earlier anomalies. And the revision is likely to be large-scale, despite the confinement of consciousness to certain small pockets of the natural world. This is because space is such a fundamental feature of things that anything that produces disturbances in our conception of it must cut pretty deeply into our world-view.

No doubt this is all very mind-stretching and obscure; and it is of course not a theory but an indication of where the correct theory might lie. There is a rather Kantian ring to it, what with noumenal space containing all the answers that phenomenal space cannot provide. But I am not really distressed by the lack of transparency of the conjecture, because I think that it is quite *predictable* that our intellects should falter when trying to make sense of the place of consciousness in the natural order. (See McGinn 1991; 1993b.) And here is where the bitter pill beneath the sweet coating begins to seep through. For to suggest that we need a radically new conception of space is not to imply that we *can achieve* any such conception, even in principle. It may be merely to point to the place at which we are incurably ignorant. To explain what I mean let us back up for a while to consider the question of human epistemology — the question of what we can and cannot know.

IV. The Limits of Human Knowledge

It is easier not to know than to know. That truism has long had its philosophical counterpart in rueful admissions that there are nontrivial limits on what human beings can come to grasp. The human epistemic system has a specific structure and mode of operation, and there may well be realities that lie beyond its powers of coverage. Chomsky, in particular, regards our cognitive system as a collection of special-purpose modules that target specific areas of competence, and fail to target others. (See Chomsky 1976; 1988.) The language faculty is one of these, which itself breaks down into a number of sub-modules. It is targeted away from certain possible languages as a by-product of its positive targeting: human languages, yes; Martian languages, no. Chomsky adopts essentially the same conception of what he calls our 'science-forming' faculties: they too are just a collection of contingent cognitive structures, biologically based, that have arisen in us over the course of evolution. They have a phylogeny and an ontogeny, and they operate according to certain specific principles, these being realised by machinery in the brain. They are as natural as any organ of the body. Given this, there is absolutely no reason to believe that the faculties in question are capable, at this period in our evolution, of understanding everything there is about the natural world. Viewing the matter in a properly naturalistic spirit, with the human species counted as just one evolved species among others, the overwhelming probability is that we are subject to definite limits on our powers of understanding, just as every other species is. We hardly suppose that the bipedal species who preceded us, traces of which sometimes show up in the fossil record, were themselves as intellectually advanced as we are, with our massively protruding frontal lobes and impressive manual dexterity. We just need to project ourselves into the position of the species that might *succeed* us to see how contingent and limited our capacities are.

This general viewpoint makes one open to the possibility that some problems may simply exceed our cognitive competence. But I think something more specific is suggested by our discussion so far: namely, that our troubles over space and consciousness arise from certain deep-seated features of the way we represent space to ourselves. We are, cognitively speaking as well as physically, spatial beings *par excellence*: our entire conceptual scheme is shot through with spatial notions, these providing the skeleton of our thought in general. Experience itself, the underpinning of thought, is spatial to its core. The world as we find it — the human world — is a preeminently spatial world. This is a line of thinking powerfully advocated by P.F. Strawson, who focuses particularly on the rôle of space in our practices of identification. (See Strawson 1959; 1974.) The guiding Strawsonian thesis is that the distinction between particular and universal, and hence between subject and predicate, is founded on the idea, or experience, of spatial distinctness. We regard x and y as distinct particular instances of the same universal P just in so far as we acknowledge that x and y are *at distinct places*. That is what the non-identity of particulars fundamentally consists in for us. Without that spatial resource we should not be able to frame the conception of multiple instances of a single property. And this implies that the very notion of a proposition presupposes the notion of spatial separation, and hence location. At root, then, our entire structure of thought is based upon a conception of space in which objects are severally arrayed; though once this structure is in place we can extend and refine it by means of analogy and relations of conceptual dependence.

Now consider thought about consciousness. The non-spatiality of consciousness presents a *prima facie* problem for our system of thought: how, if the Strawsonian thesis is right, do we contrive to think about consciousness at all? It ought to be impossible. The answer lies in those analogies and dependencies just mentioned. We go in for spatialising metaphors and, centrally, we exploit relations to the *body* in making sense of numerically distinct but similar conscious episodes. We *embed* the mental in the conceptual framework provided by matter in space. We don't *reduce* it to that framework; we appeal, rather, to systematic relations that the two realms manifest. But — and this is the crucial point for me — this is to impose upon conscious events a conceptual grid that is alien to their intrinsic nature. It is as if we must resort to a spatial scheme because nothing else is available to us, given our *de facto* reliance on spatial conceptions. It is not that this scheme is ideally fitted to embed the target subject-matter. Thus we get a kind of partial fit in which location is causally based and notions of extension find no purchase at all. Consciousness comes out looking queasily quasi-spatial, a deformed hybrid. Deep down we know it isn't just extended matter in space, but our modes of thought drag it in that direction, producing much philosophical confusion. We represent the mental by relying upon our folk theory of space because that theory lies at the root of our being able to represent at all — not because the mental itself has a nature that craves such a mode of representation.[12]

To represent consciousness as it is in itself — neat, as it were — we would need to let go of the spatial skeleton of our thought. But, according to the Strawsonian thesis, that would be to let go of the very notion of a proposition, leaving us nothing to think with. So there is no real prospect of our achieving a spatially nonderivative style of thought about consciousness. But then, there is no prospect of our developing a set of concepts that is truly adequate to the intrinsic nature of consciousness; we will always be haunted by the ill-fitting spatial scheme. No doubt this lies behind the sense of total theoretical blankness that attends our attempts to fathom the nature of consciousness; we stare agape in a vacuum of incomprehension. Our conceptual lens is optically out of focus, skewed and myopic, with too much space in the field of view. We can form thoughts *about* consciousness states, but we cannot articulate the natural constitution of what we are thinking about. It is the spatial bias of our thinking that stands in our way (along perhaps with other impediments). And without a more adequate articulation of consciousness we are not going to be in a position to come up with the unifying theory that must link consciousness to the world of matter in space. We are not going to discover what space must be like *such that* consciousness can have its origin in that sphere. Clearly, the space of perception and action is no place to find the roots of consciousness! In that sense of 'space' consciousness is not spatial; but we seem unable to develop a new conception of space that can overcome the impossibility of finding a place for consciousness in it.[13]

In saying this I am presupposing a robust form of realism about the natural world. That we are constrained to form our concepts in a certain way does not entail that reality must match that way. Our knowledge constitutes a kind of 'best fit' between our cognitive structure and the objective world; and it fits better in some domains than others. The mind is an area of relatively poor fit. Consciousness occurs in objective reality in a perfectly naturalistic way; it is just that we have no access to its real inner constitution. Perhaps surprisingly, consciousness is one of the more knowledge-transcendent constituents of reality. It must not be forgotten that knowledge is the product of a biological organ whose architecture is fashioned by evolution for brutely pragmatic purposes. Since our bodies are extended

[12] The inadequacy of spatially-based identification of conscious particulars is a contention of mine, not Strawson; he seems far more sanguine that the spatial scheme is a satisfactory framework for talk of the mental.

[13] Compare cognitive beings who have mastered Euclidean geometry but who constitutionally lack the mathematical ability to develop non-Euclidean geometry. An instructive parable on cognitive limitation, with special reference to space and geometry, is Abbott 1884. I am saying that we too are Flatlanders of a sort: we tend to take the space of our experience as the only space there is or could be.

objects in space, and since the fate of these bodies is crucial to our reproductive prospects, we need a guidance system in our heads that will enable us to navigate the right trajectory through space, avoiding some objects (predators, poisons, precipices) while steering us close to others (friends, food, feather beds). Thus our space-representing faculties have a quite specific set of goals that by no means coincide with solving the deep ontological problems surrounding consciousness and space. Many animals are expert navigators without having the faintest idea about the true objective structure of space. (The eagle, for one, still awaits its sharp-beaked Newton.) There is simply no good reason to expect that our basic forms of spatial representation are going to lead smoothly to the ideal theory of the universe. What we need from space, practically speaking, is by no means the same as how space is structured in itself.

I suspect that the very depth of embeddedness of space in our cognitive system produces in us the illusion that we understand it much better than we do. After all, we *see* it whenever we open our eyes and we *feel* it in our bodies as we move. (Time has a similar status.) Hence the large cognitive shocks brought about by the changes in our view of space required by systematic science. We are prone to think that we *can't* be all that wrong about space. I have been arguing that consciousness tests the adequacy of our spatial understanding. It marks the place of a deep lack of knowledge about space, which is hard even to get into focus. No doubt it is difficult to accept that two of the things with which we are most familiar might harbour such intractable obscurities. Irony being a mark of truth, however, we should take seriously the possibility that what we tend to think completely transparent should turn out to transcend altogether our powers of comprehension.

References

Abbott, E.A. (1884). *Flatland: A Romance of Many Dimensions*. New York: Signet Classic.
Chomsky, N. (1976). *Reflections on Language*. London: Fontana.
Chomsky, N. (1988). *Language and Problems of Knowledge*. Cambridge, MA: MIT Press.
Cottingham, J., Stoothoff, R., Murdoch, D. (1985)[eds]. *The Philosophical Writings of Descartes, Volume I*. Cambridge: Cambridge University Press.
Fodor, J. (1974). Special Sciences. *Synthese*, **28**, 77–115.
McGinn, C. (1991). *The Problem of Consciousness*. Oxford: Basil Blackwell.
McGinn, C. (1993a). Consciousness and cosmology: hyperdualism ventilated. In Davies & Humphreys 1993.
McGinn, C. (1993b). *Problems in Philosophy*. Oxford: Basil Blackwell.
Nagel, T. (1986). *The View from Nowhere*. Oxford: Oxford University Press.
Penrose, R. (1989). *The Emperor's New Mind*. Oxford: Oxford University Press.
Strawson, P.F. (1959). *Individuals*. London: Methuen.
Strawson, P.F. (1974). *Subject and Predicate in Logic and Grammar*. London: Methuen.

Eva Ruhnau

Time Gestalt and the Observer

Reflections on the 'tertium datur' of Consciousness

'Mind is a process, not a thing.'
(William James)

Cartesian dualism, the division of reality into two basic kinds of substances, *res cogitans* and *res extensa*, is increasingly thought to be outdated, albeit some forms of property dualism are still under discussion. In most cases, the abandonment of substance dualism is linked to the idea that the results of the neurosciences will lead to the identification of mental states with material states of the brain. However, this new 'solution' of the old mind–body problem rests on Cartesian dualism in its very formulation. Materialistic monism is not even conceivable without this foundation.

The modelling of reality requires at least two concepts: constancy and change. To perceive change, something has to be invariant. Conversely, constancy needs change as its background to be observed. Within the conceptual realm of western philosophy, however, the complementarity of constancy and change is turned into a hierarchy. The staticity of being is chosen as dominant, the dynamics of change becomes a derived and secondary concept. This transformation of complementarity into hierarchy is the essential (though in general unacknowledged) precondition of scientific realism and objectivism. Consequently, the purpose of knowledge is the construction of a perceptual entirety of objects and properties — rather than the comprehension of a world created by the dynamical unity of opposites.

Consciousness, the 'stream of thought' (William James 1890), can be characterized in the following way: it is personal, always changing, nevertheless continuous, turned towards objects independent of itself and selective with respect to object properties (see also Picton & Stuss 1994).

165

'Consciousness' includes *three* components: objects, knowledge, and someone knowing this knowledge, an accessory or accomplice ('*con*scientia'). We have *one* material world: being, the facts. And we are confronted with an *ambiguity* of knowledge. Here, I suggest that this ambiguity of knowledge prevents us from identifying knowledge and being in a definite (unambiguous) way, thus generating ultimately the old ideal, the static unity of one context or universe of discourse. If we want to attain this ideal in all circumstances, the accessory, the 'I' of 'I know' has to be eliminated.

The ambiguity of knowledge is caused by a twofold move of thinking. Thinking can point towards things and objects. And it can point at itself, the thinking of thinking. But this yields the question: is thinking itself an object of thinking, just as things are objects of thinking? In general, we do not categorize thinking as thing or substance in such an obvious, naive manner. Instead, we talk about functions and processes. Nevertheless, we try to get a grasp of processes with the same formal equipment we use to classify things. Actually, we do not treat processes like objects — which are considered to be identical with themselves in time — yet we do deal with processes as successions of states in time. With the exception of the dimension of time, the formal apparatus we apply to describe states is the same which we use to define objects. But processes cannot be reflected as non-temporal like objects; time is constitutive in comprehending processes. However, processes are usually described as temporal successions of objective states. That is, they are defined as objects plus time.

As a result of such a classification of processes — in addition to the formalism of the two-valued logics of being, i.e. the three logical principles (the Law of Identity, the Law of Contradiction and the Law of Excluded Middle, the tertium non datur) — the concept of time appears. Time appears as a necessary background to objectify processes. In other words, within time the concept of change escapes its fixation as object.

However, if time is separated in such a way from thinking, suddenly time itself is accessible for objectification. Time is now considered to be a continuum, appearing as an unlimited divisibility. Such a conception, I want to assert, is not the genuine nature of time; it is the inevitable consequence of the subordination of reality to objective categories of being. If this effort were successful, thinking would be dissolved in the identity of the objective, yielding plain materialistic monism. Yet the bivalence of the formalism, and its symmetry, admit another solution: the revocation of the objective into an absolute subject. This would be plain idealistic monism. Both solutions are equivalent to each other. The oscillation between materialism and idealism, and the bitter opposition of both, are based on this equivalence.

Is the solution therefore dualism? Not at all. Tertium datur, the Third exists and it exists in the Gestalt as the accomplice of being and thinking, in the Gestalt of the 'I' of consciousness. This Third is between matter and mind: it is their connecting link. I suggest that this Third is not a pure cognitive construct but is founded in the biological or, to be more precise, the ecological functioning of an organism in its environment. This Third, which does not yet play an adequate role in the categoric scheme of concepts: what does it know about time, how does it experience time?

I. Consciousness and Time

How does time appear to the 'I'? Is time an absolute given entity, is it tied to the observing I and its analysis, is it created by the I? On the one hand, most of us believe that time flows continuously and is independent of all events. This view is the foundation of the Newtonian concept of time and is therefore the basis of all classical physics. On the other hand, we know that inner temporal experience and the external time of a clock do not necessarily coincide. There is no simple and unique mapping between internal experience of time and external physical time (see also Dennett & Kinsbourne 1992). The physical duration of time may be over- or underestimated. The externally given temporal order of events may not be reflected in perception. Time in physics is treated as a continuous parameter; but the nature of the temporal organisation of subjective awareness reveals essential discontinuities. In the following, I want to demonstrate which temporal constraints shape our conscious experience.

External initial conditions are the presentation of two stimuli (flashes of light or tones) in a well-defined temporal order with (external) temporal distance Δt. Through linear variation of Δt, the *internal* experience of these stimuli (which I call atomic events; with respect to sensory perception, atomic events are not further divisible and not evaluable) reveals a whole hierarchy of elementary temporal percepts.

If the external temporal interval Δt is below a certain value, the *coincidence* threshold, the two stimuli coincide and only one atomic event is observed. This coincidence threshold is different for different sensory modalities, and is connected to the different transduction times (acoustic 2–3 msec; tactile approximately 10 msec; visual approximately 20 msec).

If Δt exceeds the coincidence threshold, two atomic events are observed. However, it is not possible to decide which atomic event is the first and which is the second. Only if Δt exceeds an *order* threshold is a before–after relation experienced, so that the temporal direction can be perceived. It is important to note that the order threshold (of approximately 30 milliseconds), defined as the minimum temporal distance needed to identify the order of stimuli, is the same for all modalities (Hirsh & Sherrick 1961). The perception of temporal order, then, seems to be connected to a central processing mechanism.

This leads to the following hypothesis (Pöppel 1985/1988; Pöppel *et al.* 1990; Ruhnau & Pöppel 1991; Pöppel 1994):

The brain creates and is structured by *adirectional temporal zones* or zones of co-temporality. With respect to external time such 'temporal windows' appear as time quanta. Their duration (of about 30 msec) characterizes the functional level of the operating system.

Besides the order threshold, further experimental results suggest the existence of such temporal neutral zones. In reaction time measurements to visual or acoustic stimuli one often observes multimodal shapes of the response curves. Multimodal distribution of reaction time histograms can be registered if the reaction to stimuli is triggered in definite phases of neuronal activity only. Multimodalities can only be observed if the response is temporally related to stimulus onset, i.e. it is stimulus locked, not only stimulus induced (see also Ruhnau & Haase 1993). Another example yielding evidence for temporal windows is finger-tapping experiments. The task is to synchronize a regular stimulus sequence with motor taps. In general, stimulus anticipation of about 30 msec is observed corresponding to one zone of co-temporality (Müller *et al.* 1990). But this effect occurs only if the interstimulus interval is shorter than 3 seconds (Mates *et al.* 1994). This experimental fact already points to further levels of time perception.

What is described so far is the succession of perception, but not the perception of succession. It is characteristic for human perception (and action) that successive events can be bound together to generate a new perceptual content — for example a musical theme. To be more precise, two further mechanisms have to be distinguished.

Temporal integration of successive temporal windows — the Now:

At a basic level, an automatic temporal integration process is observed that links several successive time windows (of 30 msec) together, up to intervals of approximately 3 seconds, providing the foundation for the formation of perceptual units. Such processes constitute the formal basis of the experienced subjective '*Now*'. Experimental support for such an automatic integration process comes from reproduction studies of temporal intervals (Pöppel 1978). When subjects are asked to reproduce the duration of intervals, intervals of approximately 3 seconds are reproduced accurately. Shorter intervals are slightly overestimated, whereas longer intervals are underestimated. Temporal segmentation in the 3 second range is also discovered in language processing (Pöppel 1985/1988; Turner & Pöppel 1983) and in the temporal organization of intentional acts (Schleidt *et al.* 1987). All these results, based on different experimental paradigms, provide clear evidence that the conscious Now is — language and culture independent — of the duration of approximately 3 seconds. The experienced Now is not a point, but is extended (for further details see also Pöppel 1994).

Semantic integration of contents of consciousness — duration:

On this highest level of temporal integration, perceptual units of conscious-ness are linked together. The integration intervals of 3 seconds, the Now-moments, serve as a formal basis for the representation of these contents. Yet these do not define what is represented or how the represented informa-tion is bound together. The subjective continuity of experience is presum-ably the result of a *semantic* connection of the Now-moments. The observation that continuity can break down, as in the case of schizophrenia, implies that under normal circumstances a specific neuronal process is responsible for the semantic nexus.

In summary: on a formal level, time appears to be discrete; but in regard to content, time seems to be continuous, as a consequence of semantic binding operations. The tertium datur of consciousness experiences time not only as continuous. Continuity of experience seems to require some semantic aspects, i.e. the concept of meaning. Syntactically constitutive for time are however two temporal discrete mechanisms:

- a high frequency mechanism providing *elementary temporal win-dows*; the external duration of these adirectional zones is of the order of 30 msec;

- a low frequency mechanism defining *intervals of integration* of 3 sec; within these intervals sequential information is bound together independent of context.

In this way, we have a temporal syntax at our disposal, i.e. windows of co-temporality (without internal temporal succession) and a limited capacity of integration of successive units of co-temporality ('Nows'). What is the point of these syntactic constraints? What is their functional significance?

II. Time and Gestalt

To obtain a subjective representation of mental phenomena, specific logis-tical requirements have to be met. In order to function, a brain has to reach a certain level of *activation*. Another logistical requirement is the *organi-zation* of the spatially distributed mental functions. Specific mental func-tions are represented *locally* in the brain. Localization of function means that a defined neuronal process (inter alia characterized by specific neuro-chemical mechanisms) relates a mental function to a spatially defined area. Mental functions are available in modules (see Fodor 1983). Experimental verifications of this thesis are mainly based on observations with brain-injured patients. Pieces from the entire repertoire of mental functions can be lost if specific neuronal algorithms are no longer available. In other words, specific lesions of the brain result in defined — *inter*individually similar — functional losses. The loss of mental functions is their proof of existence.

The spatial segregation of mental functions throughout the brain leads to the question of how integrated subjective experiences are possible. Each mental act is characterized by ('simultaneous') activities in different areas of the brain. In particular, PET (positron emission tomography) studies show that always *several* spatially distinct areas of the brain exhibit higher activity during defined psychological tasks (for example, reading a text). In general, each mental act can be characterized by a specific pattern of spatially distributed activities within neuronal assemblies. This observation indicates that neuronal mechanisms are required which provide the integration between the distributed activities in order to result in the experience that each subjective phenomenon is *just one* — not many.

It is useful to distinguish different operational levels of integration. This is demonstrated briefly with the following picture:

differentiation		**integration**
space, motion	→	*intra*sensory
intensity	→	(quantitative)
form	→	*intra*sensory
colour	→	(quantitative)
visual	→	*inter*-
acoustic	→	sensory

The problem of integration is already met at the *intra*sensory level. Perceived objects usually cover different intensities of brightness or tones. But reaction times depend on the intensity of the given stimuli. For example, a difference of light intensity of approximately two logarithmic units corresponds to a difference in transduction time of about 20 msec, with decreasing transduction time corresponding to increasing intensity. In the auditory domain, a difference in transduction time of about 20 msec occurs with respect to intensities of 45 and 90 db (Pöppel *et al.* 1990). In addition, intrasensory object integration of different qualities like colour or form has to be ensured.

However, *inter*sensory integration is also necessary. It is known from reaction time experiments that simple auditory reaction time is considerably shorter than simple visual reaction time (with a difference of about 30 msec). This can be traced back to the biophysical difference of transduction for both sensory modalities. Furthermore, the distance of the sound source from the subject is important in the auditory case, and affects auditory reaction time. Auditory reaction time is lengthened if the stimulus is removed from the subject. This lengthening is due to the time the sound wave takes to reach the subject. In the visual case, however, the time the light wave needs from source to target can be neglected because of the immense velocity of light. Because of the difference in sound and light velocities and the different transduction times, it is calculated that at approximately 10 metres distance, auditory reaction time corresponds to visual reaction time. This distance can be called the 'horizon of simultaneity' (Pöppel 1985/1988). The temporal central availability in the two sensory domains is co-temporaneous for objects at this distance from the perceiving subject. Therefore, perception of an object as *one* by means of auditory and visual stimuli requires intersensory integration.

In summary, these results indicate that the central temporal availability of stimuli within one sensory modality and between different modalities is constantly changing. Why then do we perceive the identity of objects, why not the disintegration of object identity into many separate identities corresponding to different contexts of perception? Perhaps 'time' is the glue, and the clue in solving this problem.

As a solution of the integration or binding problem, the following hypothesis is suggested:

> The adirectional temporal zones or zones of co-temporality (of 30–40 msec duration in external time) define *elementary integration units* (EIUs). Within these zones activation from different functional units of the brain is correlated.

The concept of elementary integration units might be the logistical basis for the implementation of binding operations, hence a possible solution of the integration problem. Which kind of processes could yield such specific temporal structures of information processing? One has to distinguish between stimulus-independent internal periodic processes ('running clock' models, cf. for example Stroud 1955), and stimulus-locked periodicities (see Harter 1967; Pöppel 1972; Pöppel *et al.* 1990). For a detailed discussion of both classes of models, see Jokeit 1991.

The model proposed here belongs to the second class (Pöppel 1968). It is assumed that the occurrence of adirectional temporal zones is based on the relaxation of oscillations of neuronal assemblies (connected via mutual re-entrant maps between different modules). Suprathreshold stimuli reaching the sensory surface initiate such neuronal oscillations. The elementary integration units are defined as successive periods of these oscillations. Thus each period corresponds to a temporal window of the brain. Within such a window all available information is treated as co-temporaneous, thus obtaining intra- and intersensory integration. Within such elementary integration units, no direction of time can be perceived. A before–after relation is obtained only if at least two temporal windows are provided.

Recent electrophysiological findings of coherent oscillations in the gamma frequency range, around 30–60 Hz (Eckhorn & Reitboeck 1989; Eckhorn *et al.* 1988; 1993; Engel *et al.* 1991; Gray and Singer 1989; Gray *et al.* 1989; Singer 1994; Sporns *et al.* 1989), force the idea that via coherent cortical oscillations, spatially segregated activities of the brain might be integrated. Let us take, for example, a moving object. Those parts of the visual scene belonging to the object are distinguished through spatiotemporal coherences of motion, contours and colour, for example. How does the brain 'know' that spatiotemporal coherence is a property of objects which can be used to differentiate (figure from ground) and to integrate (different features)?

In the development of cognitive structures, those connections between neurons are stabilized whose patterns of activity are correlated with each other. Such selective coupling is generated because neurons which are activated simultaneously (via spatio-temporally coherent features of objects) tend to strengthen their synaptic connections. Such groups of nerve cells form feature detectors; they are, so to speak, measuring apparatuses of the relevant features. This is the aspect of *differentiation*. The associated neurons oscillate with a frequency of about 40 Hz if the appropriate features of an object are available. Spatially segregated feature detectors can, in the case of coherent properties of the perceived object, synchronize their rhythmic activities. This is the aspect of *integration* or binding (see also Singer 1993).

The different experimental results vary with respect to spatial resolution (from single unit to EEG activities) and with respect to temporal relations to stimulus onset (strictly stimulus-locked, or stimulus-induced only). An excellent overview concerning the experimental issues and findings can be found in Neven & Aertsen 1992; Aertsen & Arndt 1993. It is important to note that in case synchronized oscillations are supposed to provide a solution of the binding problem, the question of their functional effectiveness arises. If we do not want to postulate the existence of a homunculus in the brain overseeing synchronisation, the mass activity generated by the synchronized activities of neurons has to be functionally effective. What could be an appropriate experimental paradigm to study the functional relevance of coherent oscillatory phenomena?

The data supporting the proposed model of elementary integration units are mainly results of reaction time studies, and strictly time-locked to stimulus onset. This suggests that the appropriate paradigm might be to take into account *complete* sensory-motor cycles. If coherent oscillations are functionally effective, this effectiveness should be relevant and prove itself on the *output* side. In the last decades, there have been significant experimental and theoretical prejudices in favour of cognition and the sensory part of awareness. This, I claim, makes the homunculus unavoidable. In the context of the cognitive paradigm, neuronal patterns of activity cannot reflect holism per se, but necessarily and immediately lead to the question, 'holism for whom or what?' Correction of the cognitive prejudice, and appropriate consideration of the motor aspect, could presumably solve the problem. Functional effectiveness should be relevant at the efferent side. The homunculus dissolves with sensory-motor integration. In brief: perception and motion constitute an inseparable unity.

At the phenomenological level we usually observe (!) observation and action as separated. It seems that in the flow of action the actor cannot constitute himself also as an observer. Observation has to interrupt, to break the flow, to establish objects. However, replacing the observer by the accomplice, the 'con' of consciousness, the 'I' of 'I know', turning attention away from objects and toward units of action or action-Gestalts, could provide us with a totally different picture. To make this more precise, in the following I want to distinguish between object and Gestalt.

III. Gestalt and Observer

Definition III. 1

A non-empty set T and a two-valued relation over T form a *strictly ordered set* $(T,<)$ if and only if the relation $<$ is (1) asymmetric and (2) transitive; i.e. for all elements t, t', t'' of T the following holds:

(1) if $t < t'$, then not $t' < t$
(2) if $t < t'$ and $t' < t''$, then $t < t''$.

The strictly ordered set $(T,<)$ is called a *time order* if the elements of T are called *time positions* and the relation $<$ is called a *before–after* relation.

Definition III. 2

The time order $(T,<)$ is called *external time* if T is the set of real numbers. It is symbolized by $(T_{ext},<)$. The elements of T_{ext} are called *time points*.

Definition III. 3

The time order $(T,<)$ is called *internal time* if T is the set of natural numbers. It is symbolized by $(T_{int},<)$. The elements of T_{int} are called *time windows*.

The class of atomic events within one elementary integration unit (EIU) can be characterized in the following way: the symbol E_a^i marks an atomic event where 'a' denotes the 'external temporal index' and 'i' the 'internal temporal index'. E_a^i with $i = 0$ are external stimuli. The choice of indices reflects the fact that the atomic events are represented within the different time orders. The 'internal extension' of an elementary integration unit is reflected as a temporal window of duration D of about 30 msec. Extension of subjective presence is given by mD, where m (of the order of 10^2) denotes the maximal number of EIUs creating the experienced Now of approximately 3 sec. Events $E_a^n : (n-1)D < a < nD$, $n = 1, \ldots, m$ belong to the nth EIU. Duration D corresponds to an interval I_n of external time, duration mD of subjective presence to the union of the intervals I_1 to I_m.

Definition III. 4

An atomic event E_a^i is called *co-temporaneous* with an atomic event E_b^j if and only if $i = j$ $(i,j>0)$ and there exists a number n with the following property: $1 \le n \le m$ and $(n-1)D < a,b < nD$. This relation is symbolized as $E_a^i \; ct \; E_b^j$.

Proposition III. 1
The relation ct is an *equivalence relation*. The eqivalence class containing E_a^i will be denoted by (E_a^i).

To prove this statement one has to show that the relation ct fulfils the following properties:

  reflexivity: E_a^i ct E_a^i
  symmetry: E_a^i ct E_b^j implies E_b^j ct E_a^i
  transitivity: E_a^i ct E_b^j and E_b^j ct E_c^k implies E_a^i ct E_c^k .

The proof is straightforward. The equivalence relation ct is a formal expression of the partition of the set of atomic events into mutually exclusive EIUs.

The perception of a stimulus is always correlated with a state of activity of the brain. To be more precise, it is correlated with quite a number of such states. In general, talking about the state of a system denotes the present condition of the system, i.e. states correspond to time points and therefore to elements of T_{ext}. If a state lasts for a while, it corresponds to several time points, i.e. to an interval of T_{ext}. To distinguish this duration in external time from the 'internal extension' of elementary integration units, the concept of time Gestalt is introduced (see also Ruhnau 1995a).

Definition III. 5
Let $(T,<)$ denote a time order and I an interval of T. An attribute P which holds for the interval I if and only if it holds for all subintervals of I is called *homogeneous* over I.

Remark: This mathematically defined concept of homogeneity corresponds via simple mapping to the concept used in the philosophical discussion of qualia.

Definition III.6
Let $(T,<)$ denote a time order, I an interval of T, and P an attribute on I. I is called a *maximal interval* with respect to P if and only if there exists no interval I' on which P holds and I is a proper subinterval of I'.

Definition III. 7
Let $(T,<)$ denote a time order, I an interval of T, and P an attribute on I. P is called *Gestalt-generating* with respect to I if and only if the following holds: P is homogenous over I, and I is maximal interval with respect to P.

Definition III. 8
Let $(T,<)$ denote a time order, I and I' two mutually exclusive, consecutive intervals of T, and P an attribute which holds for both intervals. P is called *concatenable* if and only if it holds for the union of I and I'.

The characteristics of the equivalence relation ct yield the following two propositions:

Proposition III. 2

The attribute P: (for two atomic events $E_a{}^i$ and $E_b{}^j$ the following holds, $E_a{}^i$ ct $E_b{}^j$) is homogeneous over the intervals defined by ct of the external time order $(T_{ext}, <)$; these intervals are maximal, i.e. P is Gestalt-generating with respect to these intervals. Furthermore, P is not concatenable.

Proposition III. 3

The attribute P: (for two atomic events $E_a{}^i$ and $E_b{}^j$ the following holds, $E_a{}^i < E_b{}^j$, i.e. $i < j$) is concatenable and not homogeneous over the union of the intervals I_1 to I_m of the external time order (i.e. with respect to the Now of 3 seconds).

Usually the concept of Gestalt is related to spatially extended and delimited entities. The atomic events of an equivalence class are extended with respect to external time, delimited with respect to the before-after relation, and identified with respect to internal time. In a certain sense, they generate a Gestalt in time.

Definition III. 9

An equivalence class of the equivalence relation ct of atomic events is called *time Gestalt*.

Time Gestalt as defined above is not just a simple succession of time points. The actual time window in its entirety constitutes a time Gestalt. The binding together of atomic events to classes of co-temporality is an expression of an internal dynamic of the brain. With respect to the representation of atomic events in internal or external time order, the concept of homogeneity is connected to co-temporality, and the concept of concatenation is connected to the before–after relation. The linkage within the Now of 3 seconds may be a necessary prerequisite for the experience of *causality*. However, causal connections grasp more than a syntactical structure. The meaning of the entities which are to be connected in a certain context turns out to be essential. This does not exclude the possibility that meaning emerges from a syntax adapted to spatio-temporal coherence. Nevertheless, once a perceptual apparatus internalizing this external coherence in its functioning has been built up, coherence (or its change) is meaningful for the system.

   In the following, I want to associate the concept of meaning with the question, 'What constitutes an event for a system (a brain)?' As a time Gestalt differs from the mere succession of time points, similarly an event should be distinguished from the mere occurrence and stringing together of atomic events. (Actually, the terms atomic percepts or atomic incidents would be preferable.) Also, in this case, the linkage (to a temporal chain) is essential for the functioning of the system, but the mapping on to a time axis which is external to the system is not. In other words, (dynamical) time is created by the system itself. The syntax necessary for the concatenation of atomic events is given by the extension of the Now.

Definition III. 10

Let $(T,<)$ denote a time order. A non-empty subset H of T is called a *happening* if and only if H is (1) connex and (2) dense; i.e. for all elements t, t', t'' of H and all t^* of T the following holds:

   (1) $t < t'$ or $t' < t$ or $t = t'$
   (2) if $t' < t^*$ and $t^* < t''$, then t^* is an element of H.

Two arbitrary elements of T are not necessarily in the relation <. Connexity ensures the complete order of H. Such a complete ordered set is also called a *chain*. The interpretation of the density of a happening is especially interesting when the happening is based on several atomic events. Even if temporal gaps between atomic events exist, some connection has to be guaranteed. In other words, a (generally defined) memory has to be in effect. For the syntactical level considered here, such a memory could be associated with the relaxation of the synchronous activity of neurons. (There is an interesting overlap of these ideas with Husserl's phenomenological theory of temporal experience, especially with the concept of retention; see Husserl 1928; 1955.)

From the definition of a happening it immediately follows that the property of elements of $(T,<)$ to form a happening is concatenable. However, an event should not be divisible into parts of the same event type. An event must be unitary. This leads to

Definition III. 11

Let $(T,<)$ denote a time order, I an interval of T, and P an attribute on I. I is called a *minimal interval* with respect to P if and only if there exists no interval I' on which P holds and I' is proper subinterval of I.

Definition III. 12

Let $(T,<)$ denote a time order, I an interval of T, and P an attribute on I. P is called *event-generating* with respect to I if and only if the following holds: P is a happening, and I is a minimal interval with respect to P.

Definitions III.7 and III.12 comprise the syntactical preconditions to generate Gestalts or events. The transition to the actual Gestalt or event requires semantics in a general sense, i.e. decisions or a context of meaning or evaluation. The Gestalt-generating co-temporality of atomic events is an actual Gestalt only if the before-after relation determines the maximal homogeneity. In analogy, the transition from an event-generating happening to an actual event requires the determination of the minimal happening through imbedding into a context of meaning or a value context.

Connecting the concepts of Gestalt or event with the before–after relation, or with a context of meaning or evaluation, respectively, leads to the questions of how the direction of time, or the value defining system, are related to the Gestalt or event-generating syntactical process itself. The direction of time is based on irreversibility. Irreversibility is linked to the concept of observation or — in other words — to the facticity of the past and the possibility of the future (see Görnitz *et al.* 1991; Haag 1990; Weizsäcker & Görnitz 1990). This is clearly recognizable in quantum theory, where quantum systems are subjected to a measurement within a context of meaning set up by the observer.

Here, a remark is appropriate. Reference to quantum theory does *not* endorse the (at the moment fashionable) combination of this theory with the phenomenon of consciousness. I do not want to support hypotheses *à la* Penrose (Penrose 1986; 1989; 1994). It seems to me that the connection of the experience of consciousness with a still unknown theory of quantum gravity is based on a category mistake. Nevertheless, I think that the quantum mechanical measurement process is interesting, and relevant for the description of consciousness. The analogy which is pursued here may point to fundamentally similar processes to create objects and meaning in the contexts of matter and mind. However, this is true for an abstract interpretation and theory of observation and meaning only. To examine this, I will next define the concept of an observer.

IV. Observer and time

Here, I want to consider in more detail the decisive act, fundamental to any theory of cognition and knowledge, of dividing a whole into a part which observes, and a part being observed. One way to approach this task is by the investigation of internal and external perspectives (see also Ruhnau 1994a). In the following, the term 'system' denotes the entity being referenced within a theoretical discourse.

Definition IV.1

An attribute of a system, defined by the description of an apparatus to measure it, is called an *observable*. An observable whose measurement yields a value of the set $(0,1)$ is called a *proposition*.

Definition IV.2

Let S_1 denote a system. Let S_2 be a system together with a measuring apparatus A. If S_2 registers the truth values of propositions of S_1 defined by A, then S_2 is called an *observer* of S_1.

An observer is not necessarily a human being; S_2 may be identical with A. Note that an observer registers the final outcome of a yes/no inquiry and not a superposition of possible results. In the following, the definition of an observer is connected to the differentiation between external and internal perspective.

Definition IV.3

A system without an external observer is called an *endosystem*.

This definition refers to the ontic aspect of a system. An endosystem is an entity existing independently of an observer's knowledge about it. Furthermore, an endosystem cannot be observed from outside. In other words, it cannot be observed as a whole. But an internal observer is not excluded by definition.

Definition IV.4

An observer external to a system is called an *exosystem*.

This definition refers to the epistemic aspect. Note that because of definition IV.3. an exosystem cannot observe an endosystem defined within the same conceptual frame.

Definition IV.5

An endosystem containing one or more exosystems is called a *universe of discourse*. The systems observed are called *objects*.

This act of separation into observer and object of observation may be carried out in different ways. One and the same endosystem may be represented as a variety of universes of discourse. However, it can be shown that the act of partition cannot be verified within the endosystem. Its status is that of a hypothesis whose truth value can be fixed on a meta-level only. In other words, representation of an endosystem as a universe of discourse opens an infinite regress.

Closely related to this problem of infinite regress are the measurement problem in quantum theory, or the transition from possibilities to facts; and the problem of an observer (homunculus) within the brain, or the existence of an integrative brain centre. Both topics can be embodied in the question, 'How do objects come into existence?' As in classical physics, regarding an object and a brain as obviously separate entities escapes this crucial question. To attack this topic, it is useful to think of the brain of a newborn organism as a network of unspecified neurons receiving stimuli from the environment. But the environment is not yet known to be separated. In the context of the discussion here, the basic structure of a net together with its chaos of changes forms an endosystem. Can it specify itself into a universe of discourse?

At this early stage, the brain does not have any measuring apparatus (feature detector) at its disposal. However, the brain does not operate in an empty space. To a certain extent, the environment provides spatiotemporal continuities and further symmetries to which the organism must adapt to behave adequately. The chaos of neuronal changes caused by stimuli from external sources has to be categorized. Systems external to the brain must be 'measured' by the brain. How could this be achieved?

As mentioned above, there is evidence for coherent states of the brain which facilitate differentiation and integration. These coherent integrative states of the brain can be described as temporal correlations of neurons established by re-entrant processes. Different levels of integration correspond to symmetries and unities of external objects. The brain considered as endosystem constitutes a 'measuring apparatus' adapted to (and partially reflecting) spatiotemporal continuities and symmetries of its environment.

But a measuring apparatus is not yet an observer. Registration of coherence in a yes/no manner is necessary. This could be modeled by effectors being realized as threshold units (combined with motor neurons), connecting occurrence of synchronization to behaviour. This would imply that the endosystem brain has become a universe of discourse containing exosystems that observe objects. Note that these objects are *inherent in* the endosystem brain!

The definition of objects in the context of endo/exo descriptions is the result of current discussions concerning the problem of object formation in quantum theory (see Finkelstein 1988; Primas 1994; Rössler 1987; Ruhnau 1994a). Yet it was argued in the last section that time Gestalts and events are more adequate concepts with respect to the brain. Time Gestalts as homogeneous entities of co-temporality, and events as happenings bearing meanings get their maximal or minimal extension in the time order $(T, <)$ by a direction of time, that is the before–after relation, or a closure within a context of meaning, respectively. Concerning object definition in physics, the closure, the irreversibility, is given via measurement, i.e. registration of a yes/no decision. In physics, the measurement receives its meaning within the theory of the observer. Such meaning defined by the observer may be meaningless for the system under consideration. In the case of the brain, the brain, so to speak, is measuring itself; it is its own measuring apparatus. The primary preconditions for action units (i.e. events) are not objects or instantaneous irreversibilities, but time Gestalts and the before–after relation. Only in a second step are objects categorized. The complete sensory motor cycle is decisive. Sensory and motor activity, perception and action, develop in parallel.

To examine the structural relation between the valuation system and the system being evaluated, some relevant aspects from quantum theory are discussed briefly. Quantum theory deals with isolated systems which are observed through interaction with a measuring apparatus. The quantum state (the wave function) of a quantum system comprises all contingent statements about the system which are true at a time t. The superposition of two possible states is again a possible quantum state. The time evolution of such a superposition of quantum states is governed by the Schrödinger equation. This equation is symmetric with respect to time inversion (or to be more precise, with respect to inversion of motion) and covers the deterministic and linear part of time development. There is also a stochastic and nonlinear part. Quantum states exist as superpositions of possible states as long as the probabilistic wave function does not collapse via measurement. After a collapse, there is no longer a superposition of possible states; one state has become factual. The nonlinear transition process from the superposition of possible quantum states to one actual quantum state is not understood within the formalism of quantum theory. The transition breaks the time symmetry, and causes irreversibility.

The superposition of possible quantum states is transformed through observation to a factual existing state. However, what happens if the system is constantly observed, i.e. the time intervals between successive observations are steadily decreased? Quantum theory predicts that such a system under permanent observation cannot change its state, even though such a state might be extremely unstable. This is called the quantum Zeno effect (see for example Omns 1992). Continuous observation, i.e. observation not allowing zones free of time, results in a fixation of the state of the system.

In contrast to the isolated systems of quantum theory, brains are open systems embedded into a specific environment. Permanent observation or measurement would correspond to a continuous transposition of incoming (afferent) into outgoing (efferent) patterns of activity. This flow of motion would make the goal-oriented behaviour of the organism as a whole impossible. Therefore, I want to suggest that coordinated action of the whole organism requires zones free of observation, or zones of co-temporality (compare section II). In this case, observation is defined as effectiveness of the appropriate neuronal coherences.

One could also speculate that windows of co-temporality or time Gestalts are necessary preconditions for *any* kind of integration capacity. It is conceivable that conceptual abstraction (the creation of symbols) is based on processes to generate such time Gestalts. The external duration of these atemporal windows would not be limited to the range of 30–40 milliseconds, but would vary. In this context, the question of repetition or succession of time Gestalts would be of great importance. Time Gestalts which (re)iterate themselves and which can be strung together up to several seconds — as in case of the 30 msec windows — are constitutive for the system under consideration. They could be regarded as the syntactical basis — materialized as neuronal connections — of memory.

V. Time and consciousness

On the one hand, the concept of time Gestalt has been connected to the concept of co-temporality. On the other hand, co-temporality or simultaneity can only be defined with respect to a before–after relation, that is, with respect to a time passing. Now, I want to complete the perspective in a certain way. The starting point is not only a world of objects and states which keep their identity in time and develop in time; not only a vision of reality as objects plus time; but a reality whose dynamics *create* objects and time.

Time: is it created or given, discrete or continuous? Both aspects of time are complementary. With respect to operations of the brain, time appears to be discrete; an operational closure constitutes a discretization which is represented as discontinuity of extended time windows. With respect to observation, as a consequence of semantic binding operations, time appears to be continuous. One can formalize this point of view in such a way that the continuity of time is the result of the separation of an (abstract) defined observer from the object of observation. Continuity turns out to be an abstraction, the construction of a meta-level of observation. With respect to this meta-level, the underlying processes appear as formal and free of content. This then leads to the idea of a homogeneous quantifiable construct called continuous time, which I define as an abstract structure of unlimited observability. In this way, I propose that the familiar continuity of time is a construct.

Could these considerations concerning the concept of time be applied to consciousness? I claim that this is so. My point of view (for formalization see Ruhnau 1994b; 1995b) is similar to a theory proposed by Edelman (Edelman 1989; 1992). Edelman uses the concepts of primary and higher-order consciousness. In summary, I want to suggest the following five hypotheses:

- Consciousness — created or given, discrete or continuous? Both aspects of consciousness are complementary.

- Two types of consciousness must be distinguished: consciousness which is constituted through brain functioning, and consciousness which is based on the observation of these functions. The first is identified with I-consciousness, the second with self-consciousness.

- In both cases, a closure is necessary for functioning and for the observation of processes. The limbic system is assigned as evaluating system to consciousness of the first kind. The selection of hypotheses in the context of internally generated universes of discourse, or consistency checking as a decision system, is assigned to consciousness of the second kind.

- The Now of 3 seconds is associated with consciousness of the first kind; the chain past–present–future with consciousness of the second kind.

- The continuity of the self is a construction based on the abstract structure of unlimited observability of processes.

182   E. RUHNAU

References

Aertsen, A. & Arndt, M. (1993). Response synchronization in the visual cortex. *Current Opinion in Neurobiology,* 3, 586–94.

Dennett, D. & Kinsbourne, M. (1992). Time and the observer: the where and when of consciousness in the brain. *Behavioral and Brain Sciences,* 15, 183–247.

Eckhorn, R., Bauer, R., Jordan, W., Brosch, M., Kruse, W., Munk, M. & Reitboeck, H.J. (1988). Coherent oscillations: a mechanism of feature linking in the visual cortex? *Biological Cybernetics,* 60, 121–30.

Eckhorn, R. & Reitboeck, H.J. (1989). Stimulus-specific synchronizations in cat visual cortex and their possible role in visual pattern recognition. In H. Haken (ed), *Synergetics of Cognition* (Springer Series in Synergetics, Vol. 45). Berlin: Springer.

Eckhorn, R., Frien, R., Bauer, R., Kehr, H., Woelbern, T. & Kruse, W. (1993). High frequency (50–90 Hz) oscillation in visual cortical areas V1 and V2 of an awake monkey are phase-locked at zero delay. *Society Neuroscience Abstracts,* 19, 1574.

Edelman, G.M. (1989).*The Remembered Present: A Biological Theory of Consciousness.* New York: Basic Books.

Edelman, G.M. (1992). *Bright Air, Brilliant Fire: On the Matter of the Mind.* New York: Basic Books.

Engel, A.K., Knig, P., Kreiter, A.K. & Singer, W. (1991). Interhemispheric synchronization of oscillatory neuronal responses in cat visual cortex. *Science,* 252, 177–9.

Finkelstein, D. (1988). Finite physics. In R. Herken (ed), *The Universal Turing Machine: A Half-century Survey.* Oxford: Oxford University Press.

Fodor, J.A. (1983).*The Modularity of Mind.* Cambridge, MA: MIT Press.

Görnitz, Th., Ruhnau, E. & v.Weizsäcker, C.F. (1991). Temporal asymmetry as precondition of experience — the foundation of the arrow of time. *International Journal of Theoretical Physics,* 31, 37–46.

Gray, C.M., König, P., Engel, A.K. & Singer, W. (1989). Oscillatory responses in cat visual cortex exhibit intercolumnar synchronization which reflects global stimulus properties. *Nature,* 338, 334–7.

Gray, C. M. & Singer, W. (1989). Stimulus-specific neuronal oscillations in orientation columns of cat visual cortex. *Proceedings of the National Academy of Sciences USA,* 86, 1698–702.

Haag, R. (1990). Fundamental irreversibility and the concepts of events. *Communications in Mathematical Physics,* 132, 245–51.

Harter, M.R. (1967). Excitability cycles and cortical scanning. *Psychological Bulletin,* 68, 47–58.

Hirsh, I.J. & Sherrick C.E.J. (1961). Perceived order in different sense modalities. *Journal of Experimental Psychology,* 62, 423–32.

Husserl, E. (1928). Vorlesungen zur Phänomenologie des inneren Zeitbewuβtseins. M. Heidegger (ed), *Jahrbuch für Philosophie und Phänomenologische Forschung, Bd. IX,* 367–498.

Husserl, E. (1985). *Texte zur Phänomenologie des inneren Zeitbewuβtseins (1893-1917).* Hamburg: Felix Meiner.

James, W. (1890). *The Principles of Psychology.* Reprint. New York: Dover. 1950.

Jokeit, H. (1991). *Analyse von Periodizitten in Reaktionszeitdaten.* Humboldt-Universität Berlin.

Madler, C. & Pöppel, E. (1987). Auditory evoked potentials indicate the loss of neuronal oscillations during general anaesthesia. *Naturwissenschaften*, **74**, 42–3.

Mates, J., Müller, U., Radil. T. & Pöppel, E. (1994). Temporal integration in sensorimotor synchronisation. *Journal of Cognitive Neuroscience.*

Müller, U., Ilmberger, J., Pöppel, E., Mates, J. & Radil, T. (1990). Stimulus anticipation and the 30 ms basic timing unit during rhythmic tapping. *Activ. nerv. super.*, **32**, 144.

Neven, H. & Aertsen, A. (1992). Rate coherence and event coherence in the visual cortex: a neuronal model of object recognition. *Biological Cybernetics*, **67**, 309–22.

Omns, R. (1992). Consistent interpretations of quantum mechanics. *Reviews of Modern Physics*, **64**, 339–82.

Penrose, R. (1986). Gravity and the state vector reduction. In R. Penrose & C.J. Isham (eds), *Quantum Concepts in Space and Time*. Oxford: Oxford University Press.

Penrose, R. (1989). *The Emperor's New Mind.* Oxford: Oxford University Press.

Penrose, R. (1994). *Shadows of the Mind.* Oxford: Oxford University Press.

Picton, T.W. & Stuss, D.T. (1994). Neurobiology of conscious experience. *Current Opinion in Neurobiology*, **4**, 256–65.

Pöppel, E. (1968). Oszillatorische Komponenten in Reaktionszeiten. *Naturwissenschaften*, **55**, 449–50.

Pöppel, E. (1972). Oscillations as possible basis for time perception. In J.T. Fraser (ed), *The Study of Time*. Berlin: Springer.

Pöppel, E. (1978). Time perception. In R. Held, H.W. Leibowitz & H.L. Teuber (eds), *Handbook of Sensory Physiology, Vol. VIII*. New York: Springer.

Pöppel, E. (1985/1988). English: *Mindworks: Time and Conscious Experience.* New York: Harcourt Brace Jovanovich.

Pöppel, E., Ruhnau, E., Schill, K. & Steinbüchel, N.v. (1990). A hypothesis concerning timing in the brain. In H. Haken & M. Stadler (eds), *Synergetics of Cognition* (Springer Series in Synergetics, Vol. 45). Berlin: Springer.

Pöppel, E. (1994). Temporal mechanisms in perception. *International Review of Neurobiology*, **37**, 185–202.

Primas, H. (1994). Endo- and exo-theories of matter. In: H. Atmanspacher and G. Dalenoort (eds), *Inside versus Outside. Endo- and Exo-Concepts in the Sciences.* Berlin: Springer.

Rössler, O.E. (1987). Endophysics. In J.L. Casti & A. Karlqvist (eds), *Real Brains, Artificial Minds* . New York: North Holland.

Ruhnau, E. (1994a). The Now — a hidden window to dynamics. In: H. Atmanspacher and G. Dalenoort (eds), *Inside versus Outside. Endo- and Exo-Concepts in the Sciences.* Berlin: Springer.

Ruhnau, E. (1994b). The Now — the missing link between matter and mind. In: M. Bitbol & E. Ruhnau (eds), *The Now, Time and the Quantum.* Gif-sur-Yvette: Editions Frontières.

Ruhnau, E. (1995a). Which logical and temporal concepts should be used in neurocognitive modelling? In H.J. Herrmann, D.E. Wolf & E. Pöppel (eds), *Workshop on Supercomputing in Brain Research: from tomography to neural networks, HLR7, KFA, Jülich.* Singapore: World Scientific.

Ruhnau, E. (1995b). Loop structure and time, in preparation.
Ruhnau, E. & Haase, V.G. (1993): Parallel Processing and integration by oscillations. *Behavioral and Brain Sciences*, **16**, 587–8.
Ruhnau, E. & Pöppel, E. (1991). Adirectional temporal zones in quantum physics and brain physiology. *International Journal of Theoretical Physics*, **30**, 1083–90.
Schleidt, M., Eibl-Eibesfeldt, I. & Pöppel, E. (1987). A universal constant in temporal segmentation of human short term behavior. *Naturwissenschaften*, **74**, 289.
Singer, W. (1993). Synchronization of cortical activity and its putative role in information processing and learning. *Annual Review of Physiology*, **55**, 349–74.
Sporns, O., Gally, J.A., Reeke, G.N. Jr. & Edelman, G.M. (1989). Reentrant signaling among simulated neuronal groups leads to coherency in their oscillatory activity. *Proceedings of the National Academy of Sciences USA*, **86**, 7265–9.
Stroud, J.M. (1955). The fine structure of psychological time. In H. Quastler (ed), *Information Theory in Psychology*. Glencoe: The Free Press.
Turner, F. & Pöppel, E. (1983). The neuronal lyre: poetic meter, the brain and time. *Poetry (USA)*, **August**, 277–309.
Weizscker, C.F.v. & Görnitz, Th. (1990). Quantum theory as theory of human knowledge. In P. Lathi & P. Mittelstaedt (eds), *Proceedings of the Symposion on the Foundations of Modern Physics, Joensuu 1990*. Singapore: World Scientific.

Rick Grush and
Patricia Smith Churchland

Gaps in
Penrose's Toilings

I. Introduction

Consciousness is almost certainly a property of the physical brain. The major mystery, however, is how neurons achieve effects such as being aware of a toothache or the smell of cinnamon. Neuroscience has not reached the stage where we can satisfactorily answer these questions. Intriguing data and promising research programmes do exist,[1] but no one would say we pretty much understand the neurobiological mechanisms of awareness.[2] Much more work, both experimental and theoretical, needs to be done. What available data do suggest is that awareness and subjectivity are probably *network* effects, involving many millions of neurons in thalamic and cortical structures. But there are other possibilities. Dualism aside, a different possibility is that consciousness emerges from quantum-mechanical goings-on in subneuronal structures.

Quite a lot is known about how single neurons work. The biophysics of the synapse, the neuronal membrane, neuron-to-neuron interactions,

We would like to thank the following people for valuable discussions, advice and insights: Oron Shagrir, David Chalmers, Paul Churchland, Francis Crick, Mark Ellisman, Andrew Hibbs, Brian Keeley, Christof Koch, Steve Quartz, Terry Sejnowski, Chuck Stevens, Timothy van Gelder, Hal White, Robin Zagone, the participants of EPL (Experimental Philosophy Lab, UCSD), and three helpful anonymous reviewers.

[1] Cf. Logothetis & Schall 1989; Llinás & Paré 1993; Llinás & Ribary 1993; Crick 1994; Damasio 1994; Damasio & Damasio (forthcoming); Churchland 1995; Bogen 1995.

[2] Although Dennett's book title, *Consciousness Explained* (Dennett 1991), rather misleadingly suggests otherwise.

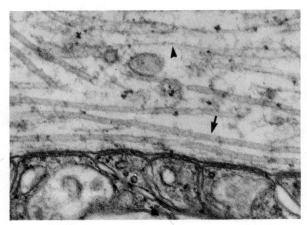

Figure 1: Electron micrograph of a longitudinally oriented ultrathin section (>500 Ångströms) through a myelinated axon near a node of Ranvier in rat optic nerve. The preparation is stained with Mg uranyl acetate and Pb citrate to highlight cytoskeletal structures and membranes. Microtubules are clearly delineated (arrow) as are the smaller neurofilaments (arrowhead). (This micrograph was kindly provided by Mark Ellisman at UCSD.)

enzyme–gene interactions and organelle behaviour (e.g. mitochondria, microtubules), is known in impressive, though not complete, detail.[3] Given what is known, 'very remote' is the label typically stamped on the possibility that quantum-mechanical effects play any explanatorily significant role in neuronal function.[4] 'Very remote' is not equivalent to 'certainly not', of course. The possibility that quantum-mechanical effects give rise to conscious awareness remains alive, especially in certain quarters of physics and mathematics. An otherworldly, gaze-averting fondness for Platonism in mathematics, twinned to a fascination for the counter-intuitive aspects of quantum physics, can foster the hunch that something really uncanny — and completely unkenned — is going on in the brain. Hoisting its status from 'campfire possibility' to 'scientific possibility' is problematic, however, given that quantum-level effects are generally agreed to be washed out at the neuronal level. Roger Penrose, nonetheless, has gallantly taken up the challenge in his widely discussed book, *The Emperor's New Mind* (Penrose 1989, henceforth *Emperor*) and in its successor, *Shadows of the Mind* (Penrose 1994b, henceforth *Shadows*).

   The crux of the Penrose idea is that quantum-mechanical effects exist at the *sub-neuronal* level — the level of cell organelles, in particular, in microtubules, whose pore diameter of about 14 nanometers, as well as other physical properties, make them candidates for the possibility of harnessing quantum-level effects. This is the tactic to avoid the aforementioned

---

[3] Cf. the classic Bray 1992; also Hall 1992; Sossin, Fisher & Scheller 1989.

[4] 'Quantal release' at the synapse means that either a vesicle of transmitter is released or it is not. It means that when there is release, the whole vesicle opens and all its transmitter is emptied into the synaptic cleft. This is in no sense a quantum-mechanical effect. Also, by 'explanatorily significant' we mean any effect which is not capturable by a classical biochemical explanation.

'washed out' objection. Why expect a quantum-level effect *anywhere* in the brain? Because, avers Penrose, certain cognitive processes — including those responsible for mathematical knowledge — are nonalgorithmic (in a sense to be discussed below), while all classical-level biochemical processes are algorithmic. The central motivation underpinning Penrose's whole argument structure is therefore a problem in the *epistemology of mathematics*. It is the problem of how we understand mathematics if understanding does not *consist* in following a rule, but involves understanding the meaning of mathematical concepts (see below). This is a rather more arcane starting point than, say, the awareness of a toothache or the sleeping/dreaming/wakefulness cycle, which are pretty robust phenomena with a nontrivial log of well-researched data from psychology and neuroscience.[5]

In what follows we present a compact version of Penrose's argument as we understand it from *Emperor* and *Shadows*. Support for the quantum–consciousness connection is drawn chiefly from three sources: (1) Gödel's incompleteness result and the fact that mathematical understanding exists; (2) the properties of microtubules, long protein structures found in *all* cells, including neurons; and (3) heretofore unrecognized physical processes, perhaps exemplified in a kind of physical structure known as a 'quasi-crystal'. Bringing these three together in such as way as to make a case for the role of quantum-level processes in consciousness is the task Penrose sets himself. Our task will be to analyse and evaluate the argument.

To avoid standing in shadowy places we wish to state at the outset that, in our view, the argument consists of merest possibility piled upon merest possibility teetering upon a tippy foundation of 'might-be-for-all-we-know's. It also rests on some highly dubious assumptions about the nature of mathematical knowledge. Our assessment is not that the Penrose hypothesis is demonstrably false, in the way that molecular biologists can confidently say that the hereditary material is not a protein; it is DNA. Neurobiology is simply not far enough along to rule out the Penrose possibility by virtue of having a well-established, well-tested, neurobiological explanation in hand. Rather, we judge it to be completely unconvincing and probably false.

---

[5] There is a very simple — and fallacious — argument sometimes tugging at the physicist's intuitions. Its clearest formulation is, to our knowledge, owed to the philosopher of science and mathematics, Itamar Pitowski, in honour of whom we call this the *Pitowski Syllogism*: (1) we really do not understand the nature of consciousness; (2) the only things in the physical world we really do not understand are quantum-level phenomena; (3) therefore, these are probably the same mystery. As Pitowski is quick to point out however, premise 2 is clearly false.

II. Compact Version of the Penrose Argument[6]

Part A: Nonalgorithmicity of human conscious thought

A1 Human thought, at least in some instances, is sound[7] yet nonalgorithmic (i.e. noncomputational). (Hypothesis based on the Gödel result.)

A2 In these instances, the human thinker is aware of or conscious of the contents of these thoughts.

A3 The only recognized instances of nonalgorithmic processes in the universe are perhaps certain kinds of randomness; e.g. the reduction of the quantum-mechanical state vector. (Based on accepted physical theories.)[8]

A4 Randomness is not promising as the source of the nonalgorithmicity needed to account for A1. (Otherwise mathematical understanding would be magical.)

Therefore:

A5 Conscious human thought, at least in some cases, perhaps in all cases, relies on principles which are beyond current physical understanding, though not in principle beyond any (e.g. some future) scientific physical understanding. (Via A1–4.)

Part B: Inadequacy of current physical theory, and how to fix it

B1 There is no current adequate theory concerning the 'collapse' of the quantum- mechanical wave function, but an additional theory of *quantum gravity* might be useful to this end.

---

[6] At least this is our best, most sympathetic, and long-pondered shot at it. We do acknowledge that the presentation of the argument in *Shadows* is complex, the issues are complex, and that the compact account is a simplification. We have no interest in merely setting up a straw man, but there is value in having the crux of the argument clear.

[7] For purposes of this paper, soundness is a property of procedures or mechanisms or the exercise of capacities. Soundness can be taken to be roughly equivalent to 'truth producing', meaning that given true premises, when the normal functioning of the procedure or mechanism or capacitiy produces conclusions, they are true ones, not false ones. Soundness should thus not be thought of as necessarily tied to algorithmic or syntactic procedures, though of course these too might be sound. More generally: statements can be true or false, arguments can be valid or invalid, procedures etc. can be sound or not. Though our expression, 'truth-producing', is less conventional than 'truth-preserving' in this context, it is called for in order to accommodate Penrose's very interesting idea that things other than algorithms, formal systems and the like, might be sound.

[8] Penrose does argue that chaotic processes are themselves algorithmic (Penrose 1994b: 177–9), in that they can be simulated to any desired degree of accuracy by digital computational mechanisms. While some may feel that this subsumption of chaotic systems to algorithmic ones is unjustified, we propose to grant this premise.

B2 A more adequate theory of wave-function collapse (a part, perhaps, of a quantum gravity theory) could incorporate nonalgorithmic, yet non-random, processes. (Penrose hypothesis.)

B3 The existence of quasicrystals is evidence for some such currently unrecognized, nonalgorithmic physical process.

Therefore:

B4 Future theories of physics, in particular quantum gravity, can be expected to incorporate nonalgorithmic processes. (Via B1–3.)

Part C: Microtubules as the means of harnessing quantum gravity

C1 Microtubules have properties which make certain quantum-mechanical phenomena (e.g. super-radiance) possible. (Hameroff/Penrose hypothesis.)

C2 These nonalgorithmic nonrandom processes will be sufficient, in some sense, to account for A5. (Penrose hypothesis.)

C3 Microtubules play a key role in neuronal functioning.

C4 Neurons play a key role in cognition and consciousness.

C5 Microtubules play a key role in consciousness/cognition (by C3, C4 and transitivity).

Therefore:

C6 Microtubules, because they have one foot in quantum mechanics and the other in conscious thought, provide a window for nonalgorithmicity in human cognition.

THEREFORE:

D *Quantum gravity, or something similar, via microtubules, must play a key role in consciousness and cognition.*

Briefly, our analysis of this argument indicates that A1 is most likely false, and Section III below provides some reasons for denying it. This undercuts the case for A5, and hence Part A. B3 is almost certainly false (this is the subject of Section IV), and given its falsity B2 is entirely speculative as well. This undercuts the case for B4, and hence the conclusions of Part B are exposed as entirely speculative. C1 is quite speculative, C2 is no more than a guess and C5 is simply a bad inference (these are discussed in Section V), hence Part C looks tenuous. In short, it appears to us that even if D did happen to be true, the argument embodied in parts A, B and C provides no reason to believe that it is. In Section VI we provide independent reasons for thinking that D is probably false.

III. Are there Instances of Conscious Human Reasoning that are Sound and Nonalgorithmic? Analysis of Premise A1

Insight, pattern recognition and artificial neural nets

The Gödel result forms the springboard of the reasoning underlying Penrose's premise A1, and we restate his argument below. As a preliminary, note that by nonalgorithmic is meant 'noncomputable'.[9] This implies that the performance of the system could not be produced by any algorithmic procedure; more, it could not be *approximated* by an algorithmic procedure.[10] The behaviour of a river eddy is weakly nonalgorithmic insofar as it is a complex system and its states are continuous. It could, however, be *approximated* by an algorithm, *to any desired degree of accuracy*, and given Penrose's conventions this entails that its behaviour is algorithmic. 'Nonalgorithmic' in the sense Penrose quite reasonably intends is, therefore, a *very* strong constraint; so strong in fact, that whether there exist any physical systems in the real world whose behaviour is noncomputable in this strong sense remains very much an open question. Penrose conjectures[11] that quasicrystals may be such phenomena. As for consciousness, the Penrose hypothesis is that given human mathematical performance we can tell that the brain must be such a (deeply) noncomputable system.

Here is Penrose's own summary of the argument:

> It is a kind of *reductio ad absurdum* argument, in which I try to show what would happen if we tried to construct robots with the kind of ability to understand that we have. Because the Gödel argument is basically about understanding; it tells us how to move from one formal system to a system outside that, from the understanding of what that system is trying to say. It is concerned with the question of the *meanings* of the symbols, which is a dimension that a computational system does not have; a computational system just has the rules which it follows. What one can do in mathematics is, by understanding the meanings of the symbols, one can go beyond the formal rules, and see what new rules must apply from those things, and one does this by understanding their meanings (Penrose 1994a: 19).

Granted that some instances of understanding and extending understanding do not involve *explicit* rule following, is there any framework for approaching such cognition? Indeed there is, and famously so. Artificial neural nets (ANNs) are capable of learning complex pattern recognition tasks as well as sensorimotor integration tasks.[12] Once the weights have

---

[9] For a brief but powerful criticism of Penrose on the Gödel result, see Putnam 1994.

[10] Thus we will follow Penrose in using the term nonalgorithmic only for those processes which cannot even be approximated with an algorithm. This will contrast with 'weakly' nonalgorithmic, which just means not following explicit rules.

[11] See footnote 34, below.

[12] Cf. Churchland & Sejnowski 1992; Churchland 1995; Jordan 1989.

been set, typically by training on a range of cases, networks can perform very well on new cases, even giving 'good' answers in cases that are nonstandard or missing bits or presented in unusual conditions. Given recurrent connections between units ANNs can recognize sequences, for example sequences of sounds. Training a network is not programming with an explicit algorithm. The only algorithms in the neighbourhood are relatively simple ones used to adjust the weights, in reinforcement learning or via a Hebbian learning rule, for example. In any case the ANN has no *explicit* rules that govern its performance, any more than a child does when it successfully extends 'dog' beyond the family retriever to the neighbour's poodle and grandma's great dane. The same applies for concepts such as 'chair', 'cold front', 'promising student', 'fair', 'reasonable', and so forth.

Pattern recognition has been argued[13] to be the key cognitive function of nervous systems, underlying not merely capacities such as recognizing a dog or a chair but also, in the cognoscenti, recognizing a chess configuration and a theorem in the predicate calculus. In logic or mathematics, insight-cum-recognition can be followed up with a proof to determine whether one's insight was correct. On the other hand, for other highly complex patterns such as instances of injustice or insanity, for example, verifying insight may involve nothing so straightforward as application of a proof procedure. The general point, however, is that what gets called 'insight' and 'intuition' could very well be complex pattern recognition performed by recurrent neural networks.

The ANN processes are analogue and parallel; the machine is flexible and plastic.[14] These are indeed very striking capacities, and they are what make ANNs so exciting to robotics, artificial vision and so forth, and what makes them relevant to real nervous systems. 'Computing without rules' was indeed the popular watchword in early stages of connectionist research.[15] That ANNs can learn, rather than be programmed, that they have analogue properties, that they are flexible, fault tolerant and can give answers to degraded inputs are, *inter alia*, what make ANNs far more suitable and powerful than classical programming techniques for many problems in the simulation of nervous system capacities. But uncanny they are not. Are their input–output functions *non*computable in the weak sense of not being instances of explicit rule following or discrete state transitions? Yes. Can the behaviour of neural nets (artificial and otherwise) be *approximated by an algorithm*? So far as anyone knows, yes. This may, certainly, be a strained, semi-fictional sense of computable if no algorithm can execute the function in real time. Nevertheless, the 'approximatability' does mean that

---

[13] Cf. Churchland 1995.

[14] Cf. Mead 1989.

[15] Cf. Churchland & Sejnowski 1992; Churchland 1995.

they fail to have the property Penrose is after, namely being noncomputable *and* 'nonapproximatable'. That is, they *are indeed computable and algorithmic, in the sense Penrose intends.* Now *if* Penrose is right in supposing human thought cannot be even approximated by an algorithm, then the success of ANNs is not, by itself, enough to subvert Penrose. At the risk of repeating ourselves we do emphasize that it is not known whether *any* physical processes exist that are strongly noncomputable in the sense Penrose seeks. (See also below, Section IV.) *Even if they are not counterexamples to Penrose's hypothesis,* the success of ANNs teaches us that phenomena that appear intractable to conventional programming on a classical machine might very well be managed elegantly by a nonclassical, analogue device.

What is Penrose's argument for Premise A1?

A1a In order to ascertain mathematical truth, human mathematicians are not using a knowably sound algorithm.[16]

A1b The brain procedure that does underlie this 'ascertaining mathematical truth' is sound.

A1c If human mathematicians were using a sound *algorithm*, this algorithm would be knowable.

A1d Therefore, human mathematicians do not use an algorithm in order to ascertain mathematical truth.

A1e The understanding mathematicians employ is not different in kind from everyday human understanding and conscious thought.

Therefore Premise A1:

Human thought, at least in some instances, *perhaps in all,* is sound, yet non- algorithmic.

Critical analysis of Penrose's argument for Premise A1

Penrose's arguments in favour of A1a and A1c are where most of the technical machinery is brought to bear. It may therefore be a relief that we propose, for convenience of strategy, to grant both of these premises, and focus rather on A1b.

---

[16] In brief, what Gödel showed was that for any sufficiently powerful consistent formal axiomatic system F, there will be true statements, expressible in F, yet not provable in F. In particular the statement that F is consistent, call this G(F), will not be provable in F, provided that F is in fact consistent. Curiously, G(F) will be provable in F if F is in fact inconsistent, i.e. if G(F) is false. In a nutshell, the argument for A1a is that since humans are sound (hence consistent), and since we can know that we are sound, we cannot be relying on any formal system for our knowledge. This is because if we were exclusively using some sound formal system, we could never know (prove) our own soundness. Penrose's treatment of this argument is much more complete (Penrose 1994b).

Our point is this: *even if* humans are using some sort of algorithm, *and* that algorithm is knowable, A1a presents a problem *only if we assume that this algorithm is sound*. This is supposed to be not worth considering because an unsound procedure would license entailment to anything, and we can be sure that (p & ~p) is not true. Matters are not quite so simple, however, because these are questions about human knowledge, not about what Eternal Immutable Truths really are on display in Plato's heaven. By definition, Plato's realm has only Truths. What is in the human mind/brain is a matter not of definition but of empirical fact. Our only access to Plato's realm is through our brains, and our brains have to use cognitive procedures to figure things out. Were our knowledge system to contain an inferentially remote falsehood, some far-flung plausible but false proposition, we might have a hard time deploying the cognitive machinery to force it to the surface or to recognize it to be false. It is conceivable that one's mathematical understanding sequesters somewhere a false, but practically isolated, proposition masquerading as a truth. Thus we have to consider this possibility: humans could be using a cognitive procedure(s) which is unsound[17] but *benignly* so — perhaps because it includes the axiom of choice (explained below) — or perhaps because it includes the negation of the axiom of choice, or for some other reason altogether.[18]

To make Premise A1 plausible Penrose must do three things: first, identify some range of phenomena — some cognitive procedures, or set of insights or whatever — which are uncontroversially sound and which are not known to be algorithmic. Let us call such a procedure (*or insight*) an S-procedure. Second, he must then invoke A1a to claim that in fact S-procedures cannot be supported by a knowable algorithm or approximated

---

[17] As Penrose himself notes, this seems to be what Turing thought was the real moral of the Gödel result. Turing is worth quoting at length:

> It might be argued that there is a fundamental contradiction in the idea of a machine with intelligence. It is certainly true that 'acting like a machine', has come to be synonymous with lack of adaptability . . . It has for instance been shown that with certain logical systems there can be no machine which will distinguish provable formulae of the system from unprovable . . . Thus if a machine is made for this purpose it must in some cases fail to give an answer. On the other hand, if a mathematician is confronted with such a problem he would search around and find new methods of proof, so that he ought to be able to reach a decision about any given formula. Against it I would say that fair play must be given to the machine. Instead of it sometimes giving no answer we could arrange it so that it gives occasional wrong answers. But the human mathematician would likewise make blunders when trying out new techniques. It is easy for us to regard these blunders as not counting and give him another chance, but the machine would probably be allowed no mercy. In other words then, if a machine is expected to be infallible, it cannot also be intelligent. There are several mathematical theorems which say almost exactly that. But these theorems say nothing about how much intelligence may be displayed if a machine makes no pretense at infallibility. (Turing 1986.)

[18] See footnote 24, below.

by a knowable algorithm. Third, he must argue for a presumed counterfactual: if S-procedures were supported by an algorithm, this algorithm *would in principle* be knowable. How successful is Penrose in satisfying the first of these three conditions? Not very, for the simple reason that there do not appear to be any S-procedures. Notice that anything which is knowably algorithmic cannot be an S-procedure, and so this rules out inference rules like *modus ponens*,[19] anything formalizable in predicate logic or Zermelo-Fraenkel axiomatic set theory (ZF), and the like. As we shall see, when these are excluded there is reason to doubt that any procedures for mathematical deliberation are sound.

Mathematical thought, at least in some instances, is Penrose's prime candidate for a sound, noncomputable S-procedure. Errors in workaday human cognition are legion, belying any suggestion that sound procedures might be operative in nonmathematical reasoning, and Penrose clearly doesn't want to deny this.[20] Is the case for mathematical thought better? Even in the domain of mathematics, mathematicians do make errors, errors that mathematicians themselves confess to be errors. Such errors are likely to be inobvious, and it can take months to determine whether a putative proof of, e.g. Fermat's Last Theorem, is free of errors. To avoid impugning the underlying procedures Penrose adopts the equivalent of a performance/competence distinction. Granted, the argument goes, mathematicians make mistakes, but these mistakes are merely performance mistakes resulting from the misapplication of an *underlying sound competence*.

In linguistics, where Chomsky made famous the performance/competence distinction, many difficulties dog the task of rendering it precise. Crudely, one problem is that there does not appear to be any principled way to distinguish between these two cases: (1) the sentence Q is really grammatically correct but the native speakers have limitations on memory, attention etc. and hence conflict in judgment; (2) Q is not really grammatical because native speakers conflict in judgment. The trouble arises when trying to adjudicate between competing theories of syntax, since the performance/competence distinction can always be invoked to insulate aspects of a formal syntactic theory from empirical disconfirmation. Restricting application of the distinction to unproblematic cases helps enormously.[21] Thus it is important to identify sentences that both exhibit the relevant properties but are simple enough so that judgment discrepancies cannot fairly be attributed to limitations in attention, memory, and so on. In other words, application is restricted to cases where the distinction does not obviously subvert experimental testing.

[19] *Modus ponens* has the form: if P then Q, P, ∴ Q. *Modus tollens* has the form: if P then Q, not Q so not P.

[20] Cf. Penrose 1994b.

[21] Cf. Bates & MacWhinney 1989.

Comparably, to protect himself from begging any questions, Penrose must identify some set of mathematical capacities/abilities (our S-procedures) that are not only sound but are simple enough, or short enough, such that performance errors are minimized or eliminated altogether. The secondary assumption is that performance on these tasks will result from deployment of the underlying sound procedures which support more complex and lengthy episodes of mathematical reasoning. So circumscribed, this set of capacities/ abilities seem to be what Penrose intends by the phrase 'the perception of unassailable mathematical truth'. The danger in failing thus to circumscribe is that one may presume the actual truth of what is merely believed-to-be-true, and in consequence postulate capacities the brain does not actually have. These capacities/abilities and their underlying brain procedures are now our S-procedure candidates (or simply S-candidates). Do we know *they* are sound?

Trying to delimit instances of 'the perception of unassailable mathematical truth' uncovers deep and troubling issues in the epistemology of mathematics generally. First, and most notoriously, what counts as unassailable in mathematics differs from century to century and from mathematician to mathematician. The brilliant nineteenth-century mathematician Cauchy, for example, denied the existence of infinite sets. Infinite sets, he correctly reasoned[22] (and he was not alone), would have proper subsets with which they could be put into one-to-one correspondence. His mathematical intuitions led him to conclude that this would be a contradiction, and hence that the existence of such sets should be rejected as false. Thanks to Cantor it can be shown that there is no contradition, however much our intuitions bid us believe otherwise. The statement that Cauchy 'clearly perceived' as contradictory is now taken as a right and proper — an unassailable, noncontradictory, teach-to-undergraduates — *definition* of an infinite set. Why not view this as a development in mathematical understanding, not unlike progress in physics, chemistry and biology?[23]

Discrepancies in judgment (differences of opinion) are not merely a thing of the hoary old past, but exist today. One instance concerns the axiomatic status of the so-called axiom of choice, which is quite easy to state and understand: for any collection of non-empty sets there exists another set that contains exactly one element from each set in the collection. Thus, as in the case of Cauchy's insight, when careful, sober, mathematical intuitions fail to coincide about the truth of the axiom of choice, the failure does not seem to be explainable on grounds of performance errors. Sound[24] procedures (to

[22] Cf. Boyer 1959: 296.

[23] Cf. Bloor 1976: 131–56; Boyer 1959.

[24] Notice that the emphasis here is on *soundness*, and not just consistency. While it of course has been proven that the axiom of choice (and hence its denial) are independent of ZF, and thus consistent with it, it does not follow that both are *sound* when added to ZF. In fact, on any reasonable account of what soundness means, they cannot both be so.

a first approximation, truth-producing procedures) cannot yield *both* a given result (S is true) and that result's denial (S is false), for if they do they simply are not *truth-* producing. Nevertheless some mathematicians' mathematical intuitions lead them to embrace the axiom of choice, while others' lead them to deny it.[25] Some mathematicians, typically Platonists, have 'perceived' the unassailable truth of propositions about transfinite sets, while constructivists 'perceive' the contradictory nature of transfinite sets. For constructivists the law of the excluded middle (p v ~p) is not universally true and hence not a law; for *a priorists*, it is — and so on.[26]

Penrose has a problem for his assumption regarding the 'soundness' of human mathematical capacities when the careful, reflective performance of mathematicians on relatively simple statements, such as (p v ~p), the axiom of choice, and the existence of infinite sets, is discrepant. He has essentially three options. (1) He could claim that some of the mathematicians (which ones — the constructivists?) are making performance errors in these and similar cases, care and IQ notwithstanding. This is unconvincing because the examples involved do not make heavy demands on attention and understanding, compared to many mathematical statements. (2) He could claim that *some* mathematicians do lack underlying sound procedures (competence), while others luckily have them. This is not an attractive option either, because those who allegedly depend on an unsound procedure (from a Platonists' point of view that might be Cauchy or Dummett, for example) do in fact make significant insightful contributions to mathematics. At the very least it is safe to say they understand Gödel's theorem. Now if some mathematicians (e.g. the constructivists and intuitionists) can do brilliant mathematics while having unsound mathematical understanding, how can we be sure this does not hold generally? (3) He could claim that these are not good examples of what he has in mind as S-candidates. This looks embarrassingly *ad hoc*, especially when something like the truth of an old saw like (p v ~p) can be reasonably assailed, albeit with complicated background argument. Moreover, if *these* examples will not do, if anything knowably algorithmic including simple inferences, such as *modus ponens* or anything else formalizable in first order logic or ZF will not do, what will?

Disappointingly, Penrose fails to provide any actual examples of background mathematical understanding which can be known to be sound. In

---

[25] A particularly striking example of the tenuousness of the Penrose assumption concerning mathematical intuitions was encountered when one of us (Grush) was discussing these issues with a mathematics graduate student who admitted, in good faith, the following: 'I firmly believe that Zorn's lemma is true, and I'm convinced that Zorn's lemma is equivalent to the axiom of choice, and yet I am certain that the axiom of choice must be false.'

[26] For a lucid and compelling discussion of a non-Platonist approach to mathematics, see Kitcher 1984.

fact *Shadows* is rife with admissions of the form '. . . as mathematicians gain in experience, their viewpoints may well shift with regard to what they take to be unassailably true — if they indeed ever take anything to be unassailably true'.[27] Given such admissions, why does Penrose still cling to the belief that mathematical performance is backed by sound procedures as opposed to usually reliable, or heuristically useful, procedures?

His core argument is: 'It would be an unreasonable mathematical standpoint that allows for a disbelief in the very basis of its unassailable belief system!'[28] That is, if a mathematician (or anybody else) has unassailable beliefs, then that person must believe that the procedures which support or result in those beliefs are sound. But does 'A is unassailable' mean 'A is certainly true' or does it mean 'one is convinced that A is true'? Is (p v ~p) really unassailable for a Platonist, or is it rather that she is convinced that it is true while recognizing that some of her esteemed intuitionist colleagues do not take it to be true. She also knows full well that being utterly convinced that A is true is not a Divine Guarantee of the truth of A. This matters, because if there is any doubt at all, even a tiny doubt, that any of her beliefs really are true, then the inference to the soundness of their source is blocked. This does not mean she thinks that the underlying procedures must be hopelessly flawed, but only that there are some puzzling propositions where the reasonable person realizes there can be a difference of opinion.

Now it would seem a perfectly reasonable view, one often adopted by cautious, reflective humans, that some sources of information should be taken to be generally reliable, yet not entirely infallible, and that any of its entailments can be adopted with *very high confidence*, but not with the complete certainty a stroll in Plato's heaven might provide. Bus schedules, phone books, newspapers, college textbooks, mathematics textbooks, scholarly publications, eyewitness testimony, expert opinions, etc. etc., are all *known to be flawed from time to time, and hence known to be unsound.* Perhaps the *un*reasonable position is the one with standards so high as to *reject* any sources of information that might be flawed. On the contrary, it seems reasonable to admit the fallibility and retain some (perhaps quite high) measure of confidence in them.

Although respected mathematicians have undergone changes of mind, even on core foundational issues, Penrose's Platonism leads him to say, '. . . it is an unreasonable mathematical standpoint that allows for a disbelief in the very basis of its unassailable belief system'. (1994b: 131) Notice, finally, that 'M does not believe that A is unassailably true' does *not* entail 'M *dis*believes A'. It might merely mean that M is not certain, even though M takes A to be highly likely, and in daily life M acts as though it were

[27] Penrose 1994b: 193 (emphasis original).

[28] Penrose 1994b: 131.

unassailable. For example, consider the axiom of choice. One may be convinced of its truth, while not being prepared to stake one's life on it as an unassailable truth.

To make the point a bit more strongly, the inference from 'I really believe that A is true', or 'I don't see how A could *possibly* be false', to 'A *is* unassailably true' is an inference rule known to be unsound. To take but one example, Kant thought it a necessary truth that Euclidean geometry described physical space. That very rule *has*, in fact, led to falsehoods. Now either our mathematician does have beliefs that she takes to be absolutely unassailable, in which case she is unsound, because such a belief could only be the result of the unsound inference rule (or something similar) specified three sentences back, or the mathematician has beliefs held only with very great confidence, in which case her inference to the soundness (as opposed to reliability) of the source of those beliefs is not licensed.[29]

Are there any alternatives to a Platonist ontology of mathematical objects (abstract, immutable objects — truths, numbers etc.) and its usual companion, an *a priori* epistemology of mathematics (grasping with the intellect the absolute and immutable truths in Plato's heaven)? Indeed there are.[30] A major motivation for seeking a more satisfactory epistemology is just this: what are supposed to be the nature of the interactions between the Platonic realm and the thinker's brain? If the denizens of the realm cannot causally interact with anything, let alone human brains, how on earth can mathematical understanding be acquired by the human brain? Plato's own answer, that we do not learn we only remember our soul's pre-birth observations with Truths in the realm, is less than satisfactory.

Even supposing we retrofit Plato's account with supports from evolutionary biology, the idea still founders. Evolution may have wired in a variety of capacities, but in the life of primates and early hominids there was no evolutionary pressure to acquire fancy mathematical knowledge (e.g. infinitesimal calculus), and some of mathematics surely had to be discovered by some and learned by others. Doubtless the struggle for survival meant that skills in planning, preparing, anticipating, communicating and so forth would have had great value, and brain structures subserving such skills may well be deployable for culturally-dependent skills such as reading, writing and mathematics. It is harder to see, however, why *soundness* as opposed to reliability should be selected for. (Notice too that even if mathematical

[29] Penrose might object that our argument relies on the variable or dicey mathematical competence of individual mathematicians, while his argument is couched in terms of the competence of the mathematical community as a whole (see discussion in Penrose 1994b: 97–101). This move would be rhetorically awkward, since presumably consciousness, in all its putative non-algorithmic glory, is supported by brains, and brains are supported by individuals.

[30] Cf. Heyting 1956; Lakatos 1976; Benacerraf & Putnam 1983; Dummett 1991; Quine 1970; Kitcher 1984.

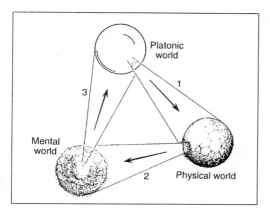

Figure 2: Penrose's Three Worlds.

The drawing schematically illustrates the idea that the physical world can be thought of as a projection from part of the Platonic world of eternal Truths, the mental world arises from part of the physical world (presumably the brain), and that the Platonic world is 'grasped' somehow during some mental activities. (From Penrose 1994b, courtesy of Oxford University Press).

capacities are hard-wired in, this is no guarantee of the soundness of mathematical understanding.) Evolution is a satisficer, not an optimizer, and 'approximately accurate' or 'accurate for most of the likely cases', is often good enough.[31] How humans come to have the conceptual and cognitive resources to develop formal systems, proof theory and mathematical certainty is a puzzle — though not, perhaps, more intractable than how we have the resources to read and write, to compose and play music, to skate, hang glide and perform eye surgery. The idea, therefore, that mathematical capacity is an independent faculty of pure reason, whose exercise yields mathematical (or any other absolutely certain) knowledge by virtue of intuitive grasping of propositions and objects in Plato's realm, is wanting in biological plausibility.

Cognitive models of higher cognitive processes in general, and mathematical cognition in particular, are not as far advanced as modelling of sensory processing and modelling of single neurons. Suffice it to say that the epistemology of mathematics has not kept pace with philosophical developments in other domains. Although the existence of the epistemological problems is well recognized amongst philosophers of mathematics, it is often of marginal interest to mathematicians themselves. One of the outstanding exceptions is the recent work by Philip Kitcher,[32] who does make a splendid attempt to bring the epistemology of mathematics up to date.

Platonism is surely a kind of convenient myth, rather like the way in which frictionless planes and ideal gases are convenient myths, or perhaps even as the 'spirit of Christmas' or 'zeitgeist' are convenient myths. As such, however, it cannot support grand metaphysical theories, such as that espoused by Penrose (Figure 2). Nor can it provide much in the way of

---

[31] Cf. Stich 1990 for an excellent critical discussion of the link between evolutionary pressures and truth.

[32] Cf. Kitcher 1984. Also, see Churchland 1995.

significant constraints on the cognitive neurobiology of understanding and consciousness. When the 'just-so' story is taken literally and used to constrain theories about natural phenomena, it positively gets in the way.[33]

IV. Quasicrystals: Argument Against B3

A consequence of Penrose's Gödel-inspired arguments for strong (no-algorithm-can-even-approximate) noncomputability in the mind/brain is that current theories in physics are fundamentally incomplete. In Penrose's view they ought to be augmented by a theory of quantum gravity. One might, however, prefer to *tollens* here rather than to *ponens*. In other words, one's confidence in current physics is a *prima facie* reason for denying the correctness of these Gödel-inspired arguments. The considerations given in the previous section mean this option is not unattractive. From Penrose's perspective, therefore, it is important to have hard evidence for the existence of such postulated nonalgorithmic processes apart from the contentious case at hand, namely the mind/brain. There are sections in *Emperor* which could be construed as attempting to provide such evidence.[34]

The reasoning behind B3 we reconstruct as follows:

B3a Because there exist sets of tiles which tile the plane only non-periodically, the question of whether a given set of tiles will tile the infinite Euclidean plane is not decidable (algorithmic).

B3b Some of these non-periodic sets tile the plane with a five-fold symmetry.

B3c There exist 'quasicrystals' whose lattice structure exhibits a similar five-fold symmetry.

B3d So the growth of these crystals depends on nonalgorithmic processes (maybe).

Therefore Premise B3:

The existence of quasicrystals is evidence for some such currently unrecognized, nonalgorithmic physical process.

The argument is unconvincing. The chief problem is that B3d and hence B3 simply do not follow from B3a–c. First, even if the analogy between the

---

[33] This is a point which we understand G. Kreisel to have made in correspondence with Francis Crick.

[34] These are pp. 132–8 and 434–9. Fixing an adequate interpretation of these sections is difficult, as it is unclear if Penrose takes quasicrystals to be evidence for nonalgorithmic processes, or simply non-local but algorithmic ones. The paragraph bridging pp. 438–9 in *Emperor* seems to favour the reading where nonalgorithmicity is at issue. Curiously, there is no mention of quasicrystals in *Shadows*, perhaps because Penrose doesn't (any longer?) take them to provide evidence of such physical actions. If this is the case then perhaps he would agree with the discussion in this section.

structure of quasi-crystals and the non-periodic tilings were close, the 'problems' whose computability is at issue in each case are different. In the case of the tiling problem, the undecidable feature is not how to put the tiles together in order to tile some region (putting the tiles together may very well be algorithmic), but whether or not given a set of tiles, and perhaps some way of putting them together, these tiles can cover the entire infinite Euclidean plane without gaps or overlaps. Second, the analogy simply does not hold. The reason is that *quasi-crystals are in fact finite*, unlike the infinite Euclidean plane, and hence their growth undoubtedly is computable. Indeed, algorithms have been proposed[35] for the growth of just such crystals (as Penrose himself notes!).[36] Although the information required to determine the appropriate arrangement might not be locally available to individual atoms in the lattice, that is not a problem as far as algorithmicity goes.

Without this premise, the whole of Part B of the Penrose argument — that there are in fact nonalgorithmic (in the strong sense characterized earlier, p. 5) processes in the universe — amounts to no more than unsupported speculation. Now it might be wondered whether we are uncharitably pillorying an argument that Penrose himself no longer favours nor deploys in *Shadows*. However that may be, the fact is that *the speculation that such processes really do exist* continues to be a crucial underpinning in the complex structure of the overarching argument. Naturally enough, identifying this claim as speculative does *not* entail that it is actually false, and we are prepared to admit that despite the absence of evidence this speculation could turn out to be correct. Our point here is practical and simple: because investment of research time and energy is often made with the background probabilities in mind, it is important to recognize a bald speculation as a bald speculation. Forewarned, one might nevertheless decide to throw one's lot in with the speculation anyhow.

V. Are Microtubules the Generators of Consciousness?

We come now to the specific hypothesis about how quantum gravity and consciousness are parts of the same mystery. As the idea that microtubules are the key originated with and is mainly articulated by Stuart Hameroff, later to be adopted by Penrose, we shall focus first on the story as it comes from Hameroff.[37]

Here is Hameroff's summary statement of the conjecture:[38]

[35] Cf. Onoda *et al*. 1988; Sasajima *et al*. 1994.

[36] Penrose 1989: 449 n.7.

[37] Cf. Hameroff 1994; Hameroff, Rasmussen & Mansson 1989; Hameroff & Watt 1982; Hameroff *et al*. 1992; Jibu *et al*. 1994.

[38] Hameroff 1994: 105.

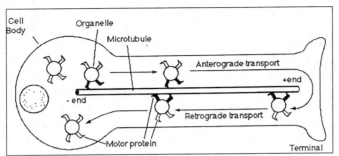

Figure 3:
Very schematic draw-
ing of a neuron, show-
ing the microtubule's
role as a structure
along which organ-
elles get transported
from the cell body to
the terminal and back.
Adapted from Hall
1992.

To summarize, cytoskeletal microtubules are likely candidates for quantum coherence relevant to consciousness because:

- Microtubule individual subunit (tubulin) conformation may be coupled to quantum-level events (electronic movement, dipole, phonon) in hydrophobic protein regions.
- Microtubule paracrystalline lattice structure, symmetry, cylindrical configuration and parallel alignment promote long-range cooperativity and order.
- Hollow microtubule interiors appear capable of water-ordering, waveguide super-radiance and self-induced transparency.

First, we note that all body cells have microtubules, where a major function is to support cell division. In neurons one of their known functions is transport, on their outside surface, of molecules such as neurotransmitters and various proteins between the cell body and the axon, and between the cell body and the dendrites (see Figure 3). Now it is generally believed that some general anaesthetics (hydrophobic ones) alter the neuronal membrane receptors and protein channels, with an effect on protein water- binding. Hameroff builds on this data by arguing that the protein constituting the microtubules (tubulin) might also have *its* water-binding properties affected. *If* it did, and *if* tubulin structures did have the quantum-mechanical properties of 'super-radiance'[39] and 'self-induced transparency', then, the argument goes, the loss of consciousness might be attributable to these changes in the microtubules. Briefly, here are some reservations:

The anaesthesia/microtubule connection

(1) There is no direct evidence that changes in microtubules in neurons are responsible for the phenomenological effects of general anaesthetics. What

[39] In the context of the present discussion, super-radiance is a quantum-mechanical effect in which water molecules within the microtubule might act in ways roughly analogous to a laser. Specifically these molecules, because they have dipole moments, could coherently emit radiation by shifting between angular momentum states. This effect, if it exists, would depend crucially on the purity of the water within the tubule, as well as on the properties of the tubule itself, such as its diameter and minute details of its electric field. See Jibu *et al.* 1994; Hameroff 1994.

the most recent data do indicate is that at surgical concentrations, ligand-gated ion channels (proteins) in the neuronal membrane are the main sites of anaesthetic effects. Relative to the quantum effects envisaged for microtubules these are *large* effects. In their review article in *Nature* (1994), Franks and Lieb state that among possible receptor targets $GABA_A$ (γ-aminobutyric acid) receptor protein has been established by electrophysiological studies to be a major target. The general anaesthetics that potentiate the GABA receptor protein include inhalational agents such as halothane, enflurane and isoflurane, as well as intravenous anaesthetics such as pentobarbitol, propofol and alphaxalone. GABA is the major inhibitory neurotransmitter in the brain, and potentiation of the GABA receptor probably up-regulates inhibition which effectively overrides excitation. This is consistent with the finding that anaesthetic interactions with the GABA receptor protein extend its open time. The other receptor that has been shown to be a target is the excitatory voltage-dependent NMDA receptor. It is inhibited by the agent, ketamine.[40] To repeat, these effects on receptors are large effects in the millivolt range.

(2) Even if disruption of microtubule function were consistently correlated with general anaesthetics, there is no reason to suppose that 'normal' microtubule functioning is anything more than a necessary *background* condition — one necessary condition among hosts of others (e.g. availability of oxygen, ATP, glucose etc.).

The microtubule/super-radiance/consciousness connection

(3) There is no evidence[41] that quantum coherence involving super-radiance (or anything else for that matter) occurs in microtubules. At best, what Hameroff has done is to show that it might be possible. This should most definitely be distinguished from providing *evidence* that it is *actual*.

(4) It is highly unlikely that the pore of the tubulin tube contains nothing but pure water, since there is no known mechanism for keeping out common cytoplasmic ions such as calcium and sodium. This is a major problem for the hypothesis because impurities are an obstacle to the postulated long-range cooperativity, especially super-radiance. It is therefore highly speculative that quantum coherence involving super-radiance occurs in microtubules.

(5) An ancient and still common palliative for the disease known as gout is the drug colchicine. This was introduced to American medical practice by Benjamin Franklin. For our purposes colchicine has the highly interesting property that, *inter alia*, it disrupts microtubules by attaching to the

---

[40] Franks & Lieb 1994; for further dicussion, see Bowdle, Horita & Kharasch 1994.

[41] In this paragraph, as well as in (1) above, we are in the awkward situation of merely stating that there is no direct evidence of such and such. This is not because we are simply discounting Hameroff's evidence, but because, so far as we can see, he doesn't offer any. His arguments take more the form of demonstrating how certain phenomena might be possible, not of providing direct evidence for them.

'add-on' end and preventing repolymerization repairs. After a period of colchicine treatment for gout, therefore, the microtubules show consider-able depolymerization.[42] This is a major monkeywrench for super-radiance,[43] a bit like the way in which breaks in fibres disrupt fibre-optic transmission. The capacity of the microtubule to support the self-focusing soliton wave[44] (which 'transmits' the super- radiance effect down the length of the tube) depends crucially on the characteristics and the uniformity of the waveguide, which is just the interior of the microtubule in this case. So any disruption as radical as depolymerization of the tubule prevents any quantum phenomena that might have been. If Hameroff and Penrose are right, then microtubule depolymerization ought to block super-radiance and hence significantly impair consciousness. Does it impair consciousness? Not that anyone has noticed, and loss of awareness is a major thing to not notice. It is known, however, that prolonged use can cause paralysis, beginning with the lower extremities. The colchicine data are surely an embarrassment for the Hameroff hypothesis.

(6) Hameroff envisages consciousness as involving a unity across diverse brain regions. Even if the interesting quantum events did occur in a single tubule, to play a role in consciousness the effect must be transmitted from one tubule to its microtubule neighbour within the cell. If big transmitter molecules are in the vicinity, making their way to and from the synapse, the prediction is that this would seriously inhibit the spread of the quantum coherence. The next-stage-up problem has the same form: to play a role in consciousness the effect must be transmitted from one *neuron* to other neurons. The problem with this step is that the principal neuromembrane

[42] Goodman, Gilman, *et al.* 1990. This was brought to our attention by Chuck Stevens. For evidence that small though 'effective' amounts of colchicine do pass the blood-brain barrier, see Bennett, Alberti & Flood 1981. A number of studies (e.g. Kolasa *et al.* 1992 and Emerich & Walsh 1991) injected colchicine directly into the brain of rats and then ran various behavioural tests on them. No such studies we have seen mention any problems associated with consciousness, including Bensimon & Chermat (1991) who injected rat brains directly with colchicine every day for ten days, Conner & Varon (1992) who directly injected the brain at several different locations, and Ceccaldi *et al.* (1990) who pumped colchicine continuously into rat brains over extended periods of time with an osmotic pump. Note that all these studies used colchicine *specifically because it depolymerises microtubules*, disrupting their transport function. It is revealing to note that many of these studies mention that the rats were anaesthetized before being sacrificed, which implies that the microtubule disruption *did not* render them unconscious, and that the normal anaesthetic *did* render them unconscious (presumably in some manner other than affecting the already-depolymerized microtubules, *contra* Penrose & Hammeroff).

[43] And probably any other putative quantum-mechanical effect supported by microtubules as well. In fact it seems also to be a problem for other accounts of the importance of microtubular computation (quantum-mechanical or otherwise) as supporting consciousness or cognition, e.g. Hameroff 1994; Hameroff & Watt 1982; etc.

[44] Cf. Jibu *et al.* 1994.

effects involving voltage changes are big — of the order of tens of micro-
volts — and it is a fair prediction that these effects would wipe out the
nanoeffects from the microtubules.[45] This is not to say it cannot be done,
but no one has the slightest evidence that it is done, nor the slightest idea
how it might be done.

(7) Given the Hameroff hypothesis one might predict that disruption of
microtubule function underlies other more routine changes in the state of
awareness, such as the daily shift from being awake to being in deep sleep.
This shift is generally regarded as a major change from being conscious of
events to not being conscious of them.[46] There is no reason to suppose that
microtubules alter function concordant with these state changes, for
example by ceasing their water-ordering, wave-guided super-radiancing
and self-induced transparency. What we do know is that certain neurons do
change in very specific ways with changes in sleep/wakefulness — in thalamic
and brain stem structures in particular.[47]

Penrose's preferred role for microtubules differs a bit from that of
Hameroff. He sees them as altering neuronal signalling via modifying
pre-synaptic efficacy. The idea seems to be this: if they can do this, then
perhaps they can shape specific patterns of activation in the brain, and these
particular patterns are what support consciousness. So what microtubules
must do is to somehow encode the information derived from sensory
structures, process it, and then modify the firing of neurons in such a way
as to support consciousness of the stimulus, and perhaps a purposeful
response as well. How plausible is this?

Here are some reservations specific to the Penrose version of the microtubule story:

(1) First, microtubules are seldom seen in close proximity to the business
end of the synaptic complex. Generally they appear to end about a micron
from the synaptic complex, which means, for the kind of effect Penrose is
talking about, the distance may as well be meters.[48]

(2) How is the microtubule supposed to communicate with the synapse to
have the Penrose effect? What precisely is supposed to be the effect on the
neuronal membrane and how is it to be achieved? Penrose does not give us
a clue. The release of neurotransmitter vesicles, for example, do not have
any characteristic association with microtubules, so far as is known.

---

[45] Of course, depending on the story told about exactly what kinds of quantum coherence are
important and how they are maintained in spatially separate regions, the presence of transmitter molecules and electric fields may not be a problem. The problem is that these details
are not provided.

[46] See Llinás & Ribary 1993, and Flanagan (forthcoming).

[47] Cf. Steriade et al. 1993.

[48] See Peters, Palay & Webster 1978.

(3) Suppose Penrose has in mind that the alleged quantum goings-on in the microtubules modify neurotransmitter release. Is this reasonable? Not very. What is known is that release of a vesicle of neurotransmitter when a spike reaches the axon terminal is highly dependent on calcium channels and on the phosphorylation rate of membrane proteins. Neuromodulators (e.g. norepinephrine, any of the various neuropeptides, caffeine, etc.) can affect calcium channels and hence affect transmitter release. Caffeine, for example, works by blocking the receptor adenosine, which acts with a second messenger to down-regulate the neuron. These are very big effects in the world of neurons. Even if microtubules did display the quantum goings-on, the effects would seem to be trivial relative to the effects of neuromodulators.[49]

(4) The encoding problem for microtubules is ignored by Penrose. If microtubules are to perform their Penrosian function they must be able to *get* the information that they then (nonalgorithmically) process. Neurons depend, for *their* signals, mostly on neurotransmitters and neuromodulators which alter the neuron membrane's permeability to various ions. Is the idea that microtubules can use *these* ion concentrations as sources of information? Maybe, but this seems to conflict with the requirement that microtubules be insulated from their ionic environment in order to support quantum coherence, etc.[50] Even if that can be resolved, how is this supposed to work?

Even with generous conjecture-granting, Penrose is still not out of the woods. As Hameroff in (3) above has problems about getting a global effect out of a highly local effect, so of course does Penrose. How is it that microtubule clusters in different neurons coordinate their activities in order to shape the overall patterns of neural activity which support consciousness? For surely changes in a single neuron will not cause the generation or loss of consciousness. No answer. Are microtubules able to support some form of long-range quantum coherence or entanglement? No answer. Quantum entanglement we assume is ruled out, because it would require that the insulated interiors or surfaces of the microtubules interact in some way, and since they will be in separate neurons across wide stretches of the brain it is not clear how this could happen. Finally, how realistic is it to predict a quantum-coherent state between the spatially-separated microtubules (or their contents)? Penrose correctly assesses the prospects when he remarks (Shadows, p. 373), 'Such a feat would be a remarkable one — almost an incredible one — for Nature to achieve by biological means.'

---

[49] See Stevens & Wang 1994.

[50] Ions in close proximity to the tubulin dimers would affect their electrical properties and hence their capacity to engage in or support these sorts of quantum phenomena. See Jibu *et al.* 1994; Hameroff 1994.

VI. Conclusions

Let's take stock of where we are. The first part of the Penrose argument (Part A) is in trouble. There is reason to doubt that human cognition or consciousness must take advantage of nonalgorithmic processes since unsound, albeit reliable, algorithmic processes escape Gödel's net. Second, Part B of the argument is entirely speculative — there is no evidence at all (including quasicrystals) that there are any (strongly) nonalgorithmic processes anywhere in the universe. Indeed, even if Penrose's quantum gravity hunch were correct (another big 'if'), it need not incorporate any non- algorithmic processes. Finally, the prospects for Part C look grim. There is no experimental evidence that microtubules do support interesting quantum phenomena and, save in the unlikely event that the water in and around them is pure, it is doubtful that they do. Water purity is not the only problem; other highly speculative conditions would also have to obtain. Even if they can support such phenomena, long-range coherence seems quite far fetched. Furthermore, because microtubules can depolymerize without noticeable effect on consciousness, it seems unlikely that they support conscious thought.

Consciousness is a problem, but it must be remembered that we are still in the very early stages of understanding the nervous system. Many fundamental questions about basic phenomena — such as the role of back projections, the nature of representation in sensory systems, whether sensory systems are hierarchically organized, precisely how memory is stored and retrieved, how sensorimotor integration works, what sleep and dreaming are all about — have not yet been satisfactorily answered. Is the problem of consciousness utterly different from all these other problems? Perhaps, but *qua* mystery it does not come with its degree or depth or style of mysteriousness pinned to its shirt. Sometimes problems that appear to be the really tough ones, such as the composition of the stars, turn out to be easier to solve than seemingly minor puzzles, such as the precession of the perihelion of Mercury. Undoubtedly many surprises await us, and for all we know some of them may involve surprises for (or from) physics. Never-the-less, before making a heavy research investment in a precarious and far-fetched hypothesis, it would be nice to have something solid to go on. This may be a matter of taste, however.

Despite the rather breathtaking flimsiness of the consciousness–quantum connection the idea has enjoyed a surprisingly warm reception, at least outside neuroscience. One cannot help groping about for some explanation for this rather odd fact. Is it not even *more* reductionist than explaining consciousness in terms of the properties of networks of neurons? Emotionally, it seems, the two reductionist strategies arouse quite different feelings. After some interviewing, in an admittedly haphazard fashion, we found the following story gathering credence.

Some people who, intellectually, are materialists, nevertheless have strong dualist hankerings — especially hankerings about life after death. They have a negative 'gut' reaction to the idea that neurons — cells that you can see under a microscope and probe with electrodes, brains you can hold in one hand and that rapidly rot without oxygen supply — are the source of subjectivity and the 'me-ness of me'. The crucial feature of neurons that makes them capable of processing and storing information is just ions passing back and forth across neuronal membranes through protein channels. That seems, stacked again the 'me-ness of me', to be disappointingly humdrum — even if there are lots of ions and lots of neurons and lots of really complicated protein channels.

Quantum physics, on the other hand, seems more resonant with those residual dualist hankerings, perhaps by holding out the possibility that scientific realism and objectivity melt away in that domain, or even that thoughts and feelings are, in the end, the fundamental properties of the universe.[51] Explanation of something as special as what makes me *me* should really involve, the feeling is, something more 'deep' and mysterious and 'other worldly' than mere neurons. Perhaps what is comforting about quantum physics is that it can be invoked to 'explain' a mysterious phenomenon without removing much of the mystery, quantum-physical explanations being highly mysterious themselves.

Now we are *not* for a moment suggesting that anything like this is behind Penrose's work, and whether our diagnosis is right or wrong has no bearing whatever on the strengths and weaknesses of his arguments. It may, however, help explain why the very possibility of a quantum-physical explanation is often warmly greeted, whereas an explanation in terms of neurons may be considered 'scary', 'degrading' and even 'inconceivable'. Why should it be less scary, reductionist or counter-intuitive that 'me-ness' emerges from the collapse of a wave function than from neuronal activity?

Nothing we have said in this paper demonstrates the falsity of the quantum–consciousness connection. Our view is just that it is no better supported than any one of a gazillion caterpillar-with-hookah hypotheses.

References

Bates, E. & MacWhinney, B. (1989). Functionalism and the competition model. In E. Bates & B. MacWhinney (eds), *The Crosslinguistic Study of Sentence Processing*. Cambridge: Cambridge University Press.

Benacerraf, P. & Putnam, H. (1983)[eds]. *Philosophy of Mathematics; Selected Readings*. Englewood Cliffs, NJ: Prentice-Hall.

Bennett, B.M., Hoffman, D.D. & Prakash, C. (1989). *Observer Mechanics*. San Diego: Academic Press.

---

[51] Cf. Bennett, Hoffman & Prakash 1989.

Bennett, E., Alberti, M.H. & Flood, J. (1981) Uptake of [^{3}H]Colchicine into brain and liver of mouse, rat and chick. *Pharmacology, Biochemistry and Behaviour*, **14**, 863–9.

Bensimon, G. & Chermat, R. (1991). Microtubule disruption and cognitive defects: Effect of colchicine on learning behaviour in rats. *Pharmacology, Biochemistry and Behaviour*, **38**, 141–5.

Bloor, D. (1976). *Knowledge and Social Imagery*. Chicago: University of Chicago Press.

Bogen, J.E. (1995). On the neurophysiology of consciousness: I. An overview. *Consciousness and Cognition*, **4**, 52–62.

Boyer, C. (1959). *The History of the Calculus and its Conceptual Development*. New York: Dover.

Bowdle, T.A., Horita, A. & Kharasch, E.D. (1994). *The Pharmacological Basis of Anesthesiology*. New York: Churchill Livingstone.

Bray, D. (1992). *Cell Movements*. New York: Garland Publishing.

Ceccaldi, P.E., Ermine, A. & Tsiang, H. (1990). Continuous delivery of colchicine in the rat brain with osmotic pumps for inhibition of rabies virus transport. *Journal of Virological Methods*, **28**, 79–83.

Conner, J.M. & Varon, S. (1992). Distribution of nerve growth factor-like immunoreactive neurons in the adult rat brain following colchicine treatment. *Journal of Comparative Neurology*, **326**, 347–62.

Churchland, P.M. (1995). *The Engine of Reason, The Seat of the Soul*. Cambridge MA: MIT Press.

Churchland, P.S. & Sejnowski, T. (1992). *The Computational Brain*. Cambridge MA: MIT Press.

Crick, F.H.C. (1994). *The Astonishing Hypothesis*. New York: Scribners.

Damasio, A.R. (1994). *Descartes' Error*. New York: Putnam.

Damasio, A.R. & Damasio, H. (forthcoming). Images and subjectivity: Neurobiological trials and tribulations. In Robert McCauley (ed), *The Churchlands and their Critics*. Oxford: Blackwell.

Dennett, D.C. (1991). *Consciousness Explained*. Boston: Little, Brown and Co.

Dummett, M. (1991). *The Logical Basis of Metaphysics*. Cambridge MA: Harvard University Press.

Emerich, D.F.& Walsh, T.J. (1991). Ganglioside AGF2 prevents the cognitive impariments and cholinergic cell loss following intraventricular colchicine. *Experimental Neurology*, **112**, 328–37.

Flanagan, O. (forthcoming). Prospects for a unified theory of consciousness, or, what dreams are made of. In J. Cohen and J. Schooler (eds), *Scientific Approaches to the Question of Consciousness: 25th. Carnegie Symposium on Cognition*. Hillsdale NJ: L. Earlbaum.

Franks, N.P. & Lieb, W.R. (1994). Molecular and cellular mechanisms of general anaesthesia. *Nature*, **367**, 607–14.

Goodman, L., Gilman, A. *et al* (1990)[eds]. *Pharmacological Basis of Therapeutics*. 8th edn. New York: Pergamon Press.

Hall, Z.W. (1992)[ed]. *An Introduction to Molecular Biology*. New York: Sinauer.

Hameroff, S.R. (1994). Quantum coherence in microtubules: a neural basis for emergent consciousness? *Journal of Consciousness Studies*, **1**, 98–118.

Hameroff, S.R., Dayhoff, J.E., Lahoz-Beltra, R., Samsonovich, A. & Rasmussen, S. (1992). Models for molecular computation: conformational automata in the cytoskeleton. *IEEE Computer* (Special issue on molecular computing), **25**, 30–9.

Hameroff, S.R., Rasmussen, S. & Mansson, B. (1989). Molecular automata in microtubules: basic computational logic for the living state? In C. Langton (ed), *Artificial Life, SFI Studies in the Sciences of Complexity*. New York: Addison-Wesley.

Hameroff, S.R. & Watt, R.C. (1982). Information processing in microtubules. *Journal of Theoretical Biology*, **98**, 549–61.

Heyting, A. (1956). *Intuitionism: An Introduction*. Amsterdam: North-Holland.

Jibu, M., Hagen, S., Hameroff, S.R., Pribram, K.H. & Yasue, K. (1994). Quantum optical coherence in cytoskeletal microtubules: implications for brain function. *BioSystems*, **32**, 195–209.

Jordan, M.I. (1989). Serial order; a parallel distributed processing approach. In J.L. Elman & D.E. Rumelhart (eds), *Advances in Connectionist Theory*. Hillsdale, NJ: Erlbaum.

Kitcher, P. (1984). *The Nature of Mathematical Knowledge*. Oxford: Oxford University Press.

Kolasa, K., Jope, R.S., Baird, M.S. & Johnson, G.V. (1992). Alterations of choline acetyltransferase, phosphoinositide hydrolysis, and cytoskeletal proteins in rat brain in response to colchicine administration. *Experimental Brain Research*, **89**, 496–500.

Lakatos, I. (1976). *Proofs and Refutations*. Cambridge: Cambridge University Press.

Llinás, R.R. & Ribary U. (1993). Coherent 40-Hz oscillation characterizes dream state in humans. *Proc. Natl. Acad. Sci.,* **90**, 2078–81.

Llinás, R.R. & Paré, D. (1993). Of dreaming and wakefulness. *Neuroscience*, **44**, 521–35.

Logothetis, N. & Schall, J.D. (1989). Neural correlates of subjective visual perception. *Science*, **245**, 753–61.

Mead, C. (1989). *Analog VLSI and Neural Systems*. Reading, MA: Addison-Wesley.

Onoda, G.Y., Steinhardt, P.J., DiVincenzo, D.P. & Socolar, J.E.S. (1988). Growing perfect quasicrystals. *Phys. Rev. Letters*, **60**, 2688.

Penrose, R. (1989). *The Emperor's New Mind*. Oxford: Oxford University Press.

Penrose, R. (1994a). Interview with Jane Clark, *Journal of Consciousness Studies*, **1**, 17–24.

Penrose, R. (1994b). *Shadows of the Mind*. Oxford: Oxford University Press.

Peters, A., Palay, S.L. & Webster, H. de F. (1978). *The Fine Structure of the Nervous System*. Philadelphia: W.B. Saunders.

Putnam, H. (1994). The best of all possible brains? Review of 'Shadows of the Mind'. *New York Times Review of Books*, November.

Quine, W.V.O. (1970). *Philosophy of Logic*. Englewood Cliffs, NJ: Prentice-Hall.

Sasajima, Y., Adachi, K., Tanaka, H., Ichimura, M., *et al*. (1994). Computer simulation of the growth process of binary quasicrystals. *Japanese Journal of Applied Physics, Part 1*, **33**, 2673–4.

Sossin, W.S., Fisher, J.M. & Scheller, R.H. (1989). Cellular and molecular biology of neuropeptide processing and packaging. *Neuron*, **2**, 1407–17.

Steriade, M., McCormick, D.A. & Sejnowski, T.J. (1993). Thalamocortical oscillations in the sleeping and aroused brain. *Science*, **262**, 679–85.

Stevens, C.F. & Wang, Y.Y. (1994). Changes in reliability of synaptic function as a mechanism for plasticity. *Nature*, **371**, 704–7.

Stich, S. (1990). *The Fragmentation of Reason.* Cambridge, MA: MIT Press.

Turing, A. (1986). Lecture to the London Mathematical Society on 20 February 1947. In B.E. Carpenter & R.W. Doran (eds), *A.M. Turing's ACE Report of 1946 and Other Papers.* Charles Babbage Institute Reprint Series for the History of Computing, **10.** Cambridge, MA: MIT Press.

Part Four

The Knowledge Argument

Introduction to Part Four

One of the basic problems in developing a theory of consciousness is the so-called 'epistemic asymmetry'. We know of conscious experiences in two essentially different ways: through direct inner acquaintance and through access from the outside, i.e. the third person perspective. For centuries, philosophers have been troubled about whether and how the introspective knowledge of phenomenal states from the first person perspective can be brought into accord with our knowledge from the third person perspective. One of the focal points in the recent discussion has been the *knowledge argument* of Frank Jackson. Jackson's anti-materialist argument claims to show that one can possess complete physical knowledge concerning a person with conscious experience and still fail to grasp an essential aspect. The argument utilizes two thought experiments starring two fictitious persons: Fred and Mary. For the reader's convenience I shall quote the central passage of the second thought experiment:

> Mary is a brilliant scientist who is, for whatever reason, forced to investigate the world from a black and white room *via* a black and white television monitor. She specialises in the neurophysiology of vision and acquires, let us suppose, all the physical information there is to obtain about what goes on when we see ripe tomatoes, or the sky, and use terms like 'red', 'blue', and so on. She discovers, for example, just which wave-length combinations from the sky stimulate the retina, and exactly how this produces *via* the central nervous system the contraction of the vocal chords and expulsion of air from the lungs that results in the uttering of the sentence 'The sky is blue'. [. . .]
>
> What will happen when Mary is released from her black and white room or is given a colour television monitor? Will she *learn* anything or not? It seems just obvious that she will learn something about the world and our visual experience of it. But then it is inescapable that her previous knowledge was incomplete. But she had *all* the physical information. *Ergo* there is more to have than that, and Physicalism is false.

What has changed in Mary's life after she has seen the blue sky and a red tomato for the first time? Did she merely acquire a new *ability*, e.g. the ability to imagine certain things? Or has she acquired a new and specific type of *inner* knowledge, of subjective experiential knowledge? If the latter, then *what sort* of knowledge is it that can only be acquired through one's own experience of certain phenomenal states? Is it a special form of factual knowledge? Philosophical discussion of the argument has continued unabated for more than two decades. The contributions in this section show, from three rather different perspectives, why philosophers are still fascinated by it.

In the title of her essay, **Martine Nida-Rümelin** alludes to the title of another well-known paper of Frank Jackson. But she is interested in the *epistemological* rather than the ontological aspects of the knowledge argument: the question is not whether there are non-physical facts but whether there is a special type of factual knowledge of phenomenal states which is only accessible to subjects who are acquainted with the states from their own experience? In the beginning of her contribution she explains why someone who lacks certain conscious colour perceptions is unable, in principle, to form certain kinds of beliefs about other people's colour perceptions. At the heart of her argument is a conceptual distinction between phenomenal and non-phenomenal beliefs, which she introduces by means of an example. After a series of possible objections has been addressed, the distinction is put to a variety of uses. First, it allows a formulation of Mary's epistemic progress that is both intuitively plausible and theoretically precise. Second, it can be demonstrated that the new concept of 'phenomenal knowledge' is more suitable than Nagel's 'knowing what it's like' to grasp the intuition underlying the knowledge argument. Third, if there is really a type of propositional knowledge about states of phenomenal consciousness which presupposes an acquaintance with the states in question, then Jackson's argument gains further support: every description of conscious creatures using physical but not phenomenal terminology must remain epistemically incomplete. If an empirical science is to aim for such completeness, then it cannot do without phenomenal vocabulary.

In his contribution, **William Lycan** investigates two much-discussed strategies for the defence of materialism against Nagel's and Jackson's arguments. These strategies have been put forward by Laurence Nemirow and David Lewis. These authors deny that there is such a thing as intrinsic subjective, phenomenal information or a propositional form of phenomenal knowledge in the sense of a subjective 'knowledge that'. There are only certain abilities, such as abilities of imagination or of memory. Lycan argues against this reduction of experiential knowledge to non-propositional abilities, defending the concept of *phenomenal information* according to which Mary really acquires propositional knowledge when she has a colour experience for the first time. Lycan starts by presenting nine critical arguments against Nemirow and Lewis, and then introduces a strict definition of qualia as a certain type of intentional object. Next he applies Frege's distinction between reference and mode of presentation to a meta-representational theory of introspective knowledge as a type of inner perception. From this it follows that there are no coarse-grained phenomenal facts in Nagel's and Jackson's sense, but there is (contrary to Nemirow and Lewis) a sort of fine-grained phenomenal information, individuated not through facts but through inner, functional modes of presentation. In the last two sections of the article, Lycan uses this distinction to analyse the nine arguments given at the start as well as two further arguments given by Lewis against the concept of phenomenal information.

Why does the idea that consciousness is physical run so stubbornly aginst our intuitions? **David Papineau** holds the 'antipathetic fallacy' responsible: We believe that we could never refer to subjective states through the external perspective, because third person thoughts about the conscious states of others mention these states but do not *use* any secondary versions or re-creations of such states. This notorious conflation of use and mention on the mental level makes it seem implausible that certain parts of nature as such could possess conscious experience. But if this is true, there may be no such thing as a well-defined object of scientific theories of consciousness: There is only the class of states which creatures like us can re-create in the imagination, combined with the illusory property that their owners possess a certain type of inner illumination.

Further Reading

Jackson, F. (1982). Epiphenomenal qualia. *Philosophical Quarterly*, **32**, 127–36. Reprinted in Lycan 1990 and in Block *et al.* 1996.

Jackson, F. (1986). What Mary didn't know. *Journal of Philosophy*, **83**, 291–5. Reprinted in Rosenthal 1991 and Block *et al.* 1996. Reprinted with a postscript in Moser, P.K. & Trout, J.D. [eds], *Contemporary Materialism*. London: Routledge.

Lewis, D. (1983). Postscript to 'Mad Pain and Martian Pain'. In *Philosophical Papers*, Vol. I. Oxford: Oxford University Press.

Lewis, D. (1990). What experience teaches. In Lycan 1990.

Lycan, W.G. (1987). *Consciousness*. Cambridge, MA: MIT Press.

Lycan, W.G. (1990)[ed]. *Mind and Cognition*. Cambridge, MA: MIT Press. (Especially part VII)

Lycan, W.G. (1996). *Consciousness and Experience*. Cambridge, MA: MIT Press.

Nagel, T. (1974). What is it like to be a bat? *Philosophical Review*, **83**, 435–50.

Nemirow, L. (1980). Review of Nagel's *Mortal Questions*. *Philosophical Review*, **89**, 475–6.

Nemirow, L. (1990). Physicalism and the Cognitive Role of Acquaintance. In Lycan 1990.

Nida-Rümelin, M. (1993). *Farben und phänomenales Wissen*. St. Augustin: Academia Verlag.

Nida-Rümelin, M. (1995). Pseudonormal vision. An actual case of qualia inversion? *Philosophical Studies*, Supplement.

Nida-Rümelin, M. (1996a). Is the naturalization of qualitative experience possible or sensible? In Carrier & Machamer 1996.

Nida-Rümelin, M. (1996b). The character of color predicates. A phenomenalist view. In M. Anduschus, W. Künne & A. Newen (eds), *Direct Reference, Indexicality and Propositional Attitudes*. Stanford: CSLI.

Papineau, D. (1993). *Philosophical Naturalism*. Oxford: Basil Blackwell.

Papineau, D. (1993). Physicalism, consciousness and the antipathetic fallacy. *Australasian Journal of Philosophy*, **71**, 169–83.

Additional references regarding the knowledge argument and the problem of the general relationship of consciousness to the physical world can be found in the bibliography at the end of this volume. Section 3.7 offers a selection of texts which are directly concerned with Frank Jackson's argument. Further works which contain specific discussions of the relationship between consciousness, physicalism and the mind-body problem are listed in section 3.2.

Martine Nida-Rümelin

What Mary Couldn't Know: Belief about Phenomenal States

I. Introduction

Everyone familiar with the current mind–body debate has probably heard about Frank Jackson's neurophysiologist Mary.[1] So I tell her story very briefly. Mary knows everything there is to know about the neurophysiological basis of human colour vision but she never saw colours herself (she always lived in a black-and-white environment). When Mary is finally released into the beauty of the coloured world, she acquires new knowledge about the world and — more specifically — about the character of the visual experiences of others. This appears clear at first sight. In the ongoing philosophical debate, however, there is no agreement about whether Mary really gains new knowledge and about whether this would, if it were so, represent a problem for physicalism. Those who defend the so-called argument from knowledge (or 'knowledge argument') think that it does.[2]

Most participants in the debate agree that there is a strong inuition in favour of the thesis that Mary makes a genuine epistemic progress after her release. But there is disagreement about whether this intuition survives critical investigation and also about how the apparent or genuine epistemic progress can be adequately described. Most work about the argument from knowledge has focussed on the question whether it leads — as was originally intended — to the ontological result that there are non-physical facts.

[1] For the title compare Jackson 1984b. The example of Mary is presented in Jackson 1984a.

[2] The assumption in the example is, more exactly, that Mary knows everything there is to know about human colour perception except for what she cannot possibly know given her colour deprivation.

219

The epistemologically interesting questions raised by the Mary-example, however, have not yet been considered in much detail. It seems clear to me that an intuitively adequate theoretical description of what Mary learns after her release has not been proposed so far — neither by those who attack nor by those who defend the knowledge argument. Such a description requires, I think, the use of an epistemological distinction (between phenomenal and nonphenomenal belief) that will be proposed in the present paper. Using this distinction it will be possible to say in a precise manner what Jackson's Mary learns, when she finally is allowed to see colours and why she could not have learned all this before. Most philosophers use Nagel's term of 'knowing what it's like' in this context.[3] But this metaphorical locution is misleading and does not capture the intuition underlying the knowledge argument.

I have been considering Mary's specific epistemic situation so far. But, of course, the controversy addressed in this paper is not — or only at a superficial level — about how we should describe the counterfactual situation of a fictitious person. One of the deeper questions behind this is, whether there really is — as Mary's example seems to suggest — a specific kind of factual knowledge about the experiences of others that is only accessible to an epistemic subject who is acquainted by personal experience with the type of mental state at issue. The answer to this question is 'yes' for phenomenal knowledge as introduced below. Once we accept that there is such knowledge (knowledge that presupposes acquaintance with certain specific phenomenal states), then it appears that any description of a conscious being capable of phenomenal experience that uses only terms that the physicalist accepts as unproblematic will be — in a sense — epistemically incomplete, since it is characteristic for such a description that it can be understood and believed to be true by any rational epistemic subject independently of the specific kinds of phenomenal qualitites it is able to experience given its physiological 'apparatus'. (See Nagel 1986: 13 ff.)

My main concern in this paper is to convince the reader that the epistemological distinction I propose between phenomenal and nonphenomenal belief concerning the experiences of others makes sense and that it is useful for certain philosophical purposes. I hope to show this by using the distinction in the following. (I will introduce the distinction only for the special case of belief and other propositional attitudes concerning colours and colour experiences, but the distinction naturally carries over to belief about other phenomenal states.[4]) You might convince yourself of the usefulness of this distinction, e.g. for explicating certain philosophical intuitions, even

---

[3] The term was introduced by Thomas Nagel, see his famous paper Nagel 1974.

[4] The conditions that must be fulfilled in general in a case where the distinction makes sense are discussed in Nida-Rümelin 1996b, section 3.

if you do not — in the end — agree with the view here presented about the knowledge argument.

II. An Unusual Epistemic Situation

To introduce the distinction between phenomenal and nonphenomenal belief, I will change Mary's example. Like Mary, Marianna has always lived in a black-and-white environment. Also, there are no colours, we may suppose, in her dreams and visual phantasies and imaginations. Maybe Marianna has — like Mary — detailed knowledge about physiology, but this is of no importance for the following.[5] Marianna has agreed to participate in a psychological experiment which requires that she does not leave the house where she has always been living. But the interior decoration is now radically changed. She sees artificial objects (walls, tables etc.) of all colours, but is not taught the names of these colours. She already knows of a number of natural objects (like leaves, sunflowers, etc.) that they are called 'green', 'yellow' etc. But she is not allowed to see any of these objects (she is not allowed to see ripe tomatoes, photographs of landscapes or realistic paintings, she is somehow prevented from seeing the natural colours of her own body, she does not see the sky, etc.). In the course of the psychological experiment Marianna undergoes the following test: She is visually presented with four slides showing clear cases of blue, red, green and yellow, and she is asked which of the four slides shows a clear case of the colour she believes to be experienced by normal people when they look at the sky. Marianna is especially impressed by the beauty of the red slide. Having been told about the beauty of the sky on a sunny summer day she says after some reflection, pointing to the red slide: 'I believe it's this one.' Two more details are relevant for the following discussion: Marianna believes herself to be normally sighted and this belief is correct.[6]

Already, before she has been presented with colours for the first time, Marianna has acquired the belief that the sky appears blue to people with normal colour perception. It appears correct to ascribe this belief to her since a number of those conditions are clearly fulfilled which normally — according to the usual practice of belief ascription — lead us to the claim that a person believes that p: Marianna would say (when asked the appropriate question) 'the sky appears blue to normally sighted people'; she intends to thereby express the belief that is normally expressed using these

[5] The example is used here only to introduce an epistemological distinction and, contrary to Jackson's use of his example, it does not serve for a direct attack on physicalism. This is why I do not need the assumption of 'complete physical' knowledge about human colour perception.

[6] Only under this assumption we are allowed to draw the conclusion that will be drawn in the following, namely that Marianna believes — in a certain sense — that the sky appears red to normally sighted people. If Marianna were red/green blind or pseudonormal (for pseudonormality see footnote 13), it would be a mistake to conclude this.

words and she belongs to a language community where people normally use the above sentence to claim that the sky appears blue to normally sighted people.[7] So, if we wish to describe the beliefs Marianna holds before her acquaintance with colours, then we have reason to claim:

(1)   Marianna believes that the sky appears blue to normally sighted people.

But, when she was finally presented with colours, Marianna did not give up this original belief. Her answer in the above described experiment is not accompanied by a revision of her original opinion about how the sky appears to normally sighted people. Therefore, (1) is still correct when claimed about Marianna with respect to the later moment considered. In a sense, Marianna still believes that the sky appears blue to normally sighted people. She still trusts those who told her that this is so. Furthermore, Marianna would therefore contradict the verbally (and without ostension) expressed opinion that the sky appears red to normally sighted people. So we also have reason to claim (with respect to her later epistemic situation):

(2)   Marianna does not believe that the sky appears red to normally sighted people.

On the other side, there are strong intuitions against (1) and (2). Marianna believes herself to be normally sighted and she is normally sighted. The red slide appears red to her and she is right in assuming that she has the same type of colour experience when looking at the slide as other people with normal colour vision.[8] In a sense she believes, therefore, that the slide appears to others like it appears to her, namely red. And she believes that the sky appears to normally sighted people with respect to colour like this slide, red therefore, and not blue. Viewed in this way it appears correct to ascribe to Marianna the following beliefs:

(3)   Marianna believes that the sky appears red to normally sighted people.

(4)   Marianna does not believe that the sky appears blue to normally sighted people.

So, on the one side, there is a tendency to claim that Marianna believes that the sky looks blue and not red to normally sighted people, where this intuition is based on the fact that Marianna belongs to a certain language

---

[7] More precisely, this sentence is normally used to claim that the sky appears blue$_p$ to normally sighted people (see Nida-Rümelin 1996c: section 5). But I have not yet introduced the subscripting convention to distinguish phenomenal and nonphenomenal belief at this point of the present paper.

[8] By assuming that normally sighted people have the same type of colour experience when looking at the slide I do not mean to claim that they experience exactly the same shade of red. I just assume that for every normally sighted person the slide appears in the same basic hue (red). In every such case, what is seen is a clear case of red.

community. On the other side, it appears obvious that Marianna believes of the wrong visual quality (namely with respect to red) that it is the colour experienced by normally sighted people, when looking at the sky on a sunny day. She clearly has, in a sense, mistaken beliefs about the character of the colour experiences of others. When imagining the sky in the way it appears to others, she would imagine a red sky. In a certain sense she does not know, which colour is the colour of the sky.

To account for these conflicting intuitions with respect to Marianna's epistemic situation, we should distinguish two readings of belief descriptions containing colour terms in their that-clause. One quickly realizes that the distinction makes sense not just for cases where the that-clause contains a 'colour appearance term' like 'appears red to . . .' but for any occurrence of a colour term (as in 'Marianna believes that the sky is red' or in 'Marianna believes that Peter saw a red flower in his dream last night').[9] A first attempt to resolve the conflict between (1) and (4) and (2) und (3) could consist in distinguishing phenomenal and nonphenomenal belief in the following way:

(1') Marianna believes nonphenomenally that the sky appears blue to normally sighted people.

(2') Marianna does not believe nonphenomenally that the sky appears red to normally sighted people.

(3') Marianna believes phenomenally that the sky appears red to normally sighted people.

(4') Marianna does not believe phenomenally that the sky appears blue to normally sighted people.

But consideration of examples with several occurrences of colour terms in the belief context shows that we need to distinguish for every occurrence of a colour term in the that-clause whether it is used to ascribe phenomenal or nonphenomenal belief (compare belief description (5) below). I therefore propose to attach the subscripts 'p' (for 'phenomenal') and 'np' (for 'nonphenomenal') to colour terms within belief contexts to express the intended distinction. Using this subscripting convention we may describe Marianna's epistemic situation by the following claims:

(1') Marianna believes that the sky appears $blue_{np}$ to normally sighted people.

(2') Marianna does not believe that the sky appears red_{np} to normally sighted people.

---

[9] The relation between belief about colour properties of concrete objects ('x believes that roses are red') and belief about colour appearances ('x believes that roses appear red to normally sighted people') is discussed in Nida-Rümelin 1993, chapter 5.

(3') Marianna believes that the sky appears red$_p$ to normally sighted people.

(4') Marianna does not believe that the sky appears blue$_p$ to normally sighted people.

(5) Marianna believes that blue$_{np}$ objects appear red$_p$ to normally sighted people.

Colour terms should only be thus subscripted within belief contexts and — more generally — within the description of propositional attitudes and they are used to distinguish different possible readings of the description as a whole. Accepting this subscripting convention within the description of propositional attitudes does not force us to introduce subscripts for colour terms also outside such contexts. In my view, there is no way to introduce a corresponding distinction for colour terms outside propositional attitudes.[10]

I have been assuming and will argue below that phenomenal belief (and nonphenomenal belief as well) is belief about something that may or may not be the case. Most contemporary philosophers think of such beliefs as having propositions as their content. Therefore, for them the question immediately arises how we should describe the propositions believed in phenomenal and in nonphenomenal belief. Furthermore, who thinks that believing is a relation between a believer and a proposition will ask whether the distinction here introduced is meant as a distinction between two kinds of belief relations (in this case there would be different ways of believing a proposition) or whether the distinction is concerned with the second *relatum* of the belief relation and thus is meant as a distinction between different kinds of propositions. What ontological consequences result from the knowledge argument depends on the view one takes about this question. But

---

[10] If there were a 'corresponding distinction' (in the sense here intended) between 'red$_p$' (which would be a colour term taken on its 'phenomenal reading) and 'red$_{np}$' (colour term on its nonphenomenal reading), then this distinction between phenomenal and nonphenomenal interpretations of colour terms could be used to distinguish the content of phenomenal and nonphenomenal beliefs. The content of the belief that the sky appears blue$_{np}$ would then be given by the content of the sentence 'the sky appears blue$_{np}$' and analogously for phenomenal belief. The reason why I think this picture is completely misguided, is — very roughly — that there is no nonphenomenal concept of red such that whoever believes something of the colour red nonphenomenally, believes it about red 'under this nonphenomenal concept'. What people who have nonphenomenal beliefs about a colour share is not their conceptual access to the colour at issue but rather the way their belief is acquired and the way it is thereby embedded in a certain social context of a specific language community. I do not deny that it might make sense to distinguish different senses of colour terms outside belief context. I just deny that such a distinction would correspond, in the simple way sketched above, to the epistemological distinction here proposed.

a clear understanding of the distinction does not presuppose a decision between the two views about it sketched above.[11]

The distinction is not meant as a diagnosis of a normal kind of ambiguity that is already there in natural language.[12] By a 'normal kind of ambiguity in natural language' I mean cases where a hearer of a sentence containing the ambigious term has first to find out, e.g. by the context or by asking, in which of the two senses the term is presently used, before he can possibly understand the assertion at issue. This is not so in the case of sentences that describe propositional attitudes with respect to colour. If someone says in a normal life situation about a person who refuses to buy green salad tomatoes 'she thinks that green tomatoes are immature', we can understand what he asserts without disambiguating. There is no need to ask 'in which of the two senses do you mean this belief description?' So, the distinction between phenomal and nonphenomenal belief (and the corresponding distinction for other propositional attitudes) does not correspond to a normal ambiguity in natural language in the sense explained above. The reason for this is, simply, the following: in normal life situations the truth conditions for phenomenal and those for nonphenomenal belief are always simultaneously fulfilled, or at least we normally implicitly assume that this is so. Unusual epistemic situations that are in relevant respects analogous to the one of Marianna normally do not occur.[13] But it is only in these unusual situations that the truth conditions for phenomenal and nonphenomenal belief may 'fall apart', and only when this may happen is it necessary to add what reading is meant in the relevant belief descriptions.

[11] An analogous question arises in the case of *de se* belief. Some have claimed that *de se* belief has a special content (*de se* propositions), others think that *de se* attitudes involve a specific relation to the proposition at issue, still others claim that *de se* belief is not propositional at all. In this case too, one must — in a sense — have gained a clear understanding of what is meant by '*de se*' beliefs before one can start to discuss these issues (see e.g. Perry 1979; Chisholm 1981; Sosa 1983).

[12] I owe this insight to a discussion with Andreas Kemmerling.

[13] An exception would be the case of pseudonormal people if they really exist which is presented and discussed at length in Nida-Rümelin, 1995. I will use this example several times in the following and therefore I here explain the case briefly. According to an empirical hypothesis about the inheritance of red/green blindness, there are people who have their receptors on the the retina filled with photopigments in a specific unusual way. For this specific unusual distribution of photopigments, the so-called opponent process theory of colour vision predicts an 'inversion' of red and green, that is to say: what appears greenish to normal people appears reddish to them, and vice versa. Pseudonormal people would call those objects red that appear green to them (and vice versa). They would express the opinion that something appears $green_p$ to a person, using the term 'red'. To describe the epistemic states of pseudonormal people the distinction between phenomenal and nonphenomenal belief is needed (for a discussion of this thesis and its consequences for the philosophy of language see Nida-Rümelin, 1996a). The assumption that pseudonormal people exist does not imply the possibility of undetectable qualia inversion, nor the possibility of qualia inversion in a case of functional 'equivalence'. For scientific literature about the empirical hypothesis of pseudonormal vision see Piantanida 1974 and Boynton 1979.

III. A Few Remarks About the Status of the Proposed Distinction

This section adresses questions that are likely to occur to readers familiar with the discussion of propositional attitudes within the analytical tradition when they are first confronted with the present epistemological proposal. The results of this section are only presupposed in the following discussion in the sense that they answer objections that are likely to be raised against the proposed distinction between phenomenal and nonphenomenal belief.

One might be tempted to think that the phenomenal / nonphenomenal distinction here proposed is only a special case of the so-called *de re / de dicto* distinction. On this view, phenomenal beliefs would be *de re* beliefs that have a special kind of entity, namely colours, as their objects. But this interpretation is likely to evoke misunderstandings. One might erroneously conclude that the well-known problems of the *de re / de dicto* distinction need to be solved before one can reasonably accept the distinction between phenomenal and nonphenomenal belief. Also, one might be tempted to conclude that the proposals for a precise account of the *de re / de dicto* distinction proposed in the literature could simply be taken over to account for the phenomenal / nonphenomenal distinction. I cannot discuss these possible claims in detail here, but I wish to explain briefly how I think one should see the interconnection between the phenomenal / nonphenomenal and the *de re / de dicto* distinction.[14]

The intuition behind the *de re / de dicto* distinction can be seen by a comparison of the following two cases. Anna believes that the best dolphin swimmer of Munich is broad-shouldered and her reasons to believe this are certain general convictions: She believes that every good dolphin swimmer is broad-shouldered, she thinks there is one person who is the best at this swimming discipline in the Bavarian capital and she thinks that there are good dolphin swimmers in Munich. Anna has no idea who is the best dolphin swimmer in this city. Maria, by contrast, knows the best dolphin swimmer of Munich (without however knowing that he is the best). Maria saw this person in a swimming competition and she saw that he is broad-shouldered. So Maria too believes (in a certain sense) that this person (the best dolphin swimmer in Munich) is broad-shouldered. Maria's belief is — in a sense — about this individual person (about this 'thing', this 'res', the belief is a paradigm case of so-called '*de re* belief'). Anna, by contrast, does not seem to have any opinion about this particular person. Her belief is a typical example for the idea underlying the notion of a 'mere' *de dicto* belief.

It is common to distinguish between the *de re / de dicto* dichotomy on the level of belief descriptions on the one side and the corresponding dichotomy on the level of the beliefs themselves on the other. The difference between *de re* and *de dicto* belief descriptions can be explained by their hidden

---

[14] For a concise and clear presentation of the *de re / de dicto* debate see Haas-Spohn 1989.

logical structure. Thus the following belief description (6) if interpreted on its *de dicto* reading can be paraphrazed by (6'):

(6) Anna believes that the best dolphin swimmer of Munich is broad-shouldered.

(6') Anna believes that there is someone who is the best dolphin swimmer of Munich and who also is broad-shouldered.

By contrast, the assertion (7), if interpreted on its *de re* reading can be paraphrased by (7'):

(7) Maria believes that the best dolphin swimmer of Munich is broad-shouldered.

(7') There is a person who is the best dolphin swimmer of Munich and who is believed by Maria to be broad-shouldered.

The quantifier ('there is someone who . . .') appears within the range of the belief predicate in (6') (the quantifier has 'narrow scopus') whereas in (7') it appears outside the belief predicate (the quantifier has wide scopus). It is sometimes claimed that there is nothing more behind the so-called *de re / de dicto* distinction than this syntactic ambiguity. Whoever tends to think that way, might suspect that there is nothing more to the phenomenal / nonphenomenal distinction here proposed either. If this were true then the phenomenal reading of (8) could be captured by paraphrasing with 'wide scopus' — see (8').

(8) Maria believes that the sky appears blue$_p$ to normally sighted people.

(8') There is a colour such that it is the colour blue and it is believed by Marianna to be the colour in which normally sighted people see the sky.

But this reformulation of (8) does not exclude a nonphenomenal reading. Marianna has learned the term 'blue' by people who refer to the colour blue using this term. Her nonphenomenal belief that the sky appears blue$_{np}$ to normally sigthed people, is, therefore, in a sense a belief about this colour, namely about blue. So the phenomenal / nonphenomenal distinction cannot be captured simply by pointing out the syntactic ambiguity at issue and the latter ambiguity cannot replace the distinction between phenomenal and nonphenomenal belief.

De re belief descriptions face the well-known problem that Quine pointed out using his famous Ortcutt-example:

> There is a certain man in a brown hat whom Ralph has glimpsed several times under questionable circumstances on which we need not enter here; suffice it to say that Ralph suspects he is a spy. Also there is a gray-haired man, vaguely known to Ralph as rather a pillar of the community, whom Ralph is not aware

of having seen except once at the beach. Now Ralph does not know it, but the men are one and the same. (Cited from Quine 1953.)

It would be natural to describe Ralph's beliefs as follows:

(9)   Ralph believes that the man with the brown hat is a spy.

(10) Ralph does not believe that the man at the beach is a spy.

These beliefs are beliefs about one and the same person whose name is 'Ortcutt' in Quine's story. Interpreted as *de re* belief descriptions (9) and (10) would have to be paraphrased by (9') and (10')[15]:

(9')   There is a man named Ortcutt who is believed by Ralph to be a spy.

(10') There is a man namend Ortcutt who is believed by Ralph to be no spy.

We thus have arrived at ascribing conflicting beliefs to Ralph which already appears problematic. Serious problems arise if one further accepts the following belief description (11) for the epistemic situation at issue and then paraphrases (11) with 'wide scopus' like in (11'):

(11) Ralph does not believe that the man at the beach is a spy.

(11') There is a man named Ortcutt who is not believed by Ralph to be a spy.

As is well-known, there is a controversy about whether (11') should be accepted for Ralph's epistemic situation. I cannot enter the debate about Quine's example here. I only recalled Quine's problem because it can help to gain a better understanding of how the phenomenal / nonphenomenal distinction and the *de re / de dicto* dichotomy are related to one another.

Confronted with Quine's problem one might at first think that the problem can be avoided by restricting *de re* belief descriptions to cases where the epistemic subject has a sufficiently direct epistemic access to the object of his or her belief. The reason why the difficulty arises in Quine's example is obviously the fact that Ralph does not recognize a person he already knows in new circumstances. So the relation of a person to the object of his or her belief should be so intimate that such a case is excluded. Restricting *de re* belief descriptions to such cases would therefore solve Quine's problem. But one quickly realizes that there does not seem to be any way to give a general characterization of the 'epistemic intimacy' required which is not *ad hoc* and which still allows *de re* belief descriptions to be at least sometimes adequate. This is so since 'it is in principle always thinkable that we do not recognize even the most familiar object in unusual circumstances

---

[15] In the formulations with 'wide scopus' the terms 'the man with the brown hat' and 'the man at the beach' occur outside the belief context and therefore can be replaced by an expression that designates the same person without thereby changing the truth value.

and thus mistake one thing for two'.[16] The situation is different in the case of belief about colours. Quine's problem can here be avoided in a natural way by simply restricting *de re* belief descriptions to phenomenal belief about colours. It is impossible for a rational person to have conflicting beliefs about one and the same colour. One will immediately see that this is so when trying to find counterexamples.[17] One might describe the situation as follows: We could say that a genuine *de re* belief in an intuitively obvious sense is a belief where the subject is so intimately related to the object of his or her belief that he or she is just incapable to commit the mistake that gives rise to Quine's problem. Phenomenal beliefs about colour are genuine *de re* beliefs in this sense and maybe phenomenal beliefs in general are the only kind of beliefs that are in this sense 'genuinely *de re*'. (This thesis and similar ones about the relation between the two epistemological distinctions at issue obviously can be considered only after having introduced the phenomenal / nonphenomenal distinction independently, without thereby already using the *de re* / *de dicto* distinction).

The above considerations should have shown among other things: (1) The precise relation between the two epistemological distinctions is a theoretical question that requires detailed examination. (2) It is possible to introduce the phenomenal / nonphenomenal distinction without thereby presupposing the *de re* / *de dicto* distinction and without thereby being committed to solving first the well-known problems of the latter.[18]

I will not assume in the following (although I think the claim can be defended) that phenomenal belief about colours is *de re* belief about colours. One more reason for not doing so is that this thesis seems to commit its proponent to saying something clarifying about the difficult question of what 'res' these special beliefs are about. But no special philosophical theory about the ontological status of colours is needed for a clear understanding and for a precise account of the epistemological distinction between phenomenal and nonphenomenal belief.

One might furthermore be tempted to think that phenomenal belief about the experiences of others is just a special kind of *de se* belief (of belief about oneself). When Marianna learns that the sky appears blue$_p$ to normally sighted people, she thereby acquires the belief that the sky appears to those people with respect to colour like this slide (the blue one) appears to her*.[19]

---

[16] Cited from Haas-Spohn 1989: S. 64 (my translation).

[17] This thesis is discussed in more detail in Nida-Rümelin 1993, 61 f. The idea underlying this solution of Quine's problem for belief about colours if of course related to the old idea that colours (and phenomenal qualities in general) are in a sense directly presented to the perceiver in his or her perception (or more general to the subject in his or her experience).

[18] Whoever makes a conceptual proposal should of course relate this proposal to concepts that are already commonly accepted. There is no room to do this here (but see Nida-Rümelin 1993: 48–63).

[19] I use Castañeda's '*' to indicate *de se* belief. See e.g. Castañeda 1967.

It might therefore appear as if Marianna's progress could be described in the following way: If we select an object that appears blue to Marianna, then we can describe her epistemic progress as consisting in having learned that the sky appears to others with respect to colour like this object appears to her*.

This thesis is interesting in the context of the argument from knowledge if combined with the view that the locution 'O appears to S in the same colour as O' appears to S'' or 'O appears to S with respect to colour like O' appears to S'' can be explicated in purely physicalist terms. Let us call 'physical *de se* knowledge', knowledge that involves self-attribution of physical properties (or of properties that can be explicated in physicalist terminology). Then according to the thesis at issue, phenomenal knowledge about the experiences of others would be physical *de se* kowledge. But, it is common opinion that *de se* belief and *de se* knowledge does not represent a problem for physicalism.[20] It would follow that the notion of phenomenal belief cannot help much in a defence of the knowledge argument.

But the thesis that phenomenal belief (in the sense here introduced) is nothing but physical *de se* belief is untenable. This thesis assumes the equivalence of the following two assertions:

(12) Marianna believes that the sky appears red$_p$ to Peter.

(13) Whenever Marianna is visually presented with a red object she forms the *de se* belief that the sky appears to Peter with respect to colour like this object presently (*de nunc*) appears to her*.[21]

But the equivalence between (12) and (13) only holds under the assumption that the red object actually appears red to Marianna in the given circumstances. It does not hold if Marianna is pseudonormal or if she is visually presented with the object at issue under unusual lighting conditions that make it appear e.g. brown.[22] So (13) must be changed into (13') in order to get an assertions that is true just in case (12) holds of Marianna:

(13') When Marianna is visually presented with an object that appears red to her under the then prevailing conditions, she forms the *de se* (and *de nunc*) belief that this object presently (*de nunc*) appears to her* (*de se*) with respect to colour like the sky appears to Peter.

Now, quite obviously, the equivalence between (12) and (13') is to be explained in the following way: When Marianna is visually presented with an object that appears red to her under the then prevailing cirumstances, she

[20] It do not subscribe to this view here but it would be bad for my argument if I first had to show that this view is false.

[21] *De nunc* belief is belief we normally express using the term 'now'. For a discussion of *de nunc* belief see e.g. Sosa 1983.

[22] For pseudonormality see footnote 13.

knows that the object presently (*de nunc*) appears red$_p$ to her* (*de se*). That the epistemic subject does have this *de nunc–de se* belief in the circumstances at issue is implicitly assumed in the claim that (12) and (13') are equivalent. This is not a decisive argument but a hint at what is wrong with the claim under consideration. A genuine refutation of the claim that phenomenal belief is physical *de se* belief can be accomplished using a more complex thought experiment (there is no room, however, to present it here).[23]

Furthermore, phenomenal belief is not just a kind of indexical belief. This idea might appear plausible since we could inform Marianna about what she did not yet know (in the phenomenal sense about the experiences of others, e.g. when they look at the sky) by 'ostensive teaching' (e.g. by pointing to a blue object saying 'this is what we call "blue"'). This might lead to the conclusion that (12) can be paraphrased by (15):

(15) Every red object **O** is such that the the following holds: If Marianna is visually presented with **O**, then she will form an indexical belief that she could express saying while demonstratively refering to **O** (e.g. by pointing): 'The sky appears to Peter with respect to colour like *this*'.

However, neither the conclusion of (15) from (12), nor the conclusion of (12) from (15), is valid in general. For example, if Marianna is pseudonormal (green objects appear red to her and red objects appear green to her), (15) can be true and (12) false: If Marianna does not know that she* is pseudonormal then she will express her phenomenal belief that the sky appears red$_p$ to Peter by demonstrative reference to green objects (that appear red to her) and she will have no tendency to express the relevant indexical belief when presented with red objects. The same example refutes the claim that (15) implies (12). The non-equivalence of (12) and (15) can be seen in another way: Suppose there is a measuring instrument that allows blind people to identify the colour of objects on the basis of their physical surface properties. Then a blind person who is allowed to use this instrument when confronted with a coloured object can fulfill the property ascribed to Marianna in (15) although he or she does not have the belief ascribed to Marianna in (12).[24]

Having this last counterexample in mind a proponent of the indexical interpretation of phenomenal belief might try to defend his position requiring a visual confrontation of the subject with the object at issue in a revised version of (15). But this move does not help for a defence of the claim that phenomenal belief is just a special kind of indexical belief. If phenomenal

---

[23] This refutation is presented in Nida-Rümelin 1993, section 4.3.

[24] I owe this example to a comment of Michael Pietroforte. The two articles Spohn 1996 and Nida-Rümelin 1996a discuss in detail the related question whether colour terms are hidden indexicals.

beliefs were nothing but indexical beliefs then the way in which the corresponding demonstrative reference is achieved should not matter.

IV. Marianna's Epistemic Progress

Jackson's example appears in a new light when reconsidered having Marianna's case in mind. When Mary is finally released she acquires new knowledge about the experiences of others (she learns e.g. that the sky appears blue$_p$ to people with normal colour perception). But Mary does *not* gain this item of knowledge simply by gaining sight and thereby acquaintance with colours. A disadvantage of Jackson's example is that it fails to distinguish two steps of epistemic progress that can be distinguished clearly in Marianna's case. When Marianna gains sight and thereby acquaintance with blue, green, yellow and red she takes a first step of epistemic progress which consists in her gaining *epistemic access* to questions that she could not have considered before. Only after this first step, namely when she knows red, green, blue and yellow by personal experience, can she consider the question whether the sky appears blue$_p$ or red$_p$ or yellow$_p$ or green$_p$ to normally sighted people. She can weigh these four possibilities against each other, she might assign subjective probabilities to these alternatives. These four possibilities were epistemically inaccessible to her before she left her black-and-white environment. Having gained epistemic access to questions she could not have considered before, is already a kind of *epistemic progress* — although she has not yet gained any new item of the relevant propositional knowledge.

A second step of epistemic progress is required to find out which of the hypotheses she is now able to consider is in fact true. Jackson's Mary seems to take these two steps at once. This is why Jackson's case fails to show explicitly that there is a kind of knowledge inaccessible to blind Mary which *does* involve the elimination of 'hitherto open possibilities'.[25]

Using the notion of phenomenal belief we can describe more in detail what happens when Marianna takes the second step of epistemic progress. Before her release Marianna believes that the sky appears red$_p$ to normally sighted people. She expects the sight of a red$_p$ sky for the moment in which she will leave the house. She entertains — in other words — the *de se* expectation that the sky will appear red$_p$ to her*. When she finally leaves the house on a sunny day she will realize with surprise that her *de se* expectation was mistaken. She will then rationally conclude (since she believes herself to be normally sighted) that — contrary to what she had

---

[25] David Lewis (1988) has objected to the view that Mary gains propositional knowledge after her release by pointing out that the acquisition of 'knowledge of what it's like' does not seem to be connected with an elimation of hitherto open possibilities. Using the notion of phenomenal belief to describe Mary's epistemic progress allows for an answer to this objection. Every acquistion of an item of phenomenal knowledge involves the exclusion of other hitherto open *epistemic* possibilitities.

thought — the sky appears blue$_p$ to normally sighted people. When Marianna finally sees the sky she also detects an error in her former assumptions about the normal use of language. When she still believed that the sky appears red$_p$ to normally sighted people, she thought — so to speak — of the wrong colour that it was the colour referred to by 'blue'. More precisely her mistake about language should be described this way: She believed that red$_p$ objects are called 'blue' and she believed that 'object **O** appears blue to person **S**' is truely asserted of a person **S** just in case **O** appears red$_p$ to that person. Note that a precise formulation of her mistake about language already requires the use of the notion of phenomenal belief. Marianna can make this mistake only when she is capable of entertaining phenomenal belief, so only after she has taken the first step of epistemic progress described above. (Her epistemic progress involves the capability to make new errors, which might seem paradox at first sight but is not on a second: who gains epistemic access to new questions also acquires the new ability to believe in the wrong answers). In the present context it is important to see the following: Marianna's second step of epistemic progress does not *consist* in her revision of a mistake about language (although it goes along with such a revision). It would be a mistake to think that Marianna, when she finally sees the sky, does not learn more than that blue$_p$ objects are called 'blue' and that somthing is said to appear 'blue' just in case it appears blue$_p$. Given her rich background knowledge this new knowledge about language is necessarily accompanied by the acquisition of a rich body of new phenomenal knowledge. Suppose she had learned that objects appear blue$_{np}$ to a person iff certain physiological conditions are fulfilled. Then her new knowledge about language goes along with the acquistion of the new item of phenomenal belief that things appears blue$_p$ to human beings iff these conditions obtain.

V. Phenomenal Knowledge as Knowledge about What is the Case

Before I answer possible objections against the view that phenomenal knowledge is knowledge in the strict sense about something that is the case, I will briefly sketch a few positive reasons for this claim.

(1) The epistemological notion here introduced allows for the distinction between belief and knowledge. Marianna believes e.g. that the sky appears red$_p$, but she does not know this, since what she believes is false. There is no analogous pair of notions (phenomenal belief on the one hand and phenomenal knowledge on the other) in the case of practical capacities, nor is there any such analogous pair of notions in the case of so-called knowledge of what it's like. That there is a corresponding notion of belief is of course typical for knowledge in the full-fledged sense.

(2) In normal cases of belief about something that is the case we can specify the conditions under which the belief of the person is correct using normal assertive sentences. For the case of 'knowing what it's like to have a perception of blue' it is hard to see how one could fulfil this possible requirement. First of all, one would have to explain what could be meant by a corresponding notion of belief about 'what it is like to have a perception of blue', second one would have to find a sentence S such that S is true iff the corresponding belief is true. This task appears almost unsolvable in the case of knowing what it's like. For most cases of phenomenal belief, by contrast, it does not represent any problem.[26] Marianna's phenomenal belief that the sky appears red_p to Peter would be true iff the sentence 'the sky appears red to Peter' were true.

(3) Phenomenal belief and phenomenal knowledge can be ascribed in the normal way, by using that-clauses, which again is typical for belief and knowledge about something that is the case. Also — as in the case of *de re*, *de dicto*, *de se* and *de nunc* beliefs — the distinction naturally carries over to other propositional attitudes: Marianna may hope that the sky appears red_p to normal perceivers, she may wonder whether the sky appears red_p or she may doubt that it appears red_p to normal perceivers, etc.

(4) Also, as in the case of other opinions about what is the case, one can easily construct situations in which Marianna might rationally assign some specific subjective probability to the alternative that the sky appears red_p to normal perceivers. This observation too strengthens the intuition that phenomenal belief is belief about something that might or might not be the case.

(5) It makes sense to ask whether a specific phenomenal belief is rationally justified. Consider the following case. Marianna has seen a painting showing a landscape with a red sky. She has reason to think that the painting is naturalistic. She has reason to think that she* is normally sighted and that she saw the painting under normal lighting conditions. In this case Marianna may have good reason to think that the sky appears red_p to normally sighted people. The fact that there is room for the notion of rational justification is one more reason to think that phenomenal belief is belief in the full sense of belief about a state of affairs.

The above arguments in favour of the thesis that phenomenal knowledge is factual knowledge would have to be defeated by a proponent of the view

---

[26] An exception is e.g. the belief that $blue_{np}$ things appear $blue_p$ (for a discussion of this see Nida-Rümelin, 1996b, section 6).

that Mary only gains a bundle of practical capacities after her release. But, all the same, I wish to examine this kind of objection more closely (I will call this objection the 'ability objection'). The reason why the ability objection seems to me to deserve a more detailed discussion is the observation that it appears to be surprisingly resistant against counterarguments and conflicting intuitions in discussion with many people (maybe one main cause for this is the celebrity of one of its proponents). The above mentioned properties of phenomenal knowledge that are typical for genuine knowledge are not shared by knowledge of what it's like.[27] This counts against the thesis that knowledge of what it's like is genuine knowledge. So the ability thesis may actually appear plausible as long as one starts from the assumption that Marianna's progress after her release is properly described by saying that she acquires knowledge of what it's like. Let us now see how the analogous objection would have to be formulated once it is accepted that the notion of phenomenal knowledge provides a more adequate account of Mary's real or apparent epistemic progress.

Some of these abilities normally mentioned in this context can quickly be excluded as a possible basis for an analysis of phenomenal knowledge, because Marianna already acquires these abilities after her first step of epistemic progress when she still has not acquired the relevant items of phenomenal knowledge at issue. Marianna is able, for instance, to imagine something blue at will or to remember something blue before she learns that the sky appears $blue_p$ to human beings with normal colour perception.

A first answer to this defence against the ability objection could be the following: The relevant sense of 'ability to imagine (or to remember) something blue' is the ability to obey to the verbally given imperative 'imagine something blue' or 'remember an occasion when you saw something blue'. Marianna indeed gains this capacity only after her second step of epistemic progress. At a point of her history when she still believes that the sky appears red_p to normally sighted people she will imagine something red or remember an experience of red when trying to obey to the above imperatives. So the defence above cannot be repeated here. But this does not show that Marianna's progress (after her second step) is not a genuine epistemic one that involves new knowledge of facts. It is quite common that the gaining of factual knowledge goes along with the acquisition of the practical ability to obey to certain imperatives (consider: 'point to the person who is the thief!' or 'choose the right answer!'). In these normal cases the new factual knowledge explains why the person has acquired the capacity at issue. Now, quite obviously, this also applies in the case presently under consideration. Marianna is able to obey to those imperatives after her second step of epistemic progress *because* she now has acquired

[27] An analysis of 'knowing what it's like' in terms of phenomenal belief is proposed in Nida-Rümelin 1996b: section 6 and in Nida-Rümelin 1993: 70–6.

the phenomenal knowledge needed for this practical ability. Before Marianna corrects her mistake about the normal use of language she believes that a person who wishes to obey to the imperative 'Imagine something blue!' must imagine something red_p and that a person must remember an experience of red_p in order to obey to the second imperative mentioned above. So her incapacity to obey to these imperatives is due to a lack of phenomenal knowledge and her capacity to do so after her second step of epistemic progress is due to an acquisition of new phenomenal knowledge.

There is a further interesting capacity sometimes mentioned in this context, namely the capacity to predict the behaviour of others by imaginative experiments. (See Nemirow 1979; 1980.) Now there certainly is an interesting connection between the capacity to make such predictions on the basis of 'correct empathy' on the one hand and phenomenal knowledge on the other, but in this case too it appears obvious to me that the capacity at issue does not constitute the kind of knowledge at issue, but is, rather, in fortunate cases the *result* of phenomenal knowledge. Unfortunately, there is no room for further elaboration of this point in the present paper.[28]

Whoever claims that phenomenal knowledge is nothing but a bundle of practical capacities, should propose a concrete analysis of phenomenal knowledge in terms of such abilities. How could such an analysis look like? A proponent of this view might propose (17) as an analysis of (16):

(16) Marianna knows that ripe tomatoes appear red_p to normally sighted people.

(17) Marianna has acquired the practical capacity to select (on the basis of visual perception) those objects that appear to normally sighted people with respect to colour like ripe tomatoes.

But this proposal can again be refuted by considering the case of pseudonormal people. (See footnote 13.) If Marianna were pseudonormal without knowing that she is, she could fulfil (17) and still believe that ripe tomatoes appear $green_p$ (and do not appear red_p) to normally sighted people. Again, this counterexample renders intuitively quite obvious what is wrong with the analysis considered here. Under normal conditions, when Marianna has acquired the item of phenomenal knowledge ascribed to her in (16), then she also has the capacity described in (17) since, when presented with red objects, she knows that these objects appear red_p to her and she believes herself to be normally sighted. The practical capacity described in (17) is only a symptom for her having the phenomenal knowledge at issue but it can be — in unusual circumstances, as is shown by the example of pseudonormal vision — a symptom of a different phenomenal belief as well.

---

[28] A precise account of the relation between phenomenal knowledge and successful empathy (correct imagination of what other people experience) is proposed in Nida-Rümelin 1996c.

The proponent of the ability objection against the claim that phenomenal knowledge is genuine knowledge, also has to give an analysis of phenomenal belief (not just of phenomenal knowledge). So the question arises how he could interpret for instance (18):

(18) Marianna believes that the sky appears red$_p$ to normally sighted people.

He might consider the following proposal (19):

(19) If Marianna were asked to select those objects (out of several differently coloured objects) that have the colour that normally sighted people experience when looking at the sky, then she would select the red objects.

But again, (19) could be true of Marianna and (18) false, if Marianna is pseudonormal but does not know that she is.

I wish to leave the development of more sophisticated versions to the proponent of the ability objection. I hope to have convinced the reader that the ability objection loses its intuitive appeal once one accepts that Mary's epistemic progress is adequately described in the way here proposed (as an acquisition of phenomenal knowledge and not as an acquisition of 'knowing what it's like') and that it certainly is not obvious how the claim that phenomenal knowledge too is nothing but a bundle of practical abilities could be argued for in a convincing manner.

VI. A New Look at the Argument from Knowledge

Assuming that phenomenal knowledge is a special kind of factual knowledge about phenomenal states (knowledge about something that is the case), the argument from knowledge can be stated quite simply in the following way: There is a kind of knowledge about phenomenal states that is accessible only to an epistemic subject who knows the kind of phenomenal state at issue (the kind of state the relevant item of knowledge is about) by personal experience (by having been in that kind of state). But it is commonly accepted that an understanding of a description given in purely physicalist terms does not presuppose being acquainted with any special kind of phenomenal state by personal experience.[29] Therefore, a description of a conscious being given in purely physicalist terminology is epistemically incomplete in the following sense: A rational epistemic subject who is able to understand any physicalist description of whatever kind, may lack

[29] As is common in the discussion 'physicalist' terminology is used here in a very broad sense that includes not just the terms of physics but also of e.g. chemistry and neurobiology. Functionalist and behaviourist terminology is included as well. 'Physicalist terminology' also includes the terminology used in future developments of the mentioned empirical disciplines as long as they do not use mentalist vocabulary in an irreducible manner. 'Physical' knowledge is all knowledge that can be conveyed using physicalist terminology.

specific items of knowledge about another conscious being that in principle cannot be communicated to the subject at issue by any physicalist description, no matter how detailed and complex this description may be.

Note that for this formulation of the argument it is unnecessary to speculate about the epistemic situation of a person who has 'complete knowledge' in some relevant respect. Instead, it is sufficient to assume that the kind of knowledge at issue (contrary to so-called physical knowledge) presupposes having had certain specific kinds of experiences. When formulated this way several objections raised against the original version of the knowledge argument can be immediately rejected as irrelevant. This is true for those objections that are based on the claim that a physiologist who really knew everything 'physical' there is to know about human colour vision could immediately decide which colour is the red one when visually confronted with colours for the first time. (Cf. Churchland 1985; Hardin 1992.) The debate about this claim is irrelevant since the argument is already saved if it is accepted that e.g. a person born blind cannot have phenomenal knowledge about the experiences of others although he or she can acquire every kind of 'physical knowledge'. The question when and under what conditions a person born blind would *acquire* phenomenal knowledge when she finally gains sight is then, obviously, of no importance.

I have argued that Mary gains new factual knowledge after her release. But, in general, new factual knowledge does not necessarily involve knowledge of new facts. This can be seen by the example of *de se* knowledge: Maria might know that Maria is in Munich and yet not know that she* is in Munich (she might have forgotten that she* is Maria). When she finds out that she* is in Munich she certainly gains new knowledge. But there is good reason to doubt that she thereby has gained knowledge of a new fact, a fact she did not know before in some other way. After all, what she believes in her belief that Maria is in Munich is true iff Maria is in Munich and the same holds for her *de se* belief: Maria's belief that she* is in Munich is true just in case Maria is in Munich. This observation seems to support the view that in gaining the new item of knowledge that she* is in Munich Maria gets to know an old fact (that she already new before) in a new way, namely in what one might call the '*de se* mode'.

One might consider the view that the analogous claim holds for phenomenal belief. Many philosophers have argued that Mary gains new factual knowledge but thereby gains knowledge of old facts that she already knew before in some other way.[30] The original intention of the knowledge argument was to show that there are non-physical facts, facts that cannot be expressed in a physicalist language. But the above version of the argument

---

[30] The thesis that Mary gains new knowledge about facts she already knew before in another way has been sustained by several authors (see e.g. Horgan 1984; Loar 1990; Tye 1986).

only has an epistemological result that does not yet lead to the intended ontological conclusion. What is needed is a further assumption that can take the following form: The content of phenomenal beliefs are special propositions that cannot be believed in a 'nonphenomenal' way and what is known in phenomenal knowledge are facts that cannot be known otherwise. The following thesis (20) is one possible version of this additional assumption.

(20) Marianna has knowledge of the fact expressed by 'the sky appears blue to Peter' iff Marianna knows that the sky appears blue$_p$ to Peter.

A possible formulation of the contrary opinion could be based on some version of the view that types of mental states are identical with certain types of physiological states. The proponent of such an identity thesis could base his rejection of (20) on the following claim: for an appropriately chosen brain state S the two sentences 'the sky appears blue to Peter' and 'the sky causes under appropriate circumstances a brain state of kind S in Peter's brain' express one and the same fact. If Marianna knows that the sky produces this kind S of a physiological state in Peter's brain, then she has knowledge of the same fact that is also the content of her item of phenomenal knowlege that the sky appears blue$_p$ to Peter. Therefore, according to the identity theorist, (20) is unacceptable and the argument from knowledge does not lead to the ontological result that was originally intended.[31]

I do not wish to comment this possible objection of the identity theorist here which would require a detailed discussion. Let me just note the following: the claim that new phenomenal knowledge does not involve knowledge of new facts is considerably more problematic than the analogous thesis sketched above for *de se* knowledge. In both cases the claim implicitly assumes a specific view about the conditions under which facts that are verbally expressed in different ways are numerically identical. In the case of the claim at issue for *de se* knowledge, the implicitly accepted sufficient condition for identity of facts is based on the notion of identity of individuals (the facts at issue are considered identical because Maria is identical with the person Maria refers to using the term 'I'). The sufficient condition for 'fact identity' presupposed in the corresponding claim about phenomenal knowledge, by contrast, is based on a notion of identity between properties (between the property of being in a specific brain state and having an impression of blue). Numerical identity is certainly applicable to concrete individual things. It is, however, questionable whether numerical identity between properties is an acceptable notion at all and how — if the answer is positive — identity between properties should be explicated.[32]

---

[31] For a discussion of (20) and other versions of a further assumption that can be used to get to the ontological consequence at issue see Nida-Rümelin 1996b, sections 7 and 9.

[32] For a recent discussion of identity theories see Bealer 1994.

So I will content myself with the weaker, only epistemological result of the argument from knowledge here. Actually, it is possible to show that this result is stonger than it might appear at first sight. The result is sufficient for the defence of several central antimaterialist intuitions. For example, using this epistemological result it is possible to argue for the indispensability of phenomenal vocabulary in the empirical sciences of conscious beings. Contrary to a wide-spread opinion among materialists, certain well-founded epistemic interests that the empirical sciences can and should respond to, cannot be satisfied by these sciences unless they make use of phenomenal terminology. A precise account of this claim and of how it can be argued for can be based on the here proposed version of the argument from knowledge. But there is no room left here to elaborate this point.[33]

References

Bealer, G. (1994). Mental properties. *Journal of Philosophy*, **91**, 185–208.

Boynton, R.M. (1979). *Human Color Vision*. New York: Rinehart and Winston.

Castañeda, H-N. (1967). Indicators and quasi-indicators. *American Philosophical Quarterly*, **4**, 85–100.

Chisholm, R.M. (1981). *The First Person*. Brighton: Harvester Press.

Churchland, P. (1985). Reduction, qualia and the direct introspection of brain states. *Journal of Philosophy*, **82**, 8–28.

Haas-Spohn, U. (1989). Zur Interpretation von Einstellungszuschreibungen. In G. Falkenberg (ed): *Wissen, Wahrnehmen, Glauben*. Tübingen: Max Niemeyer Verlag.

Hardin, C.L. (1992). Physiology, phenomenology and Spinoza's true colors. In Beckermann *et al.* 1992.

Horgan, T. (1984). Jackson on physicalism and qualia. *Philosophical Quarterly*, **34**, 147–52.

Jackson, F. (1984a). Epiphenomenal qualia. *Philosophical Quarterly*, **34**, 127–36.

Jackson, F. (1984b). What Mary didn't know. *Journal of Philosophy*, **83**, 291–5.

Lewis, D. (1988). What experience teaches. *Proceedings of the Russellian Society*, University of Sidney. Reprinted in Lycan 1990.

Loar, B. (1990). Phenomenal States. *Philosophical Perspectives 4: Action Theory and the Philosophy of Mind*, 81–107.

Nagel, T. (1974). What is it like to be a bat? *Philosophical Review*, **83**, 435–50.

Nagel, T. (1986). *The View from Nowhere*. Oxford: Oxford University Press.

Nemirow, E.L. (1979). Functionalism and the subjective quality of experience. Dissertation at Stanford University Press, unpublished.

Nemirow, E.L. (1980). Review of Thomas Nagel 'Mortal Questions'. *Philosophical Review*, **LXXXIX**, 473–7.

Nida-Rümelin, M. (1993). *Farben und phänomenales Wissen*. St. Augustin: Academia.

Nida-Rümelin, M. (1995). Pseudonormal vision. An actual case of qualia inversion? *Philosophical Studies*.

---

[33] A detailed presentation of this argument is the topic of Nida-Rümelin 1996b.

Nida-Rümelin, M. (1996a). The character of color predicates: A phenomenalist view. In M. Anduschus, A.Newen & W.Künne (eds), *Direct Reference, Indexicality and Propositional Attitudes*. Stanford: CSLI.

Nida-Rümelin, M. (1996b). On belief about experiences: An epistemological distinction applied to the knowledge argument (submitted).

Nida-Rümelin, M. (1996c). Is the naturalization of qualitative experience possible or sensible? In Carrier & Machamer 1996.

Piantanida, T.P. (1974). A replacement model of X-linked recessive colour vision defects. *Annals of Human Genetics*, **37**, 393–404.

Perry, J. (1979). The problem of the essential indexical. *Noûs*, **XIII**, 474–97.

Quine, W.V. (1953). Quantifiers and propositional attitude. *The Journal of Philosophy*, **53**, 177–87.

Sosa, E. (1983). Consciousness of the self and of the present. In J.E. Tomberlin (ed.), *Agent, Language and the Structure of the World*. Indianapolis: Hackett Publishing Company.

Spohn, W. (1996). The character of color predicates: A materialist view. In M. Anduschus, A.Newen & W.Künne (eds), *Direct Reference, Indexicality and Propositional Attitudes*. Stanford: CSLI.

Tye, Michael (1986). The subjective qualities of experience. *Mind*, **45**, 1–17.

William G. Lycan

A Limited Defence of Phenomenal Information

As is no great secret, Thomas Nagel (1974) and Frank Jackson (1982) have argued that a complete scientific psychology must forever elude us, because, in particular, the subjective phenomenal character of a sensory experience resists explanation or even description in scientific terms: one might know every 'objective', third-person scientific fact there was to know about a human subject — her/his physics, chemistry, neurobiology, functional organization, whatever — and still not know 'what it's like' for that subject to experience the sensation in question. It seems to follow that familiar versions of scientific physicalism or materialism are false.[1]

My purpose in this paper is to assess one distinctive and important defence of materialism against the Nagel-Jackson argument, that of Laurence Nemirow (1980; 1990) and David Lewis (1983; 1990). I shall argue that, as advertised, it is unsuccessful, though it can be reconstructed to advantage.

I. The Dialectic

Jackson offers the now familiar example of Mary, the brilliant colour scientist trapped in an entirely black-and-white laboratory (even she herself is painted black and white). Working through her modem and her television

---

[1] This objection to materialism originated (so far as I am aware) with Farrell (1950), though Farrell also provided what he believed to be an adequate rejoinder.

It should be noted that Nagel chooses not to infer the final conclusion, the falsity of materialism, but only that 'we cannot understand [materialism,] because we do not at present have any conception of how it might be true' (Nagel 1974: 446).

In two previous works (Lycan 1987; 1990a) I have rebutted Nagel and Jackson in my own way, and provided what I think is quite an attractive conception of how materialism accommodates the subjective character of sensory experience, but my concern here is with a different line of response.

monitor, she becomes scientifically omniscient as regards the physics and chemistry of colour, the neurophysiology of colour vision, and every other conceivably relevant scientific fact; we may even suppose that she becomes scientifically omniscient, period. Yet when she is finally released from her captivity and ventures into the outside world, she sees colours for the first time, and learns something: namely, she learns what it is like to see red, blue, ochre and the rest of the gang. Thus she has acquired information that is (by hypothesis) outside the whole domain of science — intrinsically subjective phenomenal information.

Nemirow and Lewis (hereafter N-L) respond by agreeing that Mary learns something new, adequately expressed by the now cant phrase 'what it's like', but then they move to deny that to know what it's like to be in a particular sensory state is a propositional matter, a knowing-that. Rather, according to N-L, 'knowing what it's like' is only a knowing-how, an ability. Nemirow thinks it is an ability to imagine — in the case of a colour, the ability to visualize that colour. Lewis adds (1990: 515–16) that it can also comprehend abilities to remember experiences, to recognize similar ones when they occur, and to imagine related experiences that one has never had. Thus, what Mary gains is not a special, perspectival sort of phenomenal information; it is not information at all.

I could live with N-L's bold contention; indeed I think they are half right. But for what it is worth, I believe they are also and importantly half wrong. I shall argue that they have posed a false dichotomy, between phenomenal information in a materialistically objectionable sense and mere non-propositional abilities.

To begin, let me set out some positive arguments for the claim that what Mary gains is indeed propositional knowledge and not just a set of abilities. Later we shall evaluate those arguments in light of two distinctions that N-L have ignored.

II. Nine Arguments Against N-L

1. From meaning and syntax

Indirect-question clauses are closely related to 'that'-clauses, both in meaning and grammatically. In particular, instances of 'S knows wh—' are related to 'S knows that': 'S knows where X Vs' is true in virtue of S's knowing that X Vs at p, where 'p' suitably names some place; 'S knows when X Vs' is true in virtue of S's knowing that X Vs at t, where 't' suitably names some time; 'S knows who Vs' is true in virtue of S's knowing that N Vs, where 'N' suitably names some person.[2] There are close syntactic

---

[2] 'Suitably' in these formulations hides a multitude of technicalities (see Boër & Lycan 1986), but they do not affect the present issue.

relations as well (consider 'when'/'then', 'where'/'there', 'whither'/'thither' *et al.*).[3]

On this model, 'S knows what it's like to see blue' means roughly 'S knows that it is like Q to see blue,' where 'Q' suitably names some inner phenomenal property or condition. Therefore, N-L cannot strictly and literally use the 'knowing what it's like' locution; they must say that the Farrell-Nagel-Jackson formulation is erroneous and that those authors have mistaken a knowing-how *for* a knowing-what. If the rest of us continue to think that what Mary learns is *literally* what it is like to see the various colours, we should resist N-L.

Nemirow anticipates a similar point and responds (1990: 494–5) that the phrase 'what it's like' is

> a 'pseudo-singular term' . . . that has the grammatical form of a singular term but, on analysis, does not even purport to refer. Like . . . the term 'sake' in the sentence, 'she did it for her country's sake' . . . [T]he [ability] analysis should forestall the temptation to treat the expression 'what it's like' as a referring expression in virtue of its grammatical form.

Well. True, the ability analysis should forestall that temptation, *if* the analysis is supported by convincing syntactic and semantic evidence. Grammatical appearance can mask a strikingly different underlying logical reality. But, here as elsewhere, the burden of proof lies with the theorist who insists that reality differs from appearance. And in the present case the topic is grammar and logic, so the relevant evidence would be syntactic and semantic, of the sort deployed by linguists and linguistic semanticists; purely philosophical wish-fulfilment does not count. Yet Nemirow has provided no counter-evidence at all to the standard linguistic grounds for thinking that 'wh—'-complements are derived from 'that'-clauses. So my temptation to treat 'what it's like' as a referring expression rages on unhindered.

2. From possibility-elimination

As Lewis himself says (1990: 505), the acquisition of 'information' is often conceived as the elimination of possibilities: to receive a piece of information is to rule out a particular class of possible worlds as candidates for being *one's own* world. (Finally to narrow the candidates down to just one would be to become omniscient.) Sets of possible worlds constitute, or at least correspond to, propositions: intuitively, a given set corresponds to proposition P iff[*] it is the class of worlds at which P holds.

---

[3] For some relevant syntactic work, see Karttunen 1977, Hirschbühler 1979, and Groenendijk & Stokhof 1982.

[*] The term 'iff' is shorthand for the phrase 'if, and only if,' in logical argument.

But when Mary is released from her colourless room and undergoes her epiphany, surely she does eliminate some possibilities, e.g. that visual yellow might look phenomenally one way or another (say what we call 'pink') instead of the way it actually does look. The possible worlds she rules out form a set. A set of worlds is a proposition. So, for some proposition P_q, she has learned that P_q.

Though Lewis himself suggested this argument, he does not rebut it directly. He does say (1990: 512) that 'the alternative possibilities must be unthinkable beforehand':

> I cannot present to myself in thought a range of alternative possibilities about what it might be like to taste Vegemite. That is because I cannot imagine either what it *is* like to taste Vegemite, or any alternative way that it *might* be like but in fact isn't ... I can't even pose the question that phenomenal information is supposed to answer: is it this way or that?

But this does not address the point made above, which was just that *there are* multiple possibilities. My argument does not require that Mary or anyone else have imagined those possibilities in advance, or even that anyone would ever be able to do so.

3. From theoretical knowledge

> ... [I]t would be perverse to claim that bare experience can provide us *only* with various practical abilities, and never with theoretical knowledge. By being shown an unfamiliar color, I acquire information about its similarities and compatibilities with other colors, and its effects on other of our mental states: surely I seem to be acquiring certain facts about that color and the visual experience of it (Levin 1986: 479).[4]

Nemirow obliquely responds to this:

> In reasoning from what an experience is like, a person begins by imagining particular experiences, and draws specific inferences about actual or future sensory experiences, none of which is itself critical to the function of the imagination. Such lines of inference in turn begin to account for the general utilities of imagining that cause imagining to appear to grant direct access to the essential qualities of experience (1990: 496).

Nemirow seems to grant that we 'draw inferences' from our imaginings. Why does this not amount to endorsing Levin's argument, rather than refuting it? Perhaps the point is (in Sellarsian jargon) that it is the imagin-*ings* or events of imagining that serve as premises in the inferences, rather than the imagin*eds* or propositional contents imagined. But when Levin suggests that by being shown an unfamiliar colour, we acquire information

---

[4] Of course *Mary* would acquire no such facts, since, being scientifically omniscient, she would already have known them. Levin is speaking of the rest of us.

about its relations to other colours etc., she could not mean that the event of our *doing the imagining* shows us those things and licenses the relevant inferences; rather, it is (for all N-L have argued) *what* we succeed in imagining that does that. And, one would think, contents that afford inferences to propositional conclusions are themselves propositional.

4. From the empiricist residue (Levin 1986: 479)

The British empiricists believed that all empirical knowledge was based on purely phenomenal knowledge involving phenomenal concepts. Now, although there are few British empiricists left these days, why should we reject even the last vestige of their view? Is not *some* empirical knowledge, even the smallest occasional bit, based on beliefs about the phenomenal character of one's experience? If so, then there are such beliefs; and, plausibly, Mary could not have had phenomenal-colour beliefs before her release, because as the empiricists argued, one must have phenomenal experience in order to have phenomenal concepts, and one must have phenomenal concepts in order to have phenomenal beliefs.

5. From 'important cognitive differences' (Levin 1986: 479–80)

Levin defines what she calls a 'direct recognitional capacity' as 'an ability to know that one is in a particular [mental] state without making inferences . . . simply by applying one's concept of that mental state to the experiences at hand,' and she points out that people do sometimes have such knowledge.[5] If we have direct recognitional capacities that other species, or even other human beings, do not have, then is it not reasonable to explain those differences *in factual knowings* by appeal to differences in our knowledge of phenomenal facts about experience?

6. From best explanation of the abilities

For that matter, our imaginative (etc.) abilities themselves call for explanation. Is not our ability to visualize red or blue best explained by our factual knowledge of what it is like to see those colours? Consider our more familiar quotidian imaginative abilities. For example, I can visualize my mother-in-law's face when she is not present, or the front of my house when I am out of town. Those abilities are well explained by the uncontroversial fact of my knowing what my mother-in-law and the front of my house look like; and there is nothing mysterious about those items of knowledge, since I can express them descriptively in some detail. Why should my knowing what it is like to see red or blue be explained differently?[6]

[5] Levin goes on to distinguish a strong from a weak sense of 'direct,' but that distinction does not matter to the present point, vital though it is to her own main argument against Nagel and Jackson.

[6] Conee (1985: 298) adds that in some abnormal cases, the abilities might be explained otherwise; e.g. without knowing what it is like to see red or blue, Mary might be surgically

There is one difference that might be thought relevant. Though mothers-in-law and houses can be described in public natural languages, what it is like to experience a sensation of red or of blue cannot, except at best in comparative or analogical terms. As Nemirow points out (1990: 493), that ineffability is well explained by N-L's 'ability' thesis. But it can also variously be explained by friends of phenomenal information — notoriously by Russell, for example. N-L have no monopoly on ineffability.[7] So the ineffability difference has not yet been shown to impugn our explanation of the imaginative abilities.

7. From attempting-to-describe

One can *try* to convey the taste of pineapple to someone who has never eaten pineapple, though probably without much success. It certainly feels as though there is something to describe, if only we could find the words, and some of the descriptions we offer get at the taste better than others do. If N-L are right, this sort of attempt is utterly misguided and its seeming partial success is completely illusory, for there is nothing to describe; description is propositional. N-L owe us at least an explanation of the illusion.

8. From comparisons

Consider explicitly comparative descriptions of phenomenal qualities. Carbon disulphide smells (as I recall) like rotten eggs.[8] Assuming that statement to be true, what is its truth-maker? Presumably just that rotten eggs smell a certain way and that carbon disulfide smells the same way. This could be relativized to a person and a brief period of time: what it is like for S to smell carbon disulphide during a time interval Δt is exactly what it is like for S to smell rotten eggs during Δt. But that formulation seems to treat 'what it's like' as a matter of fact, even if ineffable fact; and the facts in question are *per se* not about imagining, but about actually smelling. And what is factual is propositional.

---

given the *ability* to visualize those colours even though she never goes on to exercise that ability. Nor do the various abilities seem necessary for 'knowing what it's like': Mary might know what the blue of sky looks like while she is seeing the sky, but through neurological deficit be deprived of any ability to visualize, to compare, or the like. See also Conee 1994: 138–9.

[7] Nemirow (1990: 493) says that the ability hypothesis affords a 'more elegant' explanation of the ineffability than does bare reference to 'the inexpressible qualities of experience'. I vigorously agree that it does; what I dispute is that it gives a more elegant explanation than does Russell's explanation, or a functionalist one, or any of a number of other possible substantive explanations. For my own explanation of the ineffability, see secs. 6–8 of Lycan 1990a.

[8] I almost used a different example, the taste of Vegemite, for I have a Vegemite comparison that is both vivid and deadly accurate, but if I had expounded it and David Lewis were to read this paper, he would lose his vaunted innocence and it would be all my fault.

9. From success and failure

As Nemirow concedes (1990: 497), imagining can be successful or unsuccessful, indeed correct or incorrect. I can visualize my boyhood home in New Jersey, and be fairly certain that the house did look as I am imagining, but find upon checking a period photograph that I have got it wrong. Imagining is a form of representation. Therefore, if to know 'what it's like' to experience phenomenal red is in large part to be able to imagine experiencing red, presumably this means imagining correctly rather than incorrectly. I would not be counted as knowing what it is like to see red — especially by a proponent of N-L's ability hypothesis — if when I tried to imagine such an experience, I always visualized what is in fact blue or yellow. And therefore, there is such a thing as getting 'what it's like' right, representing truly rather than falsely, from which it seems to follow that knowing 'what it's like' is knowing a truth.[9]

Thus a vigorous case can be made against N-L. But now let us seek the middle path.

III. Two Distinctions

I begin with the notion of a *quale*, in a carefully strict sense of that unhappy word. The sense I have in mind is roughly C.I. Lewis' original sense, in which a 'quale' is the introspectible monadic qualitative property of what seems to be a phenomenal individual, such as the colour of what Bertrand Russell called a visual sense-datum. For example, if S is visually healthy and looking at a ripe tomato in good light, the tomato will look red to S, and if S focusses her introspective attention on the corresponding subregion of her visual field, S will see that subregion as an individual red patch having a roundish shape. The redness of that phenomenal patch is the quale of the containing visual sensation.[10] One registers such a quale whenever one perceives a coloured object as such.

And on my view, a quale is a represented property, an intentional object; S's visual sensation represents the tomato (whether correctly or falsely) as having the colour red. Why only an intentional object? Because if it were an *actual instance* of redness present in the mind, then there would have to be a mental object that really is red — i.e. an actual Russellian sense-datum — which there surely is not. Rather, the visual sensation represents a state of affairs in which an external object, or its physical surface, has a certain intrinsic property. Perhaps that property is real, objective physical redness

---

[9] Though it starts from the same premise, this argument differs from the 'second objection' Nemirow anticipates on p. 497.

[10] One need not endorse Russellian sense-datum metaphysics or epistemology in order to use the term 'quale' in this way; just think of the colour that suffuses a particular subregion of one's visual field at such-and-such a time.

that could be described and investigated by physics. Or perhaps there is not really any such property as 'objective physical redness', but in that case S's sensing is unveridical and portrays something that does not exist.

Yet the term 'registers' (as in 'One registers such a quale') is to be understood very weakly. For some of our perceivings are un- or subconscious in the sense that we are unaware of achieving them. Armstrong (1980) gives the well-known example of the long-distance truck driver who is absent-mindedly driving on (so to speak) automatic pilot while thinking of something entirely different; the driver 'comes to' and suddenly realizes that he has driven for miles without any awareness of what he is doing. Yet he must have perceived the bends in the road, the road signs, the stop lights, and so on. Suppose he did in fact stop at a red light. Presumably the light looked red rather than green to him; that is the only reason he would have stopped. So, in our present strict sense of the term, he was presented with a red quale; a subregion of his visual field had redness as its phenomenal or qualitative character. But the driver was not aware of any such thing; it was an un- or subconscious perceiving, entirely unintrospected. (Rosenthal 1991 makes a similar point.)

Yet some philosophers, at least, might be loath to credit the truck driver with having had a sensory *experience* of red; after all, he was entirely unaware of his perceptual encounter with the stop light. Certainly there is a sense in which one has not experienced phenomenal red, or *felt* pain, unless one is aware of the redness or the pain. To experience a sensation in that fuller sense, one must both have the relevant quale and notice it introspectively.

What, then, of 'what it's like'? That phrase is now ambiguous, as between phenomenal character, i.e. a quale in our strict sense, and the conscious experience of such a quale. That is my first distinction.[11]

Now, consider the business of internal awareness or introspection. Following Locke and Armstrong,[12] I think of introspection as the operation of one or more internal monitors or scanners, 'inner eyes'. These operate, sometimes not at all (as in the case of the truck driver), sometimes spontaneously without direction, sometimes at will.[13] Further, in my view, when they do operate, a human being's internal monitors emit representations as

---

[11] It is important, both for psychologists and for philosophers, to separate questions about qualia from questions about awareness and introspective consciousness; and failure to notice the difference has led to some considerable confusion in research on consciousness; see Lycan: forthcoming.

[12] Locke 1690/1959, Book II, Ch. I, sec. 3, p. 123; Armstrong 1980; Lycan 1987, Ch. 6; forthcoming.

[13] Perhaps only in the latter case should we speak of introspecting. On this usage, awareness or 'introspective' consciousness may or may not be a result of introspecting. Armstrong himself makes a similar distinction between 'reflex' introspective awareness and 'introspection proper'.

their output, second-order representations of the subject's own first-order psychological states.

And here comes my second distinction: If indeed there is second-order representing of first-order states including states that include qualia in our strict sense, then as in any case of representation, each introspective second-order representation has both a *referent* and a *mode of presentation* under which the referent is exhibited; it presents a feature of the first-order state in question but also presents that feature in a certain way, under a particular guise. But let me back up and illustrate the general idea before applying it to my very special case of introspective representations.

For present purposes the most obvious illustrative examples of the distinction between a representation's referent and the mode of presentation under which the representation picks out that referent, are *a posteriori* scientific identifications of the sort materialists have touted since U.T. Place's time: water with H_2O, lightning with electrical discharge in the sky, genes with segments of DNA molecules (and, many now believe, sensings with brain events). Such cases show that knowledge of any fact is knowledge under a representation; one and the same fact may be known or unknown to a subject depending on that subject's mode of representing that fact. For example, knowledge of the fact that a flagon of water is being poured over one's head by an eccentric graduate student is not in itself knowledge that H_2O is being poured over one's head, even though the pouring of the water just is the pouring of the H_2O. Modes of representation are individuated far more finely than by extension, even when 'extensions' are taken to be full-blown states of affairs rather than just truth-values or 'tuples of objects. This is why one may not know a fact F_1 even though one knows F_2 and $F_1 = F_2$.

McGinn (1983: 21) makes a closely related point, but in terms of indexical pronouns:

> [A] difference of representation does not imply a genuine disagreement . . .
> [T]wo people in different places do not disagree if one calls 'here' what the other describes as 'there'; there would be disagreement only if they *both* referred to the same place as 'here'.

Similarly, one can know that something is happening *here*, and not know that that thing is happening *there*, even if 'here' and 'there' turn out to be one and the same place. More generally, this brings up the matter of 'essentially indexical' reference, as called to our attention by Geach (1957), Castañeda (1966) and Perry (1979).

Consider my own (entirely false) belief that *I myself* am underpaid and my colleague's belief that *he himself* is underpaid. Like Nagel's and Jackson's issue, the matter of essentially indexical beliefs also features apparent 'perspectival information' in some form, since the belief 'contents' in question cannot be rendered in any third-person way: If someone else were to say of me that 'WGL is underpaid,' this would not express the same thought as my own, for if I were amnesic I might share that opinion without having the very thought that *I myself*, as opposed to that person WGL, was underpaid.

Some philosophers have read great ontological significance into such data. But, properly understood, those facts are ontologically harmless and not even particularly surprising. The difference between an ordinary third-person thought and the corresponding first-person thought is not, I suggest, in the referents of the subject's representations, but in the representations' functional role.[14]

Knowings are believings, and beliefs (I shall continue to assume) are inner, representational states of people.[15] As such, they have properties of two distinctive sorts: they have referential truth-conditions, and they have inferential or computational or otherwise functional roles in their hosts' behavioural economies. Beliefs' constituent concepts, both general and individual, share this dual nature. A concept has both an extension (a set of items to which it applies) and a functional profile within its owner's psychology. Moreover, a concept's functional role and the same concept's extension are not only independent of each other but far less conditioned by each other than one might think; this is shown by twin-earth-style examples (Putnam 1975; Stich 1978; Fodor 1980; Burge 1979.) and, more vividly, by indexical cases. Concepts that are functionally very different may coextend *even throughout logical space*, and concepts that are functionally just alike — even shared by all molecular duplicates — may differ in extension. The concept 'water' has an *inferential* role, in particular, quite distinct from that of 'H_2O', and no doubt other diverging computational features; so knowing that water is being poured can differ sharply from knowing that H_2O is being poured. Similarly, believing that I myself am underpaid can differ even more dramatically from believing that WGL is, though the fact known is the same in each case and the two beliefs are alike in truth-value throughout all possible worlds.

And so does knowledge that one is having such-and-such a sort of sensation differ from knowledge that one is in brain state so-and-so, even though (as I believe) one's having that sort of sensation just is one's being in brain state so-and-so. Now to apply our second distinction to qualia and consciousness of them.

---

[14] In what follows I shall merely summarize the view I have developed in some previous works, particularly Lycan 1985; Boër and Lycan 1986; Chapter 4 of Lycan 1988; and especially Lycan 1990a. For some cognate ideas mobilizing the distinction between referent and mode of presentation, see McGinn 1983; McMullen 1985; Loar 1990; and especially Rey 1991; 1993.

[15] This commonsensical view is of course controversial on each of several fronts. But I have defended it at length elsewhere, particularly in Lycan 1988.

IV. Introspective Modes of Presentation

Think of an *introspective* representation as a token in one of the subject's languages-of-thought, her/his Introspectorese. As an immediate consequence of the operation of one of S's internal monitors, we might say, S tokens a mental word for the type of first-order state being inwardly sensed. Now, that word would not be lexically composite; its meaning would not be the compositional result of a semantic compounding operation performed on the prior meanings of its morphologically proper parts. It would be semantically primitive. And since its inferential and/or conceptual role would be unique to its subject, in that no other subject could deploy a functionally similar representation whose designatum was that (the subject's) very same first-order state-token, the introspective word would certainly not be synonymous with any primitive or composite expression of public English, even though it would *corefer* with some English expressions. In that sense it would be a private name as well as semantically primitive, a name that only its actual user could use to name its actual referent.[16]

It will help to turn to Farrell's and Nagel's famous example of the sonar sensations of bats: if (however fancifully) we imagine that a bat can be consciously aware of having a sonar sensation at all, we may naturally suppose the bat to have conceptual resources alien to us and in particular to apply a concept to the sensation that is not even potentially available to humans. Thus the bat would think something that we cannot and never could understand. It seems to follow that there is something to understand, something that outruns all the scientific and other third-person facts that we and our chiropterologists do understand.

If our human introspective concepts are semantically primitive lexemes of our languages-of-thought, and if we do think of the bat as mobilizing concepts at all, then it is only fair to grant that the bat's sonar-sensation concept is likewise a semantically primitive lexeme of its language-of-thought also. And certainly that mental word will be synonymous neither with any public word of English nor with any word of any human being's language-of-thought. Thus, just as I can refer to my pain using a concept that no one else can use to refer to my own very pain, the bat can refer to its sonar sensation using a concept that no human could use (for that matter) at all. But as before, it does not follow that the bat knows or understands a *different fact*. The bat 'understands something that we cannot' only in the same sense as that in which the chemist knows something that a chemical illiterate cannot when both see the water poured over my head.

One might of course insist on a notion of 'fact' or 'state of affairs' that incorporated mode of presentation, in such a way that such items did obey

---

[16] That distinctive sort of privacy, Lycan (1990a) argues, is what constitutes the subjectivity or Nagelian perspectivalness of a mental state.

Leibniz' Law as regards being known. In that fine-grained sense, the fact of one's having that sort of sensation would be distinct from one's being in brain state so-and-so. But so would the fact of water's being poured be distinct from that of H_2O's being poured, and lightning be distinct from electrical discharge; yet no one would on that account become a dualist or a vitalist about water or lightning. It seems to me entirely proper to persist in using 'fact' in our original coarse-grained way.

V. Phenomenal Information

And now we can see why N-L are both right and wrong about phenomenal information. They are right in that no special phenomenal facts, in the coarse-grained sense, are introduced by the 'what it's like' locution. For all that has been shown by Nagel and Jackson, neither qualia nor our awareness of qualia require any surd in nature or any unscientistic ontology.

But N-L are also wrong, in that there is a perfectly good sense of 'information', more finely grained than that of 'fact,' in which there is after all phenomenal information, indeed (!) phenomenal information inaccessible to objective, third-person science.[17] Upon her release, Mary learns that actually to experience red is like . . . ploiku! — where my sign-design 'ploiku' stands in lieu of whatever mental morpheme is actually tokened by Mary's introspector in making its report. (Again, that morpheme cannot be expressed in standard English, even though it corefers with expressions like 'Mary's being appeared to redly' and 'Mary's being in [such-and-such a] perceptual state of the red-presenting sort' and 'Mary's hosting cognitive goings-on [so-and-so].') Think again of my coming to believe, upon recovering from my amnesia, that *I* am underpaid, even though (on the basis of reading the standard biographies) I have always believed that WGL is underpaid. In the functional and/or computational sense, I certainly do acquire some new information and my cognitive powers are greatly enhanced, even though in our coarse-grained sense I have not learned any new fact. I relearn the same fact in a new, behaviour-affecting guise. And propositional-attitude constructions in natural language mark this phenomenon by offering a choice between two starkly different complement clauses — in that perfectly good sense, different information ascribed. Hereafter I shall speak of 'computational information,' meaning the fine-grained type distinguished by functional modes of presentation, as opposed to 'coarse-factual information', the information corresponding to facts in our coarse-grained sense that ignores modes of presentation.

---

[17] Also, there is also the 'explanatory gap' explored by Levine (1983); but that is another question, addressed at length in Lycan 1990a.

VI. The Arguments

Multiplied by each other, my two distinctions require a fourfold approach to arguments for and against phenomenal information. For in any case of sensing, there is (1) at least one quale (strictly so called), a qualitative intentional object, such as the alleged objective redness of S's tomato. There is also (2) the mode of presentation under which the represented property is represented (in S's case the visual-redness mode, as opposed, say, to some scientific description of the colour property, if the property is indeed a real property of objects and has a scientific description). If the subject is consciously aware of doing the sensing, there will also be (3) her/his introspector's internal representation of the sensing itself, and (4) the special introspective mode of presentation under which the sensing is represented, as opposed to a third-person computational or neurobiological description.

Thus, there are potentially four types of information involved in any sensing: coarse-factual information as represented in the form of a quale; the computational information that incorporates the distinctive sensory mode of presentation; the coarse-factual information recorded by one's introspector; and the computational information that incorporates the introspector's special mode of presenting the latter. In the case of S and her tomato, these are, respectively: that the tomato is red, where 'red' occupies an extensional position and could be replaced by any correct description of objective redness if any; that the tomato is red *qua* red as opposed to *qua* something from physics; that S herself is sensing in a visual-red way, where 'sensing in a visual-red way' could be replaced by any correct description of the same state of affairs, such as a psychophysical description; and that S is having one of those . . . well, *those* sensations again, where the frustrated demonstrative can be replaced by nothing in English but only (*per impossibile*) by a lexeme of S-introspectorese such as 'ploiku'.

We saw in section III that the phrase 'what it's like' is ambiguous as between phenomenal character, i.e. a quale, and the conscious experience of such a quale. But the issue of 'phenomenal information' as discussed by Farrell, Nagel and Jackson and addressed by N-L was raised as having to do with a *knowing*, and a knowing whose object is already something mental, e.g. knowing what it is like to experience red; so the issue concerns only our third and fourth kinds of information.

Space limitations force me to bring this paper to a close. And that means we must leave some business unfinished, though the business is not difficult. One would like to run through the nine arguments of section II, and see to what extent and exactly how their conclusions are vindicated by the present model. Also, Lewis (1990: 512–14) has offered two direct arguments against phenomenal information, which would need to be rebutted in light of the model I have offered.

It is a fairly routine exercise to see that my notion of 'computational information' does vindicate most of the nine arguments' conclusions, for as I have noted, 'that'-clauses are sometimes specialized for computational as opposed to merely coarse-factual information. (Recall knowing 'that H_2O is being poured' as opposed to 'that water is being poured,' or believing 'that he is underpaid' as opposed to 'that I am underpaid' when 'he' and I are in fact the same person.) Most of the nine arguments militate just for 'that'-clauses of the fine-grained computational sort, not for distinctive 'phenomenal information' in the more alarming sense of coarse-factual information, i.e. new facts. I shall comment on just the first two of the arguments, which have special features.

(1) My introspective model more or less explains the data that afford the argument from meaning and syntax. To know 'what it's like' to experience visual red is to know introspectively that experiencing red is like . . . *that*, or like ploiku, to have computational information that has no English expression.

(2) The argument from possibility-elimination requires qualification. For the possibility Mary eliminates, say that visual yellow might look phenomenally like what we call 'pink' instead of the way it actually does look, is not a metaphysical possibility that outruns total science, but supervenes on total science. So the worlds Mary rules out form at best a set of metaphysically impossible worlds, if such there be, and it is questionable whether a set of metaphysically impossible worlds constitutes propositional information in any decent sense.

But computational information does come to the rescue. Recall our pronominal examples. I can newly learn that the meeting will be held *here*, even though I already knew that the meeting would be held in Room 215 and this room is in fact Room 215; and I can newly come to believe that I am underpaid even though I already believed that WGL is underpaid. In each case, the 'possibility' that I eliminate is a metaphysical impossibility. As we have seen, computational information is finer-grained than is coarse-factual information, and its grain distinguishes between guises presenting the same fact. So the argument's premise is not strictly true: Mary does not eliminate any genuine metaphysical possibility. But to do that is not the only way of acquiring information; one can acquire computational information, expressible in a perfectly well-formed 'that'-clause of the kind that is marked for fine computational individuation.

A momentary concluding word against Lewis' two arguments aforementioned (1990:512–14). They are arguments from queerness — specifically, charges that phenomenal information would have to be epiphenomenal in an objectionable sense: differences in phenomenal information would (at best) find it hard to make a difference to the subject's behaviour. If it were coarse-factual information that were being defended against N-L, those charges would have considerable force. (However, see the excellent discussion in Robinson 1993.) But computational information is itself individuated functionally, in terms of some of its causes and causal powers themselves, rather than solely in terms of its referents. (It is hardly surprising that I behave differently once I come to believe that I am underpaid, and the computational information 'that I am underpaid' is distinguished from 'that WGL is underpaid' precisely in terms of functional differences.) So I doubt the reader will find that Lewis' arguments impugn the fine-grained sort of phenomenal information I have defended here.

References

Armstrong, D.M. (1980). What is consciousness? In *The Nature of Mind and Other Essays*. Ithaca, NY: Cornell University Press.

Boër, S. & Lycan, W. (1986). *Knowing Who*. Cambridge, MA: MIT Press.

Burge, T. (1979). Individualism and the mental. In P. French, T.E. Uehling & H. Wettstein (eds), *Midwest Studies in Philosophy, Vol. IV: Studies in Metaphysics*. Minneapolis: University of Minnesota Press.

Castañeda, H-N. (1966). 'He': A study in the logic of self-consciousness. *Ratio*, **8**, 130–57.

Conee, E. (1985). Physicalism and phenomenal qualities. *Philosophical Quarterly*, **35**, 296–302.

Conee, E. (1994). Phenomenal knowledge. *Australasian Journal of Philosophy*, **72**, 136–50.

Farrell, B. (1950). Experience. *Mind*, **59**, 170–98. Reprinted in V.C. Chappell (ed), *The Philosophy of Mind* (Englewood Cliffs, NJ: Prentice-Hall, 1962).

Fodor, J.A. (1980). Methodological solipsism considered as a research strategy in cognitive psychology. *Behavioral and Brain Sciences*, **3**, 63–73.

Geach, P. (1957). On belief about oneself. *Analysis*, **18**, 23–4.

Groenendijk, J. & Stokhof, M. (1982). Semantic analysis of *wh*-complements. *Linguistics and Philosophy*, **5**, 175–234.

Hirschbühler, P. (1979). *The Syntax and Semantics of Wh Constructions*. Bloomington, IN: Indiana University Linguistics Club Publications.

Jackson, F. (1982). Epiphenomenal qualia. *Philosophical Quarterly*, **32**, 127–36. Reprinted in Lycan 1990b.

Karttunen, L. (1977). Syntax and semantics of questions. *Linguistics and Philosophy*, **1**, 3–44.

Levin, J. (1986). Could love be like a heatwave? Physicalism and the subjective character of experience. *Philosophical Studies*, **49**, 245–61. Reprinted in Lycan 1990b.

Levine, J. (1983). Materialism and qualia: the explanatory gap. *Pacific Philosophical Quarterly*, **64**, 354–61.

Lewis, D. (1983). Postscript to 'Mad pain and Martian pain'. In *Philosophical Papers, Vol. I*. Oxford: Oxford University Press.

Lewis, D. (1990). What experience teaches. In Lycan 1990b.

Loar, B. (1990). Phenomenal states. In Tomberlin 1990.

Locke, J. (1690/1959). *An Essay Concerning Human Understanding*. Ed. A.C. Fraser. New York: Dover Publications.

Lycan, W.G. (1985). The paradox of naming. In B-K. Matilal & J.L. Shaw (eds), *Analytical Philosophy in Comparative Perspective*. Dordrecht: D. Reidel.

Lycan, W.G. (1987). *Consciousness*. Cambridge, MA: MIT Press.

Lycan, W.G. (1988). *Judgement and Justification*. Cambridge: Cambridge University Press.

Lycan, W.G. (1990a) What is the 'subjectivity' of the mental? In Tomberlin 1990.

Lycan, W.G. (1990b)[ed]. *Mind and Cognition*. Oxford: Blackwell.

Lycan, W.G. (forthcoming). Consciousness as internal monitoring, I. *Philosophical Perspectives*.

McGinn, C. (1983). *The Subjective View*. Oxford: Oxford University Press.

McMullen, C. (1985). 'Knowing what it's like' and the essential indexical. *Philosophical Studies*, **48**, 211–34.

Nagel, T. (1974). What is it like to be a bat? *Philosophical Review*, **83**, 435–50.

Nemirow, L. (1980). Review of Nagel's 'Mortal Questions'. *Philosophical Review*, **89**, 475–6.

Nemirow, L. (1990). Physicalism and the cognitive role of acquaintance. In Lycan 1990b.

Perry, J. (1979). The problem of the essential indexical. *Noûs*, **13**, 3–21.

Putnam, H. (1975). The meaning of 'meaning'. In K. Gunderson (ed), *Minnesota Studies in the Philosophy of Science, Vol. VII: Language, Mind and Knowledge*. Minneapolis: University of Minnesota Press.

Rey, G. (1991). Sensations in a language of thought. In Villanueva 1991.

Rey, G. (1993). Sensational sentences. In Davies & Humphreys 1993.

Robinson, D. (1993). Epiphenomenalism, laws & properties. *Philosophical Studies*, **69**, 1–34.

Rosenthal, D. (1991). The independence of consciousness and sensory quality. In Villanueva 1991.

Stich, S.P. (1978). Autonomous psychology and the belief-desire thesis. *Monist*, **61**, 573–91. Reprinted in Lycan 1990b.

Tomberlin, J. (1990)[ed]. *Philosophical Perspectives, Vol. 4: Action Theory and Philosophy of Mind*. Atascadero, CA: Ridgeview Publishing.

David Papineau

The Antipathetic Fallacy and the Boundaries of Consciousness

I. Introduction

There is strong argument for identifying conscious states with physical states. After all, conscious states clearly have physical effects, in particular behavioural effects.[1] And it is a central and well-confirmed part of our world-view that all physical effects have complete physical causes. So either all behavioural effects are overdetermined by separate conscious and physical causes, which seems absurd, or conscious states are identical with physical states.[2]

Despite the above argument, however, the idea that consciousness is physical runs counter to widespread and deep-seated intuitions. My first aim in this paper is to explain these intuitions away. I shall attribute them to an extremely seductive fallacy, which I call the 'antipathetic fallacy', and which I think is responsible for much confusion both inside philosophy and without. The identification of this fallacy will explain why anti-physicalist intuitions are widespread even though they are false, and will thus leave the above argument for a physicalist view of consciousness uncontested.

My second aim in this paper will be to consider how we should then think of consciousness from a physicalist point of view. The antipathetic fallacy is important for this issue too, for it is apt to confuse even those who profess

[1] All right, epiphenomenalists deny this (because they realize it is the only way of evading the argument for physicalism). Still, I take epiphenomenalism to be *ad hoc*, and therefore to be avoided if there is a better alternative, as I shall argue there is.

[2] I am here assuming that the relata of causation are facts, or 'states', rather than events (cf. Mellor 1987). This assumption isn't essential, in that versions of my argument can be run in terms of causal *explanation*, even if causation itself is a relation between events.

DAVID PAPINEAU

a physicalist view of consciousness, making them look for explanations where there is nothing to explain. I shall argue that once we are properly free of the fallacy, we need to reconsider whether the category of conscious states constitutes a serious natural kind.

Before proceding, perhaps I should be a bit more specific about the sense in which the causal argument I started with shows conscious states to be identical with physical states. Strictly speaking, I don't think it does show this, so much as that conscious states are identical with *or realized by* physical states.[3] Of course, if we interpret 'physical' broadly, as signifying *either* states identifiable in strictly physical terminology *or* higher-order states which are realized by such physical states, then we can continue to maintain that the causal argument establishes the identity of conscious with 'physical' states. This usage is in fact quite common in this area of debate,[4] and I shall adopt it in most of what follows, except where greater precision is needed.[5]

II. The Antipathetic Fallacy

My aim in this section is to show how the existence of anti-physicalist intuitions about consciousness is explicable even if physicalism is true. Since we have good independent reason to suppose physicalism *is* true — namely the causal argument with which I started — I take this to show that we should stand by physicalism and reject the intuitions.

Since I want to show what physicalism can explain, I shall assume physicalism for the sake of this section's argument. My thesis will be that that anti-physicalist intuitions about consciousness arise because there are two ways of thinking about conscious states. One way is to think of conscious states as brain states, or as causes of behaviour, in some other

---

[3] This is because the causal argument needs 'cause' to be understood in the sense which allows that higher-order states cause what their realizations cause. For a more detailed analysis of this point, see section 1.7 of my *Philosophical Naturalism* 1993, or, better, my 'Arguments for Supervenience and Realization' 1994.

[4] Cf. Horgan 1984: 147–8; Tye 1986: 1. Perhaps it is worth noting that I do not regard fuctional states as the only species of physically realized higher-order states; the state of having-some-state-which-has-biological-function-F would be another such; and there are other possibilities.

[5] The reason why this usage is common in this area, and why greater precision is not normally needed, is that intuitions about the distinctness of conscious states count as strongly against the view that conscious states are physically realized higher-order states as against the view that they are strictly physical. This is because, to be physically realized, a conscious state would need to be in essence a state of having-some-state-with-feature-R (with some physical state with feature R then fitting the bill). Yet intuition seems to preclude physical states from sharing the essential features R of conscious states in this way, just as much as it precludes their being identical with them.

such 'third person' way. The other way is to use our powers of imagination to represent conscious states from the 'first person' perspective.

This contrast applies to a wide range of mental acts. The most obvious is imagination itself. I can imagine you are in pain is by imagining your C-fibres are firing.[6] This is third person imagining. But I can also imagine your pain in a first person way. I can imagine *having* the pain, from the 'inside', as it were. There is a similar contrast for remembering (I can remember that my C-fibres fired, and I can remember *having* the pain), for judging (I can judge that your C-fibres are firing, and I can judge that you feel something like *this*), and perhaps for other kinds of mental acts too.

It is a striking feature of first person ways of thinking about conscious experiences that they are by and large only available to people who have had those experiences. You can only imagine the smell of thyme if you have yourself once smelt thyme.

Dualists explain this by supposing that, when you have a conscious experience, you become acquainted with some non-physical feature of the experience, and that this knowledge is then deployed in first person ways of thinking about experience. As it is sometimes put, you find out 'what it is like' to smell thyme, and thereby learn how to imagine this smell.[7]

However, physicalists have an equally good explanation for the fact that you can only imagine experiences after you have had them. Suppose, as is fairly well evidenced, that imagining an experience is literally *re-creation*, in the sense that in imagination the same parts of the brain are activated as in the original experience (though the activation will obviously not be identical, and in particular the normal links to behaviour will be absent). This then suggests an obvious explanation for why you can only imagine experiences after you have had them — namely that the brain needs an original mould to be able to form replicas of the relevant state.

Note that this explanation dispenses with the dualist assumption that people become acquainted with distinctive non-physical features of conscious states when they first have experiences.[8] Physicalists can continue to allow that people need to have an experience in order to find out 'what it is like', but they will say that this phrase simply signifies the acquisition of a new ability, namely the ability to recreate the experience at first hand, as opposed to thinking about it in some third person way.[9]

[6] I intend this talk of C-fibres only as a place holder for an adequate physicalist analysis of pain.

[7] This is of course the basis of Frank Jackson's 'knowledge argument' for dualism; cf. Jackson 1982; 1986. Jackson points out that someone who knows every physical truth about a type of experience need not 'know what it is like', and so concludes that there are non-physical features of experience.

[8] And thereby blocks Jackson's knowledge argument.

[9] For a more careful physicalist account of the changes produced in people as a result of new experiences, together with references to the literature on this topic, see Papineau

Note also that the physicalist explanation suggests an explanation of why an imagined experience feels like the original experience itself — namely that such imaginings literally involve a physical copy of the original experience.[10] Some readers may feel there is an explanatory gap here. Why should the fact that two brain states are physically similar make them phenomenologically similar? As it happens, I think there is less of a gap here than there seems, and some of the observations made later in this paper will indicate why. But in any case the precise point is not essential to the argument of this section. At this stage I need assume only that imaginings *are* experientially similar to original experiences, whether or not this is explained by their physical similarity.

D.H. Mellor (1992: 11) uses the term 'secondary' to refer to the kind of experience which ocurs when we recreate in imagination those primary experiences we have previously undergone. Adopting this terminology, we can draw the contrast between first and third person ways of thinking about experiences by saying that the first person ways deploy secondary versions of those experiences, whereas third person ways do not. Thus when you imagine, or remember, or judge — in a first person way — that someone is in pain, your thought contains an element, the secondary experience, which to some slight extent shares the unpleasantness of pain. By contrast, third person thoughts about people being in pain do not contain this element.

It is this specific aspect of the difference between first person and third person thoughts about experience that I think gives rise to the widespread intuition that conscious states are non-physical. For it is all too easy to conclude, when we reflect on this difference between these two kinds of thoughts, that only the first person thoughts really refer to experiences, while the third person thoughts refer to nothing except physical states.

The route to this conclusion begins with the perfectly accurate observation that first person thoughts include an experiential element which is absent from the third person cases. first person thoughts portray the relevant experience directly, so to speak, by giving the thinker a simulacrum, by recreating in the thinker a version of the experience being thought about. third person thoughts, on the other hand, do not do this, since they do not involve secondary experiences.

So there is a sense in which third person thoughts do indeed 'leave something out': they do not *give* us (secondary versions of) the experience being referred to. And this observation can then easily lead to the further conclusion that third person thoughts are about something different from

---

1983: 4.3–4.4. Some of the other material in this paper also receives more detailed treatment in Papineau 1983: ch 4.

[10] It is a moot point whether the alternative dualist explanation, in terms of non-physical properties of experience, offers any competing explanation of why an imagining feels similar to the original experience. In general, thinking of something as an event with some property can have any experiential nature, or none at all.

first person thoughts: where first person thoughts refer to the experience itself, in all its conscious immediacy, third person thoughts merely refer to the external trappings of the conscious event, the physical goings-on which accompany it.

But of course this last step is a fallacy. The fact that we do not *have* certain experiences when we think third person thoughts does not mean that we are not *referring* to them. To make this move is to succumb to a species of the use–mention confusion: we slide from (a) third person thoughts, unlike first person thoughts, do not *use* (secondary versions) of conscious experiences to portray conscious experiences to (b) third person thoughts, unlike first person thoughts, do not *mention* conscious experiences. There is no reason, however, why third person thought about experiences, like nearly all other thoughts about anything, should not succeed in referring to items they do not use.

I propose to call the above fallacy the 'antipathetic fallacy'. Ruskin coined the phrase 'pathetic fallacy' for the poetic figure of speech which attributes human feelings to nature ('the deep and gloomy wood', 'the shady sadness of a vale'). I am currently discussing a converse fallacy, where we refuse to recognize that conscious feelings inhere in certain parts of nature, namely, the brains of conscious beings.

Some other writers have observed that the existence of two ways of thinking about experiences might lead us to think that there are two things being thought about (cf. Nagel 1974: 446–7; Lycan 1987: 76–7). What they have generally failed to emphasize, however, is the feature that makes the antipathetic fallacy both so distinctive and so seductive: namely that one way of thinking about experiences — the first person way — deploys elements that *feel like* the experience being thought about, and so makes us think that the other way — the third person way — *leaves out* the feeling itself. In general, when two different modes of thought create the impression that two things are being thought about, the illusion is easily enough dispelled by evidence that there is in fact only one referent. But in the mind–body case the impression of difference continues even in the face of any amount of evidence, precisely because of the special feature — the first person modes of thought *feel like* the experience being thought about — that makes it seem as if the third person modes of thought omit mention of that experience altogether.

III. Identities Need No Explanation

It is worth being clear what the identification of the antipathetic fallacy is supposed to explain. It is supposed to explain why so many people have strong *intuitions* that conscious states are *non-physical*. It *not* supposed to explain why some *physical* states are conscious, in the sense that it feels like something to have them. (Indeed it takes for granted one instance of this, in

264

DAVID PAPINEAU

assuming that first person imaginings feel like the experience being imagined.)

The identification of the antipathetic fallacy does, however, cast some light on this latter issue, the issue of why some physical states feel like they do. Note first that this issue arises at two levels. There is a generic question, about consciousness-as-such: why are some physical states conscious, but others not? Why is there something that it is like to be in some in some physical states, but not in others? Then there is a question about specific conscious states: why does such-and-such a physical state give rise to the conscious experience of seeing red, say, or of feeling pain? We can think of the first issue as focusing on the determinable property, consciousness, while the second focuses on the determinates, seeing red, feeling pain, and so on.

Both the generic and the specific questions can seem deeply ineffable. Physicalistically-minded philosophers and psychologists often aspire to physicalist acceptable 'theories' both of consciousness-as-such and of specific modes of consciousness. That is, they seek to identify some physical characteristic (in the broad sense that includes higher-order physically realized characteristics) that is common to conscious states as such, and they also seek to identify physical characteristics common to experiences of seeing red, feeling pain, and so on. However, a natural response to both these kinds of 'theory' is that they simply fail to address the deeper philosophical questions. Even if they yield extensionally adequate physical indicators of the relevant conscious states, they seem to offer no explanation of *why* those conscious states arise in those physical circumstances. Why, that is, should the firing of a system's C-fibres give rise to the conscious experience of pain? Or why, to take one popular theory of consciousness-as-such, should consciousness emerge in just those computational systems that can represent their own internal states, but not elsewhere?

I think these questions only seem ineffable because they are bad questions. They are like asking *why* was Cicero the same man as Tully, or *why* is water the same stuff as H_2O? You cannot *explain* why the two terms of a true identity coincide, since the truth of the identity means there is only one item in reality, and so no possibility of 'them' diverging. Similarly with the identification of conscious states with physical ones. If physicalists are right to assert such identities, as I am arguing, then there is no further question of why their two terms are always found together. Such an equation refers to a single state, and so no there is nothing further to explain.[11]

Some philosophers who profess an openness to physicalism have hypothesized that there may nevertheless be insuperable obstacles to our

[11] Of course we can ask why we should *believe* such physical identities, just as we can ask why we should believe Cicero = Tully or water = H_2O? But this is a different question, which can be answered by the causal argument I began with.

ever explaining why some physical states give rise to conscious experience. Thus Colin McGinn has suggested that this task is simply beyond human cognitive powers. And Scott Sturgeon has argued that the special relation of conscious states to our awareness of them means there is no room for the kind of reductionist explanation in terms of physical properties that we often give for other kinds of states (cf. McGinn 1991; Sturgeon 1994).

In my view, these authors are offering solutions to a problem that does not exist. The reason physicalism can't offer any explanation of why physical states gives rise to conscious experience is simply that there is nothing to explain. To think otherwise is to fail to grasp physicalism properly. The real puzzle is not that some physical states yield experiential states (if they are identical, what else would you expect?) but that it continues to seem that there is something to explain, even to those who are otherwise ready to countenance physicalism.

My answer to this last puzzle, as you would expect, is the antipathetic fallacy. It is harder to countenance physicalism than we might suppose. We imagine the experience of pain in the first person, and then think of C-fibres firing (or whatever), and then the antipathetic fallacy persuades us that the experience is extra to the physical goings-on, some kind of additional inner light which illuminates the minds of conscious beings. But this is a mistake. There aren't any such extra inner lights whose emergemce stands in need of explanation. There are just the physical states, and that's all.

This last remarks might make it sound as if I am, absurdly, denying the existence of consciousness, denying that there is something that it is like to be in certain physical states. Not at all. What I deny is that there are any *extra* inner lights, any states *additional* to the physical states. I don't deny that it's like something to be in those physical states, nor that what it's like is often very important, especially for the beings that are in those states. Of course it is like something to smell thyme or feel depressed. All I say is that this isn't anything different from being in the relevant physical states. The phrase 'what it's like' doesn't refer to anything non-physical, but just to the presence of the physical state *for* the individual that has it.

IV. Prospects for a Physicalist Theory of Consiousness

In this last section I want to look a bit more closely at the prospects for physicalist 'theories' of conscious states. It is not clear to me that such theories will necessarily be available, even if we embrace physicalism. The antipathetic fallacy, with its associated picture of extra inner lights, matters here too. Many enthusiasts for physicalism take it to be uncontentious that consciousness is the kind of thing for which we can give a physical analysis. But I shall argue much of this optimism derives from the picture of inner lights, which makes consciousness seem a much more definite phenomenon than it necessarily is.

DAVID PAPINEAU

In this section I shall focus on consciousness-as-such, rather than on specific kinds of conscious state. Though I think that similar issues arise in both cases, the kind of points I want to make can be put more clearly in connection with the generic state than its more specific determinates.[12]

What we want of a physical 'theory' of consciousness will depend in part on what we take the concept of consciousness to involve. Suppose, for example, that it were part of our concept of consciousness that consciousness consists of an extra inner light which arises in certain physical circumstances. Then a satisfactory physical theory of consciousness would presumably need to identify the kind of physical circumstance which gives rise to this extra inner light, and presumably would also need to give some physicalisically acceptable explanation of why this light is present in those circumstances.

I take it that no theory of this kind is possible. If there are no inner lights, as I have argued, then there are no physical circumstances that give rise to them. (And even if there were, there wouldn't be any physicalistically acceptable explanation of why they were then present.)

Is the idea of an extra inner light part of our concept of consciousness? I certainly think that the antipathetic fallacy leads nearly everybody (including physicalists in unguarded moments) to *believe* that consciousness involves an extra inner light. But beyond that I doubt that it is determinate whether or not this idea is part of the *concept* of consciouness. As a general rule, it is unnecessary that there be any fact about which of the central beliefs surrounding a given concept are part of that concept or not. (In this sense most of our concepts involve an element of vagueness.) It is only when these central beliefs are called in question that decisions need to be made, and then the issue can usually be resolved on pragmatic grounds. What else, apart from pragmatic grounds, should tell us how to refine some vague term, when it turns out that some such refinement is necessary?[13]

I propose to proceed, then, on the assumption that the idea of an extra inner light is *not* part of our concept of consciousness. We could cover most of the ensuing points on the basis of the contrary assumption, but it would be inconvenient, and would make physicalism seem even stranger than it is.

The trouble, however, is that once we drop the association with an inner light, the concept of consciousness we are left with is a fairly minimal one. There is certainly an effective procedure governing the application of the concept to humans beings. But it should not be taken for granted that the concept fixed by this procedure corresponds to any natural kind, nor even that it has a clear application outside the realm of human beings.

The procedure we use to decide which human states are conscious is to consider whether they can be recreated from the first person perspective.

---

[12] For my views on specific conscious states, see Papineau 1993: 4.10.

[13] These ideas about concept identity and vagueness are developed in Papineau forthcoming.

We judge that seeing red and feeling elated are conscious because, when the question is raised, we can recreate (secondary versions of) these states in memory and imagination. By contrast, being anaesthetized or having high blood pressure are not recreatable in this way.

This might seem a somewhat dubious claim. Couldn't a state *be* conscious, in that it is like something to have it, even though we cannot afterwards recreate it in memory or imagination? Maybe so, and I shall come back to this possibility later. But there seems little doubt that in such a case we would not *think* that the state is conscious, even though it is. Suppose, for example, that it is like something for humans to hear ultrasonic whistles, at the moment when they hear them, but that afterwards they have no ability to recreate the experience (they forget 'what it's like'). If they are then asked whether they are ever conscious of ultrasonic whistles, they will think back to what it was like on occasions when they know such whistles were present — and by hypothesis will simply draw a blank. The obvious upshot will be that they will clasify hearing ultrasonic whistles with having high blood pressure, as outside the realm of consciousness. (And if there is evidence that humans do respond behaviourally to these whistles, they will classify them as another species of unconscious perception, along with blindsight, subliminal vision, and the like.)

Let us assume, then, that first person recreatability is the test which we use in practice to identify which human states are conscious (though perhaps it is a test that misses some conscious states). What are the prospects for a physical 'theory of consciousness' consistent with this? Think of such a theory as aiming to identify some physical (including physically realized higher-order) characteristic common to the states the test identifies as conscious. There seem two natural ways of doing this. One is simply to identify the property of being conscious with first person recreatability itself. The other way is to view first person recreatability as akin to a description that fixes the referent of 'conscious', with consciousness itself then being whichever physical property is common to all the states that the test picks out. I shall consider these two suggestions in turn.

The first suggestion faces an initial hurdle, in that it needs to show that first person recreatability is indeed a well-defined physical characteristic (in the broad higher-order sense). This would require rather more careful attention than I have given to what kinds of recreation, and of what kinds of states, are required for first person recreatability. But even if we suppose that this initial hurdle can be cleared, there are other objections to this first suggestion. It seems unnatural to view first person recreatability as the essence of consciousness itself, rather than as a way of detecting some *other* property. Consider the thought experiment about ultrasonic whistles again, which took as its starting point the idea that it makes sense for a state to be conscious, in that it is like something to have it, even though it is not first person recreatable.

This thought can be reinforced by considering the question of animal consciouness. If we identify consciousness with first person recreatability, then it seems to follow that all animals, apart from humans and a few other higher mammals, lack conscious states, since they do not think about their own mental states in first person ways. This seems unsatisfactory. We surely want to allow that some animals can be 'sentient', even if they are not 'self-conscious'. It seems wrong to hold that chickens, say, cannot feel pain, simply because they cannot imaginatively anticipate or recall having been in pain.

So there seems good reason to reject the equation of consciousness with first person recreatability. This leaves us with the other suggestion, which identifies the property of being conscious with whichever other physical characteristic is common to all the states picked out by the test of first-person recreatability. The obvious danger facing this suggestion, however, is that there may be no such common characteristic. Why expect that there is something physically in common to all the things that are first person recreatable, over and above the fact that they are first person recreatable? After all, the class of states which we humans can think about in first person ways is extremely heterogeneous. As well as pains, itches, tickles, and the various modes of sense experience, there are emotions, cogitations, and moods. There seems no obvious reason, on the face of it, why there should be any physical property (even in the broad higher-order sense) common to this whole genus. Even if each species within the genus of conscious human states shares some explanatorily significant physical property, why suppose that there is some further such characteristic, common to members of all these species, which binds them all together?

Perhaps there is some common evolutionary explanation of why all these states are first person recreatable. For example, it may be that this aids our decision-making capabilities in a certain way. This would then give us a common functional characteristic. But this wouldn't be a common charac- teristic of the states themselves, but rather of their first person recreatability. And since we have already rejected the identification of consciousness with first person recreatability itself, we certainly won't want to identify it with this common functional characteristic of first person recreatability.

I see no reason to suppose that there is any serious physical characteristic (in however broad a sense) for a physical 'theory of consciousness' to identify. Instead I suspect that consciousness is like many other categories that we use to classify the world: we can identify a range of central instances by means of an effect they produce, but beyond that the category corre- sponds to no further natural kind. This doesn't mean that it is not an important category. In human affairs it certainly matters whether a state is conscious or not. But it does mean that this category fails to cut nature at the seams, and that its application to beings unlike ourselves may be quite indeterminate.

By way of analogy, consider categories like *intelligent*, or *angry*. These are perfectly useful concepts, and indeed ones that play an important rôle in human affairs. But no one would think that they picked out important natural kinds, or that it made any great sense to apply them to beings that are not significantly similar to humans (cf. Horgan 1994).

V. Concluding Remarks

There may seem to be an obvious objection to the position I have reached. What about the difference between states *that are like something*, and the rest? Surely this is a difference that cuts nature at the seams, if anything does. And if physicalism cannot find any corresponding physical property, as I have argued, then surely this shows there is something wrong with physicalism, not with the idea of consciousness.

I doubt that the phrase 'what it is like' can bear the weight of this line of argument. I said earlier that physicalists will regard this phrase as simply referring to the presence of a physical state *for* the individual that has it. Accordingly, they will accept that how it is for a given being will vary depending on which physical states it is in. What they do not have to accept, it seems to me, is that there need be any kind of meaningful line between cases where 'how it is' equals something and those where it equals nothing.

Of course, they should also recognize, since it is true, that the belief in such a line is widespread and deep-seated. But this they can attribute to the antipathetic fallacy. This fallacy makes nearly everybody think that first person thoughts about experiences refer to something non-physical, to the extra inner lights which illuminate the inner world. And once they think that, then of course they think that there is a clear line between cases where a light is on, and those which lack all illumination. Thus we find Colin McGinn, for instance, holding that 'the emergence of consciousness must . . . be compared to the *sudden* switching on of a light . . .' (McGinn 1982, italics mine).

However, if the antipathetic fallacy is a fallacy, and there are no inner lights, then this argument for a well-defined category falls away. Instead we are left with an explanation of why nearly everybody *thinks* there is a sharp line between states which are like something and those which aren't, even though there isn't.

But don't we know, from our own introspective experience, that there is a sharp line? What about the difference between seeing red and feeling pain, on the one hand, and being anaesthetized or having high blood pressure, on the other? Doesn't this give us a direct acquaintance with the difference between states that are like something and those that are not?

Here too, however, there is an explanation of why there will seem to be a sharp line, even if there isn't. Namely, that we use the test of first person recreatability to decide which of our states are conscious. Suppose it were indeterminate whether some state of ours were conscious (or 'sentient').

The application of the first person recreatability test will still yield a determinate yes-no answer, depending on whether we can imaginatively recall the state . Recall the example of hearing ultrasonic whistles. Even if this state is definitely conscious (as the earlier thought experiment supposed), or even it is indeterminate whether it is conscious, the first person recreatability test will still make us think it is definitely not conscious, if we can't imaginatively recall it.

What our introspective experience shows is that the test of first person recreatability draws a sharp line among our states, not that the concept of consciousness itself does. Given the earlier reasons for distinguishing consciousness itself from first person recreatability, there is no way of inferring the determinacy of consciousness from the determinacy of first person recreatability.

If the argument of this paper is right, then the current enthusiasm for scientific theories of consciousness (cf. Horgan 1994) is fated to end in disappointment. For it is an illusion, fostered by the antipathetic fallacy, to suppose that there is a well-defined object for such theories to explain. In reality there is only the class of states which we are able imaginatively to recreate. The special structure of imagination creates the illusion that these states possess a distinctive quality of inner illumination, and so engenders the desire to identify and explain this quality. But in fact there is no such quality, nor any other reason to suppose anything scientifically important binds these states together.

References

Horgan, T. (1984). Jackson on physical information and qualia. *Philosophical Quarterly*, **34**, 147–52.
Horgan, J. (1994). Can science explain consciousness? *Scientific American*, **271**, 72–8.
Jackson, F. (1982). Epiphenomenal qualia. *Philosophical Quarterly*, **32**, 127–36.
Jackson, F. (1986). What Mary didn't know. *Journal of Philosophy* **83**, 291–5.
Lycan, W. (1987). *Consciousness*. Cambridge, MA: MIT Press.
McGinn, C. (1982). *The Character of Mind*. Oxford: Oxford University Press.
McGinn, C. (1991). *The Problem of Consciousness*. Oxford: Basil Blackwell.
Mellor, D.H. (1987). The singularly affecting facts of causation. In P. Petit, R. Sylvan & J. Norman (eds), *Metaphysics and Morality*. Oxford: Basil Blackwell.
Mellor, D.H. (1992). Nothing like experience. *Proceedings of the Aristotelian Society*, **93**, 1–16.
Nagel, T. (1974). What is it like to be a bat? *Philosophical Review*, **83**, 435–50.
Papineau, D. (1993). *Philosophical Naturalism*. Oxford: Basil Blackwell.
Papineau, D. (1994). Arguments for supervenience and realization. In E. Savellos & U. Yaçin (eds), *Supervenience: New Essays*. Cambridge: Cambridge University Press.
Papineau, D. (forthcoming). Theoretical definitions. *Philosophy of Science*.
Sturgeon, S. (1994). The epistemic view of subjectivity. *Journal of Philosophy*, **91**, 221–35.
Tye, M. (1986). The subjective qualities of experience. *Mind*, **95**, 1–17.

Part Five

Qualia

Introduction to Part Five

Within the philosophy of mind, qualia are understood as mental states which possess a special sort of content: a subjective quality of experience, only accessible to the person who *has* these experiences. States of sensory consciousness in particular have such a quality: The subjective quality of *Pantone Blue 72* in a colour experience or the *painfulness* in a pain experience are examples of this. This type of content, however, generates a series of problems. It seems to be directly and immediately given, but only from the first person perspective (whatever that may mean). It appears to be the essential core of the conscious states in question. This core, however, eludes every necessary connection to the causal matrix of the physical world. The qualitative content seems to be tied at best only indirectly to the causal role or the functional profile of any correlated bodily states. Moreover, the information contained in the qualitative content can be transported into the public space only with extreme difficulty, because it is easily lost in linguistic forms of representation. This generates a strong intuition according to which phenomenal content is ineffable. These properties, among others, render even simple types of phenomenal content such as *Pantone Blue 72* or *painfulness* problematic for every theory of consciousness that aims to both assign them a place in the natural order of things and to take the first person perspective as seriously as possible. Of course it is controversial whether the characteristics of qualia as enumerated above exist at all.

Intuitively the quality of redness, e.g. in the conscious visual experience of a ripe tomato, seems to be what philosophers call an *intrinsic* property: the inner structureless core of experience. In order to reduce this core successfully to a deeper descriptive level, it would have to be dissolved into relations between some entities of this descriptive level. *Redness* would then have to be analysed as a relational property, e.g. as a relation between the elements of a neurophysiological or computational description of the activity of the brain or as a certain *causal* property of the brain. Many philosophers find this extremely implausible. Phenomenal consciousness is so very interesting in the first place, it appears, because intrinsic properties are instantiated in it.

In his contribution, **Joseph Levine** provides a lucid account of the resulting dilemma. This dilemma is one of the focal points of the philosophical discussion of qualia. In an important and influential paper published in 1982, Levine diagnosed the root of the dilemma as an 'explanatory gap'. Although general epistemic arguments such as the familiar *absent qualia argument* do not permit metaphysical conclusions, he argued, they pose a fundamental obstacle which besets any explanatory attempt which aims at assigning a definite place in the natural order of things to qualia. The problem consists in the fact that in this case there seems to be no difference between being and appearance, because we introspectively pick out phenomenal properties *through themselves*. The phenomenal character of *redness* does not provide any information concerning the causal role which could be played by such states. In virtue of this fact, these states seem to resist for fundamental reasons any physicalist strategy of reduction which tries to identify them with those mechanisms that physically realize their role. Against the background of these difficulties Levine analyses the philosophical options which we could choose in the face of the dilemma. Levine does not believe that any of these options is promising in the end. However, he offers a very clear account of the arguments for and against each of them.

One of the most difficult philosophical puzzles results from the widespread thesis that the qualitative content of conscious experiences is *ineffable*. This ineffability might seem to pose an insuperable obstacle for the analytic philosophy of mind. But what exactly does this mean? On the one hand we cannot explain to a blind person what *redness* is. On the other hand we all talk to each other about the subjective qualities of our conscious experiences, and it seems as if this kind of communication by means of folk psychological categories is thoroughly successful. So what theoretical significance do claims have which represent qualia as inexpressible in principle? **Diana Raffman** has already advanced an interesting and original view on this problem in earlier works. Here she develops her argument using the example of colour vision. This argument is directed against a certain group of theoretic strategies whose central point is that *subjective facts* about qualia do not exist, and that instead there are only different ways of epistemic access to physical or functional facts within the brain. According to this account, there is no logical or metaphysical difference between two kinds of facts, i.e. between subjective and objective facts, but only an *epistemic* difference between different modes of presentation, perspectives or ways of representation.

Raffman terms this the 'materialist line' and then uses results from the psychology of perception to argue that this line is empirically implausible owing to drastic limits on our perceptive memory. Because our ability to recognize colours is much less fine-grained than our ability to *discriminate* colours and visual nuances, we cannot categorize perceptive values which are given and definite in direct experience. It seems that we cannot analyse phenomenal representation-processes as predications from a first-person point-of-view. Finally, Raffman extends her arguments to demonstrative variants of the materialist line, and concludes that none of the contemporary attempts to eliminate subjective facts by an appeal to different modes of epistemic access can be successful. In doing this, she also provides an important contribution to the clarification of the question of what we could really mean when we say that certain realms of subjective space are so rich, subtle and elusive that their content is in principle linguistically inexpressible.

David J. Chalmers uses two thought experiments which are as sophisticated as they are entertaining to argue that conscious experiences are nomologically completely determined by the functional organization of the underlying system. That is to say: It is empirically impossible that a system with the same abstract pattern of causal interactions between its parts as a conscious system, could *lack* qualia or possess *inverted* qualia. The argument has the logical form of a *reductio ad absurdum*: Chalmers develops the familiar absent qualia argument and the inverted qualia argument further in his two new thought experiments to draw out absurd consequences. A crucial aspect of the discussion is that only a weak version of functionalism can be defended in this way: Although the appropriate functional states are *nomologically sufficient* for conscious experience, they need not be *constitutive* of conscious experience. This leads to an interesting position which Chalmers calls *non-reductive functionalism*, which is compatible both with property dualism and with some forms of physicalism. At the same time, his discussion contributes to a more precise description of the physical basis of phenomenal consciousness. In this way the aims of cognitive science, AI research and computational neuroscience are supported, even though Chalmers' associated theory of consciousness is non-reductionist.

Further Reading

Chalmers, D.J. (1995). Facing up to the problem of consciousness. *Journal of Consciousness Studies*, **2**, 200–19. Also in Hameroff *et al.* 1996.

Chalmers, D.J. (1996). *The Conscious Mind*. New York: Oxford University Press.

Chalmers, D.J. (1996). Availability: the cognitive basis of experience? In Block *et al.* 1996.

Dennett, D.C. (1988). Quining qualia. In Marcel & Bisiach 1988. Reprinted in Block *et al.* 1996.

Levine, J. (1983). Materialism and qualia: The explanatory gap. *Pacific Philosophical Quarterly*, **64**, 354–61.

Levine, J. (1989). Absent and inverted qualia revisited. *Mind and Language*, **3**, 271–87.

Levine, J. (1991). Cool red. *Philosophical Psychology*, **4**, 27–40.

Levine, J. (1993). On leaving out what it's like. In Davies & Humphreys 1993.

Raffman, D. (1988). Towards a cognitive theory of musical ineffability. *Review of Metaphysics*, **41**, 685–706.

Raffman, D. (1993). Qualms about Quining qualia. In D. Raffman, *Language, Music, and Mind*. Cambridge, MA: MIT Press.

A selection of monographs and collections of essays about qualia is listed in sections 1.1 and 2.1 of the bibliography at the end of this volume. In section 3.7 individual articles can be found which directly concern themselves with Thomas Nagel's famous essay 'What is it like to be a bat?' and Frank Jackson's knowledge argument. Section 3.8 contains a selection of texts which deal with the arguments of absent or inverted qualia. In section 3.9 a number of works are given regarding qualia and phenomenal properties which cannot easily be grouped into any of the other thematic sections. Further texts, which centre on the relation between consciousness and the physical world, can be found in section 3.2.

Joseph Levine

Qualia: Intrinsic, Relational or What?

I

Qualitative character is a troublesome property. For instance, take the reddish quality of my current visual sensation as I stare at the red diskette case sitting on my computer table. Is it an intrinsic property of the sensation? It certainly seems to be. But then there's a real problem about which intrinsic property it is, at least if we assume a materialist metaphysics. On the other hand, perhaps it's a relational property, in which case the problem of identifying the appropriate physical intrinsic property evaporates. But then there's a problem too; namely, it's just too implausible. So what sort of property is qualitative character? I don't know, which is why I think it's so troublesome.

It seems to me that a lot of the literature about qualia over the past two decades comes down to the dilemma posed above, with various proposals bouncing back and forth but none overcoming the basic structure of the dilemma. Qualia as intrinsic properties can't be integrated into a naturalistic framework, but no proposal to treat them as relational seems at all compelling. I have no solution to this dilemma to offer in this paper. What I hope to do, rather, is to make the case that it really is as difficult a dilemma as I claim it is.

II

Let's begin with the intrinsic side, since this is the intuitive starting point. It seems plausible to think of visual experience as having an intrinsic qualitative character. The reddishness of my visual experience of the diskette case seems to be a property of my experience. Let's dub this property 'QR'. We needn't expect *a priori* to know what sort of property it is, but that my experience has it seems apparent. (I am not appealing to privileged access, or any sort of hyper-certainty. I'm just saying let's not doubt the obvious until we have to.)

If we claim that qualitative character is an intrinsic property of an experience, then immediately we want to know what sort of property it is; i.e. whether it is physical or not. According to the classical identity theory, it is a type of neurophysiological property — call it 'PR'. Two sorts of challenges have been mounted against this identification: the multiple realizability argument and the conceivability argument. According to the first, QR can't be identical to PR because it seems possible that there could be creatures with a different sort of physical constitution (say, Martians, or robots) that nevertheless could experience reddish visual sensations like ours. The conceivability argument also trades on intuitions about what's possible. It goes like this. It certainly seems possible that one could be having an experience of type QR and yet not be in state PR, the neurophysiological state in question. Therefore, since what is conceivable is possible, it is possible to be in QR without being in PR. But if it is possible that $\sim (PR = QR)$, then in fact $\sim (PR = QR)$.

I want to suggest that both arguments stem from the same source, what I call the 'explanatory gap' argument.[1] That is, the basic problem for materialists with treating qualitative character as an intrinsic property is that there is then no way to explain how it arises from the material processes of our nervous system.

To see how the explanatory gap underlies both challenges to the identity theory, consider the following response to the conceivability argument. One could just deny that what is conceivable is possible. Or, to put it another way, deny that epistemological possibility is a guide to metaphysical possibility. Once we deny that premise of the conceivability argument, we make room for the possibility that indeed, despite what seems possible, QR is identical to PR. But now we have an answer as well to the multiple realizability argument. After all, what makes us so confident that QR could be realized in a variety of different ways? Isn't it just the same conceivability we appealed to in the conceivability argument? If we're convinced that qualitative character is an intrinsic property of experience, and we're also confirmed materialists, then we must just stand our ground and say that only creatures with *our* neurophysiological constitution are capable of experiencing QR.

Indeed, it does seem right to say that the original conceivability argument and the more contemporary multiple realizability argument are of a piece. In both cases it is open to the identity theorist to deny the metaphysical implications of the argument. That is, to say that, despite strong intuitions to the contrary, it is not possible for a creature to experience QR without

---

[1] See Levine 1983 and 1993a for a more extensive presentation of this argument.

occupying state PR. However, the epistemological implications are bad enough. The very fact that QR and PR are so separable in conception, if not in fact, is a symptom of the lack of an explanatory connection between them. If, for instance, it were possible to explain the particular qualitative character definitive of QR by reference to the neurophysiological property PR, then it wouldn't be conceivable that something that instantiated PR could lack QR; or that there could be a wide variety of physical mechanisms that would instantiate QR.[2]

It has been objected to this sort of consideration that the apparent explanatory gap between the neurophysiological and the qualitative is merely that — apparent. It is an artifact of our current ignorance of the neurophysiological mechanisms underlying conscious experience. As we learn more about the brain and the various sensory mechanisms responsible for our qualitative experience we'll come to understand why being in various neurophysiological states is experienced the way it is.[3]

Of course it is always open to someone to appeal to what may yet be discovered — who knows what that may be. But if we assume that we're dealing with the sort of neurophysiological properties with which we are already familiar — the sorts of electro-chemical properties exhibited by the firings of neurons, along with the excitatory and inhibitory connections among them — then I don't see how appeal to such properties could explain qualitative character, so long as it's considered an intrinsic property of experience. To put the point starkly: what is it about the firing of a neuron, or the nature of a synaptic connection from one neuron to another, or any complicated assembly of such connections and firings, that could explain the reddishness of my experience of the diskette case? It seems to me that there are only four options available in response, none of which works.

Option one is to admit that no progress can be made if we consider qualitative character to be an intrinsic property of experience, and to argue that it ought to be analysed as a relational/functional property instead. This of course just means confronting the other horn of the dilemma, and we'll do that in the next section.

Option two is to appeal to correlations as the basis for identification. For instance, suppose we find that whenever someone is experiencing a visual sensation of type QR, there is a particular pattern of neural firing occurring

[2] Of course there could be more than one. The point is that if we were able to say what it is about PR that explained its being experienced as QR, we would have a principle for determining when other candidate physical states were also experienced as QR. Another way to put it is this: with the right sort of explanatory connection, we would be able to determine the right level of abstraction or aggregation at which to define PR.

[3] See Churchland 1985 and Flanagan 1992 for arguments along these line. Though I don't claim really to understand what Searle's position is on this question, it seems to me that the arguments that follow also address his attempt to establish that there is no problem in identifying consciousness with a 'higher-order' property of the brain. See Searle 1992.

in their visual cortex. Or suppose that whenever someone is having a conscious sensation, a 40 hz oscillation pattern is occurring in the relevant cortical areas. (Cf. Crick and Koch 1990.) We might then appeal to this discovery as a basis for the claim that to have an experience of type QR is just to have the relevant pattern of firing in the visual cortex (similarly for having a conscious sensation and the presence of the 40 hz oscillation pattern).

While a robust correlation of the sort envisaged might provide grounds for identifying the properties in question, it certainly doesn't explain anything on its own. Is it really just a brute fact that certain neurophysiological states constitute qualitative experiences? That seems very hard to swallow. Instead of resting on brute correlation, option three is often preferred. According to this view, what legitimates the identification of QR with PR is the fact that PR provides the mechanisms by which the functions we associate with QR are performed. Colour perception involves selective sensitivity to fairly complicated properties of the light reflected from physical surfaces, and we now know a lot about how that sensitivity is implemented in neural hardware.

The problem is that the theory of neural implementation, as important and interesting as it is, basically comes down to the theory of how certain states bear information about other states. What we find out from studies of the neural pathways leading from the retina to the visual cortex is how information about various properties of the light are processed. But informational content is a relational property *par excellence*. If we are still committed to treating qualitative character as an intrinsic property of experience, then it isn't reducible to the property of bearing such-and-such information about the distal (or even the proximal) stimulus. It may in fact bear such information (presumably it does, or what's it good for?), and indeed the description of the neurophysiological mechanisms underlying vision may explain its ability to carry such information, but that doesn't amount to there being a neurophysiological explanation of qualitative character itself.

Option four for closing the explanatory gap is to build the explanatory connection out of isomorphic structure. For instance, Hardin and Van Gulick have argued that one reason qualia are thought to be inexplicable is that they are thought to have no structure. (Cf. Hardin 1988; Van Gulick 1993.) The idea is that the only way to explain the instantiation of one property in terms of the instantiation of other properties is to exhibit the structure of the explanandum property and show how the explanans properties realize that structure. If the property to be explained is simple, then the most you get from the alleged explanation is a brute correlation between that property and the ones in terms of which it is supposed to be explained. They then argue that though qualia appear at first blush to be simple properties, they are in fact quite complex, structured states, and therefore susceptible of an explanatory reduction to neurophysiological states.

A very simple example of the sort of thing they have in mind is this. A visual experience of orange might at first blush appear simple in character. Yet, upon reflection it seems to have a reddish and a yellowish component. Now, suppose we find that light reflected from orange objects tends to excite both the neural correlates of red and of yellow (something like this appears to be the case), then we could see why such light would cause the experiences it does. If we could analyse every experience of colour into a complex, multidimensional property,[4] then perhaps we could see how it is that its neurophysiological correlate constituted the type of experience it did. We would have transcended brute correlation for genuine explanation.

My problem with option four — I call it the 'complexity gambit' — is that it either doesn't address the real challenge, or else it reduces to option one. The idea is supposed to be that by finding structure inside qualia we will better be able to connect qualia to their underlying neurophysiological realizations. But why is this *internal* structure necessary anyway? Why isn't it sufficient that each quale maintains a complicated set of external relations to other qualia (as well as to stimuli, behaviour, and other mental states)? We can then link each quale to its neurophysiological correlate by exhibiting how the properties of the latter explain the external relations maintained by the former.

Obviously, the problem is that if we intend to get our explanatory punch from the external relations maintained by a type of qualitative character, then we are back to options one and three. Either we've given up on analysing qualitative character as an intrinsic property, or we have to admit that though we can explain the way a state with property QR relates to other states by appeal to PR, we still cannot explain the nature of QR itself in this manner. Hence the move to find structure *internal* to qualia, so that there will be more for those explanatory hooks to grab onto.

The problem is that this just displaces the explanatory gap, instead of removing it. Structure is a matter of relations among elements, which are themselves either structured or simple. To avoid an infinite regress, it is clear that whatever set of relations individual qualia are analysed into, the relata must themselves be simple elements of experience. Whether red is a simple, or warmth is, something experiential has to be. So long as the experiential primitives are themselves intrinsic properties of experience, the explanatory gap will remain.

I have argued that if qualitative character is an intrinsic property of experience, then we can't explain its presence in physical terms. The point is that descriptions of neurophysiological mechanisms can explain how information is processed, or, more generally, how various relational, or higher-order properties are realized. If we are to explain the presence of

---

[4] Hardin (1988: 134–42) proposes (by way of a speculative example) that aspects of colour experience like the 'warm/cool' distinction might be useful in supplying the requisite structure. For my critique and Hardin's reply, see Levine 1991 and Hardin 1991.

qualitative character in terms of such mechanisms, then we will first have to analyse it as a relational property of experience. If we can do this, then we can show how the relevant neurophysiological mechanisms that realize the experience stand in the appropriate relations, and there will be no explanatory gap.

III

So now we confront the other horn of the dilemma. It seems that the only way to explain qualitative character is to first analyse it as a relational property and then show how our neurophysiological mechanisms realize the appropriate relations. But, as I claimed at the start, the problem is that relational accounts of qualia are so plainly implausible. In this section I want to explore the reasons for this (allegedly) patent implausibility, extracting certain general themes from the arguments and counterarguments that have been presented over the last two or three decades.

Functionalism is the view that mental states, including qualia, are definable in terms of their causal roles, their causal relations with stimuli, behaviour, and other mental states.[5] So a state would have the property QR just in case it was normally caused by viewing red things, it tended to cause judgments to the effect that something was red, and it generally related to other mental states — in particular through similarity judgments — in the way that is typical of experiences of red. Let's call the functional role in question 'FR'.

The basic objection to functionalism is that it just seems intuitively plausible that FR and QR could come apart. The mismatch goes in both directions. That is, according to the famous absent and inverted qualia hypotheses, it seems quite possible that a creature could satisfy the conditions for being in FR even though not experiencing QR, or, for that matter, having any qualitative experience at all. On the other hand, and this is less emphasized in the literature, it also seems quite possible that a creature could experience QR even though most of the causal relations normally maintained by QR were absent.[6]

An example of the first sort of problem is the famous inverted spectrum thought experiment. If we assume that colour space is appropriately symmetrical, then if one person's experience underwent a transformation so that she experienced the complement of what everyone else experienced, she would satisfy the same functional description yet her experience would possess a different qualitative character.

An example of the second sort could occur if someone's normal functioning were disturbed, so that various relations between her colour experience

---

[5] For a presentation of the functionalist position, along with the objections that follow, see Block & Fodor 1972 and Block 1980.

[6] Antony (forthcoming) and Maudlin (1989) mount convincing arguments along these lines.

and memory, belief, and the like no longer held. It seems possible that this could happen while the qualitative character of her experience remained as it were. One concrete case of this is colour blindness. The fact that someone can't distinguish red from green obviously affects the structure of their colour space, yet it isn't obvious that this makes their experiences of blue any different from mine. In fact, I think we could take this to an extreme and imagine someone whose entire visual experience involved just one hue, and that one was qualitatively similar to the one involved in my experiences of type QR. Why shouldn't this be (at least conceptually) possible?

There have been two basic responses to these anti-functionalist arguments. The first is to grant their cogency and claim that for qualia, as opposed to cognitive states like belief, functionalism is wrong and the traditional type-identity theory is right.[7] But then one must confront the explanatory gap, as argued above.

The second sort of response is to attempt to undermine the intuitive resistance to a relational account represented by the absent and inverted qualia hypotheses. Numerous such attempts have been made, but I want to focus on two, related strategies in particular. I think they both fail, but their failure is especially instructive.

The basic idea behind the first strategy is to argue that an appropriately chosen and sufficiently rich relational description can uniquely identify a type of qualitative character, and thereby get around the sorts of counter-examples just discussed. So Austen Clark argues that each type of colour quale can be identified with a point in a multidimensional colour space, so that it is defined by its relations to other colour experiences, and nothing else (Cf. Clark 1993.) It may well be that only that particular type of colour quale could occupy that point in the space. If so, then there can't be inverted colour qualia.

The second strategy is exemplified by Van Gulick, in his discussion of the absent qualia argument. (Cf. Hardin 1988; Van Gulick 1993: 147–9.) He notes that the absent qualia hypothesis seems to assume that a state's being conscious is not necessary for playing its functional role. In fact, there is some evidence, for example, from blindsight cases, that consciousness is necessary. For instance, blindsight patients tend not to initiate action with respect to the objects that they can passively detect in their blind field. If, as such cases suggest, consciousness is essential to the performance of certain functional roles, then it isn't possible for a non-conscious state to play the same functional role.[8] Hence, absent qualia aren't possible.

[7] Shoemaker proposes an interesting in-between theory on which the property of having some qualitative character or other is a functional property, but the particular type of qualitative character is determined by the identity of the physical realization. See Shoemaker 1984, chapters 9, 14, and 15, and Levine 1989 for a critique of his position.

[8] Ned Block 1995 criticizes arguments of this sort. My objections here are slightly different from his, though I'm sympathetic to his critique as well. I discuss the relation between our views in Levine 1995.

Both strategies, finding a function that a quale is uniquely suited to perform and finding a definite description sufficiently rich to uniquely specify it, suffer from the same defect: namely, an unwarranted assimilation of role-player to role. However complex the description of the functional role played by, or network of relations maintained by, my reddish visual experience of the diskette case, it seems like the right way to characterize the situation is that the reddish experience is *playing* a certain role, not that it *is* a certain role. The point is that you don't show that a property is itself relational merely by finding a relational description that uniquely identifies it. It might still be that the property is itself intrinsic, it just turns out that only it satisfies the relevant description.

Thus, in response to Van Gulick, I grant, for the sake of argument, the possibility that there may be jobs, or roles, that only conscious states can fill. That still doesn't mean that filling that role is what it is to be conscious. In fact, that very way of putting it — that being conscious is essential, or necessary to playing the role — seems to imply just the reverse; that being conscious is one thing, playing the role quite another. Suppose it turned out that being red was essential to some plant's playing the ecological role it played; nothing that was not red could do it. We wouldn't say that being red *is* to play that role, but rather that being red is what makes the plant in question especially suited to play that role. It seems to me the same goes for being conscious in the scenario envisioned.

There is an interesting similarity here between the way that being conscious fills a role and the way that neurophysiological properties fill a role. In both cases, it seems, we have a role, relationally defined, and then we find something that plays it and determine that certain of its intrinsic properties are the ones that enable it to play the role. Whether it's being conscious or resonating at 40 Hz, the explanatory structure seems to be the same. In fact, this very similarity in the way that qualitative and neurophysiological states enter the explanatory picture is just what makes the identity theory so tempting in the first place.

So, for instance, suppose the role in question is the 'binding' of different features of a percept into a unified visual experience. On the one hand, as some speculate, the resonating at 40 hz might be the relevant neurophysiological cross-referencing property. On the other, conscious awareness certainly also seems to bring the various perceptual features together into a unified experience. Thus identification of the consciousness with the resonating seems almost irresistible. Of course, as I argued above, so long as consciousness is understood as the role *player*, and not the role itself, we can't explain *its* character by reference to the neurophysiological property. All that we could explain by identifying it with the neurophysiological property would be its ability to play the role.

This sort of confusion between role and role player, and the way this clouds discussion of the explanatory adequacy of neurophysiological reductionist accounts of qualitative character, is exhibited in Owen Flanagan's (Flanagan 1992, chapter 3, section 6.) discussion of the neural coding of sensory qualia, and in the way he employs his distinction between 'informational' sensitivity and 'experiential' sensitivity. Informational sensitivity is an organism's ability to respond selectively to stimuli. So, in the case of blindsight, though the subject claims to be unable to see anything in a certain region of her visual field, she displays informational sensitivity by 'guessing' correctly at the identity of objects displayed there. Experiential sensitivity is the ability of an organism to respond to stimuli with phenomenal experience, a state that has not only an informational content but also a qualitative character. It is the presence of this sort of sensitivity that distinguishes normal sight from blindsight.

Now, with respect to qualia, Flanagan proposes the following. Each qualitative difference to which we are capable of consciously responding (like the difference in taste between Coke and Pepsi) — an instance of experiential sensitivity — must correspond to a difference in the activation vector of the relevant sensory pathway. Now this seems right, since the only way the difference can be detected is by way of its effect on sensory mechanisms. No difference in the latter, no difference in experience.

But then Flanagan goes on to propose that we take the next step and identify the relevant quale with its corresponding sensory vector. The reasoning seems to be that since the ability to distinguish between the tastes of Coke and Pepsi is explained by the difference in activation vectors, these vectors explain the nature of the experienced tastes themselves.

But this is wrong. What the vectors explain is precisely informational sensitivity, because they provide avenues for preserving information about the difference in chemical composition between Coke and Pepsi. Of course *any* system of units capable of taking on the activation vectors that neurons take on, and capable of responding with just those vectors to just those chemical properties, would do the job just as well. What's essential here is precisely the job of information transfer, not the means by which it is done. Furthermore, we can think in the same terms about our experiential sensitivity. That is, what our consciousness of the difference between the taste of Coke and the taste of Pepsi enables us to do is to detect a difference in the stimuli — between Coke and Pepsi. That is, the qualitative difference serves to preserve, or transfer information concerning the chemical difference. Again, the qualitative character is here playing the role of information carrier, it isn't reducible to the very fact of information carrying itself. The qualitative difference and the vector difference are on a par here, as implementations of a task. They both explain how we detect the difference between Coke and Pepsi. That they are correlated in doing this job is undeniable. But what I do deny is (1) that the activation vector itself explains the qualitative character; and (2) that the qualitative character is identifiable with the job it is carrying out.

I have not tried directly to engage the debate over the inverted and absent qualia hypotheses. Some think these cases represent genuine possibilities, while others doubt this. My strategy has been to explore the intuitive domain surrounding the controversy. What I do hope to have established is not that qualia are definitely intrinsic properties, but that at least one sort of strategy for convincing us otherwise is inadequate. That is, devising definite descriptions in relational terms for identifying qualia is not suffi- cient for establishing that the properties themselves are relational. An inherently intrinsic property may be uniquely describable in relational terms. In particular, I have argued that many functionalist moves only work if we blur the distinction between *role* and *role-player*. If we keep these two notions distinct, then the functionalist moves lose much of their claim to plausibility.

In addition to the role/role-player argument just presented, I think there's another way of looking at what seems wrong about the case for treating qualitative character as a relational property. Earlier I argued that it cer- tainly seemed possible that someone could experience a sensation with a reddish quality even if they were incapable of experiencing sensations of other chromatic types. In response the relationalist might argue that red- dishness is essentially a matter of occupying a certain point in colour quality space. Not to be related to other colour qualities in this particular way is just not to be reddish.

But even if we grant that the structure of colour quality space is somehow essential to its occupants, it still doesn't follow that there couldn't be creatures who experience only a subset — perhaps even only a singleton subset — of the entire set of colour qualities. Perhaps the abstract property QR is necessarily related to the abstract property QG (greenishness) in a certain way. That doesn't entail that someone who experiences QR must also be capable of experiencing QG. It might mean that if they do experi- ence both, these experiences must be related in a certain way, but nothing requires that the antecedent of this conditional be satisfied.

It's illuminating to draw an analogy between the debate about colour qualia and the debate over holism with respect to intentional content. A standard holist argument starts from the premise that certain propositions are necessarily related to certain others; e.g. the proposition that John is a bachelor is necessarily related to the proposition that John is not married. The inference is then drawn that no one could represent that John is a bachelor without also representing (or being capable of representing) that he is not married.

The atomist, however, can resist this conclusion while granting the premise.[9] Suppose the two propositions are necessarily related just as the

---

[9] For this argument I'm indebted to Jerry Fodor. For a general treatment of the holism debate, see Fodor & Lepore 1992; 1993.

holist claims they are. Still, this doesn't mean that a creature couldn't be capable of representing one without being capable of representing the other. Jones may have the purely punctate thought that John is a bachelor, and his thought may entail that John is not married. But still, Jones may not himself be able to notice the entailment. Perhaps this situation is not really possible. The point remains that to argue that it isn't requires more than demonstrating the entailment relation between the two propositions.

I think the situation is similar with colour qualia. I can see that in some sense it may be essential to red that it be similar to orange, a complement of green, etc. I'm not sure this is true, but let's grant it for the sake of argument. So we can be holists about the space of colour qualia. Still, individual experiences may be of the requisite type — say QR — without the subject of that experience herself being capable of experiencing more than a limited range of all the possible colour qualia. But if so, then how does the relational analysis of QR as a point in colour quality space help us with our dilemma? It turns out that Jones, who, to take an extreme case, can only experience QR and QG, is not herself in a state that satisfies the rich relational description which characterizes QR's position in colour quality space as a whole. So it can't be in virtue of occupying a state within such a structure that she counts as having such an experience. Hence, QR itself, as a property of her experience, has not been shown to be a relational property and we're back where we started.

My purpose in this section has been to explore the reasons why relational analyses of qualia are so intuitively unconvincing. In the spirit of this exploration of the intuitive domain, it might be informative to investigate other cases where what seemed intuitively to be intrinsic properties were reanalysed in relational terms. Consider two in particular: weight and colour.

At first it seems as if an object's weight is intrinsic to it. The only way to change it would be to alter the object itself. But then we learn that weight is a matter of the attractive force between the Earth and an object near its surface, so it turns out to be a relational property. In other words, I can change the weight of my red diskette case both by changing it and also by changing the mass of the Earth (or its distance from the center of the Earth). Of course what is intrinsic to the diskette case, and in some sense captures what was originally thought to be the intrinsic property weight, is its mass.

Let's turn to colour, which is closer to our primary interest here. The diskette case is red. It's also three inches from the computer. Again, normally I would say its redness is an intrinsic property and its distance from the computer is a relational property because to change its colour something would have to be done to it, whereas I could change the distance from the computer by moving the computer and leaving the case where it is. But now along comes a colour theorist who tells me that colour is itself a relational property. How so? Well, to be red is to be such as to excite certain visual experiences in normal observers under appropriate circumstances. We can change the colour of the case, then, by changing the human visual system.

Here too, as in the case of weight, the reanalysis of colour from an intrinsic property to a relational one involves substituting another intrinsic property that captures what was originally thought to be intrinsic about colour. In this case, it's the colour-quality of the visual experience. We can put it this way. We've pushed the colour, what we originally took to be intrinsic, back into the head. As far as the relational analysis of objective colour is concerned, this subjective colour, which was pushed back into the head, is still intrinsic.

It seems that when we start with an intuitively intrinsic property and reanalyse it as a relational property, that the process involves an intrinsic residue. In the case of colour it's our visual response to the light coming from the object. In the case of weight, it's mass. These are plausible intrinsic substitutes for the original intrinsic properties. Perhaps what seems so problematic about the case of making qualia relational is that there isn't a plausible intrinsic substitute. The intrinsic buck seems to stop here.

To see the force of this problem, consider the sorts of intrinsic substitutes that have generally been offered for qualia. According to traditional functionalist theories, a quale is defined by its relations to inputs, outputs, and other mental states by a Ramsey-style method of definition. Here the intrinsic residues are the inputs and outputs — stimuli and behaviour.

Despite the appeal to other mental states, this sort of functional analysis suffers from its behaviouristic flavor. It displaces the core of the identity of an experience from what is going on inside to how it contributes to behaviour. It just seems to be a contingent, not a criterial fact that experiences with a reddish quale cause me to say 'red'. And qualifying the conditions under which it causes me to say this with reference to attention, understanding, desire, etc., doesn't really help. I see the inverted qualia hypothesis as just a concrete way of expressing the contingency of this relation.

Of course there are other versions of functionalism which don't take stimuli and behaviour to be the ultimate points by which functional identity is pinned down. For instance, one might view qualia as primarily representational. So, to occupy a state of type QR is to represent an object as having a certain property — presumably, being red. The intrinsic residue, then, is redness itself. But there are two problems with this move. First, redness itself was analysed as a power to cause QR experiences, so now circularity threatens. Also, we need to distinguish representational experiences from plain representational states, such as beliefs that something is red.

With regard to the threatened circularity, there are two possible responses. First, maybe redness isn't itself a power after all. Maybe it can be identified with something like a surface reflectance.[10] Secondly, even if it

[10] See Hilbert 1987 for a defence of this view, and Hardin 1988 for objections to it.

is understood to be a power, so long as we can analyse what is distinctive about an experience of type QR in terms of conditions internal to the subject, it's still possible to count the relational property of the external surface as the intentional object of the experience. Of course this gets us out of the circularity, but at the price of removing the property of the external surface as the intrinsic residue for which we're searching.

So it all comes down, then, to the nature of the internal response. Well, what makes a visual response experiential, as opposed to merely judgmental, or cognitive? There are two possibilities. One, pin the experiential nature on the particular neurophysiological mechanisms that subserve the response. Second, pin it on the pattern of relations to judgment, memory, emotion, and the like that is characteristic of visual experience.

On the first option we are essentially giving up on the relational analysis and back to identifying qualitative character with a neurophysiological property. On the second option, the intrinsic residue is to be found in judgment, memory, and the like. But surely analyses of these states will lead us right back out to either stimuli and behaviour or properties of external objects, none of which provide plausible candidates for the intrinsic residue we're looking for.

Another source, then, for the implausibility of relational analyses of qualitative character is revealed by our comparison with the cases of colour and weight. Unlike these cases, with qualitative character there is no plausible intrinsic substitute for the original. Mass does seem sufficiently like what we took weight to be for the relational analysis of weight to make a lot of sense. Properties of visual experience — subjective colour — also serves as an intelligible, plausible replacement for the intrinsic objective colour. But judgment, memory, behaviour, or any of the other functionalist candidates, seem totally foreign to experience itself. Rather than an analysis of qualitative character, it amounts more to an elimination of it.

In this section I've presented various reasons why relational treatments of qualia are not intuitively compelling. These considerations do not constitute knock-down arguments, nor were they intended to be. Rather, what I've attempted here is a fleshing out of the strong intuitive resistance to functionalist treatments, and to show that they have a basis. So let me now turn to the question of the state of play, or burden of argument.

First of all, a word about the role of intuition is in order. When speaking of 'intuitive resistance', it's tempting for one's opponent to accuse one of 'mere intuition mongering', or even mysticism. On my view, intuition has no special epistemic status; it's not a faculty in its own right, nor are its dictates to be treated as incorrigible. As far as I can see, intuition is just reasonableness. That is, to say that something is intuitively wrong, or odd, is to say that it strikes one as unreasonable, implausible. One could be wrong about this, and the basis for this response should always be sought out to the degree possible, but sometimes one just has to rest on the fact that some hypothesis seems blatantly implausible. In the philosophy of mind there is often a tendency to take the anti-Cartesian denial of epistemic privilege for intuition to an unwarranted extreme.[11]

But now what about the case of our intuitions about qualia? I agree in principle that it could turn out — intuition notwithstanding — that qualia are actually relational properties. This follows for me from the general (and anti-Cartesian) principle that I accept — namely, that *anything* (perhaps excluding outright contradictions) could turn out to be the case. But on what basis ought we to accept a relational analysis of qualitative character in the face of its apparent implausibility? I can see only two, neither of which, at this stage in the process (and philosophers have been attempting to make the materialist world safe for qualia for a long time now), seem very promising. The first is conceptual analysis, and the second is theoretical analysis.

I don't mean to claim that there is a very sharp line between these two forms of analysis; sometimes it's quite hard to draw a line. Furthermore, it's not even clear to me that there really is such a thing as conceptual analysis.[12] But it does seem to me that there are basically two avenues along which to discover that the way we originally characterized a property has to be changed. Either, through reflection on what we had in mind, we become clear that it is really different from what we originally thought; or we make a theoretical discovery to that effect. What else could there be?

If we consider the various relational analyses of qualia that have been discussed above, it doesn't look like they could be convincingly established in either way. As conceptual analyses they just don't capture what we have in mind by our notion of qualitative character. This is the burden of the sorts of considerations that I've advanced above, as well as the point of the inverted and absent qualia hypotheses that go hand in hand with those considerations. To say that my conception of QR is really a conception of a functional role is just not credible. As I have tried to show in this section, the standard arguments that have been advanced on its behalf are unconvincing, once we make the necessary distinctions.

Perhaps, then, it's a matter of theoretical discovery. But what sort of discovery is this? Suppose we have discovered precisely what information about the light hitting the eye is registered by an experience of type QR, and also by what neurophysiological mechanisms this information-processing feat is accomplished. In what sense does this constitute a theoretical discovery to the effect that to be in state QR is just to register this information? What the theory tells us is that information of such-and-such a sort is

---

[11] I discuss this issue in more detail , especially with respect to eliminativist arguments, in Levine forthcoming.

[12] In fact, in Levine 1993b I argue against recent attempts to revive the notion of analytic or conceptual truth.

registered, and how it's done. But how can it tell us that doing so captures the essence of property QR?

The theory could do this if it explained why QR was experienced as it was. It could do this, in turn, if we already had an analysis of QR in relational terms. If we knew pretheoretically that QR was a state that interacted with light, the eyes, memory, belief, etc., and we just needed to know precisely what information about the light it detected, and just how it interacted with these other systems, then the theory would explain how we experienced QR as we do. Of course this whole scenario depends upon a prior analysis of experiencing QR in functional–relational terms. If we don't have such an analysis ready to hand, then I don't see how the theory is going to provide it. It can tell us a lot about the functional role that QR plays, and by what mechanisms that role is realized. It can't tell us that that's what QR *is*.

IV

I started this paper with the claim that qualitative character is troublesome. If treated as an intrinsic property, it doesn't seem to have a natural home in the naturalistic world everything else seems to inhabit. On the other hand, the prospects for analysing it as a relational property are not promising. Hence, when it comes to the question posed by the title of this paper, I have to opt for the third alternative.[13]

References

Antony, M. (forthcoming). Against functionalist theories of consciousness. *Mind and Language*.

Block, N. (1980). Troubles with functionalism. In Block 1980.

Block, N. (1995). On a confusion about a function for consciousness. *Behavioral and Brain Sciences*, **18**, 227–47.

Block, N. & Fodor, J.A. (1972). What psychological states are not. *Philosophical Review*, **81**, 159–81.

Churchland, P. (1985). Reduction, qualia, and the direct introspection of brain states. *Journal of Philosophy*, **82**, 8–28.

Clark, Austen (1993). *Sensory Qualities*. Oxford: Oxford University Press.

Crick, F. & Koch, C. (1990). Towards a neurobiological theory of consciousness. *Seminars in the Neurosciences*, **2**, 263–75.

Flanagan, O. (1992). *Consciousness Reconsidered*. Cambridge, MA: MIT Press.

[13] An earlier version of this paper was presented at Wake Forest University's Conference on Consciousness, May, 1993. I would like to thank the participants in that conference for their helpful comments.

292   JOSEPH LEVINE

Fodor, J. & Lepore, E. (1992). *Holism: A Shopper's Guide*. Oxford: Blackwell.

Fodor, J. & Lepore, E. (1993)[eds]. *Holism: A Consumer Update*. Special issue of *Grazer Philosophische Studien*, vol. **46**.

Hardin, C.L. (1988). *Color for Philosophers: Unweaving the Rainbow*. Indianapolis/Cambridge: Hackett Publishing Company.

Hardin, C.L. (1991). Reply to Levine. *Philosophical Psychology*, **4**, 41–50.

Hilbert, D. R. (1987). *Color and Color Perception: A Study in Anthropocentric Realism*. Stanford University: Center for the Study of Language and Information.

Levine, J. (1983). Materialism and qualia: the explanatory gap. *Pacific Philosophical Quarterly*, **64**, 354–61.

Levine, J. (1989). Absent and inverted qualia revisited. *Mind & Language*, **3**, 271–87.

Levine, J. (1991). Cool red. *Philosophical Psychology*, **4** , 27–40.

Levine, J. (1993a). On leaving out what it's like. In Davies & Humphreys 1993.

Levine, J. (1993b). Intentional chemistry. In Fodor & Lepore 1993.

Levine, J. (1995). Phenomenal access: a moving target. Commentary on Block in *Behavioral and Brain Sciences*, **18**, 261.

Levine, J. (forthcoming). Out of the closet: a qualophile confronts qualophobia. *Philosophical Topics*.

Maudlin, T. (1989). Computation and consciousness. *Journal of Philosophy*, vol. **LXXXVI**, no. 8.

Searle, J. (1992). *The Rediscovery of the Mind*. Cambridge, MA: MIT Press.

Shoemaker, S. (1984). *Identity, Cause, and Mind*. Cambridge: Cambridge University Press.

Van Gulick, R. (1993). Understanding the phenomenal mind: are we all just armadillos? In Davies & Humphreys 1993.

Diana Raffman

On the Persistence of Phenomenology

Anyone working in the philosophy of mind today has heard about the trouble with *qualia* — the supposed raw feels, phenomenal properties, immediate felt qualities of conscious experiences. According to tradition, qualia are (among other things) homogeneous intrinsic properties immediately presented to us in introspection; indeed, they are essentially subjective properties accessible *only* from an introspective or first-person 'point of view' (e.g. Nagel 1974; Jackson 1982). Thus it is claimed that introspection delivers knowledge, or at least awareness, of essentially subjective facts about one's conscious experiences: one is aware that they have this or that determinate qualitative character.

Qualia pose an obvious problem for materialist theories of mind: physical matter is paradigmatically objective stuff, so how could a material brain have subjective properties? Not surprisingly, the literature is rife with eliminative (or anyway highly revisionary) approaches. Indeed the past five or so years have seen the emergence of what deserves to be called a received view among materialists. The shared insight is that there are no subjective facts; rather, there are simply different *ways of knowing* ordinary physical or functional facts about the mind-brain.[1] On this view, introspection is a distinctive first-person way of knowing objective physical facts — the only kind of facts there are — about one's own mind-brain. Thus traditional qualia theorists have mistaken a mere epistemic difference between ways of knowing (ways of thinking, modes of presentation, perspectives, con-

---

My title is a play on the title of Daniel Dennett's classic essay 'On the Absence of Phenomenology' (1979). The present paper is based on an invited talk delivered at the APA Eastern Division meetings in December 1994. My commentator on that occasion was Michael Tye, to whom I am indebted throughout and, especially, in section IV below.

[1] I shall call these latter 'physical facts', following Frank Jackson's (1982) sensibly liberal usage of the term.

cepts, representations, mentalese predicates) for a metaphysical difference between types of facts. Call this received materialist view the *materialist line*.

I shall not here take sides in the ongoing debate over the existence and nature of qualia. Instead I shall argue that, though there may be no subjective facts, the materialist line *per se* is untenable. Or, at least, its most prevalent variants are untenable. Specifically, the materialist line is so implausible on *empirical* grounds that it fails to license any conclusion about qualia one way or the other. Thus my principal claim will be negative: subjective facts cannot be eliminated in the manner envisioned by the materialist line. I do not pretend that my story dissolves or even bypasses the intuitive gridlock characteristic of discussions about qualia. (By now we are all familiar with that schoolyard dialectic: 'You've left something out!' 'No I haven't.' 'Yes you have.' 'No I haven't.' 'Yes you have.' etc. etc.) My hope, though, is that a consideration of certain empirical factors — specifically certain limitations on perceptual memory — will serve to relocate the intuitive impasse, or at least to approach it by a different route, and thereby shed some new light on the problem.

Since my case against the materialist line will proceed from empirical psychological considerations, I had better begin by saying what those are.

I. The Memory Constraint

It is a truism of perceptual psychology and psychophysics that, with rare exceptions,[2] discrimination along perceptual dimensions surpasses identification. In other words, our ability to judge whether two or more stimuli are the same or different in some perceptual respect (pitch or colour, say) far surpasses our ability to type-identify them. As Burns and Ward explain, '[s]ubjects can typically discriminate many more stimuli than they can categorize on an absolute basis, and the discrimination functions are smooth and monotonic' (Burns & Ward 1977: 457. For instance, whereas normal listeners can discriminate about 1400 steps of pitch difference across the audible frequency range (Seashore 1967: 60), they can type-identify or recognize pitches as instances of only about eighty pitch categories (constructed from a basic set of twelve).[3] In the visual domain, Leo Hurvich observes that 'there are many fewer absolutely identifiable [hues] than there are discriminable ones. Only a dozen or so hues can be used in practical

---

[2] The exceptions are cases of so-called categorical perception; see Repp 1984 and Harnad 1987 for details.

[3] Burns & Ward 1977; 1982; Siegel & Siegel 1977a, b, for example. Strictly speaking, only listeners with so-called perfect pitch can identify pitches *per se*; listeners (most of us) with relative pitch can learn to identify musical *intervals* if certain cues are provided. This complication touches nothing in the present story.

situations where absolute identification is required' (Hurvich 1981: 2). Hurvich cites Halsey & Chapanis in this regard:

> . . . the number of spectral [hues] which can be easily identified is very small indeed compared to the number that can be discriminated 50 per cent of the time under ideal laboratory conditions. In the range from 430 to 650 [*nm*], Wright estimates that there are upwards of 150 discriminable wavelengths. Our experiments show that less than one-tenth this number of hues can be distinguished when observers are required to identify the hues singly and with nearly perfect accuracy (Halsey & Chapanis 1951: 1058).

The point is clear: we are much better at discriminating perceptual values (i.e. making same/different judgments) than we are at identifying or recognizing them. Consider for example two just noticeably different shades of red — red_{31} and red_{32}, as we might call them. *Ex hypothesi* we can tell them apart in a context of pairwise comparison, but we cannot recognize them — cannot identify them as red_{31} and red_{32}, respectively — when we see them. For present purposes I shall take colour (hue) perception as my case in point; but the line I'll be defending should apply equally to other perceptual dimensions.

Inevitably, there is disagreement over just how the relevant colour naming data should be interpreted, how many categories perceivers are actually employing, to what extent the categories in question are universal, and so on. We can ignore those controversies here, however. All my argument will require is this: even if it turns out that perceivers are able, or could learn, to type-identify colour stimuli more finely (i.e. as tokens of types more fine-grained) than is commonly supposed, it remains overwhelmingly unlikely that they could learn to identify them as finely as they can discriminate them. The reason has to do with limitations on perceptual memory. Let me explain.

It seems safe to assume that you can recognize only what you can remember. For example, in order to recognize or type-identify an object as red, upon inspection, you must remember what red looks like. A 'classical' cognitivist model of perceptual memory is helpful here (though by no means requisite; see note 6 below). Roughly, on this sort of view, enduring psychological structures called *schemas* store perceptual information about how colours look, together with linguistic information about what they are called. When you see a red object, the RED perceptual node[4] in your colour schema is activated, therein constituting your recognition of the object as red; activation then spreads to your 'red' word node, enabling you to call the object 'red' (e.g. Anderson 1980).

---

[4] I shall use upper case letters throughout for names of psychological entities like concepts, mentalese terms, schematic structures, network nodes, and so forth.

The obvious thought, then, is that the limited nature of our ability to identify shades of colour results from the limited nature of our colour schemas: the grain of our schemas is evidently a good deal coarser than the corresponding discrimination thresholds. Such a result is hardly surprising inasmuch as the point of schemas is to reduce information load; as Burns and Ward explain,

> [n]umerous studies have indicated . . . that when faced with high information signals and/or high information rates, observers tend to encode the information into categories as a means of reducing the information load (Burns & Ward 1982: 245).

In particular, schemas are thought to provide a way of reducing the information load imposed precisely by our fine-grained perceptual discriminations. It would be maladaptive, at the least, for us to remember and be able to recognize every type of stimulus we can discriminate. Hence we have evolved to ignore such fine-grained differences in the interest of simple and speedy responses.

Be the evolutionary pressures as they may, the coarse-grained character of perceptual memory explains why we can recognize 'determinable' colours like red and blue and even scarlet and indigo *as such*, but not 'determinate' shades of those determinables; we cannot recognize red_{31} or $indigo_{372}$ as such.[5] This asymmetry between our representations of red and red_{31}, of determinables and their determinates, manifests itself in telling ways.[6] In particular, because we cannot recognize determinate shades as such, ostension is our only means of communicating our knowledge of them. If I want to convey to you the precise shade of an object I see, I must point to it, or perhaps paint you a picture of it; in other words, I must somehow present an instance of the shade in question. More importantly still, since our shade *perceptions* are individuated one-to-one with the shades we can discriminate, ostension is also our only means of communicating the contents of our perceptions of determinate shades. If I want to convey to you the content of my perception of a certain shade, I must present you with an instance of that shade. You must have the experience yourself.[7]

---

[5] Lest there be any confusion: by 'determinate shades' or 'determinate hues' I shall mean the finest colours we can discriminate.

[6] That is 'representations' in its most innocent sense. In particular, the issues I address here should be resolvable independently of any conflict between classical computational and PDP architectures. If dyed-in-the-wool Gibsonians or behaviourists disapprove of even this anemic sense of the term, they can transcribe my story in whatever terms they prefer; transcription is all that will be required.

[7] For present purposes I shall use the terms 'perception', 'perceptual experience', and 'experience' interchangeably.

The significance of this limitation on perceptual memory — call it the *memory constraint* — is often overlooked by philosophers writing about consciousness. In what follows, I shall argue that our inability to type-identify determinate perceptual values, and the resulting requirement that we ostend or present them in order to communicate our knowledge of them, pose a serious problem for the materialist line. First, though, we need to hear more about the latter view. It is advanced in many forms; at present I shall focus on two of these — what I call its *predicative* and *demonstrative* forms — but my suspicion is that the difficulty cited here attends the other forms as well.

II. The Materialist Line: Predicative Variants

As I said earlier, materialist liners claim that no subjective fact is known or otherwise grasped in introspection; rather, an ordinary physical property of a perceptual state — a perception of red tomatoes, for example — is represented or 'thought of' in an idiosyncratic but materialistically unproblematic way. William Lycan writes:

> [K]nowledge involves the mode under which the knower represents the fact known, and . . . this is no less true for mental facts than for ordinary physical ones . . . [K]nowledge that one is having this sort of sensation differ[s] from knowledge that one is in brain state so-and-so, even though one's having this sort of sensation just is one's being in brain state so-and-so (Lycan 1990: 113, 120).

Specifically, the relevant neural property causes the tokening of a first-person introspective concept. On Lycan's account, this concept is a mentalese predicate tokened as the result of a process of self-scanning: mentalese 'RED-EXPERIENCE', say, is tokened as a result of the 'operation of one of [the subject's] internal scanners' upon the perceptual state in question.

Stumping for another predicative variant of the materialist line, Brian Loar argues that in introspection, some physical property of the brain triggers the tokening of a special phenomenal concept with a 'distinctive cognitive content' expressible as '*this*' or '*that*'. This concept refers directly to the causative physical property in a judgment of the form (e.g.) 'I AM NOW IN A STATE THAT FEELS LIKE *THIS*', unmediated by any higher order reference-fixing property.[8] Indeed, although Loar is more explicit than many of his colleagues on this score, presumably any version of the materialist line must require that the introspective concepts or 'ways of knowing' one's first-order perceptual state refer directly. That is because the invocation of a higher order reference-fixing property would only

---

[8] Loar 1990: 86–7. Actually, Loar claims to be agnostic: he says that *for all the qualia defenders have shown*, consciousness could be as he describes it. I ignore this dialectical fine point here.

reintroduce the original problem and thereby threaten a regress. The higher order property would itself be a physical property, as required by the materialist line, and so in turn would be apprehended under a phenomenal concept: as Loar himself points out, 'introspection delivers up no physical-functional description'. (Loar 1990: 82.) But then, presumably, this higher order phenomenal concept would itself refer via a still higher order reference-fixing property; and so on, *ad indefinitum*.

Although Loar typically characterizes his introspective concepts as demonstratives, they are in fact mentalese predicates — 'phenomenal recognitional concepts', he calls them. These terms presumably enter introspection indexed, as for example 'FEELS LIKE THIS$_1$', 'FEELS LIKE THIS$_2$', and so forth, so as to reflect their differential contents. Evidently there will be such a recognitional term for every distinct content of which we can be introspectively aware:

> We have phenomenal recognitional concepts of various degrees of generality. Some are of highly determinate qualities, and others are of phenomenal determinables: crimson, dark red, red, warm-colored, colored, visual. There is the recognitional conception of a whole sensory modality. And there is the most general of all, the recognitional concept *phenomenal* (state, quality), the highest ranking phenomenal determinable (Loar 1990: 95).

One can begin to see how these predicative views would eliminate the need for any presentation of phenomenal properties in introspection. Just what such presentation could consist in is notoriously difficult to say; but for present purposes an intuitive characterization will do. A presentational representation is one that does something more like showing than telling, more like exemplifying than merely standing for, more like instantiating than merely designating, its content. Here is a presentational representation of (let us suppose) red$_{31}$: ● . On the traditional qualia view, a perception of ripe tomatoes is a presentational representation insofar as it represents the redness of the tomatoes by being itself, phenomenally, red — in other words, by 'showing' what the tomatoes look like. In introspection, then, one is presented with that intrinsic redness.

The materialist line rejects any presentation of phenomenal colour. Here the perception is just a 'physically acceptable' state of the brain to which first-person concepts are applied in introspection. Nothing is red — objectively, phenomenally, or otherwise. The brain isn't red, and the introspective concepts neither are, nor need otherwise introduce, phenomenal red. Just as tokens of the English predicate 'red' can represent objects as red without themselves being, or otherwise needing to present, red, tokens of the mentalese predicate 'RED' can represent red-perceptions as red-perceptions without themselves being, or otherwise needing to present, phenomenal red. Representations of this latter kind are nonpresentational representations; for lack of a better term I shall call them *coded* representations. They represent in a manner more like telling than showing; they merely designate, rather than present, their content.[9]

I have been riding roughshod over many exegetical fine points (and some not so fine) in the literature discussed above; but on the face of it, predicative versions of the materialist line appear to offer a neat dismissal of the trouble with qualia. What then is the problem?

III. The Problem

As we have seen, both Lycan and Loar characterize the first-person concepts tokened in introspection as *predicates*. And like any predicates, their application effects the type-identification or recognition of things as being of certain kinds. Loar writes:

> a phenomenal concept . . . involves the ability to re-identify a feeling of a certain type, for example, feeling like *this* . . . [P]henomenal concepts are recognitional concepts, involving the ability to classify together certain states in the having of them' (Loar 1990: 97–8).

Lycan characterizes the introspective mentalese predicate as a mental 'word for the type of first-order state' being scanned (Lycan 1990: 121).

By now it must be obvious where my argument is going: the materialist line collides with the memory constraint. When it comes to our perception of a determinate shade like red_{31}, Lycan will need to say that introspection consists in the (appropriately caused) tokening of a mentalese predicate 'RED$_{31}$-EXPERIENCE', Loar that it consists in the tokening of a mentalese predicate 'THIS$_{31}$' (or something thereabouts). The looming problem is that human psychological design precludes the acquisition of a recognitional schema, *eo ipso* a recognitional concept, for such a determinate value. One might put the point this way: contrary to the materialist line, we have no phenomenal concepts, no type-identifying mental terms, corresponding to our determinate perceptual contents. We have a phenomenal concept of red — namely our red schema — and therewith a phenomenal concept of a red-perception, but no phenomenal concept of red_{31} or a red_{31}-perception. We have phenomenal *representations* of red_{31} — namely our perceptions of red_{31} — and *non*phenomenal concepts of red_{31} and red_{31}-perceptions;[10] but no phenomenal concepts of these fine-grained values. Thus it would appear psychologically impossible that introspection of our red_{31}-perceptions should consist in representing them to ourselves as, mentally 'referring' to them as, RED$_{31}$-PERCEPTIONS.

[9] If I understand him correctly, Norton Nelkin endorses a similar version of the materialist line. According to Nelkin, a ('phenomenologically') conscious mental state is an imagistic first-order state that is being introspected; and introspection is 'second-order, direct, non-inferential accessing and awareness' (1989: 133) that is sentential in nature.

[10] By 'nonphenomenal concepts' I mean concepts that can be possessed by blind and sighted subjects alike. These representations have, as it were, no strictly *perceptual* content.

Three related points want immediate emphasis. First, I do not deny that perceptual and other mental contents could be rendered in predicative or other coded form at a 'sub-personal' level of processing. For all I have said, predicative modes of presentation may be the brain's standard currency. (What that would mean, of course, is that sub-personal parts of the brain are making sub-personal type-identifications.) My point is only that predicative modes of presentation cannot be the currency of personal-level introspection: they cannot be the way *you* represent your own mental states *to yourself*. Second, the difficulty I have isolated does not depend upon an identification of introspective concepts with terms in a language of thought. On the contrary, the problem will arise for any view on which introspection requires the type-identification of properties (be they physical, functional, phenomenal, or otherwise) of internal states. Third, I am not here merely reaffirming the claim, often voiced by materialist liners, that because of its peculiar functional role, the content of a first-person introspective concept is not expressible in any natural language (e.g. Rey 1993: 249–50). In other words, the problem is not that you can't report the determinate content of your introspection because that content is not expressible in natural language. Rather, it's that you can't report that content because you can't recognize it when you have it; you can't learn to say so much as, 'There it is again.' Consider that you also can't report the determinate shades you see, and there is no problem about the natural language expressibility of shades: we can call them 'red$_{31}$', 'indigo$_{372}$', and so forth.

Think of it this way. The cornerstone of the materialist line is a distinction among different ways of knowing or representing physical facts. One of these ways of knowing, namely the first-person introspective way, is supposed to capture how I myself represent my own first-order perceptual states. So, for example, the mentalese predicate 'RED$_{31}$' is supposed to express how I represent to myself my own red$_{31}$-experiences: I represent them *as* RED$_{31}$-EXPERIENCES. But that is just what the memory constraint precludes: I cannot represent my own experiences to myself, in introspection, *as* RED$_{31}$-EXPERIENCES.

Keep in mind throughout that none of the relevant evidence supports the predicative view. What kind of evidence could support it? Only evidence of the ability to engage in 'type-identifying' behaviours: for example, to say 'red$_{31}$-experience' when and only when we have a red$_{31}$-experience, or to say 'There it is again' when and only when we have a red$_{31}$-experience, or to press a buzzer when and only when we have one. But we can do none of these things. We cannot even learn to do them. And apart from evidence of such behavioural dispositions, there is no reason to believe that we represent our red$_{31}$-experiences as such. I cannot exaggerate the importance of this point: absent the requisite behavioural evidence, a hypothesis of predicative introspective representation is entirely *ad hoc*.

Before turning to the second strand of the materialist line, what I call its *demonstrative* form, let me pause here to address a pair of objections to what I've said so far.

IV. Objections and Replies

Perhaps the materialist liner will object that a mentalese 'RED$_{31}$' could enter introspection automatically at the requisite times (i.e. when triggered by the relevant physical property) but then be irretrievable by 'personal-level' memory. Michael Tye frames the proposal in this way:[11]

> I am so built that I cannot store the concept, red$_{31}$. So, I can't learn to reidentify [red$_{31}$]. But the fact that I cannot *re*-cognize red$_{31}$, does not mean that I cannot cognize it when I see it . . . [P]erhaps I even cognize [my perceptual state] under a syntactically structured predicate like 'red$_{31}$'. . . . Perhaps what happens is that I manufacture this predicate on the spot and then mechanically chop off the subscript before placing what is left in memory . . . So, I cognize my state as a red$_{31}$ experience for as long as it lasts, but I don't remember what red$_{31}$ looks like.

The idea seems to be that we can identify our red$_{31}$-experiences as such, but only while we are having them.

One is hard pressed to make sense of this proposal, for at least two reasons. First, how is it supposed to be that we are at once able to identify our red$_{31}$-experiences whenever we have them, yet unable to re-identify them? This seems to verge on a contradiction in terms: if we can identify something whenever we encounter it, then *ipso facto* we can re-identify it. Keep in mind that the problem isn't merely that we cannot *report* our red$_{31}$-experiences as such; the latter inability is only symptomatic of the true problem, namely our inability to *identify* or *recognize* the values in question. Second, as before, there is no evidential support for a claim of type-identification in the scenario Tye describes. All of the verbal and nonverbal behavioural evidence indicates that we are not making an identification. Thus the hypothesis that we are identifying our red$_{31}$-experiences as such, even while we are having them, is *ad hoc*.

On the other hand, perhaps the materialist liner will contend that I am mistaken about the degree to which the content of experience is determinate. Rather, he may insist, experience is only as fine-grained as what we can conceptualize and hence say — for instance, only as fine-grained as 'orangey vermillion' or 'brighter red than that other patch'. The idea is that experience is only 'determinable', not 'determinate'; so the grain of expe-

---

[11] What follows is excerpted from Tye's APA commentary (see note at the beginning of this chapter). Tye himself does not endorse such a view; in fact he favours a version of what I here call the 'demonstrative' materialist line. See Tye 1995.

rience does not outrun the grain of our concepts and the memory constraint poses no problem.[12]

This second proposal too is untenable, on empirical grounds. It turns out that a small number of determinate shades are memorable and hence re-identifiable across time: the four unique hues, for example.[13] We have determinate phenomenal *concepts* of red₁, blue₁, green₁, and yellow₁, as we might call them.[14] Furthermore, a quick look at the full spectrum of hues shows that our experiences of these unique hues are no different, in respect of their 'determinateness', from those of the non-unique hues: among other things, the unique hues do not appear to 'stand out' from among the other discriminable hues in the way one would expect if our experience of them were more determinate. On the contrary, the spectrum appears more or less continuous, and any discontinuities that do appear lie near category boundaries rather than central cases. In sum, since our experiences of unique and non-unique hues are introspectively similar in respect of their determinateness, yet conceptualized in radically different ways, introspection of these experiences cannot be explained (or explained exhaustively) in conceptual terms. In particular, it is not plausible to suppose that any discriminable hue, unique or otherwise, is experienced or introspected in a less than determinate fashion.

V. The Materialist Line: Demonstrative Variants

Perhaps the difficulties encountered by predicative variants of the materialist line can be avoided by replacing the predicates with demonstratives. In other words, maybe introspection should be thought of as the application, to a first-order perceptual state, of a demonstrative representation rather

[12] This objection has been raised in one form or other by Michael Tye, Alex Byrne, and Daniel Dennett.

[13] A unique hue is a 'pure' example of its kind — *viz.* a red that contains no blue or yellow, a yellow that contains no red or green, a green that contains no yellow or blue, or a blue that contains no green or red.

[14] Even allowing for a standard deviation of about 1.3 *nm* in our unique hue settings from trial to trial (for reasons I won't elaborate here, it is debatable whether this variability need be taken into account at all in the present connection), and also for the high number (28) of identifiable hue categories postulated by Kintz, Parker, & Boynton (1969), our unique hue categories are significantly narrower (i.e. more fine-grained) than our finest schemas for non-unique hues — at least twice as narrow. See for example Hurvich, Jameson, & Cohen 1968 and Kintz, Parker, & Boynton 1969 for relevant discussion. (The figure of 1.3 *nm*, obtained from Hurvich, Jameson, & Cohen 1968, is for unique green. Unfortunately the experiments establishing unique hue loci typically employ an adjustment task, whereas the experiments establishing numbers of hue categories typically employ an absolute identification task. As this paper goes to press, I have not yet been able to locate a study comparing performance as between unique and non-unique hues on the same task. Though I am assured by my colleagues in visual psychophysics [Carl Ingling and Del Lindsey, in particular] that the view I advance here is correct, ideally one wants a study showing that the average standard deviation for non-unique hue settings is larger than that for unique hues.)

than a predicative one. Then the first-order state would be thought of in a 'special first-person way' — but a way that doesn't require its type-identification. Terence Horgan, for one, urges that the phenomenal colour property or quale one experiences in seeing ripe tomatoes is just a physical property of one's brain apprehended from 'the first-person ostensive perspective' (Horgan 1984: 151). The content of this perspective is express-ible in a judgment of the form (e.g.) 'SEEING RIPE TOMATOES HAS *THIS* PROPERTY', where '*THIS* PROPERTY' refers to the relevant neural feature. As before, no subjective facts need enter in, consciously or otherwise. Making a similar move, David Papineau proposes that introspec-tion is not the apprehension of subjective facts but rather the application of a demonstrative concept, the concept '*THAT* EXPERIENCE', to some 'physically acceptable characteristic' of the brain.[15]

The chief difficulty with this initially appealing line is that it gives rise to what I'll call the 'differentiation problem'. In its crudest form, the demon-strative line has it that we introspectively think of all of our experiences as, simply, *this* (property or experience). In other words, it renders all experi-ences introspectively identical. But of course our experiences are not introspectively identical. They stand in myriad relations of similarity and difference along their respective perceptual dimensions (hue, shape, pitch, etc.): for example, a red_{31}-experience is introspectively identical to other red_{31}-experiences but introspectively different from red_{32}-experiences. So perhaps a less crude formulation is intended — say, that the introspective judgment is something like 'SEEING TOMATOES HAS *THIS* DETERMINATE DARK-ORANGEY-SCARLET PROPERTY'. Even augmenting the demonstrative with descriptive content in this way fails to solve the differentiation problem, however, for the latter beefed-up repre-sentation will still be satisfied by tokens of different experience types (*viz.* experiences as of discriminably different shades of dark orangey scarlet). Indeed, for reasons now familiar, any such augmentation, however precise or informative, will fall short of a determinate type-identification, and hence will be satisfied by experiences as of discriminably different shades.

The materialist liner might reply that the content of introspection is given by an ordered pair consisting of the mental demonstrative plus the first-order state to which the demonstrative refers on a given occasion.[16] The neural state is the object, and the demonstrative the 'mode of presentation',

---

[15] Papineau 1993, chapter 4. It may be that Papineau's position shares more with the predicative materialist line than I make it seem; for instance, he writes of Frank Jackson's Mary that she 'acquires a new *introspective* power to re-identify that [red-]experience when she has it again' (110). I don't propose to worry over this exegetical question, however. My principal concern is the plausibility of the demonstrative line, not whether any particular philosopher endorses it. So I employ Papineau's elegant discussion, with apologies as needed, for my own purposes.

[16] Tye has suggested this response (in conversation) on behalf of the materialist liner.

of introspection. The differentiation problem is solved, he might insist, because our introspective ways of thinking are differentiated by the differences among their referents: our introspect*ive* states are differentiated by our introspect*ed* states.

This reply misses the mark, however. The differentiation problem just is the absence of differences in our ways of thinking of our first-order states. While differences among those states constitute differences among the *objects* of introspection, they precisely do not constitute or otherwise underwrite differences in our ways of thinking of those objects. Hence the inclusion of first-order states in the described ordered pairs does nothing to cure what ails us — that is, nothing to differentiate those states 'from the first-person ostensive perspective'. When we use natural language demonstratives to refer to ordinary material objects, we have independent epistemic (e.g. perceptual) access to those objects, and so the differentiation problem does not arise. On the view presently under consideration, though, the mental demonstratives provide our *only* access to our first-order states. Intuitively speaking, introspection has no access to those states, except as so many of *these*.[17]

Citing the fact that we ourselves instantiate the relevant first-order states, or even that we *know* we are using our mental demonstratives to refer to them, doesn't solve the problem. Such a strategy is implicit in Horgan's remarks about scientifically omniscient but chromatically challenged Mary (Jackson 1982):

> Does (4) ['Seeing ripe tomatoes has *this* property'] by itself convey the information which Mary expresses by using (4)? I think not. Rather, since (4) employs an indexical term essentially, it seems that in order to obtain the information which Mary expresses by (4), a member of Mary's audience would have to experience phenomenal redness himself, and would have to know that Mary is using 'this property' to designate the same property that he experiences. Knowledge about what qualia are like cannot be obtained by descriptive means alone, but requires the experiencing of those qualia (Horgan 1984: 151n).

---

[17] It may be suggested that the differentiation problem is solved by thinking of the mental demonstrative rather on the model of the first-person indexical 'I' in the natural language. The idea is that, just as in using the word 'I' we refer, and *know what we refer to*, absent any 'independent epistemic access' to that referent (see e.g. Perry 1979), in using a mental demonstrative we refer, and *know what we refer to*, absent any independent epistemic access to that referent. The analogy breaks down, however. A speaker's uses of 'I' refer to the same thing (in the sense of 'same token', namely the speaker himself) on each occasion; so of course no differentiation problem can arise. An introspective subject's uses of mental '*THIS*', on the other hand, refer to tokens of different experience types on different occasions. Consider that, absent independent epistemic access to the identities of the relevant speakers, we are equally unable to differentiate among referents of uses of 'I' by different speakers. I thank Stephen White for extremely helpful discussion on this point.

(Since any red-experience is an experience of some determinate shade of red — i.e. it is either a red_{31}-experience, or a red_{32}-experience, or a red_{33}-experience, etc. — we can read Horgan as requiring that Mary's audience experience, say, phenomenal *redness*$_{31}$. Presumably he would not object to this refinement of his view.) Horgan is right to say that by itself, (4) fails to express the content that Mary expresses using (4); and citing the instantiation of the relevant physical property as referent does fill the informational gap — but only from a third-person point of view, as it were. The trouble is that the physical property instantiation cannot supply the requisite content *from a first-person introspective point of view*. Or, better: although it supplies the requisite content, it does not supply it under the right mode of presentation; it does not supply that content under a mode of presentation that makes it accessible by introspection — in either Mary or her audience.

Taking a similar tack, Papineau writes that in introspection, 'Mary think[s]: THAT experience is vibrant, accompanied by a secondary version of seeing red; [she] thereby secure[s] reference to the experience of seeing red' (Papineau 1993: 113). This secondary version of seeing red is a 'copy' or 'recreation', in imagination or memory, of the actual experience of seeing red. (Again, since any red-experience is an experience of some determinate shade of red, we may suppose that Mary's demonstrative thought is in fact accompanied by a secondary version of seeing a particular determinate shade.)

As far as I can see, this appeal to secondary copies of experience too is ineffective. In order to solve the differentiation problem, the content supplied by such a copy would need to be accessible to introspection. In order to be accessible to introspection, it would need to be represented under the right concept or way of thinking. (For example, the content in question would not be accessible to introspection under a physicalistic concept.) But on the view at issue, the only concept under which that content would be accessible to introspection is the demonstrative '*THAT*'. And then we are back where we started with the differentiation problem. Or think of it this way: for the materialist, any such copy of an experience would itself be the instantiation of some further physical properties; and introspection has no access to any physical properties as such. So the original question would simply recur: what is introspection's mode of presentation or way of thinking of those properties?

Maybe the demonstrative view can be modified so as to build in the requisite distinctions. Notice that we often differentiate among our experiences by comparing them — for instance, by noting that one of them is redder, or darker, or louder, than another. Perhaps, then, our introspective demonstratives can serve as 'placeholders' for the differentiating representations we would token were we in a position to make the relevant comparisons. Consider for example a current red_{31}-experience and a red_{32}-

experience of five minutes ago. The idea is that, were we to have the two experiences simultaneously, and compare them, we would represent them under different modes of presentation — say, the red$_{31}$-experience under the mode 'the more red of the two red-experiences I am currently having', and the red$_{32}$-experience under the mode 'the less red of the two red-experiences I am currently having'. Then the two experiences would be introspectively differentiated, but via purely comparative or discriminatory, rather than type-identifying, representations. So if the demonstratives that refer to the two experiences are 'placeholders' for those hypothetical comparative representations, they in fact introduce distinct modes of presentation and the differentiation problem dissolves. In this way the placeholder view threads a careful path between the predicative and straightforwardly demonstrative approaches, invoking representations neither so fine-grained as to violate the memory constraint nor so coarse-grained as to generate the differentiation problem.[18]

Unfortunately it faces a panoply of problems of its own. Chief among these is the fact that since the comparative representations are not (typically) actually tokened, claiming that the demonstratives introduce distinct modes of presentation is so much empty posturing. What the placeholder view comes to, really, is the claim that experiences are introspectively different just in case we would represent them differently were we to have them simultaneously and compare them. And that won't do: according to the materialist line, introspective differences between experiences consist in their being represented differently, not in their being such that they would be represented differently under certain counterfactual circumstances. Red$_{31}$- and red$_{32}$-experiences *actually are* introspectively different; so on the materialist line, they must *actually be* represented under different modes of presentation. To its credit, the materialist line takes seriously the occurrent character of introspection: introspection is not a dispositional phenomenon.

Of course, there is in general no question of our actually tokening such distinguishing comparative representations, i.e. no question of our actually representing our current (red$_{31}$) experience as being different from our (red$_{32}$) experience of five minutes ago. Again, the reason is familiar: given the coarse grain of perceptual memory, we cannot remember, and so cannot now represent, our experience of five minutes ago with sufficient precision to permit a discrimination, in respect of determinate hue, between it and the slightly different one we are currently having.[19] To all intents and purposes, once an experience has ended, we cannot remember its determinate hue content and so cannot represent it either as similar to or as different from

---

[18] The idea of such an appeal to comparative representations was originally suggested to me by Jonathan Vogel; I first consider it explicitly in 1993: 141.

[19] Unless they are experiences of unique hues; see note 20 below.

other experiences. Only simultaneous experiences can be so compared. Hence if actual tokening of comparative representations were required for introspective differentiation, only simultaneous experiences would bear relations of introspective similarity and difference one to another. Such a result is unacceptable: if any experiences stand in such relations, all of them do.[20]

VI. Conclusion and Caveat

If the memory constraint is indeed the impediment I have made it out to be, then the dreaded subjective facts of the traditional qualia theorist may not be eliminable, as the materialist line would have it, by appeal to a distinction among ways of thinking. Of course, I have here examined only two variants of the materialist line, so a general conclusion awaits further investigation; but insofar as the predicative and demonstrative views are the dominant variants, the outlook is bleak. Let me emphasize that the memory constraint need not pose a problem for materialism *tout court*. At most, the argument advanced here shows that one family of materialist theories — namely those that traffic in coded representations in the ways detailed above — are faulty.[21] I suspect that certain elements of the present account could be mobilized to challenge materialism broadly construed, but that is a project for another occasion.[22, 23]

References

Anderson, J. (1980). *Cognitive Psychology*. San Francisco: W.H. Freeman.
Burns, E.M. & Ward, W.D. (1977). Categorical perception — phenomenon or epiphenomenon: Evidence from experiments in the perception of musical intervals. *Journal of the Acoustical Society of America*, **63**, 456–68.

[20] The exceptional case of the unique hues (determinate yet memorable) rules out biting the bullet on this point. For example, in theory I can always judge whether the unique hue I am experiencing now is similar to or different from some hue I experienced earlier (provided only that I attended to whether the earlier hue was unique); and there is no reason to think that non-unique hues differ from unique ones in respect of their instantiation of introspective similarity and difference relations.

[21] I thank Ivan Fox for bringing this point home to me. See Fox 1995 for a materialist dissolution of the qualia problem that eschews a representational theory of mind.

[22] I begin to develop such a challenge in another paper, 'The long and short of perceptual memory: a new argument for qualia' (manuscript, 1995).

[23] I am indebted to audiences at Dartmouth College, MIT, Northwestern University, and Ohio State University, and also to William Lycan, William Taschek, Steven Boer, Ivan Fox, Simon Blackburn, Ruth Barcan Marcus, Nikola Grahek, Robert Kraut, George Pappas, Ned Block, Alex Byrne, Jefferson White, Walter Sinnott-Armstrong, Meredith Williams, Joseph Salerno, Carl Ingling, Del Lindsey, and especially Stephen White and Daniel Dennett, for helpful commentary.

Burns, E.M. & Ward, W.D. (1982). Intervals, scales, and tuning. In Diana Deutsch (ed), *The Psychology of Music*. New York: Academic Press.

Dennett, D.C. (1979). On the absence of phenomenology. In Gustavson & Tapscott (eds), *Body, Mind, and Method*. Dordrecht: D. Reidel.

Fox, I. (1995). Our knowledge of the internal world. *Philosophical Topics*, 22, 59–106.

Halsey, R.M., & Chapanis, A. (1951). Number of absolutely identifiable hues. *Journal of the Optical Society of America*, 41, 1057–8.

Harnad, S. (1987)[ed]. *Categorical Perception*. Cambridge: Cambridge University Press.

Horgan, T. (1984). Jackson on physical information and qualia. *Philosophical Quarterly*, 34, 127–32.

Hurvich, L.M. (1981). *Color Vision*. Sunderland, MA: Sinauer Associates.

Hurvich, L.M., Jameson, D. & Cohen, J.D. (1968). The experimental determination of unique green in the spectrum. *Perception & Psychophysics*, 4, 65–8.

Jackson, F. (1982). Epiphenomenal Qualia. *Philosophical Quarterly*, 32, 127–32.

Kintz, R.T., Parker, J.A. & Boynton, R.M. (1969). Information transmission in spectral color naming. *Perception & Psychophysics*, 5, 241–5.

Loar, B. (1990). Phenomenal states. *Philosophical Perspectives, 4: Action Theory and Philosophy of Mind*: 81–108.

Lycan, William, 1990. What is the 'subjectivity' of the mental? In Tomberlin 1990.

Nagel, T. (1974). What is it like to be a bat? *Philosophical Review*, 83, 435–50. Reprinted in *Mortal Questions*. Cambridge: Cambridge University Press.

Nelkin, N. (1989). Unconscious sensations. *Philosophical Psychology*, 2, 129–41.

Papineau, D. (1993). *Philosophical Naturalism*. Oxford: Basil Blackwell.

Perry, J. (1979). The problem of the essential indexical. *Noûs*, 13, 3–21

Raffman, D. (1993). *Language, Music, and Mind*. Cambridge, MA: MIT Press.

Repp, B. (1984). Categorical perception: issues, methods, and findings. In N. Lass (ed), *Speech and Language, vol.10: Advances in basic research and practice*. Orlando: Academic Press.

Rey, G. (1993). Sensational sentences. In Davies & Humphreys 1993.

Seashore, C. (1967). *The Psychology of Music*. New York: Dover.

Siegel, J.A. & Siegel, W. (1977a). Absolute identification of notes and intervals by musicians. *Perception & Psychophysics*, 21, 143–52.

Siegel, J.A. & Siegel, W. (1977b). Categorical perception of tonal intervals: Musicians can't tell *sharp* from *flat*. *Perception and Psychophysics*, 21, 399–407.

Tye, M. (1995). *Ten Problems of Consciousness*. Cambridge, MA: MIT Press.

David J. Chalmers

Absent Qualia, Fading Qualia, Dancing Qualia

I. The Principle of Organizational Invariance

It is widely accepted that conscious experience has a physical basis. That is, the properties of experience (phenomenal properties, or qualia) systematically depend on physical properties according to some lawful relation. There are two key questions about this relation. The first concerns the strength of the laws: are they logically or metaphysically necessary, so that consciousness is nothing 'over and above' the physical, or are they merely contingent laws like the law of gravity? This question is the basis for debates over physicalism and property dualism. The second question concerns the shape of the laws: precisely how do phenomenal properties depend on physical properties? What sort of physical properties enter into the laws' antecedents, for instance; consequently, what sort of physical systems can give rise to conscious experience? It is this second question that I address in this paper.

To put the issue differently, even once it is accepted that experience arises from physical systems, the question remains open: in virtue of what sort of physical properties does conscious experience arise? Properties that brains can possess will presumably be among them, but it is far from clear just what the relevant properties are. Some have suggested biochemical properties; some have suggested quantum-mechanical properties; many have professed uncertainty. A natural suggestion is that when experience arises from a physical system, it does so in virtue of the system's *functional organization*. On this view, the chemical and indeed the quantum substrates of the brain are not directly relevant to the existence of consciousness, although they may be indirectly relevant. What is central is rather the brain's abstract

causal organization, an organization that might be realized in many different physical substrates.

In this paper I defend this view. Specifically, I defend a principle of
organizational invariance, holding that experience is invariant across
systems with the same fine-grained functional organization. More
precisely, the principle states that given any system that has conscious
experiences, then any system that has the same functional organization at a
fine enough grain will have qualitatively identical conscious experiences.
A full specification of a system's fine-grained functional organization will
fully determine any conscious experiences that arise.

To clarify this, we must first clarify the notion of functional organization.
This is best understood as the *abstract pattern of causal interaction* between the components of a system, and perhaps between these components
and external inputs and outputs. A functional organization is determined by
specifying (1) a number of abstract components, (2) for each component, a
number of different possible states, and (3) a system of dependency
relations, specifying how the states of each component depends on the
previous states of all components and on inputs to the system, and how
outputs from the system depend on previous component states. Beyond
specifying their number and their dependency relations, the nature of the
components and the states is left unspecified.

A physical system *realizes* a given functional organization when the
system can be divided into an appropriate number of physical components
each with the appropriate number of possible states, such that the causal
dependency relations between the components of the system, inputs, and
outputs precisely reflect the dependency relations given in the specification
of the functional organization. A given functional organization can be
realized by diverse physical systems. For example, the organization
realized by the brain at the neural level might in principle be realized by a
silicon system.

A physical system has functional organization at many different levels,
depending on how finely we individuate its parts and on how finely we
divide the states of those parts. At a coarse level, for instance, it is likely
that the two hemispheres of the brain can be seen as realizing a simple
two-component organization, if we choose appropriate interdependent
states of the hemispheres. It is generally more useful to view cognitive
systems at a finer level, however. For our purposes I will always focus on
a level of organization fine enough to determine the behavioural capacities
and dispositions of a cognitive system. This is the role of the 'fine enough
grain' clause in the statement of the organizational invariance principle; the
level of organization relevant to the application of the principle is one fine
enough to determine a system's behavioural dispositions. In the brain, it is
likely that the neural level suffices, although a coarser level might also

work. For the purposes of illustration I will generally focus on the neural level of organization of the brain, but the arguments generalize.

Strictly speaking, for the purposes of the invariance principle we must require that for two systems to share their functional organization, they must be in corresponding states at the time in question; if not for this requirement, my sleeping twin might count as sharing my organization, but he certainly does not share my experiences. When two systems share their organization at a fine enough grain (including the requirement that they be in corresponding states), I will say that they are *functionally isomorphic* systems, or that they are *functional isomorphs*. The invariance principle holds that any functional isomorph of a conscious system has experiences that are qualitatively identical to those of the original system.

II. Absent Qualia and Inverted Qualia

The principle of organizational invariance is far from universally accepted. Some have thought it likely that for a system to be conscious it must have the right sort of biochemical makeup; if so, a metallic robot or a silicon-based computer could never have experiences, no matter what its causal organization. Others have conceded that a robot or a computer might be conscious if it were organized appropriately, but have held that it might nevertheless have experiences quite different from the kind that we have. These two sorts of objections are often known as the *absent qualia* and *inverted qualia* objections to broadly functionalist theories of consciousness.

Arguments for the absent qualia objection usually consist in the description of a system that realizes whatever functional organization might be specified, but that is so outlandish that it is natural to suppose that it lacks conscious experience. For example, Block (1980) points out that the functional organization of the brain might be instantiated by the population of China, if they were organized appropriately, and argues that it is bizarre to suppose that this would somehow give rise to a group mind. In a similar way, John Searle (1980) notes that a given organization might be realized by 'a sequence of water-pipes, or a set of wind-machines' but argues that these systems would not be conscious.

Arguments for the inverted qualia objection are often illustrated by considerations about experiences of colour. According to this line of argument (taken by Shoemaker 1982 and Horgan 1984, among others), it is possible that a system might make precisely the same colour discriminations that I do, but that when confronted by red objects it has the kind of experience that I have when confronted by blue objects. Further, it is argued that this might happen even when the systems are functionally isomorphic. If this argument succeeds, then even if the appropriate functional organization suffices for the existence of conscious experiences, it does not determine their specific nature. Instead, the specific nature of experiences must be

dependent on non-organizational properties, such as specific neurophysiological properties.

Sometimes these arguments are intended as arguments for 'possibility'
only in some weak sense, such as logical or metaphysical possibility. These
less ambitious forms of the arguments are the most likely to be successful.
It seems difficult to deny that the absent qualia and inverted qualia scenarios
are at least intelligible. With the aid of certain assumptions about possibility, this intelligibility can be extended into an argument for the logical and
perhaps the metaphysical possibility of the scenarios. If successful, even
these less ambitious arguments would suffice to refute some strong versions
of functionalism, such as analytic functionalism and the view that
phenomenal properties are identical to functional properties.

In the present paper I am not concerned with the logical or metaphysical
possibility of these scenarios, however, but rather with their *empirical* (or
natural, or nomological) possibility. The mere logical or metaphysical
possibility of absent qualia is compatible with the claim that in the actual
world, whenever the appropriate functional organization is realized,
conscious experience is present. By analogy: many have judged it logically
possible that a *physical* replica of a conscious system might lack conscious
experience, while not wishing to deny that in the actual world, any such
replica will be conscious. It is the claim about empirical possibility that is
relevant to settling the issue at hand, which concerns a possible lawful
relation between organization and experience. Mere intelligibility does not
bear on this, any more than the intelligibility of a world without relativity
can falsify Einstein's theory.

On the question of empirical possibility, the success of the absent qualia
and inverted qualia arguments is unclear. To be sure, many have found it
counter- intuitive that the population of China might give rise to conscious
experience if organized appropriately. The natural reply, however, is that it
seems equally counter-intuitive that a mass of 10^{11} appropriately organized
neurons should give rise to consciousness, and yet it happens. Intuition is
unreliable as a guide to empirical possibility, especially where a phenomenon as perplexing as conscious experience is concerned. If a brain can
do the job of enabling conscious experience, it is far from obvious why an
appropriately organized population, or indeed an appropriate organized set
of water-pipes, could not.

The debate over absent and inverted qualia tends to produce a stand-off,
then. Both proponents and opponents claim intuitions in support of their
positions, but there are few grounds on which to settle the debate between
them. Both positions seem to be epistemic possibilities, and due to the
notorious difficulties in collecting experimental evidence about conscious
experience, things might seem likely to stay that way.

I believe that the stand-off can be broken, and in this paper I will offer
considerations that offer strong support to the principle of organizational

invariance, suggesting that absent qualia and inverted qualia are empirically impossible. These arguments involve thought-experiments about gradual neural replacement, and take the form of a *reductio*. The first thought-experiment demonstrates that if absent qualia are possible, then then a phenomenon involving what I will call *fading qualia* is possible; but I will argue that we have good reason to believe that fading qualia are impossible. The second argument has broader scope and is more powerful, demonstrating that if absent qualia *or* inverted qualia are possible, then a phenomenon involving what I will call *dancing qualia* is possible; but I will argue that we have even better reason to believe that dancing qualia are impossible. If the arguments succeed, we have good reason to believe that absent and inverted qualia are impossible, and that the principle of organizational invariance is true.

These arguments do not constitute conclusive *proof* of the principle of organizational invariance. Such proof is generally not available in the domain of conscious experience, where for familiar reasons one cannot even disprove the hypothesis that there is only one conscious being. But even in the absence of proof, we can bring to bear arguments for the plausibility and implausibility of different possibilities, and not all possibilities end up equal. I use these thought-experiments as a *plausibility argument* for the principle of organizational invariance, by showing that the alternatives have implausible consequences. If an opponent wishes to hold on to the possibility of absent or inverted qualia she can still do so, but the thought-experiments show that the cost is higher than one might have expected.

Perhaps it is useful to see these thought-experiments as playing a role analogous to that played by the 'Schrödinger's cat' thought-experiment in the interpretation of quantum mechanics. Schrödinger's thought-experiment does not deliver a decisive verdict in favor of one interpretation or another, but it brings out various plausibilities and implausibilities in the interpretations, and it is something that every interpretation must ultimately come to grips with. In a similar way, any theory of consciousness must ultimately come to grips with the fading and dancing qualia scenarios, and some will handle them better than others. In this way, the virtues and drawbacks of various theories are clarified.

III. Fading Qualia

The first scenario that I will present is relatively familiar,[1] but it is important to analyse it correctly, and it is a necessary preliminary to the more powerful second argument. In this thought-experiment, we assume for the purposes of *reductio* that absent qualia are empirically possible. It follows

---

[1] Neural replacement scenarios along the lines discussed in this section are discussed by Pylyshyn (1980), Savitt (1982), Cuda (1985) and Searle (1992), among others.

that there can be a system with the same functional organization as a conscious system (such as me), but which lacks conscious experience entirely due to some difference in non-organizational properties. Without loss of generality, suppose that this is because the system is made of silicon chips rather than neurons. Call this functional isomorph Robot. The causal patterns in Robot's processing system are the same as mine, but there is nothing it is like to be Robot.

Given this scenario, we can construct a series of cases intermediate between me and Robot such that there is only a very small change at each step and such that functional organization is preserved throughout. We can imagine, for instance, replacing a certain number of my neurons by silicon chips. In the first such case, only a single neuron is replaced. Its replacement is a silicon chip that performs precisely the same local function as the neuron. We can imagine that it is equipped with tiny transducers that take in electrical signals and chemical ions and transforms these into a digital signal upon which the chip computes, with the result converted into the appropriate electrical and chemical outputs. As long as the chip has the right input/output function, the replacement will make no difference to the functional organization of the system.

In the second case, we replace two neighboring neurons with silicon chips. This is just as in the previous case, but once both neurons are replaced we can eliminate the intermediary, dispensing with the awkward transducers and effectors that mediate the connection between the chips and replacing it with a standard digital connection. Later eases proceed in a similar fashion, with larger and larger groups of neighboring neurons replaced by silicon chips. Within these groups, biochemical mechanisms have been dispensed with entirely, except at the periphery. In the final case, every neuron in the system has been replaced by a chip, and there are no biochemical mechanisms playing an essential role. (I abstract away here from detailed issues concerning whether, for instance, glial cells play a non-trivial role; if they do, they will be components of the appropriate functional organization, and will be replaced also.)

We can imagine that throughout, the internal system is connected to a body, is sensitive to bodily inputs, and produces motor movements in an appropriate way, via transducers and effectors. Each system in the sequence will be functionally isomorphic to me at a fine enough grain to share my behavioural dispositions. But while the system at one end of the spectrum is me, the system at the other end is essentially a copy of Robot.

To fix imagery, imagine that as the first system I am having rich conscious experiences. Perhaps I am at a basketball game, surrounded by shouting fans, with all sorts of brightly-coloured clothes in my environment, smelling the delicious aroma of junk food and perhaps suffering from a throbbing headache. Let us focus in particular on the bright red and yellow experiences I have when I watch the players' uniforms. ('Red experience' should be taken as shorthand for 'colour experience of the kind I usually have when presented with red objects', and so on throughout.) The final system, Robot, is in the same situation, processing the same inputs and producing similar behaviour, but by hypothesis is experiencing nothing at all.

The question arises: *What is it like to be the systems in between?* For those systems intermediate between me and Robot, what, if anything, are they experiencing? As we move along the spectrum of cases, how does conscious experience vary? Presumably the very early cases have experiences much like mine, and the very late cases have little or no experience, but what of the cases in the middle?

Given that Robot, at the far end of the spectrum, is not conscious, it seems that one of two things must happen along the way. Either consciousness gradually fades over the series of cases, before eventually disappearing, or somewhere along the way consciousness suddenly blinks out, although the preceding case had rich conscious experiences. Call the first possibility *fading qualia* and the second *suddenly disappearing qualia*.

On the second hypothesis, the replacement of a single neuron could be responsible for the vanishing of an entire field of conscious experience. If so, we could switch back and forth between a neuron and its silicon replacement, with a field of experience blinking in and out of existence on demand. This seems antecedently implausible, if not entirely bizarre. If suddenly disappearing qualia were possible, there would be brute discontinuities in the laws of nature unlike those we find anywhere else.[2] Any specific point for qualia suddenly to disappear (50 per cent neural? 25 per cent?) would be quite arbitrary. We might even run the experiment at a finer grain within the neuron, so that ultimately the replacement of a few molecules produces a sudden disappearance of experience. As always in these matters, the hypothesis cannot be disproved, but its antecedent plausibility is very low.

This leaves the first hypothesis, fading qualia. To get a fix on this hypothesis, consider a system halfway along the spectrum between me and Robot, after consciousness has degraded considerably but before it has gone altogether. Call this system Joe. What is it like to be Joe? Joe, of course, is functionally isomorphic to me. He *says* all the same things about his

---

[2] One might argue that there are situations in nonlinear dynamics in which one magnitude depends sensitively on another, with large changes in the first arising from small changes in the second. But in these cases the dependence is nevertheless continuous, so there will be intermediate cases in which the dependent magnitude takes on intermediate values; the analogy therefore leads to fading qualia, below. And in any case, the sensitive dependence in these cases generally arise from the compound effects of a number of more basic gradual dependencies. In all fundamental laws known to date, the dependence of one magnitude on another is continuous in this fashion, and there is no way to compound continuity into discontinuity. Suddenly disappearing qualia, in contrast to nonlinear dynamics, would therefore require brute discontinuities in fundamental laws.

experiences as I do about mine. At the basketball game, he exclaims about the vivid bright red and yellow uniforms of the basketball players. By hypothesis, though, Joe is not having bright red and yellow experiences at all. Instead, perhaps he is experiencing tepid pink and murky brown. Perhaps he is having the faintest of red and yellow experiences. Perhaps his experiences have darkened almost to black. There are various conceivable ways in which red experiences might gradually transmute to no experience, and probably more ways that we cannot conceive. But presumably in each of these transmutation scenarios, experiences stop being *bright* before they vanish (otherwise we are left with the problem of suddenly disappearing qualia). Similarly, there is presumably a point at which subtle distinctions in my experience are no longer present in an intermediate system's experience; if we are to suppose that all the distinctions in my experience are present right up until a moment when they simultaneously vanish, we are left with another version of suddenly disappearing qualia.

For specificity, then, let us imagine that Joe experiences faded pink where I see bright red, with many distinctions between shades of my experience no longer present in shades of his experience. Where I am having loud noise experiences, perhaps Joe is experiencing only a distant rumble. Not everything is so bad for Joe: where I have a throbbing headache, he only has the mildest twinge.

The crucial point here is that Joe is systematically *wrong* about everything that he is experiencing. He certainly *says* that he is having bright red and yellow experiences, but he is merely experiencing tepid pink. If you ask him, he will claim to be experiencing all sorts of subtly different shades of red, but in fact many of these are quite homogeneous in his experience. He may even complain about the noise, when his auditory experience is really very mild. Worse, on a functional construal of judgment, Joe will even *judge* that he has all these complex experiences that he in fact lacks. In short, Joe is utterly out of touch with his conscious experience, and is incapable of getting in touch.

There is a significant implausibility here. This is a being whose rational processes are functioning and who is in fact *conscious*, but who is completely wrong about his own conscious experiences. Perhaps in the extreme case, when all is dark inside, it is reasonable to suppose that a system could be so misguided in its claims and judgments — after all, in a sense there is nobody in there to be wrong. But in the intermediate case, this is much less plausible. In every case with which we are familiar, conscious beings are generally capable of forming accurate judgments about their experience, in the absence of distraction and irrationality. For a sentient, rational being that is suffering from no functional pathology to be so systematically out of touch with its experiences would imply a strong dissociation between consciousness and cognition. We have little reason to believe that consciousness is such an ill-behaved phenomenon, and good reason to believe otherwise.

To be sure, fading qualia may be *logically* possible. Arguably, there is no contradiction in the notion of a system that is so wrong about its experiences. But logical possibility and empirical possibility are different things. One of the most salient empirical facts about conscious experience is that when a conscious being with the appropriate conceptual sophistication has experiences, it is at least capable of forming reasonable judgments about those experiences. Perhaps there are some cases where judgment is impaired due to a malfunction in rational processes, but this is not such a case. Joe's processes are *functioning* as well as mine — by hypothesis, he is functionally isomorphic. It is just that he happens to be completely misguided about his experience.

There are everyday cases in which qualia fade, of course. Think of what happens when one is dropping off to sleep; or think of moving back along the evolutionary chain from people to trilobites. In each case, as we move along a spectrum of cases, conscious experience gradually fades away. But in each of these cases, the fading is accompanied by a corresponding change in *functioning*. When I become drowsy, I do not believe that I am wide awake and having intense experiences (unless perhaps I start to dream, in which case I very likely *am* having intense experiences). The lack of richness in a dog's experience of colour accompanies a corresponding lack of discriminatory power in a dog's visual mechanisms. These cases are quite unlike the case under consideration, in which experience fades while functioning stays constant. Joe's mechanisms can still discriminate subtly different wavelengths of light, and he certainly judges that such discriminations are reflected in his experience, but we are to believe that his experience does not reflect these discriminations at all.

Searle (1992) discusses a thought-experiment like this one, and suggests the following possibility:

> as the silicon is progressively implanted into your dwindling brain, you find that the area of your conscious experience is shrinking, but that this shows no effect on your external behavior. You find, to your total amazement, that you are indeed losing control of your external behavior. You find, for example, that when the doctors test your vision, you hear them say, 'We are holding up a red object in front of you; please tell us what you see.' You want to cry out, 'I can't see anything. I'm going totally blind.' But you hear your voice saying in a way that is completely out of your control, 'I see a red object in front of me.' If we carry the thought-experiment out to the limit, we get a much more depressing result than last time. We imagine that your conscious experience slowly shrinks to nothing, while your externally observable behavior remains the same (pp. 66–7).

Here, Searle embraces the possibility of fading qualia, but suggests that such a system need not be systematically mistaken in its beliefs about its experience. The system might have true beliefs about its experience, but beliefs that are impotent to affect its behaviour.[3]

It seems that this possibility can be ruled out, however. There is simply no room in the system for any new beliefs to be formed. Unless one is a dualist of a very strong variety, beliefs must be reflected in the functioning of a system — *perhaps* not in behaviour, but at least in some process. But this system is identical to the original system (me) at a fine grain. There is no room for new beliefs like 'I can't see anything', new desires like the desire to cry out, and other new cognitive states such as amazement. Nothing in the physical system can correspond to that amazement. There is no room for it in the neurons, which after all are identical to a subset of the neurons supporting the usual beliefs; and Searle is surely not suggesting that the silicon replacement is itself supporting the new beliefs! Failing a remarkable, magical interaction effect between neurons and silicon — and one that does not manifest itself anywhere in processing, as organization is preserved throughout — such new beliefs will not arise.

While it might just seem plausible that an organization-preserving change from neurons to silicon might twist a few experiences from red to blue, a change in beliefs from 'Nice basketball game' to 'I seem to be stuck in a bad horror movie!' is of a different order of magnitude. If such a major change in cognitive contents were not mirrored in a change in functional organization, cognition would float free of internal functioning like a disembodied mind. If the contents of cognitive states supervened on physical states at all, they could do so only by the most arbitrary and capricious of rules (if this organization in neurons, then 'pretty colours!'; if this organization in silicon, then 'Alas!').

It follows that the possibility of fading qualia requires either a bizarre relationship between belief contents and physical states, or the possibility of beings that are massively mistaken about their own conscious experiences despite being fully rational. Both of these hypotheses are significantly less plausible than the hypothesis that rational conscious beings are generally correct in their judgments about their experiences. A much more reasonable hypothesis is therefore that when neurons are replaced, qualia do not fade at all. A system like Joe, in practice, will have conscious experiences just as rich as mine. If so, then our original assumption was wrong, and the original isomorph, Robot, has conscious experiences.

[3] Searle also raises the possibility that upon silicon replacement, the system might be slowly reduced to paralysis, or have its functioning otherwise impaired. Such a scenario is irrelevant to the truth of the invariance principle, however, which applies only to systems with the appropriate functional organization. If a silicon system does not duplicate the organization of the original system, the principle does not even come into play.

This thought-experiment can be straightforwardly extended to other sorts of functional isomorphs, including isomorphs that differ in shape, size, and physical makeup. All we need do is construct a sequence of intermediate cases, each with the same functional organization. In each case the conclusion is the same. If such a system is not conscious, then there exists an intermediate system that is conscious, has faded experiences, and is completely wrong about its experiences. Unless we are prepared to accept this massive dissociation between consciousness and cognition, the original system must have been conscious after all.

We can even extend the reasoning straightforwardly to the case of an appropriately-organized population: we simply need to imagine neurons replaced one-by-one with tiny homunculi, ending up with a network of homunculi that is essentially equivalent to the population controlling a robot. (If one objects to tiny homunculi, they can be external and of normal size, as long as they are equipped with appropriate radio connections to the body when necessary.) Precisely the same considerations about intermediate cases arise. One can also imagine going from a multiple-homunculi case to a single-homunculus case, yielding something like Searle's 'Chinese room' example. We need only suppose that the homunculi gradually 'double up' on their tasks, leaving written records of the state of each component, until only a single homunculus does all the work. If the causal organization of the original system is preserved, even if it is only among a system of marks on paper, then the same arguments suggest that the system will have experiences. (Of course, we should not expect the homunculus itself to have the experiences; it is merely acting as a sort of causal facilitator.)

If absent qualia are possible, then fading qualia are possible. But I have argued above that it is very unlikely that fading qualia are possible. It follows that it is very unlikely that absent qualia are possible.

Some might object that these thought-experiments are the stuff of science fiction rather than the stuff of reality, and point out that this sort of neural replacement would be quite impossible in practice. But although it might be technologically impossible, there is no reason to believe that the neural replacement scenario should contravene the laws of nature. We already have prosthetic arms and legs. Prosthetic eyes lie within the foreseeable future, and a prosthetic neuron seems entirely possible in principle. Even if it were impossible for some technical reason (perhaps there would not be enough room for a silicon replacement to do its work?), it is unclear what bearing this technical fact would have on the principled force of the thought-experiment. There will surely be *some* systems between which gradual replacement is possible: will the objector hold that the invariance principle holds for those systems, but no other? If so, the situation seems quite arbitrary; if not, then there must be a deeper objection available.

Others might object that no silicon replacement could perform even the local function of a neuron, perhaps because neural function is uncomputable. There is little evidence for this, but it should be noted that even if it is true, it does not affect the argument for the invariance principle. If silicon really could not even duplicate the *function* of a neural system, then a functional isomorph made of silicon would be impossible, and the assessment of silicon systems would simply be irrelevant to the invariance principle. To evaluate the truth of the principle, it is only functionally isomorphic systems that are relevant.

Another objection notes that there are actual cases in which subjects are seriously mistaken about their experiences. For example, in cases of blindness denial, subjects believe that they are having visual experiences when they likely have none. In these cases, however, we are no longer dealing with fully rational systems. In systems whose belief-formation mechanisms are impaired, anything goes. Such systems might believe that they are Napoleon, or that the moon is pink. My 'faded' isomorph Joe, by contrast, is a fully rational system, whose cognitive mechanisms are functioning just as well as mine. In conversation, he seems perfectly sensible. We cannot point to any unusually poor inferential connections between his beliefs, or any systematic psychiatric disorder that is leading his thought processes to be biased toward faulty reasoning. Joe is an eminently thoughtful, reasonable person, who exhibits none of the confabulatory symptoms of those with blindness denial. The cases are therefore disanalogous. The plausible claim is not that no system can be massively mistaken about its experiences, but that no rational system whose cognitive mechanisms are unimpaired can be so mistaken. Joe is certainly a rational system whose mechanisms are working as well as mine, so the argument is unaffected.

Some object that this argument has the form of a Sorites or 'slippery-slope' argument, and observe that these arguments are notoriously suspect. Using a Sorites argument, we can 'show' that even a grain of a sand is a heap; after all, a million grains of sand form a heap, and if we take a single grain away from a heap we still have a heap. This objection is based on a superficial reading of the thought-experiment, however. Sorites arguments gain their force by ignoring the fact that some apparent dichotomy is in fact a continuum; there are all sorts of vague cases between heaps and non-heaps, for instance. The fading qualia argument, by contrast, explicitly accepts the possibility of a continuum, but argues that intermediate cases are impossible for independent reasons. The argument is therefore not a Sorites argument.

Ultimately, the only tenable way for an opponent of organizational invariance to respond to this argument is to bite the bullet and accept the possibility of fading qualia, and the consequent possibility that a rational conscious system might be massively mistaken about its experience, or perhaps to bite another bullet and accept suddenly disappearing qualia and the associated brute discontinuities. These positions seem much less plausible than the alternative, other things being equal, but they are the only way to avoid it. But there is worse to come: the argument to follow provides an even more powerful case against the possibility of absent qualia, so opponents of organizational invariance cannot rest easily.

IV. Dancing Qualia

If the fading qualia argument succeeds, it establishes that functional isomorphs of a conscious system will have conscious experience, but it does not establish that isomorphs have the *same* sort of conscious experience. The preceding argument has no bearing on the possibility of inverted qualia. For all that has gone before, where I am having a red experience, my silicon functional isomorph might be having a blue experience, or some other kind of experience that is quite foreign to me.

One might think that the fading qualia argument could be directly adapted to provide an argument against the possibility of inverted qualia, but that strategy fails. If I have a red experience and my functional isomorph has a blue experience, there is no immediate problem with the idea of intermediate cases with intermediate experiences. These systems might be simply suffering from milder cases of qualia inversion, and are no more problematic than the extreme case. These systems will not be systematically wrong about their experiences. Where they claim to experience distinctions, they may really be experiencing distinctions; where they claim to be having intense experiences, they may still be having intense experiences. To be sure, the experiences they call 'red' differ from those I call 'red' but this is already an accepted feature of the usual inversion case. The difference between these cases and the fading qualia cases is that these cases preserve the *structure* of experience throughout, so that their existence implies no implausible dissociation between experience and cognition.

Nevertheless, a good argument against the possibility of inverted qualia can be found in the vicinity. Once again, for the purposes of *reductio*, assume that inverted qualia are empirically possible. Then there can be two functionally isomorphic systems that are having different experiences. Suppose for the sake of illustration that these systems are me, having a red experience, and my silicon isomorph, having a blue experience (there is a small caveat about generality, which I discuss below).

As before, we construct a series of cases intermediate between me and my isomorph. Here, the argument takes a different turn. We need not worry about the *way* in which experiences change as we move along the series. All that matters is that there must be two points A and B in this series, such that no more than one-tenth of the system is replaced between A and B, and such that A and B have significantly different experiences. To see that this must be the case, we need only consider the points at which 10 per cent, 20 per cent, and so on up to 90 per cent of the brain has been replaced. Red and blue are sufficiently different experiences that some neighboring pairs here *must* be significantly different (that is, different enough that the difference would be noticeable if they were experienced by the same person); there is no way to get from red to blue by ten non-noticeable jumps.

There must therefore be two systems that differ in at most one-tenth of their internal makeup, but that have significantly different experiences. For the purposes of illustration, let these systems be me and Bill. Where I have a red experience, Bill has a slightly different experience. We may as well suppose that Bill has a blue experience; perhaps his experience will be more similar to mine than that, but that makes no difference to the argument. The two systems also differ in that where there are neurons in some small region of my brain, there are silicon chips in Bill's brain. This substitution of a silicon circuit for a neural circuit is the only physical difference between me and Bill.

The crucial step in the thought-experiment is to take a silicon circuit just like Bill's and install it in my head as a *backup circuit*. This circuit will be functionally isomorphic to a circuit already present in my head. We equip the circuit with transducers and effectors so that it can interact with the rest of my brain, but we do not hook it up directly. Instead, we install a *switch* that can switch directly between the neural and silicon circuits. Upon flipping the switch, the neural circuit becomes irrelevant and the silicon circuit takes over. We can imagine that the switch controls the points of interface where the relevant circuits affects the rest of the brain. When it is switched, the connections from the neural circuit are pushed out of the way, and the silicon circuit's effectors are attached. (We might imagine that the transducers for both circuits are attached the entire time, so that the state of both circuits evolves appropriately, but so that only one circuit at a time plays a role in processing. We could also run a similar experiment where both transducers and effectors are disconnected, to ensure that the backup circuit is entirely isolated from the rest of the system. This would change a few details, but the moral would be the same.)

Immediately after flipping the switch, processing that was once performed by the neural circuit is now performed by the silicon circuit. The flow of control within the system has been redirected. However, my functional organization is exactly the same as it would have been if we had not flipped the switch. The only relevant difference between the two cases is the physical makeup of one circuit within the system. There is also a difference in the physical makeup of another 'dangling' circuit, but this is irrelevant to functional organization, as it plays no role in affecting other components of the system and directing behaviour.

What happens to my experience when we flip the switch? Before installing the circuit, I was experiencing red. After we install it but before we flip the switch, I will presumably still be experiencing red, as the only difference is the addition of a circuit that is not involved in processing in any way; for all the relevance it has to my processing, I might as well have eaten it. *After* flipping the switch, however, I am more or less the same system as Bill. The only difference between Bill and me now is that I have a causally irrelevant neural circuit dangling from the system (we might even imagine that the circuit is destroyed when the switch is flipped). Bill, by hypothesis, was enjoying a blue experience. After the switch, then, I will have a blue experience too.

What will happen, then, is that my experience will change 'before my eyes'. Where I was once experiencing red, I will now experience blue. All of a sudden, I will have a *blue* experience of the apple on my desk. We can even imagine flipping the switch back and forth a number of times, so that the red and blue experiences 'dance' before my eyes.

This might seem reasonable at first — it is a strangely appealing image — but something very odd is going on here. My experiences are switching from red to blue, but *I do not notice any change*. Even as we flip the switch a number of times and my qualia dance back and forth, I will simply go about my business, not noticing anything unusual. My functional organization remains normal throughout. In particular, my functional organization after flipping the switch evolves just as it would have if the switch had not been flipped. There is no special difference in my behavioural dispositions. I am not suddenly disposed to say 'Hmm! Something strange is going on!' There is no room for a sudden start, for an exclamation, or even for a distraction of attention. My cognitive organization is just as it usually is, and in particular is precisely as it would have been had the switch not been flipped.

Certainly, on any functional construal of judgment, it is clear that I do not make any novel judgments due to the flip. Even if one were to dispute a functional account of judgment, it is is extremely implausible that a simple organization-preserving replacement of a neural circuit by a silicon circuit could be responsible for the addition of significant new judgments such as 'My qualia just flipped.' As in the case of fading qualia, there is simply no room for such a change to take place, unless it is in an accompanying Cartesian disembodied mind.

We are therefore led once more into a *reductio ad absurdum*. It seems entirely implausible to suppose that my experiences could change in such a significant way, even with me paying full attention, without my being able to notice the change. It would suggest once again an extreme dissociation between consciousness and cognition. If this kind of thing could happen, then psychology and phenomenology would be radically out of step, much further out of step than even the fading qualia scenario would imply.

This 'dancing qualia' scenario may be logically possible (although the case is so extreme that it seems *only just* logically possible), but that does not mean we should take it seriously as an empirical possibility, any more than we should take seriously the possibility that the world was created five minutes ago. As an empirical hypothesis, it is far more plausible that when one's experiences change significantly, then as long as one is rational and paying attention, one should be able to notice the change. If not, then consciousness and cognition are tied together by only the most slender of threads.

Indeed, if we are to suppose that dancing qualia are empirically possible, we are led to a worrying thought: they might be *actual*, and happening to us all the time. The physiological properties of our functional mechanisms are constantly changing. The functional properties of the mechanisms are reasonably robust; one would expect that this robustness would be ensured by evolution. But there is no adaptive reason for the non-functional properties to stay constant. From moment to moment there will certainly be changes in low-level molecular properties. Properties such as position, atomic makeup, and so on can change while functional role is preserved, and such change is almost certainly going on constantly.

If we allow that qualia are dependent not just on functional organization but on implementational details, it may well be that *our* qualia are in fact dancing before our eyes all the time. There seems to be no principled reason why a change from neurons to silicon should make a difference while a change in neural realization should not; the only place to draw a *principled* line is at the functional level. The reason why we doubt that such dancing is taking place in our own cases is that we accept the following principle: when one's experiences change significantly, one can notice the change. If we were to accept the possibility of dancing qualia in the original case, we would be discarding this principle, and it would no longer be available as a defense against skepticism even in the more usual cases.

It is not out of the question that we could actually perform such an experiment. Of course the practical difficulties would be immense, but at least in principle, one could install such a circuit in me and *I* could see what happened, and report it to the world. But of course there is no point performing the experiment: we know what the result will be. I will report that my experience stayed the same throughout, a constant shade of red, and that I noticed nothing untoward. I will become even more convinced than I was before that qualia are determined by functional organization. Of course this will not be a *proof*, but it will be hard seriously to dispute the evidence.

I conclude that by far the most plausible hypothesis is that replacement of neurons while preserving functional organization will preserve qualia, and that experience is wholly determined by functional organization.

The argument leaves open a few small loopholes, but none of the loopholes leads to an attractive position. For example, while the dancing qualia scenario is straightforwardly extendible to most functional isomorphs, there are a couple of exceptions involving speed and history. If an isomorph is much faster or slower than the original system, we cannot simply substitute a circuit from one system into the other and expect everything to function normally. We can still perform the experiment on a slowed-down or speeded-up version of the system in question, however, so at most we have left open the possibility that a change in speed might invert qualia. A similar loophole is left open for physical isomorphs that differ in their *history*: perhaps if I was born in the southern hemisphere I experience green, whereas a physical twin born in the north would experience red. History cannot be varied in a dancing qualia scenario (although it can be varied in a fading qualia scenario), so the argument does not bear on the hypothesis that qualia supervene on the past.

But neither of these hypotheses were very plausible in the first place. It is reasonable that history should affect our qualia by affecting our physical structure, but the history-dependence required above would be much stronger: there would in effect be a 'nonlocal' effect of distal history on present qualia, unmediated by anything in physical structure or nearby in space and time. As for speed, it would seem quite arbitrary that a change in speed would invert qualia when nothing else could. The hypotheses here are coherent, but there is little reason to embrace them.

Another small caveat is that the argument does not refute the possibility of a very mild spectrum inversion. Between dark red and a slightly darker red, for instance, there may be nine intermediate shades such that no two neighbouring shades are distinguishable. In such a case the dancing qualia scenario is not a problem; if the system notices no difference on flipping the switch, that is just what we might expect.

Of course, there is nothing special about the figure of one-tenth as the amount of difference between two neighboring systems. But we cannot make the figure too high. If we made it as high as one half, we would run into problems with personal identity: it might reasonably be suggested that upon flipping the switch, we are creating a new person, and it would not be a problem that the new person noticed no change. Perhaps we might go as high as one-fifth or one-quarter without such problems; but that would still allow the possibility of very mild inversions, the kind that could be composed of four or five unnoticeable changes. We can reduce the impact of this worry, however, by noting that it is very unlikely that experience depends equally on all areas of the brain. If colour experience depends largely on a small area of the visual cortex, say, then we could perform any qualia inversion in one fell swoop while only replacing a small portion of the system, and the argument would succeed against even the mildest noticeable qualia inversion.

In any case, the possibility of a mild under-determination of experience by organization is an unthreatening one. If we wished, we could accept it, noting that any differences between isomorphs would be so slight as to be uninteresting. More likely, we can note that this would seem an odd and unlikely way for the world to be. It would seem reasonable that experiences should be invertible across the board, or not invertible at all, but why should the world be such that a small inversion is possible but nothing more? This would seem quite arbitrary. We cannot rule it out, but it is not a hypothesis with much antecedent plausibility.

In a similar way, the argument leaves open the loophole that *unattended* qualia might be invertible. If we are not attending to the fringes of our visual field, for example, a qualia inversion might take place there without our noticing. But to exploit this loophole would leave one in the unattractive position that qualia are organizationally invariant when they are central enough in one's attention, but dependent on other features when they are not. (Presumably an inverted green experience on the fringe will flip back to red when one attends to it?) Such an asymmetric position would be theoretically unsatisfying in the extreme.

It should be noted that the dancing qualia argument works just as well against the possibility of absent qualia as against that of inverted qualia. If absent qualia are possible, then on the path to absent qualia we can find two slightly different systems whose experience differs significantly, and we can install a backup circuit in the same way. As before, the hypothesis implies that switching will cause my qualia to dance before my eyes, from vivid to tepid and back, without my ever noticing any change. This is implausible for the same reasons as before, so we have good reason to believe that absent qualia are impossible.

Overall, the dancing qualia argument seems to make an even more convincing case against absent qualia than the fading qualia argument does, although both have a role to play. Where an opponent might bite the bullet and accept the possibility of fading qualia, dancing qualia are an order of magnitude more difficult to accept. The very immediacy of the switch makes a significant difference, as does the fact that the subject cannot notice something so striking and dynamic. The possibility of fading qualia would imply that some systems are out of touch with their conscious experience, but dancing qualia would establish a much stranger gap.

V. Nonreductive Functionalism

To summarize: we have established that if absent qualia are possible, then fading qualia are possible; if inverted qualia are possible, then dancing qualia are possible; and if absent qualia are possible, then dancing qualia are possible. But it is implausible that fading qualia are possible, and it is extremely implausible that dancing qualia are possible. It is therefore extremely implausible that absent qualia and inverted qualia are possible. It follows that we have good reason to believe that the principle of organizational invariance is true, and that functional organization fully determines conscious experience.

It should be noted that these arguments do not establish functionalism in the strongest sense, as they establish at best that absent and inverted qualia are empirically (naturally, nomologically) impossible. There are two reasons why the arguments cannot be extended into an argument for logical or metaphysical impossibility. First, both fading qualia and dancing qualia seem to be intelligible hypotheses, even if they are very implausible. Some might dispute their logical possibility, perhaps holding that it is constitutive of qualia that subjects can notice differences between them. This conceptual intuition would be controversial, but in any case, even if we were to accept the logical impossibility of fading and dancing qualia, there is a second reason why these arguments do not do not establish the logical or meta-physical determination of conscious experience by functional organization.

To see this second reason, note that the arguments take as an *empirical* premise certain facts about the distribution of functional organization in physical systems: that I have conscious experiences of a certain kind, or that some biological systems do. If we established the logical impossibility of fading and dancing qualia, this might establish the logical necessity of the *conditional*: if one system with fine-grained functional organization F has a certain sort of conscious experiences, then any system with organization F has those experiences. But we cannot establish the logical necessity of the conclusion without establishing the logical necessity of the premise, and the premise is itself empirical. On the face of it, it is difficult to see why it should be logically necessary that *brains* with certain physical properties give rise to conscious experience. Perhaps the most tenable way to argue for this necessity is via a form of analytic functionalism; but in the context of using the fading and dancing qualia arguments to *establish* this sort of functionalism, this strategy would be circular. It follows that the fading and dancing qualia arguments are of little use in arguing for the logical and metaphysical impossibility of absent and inverted qualia.

The arguments therefore fail to establish a strong form of functionalism upon which functional organization is *constitutive* of conscious experience; but they succeed in establishing a weaker form, on which functional organization *suffices* for conscious experience with natural necessity. We can call this view *nonreductive functionalism*, as it holds that conscious experience is determined by functional organization without necessarily being reducible to functional organization. As things stand, the view is just as compatible with certain forms of property dualism about experience as with certain forms of physicalism. Whether the view should be strengthened into a reductive version of functionalism is a matter that the fading and dancing qualia arguments leave open.

In any case, the conclusion is a strong one. It tells us that systems that duplicate our functional organization will be conscious even if they are made of silicon, constructed out of water-pipes, or instantiated in an entire population. The arguments in this paper can thus be seen as offering support to some of the ambitions of artificial intelligence. The arguments also make progress in constraining the principles in virtue of which consciousness depends on the physical. If successful, they show that biochemical and other non-organizational properties are at best indirectly relevant to the instantiation of experience, relevant only insofar as they play a role in determining functional organization.

The principle of organizational invariance is not the last word in constructing a theory of conscious experience. There are many unanswered questions: we would like to know just what sort of organization gives rise to experience, and what sort of experience a given organization gives rise to. Further, the principle is not cast at the right level to be a truly *fundamental* theory of consciousness; eventually, we would like to construct a fundamental theory that has the principle as a consequence. In the meantime, the principle acts as a strong constraint on an ultimate theory.

References

Block, N. (1980). Troubles with functionalism. In Block 1980.

Cuda, T. (1985). Against neural chauvinism. *Philosophical Studies,* **48**, 111–27.

Horgan, T. (1984). Functionalism, qualia, and the inverted spectrum. *Philosophy and Phenomenological Research*, **44**, 453–69.

Pylyshyn, Z. (1980). The 'causal power' of machines. *Behavioral and Brain Sciences,* **3**, 442–4.

Savitt, S. (1982). Searle's demon and the brain simulator reply. *Behavioral and Brain Sciences,* **5**, 342–3.

Searle, J.R. (1980). Minds, brains, and programs. *Behavioral and Brain Sciences,* **3**, 417–57.

Searle, J.R. (1992). *The Rediscovery of the Mind.* Cambridge, MA: MIT Press.

Shoemaker, S. (1982). The inverted spectrum. *Journal of Philosophy,* **79**, 357–81.

Part Six

Consciousness and Higher-Order States

Introduction to Part Six

In the philosophical tradition consciousness has often been understood as a type of higher-order knowledge: a form of inner knowledge which can accompany mental processes. This line of thought is also pursued by some contemporary approaches which analyse phenomenal consciousness as a specific type of meta-representation, most notably by David Rosenthal. In such an account the basic thought is often that consciousness arises when the inner states of a system, which already carry representational content, *in turn* become the content of higher-order meta-representational states. The basic problem remains of linking this terminology to introspective experience and everyday folk-psychological vocabulary with its Cartesian bias. If they are formulated in the latter form at all, such theories of consciousness typically take two forms: theories of higher-order *perception* or theories of higher-order *thought*. The first contribution in this section critically examines theories of the former type.

In the Western philosophy of consciousness, a line runs from John Locke via William James to Franz Brentano, and resurfaces recently in the works of authors such as David Armstrong, Peter Carruthers, Paul Churchland or William Lycan. What these thinkers have in common is the suggestion that consciousness may be a special kind of inner perception: the perception of one's own mental processes. In his penetrating essay **Güven Güzeldere** sketches the course this line takes in contemporary philosophy and then puts forward the critical thesis that inner perception is neither a necessary nor a sufficient condition for interesting kinds of introspective consciousness. He leads the proponents of the higher-order perception paradigm into a logical trilemma, thus shifting the onus of proof and challenging them to develop a new and consistent exposition of their central thought.

Within philosophy, **David Rosenthal's** name is associated with the theory of consciousness as *higher-order thought* (HOT). This second version of a meta-representational theory is based on the thesis that a mental state becomes a conscious state by becoming the content of a higher-order thought, viz. of the (non-conscious) thought *that* I am now in this state. In his contribution, Rosenthal examines the relation of another prominent theory, namely Daniel Dennett's *Multiple Drafts Model* (MDM), to his own approach. In doing so, he argues that one can reap the explanatory fruits of Dennett's theory of consciousness even if one develops a weaker version of this theory which does without so-called *first-person operationalism*.

The author of the last text in this thematic section is **Norton Nelkin**. Reverting to Leibniz, Norton Nelkin shows that phenomenal consciousness — contrary to widespread opinion among philosophers and psychologists — must be distinguished from *apperceptive* consciousness. In order to do this, Nelkin conceptually differentiates three types of consciousness:

phenomenal states, first order propositional states and apperception. Apperceptive consciousness, Nelkin argues, is characterized precisely through the fact that its content can be expressed by the proposition that one of the first order states (phenomenal consciousness and propositional attitudes) *is happening now*. Nelkin's thesis is the 'dissociability thesis': In any plausible theory of consciousness phenomenal states and apperception have to be clearly distinguished. The results of the empirical sciences, especially the neurosciences, play a central role in his essay: an important element of his argument is based on empirical studies of blindsight patients as carried out by Alan Cowey, Petra Stoerig and Larry Weiskrantz.

Further Reading

Armstrong, D. M. (1981). What is consciousness? In Armstrong 1981.

Carruthers, P. (1989). Brute experience. *Journal of Philosophy*, **86**, 258–69.

Churchland, P.M. (1985). Reduction, qualia, and the direct introspection of brain states. *Journal of Philosophy*, **82**, 8–28. Reprinted in Churchland 1989.

Dretske, F. (1993). Conscious experience. *Mind*, **102**, 263–83.

Gennaro, R.J. (forthcoming). *Consciousness and Self-Consciousness: A Defense of the Higher-Order Thought Theory of Consciousness*. Amsterdam and Philadelphia: John Benjamins.

Güzeldere, G. (1995a). Consciousness: What it is, how to study it, what to learn from its history. *Journal of Consciousness Studies*, **2**, 30–52.

Güzeldere, G. (1995b). Problems of consciousness: Contemporary issues, current debates. *Journal of Consciousness Studies*, **2**, 112–43.

Güzeldere, G. (1996). Consciousness and the introspective link principle. In Hameroff *et al.* 1996.

Lycan, W.G. (1996). Consciousness as internal monitoring, I. In Tomberlin 1995. Revised version in Block *et al.* 1996.

Nelkin, N. (1986). Pains and pain sensations. *Journal of Philosophy*, **83**, 129–48.

Nelkin, N. (1987). How sensations get their names. *Philosophical Studies*, **51**, 325–39.

Nelkin, N. (1987.) What is it like to be a person? *Mind and Language*, **3**, 220–41.

Nelkin, N. (1989). Propositional attitudes and consciousness. *Philosophy and Phenomenological Research*, **49**, 413–30.

Nelkin, N. (1989). Unconscious sensations. *Philosophical Psychology*, **2**, 129–41.

Nelkin, N. (1990). Categorising the senses. *Mind and Language*, **5**, 149–65.

Nelkin, N. (1993). The connection between intentionality and consciousness. In Davies & Humphreys 1993.

Nelkin, N. (1993). What is consciousness? *Philosophy of Science*, **60**, 419–34.

Nelkin, N. (1994). Phenomena and representation. *British Journal for the Philosophy of Science*, **45**, 527–47.

Nelkin, N. (1994). Reconsidering pain. *Philosophical Psychology*, **7**, 325–43.

Nelkin, N. (1996). *Consciousness and the Origins of Thought*. Cambridge: Cambridge University Press.

Rosenthal, D. (1986). Two concepts of consciousness. *Philosophical Studies*, **49**, 329–59. Reprinted in Rosenthal 1990.

Rosenthal, D.M. (1993). Higher-order thoughts and the appendage theory of consciousness. *Philosophical Psychology*, **6**, 155–67.

Rosenthal, D.M. (1993). State consciousness and transitive consciousness. *Consciousness and Cognition*, **2**, 355–63.

Rosenthal, D.M. (1993). Thinking that one thinks. In Davies & Humphreys 1993.

Rosenthal, D.M. (1996). A theory of consciousness. In Block *et al.* 1996.

Siewert, C.E. (forthcoming). *Understanding Consciousness*. Princeton: Princeton University Press.

Since the HOT theory as well as the Multiple Drafts Model play an important role in the contemporary discussion, further literature especially dealing with this topic can be found in sections 3.3 and 3.5 of the bibliography at the end of this book. A number of the philosophical monographs in section 1.1 also extensively discuss theories of consciousness, for which the assumption of higher-order states or the concept of meta-representation are of central importance. Norton Nelkin's works on the problem of phenomenal consciousness are listed in sections 1.1, 3.1, 3.4, 3.7 and 3.9.

Güven Güzeldere

Is Consciousness the Perception of What Passes in One's Own Mind?

There is a strong intuition which dates back several centuries that consciousness is not, or does not consist in, an ordinary mental state or process itself, but it is, or it consists in, the *awareness* of such states and processes. Locke epitomized this intuition in his celebrated statement: 'Consciousness is the perception of what passes in a man's own mind' (Locke 1959: 138). Various versions of this maxim have appeared in the writings of philosophers and psychologists from William James (1950) to Franz Brentano (1973)[1] and more recently received endorsement by David Armstrong

---

[1] The first instance of giving philosophical expression to this kind of an intuition could actually be said to go back to Aristotle's discussion of the 'sense that perceives other (ordinary) senses', which starts out with the reasoning that 'since we perceive that we see and hear, we must see that we see either by sight or by another sense' (Aristotle 1951, Book III, Chapter II, 584–6). James had talked about the awareness of mental states, under the name 'introspective observation', as the most fundamental method of all psychology, and characterized it as 'the looking into [of] our own minds and reporting what we there discover — states of consciousness' (James 1950: 185). But it was really Franz Brentano, more than perhaps any other philosopher psychologist, who was preoccupied with the role of higher order, 'meta-awareness' in human psychology. In the case of auditory perception, for instance, he wrote: 'The presentation of the sound and the presentation of the presentation of the sound form a single mental phenomenon . . . In the same mental phenomenon in which the sound is present to our minds we simultaneously apprehend the mental phenomenon itself' (Brentano 1973: 121–7).

These 'double-tiered' accounts of consciousness come with the threat of infinite regress (having a commitment to a third-level awareness to account for the second, a fourth for the third, and so on.) Aristotle was very much aware of this problem, and Brentano devoted a good deal of his philosophical career trying to come up with a satisfactory account that was free of such regress. The details are fascinating, but that kind of historical scholarship lies beyond the scope of this paper.

(1980), Paul Churchland (1988), David Rosenthal (1986; 1990), Peter
Carruthers (1989), and William Lycan (1987; 1996), as well as (though
rather indirectly) by Daniel Dennett (1991). Armstrong calls this form of
consciousness the 'perception of the mental', or 'introspective consciousness', and promotes it as 'consciousness in the most interesting sense of the
word':

> Introspective consciousness . . . is a perception-like awareness of current
> states and activities in our own mind. The current activities will include
> sense-perception: which latter is the awareness of current states and activities
> of our environment and our body (Armstrong 1980: 61).

Churchland echoes Armstrong's conviction in calling introspective consciousness 'just a species of perception: *self-perception*' (Churchland
1988: 74). According to Rosenthal, the awareness of mental states and
activities comes in the form of a cognitive, rather than a perceptual, state:
'[A] mental state is conscious just in case it is accompanied by a higher-
order, nondispositional, assertoric thought to the effect that one is in that
very state' (Rosenthal 1990: 7). And Lycan characterizes consciousness as
a 'perception-like second-order representing of our own psychological
states and events' (Lycan 1996: 1 in MS).

These assertions constitute the core of a substantial body of work among
the philosophical theories of consciousness today. What is common to all
these theories is the claim that consciousness is, or consists in, *some kind of*
higher-order representing of lower-level mental states and processes. This
representing may be perception-like (as Armstrong, Churchland, and Lycan
claim, after Locke), or thought-like (as Rosenthal and, to some extent,
Carruthers and Dennett claim).[2]

The psychological plausibility and philosophical merit of such accounts
depend on how well the specifics of such representings are spelled out —
whether it is the *perception of* or the *thinking about* 'what passes in one's
own mind'. Paying attention to the mechanics of higher-order
representation is important especially for the following two reasons: First,
it is these mechanics that determine the degree to which consciousness is
literally, and not just metaphorically, taken to be the 'perception (or,
thinking) of what passes in one's own mind'. Secondly, assuming a literal
reading of this conception of consciousness, it is the specifics of *just how*
certain mental states can be represented by certain others that reveal the

---

[2] There is a certain amount of terminological calibration required here. What Lycan (as well
as most others) describes under the title 'consciousness' or 'conscious awareness', Armstrong
refers to as 'introspective consciousness'. This contrasts with, for example, Armstrong's
notion of 'perceptual consciousness'. In the rest of the text, I will use 'consciousness' and
'introspective consciousness' interchangeably, and point out other uses involving the term
'consciousness' wherever necessary.

substantive differences, if any, between the perception-like and the thought-like higher-order representings of first-order mental states.

These details are what I will try to lay out in this essay. In doing so, I hope to show that the two varieties of higher-order representation accounts of consciousness, if taken literally, do not survive as two distinct competing models. In particular, I try to demonstrate that the 'higher-order perception' accounts of consciousness, upon close examination, face a serious trilemma: they either get forced to abandon their characteristic two-tiered structure, or commit themselves to what I call the 'fallacy of the representational divide', or turn into a species of their competitor.

Taking the first horn of the trilemma means simply giving up the essential introspective element of the theory. The fallacy inherent in the second horn stems from a confusion between properties of what is represented and properties of that which represents what is represented, in these accounts of second-order, introspective awareness. Avoiding this fallacy is possible only under a particular interpretation of the phrase 'perception of what passes in one's mind', which, in turn, forces the 'higher-order perception theories' to transform into a species of 'higher-order thought' theories. That is the third horn of the trilemma.

This construal can constitute only one half of a full analysis of the higher-order representation accounts of consciousness. The other half would consist in an examination of how plausible the remaining accounts of the higher-order thought variety are, and to what extent they do justice to explaining the nature and mechanism of consciousness. That half I do not attempt to give here. My goal in this essay is only to point out that the presumed distinction between the two kinds of higher-order accounts of consciousness, based on which there is a growing literature, is unfounded as it stands. In particular, the higher-order perception accounts, taken literally, can only be a species of higher-order thought accounts.[3]

---

[3] As I mentioned, the further question of whether higher-order thought accounts provide a fully satisfactory account of consciousness is one I leave unaddressed in this essay. Although I cannot pursue this question here, let me simply state my opinion. I believe that the higher-order thought models account well for certain aspects of consciousness, especially 'introspective consciousness' (which typically consists in the awareness of one's own mental states). But I take that to be only part of the whole picture. I believe that not all consciousness is of the introspective sort. More specifically, those aspects of consciousness which humans share with other animals of lesser cognitive capabilities have to be accounted for by a non-introspective, uni-level model. Although I cannot substantiate my claim here, let me mention that rudimentary elements of such a model are already present in the notion of 'attention', characterized as a limited resource in various information processing models developed in cognitive psychology.

I. The Higher-Order Representation (HOR) Theories of Consciousness

Two Senses of Consciousness

Let me start with a simple set of distinctions with respect to consciousness. Among the things that the term 'conscious' can be used to predicate upon, the two most important kinds are individual beings and mental states that belong to, or occur in, these individuals. For example, there is a difference in my being conscious (as opposed to, say, in a coma) and my having a mental state which is conscious, (as opposed to, say, subconscious).[4] The former involves one's being conscious in the sense of being awake and alert. Furthermore one's consciousness can be directed upon something, e.g. a tune coming from the radio, or a lingering thought about a past conversation. This is the *individual* sense of consciousness. (Rosenthal call it 'creature consciousness'.)

On the other hand, it makes sense to talk about whether a particular mental state is conscious or not. This is not quite the same as someone's being conscious. The *individual* sense of consciousness denotes an overall state one is in; the other one classifies one's (mental) states as of one type or another. Following Rosenthal (1990), I will call this sense of consciousness which functions as a type-identifier for mental states, *state consciousness*.[5]

Given this distinction, the natural next step is to investigate the relation between these two senses of consciousness. One way of doing this is to formulate a tighter relation between the (state-)consciousness of some particular mental state and one's (individual-)consciousness of *that* state.[6]

---

[4] Of course, none of this is really new. Variations on such distinctions can be found in James 1950 and Brentano 1973. The contemporary formulation is due to Rosenthal, e.g. 1990; 1996.

[5] There are further distinctions that I talk about elsewhere (Güzeldere 1995a,b). For instance, *individual consciousness* can be used to classify organisms (or systems) into two kinds: those that are, or are potentially, conscious (e.g. a person, even if knocked out or asleep), and those that are not (e.g. a calculator), much in the same sense as theoretical biology tries to accomplish with the predicate 'living' in drawing a line between animate and non-animate things. (See, also, the preface of Lycan 1987 for a brief but useful classification.) For the purposes of this paper, I am mainly interested in the 'intentional' sense of individual consciousness, which always involves directedness towards something, and will use it as such.

See, also, Block 1995 for another important and inherently related distinction: *access consciousness* versus *phenomenal consciousness*. Block is responsible for originally coining these terms (in the contemporary discussion), and he treats them at length in his 1995 article. Martin Davies has a carefully crafted discussion based on Block's distinction in Davies & Humphreys 1993. A somewhat related distinction, between sensational and representational properties of perceptual experience, can be found in Peacocke 1983.

[6] Here, I take the sense in which a mental state is said to be conscious as at least conceptually distinct from the subject's consciousness *of* it. Not everyone thinks so. Lycan, for instance, states: '[I] cannot myself hear a natural sense of the phrase ''conscious state'' other than as

So far, I haven't specified the domain of objects towards which individual consciousness can be directed. For the purposes of this paper, I will adopt a fairly non-detailed position: One can be individual-conscious of physical things (cups, telephones, etc.), abstract objects (relations, theorems, etc.), facts, states of affairs, and events.[7] These are all 'external', in the sense that they can be objects of other people's consciousnesses as well. Alternatively, one can be conscious of the proprioceptive states of one's own body (the muscular strain in one's leg), or, as it is generally accepted, of one's own mental states (a desire for a chocolate bar). Broadly speaking, both of these are 'internal'; only I have access to my proprioceptive states or desires, at least in the way that I do (cf. Lyons 1986).

This classification roughly corresponds to a common sense understanding of perception (seeing a cup on the counter, seeing that the cup is on the counter), proprioception (feeling one's foot getting numb), and introspection (dwelling on one's thoughts, desires, motives, etc.). That is to say, I want to spell out individual consciousness in terms of familiar mental phenomena, and remain neutral about further details at this stage. This is not to say, however, that this usage is unproblematic. In particular, the claim that mental states can be the *object* of one's individual consciousness, which makes it a 'second order' mental state, is multiply ambiguous, and it cries out for further analysis.

---

meaning "state one is conscious of being in".' So much so that he quotes a statement from Dretske (1993) that 'an experience can be conscious without anyone — including the person having it — being conscious of having it' and labels 'oxymoronic'. However, he also adds that 'the philosophical use of "conscious" is by now well and truly up for grabs, and the best one can do is to be as clear as possible in one's technical specification' (Lycan 1996: 10 in MS).

Although generally in agreement with Lycan's *latter* observation (but not the former claim), let me nonetheless note that there are various established uses that one ought to pay attention to — if not the folk psychological use, then, for instance, the use grounded in the Freudian tradition. In any case, 'giving a clear technical specification' (albeit alternative to Lycan's) is precisely what I aim at doing here. Furthermore, as evidenced from contemporary psychology literature, research on type-identifying mental states as conscious versus non-conscious, and research on the nature of consciousness of the subjects who have such states, can be, and actually are being, pursued on independent conceptual grounds.

[7] Dretske makes a distinction between 'consciousness of' *something* and 'consciousness that' *something is the case* (Dretske 1993). This distinction is in line with Dretske's earlier work in epistemology, in particular his distinction between 'non-epistemic seeing'and 'epistemic seeing', or 'seeing' versus 'seeing that', and it is fundamentally based on the lack or presence of conceptual involvement in perception (Dretske 1969). Dretske's position is not a unanimously received view. For some, perception is an affair fundamentally mingled with concepts, and hence it is always 'epistemic'. Armstrong, for instance, talks about perception as the 'acquiring of beliefs' (Armstrong 1968). I would like to remain neutral on this issue for the time being. I therefore intend my use of 'consciousness of' in a generic way, and mean it to also include the 'consciousness that' sense, *at least* when the content in question is an abstract entity, e.g. a postulate of arithmetic, or a proposition about one's beliefs.

What does 'being conscious of one's belief' mean? Being conscious of the *content* of that belief, being conscious of *the fact that one has a belief* with the content that it has, or being conscious of *the belief state qua the vehicle* that it is (i.e. the mental state that does the representing, not what it represents)? The discussion of these issues will constitute the core of my assessment of the 'higher-order perception theories' of consciousness in section II.

Linking Individual Consciousness with State Consciousness

Let me now state a canonical formulation of the relation between the state and the individual senses of consciousness. This formulation is meant to capture the thesis that underlies both the perception-like and the thought-like higher order theories of consciousness.

The Introspective Link Principle:

A mental state M in a subject S is *state-conscious*
if and only if
S is *individual-conscious* of M.

I would like to give the consciousness accounts that are built around this general linking principle a common name: the theories of Higher-Order (Mental) Representation, or in short, HOR. Implicit in the *Introspective Link Principle*, and hence in all the HOR theories, is the employment of a meta-level mental state, which is responsible for the consciousness of the lower-level states. S's (individual-)consciousness of M is itself a (second-order) mental state, M', in S, presumably directed upon M. M', then, *endows* M with state-consciousness, in virtue of being a mental state in S itself, directed upon M. In other words, M' is a second-order state which *represents* M, an ordinary first-order mental state. M may, for instance, just be a visual perceptual state whose content is a scene S is looking at, or a thought S is entertaining about her dinner plans.

Representation as Perception or Thought? HOP versus HOT

HOR comes in two main flavours, depending on the nature of the postulated higher order mental representation. This is only natural since mental representation is possible via both perceptual and (non-perceptual) cognitive states. Indeed, there is a significant number of philosophers taking each route in spelling out the 'R' of HOR.

If M' is regarded as a perception-like state, where M''s relation to its object M is somehow like the relation between a perceptual state and its object, I call this version of HOR the thesis of Higher Order Perception, or

HOP. As I noted earlier, David Armstrong, Paul Churchland, and William Lycan, following Locke, all defend this view.

Alternatively, M' can be taken to be a type of cognitive mental representation, a higher level thought-like state, the content of which is either the content of M, or (roughly speaking) a fact involving M — e.g. that S is having M. This is the thesis of Higher Order Thought, or HOT. David Rosenthal and Peter Carruthers both subscribe to the HOT thesis, and Dan Dennett comes close, though they all defend different variations of it.[8]

In either case, some form of hierarchical mental structure and of higher-order representing is the key idea for explaining consciousness in these accounts. For that reason, I call them 'double-tiered' theories. The HOR accounts constitute the orthodox line with regard to theories of 'introspective consciousness' in analytic philosophy today.[9] A forceful contemporary critique of these accounts is in Dretske 1993; 1995.[10]

II. Spelling out the 'P' in 'HOP': What's Wrong with Higher-Order Perception?

Locke, Armstrong, Churchland, and Lycan all talk about consciousness as the awareness, or perception, or monitoring, or scanning of one's mental

---

[8] In a letter to Mersenne, dated 11 June 1640, Descartes makes the following point about why he thinks animals cannot be said, strictly speaking, to feel pain:

> [I]n my view, pain exists only in the understanding. What I do explain is all the external movements which accompany this feeling in us; in animals it is these movements alone which occur, and not pain in the strict sense . . . (Descartes 1993b: 148).

Descartes seems to have an intuition here which comes very close to that which underlies the HOT thesis. Pain, or an essential aspect of it anyway, consists not in the first-order state itself, he thinks, but in a cognitive, second-level state involving (or about) it. This is basically the position Carruthers (1989) adopts in arguing for his rather baroque conclusion that animal pain cannot really count as pain due to the lack of higher cognitive faculties in animals, and hence it should not be of any moral concern to us, humans.

[9] There are of course other accounts which say interesting things about consciousness (e.g. Dennett 1991; Flanagan 1992; Searle 1992; Block 1995) but they do not always explicitly address the HOR thesis. It is instructive, however, to examine these accounts in the light of HOR, for in some cases, they turn out to be not orthogonal to it, but rather tacitly in agreement (e.g. Dennett). Hence, the discrediting of the HOR thesis may very well undermine the plausibility of some of the seemingly unrelated accounts.

[10] It is actually possible to find earlier criticisms of the 'self-perception' model of consciousness in the context of the debate on self-knowledge and self-reference. Shoemaker finds it problematic, for instance, 'to think of awareness as a kind of perception, i.e. to think of it on the model of sense perception', and denies that 'self-awareness involves any sort of perception of oneself' (Shoemaker 1984: 14–15). In a somewhat similar vein, Evans, in discussing the question of self-identification, observes that in forming a (higher-order) cognitive state about a (lower-order) informational state, the latter cannot be regarded as an *object* of the former, in analogy with perceptual states and perceived objects, for 'there is nothing that constitutes "perceiving that state".' That is, he goes on to say, '[t]here is no *informational* state which stands to the internal state as that internal state stands to the state of the world' (Evans 1992: 228).

states. There is an ambiguity inherent in all these statements concerning the nature of the proper object of such internal, perception-like, awareness. What exactly is being perceived in the 'perception of what passes in one's own mind' — the content of the mental state that happens to be 'passing through' one's mind at the time, or the mental state itself? Or the content of another thought to the effect that one is having such a mental state?

There is surprisingly little attention paid to spelling out the answer to this question in any detail. Perhaps it is because the answer seems obvious or self-evident to everyone. Or perhaps not much is thought to depend on it. I will argue that, taken literally, there is actually nothing quite obvious or self-evident about such an answer, especially when the implicit ontological assumptions underlying it are made explicit. Nor is it true that not much turns on providing such details — what is at stake is simply the plausibility of the whole class of HOP style theories.

Three Options for the HOP Theorist

So far, one of the predominant distinctions on which the discussion has been resting has been perceptual versus cognitive mental states — e.g., one's seeing a cup on the desk versus one's believing that the cup is on the desk (seeing *that* the cup is on the desk). Since vision is paradigmatic of perception, and beliefs are paradigmatic of cognitive states, let me proceed as such, assuming no loss of generality.[11]

Assume that our subject S is sitting on her desk and looking at her cup right in front of her, under all the 'normal conditions' — perfect light, veridical experience, no demons or 'evil neurosurgeons' playing tricks on S, so on and so forth. And despite the immense complexity and dynamical nature of perception, let us, in all simplicity, assume that we can capture a single instant of S's perceptual processing as she continues to eye the cup, freezing time, and thus securing a momentary state of her bodily/mental conditions — 'a polaroid snapshot of S's mind', if you will. Call the visual state S is in at this moment, the state which is in her (as well as for her) a representation of the cup, V. In other words, V is the state in virtue of which S sees the cup in the way she does. Let me denote the content of S's visual state concisely as: [cup in front].

Now, according to the HOP theorists, S's consciousness consists in her 'perception of V'. Call this S's second-order 'perception-like awareness' of V, her 'monitoring' or 'scanning' of her first-order mental state V. Whatever we may call it (and let me henceforth use the term 'awareness' to cover all these), this is a junction in the conceptual landscape where some unpacking is necessary.

---

[11] That is to say, nothing specific turns on my choice of using a visual state for my analysis; the same analysis could straightforwardly be given using a different perceptual state, or, e.g. another (first-order) belief.

I can come up with at least three different readings of 'S is aware of of her visual state V, which has the content: [cup in front]'. Let me enumerate:

1) S is aware of *the cup* in front of her, simpliciter.
2) S is aware of *her visual state V*. (i.e. she is aware of V-*qua*-vehicle, the cup-representing internal state.)
3) S is aware of *the fact that she has a visual state V*, which has the content: [cup in front].

Which one of these three readings truly reflects what the HOP theorists have in mind?

III. *Option 1:* Higher-Order Perception as Perception Simpliciter

Option 1 will not do: an (introspective) awareness of one's mental state is *not*, by the HOP theorists' definition, nothing but just having that mental state. This option would no longer leave room for higher-order representing, and hence not allow for a double-tiered account, collapsing the (first) level of an ordinary mental state and the (second) level of an introspective mental state into one.

Such an option may be available to those (single-tiered theorists of consciousness) who would like to claim that introspection is but an illusion, and that every time one tries to become introspectively aware of one's mental state, one finds oneself simply in that very mental state. But this would mean doing away with second-order representing altogether, something central to HOP accounts. *Option 1* is therefore really a non-option for the HOP theorist.[12]

---

[12] Rosenthal (1990) raises an objection to HOP theories which aims at forcing them into something like *Option 1*: All perception involves some sensory quality, he maintains, and if introspective consciousness is higher order perception, so should it. It is not obvious, however, what sort of sensory quality, if any, is involved in in higher order perceiving.

I think this is a powerful objection. One possible move for the HOP theorist could be to claim that the sensory quality involved in second order perception is the same as the one involved in the first order mental state being introspected. But this is entirely *ad hoc* as an answer to the objection. Furthermore, if all we can report are sensory qualities associated with our first order perceptions while we are trying to introspect, this constitutes fair reason to think that something like what is outlined in *Option 1* is actually the case: that the proposed double-tiered structure of introspective awareness is nothing but an illusion.

Lycan tries to counter Rosenthal's objection by stating that higher order perception is *not* like ordinary perception in every aspect. He also concedes that one can perhaps talk about a broadly construed 'mental quality' (though not necessarily a 'sensory quality', but rather some kind of 'psychological mode of presentation') associated with every higher order perceiving, and that the HOP theorist owes to give an account of this. Unfortunately, Lycan then chooses to 'leave that discussion for another time' (Lycan 1996: 14 in MS).

IV. *Option 2:* Higher-Order Perception as Perception of the Representational Vehicle

What about *Option 2*? The idea that introspective consciousness may be the direct awareness of mental states (*qua* the representational vehicles, the carriers of content) rather than of what those states represent (their content), is an interesting one. Furthermore, it can also be defended in one of two different ways, depending on the accompanying theory of mental representations. I will look at them both in some detail, but my conclusion will not be any different from what I reached for the first option: there is no reading under which 'higher order perception' can be taken literally as an account of introspective consciousness.

Two Interpretations for Option 2

Most contemporary materialist theories of mental representations, details aside, have this much in common: Mental representations are states of the nervous system which represent to the subject in whom they occur various objects in, and facts about, the subject's environment, as well as the subject's bodily states. Now, these representations, being neuronal structures interacting in various electro-chemical ways, themselves possess such properties as spiking frequencies, synaptic densities, etc. In turn, they represent the world to the subject as being a certain way, via (at least, seemingly) different properties — those properties we are all familiar with in our phenomenology: colours, textures, temperature, and so on. So, at least on the face of it, it seems that the properties of the representers and those of the represented do not always coincide — in fact, they often seem radically different.

On the other hand, there used to be a time when the relation between (what can roughly be called today) 'mental images' in the mind and objects in the world external to the mind was taken to be one of *resemblance*.[13] Under this conception of mental representation, perception was thought to involve literally 'seeing with the mind's eye.' Although it is not easy to come by anyone today who would explicitly defend the 'resemblance theory of mental representations' any more, I think that it is still an operant

---

[13] The idea that in sensation, objects produce 'resemblances' of themselves in the sensing subject, is quite common among the medieval Aristotelian scholars. Descartes describes this view as 'the intervention of "intentional forms".' (Descartes 1993a: 173–4. Cottingham *et al.* add, in an editorial footnote, that '[a]ccording to the scholastic theory referred to here, what is directly perceived via the senses is not the object itself but a 'form' or 'semblance' transmitted from object to observer.' *ibid* fn. 1.) Descartes later rejects this view in 'Sixth Set of Replies', objection 9: 'For example, when I see a stick, it should not be supposed that certain "intentional forms" fly off the stick towards the eye' (Descartes 1993a: 295).

For a modern treatment, see Cummins 1991, which argues that traces of such a 'resemblance theory', in some form or another, can be found in Aristotle and, more recently, in Berkeley's conception of mental representations as images of sorts.

intuition, albeit in disguise, in many discussions in the philosophy of perception. In fact, I will argue that one way to take the 'perception of the mental' claim literally commits the HOP theorists to such a resemblance account of mental representations.

In sum, it is possible to give two distinct interpretations of introspective consciousness construed as 'internally directed perception', depending on what the 'internal objects' of this perceptual activity are taken to be. Under the former materialist framework this would amount to, I will argue, an account of introspection as some form of 'direct access' to one's brain states, in terms of the intrinsic, physical properties of those states. In the latter version, where the introspected 'internal objects' are assumed to share the properties of the external objects they resemble, I will show that introspective consciousness in essence becomes a literal account of 'seeing with the mind's eye'. Neither account has desirable consequences, but they both deserve a more detailed treatment.

First Interpretation of Option 2:
Higher-Order Perception as 'Direct Introspection of Brain States'

Let me start with the former version. Even though the phrase 'direct introspection of brain states' exclusively belongs to Churchland (1985), I will argue that the same basic idea can be used in filling in the details of what both Armstrong (1968; 1980) and Lycan (1987; 1996) leave unspecified in their accounts. I will come back to Churchland following an analysis of Armstrong and Lycan.

Armstrong & Lycan

Armstrong (1980) contrasts introspective consciousness with ordinary perception, and talks about the consciousness of one's mental states as 'simply the scanning of one part of our central nervous system by another'. Elsewhere he states:

> [I] suggest that consciousness is no more than *awareness* (perception) of inner mental states by the person whose states they are . . . In perception the brain scans the environment. In awareness of the perception another process in the brain scans that scanning. (Armstrong 1968: 94.)

In Armstrong's view, this 'second order scanning' is just what is missing in a long-distance truck driver, who has been driving on 'auto-pilot', perceiving the road and steering accordingly, but lacking any 'inner perception' of his mental states, any introspective awareness of what he has been doing (seeing other vehicles, stopping at red lights, swerving to avoid collisions, etc.). The truck driver, Armstrong maintains, although 'perceptually conscious' of his environment, is nonetheless *unconscious* in a very important sense — he lacks 'introspective consciousness'. As a result, he will have been surprised that he has been driving for hours at the moment he (re)gains introspective consciousness, and will have no recollection of his experiences that belong to this period of introspective unconsciousness.[14]

Lycan follows suit in characterizing consciousness as 'the successful operation of an internal scanner or monitor' in the brain (Lycan 1996: 16 in MS) and asserts that 'consciousness is the functioning of internal *attention mechanisms* directed upon lower-order psychological states and events' (Lycan 1996: 2 in MS).

Unfortunately these claims, once asserted, are left at that — mere just-so stories. Neither the neurophysiological nor the psychological details of such a monitoring process are anywhere to be found in either author's account. It can perhaps be argued that Armstrong and Lycan cannot be expected actually to make a neurophysiological case; it is the job of neuroscientists to determine the validity of the higher-order scanning claim with further research. It should be noted, however, that the claim that there are self-scanners in the nervous system which are responsible for introspective consciousness, in accordance with Armstrong's and Lycan's characterization, has no solid physiological or anatomical basis in the neuroscientific literature at present, either.[15] Moreover, even if that weren't the case, there would still be a missing philosophical component in these accounts:

[14] The relation between introspective consciousness and memory is a very interesting one in its own right. Armstrong seems to think that the lack of the former would be somehow responsible for the lack of the latter, or at least the lack of long term memory, but he doesn't pursue this point any further.

Tracing this issue back in history, one encounters a passage in *New Essays* where Leibniz uses an example much like Armstrong's truck driver. Leibniz actually suggests that attention (the lack of which seems closely related to the lack of introspective consciousness in Armstrong's example) and memory must be closely related:

[T]here are hundreds of indications leading us to conclude that at every moment there is in us an infinity of perceptions, unaccompanied by awareness or reflection. [. . .] This is how we become so accustomed to the motion of a mill or a waterfall, after living beside it for a while, that we pay no heed to it. Not that this motion ceases to strike on our sense-organs . . . but these impressions . . . lacking the appeal of novelty, are not forceful enough to attract our attention and our memory, which are applied only to more compelling objects. Memory is needed for attention; when we are not alerted, so to speak, to pay heed to certain of our own present perceptions, we allow them to slip by unconsidered and even unnoticed. (Leibniz 1981: 54.)

It would probably not be too far fetched to say that Leibniz was also an early HOR theorist of sorts, given his remarks on perceptions gone unnoticed in the absence of a second-order awareness or reflection.

[15] Among the few articles that can be taken somewhat as support for such a hypothesis are Crick 1984 and Barker 1986, where the thalamic reticular complex and the basal ganglia are proposed as candidate structures in charge of processes that accomplish some form of 'selective attention' and control in the central nervous system. It is not clear whether the existence of such structures really provide evidence for the 'consciousness as self-scanning' claim, however. At best, Crick's and Barker's accounts remain sketchy and speculative to date with respect to the HOP thesis.

the construal of the nature of those properties that figure in the internal monitoring process such that their scanning gives rise to introspective consciousness.

For instance, Lycan asserts that 'to be actively-introspectively aware that P is for one to have an internal scanner in working order that is operating on some state that is itself psychological and delivering information about that state to one's executive control unit' (Lycan 1987: 72). He leaves it unspecified, however, just what kind of information about the first order states needs to be delivered to the 'executive control unit'. Surely, such information is to bear *some* relation to the state in question. It could be constitutive of the relevant state's *content*, for example, or it could just indicate the *presence* (or absence) of that state. Lycan doesn't say which.

In fact, neither of these construals can account for the 'higher order perception' hypothesis. As I tried to outline above, if the output of the second-order scanner simply provides the system with the *content* of the first-order state, this collapses the double-tiered structure of the HOP accounts into a uni-level account (transforming *Option 2* to *Option 1*). If, on the other hand, the output of the scanning process is taken merely to deliver information about whether or not the system is currently in possession of a certain first-order state, then, as I will argue below, the HOP account transforms into a species of a HOT account (transforming *Option 2* to *Option 3*). As such, neither Armstrong's nor Lycan's account provides sufficient detail to uphold the first interpretation of *Option 2* of the HOP thesis on its own.

Churchland

Churchland (1988) tries out a somewhat different tack, and his account is more explicit in its details. Furthermore, if valid, it could also provide a new way out for both Armstrong's and Lycan's accounts. As I already mentioned, Churchland, too, takes introspective consciousness as a species of perception:

> [O]ne's introspective consciousness of oneself appears very similar to one's perceptual consciousness of the external world. The difference is that, in the former case, whatever mechanisms of discrimination are at work are keyed to internal circumstances instead of to external ones . . . Self-consciousness is no more (and no less) mysterious than perception generally. It is just directed internally rather than externally. (Churchland 1988: 74.)

So what are the internal circumstances to which one's discriminatory introspective powers are keyed? Or, to put the question in another way, in virtue of what kinds of properties of internal goings on does one gain introspective consciousness of one's mental states? What sort of 'self-perception', in other words, would make the truck driver who is driving on 'auto-pilot' to become introspectively aware that he has just stopped because the traffic light turned red?

A possible answer could be found in Churchland's (1985) discussion of the direct introspection of brain states. Even though Churchland's intention there seems to be promoting a general ontological position about the mind (a blend of reductionism and eliminativism), the framework he lays out is sufficiently detailed, and it subsumes several pointers to pursue questions about the nature of introspective consciousness, especially when combined with his more specific remarks in Churchland 1988.

Churchland claims that a finer grained account of 'human subjective consciousness' can be given in the language of a matured neuroscience. Provided that we acquaint ourselves with such a new, advanced conceptual framework, he maintains, the direct introspection of brain states, which amounts to a form of 'internally directed perception', will give us greater powers of discrimination.

> Dopamine levels in the limbic system, the spiking frequencies in specific neural pathways, resonances in the nth layer of the occipital cortex, inhibitory feedback to the lateral geniculate nucleus, and countless other neurophysiological nicities could be moved into the objective focus of our introspective discrimination, just as $Gm7$ chords and $Adim$ chords are moved into the objective focus of a trained musician's auditory discrimination. We will of course have to *learn* the conceptual framework of a matured neuroscience in order to pull this off. And we will have to *practice* its non-inferential application. But that seems a small price to pay for the quantum leap in self-apprehension. (Churchland 1988: 55.)

Perhaps so. That is to say, perhaps we can indeed learn to discriminate among our brain states in terms of their intrinsic properties, and become very good at it. Note that underlying Churchland's claim is the conviction that not only are mental states identical to brain states, but also the properties of the former will turn out to be identical to, or will replace the properties of, the latter (or a combination of both). And perhaps that, too, is true. But would any amount of such 'direct access' to the neurophysiological properties of our brain states help us in gaining *introspective consciousness* of our first-order perceptual states?

The answer is no. Consider Armstrong's truck driver who, after having been driving for the last half hour with no introspective awareness, 'comes to realize' that he has just stopped because he is at a red traffic light. What does his realization, his gaining introspective consciousness, amount to? Note that the question is not whether or not spiking frequencies or dopamine levels in his brain underlay or played a causal role in his becoming introspectively conscious of his circumstances. (Of course they did.) We are rather interested in how far we can go by taking the idea of 'direct introspection of brain states' literally. Certainly the driver is now aware of *something* he wasn't before. But is it the dopamine levels or spiking frequencies in his brain that he 'perceived' and became aware of?

The Fallacy of the Representational Divide

Looking inside someone's head to find out about the content of his or her introspective awareness is a mistake. Not only does the truck driver *not* need to be aware of the intrinsic properties of his brain states in order to come to realize that he is at a red traffic light, his awareness of such properties would not necessarily suffice to wake him up to his circumstances, either. According to Armstrong, he has always been aware of the road and the traffic lights, in *some* sense of the word 'consciousness'. (Armstrong calls this 'perceptual consciousness'.) Perhaps what changes in his situation is the way he becomes aware of the red light, or the amount of attention he pays to what he is up to. All of this has a lot to do with the intrinsic properties of one's brain. But none of it has to involve one's awareness, or knowledge, of those properties *per se*.

Conversely, the driver could, in some bizzarely concocted way, 'perceive' his brain states and processes (say, through real-time fMRI — functional Magnetic Resonance Imaging — viewing), in the same non-introspective way he has been perceiving the road. Or (if we were to insist) matters could be arranged such that he could take a peek at the cheesy grey surface of his own brain with the help of a set of mirrors through his open skull. But why should any of that provide him with the sort of extra awareness Armstrong describes?

True, both an fMRI plate and a reflected image on a mirror of a brain are, in some sense, representations of that brain, or of its states. But perceiving (the states of) one's own brain this way doesn't bring about the desired effect — it neither makes those states conscious, nor does it make one introspectively conscious of what those states represent. There can be various ways to encode states of a brain in different media — whether it is in terms of magnetic resonance distribution, positron emission levels, electroencephalographic patterns, or simply light waves bouncing off of its surface. But these are representations *of* the states of a brain (in the intentional sense), not representations *in* a brain. As such, they don't play the right causal role in the cognitive economy of the brain's owner. So the truck driver can actually get to literally perceive (the states of) his own brain, thanks to recent technology or an ingenious set-up, but this doesn't help contribute to his introspective consciousness in any way. I am afraid this is nothing but just belabouring the obvious.[16]

---

[16] What is not so obvious is the specification of conditions under which a given representational state in a subject plays the right causal role in making the subject conscious of various things or facts. Van Gulick presents an insightful proposal in this direction in his attempt to secure a functional role for phenomenal states. His account is based on the notion of *semantic transparency*, which 'concerns the extent to which a system can be said to

Now, notice that what Armstrong is trying to give an account of is *some form of* (heightened? attentive? observant? but, after all,) *externally directed*, awareness. Why, then, try to explain that in terms of another form of, *internally directed*, awareness? I think that the reasoning which tries to account for the changes in the attentiveness, vividness, etc. of the externally directed ordinary perception (from the truck driver's auto-pilot mode to his attentive condition) in terms of an internally directed, higher-order perception of lower order perceptual states, is based on a fundamental mistake worthy of a name — I will call it the 'fallacy of the representational divide'.

Mental states *qua* brain states (in a materialist ontology) are the *vehicles* that represent for us the world around, as well as in, us. What we thus become aware of is what those states represent as being a certain way, i.e. their *content*, in terms of the properties of what is represented. The mistake in the reasoning I am targeting here seems to result from a tacit attempt to replace what is being represent-*ed* with that which is the represent-*er*. Armstrong talks as though we should expect the truck driver to become (attentively) aware of the red light in virtue of his 'internally perceiving' (scanning, monitoring) his ordinary perception of the light. Notice that there seems to be some causal role for the second-order perception involved in what the first-order state is about, here. The force of the example comes from the conviction that when truck driver 'comes to', he doesn't merely gain access to an inventory of what kind of internal states he is currently having, but that the *content* of one of his first-order states starts to figure in his behaviour. Perhaps this is only to be expected — that gaining access to an inventory of one's ongoing mental states automatically (by nomological necessity, etc.) makes the contents of some of those states causally relevant to one's behaviour. But this intuition, which seems crucial for rationalization of the HOP theorist's most celebrated example, has to be spelled out.

The explication of the relation of higher-order perceptions to the contents of first-order states that become the objects of such perceptions is of utmost importance, especially in the presence of close-kin, competing theories, such as HOT accounts. (Although HOT accounts are to be held equally liable for having to provide such details as well.) The underlying operative presumption in Armstrong's truck driver example seems to be that the (second-order) perception of the (first-order) perception of an object should furnish one's (first-order) perception of that object with more attentiveness. More generally, it seems to be assumed that by gaining higher-order access to the intrinsic, non-representational properties of a first-order state

---

understand the content of the internal symbols or representations on which it operates' (Van Gulick 1993: 149).

In terms of higher-order representations, Dretske (1995) talks about what makes something truly a 'representation of a representation' — a *metarepresentation* — such that it plays the right causal role, in virtue of being a metarepresentation, in one's cognitive functioning.

Both accounts are very promising, and deserve a more detailed treatment.

(a visual perception), which happens to represent something (the red light), one gains access, perhaps more attentively, to the extrinsic, representational properties of that state itself (its content, the red light). But why should that be the case? In Armstrong and Lycan, this issue is left unexpounded, though some form of the intuition I sketched above seems implicitly to be in operation on a fundamental level.

When it comes to utilizing representational states in behaviour, finding out all the facts inside the head (facts about the representations) may not suffice by itself in providing all the facts outside the head (facts about what are being represented by those representations). In other words, no matter how much we find out about the intrinsic properties of representational states, we may simply not be able to reach the other side of the 'representational divide', in virtue of this alone, and get to the extrinsic, relational properties of those states.[17]

But if it is impossible to understand one's first-order states as *intentional states* of sorts, and find out about their content simply by examining the non-relational features of those states, insisting on an Armstrongian account of introspective consciousness is a moot endeavour. Such insistence, I suspect, has its roots in a commitment to an implicit but misguided assumption — the assumption that a case can be made by using the properties of the representers when what is called for is how the representers represent what they represent, i.e. the properties of the represented. Operating on the basis of this unacknowledged assumption is somewhat like trying to figure out what a stop sign is by studying only the colour, shape, material, and mass of the actual sign. Surely, one would learn a lot of facts, but expecting to find out, in this way, what the stop sign *qua* a traffic symbol really is, would be a mistake. Making this mistake is what I have in mind by the term 'fallacy of the representational divide'.

In a similar vein, the neurophysiological properties Churchland thinks will be revealed to our discriminatory powers in the future involve only the intrinsic properties of the brain states themselves, whereas figuring out what they are about needs to bring into the picture their extrinsic, intentional properties as well. One cannot become introspectively conscious of what an ongoing perceptual state is about in terms of identifying only the neural properties of that state. Insisting that such is the case, that the direct introspection of brain states as a method will reveal not only which type of states they are, but also what they are about (e.g. a visual state, about a cup

---

[17] Here, the point I am making does not depend on Twin Earth-like scenarios. That is, I take the 'representational divide' to pose a problem for the project of giving a full account of mental states only in terms of their intrinsic properties even in the most ordinary cases human psychology. Problems about widely individuated content do, *a fortiori*, pose a further challenge to HOP accounts.

A fully externalist account of not only propositional attitudes but also sensory experience, which deal with various issues involving wide content and Twin Earth cases, can be found in Dretske 1995.

in front of the subject) is, once again, conflating the properties of the represented and those of the represented. It is almost never the case, except in iconic representation (and then only if one knows it is iconic) that one can find out about the nature of what is being represented via the properties of whatever it is that does the representing. Why should we expect, then, to find out all about the cup a subject sees by examining the neural properties of the visual state that subject happens to have in looking at that cup?[18]

In conclusion, the 'perception of what passes in one's mind', taken literally, is neither a necessary, nor a sufficient condition for the sort of introspective awareness that furnishes one with 'consciousness in the most interesting sense of the word.' But *Option 2* has yet another version, based on the 'mind's eye' model of introspective consciousness, which involves a variation of the fallacy of the representational divide. The mind's eye model is based on a defunct account of mental representation of the long gone past, but it is nonetheless worthy of examination, especially to provide contrast with the former version.

Second Interpretation of Option 2:
Higher-Order Perception as 'Seeing with the Mind's Eye'

Is there absolutely no way to make sense out of the idea of 'internally perceiving' (the properties of) one's mental states, and thereby becoming introspectively conscious of what those states are states of? That is, can't there be a plausible interpretation within which to accommodate the idea of 'perceiving one's perception' of a cup, for instance, and in virtue of this introspective awareness, becoming (attentively) aware of the cup itself?

This scheme could actually work if the properties of one's representational states resembled (or, were identical to) the properties that those states represented. This would mean taking the idea of 'seeing with the mind's eye' literally. Here is how it would go: By a first-order visual perception, the subject S forms, in her mind, a representation of the cup in

---

[18] Churchland's case may have more plausibility regarding brain states that do not have any obvious representational content, e.g. emotions and moods. Perhaps we can indeed learn to individualize such states, which do not (if such is the case) represent anything 'outside the head' via their intrinsic qualities. I think that view has some truth in it, but for the purposes of this paper, I will choose to leave this issue open, and make my point in terms of straightforwardly representational states, such as visual states and beliefs.

Let me also add that, in the present essay, I intentionally eschew the traditional debates regarding the status of Identity Theory that heavily dominated philosophy of mind in the late 1950s and in the 1960s. Not because they are irrelevant; on the contrary, the question of identity between 'mental' and 'physical' properties (properties of the mind versus those of the brain, or the body in general) lies at the heart of the matter being discussed here. However, given the gigantic literature that came out of this era, it is virtually impossible to consider the the debate in its entirety. My discussion is just one of several possible approaches to the larger 'mental/physical' question, but it proceeds on the relatively recent 'intrinsic/extrinsic' axis in the context of the representational content of mental states. For classics of this debate, see Smart 1959 and Feigl 1967, among others.

front of her — this representation is her visual state, V. By second-order introspective consciousness, she goes on to 'internally perceive' this representation. The representation of the cup has cup-like properties, that resemble properties of the cup itself. Thus, by her second-order perception, S gets to 'see the cup in her mind's eye'.

Such a story doesn't make sense unless we commit ourselves *literally* to a 'mind's eye', and to mental representations which bear a *resemblance relation* to what they represent. If S had in her mind, as Scholastic Aristotelians thought, something like a little replica of what she saw in front of her, and with the aid of a 'third eye' she were able to view this replica, and had, as a result, a conscious visual experience of the real cup . . . only then would her case have constituted a true example of this reading of the HOP account. This is all fairy tales, of course, and this interpretation of *Option 2*, not unlike the previous alternatives, is no option for the HOP theorist.[19]

Notice how both cases, the 'direct introspection of brain states' as well as the 'resemblance theory of mental representations', involve a confusion

---

[19] William Lycan pointed out to me (in a personal communication) that the interpretation of higher-order perception as 'seeing with the mind's eye' may not be 'all fairy tales' after all. 'Not all resemblance is first-order resemblance' Lycan says, 'isomorphism is resemblance too.' He then continues, 'it is not only possible but a known fact that, especially in perceptual processing, the brain constructs certain isomorphs of external scenes.'

It is indeed an interesting point to note here that there actually exist certain *topographical relations* between objects perceived and the representational brain structures involved in the perception of them, which go deeper than the receptor surfaces. That is to say, in the case vision, for example, there exist order-preserving systematic relations not only between visual stimuli and the retinal image caused by them, but also between the retinal image and the cortical areas that are responsible for processing the retinal input. Rosenzweig & Leiman report the following:

> [R]ecent examination of the cortex of the owl monkey (a New World monkey) reveals at least six visual areas, each of which is a topographic representation of the retina. No other species has yet been mapped as completely, but in the macaque (an Old World monkey) it also appears that most of the cortical visual regions consist of orderly maps of the retina. (Rosenzweig & Leiman 1989: 323; a detailed account of cortical processing topography in visual perception can be found in Woolsey 1981.)

But does this provide *any* support for the 'mind's eye' model? I think not. First, the relation between objects perceived and cortical areas involved in perception is, strictly speaking, *not* an isomorphism of any order — it is simply a topographical relation of a very crude sort, preserving only order, but not size and not really shape. (Needless to say, secondary properties are never preserved; e.g., no part of the occipital cortex ever turns red upon perceiving a red object! Also note that a similar topographical relation exists in auditory perception as well, where it is even more difficult to talk about *any* kind of resemblance.) Secondly, even if the 'representations as replicas' part of the 'mind's eye' story was correct, one would still need to account for how it was that those replicas got perceived by an 'internal eye' in the absence of any neuroanatomical evidence, and also without falling into the infinite regress of requiring yet a second 'internal eye' to account for the perception of the replicas themselves, and so forth. In short, I think that although the topography of the cortex in relation to the perceived objects is a very interesting research area to pursue, it doesn't provide any credibility, or even plausibility, to the 'mind's eye' model of perception.

about the nature of the representational divide — a conflation of the properties of that which represents and of what is represented — though in a mirror-imaged way. In the former case, the properties of the representer are taken to be the properties of the represented, identifying what is in the head with the properties of what is perceived (something outside the head). In the latter, the properties of the represented are taken to be the properties of the representer, importing the properties of what are outside the head as the properties of the representers inside the head. Under either interpretation, *Option 2* is committed to the fallacy of the representational divide.

V. *Option 3:* Higher-Order Perception as Higher-Order Thought

At the present junction of this exposition, it can perhaps be argued that all the circumlocution in the previous section was really not necessary. For isn't there just a simple, straightforward way to account for the truck driver's psychology? More specifically, I have in mind the following proposition: The driver's gaining of introspective consciousness while he was driving on auto-pilot comes down simply to the occurrence of a *thought* about his circumstances. 'Oh, there is the railroad crossing; I must have been driving for the past hour!', he thinks, and this is, in Armstrong's story, precisely what marks his transition from a state of mere perceptual consciousness to one of introspective consciousness.

This proposal is simple and straightforward, indeed. Moreover, it seems to have folk psychological plausibility. In ordinary circumstances, we are generally aware of having a variety of mental states, and can easily report the presence of 'what is passing in our minds'.[20] At least, it seems commonplace to be able to make judgements of the sort: 'I am now looking at a coffee cup with bird motifs on it that sits right in front of me, on my desk'.[21] But notice: this way of construing 'introspective awareness' as an ability to think a thought or entertain a belief about the mental state one is currently having can no longer be regarded as a case of Higher-Order Perception. As it happens, this is precisely the thesis of a competing theory — that of Higher-Order Thought (HOT). The HOP theorist cannot opt for this route, while defending an account separate from and independent of the HOT account. Thus, *Option 3* is really not an option for HOP accounts, either.

---

[20] Easily, but not necessarily accurately. Above and beyond some rudimentary ability to report what we are experiencing, human subjects are notoriously bad in making correct and accurate judgements about the causes of their reasoning and behaviour. For many 'surprising' results along these lines, see: Nisbett & Wilson 1977, Wilson & Dunn 1986, Lyons 1986.

[21] There are further issues here that are worthy of pursuing, especially regarding the nature of the relation between the ability to make judgements about the mental state one is in and the ability to verbalize or report the presence and/or the content of that state. For a detailed account which deals with such issues, see Rosenthal 1990 and 1996.

VI. The Trilemma for the HOP Theorist

Time to recapitulate. The HOP theorists are at a crossroads where neither of the directions looks promising. In fact, a serious trilemma looms: they either have to abandon the two-tiered structure of their account of introspective consciousness, or commit themselves to the 'fallacy of the representational divide', or allow the central HOP thesis to transform into the thesis of the competing HOT theory.

Options 1, 2, and 3 present the first, second, and third horns of this trilemma, respectively. Embracing either one of *Option 1* or *Option 3* simply means trading in the HOP thesis in favour of a different type of account. Accepting *Option 2* avoids this sort of a theoretical surrender, but it burdens the HOP account with a fundamental fallacy regarding the nature of representational states. Neither alternative is desirable.

In sum, there is no single construal of a HOP theory of consciousness that doesn't look substantially problematic. Furthermore, it is not clear that the four major proponents of HOP theories I talked about, i.e. Locke, Armstrong, Lycan and Churchland, would all opt for the same interpretation. In fact, everyone may be forced to take a different path, given their prior theoretical commitments.[22] If the Locke-Armstrong-Churchland-Lycan pact could thereby disintegrate under this sort of an argumentative pressure, it would be hard to say whether there was any genuine theoretical backbone in the HOP paradigm to begin with.

---

[22] For example, even though David Armstrong explicitly talks about (introspective) consciousness as a 'perception-like awareness of current states and activities of one's own mind', and Lycan locates Armstrongs in the same lineage with Locke and himself, Armstrong's position may ultimately be closer to those of the HOT theorists, such as David Rosenthal. For Armstrong thinks that 'perception is the acquiring of beliefs'. [Cf. Armstrong (1968), Chp. 10, pp. 208–44.] From the writings of these authors, it is hard to judge just how conceptually loaded Armstrong wants to view perception *vis-à-vis* Lycan. But it is at least a possibility that Armstrong may turn out to be on the same side of the fence with Rosenthal, not with Lycan, despite the *prima facie* dissimilarity of their respective vocabulary.

In fact, Armstrong kindly acknowledged (in subsequent personal communication) that he thought his position 'fell in between' the HOP and HOT characterizations. He writes:

> For me, perception, taken as a mental act, is always *propositional*, by which I do not of course mean it is in any way linguistic, but that the content of the perception will have a form **Fa** or **Rab** or . . . some state-of-affairs structure. [. . .] When the truck driver 'comes to' and introspective consciousness resumes, to [the current content of his perception] will be added the further content that 'I am perceiving these things'. [. . .] This is HOT-like. But, following Locke and Kant, I think the introspective awareness is perception-like. For instance, it is very like proprioception, and seems not to involve any linguistic capacity. Perhaps chimpanzees and even dogs have such consciousness.

It is not immediately obvious to what extent Armstrong's HOP account, under his particular characterization of perception, succeeds in avoiding the difficulties of HOP accounts in general, while actually remaining distinct from HOT accounts. Further pursuit of this issue elsewhere on the basis of both Armstrong 1968 and Armstrong 1980 would certainly be useful.

In closing, let me note that I *do* intend this analysis to be exhaustive of all possible readings, but of course there can be no saying on my part that such is the case. Nonetheless, I hope to have hereby posed a challenge to the HOP theorists — the challenge of spelling out the specifics of the 'perception of what passes in one's own mind', taken literally. Given that the HOP accounts presently lack any such analysis, it is up to the defenders of this view to fill in the gaps in order to show that they can deliver what they promise — a separate higher-order account of consciousness which does not fall into the HOT characterization.[23]

References

Aristotle (1951). *De Anima*. London: Routledge and Kegan Paul Ltd.

Armstrong, D. (1968). *A Materialist Theory of the Mind*. New York: Humanities Press.

Armstrong, D. (1980). *The Nature of Mind and Other Essays*. Ithaca: Cornell University Press.

Barker, R. (1986). How does the brain control its own activity? A new function for the basal ganglia? *Journal of Theoretical Biology*, **131**, 497–507.

Block, N. (1995). On a Confusion About a Function of Consciousness. *Behavioral and Brain Sciences*, **18**, 227–47.

Block, N., Flanagan, O. & Güzeldere, G. (1996)[eds]. *The Nature of Consciousness: Philosophical and Scientific Debates*. Cambridge, MA: MIT Press.

Brentano, F. (1973). *Psychology from an Empirical Standpoint*. A. Rancurello, D. B. Terrell & L. McAlister [trs]. New York: Humanities Press.

Carruthers, P. (1989). Brute Experience. *The Journal of Philosophy*, **86**, 258–69.

Churchland, P.M. (1985). Reduction, qualia, and the direct introspection of brain states. *Journal of Philosophy*, **82**, 8–28.

Churchland, P.M. (1988). *Matter and Consciousness*. Cambridge, MA: MIT Press.

Crick, F. (1984). Function of the thalamic reticular complex: the searchlight hypothesis. *Proceedings of the National Academy of Sciences*, **81**, 4586–90.

Cummins, R. (1991). *Meaning and Mental Representation*. Cambridge, MA: MIT Press.

Davies, M. & Humphreys, G. (1993). Introduction. In Davies & Humphreys 1993.

Dennett, D. (1991). *Consciousness Explained*. Boston, MA: Little, Brown & Co.

Descartes, R. (1993a). Objections and Replies. *The Philosophical Writings of Descartes*, II. J. Cottingham, R. Stoothoff & D. Murdoch (eds). Cambridge: Cambridge University Press.

[23] This article had its beginnings in a poster presentation and its accompanying short paper, given in the 'Toward a Scientific Basis of Consciousness' conference in Tucson, Arizona, April 1994. The original paper, titled 'Consciousness and the introspective link hypothesis', is to appear in a volume containing the conference proceedings (*Toward a Scientific Basis of Consciousness*. S. Hameroff, A. Kaszniak & A.C. Scott [eds]. The MIT Press, 1996). The present article is a much expanded version of it.

I would like to express my thanks to Fred Dretske, John Perry, Owen Flanagan, William Lycan, David Armstrong, Murat Aydede, Stefano Franchi, and Lisa Taliano for helpful discussion and correspondence, as well as valuable comments on earlier drafts of this essay.

Descartes, R. (1993b). The Correspondence. *The Philosophical Writings of Descartes*, III. J. Cottingham, R. Stoothoff & D. Murdoch (eds). Cambridge: Cambridge University Press.

Dretske, F. (1969). *Seeing and Knowing*. Bloomington: University of Chicago Press.

Dretske, F. (1993). Conscious Experience. *Mind*, **102**, 263–83.

Dretske, F. (1995). *Naturalizing the Mind*. Cambridge, MA: MIT Press.

Evans, G. (1992). Self-Identification. In J. McDowell (ed), *The Varieties of Reference*. Oxford: Oxford University Press.

Feigl, H. (1967). *The 'Mental' and the 'Physical'*. First appeared in 1958. Minneapolis: University of Minnesota Press.

Flanagan, O. (1992). *Consciousness Reconsidered*. Cambridge, MA: MIT Press.

Güzeldere, G. (1995a). Consciouness: What it is, how to study it, what to learn from its history. *Journal of Consciousness Studies*, **2**, 30–52.

Güzeldere, G. (1995b). Problems of consciouness: Contemporary issues, current debates. *Journal of Consciousness Studies*, **2**, 112–43.

James, W. (1950). *The Principles of Psychology, Vol. I*. New York: Dover.

Leibniz, G., (1981). *New Essays on Human Understanding*. P. Remnant & J. Bennett (eds). Cambridge: Cambridge University Press.

Locke, J. (1959). *An Essay Concerning Human Understanding*, Vol. I. New York: Dover Publications.

Lycan, W. (1987). *Consciousness*. Cambridge, MA: MIT Press.

Lycan, W. (1996). Consciousness as internal monitoring. In Block *et al.* 1996.

Lyons, W. (1986). *The Disappearance of Introspection*. Cambridge, MA: MIT Press.

Nisbett, R. & Wilson, T. (1977). Telling more than we can know: Verbal reports on mental processes. *Psychological Review*, **84**, 231–58.

Peacocke, C. (1983). *Sense and Content*. Oxford: Oxford University Press.

Rosenzweig, M. & Leiman, A. (1989). *Physiological Psychology*. New York: Random House.

Rosenthal, D. (1986). Two concepts of consciousness. *Philosophical Studies*, **94**, 329–59.

Rosenthal, D. (1990). Explaining Consciousness. Manuscript. New York: CUNY, Graduate School.

Rosenthal, D. (1996). A theory of consciousness. In Block *et al.* 1996.

Searle, J. (1992). *The Rediscovery of the Mind*. Cambridge, MA: MIT Press.

Shoemaker, S. (1984). Self-reference and self-awareness. In Shoemaker 1984.

Smart, J.J.C. (1959). Sensations and brain processes. *Philosophical Review*, **LXVIII**, 141–56.

Van Gulick, R. (1993). Understanding the phenomenal mind: Are we all just armadillos? In Davies & Humphreys 1993.

Wilson, T. & Dunn, D. (1986). Effects of introspection on attitude-behavior consistency: Analyzing reasons versus focusing on feelings. *Journal of Experimental and Social Psychology*, **22**, 249–63.

Woolsey, C. (1981) [ed]. *Cortical Sensory Organization. Vol. II: Multiple Visual Areas*. Clifton: Humana Press.

David M. Rosenthal

Multiple Drafts and the Facts of the Matter

Folk psychology conceives of consciousness as a unified phenomenon, which bears some essential connection to a single, unitary self. This encourages a picture on which consciousness occurs at a single place, defined by the interface of certain causes and effects. But the causes and effects of a phenomenon do not always define a unique interface. There is no single place, for example, at which the causes and effects of an enclosed volume of gas all converge. The supposition that in the case of consciousness causes and effects do define a unique interface is a substantive assumption, which might well be mistaken. It is that assumption which underlies what Dennett calls the Cartesian Theater model of mind.

I agree with Dennett that the tacit operation of this model, which is seldom explicitly acknowledged, is responsible for much that's mistaken in current thinking about mind and consciousness. For example, the most promising strategy for explaining consciousness is to build up from phenomena that are mental but not conscious. Tacit adherence to the Cartesian Theater model, however, has led many to see this strategy as unworkable. That's because the afferent pathways leading to mental states are wholly nonmental; so if we locate conscious states at the interface of afferent and efferent, it may well seem that those states literally have no mental antecedents.

For these and many other reasons, Dennett's sustained, effective effort to expose and demolish the myth of the Cartesian Theater constitutes a highly important contribution to our understanding of consciousness. Moreover,

This is a much expanded version of my 'Multiple drafts and higher-order thoughts', *Philosophy and Phenomenological Research*, **LIII** (December 1993), 911–18. An earlier draft was read at the Society for Philosophy and Psychology Symposium on Daniel C. Dennett's *Consciousness Explained*, June 1993, in Vancouver.

any correct explanation of consciousness will, as I'll argue, share much with Dennett's alternative theory, the Multiple Drafts model (MDM). Many of Dennett's rich and penetrating discussions of conscious phenomena, both mundane and esoteric, provide the essentials of how we must understand those phenomena.

Despite my extensive agreement with Dennett's treatment, however, I want to urge that we can get the substantial explanatory benefits of Dennett's MDM with a theory that, in one respect, is somewhat weaker. In what follows I shall argue that this is so, indicating along the way the many respects in which Dennett's theory is exactly on target.

I. Multiple Drafts and the Revisability of Consciousness

Perhaps the most important virtue of the MDM is its ability to accommodate the temporal anomalies Dennett discusses. In colour phi, for example, alternating red and green flashes occur, respectively, on the left and right sides of the subject's visual field, but subjects seem to see a single spot that moves and changes colour. In the so-called cutaneous rabbit, three bunches of physical taps, at the wrist, elbow, and upper arm, result in the subject's feeling a sequence of single taps along the arm separated by small distances. Why is it that one doesn't first consciously sense the initial, stationary, red flash, and the initial bunch of taps at the wrist? Dennett believes the MDM has the answer.

According to that model, consciousness is continuously revised, much as a text changes through successive drafts. Some features of a text undergoing revision will persist through many drafts; others may be so transitory as to escape notice altogether. Similarly with consciousness. When we try to determine what conscious experience a subject has, eliciting reactions from the subject at different times may well result in different reports. At successive moments we may well, as Dennett puts it, 'precipitat[e] different narratives . . . [different] versions of a portion of "the stream of consciousness"'.[1] Nor is there any privileged moment at which a report would reveal the true nature of the subject's conscious experience; even first-person, introspective impressions of our own experiences sometimes vary through time. Reporting our experiences may seem to be the last word on this matter, much like publishing a text. But even publication fixes a text only relative to a social context; post-publication revision can and does occur. Similarly with reports of conscious experiences.

These points help explain colour phi and the cutaneous rabbit. If the initial stationary flash enters the subject's consciousness at all, its presence is so transitory that it escapes notice altogether. Perhaps at some early moment we could elicit a report of the initial red flash; but if we don't, it is for the subject as though no conscious experience of that flash ever occurred.

---

[1] Dennett 1991: 135. Unless otherwise noted, page references throughout are to this work.

This much is fairly straightforward. In many cases we simply won't know, from either a first- or a third-person point of view, whether or not a particular stimulus makes it to consciousness. But Dennett goes one step farther, and

> makes 'writing it down' in memory criterial for consciousness . . . There is no reality of consciousness independent of the effects of various vehicles of content on subsequent action (and hence, of course, on memory) (132).

Accordingly, Dennett rejects both the 'Stalinesque' view, which says that the initial flash or taps are edited out prior to consciousness, and the opposing 'Orwellian' claim that the flash reaches consciousness but is immediately forgotten. Rather, he maintains, when no early reaction is elicited, there is simply no fact of the matter about whether the initial stimulus ever becomes conscious. '[T]here are no fixed facts about the stream of consciousness independent of particular probes' (138; cf. 275).

II. Temporal Anomalies and Higher-Order Thoughts

Central to the MDM is the idea that it's not fixed, from one moment to the next, what our conscious experiences are. Any satisfactory explanation of consciousness plainly must accommodate such revisability. But it's less clear that we must also adopt Dennett's *'first-person operationalism'* (132): his denial that there's any fact of the matter about whether certain stimuli reach consciousness, and about what our conscious experiences are at any particular moment.

We can explore this question by seeing whether the explanatory virtues of the MDM remain when we subtract first-person operationalism, that is, when we adopt a theory that accommodates the revisability just described but denies the operationalism. One such theory is the higher-order-thought explanation of consciousness that I've put forth elsewhere, and which Dennett discusses in chapter 10.[2]

I use 'thought' here as a term of art for any episodic intentional state with an assertoric mental attitude. When a mental state is conscious, one is conscious of being in that state. Occasionally one is conscious of the state introspectively, but typically one is conscious of it in a way that isn't at all attentive or reflective. On the higher-order-thought hypothesis, one is conscious of being in a conscious state by virtue of having a roughly contemporaneous thought to the effect that one is in that state. Because that thought is about another mental state, it's convenient to call it a *higher-order thought* (HOT).

HOTs must be episodic and their mental attitude must be assertoric, because dispositional states and nonassertoric states do not make us con-

---

[2] See Rosenthal 1986a; 1990; 1991; 1993; 1996.

scious of the things they are about. Moreover, we sometimes infer that we're in some mental state even when that state isn't conscious; so we must stipulate that the HOT is independent of any inference of which we're aware. That restriction will also account for our sense that we are conscious of our conscious mental states is in some way that is intuitively immediate. It's enough here to say why it seems that nothing mediates between our conscious states and our being conscious of them. We need not adopt a model on which nothing actually mediates between the two, since we have no reason, independent of our having the intuition about immediacy, to think that that intuition is true.

Normally, of course, we aren't conscious of any HOTs of the sort this theory posits. But that's to be expected, given the HOT hypothesis. A HOT wouldn't be conscious unless one has a third-order thought about it, and it's reasonable to think that that rarely happens. Indeed, cases in which that does happen are cases in which we are introspectively conscious of our mental states, rather than conscious of them in the ordinary, nonintrospective way.

The HOT hypothesis accommodates the various temporal anomalies no less well than the MDM. For example, the initial flash in colour phi presumably causes a sensory state of a stationary red spot. But it may well be that no HOT about that sensory state occurs; so the sensory state never becomes conscious. After the second flash occurs on the right, a new sensory state occurs, of a moving spot that changes colour. A HOT about this second sensory state then occurs, giving one the conscious experience of a moving, changing spot.

There's also, however, a second possibility. A HOT might occur about the initial sensory state of a stationary red flash, but be replaced so fast by the new HOT about the sensory state of a moving spot that the first HOT doesn't register mentally. It doesn't last long enough to affect our memory of what we saw, and it has no other noticeable effects. In particular, the HOT goes out of existence before there's time to report that one is in the first sensory state, that is, to *express verbally* the HOT in question. So the first sensory state is technically conscious, but so briefly as to make no mental difference.

These two possibilities instantiate the Stalinesque and Orwellian models, respectively. Because the two scenarios are introspectively indistinguishable, Dennett is right that introspection can't determine which of the two has occurred. And he's also right that nonverbal behavioural reactions won't help, since, as he convincingly argues, any such reaction could be due equally to a state that's conscious or to a state that's not (124).

It doesn't follow, however, that there is no way to tell which model is operative in a particular case. Suppose, for example, we have a theory about consciousness that draws the right distinctions in unproblematic cases. We might then be able to apply that theory to our puzzle cases to determine, independently of how it seems to the subject, whether a particular stimulus does or does not make it to consciousness. Indeed, the HOT hypothesis would do just that, since the Orwellian model in effect posits an initial HOT that on the Stalinesque model doesn't occur. We don't now know, of course, which model explains colour phi or the other temporal anomalies. Perhaps some anomalies are Orwellian and others Stalinesque; perhaps some have both Stalinesque and Orwellian instances. Still, explaining these phenomena doesn't require us to deny that there's a fact of the matter about which is operative in any particular case.[3]

III. Other Explanatory Advantages

Arguably, the HOT hypothesis explains the many other mental phenomena Dennett considers at least as well as the MDM. Moreover, apart from first-person operationalism, the MDM and the HOT hypothesis agree about most theoretical issues. Consider, for example, consciousness and unity. On the Cartesian Theater model, our mental lives are unified because all conscious states occur in a single place. The MDM insists instead that consciousness is a distributed phenomenon; there's no one place where consciousness occurs, and no single location to direct probes in determining what conscious state a subject is in (136). So there's no unique 'Central Meaner' and no unique 'Author of Record' (228). The HOT hypothesis agrees. Distinct mental states are conscious because of distinct HOTs, which presumably occur in different locations.

Dennett explains the apparent unity of consciousness as due to narratives we construct that represent our mental states as belonging to a single mental life. The HOT hypothesis takes a similar line; unity results from HOTs whose content subsumes groups of mental states, and from third-order thoughts whose content connects, in turn, various second-order thoughts, and makes one conscious of the reference those thoughts ostensibly make to a self.[4] Indeed, Dennett's narratives are, in effect, just the expressions in speech of these HOTs.

On the MDM, a mental state is conscious if it leaves significant traces in memory, and has other substantial mental and behavioural effects. But not all the effects a mental state has will in fact be relevant to whether it's conscious. As Dennett notes, conscious and nonconscious mental states can have exactly the same effects on nonverbal behaviour. Similarly, most of

---

[3] We often adopt first-person operationalism in designing experimental paradigms to test a theory, but once established the theories can leave such methodological operationalism behind.

[4] The self to which HOTs refer may be whatever minimal self is involved in a creature's distinguishing itself from everything else — roughly, the creature's body. Or it might instead be just a notional intentional object of those thoughts, much as the assumption of a unique Author of Record by heterophenomenological reports is, according to Dennett, just an interpretive idealization (228).

the mental traces left by conscious states could equally well have been left by mental states that aren't conscious. This is true even for effects on memory, which Dennett counts as criterial for consciousness. One sometimes sees something without being at all conscious of seeing it, even though one may later, perhaps to one's surprise, realize that one saw it. In such cases, nonconscious perceiving has a significant, lasting effect on memory.

A mental state may have many mental effects without becoming conscious, but not if it causes a HOT. Having an assertoric thought about something implies being conscious of it. So if one comes noninferentially to have a thought that one is in a particular mental state, that state is then conscious. The HOT hypothesis thus focuses more closely than the MDM on just which mental effects are necessary for a mental state to become conscious.

If a state's being conscious hinges on its having certain effects, then it isn't conscious unless certain subsequent events occur. The temporal anomalies are cases in which it seems evident that a state is conscious only if some subsequent event does occur. But we can describe this without any air of paradox. Because many mental states aren't conscious at all, it's implausible that the property of being conscious is an intrinsic property. All mental states have some sort of content properties — intentional content in the case of intentional states and sensory content in the case of bodily and perceptual sensations and most emotions. Such content properties are arguably intrinsic to mental states.[5] By contrast, mental states can be conscious at one moment and not at another; so we have no reason to regard the property of being conscious as being intrinsic to such states. Accordingly, a state's being conscious requires the occurrence of something extrinsic to it. And it may well be, therefore, that no mental state is conscious when it first occurs. But this doesn't mean there are no facts of the matter about consciousness; states are conscious when, and only when, the relevant events occur.

Suppose a person has dispositions to make conflicting reports or, equivalently, has conflicting HOTs. One HOT, or disposition to report, might represent the person as being in a particular state, while the other represents the person as not being in it. That still wouldn't show, however, that there's no fact of the matter about whether the state is conscious. A state is conscious just in case we're able to report it noninferentially, whether or not there's also a concurrent disposition to deny its existence. Or the HOTs and dispositions to report might compete in a different way, by attributing distinct properties to the state. The facts of consciousness then embrace both ways of representing the state.

---

[5] Also, some mental attitude, such as that of believing, desiring, hoping, wondering, doubting, and the like, is presumably intrinsic to each intentional state.

When one has conflicting HOTs or conflicting dispositions to report mental states, an experimental probe may settle things by causing one of the two to stop existing. The probe would in that way determine the facts of consciousness. Does that mean that a subsequent event determines, after the fact, whether a particular mental state had earlier been conscious, and with respect to which of its mental properties? The probe does retrospectively settle what conscious states one takes oneself to have been in, at least if one doesn't recall the earlier, conflicting HOT or disposition to report, which no longer exists. But the probe does not alter what the facts were prior to it. Subsequent events may make a difference to how the prior facts of consciousness now seem, but not to what those facts were.[6]

Dennett emphasizes that it's not always clear, even from a first-person point of view, whether one is conscious of something. And he vividly illustrates this by the game of 'hide the thimble' (336), in which one may look straight at an object one's trying to find and yet fail to register it. This kind of case poses a problem. The sensory states at the centre of one's visual field are normally conscious; so if one's looking at the hidden thimble, how can one fail to see it consciously? The difficulty we have in describing this kind of case from a first-person point of view seems to underwrite Dennett's claim that, independent of particular probes, there's no fact of the matter about what conscious experiences we have.

We're seldom if ever conscious of all the detail that's represented in our sensory states, even states at the centre of our visual field. And how much detail we're conscious of often changes. Moreover, it needn't be the sensory states that change, but only how we're conscious of them. The HOT hypothesis enables us to explain these things. HOTs represent sensory states in greater or lesser detail. So, one HOT might represent a sensory state as being just of a bookcase with lots of things on it, while another HOT a moment later might represent that very sensory state in greater detail, for example, as including a thimble. In the first case one is conscious of seeing the bookcase but not the thimble; in the second case one is conscious of seeing both. All this is independent of first-person operationalism.

As Dennett notes, training in such things as piano tuning and wine tasting can change what conscious experiences one has. It's hard to believe that this training, by itself, results in new kinds of sensory states; rather, we acquire new discriminatory concepts for our experiences, and the resulting HOTs provide finer detail in the way we're conscious of those experiences. Dennett speculates that if blindsight patients became self-cuing, the states in their 'blind' hemifield would become conscious. The HOT hypothesis suggests why that might happen. If one must guess about the contents of one's blind hemifield, one's intentional states about the sensory contents of that hemifield won't have the assertoric mental attitude required for HOTs.

[6] Memory helps determine how the facts of consciousness appear to one, even though "'writing it down" in memory' is not 'criterial for consciousness'.

The ability to be self-cuing would dispel the hesitant attitude involved in just guessing, leading thereby to one's having assertoric HOTs. Moreover, guessing lacks the intuitive immediacy characteristic of the way we're conscious of our conscious states. When we guess, we regard our tentative judgments as mediated by something, even if we have no idea what that mediating factor is.

Dennett convincingly argues that, given the low resolution of parafoveal vision, we see a wide area of wallpaper as being all Marilyns by representing a few foveal Marilyns and, in effect, judging that the parafoveal shapes are 'more of the same' (355). The HOT hypothesis suggests how this might happen. One's sensory states represent foveal shapes as Marilyns and peripheral shapes as largely indistinct. One's HOT cleans things up, then, by representing the shapes in both foveal and peripheral sensory states as being all Marilyns.[7] And more generally, the HOT hypothesis fits comfortably with Dennett's view that so-called 'filling in' takes place not by the brain's manufacturing the missing sensory states, but by its forming suitable judgments. (See Dennett 1993: 205–10.)

IV. The 'Objectively Subjective'

Dennett recommends his heterophenomenological method in part because it helps undercut the apparent opposition between first- and third-person viewpoints. It does this, he urges, by being neutral about whether a subject's report truly describes that subject's first-person viewpoint or simply expresses beliefs about the subject's mental states, states which may be merely notional. We'll count those reports as describing real events if what they say accords reasonably well with events we know about independently, say, brain events.[8] The HOT hypothesis achieves the same methodological neutrality, since heterophenomenological reports express HOTs, and HOTs aren't factive.[9]

---

[7] For all we now know, of course, the sensory state with foveal Marilyns might actually produce peripheral Marilyns in the sensory state itself. But as Dennett emphasizes, we typically take parafoveal vision to be far more crisp and detailed than it could be, even given saccadic movements. So it's more likely that the apparent parafoveal Marilyns result in part from the brain's interpretive activity. The same may even be true of the influence foveal colour has on what we take surrounding colours to be.

[8] Taking heterophenomenological reports to be evidentially basic might seem at first sight to make those reports incorrigible. And that in turn suggests first-person operationalism, since how consciousness subjectively seems would then be the last word about its nature. But heterophenomenological reports aren't actually incorrigible in the way needed for first-person operationalism if, as Dennett urges, we judge their truth by way of brain events (85).

[9] Accordingly, the MDM and HOT hypothesis agree about zombies (and zimboes [310–11]). Dennett denies that anything 'in principle . . . indistinguishable from a conscious person' could lack conscious states (405; cf. 282). And on the HOT hypothesis, since having HOTs is sufficient for a state to be conscious, nothing could be in all the intentional states we are in but lack conscious states. Again, this is independent of first-person operationalism.

Dennett propounds first-person operationalism in part because its denial 'creates the bizarre category of the objectively subjective — the way things actually, objectively seem to you even if they don't seem to seem that way to you' (132). Moreover, he argues that it's a failing of the HOT hypothesis that it accepts that category (316).

There are, however, good reasons to sustain a distinction between seeming and seeming to seem. Being in a sensory state defines, in one respect, how things seem to me. That's because of the connections the state has to other aspects of my mental life, even if the state fails to be conscious. But when a sensory state isn't conscious, I'm not aware of being in it; so it doesn't then seem to me that I am in it. That's the second level of seeming.[10] Dennett might deny that being in a sensory state that isn't conscious can define how things seem to one, since he holds that a state's being conscious consists in its leaving significant traces and having wide-spread mental effects. But as I argued earlier, mental states can have many mental effects without being conscious. Moreover, Dennett accepts that we're sometimes mistaken about what mental states we're in, and it's hard to see how that could happen if the way things actually seem to one always coincides with the way they seem to seem.

Dennett might urge that ascribing representational properties to sensory states incurs all the problems that face qualia and the mental 'pigment' (346) he argues against so effectively. But it's arguable that mental pigment and qualia are problematic only because we conceive of them as being intrinsically conscious. (See Rosenthal 1991.) On the HOT hypothesis, the representational properties of sensory states need not occur consciously.

Dennett notes that distinguishing mental states from the corresponding HOTs makes room for an unexpected kind of error; my HOT might misrepresent what kind of mental state I'm in (317). Moreover, any third-order thought I have might in turn be wrong about what my second-order thoughts are.[11] Even conceding that we're sometimes mistaken about our mental

---

[10] Dennett seems to say as much: the 'onsets [of content-fixations in the brain] do *not* mark the onset of consciousness of their content' (113; emphasis Dennett's). (But see p. 12 ?? below.) Not distinguishing these two levels, moreover, risks representing consciousness as an intrinsic property of mental states, which would accord poorly with Dennett's idea that consciousness is a distributed phenomenon, and with his denial that there's any fact of the matter about when a mental state becomes conscious. And, if being conscious were an intrinsic property, it's unlikely we could explain what it is for a state to be conscious without appealing to the very consciousness we were trying to explain. (One might even interpret the Cartesian Theater model as holding that consciousness is an extrinsic property: a mental state is conscious just in case it occurs in the right location, viz., the Cartesian Theater. Cf. 144.)

[11] Dennett takes the HOT hypothesis to posit not just HOTs, but also higher-order beliefs distinct from those HOTs, apparently because he assumes that that reports of conscious states express these beliefs (307; cf. 317). He concludes that error might also occur between HOT and higher-order belief. But since reports of conscious states directly express HOTs, the HOT hypothesis doesn't posit distinct higher-order beliefs at all.

states, Dennett sees these proliferating levels of possible error as another reason to reject the HOT hypothesis, since he thinks it's idle to distinguish among mistakes at all these different levels.[12]

The view that introspection 'must give exhaustive and infallible information' is, as C.D. Broad remarked, 'a curious superstition' (Broad 1925: 284). There are always features of our conscious states we might be aware of but aren't; consider our sensation of the scene that includes the thimble we don't notice. Why, then, shouldn't the way we're conscious of mental states sometimes represent them as having features they lack? There's evidence from clinical contexts and from social psychology[13] that this sometimes occurs. And many of the repressed states familiar from clinical contexts and Freudian theory are very likely not literally unconscious states, but rather states whose intentional properties subjects represent in a radically disguised way, so as to avoid having to face what states they are actually in.

Even introspective impressions, moreover, may occasionally be erroneous if one's third-order thought misrepresents the content of a second-order thought, perhaps because a theory had influenced what one expected to find introspectively. Once again, it doesn't matter if introspection can't distinguish this kind of error from errors at the first level, since in any particular case theoretical considerations should enable us to tell which has occurred.

Dennett sees the hierarchy posited by the HOT hypothesis as reflecting our folk-psychological conceptions, and so regards both as committed to these distinct levels of possible error. It's unclear, however, that these distinct levels of error are unequivocally part of our folk psychological picture.[14] In any event, the HOT hypothesis is a theoretical proposal about what it is for mental states to be conscious, and so can both supplement and depart from our folk-psychological conceptions.

---

[12] Dennett is concerned that if the HOT hypothesis allows an indefinite hierarchy of HOTs, there will be indefinitely many distinct errors. But it's unlikely that there's any reason to posit thoughts at a level higher than third-order.

Dennett also urges that a hierarchy of HOTs undermines 'the subjective intimacy or incorrigibility that is supposedly the hallmark of consciousness' (319). But the HOT hypothesis preserves the appearance of subjective immediacy, both because HOTs typically aren't conscious, and because HOTs aren't due to any conscious inference, and so we can't tell from a first-person point of view how we come to be conscious of our conscious states.

[13] Nisbet & Wilson (1977), who present evidence that subjects confabulate stories not only about what the causes are of their intentional states, but also about what intentional states they are in.

[14] Folk-psychological categories clearly allow distinguishing hierarchical levels of HOTs. But HOTs are theoretical posits not demanded by folk psychology, in part because we're typically unaware of them from a first-person viewpoint. Moreover, folk psychology seems to allow individuating intentional states solely by way of the mental analogue of performance conditions, ignoring the truth conditions and mental attitudes of the states. And that would mean that when a HOT is about an intentional state, we would identify the two.

Since subjects' reports express the HOTs that accompany conscious states and HOTs can misrepresent those states, subjects' reports may be inaccurate. So, as Dennett argues, there's no privileged moment at which a subject's report reveals the true nature of a conscious experience, since the report issued at any particular moment might be erroneous. But the occurrence of erroneous HOTs doesn't sustain first-person operationalism. The facts about what mental states we're in are distinct from the facts about how we're conscious of them, and HOTs pertain only to the latter.

Partly because we often discover what we think only as we say it (245), Dennett argues that our choice of words can influence the content of our thoughts (247). He concludes that HOTs don't always underlie reports of being in mental states (315). But our discovering what we think as we say it needn't show that our words affect our thoughts; rather, it may simply be that our thoughts often aren't conscious until we express them. And even when one's choice of words does affect what one thinks, one's speech act still expresses the resulting intentional state. So reports of mental states will always express HOTs in virtue of which those states are conscious.[15]

V. Multiple Drafts and Mental Taxonomy

Dennett sees as artificial the way we ordinarily carve consciousness and mind into discrete mental states. Worse, he thinks the folk-psychological taxonomy in terms of which we do so requires 'postulating differences that are systematically undiscoverable.' It's at bottom because the HOT hypothesis and the Stalinesque and Orwellian models all presuppose a folk-psychological taxonomy of mental states that he rejects both the HOT hypothesis and the distinction between Stalinesque and Orwellian explanations (319).[16]

---

[15] Dennett in effect agrees, when he writes that '[t]he emergence of the [verbal] expression is precisely what creates or fixes the content of *the higher-order thought expressed*' (315, my emphasis).

In Rosenthal 1993, I assumed a causal model of what it is for a speech act to express an intentional state on which, roughly, an intentional state causes the speech act that expresses it. (I argue for this in Rosenthal 1986b.) That model runs counter to Dennett's Pandemonium model of speech production, on which speech performances affect the content of the thoughts expressed. But this doesn't matter for the HOT hypothesis, which requires only that speech acts express an intentional state with the same content and a mental attitude corresponding to the speech act's illocutionary force. The hypothesis makes no assumptions about what causal relation, if any, speech acts bear to the intentional states they express.

One might urge that, although a state is conscious just in case it's reportable and reporting a state is the same as expressing a HOT that one is in that state, the HOT needn't exist until an actual report occurs. If so, unreported conscious states need not be accompanied by HOTs. But the ability to report must be based on something occurrent, and an actual HOT is the most reasonable candidate.

[16] Since a state's being conscious begins, on the HOT hypothesis, at the moment a HOT comes to exist, we can in principle tell whether revision occurs before or after that

As noted above, the HOT hypothesis isn't wedded to folk-psychological categories; rather, it uses them provisionally, in the way any theory works off our commonsense conceptions. Still, the issue about taxonomy will help to get a deeper understanding of Dennett's view.[17] Dennett often writes of such things as 'events of content-fixation' (365) 'information-bearing events' (459), and 'content-discriminations' (113). More important, these 'content-fixations . . . are [each] precisely locatable in both space and time' (113). Since Dennett denies that we can precisely locate conscious mental phenomena, content fixations plainly aren't conscious. Exactly what are they, then, and how do they relate to those mental phenomena that are conscious?

In the early stages of vision, colour, form, orientation, and motion are represented independently. There's presumably no problem about locating these representations precisely. Moreover, except possibly for pathological cases, independent representations of colour and shape do not occur consciously.[18] So it's natural to take Dennett's 'content-fixations' as being something like these early representations. Consciousness arises, then, in the course of subsequent integrative processes that represent these fragmentary representations as being interconnected. At any one time, there may be more than one interpretive process that serves to integrate a particular group of representations; the several editorial processes then constitute multiple drafts of the contents of consciousness. Each integrative process, moreover, will involve dispositions to produce narratives about one's mental life. When there are several concurrent editorial processes, the narratives they dispose one toward may well conflict. Only when 'particular probes' (138) occur will one integrative process drive out the others, thereby settling the facts of consciousness.

---

moment. But an example will make clear how taxonomy can be crucial. Suppose that these events occur in very close succession. A sensory state occurs, it becomes conscious by virtue of a HOT's coming to exist, the sensory state then undergoes an alteration, a second HOT with correspondingly revised content then comes to exist, and when it does the first HOT ceases to exist leaving no trace in memory. Does the HOT hypothesis count this as Stalinesque or Orwellian revision? Relative to the revised sensory state, the revision is Stalinesque, since the revision occurred before the revised state was conscious; relative to the original state, the revision is Orwellian. In effect, we'll count the revision as Stalinesque if we regard the revised state as a new state, distinct from the original, and Orwellian if we regard the revised and original states as two stages of a single state. Not only is there arguably no preferred way to take things; either choice reflects, in addition, a commitment to artificially precise identity conditions for mental states. This doesn't show, however, that there aren't facts of the matter about exactly when revision occurs and when states with particular content properties become conscious. Rather, the Stalinesque and Orwellian models aren't, as they stand, sufficiently precise to sustain an unambiguous contrast.

[17] For more on the following issues, see Rosenthal 1995.

[18] The evidence for independent representations of colour and shape in early visual processing is inferential, mainly from experiments in which subjects report seeing illusory conjunctions of the colours and shapes of distinct, simultaneous stimuli. Subjects do not report seeing either shape or colour independently of the other. See Treisman 1982; 1986; 1988.

Mental states, conceived folk psychologically, are whatever states, if any, conform to descriptions that occur in our heterophenomenological reports. Such states may turn out to be merely notional objects of these reports, and Dennett seems to think that all that exists are the locatable early representations and the subsequent editorial processes that integrate them.[19] If that's right, our folk-psychological taxonomy of ordinary mental states involves a highly artificial and unrealistic determinateness; in particular, there would then be no HOTs. More important, if no mental phenomena exist other than content fixations and editorial processes, there will be no facts of the matter about conscious mental states conceived in folk-psychological terms. First-person operationalism would then be true for conscious states so taxonomized.

But taxonomy aside, integrative processes do not always result in consciousness. For example, the complex processes posited by cognitive theories often serve to integrate, but are seldom if ever conscious. And many of the states these processes lead to also aren't conscious. Moreover, integrative processes won't help explain why we seem to be in conscious states, folk psychologically taxonomized. Such integrative processes may help us understand why certain properties come together, but not why we seem to ourselves to be in conscious states with those concurrent properties.

HOTs, by contrast, do help with these things. Even if there are no conscious states as folk psychology conceives of them, we could explain why we think we're in such states by positing nonconscious HOTs that have such states as their intentional objects. There would then be determinate facts about consciousness, though they would consist solely of the facts about our nonconscious HOTs. It's reasonable, therefore, to hope that we can explain consciousness by a version of the MDM that does not appeal to first-person operationalism.

References

Broad, C.D. (1925). *The Mind and Its Place in Nature*. London: Routledge & Kegan Paul.

Dennett, D.C. (1991). *Consciousness Explained*. Boston, MA: Little, Brown & Co.

Dennett, D.C. (1993). Back from the drawing board. In Dahlbom 1993.

Nisbett, R.E. & T.DeC. Wilson (1977). Telling more than we can know: Verbal reports on mental processes, *Psychological Review*, **LXXXIV**, 231–59.

Rosenthal, D.M. (1986a). Two concepts of consciousness. *Philosophical Studies* **49**, 329–59.

Rosenthal, D.M. (1986b). Intentionality. *Midwest Studies in Philosophy*, **10**, 151–84.

---

[19] The eliminativist strain here is offset by Dennett's methodological strategy of taking heterophenomenological reports being as evidentially basic, and using brain events to assess what, if anything, those reports are true of (85).

Rosenthal, D.M. (1990). *Why Are Verbally Expressed Thoughts Conscious?* Report 32, *Center for Interdisciplinary Research* (ZiF), Research Group on Mind and Brain, University of Bielefeld.

Rosenthal, D.M. (1991). The independence of consciousness and sensory quality. In Villanueva 1991.

Rosenthal, D.M. (1993). Thinking that one thinks. In Davies & Humphreys 1993.

Rosenthal, D.M. (1995). First-person operationalism and mental taxonomy. *Philosophical Topics*, **22**, 319–50.

Rosenthal, D.M. (1996). A theory of consciousness. In Block *et al.* 1996.

Treisman, A. (1982). Perceptual grouping and attention in visual search for features and for objects. *Journal of Experimental Psychology*, **8**, 194–214.

Treisman, A. (1986). Features and objects in visual processing. *Scientific American*, **255**, (November), 114–25.

Treisman, A. (1988). Features and objects: the fourteenth Bartlett Memorial Lecture. *Quarterly Journal of Experimental Psychology*, **40A**, 201–37.

Norton Nelkin

The Dissociation of Phenomenal States from Apperception

In a number of previous papers, I have argued that 'consciousness', rather than naming a single indivisible state, names three different and *dissociable* states that just in fact often occur simultaneously: phenomenal states (CS [or CN] consciousness), first-order propositional-attitude states (C1 consciousness), and apperception (C2 consciousness).[1] Because we fail to understand that these are three different states, we make difficulties for ourselves in regard to understanding consciousness.

CS states are those states that best fit Nagel's (1974; 1979; 1986) slogan that when a being is conscious there is something it is like to be that being for the being itself. There is something it 'feels' like for the organism.[2] Such 'feels' are often called 'qualia', and it is these I refer to as CS states.[3] C1 states are exemplified by judgments, desires, hopes, and so on, as in perceiving that a dog is brown. C2 states, like C1 states, are proposition-

---

[1] Nelkin 1987; 1989a; 1989b; 1993a; 1993b. In most of these papers, I labelled the state I am now calling 'apperception' as 'introspection'. I use 'apperception' now because I think it carries less baggage than does 'introspection'. I borrow the term 'apperception' from Leibniz (1714/1989: 208). I will reserve 'introspection' for an attentive, purposeful examination of one's own current mental states. As such, introspection is a kind of apperception — but only one sort of (rather uncommon) apperceptive state. 'CN' stands for 'Nagel consciousness', because Thomas Nagel (see especially Nagel 1974) got us thinking about phenomenal states once again. 'CS', which has replaced it (see Nelkin 1989a for the reasons), stands for 'sensation consciousness'.

[2] I put 'feels' in quotation marks because not all phenomenal states are generally thought of as being *felt*: there are visual, auditory, gustatory and olfactory phenomena as well. One should read 'feel' to mean phenomenal experiences of all sorts.

[3] For the purposes of this paper, CS states = phenomenal states = phenomena = qualia.

like, but their content is expressed by the proposition that one of the first order states (CS or C1) is occurring.[4] Thus, I can be apperceptively (C2) aware of experiencing a phenomenal image of a dog (a CS state) as well as being apperceptively (C2) aware that I see a dog (a C1 state). As I use the term, apperception does not require paying attention (one can be aware that one is seeing a dog while attending to the dog rather than to one's seeing it), apperception is not an incorrigible state, and it is *not* a phenomenal state.[5]

Of the dissociations I have argued for, perhaps the most controversial is that of CS from C2. Many philosophers and psychologists find it extremely difficult to understand how phenomenal states could occur unapperceived. They claim not to be able to conceive how one could experience a mental image or some other 'feeling' but not be apperceptively aware that one is in that state. My arguments for this dissociability thesis are scattered throughout the previously cited papers; and, thus, my present aim is to assemble many of those arguments here in one place, so that they work to reinforce one another. No one argument is by itself a knockdown one. Nor do all together constitute a knockdown argument. But since knockdown arguments are rarely available in theoretical matters, I am satisfied if, all together, they put the weight of evidence and argument on the side of the dissociability thesis. Even more weakly, I would be pretty satisfied if philosophers and psychologists would come to see that the question of the dissociability of CS from C2 is an open question that will have to be settled on theoretical/empirical grounds.

One word of caution: I am not claiming that there is no awareness involved in an unapperceived CS state. CS is itself a kind of awareness — *phenomenal* awareness. What I am claiming is that the two sorts of awareness, phenomenal awareness and apperceptive awareness, are dissociable.

I

While there are no knockdown arguments for the view that phenomenal states are dissociable from apperceptive states (the dissociability thesis), there are *no arguments at all*, so far as I am aware, that phenomenal states are *not* dissociable from apperceptive states (the nondissociability thesis). Those who would deny the relevant dissociability simply take their nondissociability for granted.

Perhaps one might assert that no argument is needed: it is just intuitively obvious that phenomenal states have to be at one and the same time apperceived. My only response is to deny the assertion in my own case and to point to the many other philosophers who also deny having the intuition. Intuitions that are so often denied are questionable intuitions.

---

[4] It is possible that at times C2 states have as their content that another C2 state is occurring.

[5] See all the articles previously cited, but most especially Nelkin 1994 and 1996 — especially chapter 8 — for a full discussion of apperception.

If any argument had ever been presented, it would go something like this: 'Every CS state I have apperceptively experienced, I have been apperceptively aware of; therefore, every CS state is such that one is apperceptively aware of it.' Since *no one* would knowingly use such a bad argument, I doubt if argument is driving the belief in the nondissociability thesis at all. But the 'grounds' for the belief are not much different from this argument. The only CS experiences we attentively notice *are* ones we are also C2 of. Indeed, they are the only ones we can directly attentively notice. And so it seems to us as if CS and C2 are inseparable. Introspectively, it probably does seem that way to us. So much so that we are tempted to ask, 'What would it be to "feel" an experience that is not apperceived?' But the answer to that question is, '*Exactly* what it "feels" like to experience one that *is* apperceived.' The inability to accept that simple (and correct) answer is based wholly on a prejudice that CS states can occur only when one is also C2 of them. But that very prejudice — for without argument to support it, that is all it is — is exactly what is in question.

Introspection cannot determine whether CS states *have* to be apperceived. Whatever it may seem like to introspection, introspection is possibly mistaken (and introspection's track record as a psychological *tool* hasn't exactly been a glorious one). And given that introspection is itself a form of apperception, it is quite difficult to see how introspection *could* determine whether an apperceived experience is or is not capable of occurring unapperceived.

Nor are all the intuitions on the side of the nondissociability thesis. Concentrate, for instance, on the bottoms of your feet. When you do, you experience certain phenomena. Now, concentrate on the pit of your stomach. Again, certain phenomena are experienced; and these are different from those experienced in the first case. Now, return your attention to the bottoms of your feet. I presume that phenomena similar to the original ones are once again apperceived.

How should the occurrences of this 'experiment' be described? In my view, this experiment provides instances of our *discovering* phenomena that were being experienced all along even when they were not being apperceived. This interpretation is certainly not implausible, and I would suggest (it is certainly true in my own case) that *experientially* it seems to us at the time as if we are discovering already-occurring phenomena. Moreover, the close similarity of the phenomena experienced in the two bottoms-of-the-feet cases makes good sense on this interpretation: the phenomenal state is a continuing one, so, of course, the two temporally separated apperceived instances are similar.

The upshot of this experiment is not that unapperceived phenomenal experiences exist, but that it is an open question whether they do. That we were not apperceptively aware of feelings in our stomach before we shifted attention to our stomach does not mean that these feelings didn't exist prior to our shifting our attention there. We can understand that they might have. Similarly, that we were not apperceptively aware of the feelings in the soles of our feet when we were paying attention to our stomachs does not mean that those feelings in our soles didn't continue between the two occurrences of apperceiving them. When we do return our attention to our feet, it seems as if we discover the phenomena as *still* there. So we have conflicting intuitions: we may intuitively believe that phenomena cannot exist unapperceived, but on occasions like that described we believe that phenomena 'still' continue unapperceived and we can rediscover them.

Often someone will ask us whether we still have a headache. Before we reply, we move our heads around, seem to *discover* the feeling there, and on that basis say we *still* have it. Similarly, in cases of the cocktail party effect, where we do not apperceptively hear anything of a neighbouring conversation until that conversation contains a key word or topic of interest to us, it seems experientially as if we are tapping into a phenomenal flow that was there all along. Or think about cases where, while concentrating on something else, we discover ourself scratching our arm. It is difficult in this case to think of any other reason we are scratching than to rid ourself of an itch — a phenomenal feeling — that we were not apperceptively aware of. Our feeling of discovery in all these cases is quite natural — and quite *justified* — if phenomenal states can exist dissociated from apperception. Any nondissociation view is going to have to claim that acts of attending make phenomena come into existence and shifting attention makes them cease to exist. Such an account cannot be ruled out *a priori*, but it is hard to see why it would be a *better* account than the dissociability thesis. My own intuitions are that the story that phenomena are attention-dependent is a much less psychologically and neurologically plausible account. In the end, only a well-developed and well-accepted theory will decide between the two accounts. The point, however, is that no grounds exist at present for the attention-dependent story. Its defenders simply take it for granted.

II

Several abnormal perceptual states are relevant to the dissociability issue: blindsight, commissurotomy (split-brain) cases, and visual extinction, among others. Blindsight patients, for instance, have been shown to be able to discriminate an X from an O in their 'blind' fields with nearly 100 per cent accuracy, all the while denying that they see anything and taking themselves to be merely guessing. When later told about the accuracy of their 'guesses', they seem genuinely surprised (see Weiskrantz 1977; 1986). Similarly, commissurotomy patients will often use their left hands to pick up objects, pictures of which have been tachistoscopically flashed to their left fields of view. All the while, the patients deny having seen anything on that side at all. When it is pointed out that they picked up an object with their left hand, they continue denying that they saw anything and often confabulate a reason for having picked up that object (see Gazzaniga 1970; 1977; Gazzaniga & LeDoux 1978). Similarly, yet again, for extinction patients. Although they (unlike blindsight or commissuro-tomy patients) can apperceptively see an object in either field of view, if objects are made to appear in each field of view simultaneously, they apperceptively see only one of the objects. Further, if forced to 'guess' whether the 'unseen' object matches or fails to match the one apperceptively seen, they 'guess' right at rates approaching 100 per cent (see Volpe *et al.* 1979).

One interpretation of these cases is that subjects perceive but do not experience phenomenal states. However, an alternative interpretation of these cases, *also compatible with the data*, is that the patients *do* experience phenomena in their blind field experience but are just not apperceptively aware that they do. Once more, their introspections cannot decide whether they do or do not experience phenomena in their blind fields.

Since *both* the no-phenomena-experienced view and the unapperceived-phenomena-experienced view are compatible with the evidence, the choice between them will have to be for independent empirical or theoretical reasons. However certain someone might feel that these patients do not experience 'feelings', no theoretical or empirical grounds support this sense of certainty. It should not surprise us if the mind turns out to be quite different from how we in our present state of ignorance — and relying mostly on introspection — expect it to be. At the same time, as we saw in the previous section, even our intuitions are not undivided on the issue of whether phenomenal experience can dissociate from apperception.

III

Little in the way of support exists for the nondissociability thesis. Does any positive support exist in favour of the dissociability thesis? There are two kinds: success at explaining cases at an empirical level and large-scale theoretical reasons.

The empirical evidence is thin, but what there is lends support to the dissociability view. The evidence to be presented is based on blindsight experiments involving hue perception and is weaker or stronger depending on one's view about the phenomenal status of hues. If one believes hues are essentially phenomenal (see Hardin 1988; Boghossian & Velleman 1991), or even that phenomenal experience is necessary for hue perception, then the evidence is quite compelling. If, however, one thinks hue judgments are altogether independent of phenomenal states, then the evidence will seem quite weak (though the dissociability thesis will at least be compatible with the evidence — as it is in the case of other blindsight perceptions).

We know that human blindsight subjects fail to apperceive their 'blind' visual fields even when those fields are perceptually activated (Weiskrantz

1986). We also have evidence that blindsighted monkeys, whose brains would be expected to be similar to our own, can recover many of their visual functions (Weiskrantz 1977). Among the functions reported to have been recovered by monkeys is the ability to make colour discriminations (Keating 1979). On the assumption that hues are phenomenal, or on the assumption that phenomena are necessary for hue perception, these facts about blindsight provide a reason to believe that blindsighted monkeys that make colour discriminations experience colour phenomena even though not apperceptively aware that they do. Of course, it is possible that, in recovering from the surgery, the monkeys recover apperception along with their phenomenal states; but such a result is unlikely since many of these monkeys' brains have been hemispherectomized. In any event, it is an empirical question which reading of the facts is correct. On the basis of the evidence we now possess, it is empirically *possible* that the dissociation occurs in the way outlined (and given those that are hemispherectomized, *likely* that apperception of their 'blind field' perceptual states is not recovered).*

Somewhat more direct evidence of the dissociation of phenomenality from apperception is provided by recent work on *human* blindsight subjects (Stoerig & Cowey 1989; 1992). These subjects are able to make paired hue discriminations that track normal discriminations, although when asked, they deny seeing anything. They take themselves to be guessing. Since their responses mirror those of normal colour perceivers in saying 'red' or 'blue' for appropriate wavelengths, and are in accord with an opponent-process theory of colour perception, it is not unreasonable to believe that they discriminate *hues*, though they are not apperceptively aware that they do so. Thus, these blindsight cases are at least consistent with, even provide evidence for, unapperceived phenomena being experienced.

One might object that it may only be wavelengths, and not hues, they — and the monkeys — distinguish, that 'red' and 'blue' may be no more meaningful in these contexts than 'one' and 'two'.[6] But two considerations support, though rather weakly, the hue-discrimination hypothesis. In the human cases, subjects are asked by a forced-choice question to 'guess' red or blue. If 'red' and 'blue' were like 'one' and 'two', then half the time the subjects should systematically mislabel the wavelengths. Yet, this reversal occurs only occasionally. Their failure to reverse would be quite strong evidence for the claim that hue was being discriminated except that Stoerig and Cowey primed their subjects at the beginning of the experiment as to

* I would like to thank Petra Stoerig for pointing out that the author appears to have made an error here regarding the empirical data. The monkeys in question were not hemispherectomized, but rather had all of their visual cortical areas bilaterally destroyed. However, it seems that a similar argument can still be made to the effect that it is unlikely that such monkeys recover apperception along with their phenomenal states. — Editor.

[6] Several people, in correspondence or conversation, have proposed this objection; among them, C.L. Hardin, Petra Stoerig, and Irwin Goldstein.

which hue they were 'seeing' (Stoerig, personal communication). So the nonreversal evidence is less conclusive than it may at first appear.

A second piece of evidence that hues are being discriminated is that in monkeys cells in area V4 of the optic system respond in accordance with colour constancy (i.e. even though the lights are dimmed on a blue object, say — and so the reflected wavelengths are different in the two cases — the cells that originally responded continue to respond (Stoerig & Brandt 1993)). If V4 is used in monkeys' blindsight colour discriminations, as it appears to be in their normal colour discriminations, then it is reasonable to think that for blindsighted monkeys 'colour' = 'hue', since constancy correlates more strongly to hue than to wavelength. Moreover, while it is not certain that monkey V4 has a homologue in the human brain, it is likely to (see Van Essen 1985). However, it has not yet been shown that V4 plays a rôle in blindsight colour discriminations, so I may be jumping the gun on the available evidence. Furthermore, there is evidence that not all blindsight colour discrimination involves V4, since human patients who have been hemispherectomized, and have had area V4 on the 'blind' side ablated, are among those who succeed at blindsight colour discrimination. So this evidence concerning V4 is also probably weaker than desired.

But recent evidence (Stoerig, personal communication) seems more clearly to support a hue-discrimination reading of these cases. Hemispherectomized patients (patients who had half their usual optical areas ablated!) have been studied who, on their own, not only 'guess' blue, say, but also spontaneously (nonforced-choice) 'guess' that it is the colour of the sky — that is, on their own, 'guess' the *shade* of blue. Spontaneously 'guessing' what shade of colour is being experienced displays a discriminatory ability well beyond anything like that needed for a mere 'one–two' discrimination. If this evidence holds up, it will be much more reasonable to believe that these patients *are* discriminating on the basis of hue than to believe the alternative.[7]

---

[7] Alas, in a July 1994 email message, Stoerig (if I understand her correctly) has pulled the rug out from under this evidence as well. When she investigated these patients with colleagues in Montreal, she found either that they showed no blindsight 'shade' responses or else one could not eliminate the possibility that their responses were the result of light scattering from the 'sighted' halves of the retinas. Still, four points remain that provide hope for empirical support of the dissociability thesis. (i) No empirical support has been provided for the nondissociability thesis by the failure of these cases. (ii) The fact that one recognizes that her evidence could have turned out otherwise and the fact that the claims initially made about these patients were made about them at all illustrate the *empirical* nature of the claims involved. (iii) Stoerig tells me, in the same message, that similar claims continue to be made about other patients whom she has not tested personally. So my claim in the text, 'If this evidence holds up . . .', continues to be operative (though I confess to being less hopeful that this particular evidence *will* hold up). (iv) If hemispherectomized patients are eliminated from consideration, then the material about monkey V4 discussed earlier becomes all the stronger.

IV

When we turn to the theoretical reasons, they can only be partially dealt with here because the best reasons are quite large-scale: They involve how a large-scale theory of consciousness maps on the world. But this theory is set out elsewhere (Nelkin 1996). Nevertheless, at least a couple of theoretical considerations can be reasonably discussed in this paper.

The *first* is that if phenomena are not dissociable from C2 states, they become theoretical danglers of large proportion. I have argued elsewhere that even if all CS states are also C2 states, the converse is not true: there are C2 states that are nonphenomenal. To borrow Descartes' (1641/1986: 50–1) example, when one thinks of a 1000-sided figure and, later, of a 999-sided figure, if phenomenal states are experienced at all, they may be exactly the same in the two instances; but one is apperceptively aware of the difference in the two thoughts. So the apperceptive awareness cannot *be* that of phenomenal experience. Also, as Wittgenstein (1953) pointed out, in the flow of ordinary conversation it is highly unlikely that we apperceptively experience phenomenal states for every instance of apperceptive understanding.[8]

Moreover, there would seem to be high-level neural states that are image-like representations in exactly the sense that CS states are; but on the nondissociability thesis these high-level neural states would not be phenomenal because they are not apperceived (see Nelkin 1989a). Somehow combining these states with C2 would cause the states to give way to phenomenal states that are exactly similar, in their representational aspect, to the states they replace *except* for also being phenomenal (for this view, see Natsoulas 1989; 1990). Such a transformation is, at best, highly mysterious. One is faced with the question of how turning one's attention (say) toward a nonapperceptively grasped high-level neural image-like representational state can cause a new, but phenomenal and apperceived, image-like representational state to come into existence, while at the same time missing the target of one's turn of attention altogether. That is, one would, on the nondissociability view, never become apperceptively aware of the state to which one turned one's attention. Instead, attending would create an altogether different representational state that would be exactly like the 'missed' state and *also* possess phenomenal properties.

On the other hand, if all high-level neural image-like representation states are phenomenal, though not all are apperceived, then phenomenality, while still a problem, is less of a dangler and less of a mystery. It is a property of all high-level neural image-like representation states. Apperception does not create phenomenal states where none before existed, and apperception *is* able to grasp the states one all along intended to grasp with it. The

[8] For fuller arguments on the dissociability of C2 from CS, see Nelkin 1987, 1989a, 1989b, 1993a, 1993b, 1996 (especially chapters 5 and 6).

dissociability view does not eliminate theoretical difficulties, but it does reduce their number and their air of mystery.

The *second* theoretical reason in favour of the dissociability thesis lies in the shortcomings of its alternative. It would seem that if the dissociability thesis is wrong, there would have to exist — in addition to high-level neural image-like representational states that are not phenomenal (call them CS' states), C1 states, and C2 states — a single state that incorporates the principal features of CS', C1, and C2 states and is phenomenal as well. Natsoulas (1989, 1990) commits himself to the existence of such states and calls them 'self-reflective states'.[9] However, two theoretical considerations weigh against positing self-reflective states.

The first is that if the dissociability thesis be correct, then one need not posit a fourth state at all. Co-occurrences of the three otherwise dissociable states would account for whatever self-reflective states could account for. It is important to realize that we do not have any direct way of *knowing* that self-reflective states occur at all: the belief in them is not based merely on directly apprehending them. For introspection cannot distinguish whether we are at an instance of time experiencing a single, indivisible, self-reflective state or experiencing three dissociable, co-occurrent states. Yet, if we had epistemically relevant direct access to self-reflective states, it would only be by way of introspection. That is, if self-reflective states exist, we have direct apprehension of them — by the definition of self-reflective states — but *that* apprehension cannot itself discern that they are self- reflective states rather than complexes of separate and dissociable states. Since, in fact, there is no direct way of knowing self-reflective states to exist, they are posited for theoretical reasons. But then it becomes legitimate to ask what theoretical work they are doing, especially if the occurrences they explain can be explained as well without positing their existence. We need posit only three independent states, not four, on the dissociability view.

The second shortcoming is internal to the proposed nature of self-reflective states themselves. How could a single state be a first-order image-like representation state, a first-order proposition-like representation state, a phenomenal state, and a second-order proposition-like representation state all at once? Such a state *would* certainly be a mystery. So no wonder defenders of the nondissociability thesis find consciousness such a mystery! Again, it seems much simpler to think that there is one sort of state (composed of high-level neural image-like representation states) that possesses phenomenality, than to think that besides the three other states there is a fourth sort of state (comprised of self-reflective states) that has all the principal properties of those states plus the additional one of phenomenality. That is, it is more reasonable to think that there is no CS', only CS — which may or may not be apperceived.

---

[9] Others who seem committed to self-reflective states are Searle (1989; 1990; 1992), Nagel (1979; 1986) and McGinn (1988; 1989).

V

The best reason for maintaining the dissociability thesis will be if the large-scale theory that incorporates it is the best theory of consciousness that we have.[10] Still, in this paper we have seen that the nondissociability thesis has been assumed, not defended, that whatever empirical evidence exists favours the dissociability thesis, and that less large-scale theoretical considerations of at least two kinds also favour the dissociability thesis. If there is no other lesson to be learned from this discussion, we *do* learn that theory/data — though not introspective data — must be relied on to settle this issue.[11]

References

Boghossian, P.A. & Velleman, J.D. (1991). Physicalist theories of color. *Philosophical Review*, **100**, 67–106.

Descartes, R. (1986)[1641]. Meditations on first philosophy. In J. Cottingham (ed. & trs.), *René Descartes: Meditations on First Philosophy, with Selections from the Objections and Replies*. Cambridge: Cambridge University Press.

Gazzaniga, M.S. (1970). *The Bisected Brain*. New York: Appleton-Century-Crofts.

Gazzaniga, M.S. (1977). On dividing the self: speculations for brain research. *Excerpta Medica:Neurology*, **434**, 233–44.

Gazzaniga, M.S. & LeDoux, J.E. (1978). *The Integrated Mind*. New York: Plenum Press.

Hardin, C.L. (1988). *Color for Philosophers: Unweaving the Rainbow*. Indianapolis: Hackett Publishing Company.

Keating, E.G. (1979). Rudimentary color vision in the monkey after removal of striate and preoccipital cortex. *Brain Research*, **179**, 379–84.

Leibniz, G. W. (1989)[1714]. Principles of nature and grace. In R. Ariew & D. Garber (eds), trs. D. Garber, *G. W. Leibniz: Philosophical Essays*. Indianapolis: Hackett Publishing Company.

McGinn, C. (1988). Consciousness and content. *Proceedings of the British Academy*, **74**, 219–39.

McGinn, C. (1989). Can we solve the mind–body problem? *Mind*, **98**, 349–66.

Nagel, T. (1974). What is it like to be a bat? *Philosophical Review*, **83**, 435–50.

Nagel, T. (1979). *Mortal Questions*. Cambridge: Cambridge University Press.

Nagel, T. (1986). *The View from Nowhere*. Oxford: Oxford University Press.

Natsoulas, T. (1989). An examination of four objections to self-intimating states of consciousness. *Journal of Mind and Behavior*, **10**, 63–116.

Natsoulas, T. (1990). Perspectival appearing and Gibson's theory of visual perception. *Psychological Research*, **52**, 291–8.

---

[10] See Nelkin 1996. Throughout, I have used 'theory' to mean philosophical theory. For the differences between philosophical theories and scientific theories, see Nelkin 1994 as well as the manuscript cited above.

[11] I would like to thank Keith Butler, Ed Johnson, and Carolyn Morillo, all of whom made useful comments on earlier versions of this paper.

Nelkin, N. (1987) What is it like to be a person? *Mind & Language*, **3**, 220–41.

Nelkin, N. (1989a). Unconscious sensations. *Philosophical Psychology*, **2**, 129–41.

Nelkin, N. (1989b). Propositional attitudes and consciousness. *Philosophy and Phenomenological Research*, **49**, 413–30.

Nelkin, N. (1993a). The connection between intentionality and consciousness. In Davies & Humphreys 1993.

Nelkin, N. (1993b). What is consciousness? *Philosophy of Science*, **60**, 419–34.

Nelkin, N. (1994). Patterns. *Mind & Language*, **9**, 56–87.

Nelkin, N. (1996). *Consciousness and the Origins of Thought.* Cambridge: Cambridge University Press.

Searle, J. R. (1989). Consciousness, unconsciousness, and intentionality. *Philosophical Topics*, **17**, 193–209.

Searle, J. R. (1990). Consciousness, explanatory inversion, and cognitive science. *Behavioral and Brain Sciences*, **13**, 585–642.

Searle, J. R. (1992). *The Rediscovery of the Mind.* Cambridge, MA: MIT Press.

Stoerig, P. & Brandt, S. (1993). The visual system and levels of perception: properties of neuromental organization. *Theoretical Medicine*, **14**, 117–35.

Stoerig, P. & Cowey, A. (1989). Wavelength sensitivity in blindsight. *Nature*, **342**, 916–18.

Stoerig, P. & Cowey, A. (1992). Wavelength discrimination in blindsight. *Brain*, **115**, 425–44.

Van Essen, D.C. (1985). Functional organization of the primate visual cortex. In A. Peters, and E.G. Jones (eds), *Cerebral cortex*. New York: Plenum Press.

Volpe, B.T., LeDoux, J.E. & Gazzaniga, M.S. (1979). Information processing of visual stimuli in an 'extinguished field'. *Nature*, **282**, 722–4.

Weiskrantz, L. (1977). Trying to bridge some neuropsychological gaps between monkey and man. *British Journal of Psychology*, **68**, 431–45.

Weiskrantz, L. (1986). *Blindsight: A Case Study and Implications.* Oxford: Oxford University Press.

Wittgenstein, L. (1953). *Philosophical Investigations*, trans. G.E.M. Anscombe. London: Macmillan.

Part Seven

Information-Processing and Neurobiological Approaches

Introduction to Part Seven

The importance of interdisciplinary approaches within the philosophy of mind has steadily increased in recent years. An especially active area is formed at the border between the neurosciences and philosophy (what Patricia Churchland has called *neurophilosophy*). Another area of interdisciplinary activity centres on information processing; this often intersects with the neuroscientific as well as with the neurophilosophical approach. As far as empirical research into consciousness is concerned, an intensive and productive contact between the two theoretical approaches has already been established. More than a few philosophers also think that it is concepts such as 'information', 'information processing' and 'representation' which will help us to develop a more precise and conceptually plausible theory of consciousness. The majority of philosophers who strive to *naturalize* phenomenal consciousness therefore assume that the most relevant level of natural science is that of neural information processing. So the question is: Can we better understand our own consciousness if we analyse ourselves as information processing systems?

Three articles follow which appeal to information-processing in different ways. **Robert Kirk** asks the question of how consciousness is *possible* at all. In order to answer this question, he tries to formulate a set of necessary and sufficient conditions for something being a subject of conscious perception, where these conditions are philosophically as unproblematic as possible. What does it mean when we say that information is information *for* a system? A central point of Kirk's considerations is that incoming information from the sense organs must have a direct bearing on the central processes by which the organism judges and evaluates its own situation. Moreover, a conscious system must possess what Kirk calls the 'basic package': a set of connected abilities and properties such as acquisition, storage and evaluation of information, decision making, control of behaviour, needs and goals. Using the conceptual tools he has developed, Robert Kirk then attempts to show how the familiar 'intelligibility gap' can be bridged. Finally, he critically examines the relationship of the theory of consciousness he has sketched to a number of different theories.

Ansgar Beckermann investigates the question of how visual information processing in the brain can also have a phenomenal aspect. His central thesis is that the perceptual processes that lead to phenomenal consciousness are precisely those in which a system generates a representational reconstruction of a scene from 'raw images', but does not simply discard the raw images after the primary analysis of the picture, but rather binds these into the explicit representations in a modified form. Like Kirk, Beckermann holds a structural feature of information processing in the central nervous system responsible for the emergence of phenomenal content. In his analysis he utilizes recent theoretical models from cognitive science as well as from AI research. Against this background, Ansgar Beckermann also offers a number of thoughts about what might have been the evolutionary advantage of phenomenal consciousness. On this basis he then investigates what it would mean to ascribe beliefs to a system which possesses the functional architecture he describes. It turns out that such a system would naturally also possess introspective beliefs about its own states, and in particular, could distinguish between changes in the scene itself and changes in the *image* of this scene. There would then also be a difference for the system between the reality and the appearance of external objects. In this case, then, we would have good reasons to ascribe phenomenal states to the system.

If one wants to take our experience of phenomenal consciousness seriously, one has to take its *holistic* character into account. But not only the overall structure of our conscious space possesses a holistic character. A related problem is the *homogeneity* of simple phenomenal properties: the elusive 'ultra-smoothness', 'density' or 'grainlessness' of simple experiential properties, such as *Pantone Blue 72*. **Thomas Metzinger** attempts to open up a new perspective on to these well-known problems, by first approaching them from the first-person perspective. In his second step Metzinger then approaches them from the external perspective of science, examining theoretical models from brain research with regard to their utility for philosophical questions. He focuses on the role of sychronization processes in the formation of representational objects in the brain, i.e. on the binding of perceptual features through mechanisms of *temporal* coding. The last part offers an empirical speculation on the importance of a generalizable solution to the binding problem and the superposition problem for a theory of phenomenal consciousness. However, he is not interested in the empirical speculation *per se*. Rather his overriding aim is to emphasize the significance of a widely neglected problem for any theory of phenomenal content: the problem of the *integration of mental content*.

Further Reading

Beckermann, A. (1986). Dennetts Stellung zum Funktionalismus. *Erkenntnis*, **24**, 309–41.

Beckermann, A. (1986). *Kann die Künstliche Intelligenz-Forschung Fragen der Philosophie beantworten?* In H. Stoyan, H. (ed.), *GWAI 85. 9. German Workshop on Artficial Intelligence*. Informatik Fachberichte **118**. Berlin: Springer.

Beckermann, A. (1988). Sprachverstehende Maschinen – Überlegungen zu John Searles Thesen zur Künstlichen Intelligenz. *Erkenntnis*, **28**, 65–85.

Beckermann, A. (1990). Semantische Maschinen. In *Intentionalität und Verstehen*, edited by the Forum für Philosophie Bad Homburg. Frankfurt am Main: Suhrkamp.

Churchland, P.M. (1989). *A Neurocomputational Perspective. The Nature of Mind and the Structure of Science*. Cambridge, MA: MIT Press.

Churchland, P.M. (1995). *The Engine of Reason, the Seat of the Soul: A Philosophical Journey into the Brain*. Cambridge, MA: MIT Press.

Churchland, P.S. & Sejnowski, T.J. (1992). *The Computational Brain.* Cambridge, MA: MIT Press.

Jackendoff, R. (1987). *Consciousness and the Computational Mind.* Cambridge, MA: MIT Press.

Johnson-Laird, P. (1983). A computational analysis of consciousness. *Cognition and Brain Theory*, **6**, 499–508. Reprinted in Marcel & Bisiach 1988.

Kirk, R. (1974). Zombies vs. materialists. *Aristotelian Society Proceedings*, **Supp. 48**, 135–52.

Kirk, R. (1979). From physical explicability to full-blooded materialism. *Philosophical Materialism*, **29**, 229–37.

Kirk, R. (1982). Physicalism, identity and strict implication. *Ratio*, **24**, 131–41.

Kirk, R. (1991). Why shouldn't we be able to solve the mind-body problem? *Analysis*, **51**, 17–23.

Kirk, R. (1992). Consciousness and concepts. *Proceedings of the Aristotelian Society*, Supplementary Volume **66**, 23–40.

Kirk, R. (1994). *Raw Feeling: A Philosophical Account of the Essence of Consciousness.* Oxford: Oxford University Press.

Maudlin, T. (1989). Computation and consciousness. *Journal of Philosophy*, **86**, 407–32.

Metzinger, T. (1993). *Subjekt und Selbstmodell. Die Perspektivität phänomenalen Bewußtseins vor dem Hintergrund einer naturalistischen Theorie mentaler Repräsentation.* Paderborn: Schöningh.

Metzinger, T. (1994). Schimpansen, Spiegelbilder, Selbstmodelle und Subjekte. Drei Hypothesen über den Zusammenhang zwischen mentaler Repräsentation und phänomenalem Bewußtsein. In Krämer, S. (ed), *Geist, Gehirn, Künstliche Intelligenz – Zeitgenössische Modelle des Denkens.* Berlin, New York: de Gruyter.

Metzinger, T. (1995). Phänomenale mentale Modelle. In K. Sachs-Hombach (ed.), *Bilder im Geiste: Zur kognitiven und erkenntnistheoretischen Funktion piktorialer Repräsentationen.* Reihe 'Philosophie & Repräsentation'. Amsterdam und Atlanta, GA: Rodopi.

Metzinger (1996). *Niemand* sein. Kann man eine naturalistische Perspektive auf die Subjektivität des Mentalen einnehmen? In Krämer 1996.

Revonsuo, A. & Kamppinen, M. (1994)[eds]. *Consciousness in Philosophy and Cognitive Neuroscience.* Hillsdale, NJ: Lawrence Erlbaum Associates.

Shallice, T. (1988). Information-processing models of consciousness: possibilities and problems. In Marcel & Bisiach 1988.

Velmans, M. (1991). Is human information processing conscious? *Behavioral and Brain Sciences*, **14**, 651–726.

Additional references concerning the importance of the information processing paradigm for the philosophy of consciousness can be found in the bibliography at the end of this volume. Works which approach the problem of consciousness from the stance of philosophical functionalism or from the perspective of cognitive theories of information processing are listed in sections 1.1, 1.2, 2.1, 2.2, 3.1, 3.6 and 3.11. A considerable number of the more theoretical works in the neuroscientific sections 1.3, 2.3 and 3.12 also operates in the sense of computational neuroscience within the information processing paradigm.

Robert Kirk

How Is Consciousness Possible?

I. What is the Problem?

> If we acknowledge that a physical theory of mind must account for the
> subjective character of experience, we must admit that no presently available
> conception gives us a clue how this could be done. The problem is unique. If
> mental processes are indeed physical processes, then there is something it is
> like, intrinsically, to undergo certain physical processes. What it is for such
> a thing to be the case remains a mystery (T. Nagel 1974: 392 f.).

In that statement from his influential article 'What is it like to be a bat?',
which appeared in 1974, Thomas Nagel expressed deep pessimism about
the mind–body problem.[1] I think developments since that time, in both
philosophy and the neurosciences, have done more than just 'give us a clue'
about how to account for the subjective character of experience. I will set
out some of the main ideas that I think help us to understand how a material
system could be conscious, focusing on the case of conscious perceptual
experience.

The problem is to understand how a *physical* thing could be conscious,
whether it is a naturally occurring terrestrial species, or a creature living on
a remote galaxy and physico-chemically very unlike us, or a computer-
controlled robot. For even if, contrary to all the evidence, something
non-physical were involved in human consciousness, that fact alone would
make no contribution to answering the philosophical question of what it
takes to be a conscious subject. In any case, I think it is possible to see how
a purely physical system could be conscious.

---

[1] A recent statement by Fodor (1992) is even more pessimistic: 'Nobody has the slightest
idea how anything material could be conscious. Nobody even knows what it would be like to
have the slightest idea about how anything material could be conscious. So much for the
philosophy of consciousness.'

There is something which makes the problem especially difficult. It shows up dramatically in a famous passage from Leibniz's *Monadologie*:

> We have to admit that perception . . . cannot be explained mechanically, that is, by means of shapes and movements. If we imagine a machine whose construction ensures that it has thoughts, feelings, and perceptions, we can conceive it to be so enlarged, while keeping the same proportions, that we could enter it like a mill. On that supposition, when visiting it we shall find inside only components pushing one another, and never anything that could explain a perception (G. Leibniz, *Monadologie*, sec. 17).

Such reasoning can seem very persuasive, but it begs the question. Leibniz just assumes that 'components pushing one another' could not amount to the machine's thinking, feeling, or perceiving. Why didn't he notice that he had no argument? Like countless far less powerful thinkers, he seems to have been fooled by the discontinuity between the observer's viewpoint and the subject's viewpoint. Observing the internal workings of something — whatever it may be — is not automatically going to inform you whether or not it is conscious. In addition you must have a good understanding of *what it is* for something to be conscious. It is, indeed, hard to understand how a physical system can also be a conscious subject. There is an *intelligibility gap*. But that gap will not be bridged by staring at the machinery, but by a good account of what it takes to be conscious.

What sort of account will be acceptable? It has sometimes been assumed that an account must provide the means for *translating* statements about thoughts and feelings into statements in terms of a narrow physical vocabulary, for example the vocabularies of physics plus those of chemistry and neurobiology, together with neutral words such as 'cause' and 'motion'.[2] Clearly, if such translations really were possible, the problem would be solved in a thoroughly satisfactory way. But there are good reasons to think they are not possible. One was indicated in Nagel's article. In effect he pointed out a broad distinction between two kinds of concepts. A full grasp of the first kind, which might be called 'viewpoint-relative' concepts, depends on being a certain kind of creature: one with certain kinds of perceptual experiences. No one who cannot actually see colours, for example, is capable of a full understanding of the word 'red'. No one without an experience of the taste of sweet things can fully understand 'sweet'. In contrast, a grasp of the other kind of concepts, which may be called 'viewpoint-neutral', does not depend on having any particular point of view, any particular type of perceptual capacities. The point can be illustrated if we imagine a species of intelligent language-using bats. We might be able to understand what these bats said about physics and chemistry and engineering because the concepts involved are all viewpoint-neutral. But

---

[2] By 'neutral' words here and elsewhere I mean words without troublesome ontological implications.

once they started to describe the experiences produced by their characteristic echolocatory mode of sense-perception, we should not be able to grasp the full sense of what they said. Now, I think Nagel's reasoning here is sound.[3] If so, it is impossible to produce viewpoint-neutral translations of statements involving viewpoint-relative expressions, such as statements ascribing conscious experiences. For understanding viewpoint-neutral statements does not require any particular sort of perceptual equipment, while understanding viewpoint-relative statements does. It follows that none of the former can mean the same as any of the latter.

Fortunately there is no reason to require translations. It will be enough if we can remove the sources of philosophical puzzlement by whatever means may be available. The way I favour is to work out a set of necessary and sufficient conditions for something to be a subject of conscious perception in terms which, although they are not purely physical, or even neutral, do not give rise to philosophical perplexities.[4] I shall use terms such as 'information' and 'behaviour' without providing definitions, yet with what I believe is *enough* explanation for us to see that nothing problematic is being overlooked. In that way the intelligibility gap can be bridged.

The account will not be satisfactory unless it shows how the purely physical facts could *determine* the facts of consciousness. To make this point vivid, imagine we have an idealized physics and an associated narrow physical vocabulary, and consider the set of all true statements in that vocabulary: the set of all physical truths. These truths will include all physical laws and descriptions of the positions and states of all elementary particles throughout space and time. The totality of these physical truths is a specification of the entire physical universe past, present, and future. I think those physical facts *fix* the mental facts in the strong sense that it is in no way possible that the same totality of statements should have been true, and the facts of consciousness in any respect different. In terms of a powerful image of Saul Kripke, if God had created the universe according to that purely physical specification, he would have had no 'further work to do' (Kripke 1972: 154). This means that descriptions of human mental life — for example that Napoleon had a headache on 1 May 1800, that I now smell freshly ground coffee, that you see the black print on the white page as you read this article — are redescriptions of events and processes which are also described, though very differently, in the narrow physical specification of the universe.[5] So now I can say, rather more sharply, how I

---

[3] Not everyone agrees. For the opposing view, see e.g. Dennett 1991: 441–8.

[4] Eliminative materialists will obviously not agree. See e.g. Churchland 1981. But then eliminativists will claim to have eliminated the whole problem which concerns me in this paper.

[5] So the totality of true physical statements strictly implies the facts about human and animal consciousness. For more on this 'strict implication thesis', see Kirk 1994: 71–86.

conceive the problem. It is to provide an account of what is involved in
conscious perceptual experience which removes perplexity over the fact
that a purely physical specification of the universe fixes the truths about
conscious experiences.

In this paper I shall only be able to indicate the main features of my
attempt to solve this problem. Many fascinating issues will be left unexplored.[6]

II. Information and the Basic Package

In common with many philosophers I think the solution is to be found in a
proper consideration of the fact that typical conscious subjects acquire and
use *information*. The central complex of ideas is that of a system which
controls its behaviour on the basis of the information it receives from its
environment.

The information has to be *for* the system.[7] To illustrate this vital point,
we can start with the example of blue litmus paper turning red in a certain
liquid. The fact that it turns red shows us that the liquid is acid. But this
information is not for the litmus paper itself because it cannot use it.
Another example is a camera. It is a valuable way of collecting information.
But again the information is not for the camera but for us, because nothing
could count as its using it. In contrast, a cat is able to learn. That is, it is able
to modify its patterns of behaviour as a result of interaction with its
environment. It can learn where its food is normally put out, where mice are
to be found, where there are dogs. And as it moves around it is acquiring
information that it can use: it hears a mouse squeak and looks round; it sees
the mouse and goes for it. The cat acquires information that is for it.

Those descriptions of the cat depend on its having what I call the 'basic
package' of capacities: a set of interrelated capacities which come as a
whole. Systems with the basic package not only collect information which
is for them: they store information, they have needs or goals, they engage
in some kind of assessment of their situation and some kind of decision
making, and they initiate and control their behaviour on the basis of
information. And if they are capable of doing any of these things, they are
capable of doing them all, as we shall see.

But what is information? You may think that until some explanation has
been given of that central notion, the rest is useless. But I am not assuming
a clear notion of information which is applicable to a system independently
of whether these other descriptions also apply. My point is that the whole
complex of concepts — including those of *acquiring information which is
for the system, storing information, assessing information, making decisions, controlling behaviour, needs and goals* — applies either as a whole,

---

[6] See Kirk 1994 for a fuller treatment.

[7] This valuable phrase was introduced by Dennett (1969: 46 f.).

or not at all. Suppose we start with the idea that the system acquires information which is for it. That implies it must be able both to store and to use information. But the information would be no use unless the system could assess its situation; and that would be no use unless it could decide what to do. That it turn would be impossible if it had no needs or goals to make it prefer some situations to others. Being able to act requires it to be able to control its behaviour. That in turn implies it must be able to acquire information about the scene of action. In this way the components of the basic package form an unbreakable complex. But more explanation is needed.

Since we are talking about purely physical systems, the acquisition of information is just a matter of certain kinds of physical changes. The question is, which changes amount to the acquisition of information? We know that the mere fact that the system is affected in *some* way by the outside world is not sufficient for it to acquire information in the relevant sense, even if we can use it as a source of information for ourselves. That point is illustrated by the litmus paper and the camera. The same point holds even if each of a range of different kinds of environmental impact causes a correspondingly different kind of behaviour. That pattern is exemplified by a weighing machine: each different weight causes the correlated reading to appear on the machine's scale. Such a machine is useful to *us*: it gives us information we can use. But it can do nothing with the information. It cannot assess its situation, and it cannot initiate or control its behaviour. It is what I call a 'pure stimulus-response system'. Its whole behavioural repertoire can be adequately represented by a fixed function from a set of possible inputs, or stimuli, to a set of possible outputs, or responses.

The sort of computer program sometimes called a 'look-up table' is a pure stimulus-response system. It can produce behaviour which seems remarkably intelligent. For example, suppose we were to list every possible position in a game of draughts, together with an intelligent move from that position, and programmed a computer, when it was its turn, to put out the move assigned to the current position. Although those who did not know how it had been set up would count its play as intelligent, those who did know would not.[8] Much of the behaviour of many insects seems to conform to that pure stimulus-response pattern. (However, since even the fruit-fly is able to find its way home, it is capable of learning, in which case it is not a pure stimulus-response system in my sense.[9]) For example, flies are hardwired so that if their feet break contact with a surface, their wings are automatically caused to buzz; and if their feet make contact with a surface, their wings are automatically caused to stop buzzing. Similarly, if their feet

---

[8] Draughts rather than chess because of the unmanageably large number of possible positions in chess.

[9] For the same reason, any organism capable of acquiring conditioned reflexes is not a pure stimulus-response system in my sense.

are in contact with a surface and that surface emits certain chemicals, the fly's mouth-parts are caused to go into action on it. (With luck, the surface will be decaying meat.)

It will be clear on reflection that a pure stimulus-response system does not acquire information which is for it. Although its behaviour may be well suited to its environment, and although it may have a wide repertoire of useful responses, it does not learn. Its patterns of behaviour are fixed, and there is nothing that could count as its assessing its situation, still less anything that could count as its deciding what to do on the basis of information. Suppose that in fact a fly's entire behavioural repertoire fitted the pure stimulus-response pattern. Then we could not describe it as acquiring information that was for it, any more than we could describe any other pure stimulus-response system — a piano, for example — as acquiring information that was for it. The piano cannot assess its situation and for that reason cannot be said to control its own behaviour.

So what else is needed in order for the changes in a system to constitute its acquisition of information? What is needed is for it to have the basic package. Of course that is vague; but I think it is adequate for present purposes. I cannot *define* the relevant notion of information; but I hope I have said enough to enable us to tell whether or not the concepts involved in specifying the basic package apply. Either all those concepts apply, or none of them does. So it is important to take account of the whole pattern of the system's behaviour. It is also important to take account of the nature of its internal processing, and to ensure that there are, for example, processes which constitute its *own* assessment of its situation, and its own control of its behaviour. (Notice that whatever processes constitute the system's own assessment of its situation will contribute directly to controlling its behaviour. In this respect they contrast with any processes of assessment which may be going on in some subsystem.)

It seems unlikely that the question whether a given system has the basic package will have a determinate answer for every possible case. The reason is not just that the concepts involved are vague. It is that there is no apparent limit to the variety of architectures capable of sustaining the sorts of capacities that are involved in having the package.[10]

Let me illustrate what I have been saying by reference to two possible systems which appear to have the basic package, but in fact do not. First, the pantomime horse: two people, Front Legs and Back Legs, inside a horse costume. They co-ordinate their behaviour so as to create the effect of a comical four-legged animal with a horse's head, moving about and following instructions. You would have to be very simple-minded, or else very deeply committed to a philosophical position, to say the pantomime horse has the basic package. (I have never yet met a child who thinks a pantomime

---

[10] See Sloman 1993 for discussion of the question of different architectures.

horse has thoughts and feelings; but I have met philosophers who have claimed to think so.) Nevertheless it is an instructive example. Unlike litmus paper, or even a pure stimulus-response insect, it produces interesting behaviour. And information does get into it, and makes a difference to how it behaves. It avoids obstacles; it even follows instructions. Clearly it is not a pure stimulus-response system. But that just illustrates the point that not everything which collects information in some sense, and is not a pure stimulus-response system, has the basic package. The reason the pantomime horse doesn't have the basic package is that, in a way, it is a fictional entity. The two people inside it are acting a part, rather as the actor playing Hamlet is pretending there is such a being, when there isn't. They are the controllers of a puppet, which differs from an ordinary puppet only in that they are inside it rather than outside.

The other system I want to mention was devised by Ned Block as a way of exposing the inadequacy of behaviourist conceptions of intelligence based on the Turing test. Turing originally proposed the test as a substitute for questions like 'can this machine think?' The tester is connected by means of computer terminals with a human being and a computer program, and is given a limited time (say, ten minutes) to decide which is which, purely on the basis of their responses to questions typed in.[11] Block argues that a better conception of intelligence, from the point of view of philosophical behaviourism,[12] is to say that it consists in the capacity to produce sensible responses to any verbal stimuli that may be typed in within the fixed time-limit. (It is left to the behaviourist to explain what to count as 'sensible' responses in this context.) He describes a computer program which on the one hand guarantees that the machine running it has the capacity to satisfy that condition, yet on the other hand has 'the intelligence of a toaster'. At first you might dismiss the program as a mere 'look-up table', such as the draughts-playing one described earlier. But a look-up table would not have the capacity to produce sensible responses in a conversation considered as a whole. For there is a significant difference between conversation and a game like draughts. In draughts the same position does not normally recur; but in conversation the same question may be asked again and again. Conversation with a computer program based on a look-up table can therefore quickly unmask it. Block's machine, however, is not a look-up table, nor any kind of a pure stimulus-response system. This is because it is based not on stored individual questions, but on stored whole conversations. The program contains absolutely every possible dialogue which would not exceed the time-limit, and in which the *second* partici-

---

[11] See Block 1981. Alan Turing's original formulation of the 'Turing test' was in his 1950.

[12] By 'philosophical behaviourism' (contrasted with behaviourism as a programme for psychology) I understand the view according to which there is no more to having mental states than having the appropriate behavioural dispositions and capacities.

pant's contributions are sensible in the context provided by the rest of the dialogue. The number of stored conversations is of course very large indeed, but finite. All the program has to do is to record whatever has been typed so far, match it against one of the stored conversations, and put out the next contribution assigned to the second participant in that stored dialogue. Such matching is entirely automatic, and clearly calls for no intelligence on the part of the program. Nor does the system work out its own response: that was done in advance by those who prepared the possible dialogues. So although Block's machine produces sensible responses, it is not intelligent. It does not have the basic package. Block briefly indicates how a similar scheme would allow a computer-controlled robot to produce sensible behaviour over a whole lifetime, in spite of not being genuinely intelligent (see Block 1981; Kirk 1994: 21 ff.).

I take it that considerations such as the above require us to reject behaviourist accounts of consciousness, according to which the right behavioural dispositions and capacities are sufficient for something to be a conscious subject.

III. Conscious Perceptual Experience

Since conscious perception at least involves the acquisition of information about the environment, the basic package is a necessary condition for being a conscious perceiver. But is it also sufficient? I think not, at any rate if the psychologists are right about phenomena such as subliminal perception and 'blindsight'.[13] Those are cases where information seems to get into a system with the basic package, yet where that information does not involve conscious perception. So what more is needed? Here it will be helpful to reflect on the evolutionary point of conscious perception. (But note: we are not defining our task in terms of either *self*-conscious perception or consciousness *that* one is perceiving. I take it that both are different from conscious perception.)

Various suggestions about the evolutionary purpose of conscious perception are on offer, but one seems overwhelmingly the most plausible. This is that it enables an organism to be influenced by incoming perceptual information without automatically being caused to produce any particular behaviour. Automatic responses are all very well in their way. For species in a favourable, consistent environmental niche, a built-in set of automatic responses assures survival. But for more complex organisms, especially when their environment is subject to irregular changes, survival may depend on being able to work out a response tailor-made to suit the particular current situation. Automatically eating when certain chemicals affect your mouthparts is generally a good thing if you happen to be a fly; but if you are a mouse, that sort of behaviour would risk getting you caught in a trap.

[13] On blindsight see Weiskrantz 1986.

So it looks as if the situation is this. Events which constitute the organism's acquisition of perceptual information have certain direct effects on the processes which constitute its assessment of its situation, so that those events will also influence its decision making. The effects in question are ones which enable it to do certain kinds of things, for example to guide its behaviour in ways that are appropriate to whatever things in the environment may have caused the original stimulation. It is crucial that although these effects *enable* the organism to behave in appropriate ways, they do not automatically cause it to do anything. We can say they endow it with certain capacities; though of course a capacity is not a kind of entity sitting inside the organism. To describe an organism's capacities at any one time is just to describe what it would be able to do *if* it decided to act in certain ways. I will say that when incoming perceptual information endows the system with capacities of these sorts, the events which constitute its acquisition of the information are 'directly active' on its main assessment processes. (Its 'main' assessment processes are those involved in the whole system's assessment of its situation, rather than only in whatever assessment there may be by its subsystems.) My suggestion, in brief, is that conscious perception is the action of these events on the system's main assessment processes.

Earlier I emphasized the contrast between conscious perception and mere hard-wired reflexes. We must now take account of another contrast, as the examples of subliminal perception and blindsight show. In those cases, incoming perceptual information does not act directly on the organism's assessment processes. Instead, it is stored in memory. It may then have indirect effects on subsequent behaviour, or it may just lie there, available to be recalled if for some reason the organism is moved to recall it. If, however, incoming information is acting directly on an organism's main assessment processes, the organism has a good basis for deciding how to act. A cat faced at the same time with a mouse near at hand and a dog approaching from some distance away can arrive at behaviour tailored to fit its own assessment of its situation. Contrast the position of an otherwise similar creature acquiring perceptual information that was not acting directly on its main assessment processes. Not having this information forced upon it, it would presumably acquire no motive for reconsidering its position. The information would be stored away somehow; but it would be there with masses of other information — about how things were the day before, perhaps. There would be no particular reason why it should summon up any particular piece of information at any particular time. You might suggest that perceptual information about the *present* state of the world would be somehow privileged, somehow made to impinge more directly on the organism's assessment processes than information about the state of the world at other times. No doubt. But in that case it would after all be directly active in my sense, contrary to the original assumption. It is precisely the special status of directly active perceptual information which distinguishes conscious from unconscious perception, and gives creatures with that way of collecting information their evolutionary advantage. The cat-like creature without that way of collecting information would stand a greater risk of starvation.

If that is right, I think we have what we needed. In order to be a subject of conscious perceptual experience it is necessary to have the basic package, when that is understood in the non-behavouristic way I have explained. But the basic package alone is not sufficient. At least some incoming perceptual information must be directly active. When that happens, there is something it is like to be the system in question. Those two conditions are jointly sufficient for conscious perceptual experience, or so I maintain. But of course there is more to be said.

The key idea — that events constituting the acquisition of perceptual information can be 'directly active' on the organism's main assessment processes — may perhaps seem too vague to be useful. But I think vagueness is unavoidable, given that the surrounding notions of perception, assessment, interpretation, and the rest are also vague. What matters is whether this way of putting things helps to throw light on the nature of conscious perception. I think it does, given further explanations, some of which are offered below. It would have helped if we had had detailed knowledge of the mechanisms of perception. Unfortunately we don't: there is more scientific work to be done. In any case, we are not interested only in consciousness in actual terrestrial organisms, but in possible cases too. And, as I remarked earlier, there seems no limit to the range of possible architectures for conscious perception. So although a detailed knowledge of actual mechanisms would have been useful, it would not have removed the need for philosophical explanations. For the same reason, I think it would be a mistake to try to substitute more detailed specifications for the vague phrase 'directly active'. However, we can get useful clues from recent work in psychology and artificial intelligence. Connectionist models help us to form a conception, clear enough for our purposes, of how there could be processes performing the functions I have indicated.

A couple of decades ago the only plausible model for the acquisition, storage, and use of information was provided by ordinary computer programs, which typically represented information by means of sentences or sentence-parts. The general assumption was that the appropriate level for modelling the psychological processes involved in intelligent thought was that of the processing of sentences. But there are huge difficulties for that approach. One which is particularly relevant to our problem (it is certainly not the only one) is posed by the fact that the information we get by our senses seems far richer than could be carried by means of sentences, at any rate if the concepts used in those sentences are anything like those of ordinary language. Suppose you are looking at the waves breaking on the beach. You can describe what is happening in great detail. But there is so much to describe, and the wave-patterns change so quickly and in such complicated ways, that even if the scene were to be frozen, and you were allowed all the time you wanted, any description would still fall short of specifying all the details. In spite of that, you are constantly *receiving* all that information and much more at every instant as you watch. I am not saying it is absolutely impossible for the classic AI approach to handle the problem, but that the approach seems ill-suited for its purpose. Connectionist models now offer a promising way of dealing with that difficulty among others.

Connectionist modelling enables us to see how it is possible for information of all kinds, and especially rich perceptual information, to be collected, stored and used by a system (which might be an animal or an artefact). And it enables us to put some flesh on my idea of the 'direct action' of events on a system's main processes of assessment.[14] Although connectionism still faces difficulties, it at least suggests that my conditions for conscious perception can be satisfied in ways that raise no special philosophical problems. One striking feature of connectionist models is that the behaviour of each node or unit is determined by the inputs it receives from whichever other units are directly connected to it. There is no central 'control' which monitors the state of each unit. That the total system behaves as it does results from the way vast numbers of relatively small constraints, exerted by each unit over its neighbours, eventually produce significant large-scale changes in the whole. So connectionist modelling is particular well-suited to avoid what Dennett calls 'Cartesian materialism': 'the view you arrive at when you discard Descartes' dualism but fail to discard the imagery of a central (but material) Theatre where "it all comes together"' (Dennett 1991: 106). Classic AI models tended to posit such a central control; connectionism helps to show how to do without it.

The remaining problems for connectionist modelling seem to be mainly ones of engineering (granted that good engineering calls for much imagination and ingenuity).

IV. The Intelligibility Gap has been Bridged

You may be sympathetic to the sort of account I have been sketching, yet still feel it leaves out something essential. How does it deal with 'qualia' or (as I prefer to say) 'raw feeling'? You may complain that we can easily conceive of something satisfying my conditions but without conscious experience. But that is not, so far, an objection. After all, there are plenty of things we can conceive of which are not genuinely possible. (Some people have conceived of what they described as a proof that π is a rational number.) Still, if it is even logically possible that something satisfying my

---

[14] For more on this, see Kirk 1994: 130–53.

conditions lacks conscious perceptual experience, my account is mistaken. I need to explain why I think that is not a genuine possibility. I will start with another look at the distinctive feature of conscious subjects.

This is that they occupy two very different positions at the same time. One is that they are centres of consciousness with their own needs, interests, and ways of thinking. The other is that they are objects of attention from others. We noticed when discussing Nagel's claims that these two positions have engendered two sets of concepts. As subjects, we have experiences describable in 'viewpoint-relative' terms. As objects, we are describable in 'viewpoint-neutral' terms. The discontinuity between these two sets of concepts can easily mislead us into thinking that they deal with completely different things — especially when the viewpoint-neutral concepts are those of the narrow physical vocabulary. Those concepts belong to a highly developed theory, of which most people know very little, if anything. Yet the totality of truths in terms of that theory specify, in their own way, *everything* that is involved in the perceptual experience of human beings and any other conscious creatures, or so I maintain. However, when it comes to specifying these experiences from the point of view of their subjects, the concepts used have been developed quite independently of the concepts of physics and the neurosciences. They have been developed for the convenience of the particular sort of agents that we human beings are, with our particular needs, interests, aptitudes, intelligence, memory and sensory capacities. I claimed earlier that these facts make it very unlikely that translations of true statements in terms of ordinary subjective experience and ordinary psychology could be provided in terms of physics, chemistry and neuroscience. This real gap, between viewpoint-neutral and viewpoint-relative concepts and descriptions, is a component of the intelligibility gap. And the present point is that it makes it too easy to assume wrongly, with Leibniz, that there is also a *logical* gap between the physical facts on one hand and the facts of consciousness on the other. I am trying to show how it is that exactly the same thing may be both a physical system describable in viewpoint-neutral terms, and a subject describable in viewpoint-relative terms, and so to close the intelligibility gap.

An example may help. Consider that common little freshwater fish, the stickle-back. Sometimes its behaviour appears to be pretty well automatic. Much of what it does in connection with mating seems to have been 'hard-wired'. Faced with anything like the bright red belly of a potential rival in the breeding season, the male stickleback aggressively fights it. But not all its behaviour seems to have been wired in; and for illustrative purposes I will assume it has the basic package, and that at any rate some incoming perceptual information is directly active in the sense I have indicated. Suppose, then, that a male stickleback is faced simultaneously with a piece of food — say a larva — and a female (identifiable by her silvery colour). In that case, whether or not the stickleback does anything about the female or, instead, about the larva, depends on its assessment of its overall situation, and its decision making, however rudimentary both assessment and decision making may be. The information about these two things is directly active in my sense. And the crucial point is that the creature's assessment of different but simultaneous events implies that its processing of those events must have different 'characters' for it. Its assessment depends on differences in the character for it of two sets of *internal* processes: those caused by the larva, and those caused by the silvery body of the female. These processes are typically caused by external things, so they are independent of those external causes. They could have been produced by other means (in which case the creature would be experiencing a hallucination). It is because these internal processes are not mere links in a stimulus-response chain, but are involved in processes of assessment, that they can be said to have different characters for the stickleback.

These points about 'characters for the organism' do not introduce anything new into the story. They are just redescriptions of what is involved in the direct action of perceptual information on the organism's main assessment processes. The mere fact that different sorts of perceptual information are directly active[15] ensures that certain internal processes have different characters for the system. If that is right, there is no logical gap. For to say that internal processes have characters for the system logically implies that there is something it is like for the organism, so that it is a subject of conscious perceptual experience.

You might suspect that the idea of characters for the system implies that there is a Cartesian split between an internal homunculus and a private TV screen. But that is not so. The main assessment processes of a system with the basic package are just components in a total system of processes which constitutes an experiencing subject as a whole. Certainly we can roughly mark off different levels of processing: low-level feature-detection close to the sense-receptors, then higher levels of analysis and interpretation, assessment, decision making, and action- initiation. But that doesn't imply that some of these processes make up a subject while others are the objects of its activities. Instead, we have to think of the whole complex of processes as constituting the subject's assessments, interpretations, and so on. Compare the way we must not think of having a headache as a *relation* between a homunculus and a pain, but instead as a single process: having-a-pain. It is convenient to categorize different aspects of what is going on. But the actual processes are an inextricable swirl involving complexes of units all over the system. Consideration of connectionist modelling helps to make these points intelligible (cf. Kirk 1994: 130–53).

---

[15] Strictly, what is directly active are the physical changes which constitute the acquisition of the information.

Suppose you reject my claim about characters for the stickleback, and assert that it is like *nothing* to be a stickleback seeing a female or a stickleback seeing a larva: the creature has no such conscious experiences. I want to know how, on that view, you explain its behaviour. Presumably you have to say that the different patterns of behaviour it exhibits when it sees a female and when it sees a larva are somehow automatic. The incoming information just causes that behaviour, more or less directly. Now, I concede that in the case of some animals that is so. But I am assuming the stickleback has the basic package, with some perceptual information directly active on its main assessment processes. And in that case these behavioural episodes — chasing the female, say, or going for the larva — are in fact not automatic. The information is not just being received by the creature in some way or other: it is having effects on its main assessment processes. And my point is that in that case, when the incoming information about the female and about the larva is active but not necessarily acted upon, the stickleback cannot fail to be having conscious experiences of the female and of the larva. It is only because the two external things cause processes with different characters for it that it has a basis for assessing its situation and deciding what to do. Given that the information in question is directly active, there must be something it is like to acquire it.[16]

It may be helpful to discuss an alleged counter-example: the sophisticated guided missile. One difficulty with it is that I think there could perfectly well be conscious guided missiles. If necessary you could even construct a guided missile around me, using my brain to do the necessary work. The result would be a genuine conscious subject, and therefore not a counter-example. However, the sort of system the objectors have in mind is something less exotic, such as a Cruise missile; and they assume that such systems are not genuinely conscious. But they must also assume that these missiles have the basic package, and it is not clear to me that they do. As I remarked earlier, there is scope for indeterminacy over that matter. However, let us grant for the sake of argument that Cruise missiles have the basic package. That is still not sufficient, on my account, for them to be subjects of conscious perceptual experience. In addition there must be incoming perceptual information which is directly active in the way I have indicated. From what little I know about such systems, it looks as if this condition is not satisfied, and that it is not a counter-example for that reason.

Let me emphasize, though, that it is a matter of degree. Perhaps guided missiles will eventually be devised which not only have the basic package, but also have incoming perceptual information that is directly active on their processes of assessment. I shall have to say that they have conscious perceptual experiences of some kind. However, here it is necessary to take

---

[16] This does not mean that the assessment and decision-making processes must themselves be conscious. In the case of such a relatively humble creature as a stickleback, that seems unlikely. Assessment need not imply deliberation; nor do decisions have to be spelt out.

another factor into account, which I have not yet mentioned. There is enormous scope for differences in the *volume* of information that different systems are capable of receiving at an instant. Human vision, for example, is amazingly rich, but some creatures have very restricted visual capacities. Evolution may have ensured that all naturally occurring species which have the basic package receive rich perceptual information of some kind or other. But there could be artificial systems that were capable of taking in only a few items of perceptual information at an instant. Their general architecture would still provide for the satisfaction of my conditions. But if relatively little information was ever directly active, there would not be much difference between being such a system and being altogether without conscious perceptual experience. So the guided missile case does not seem to pose a serious problem for my position.[17]

So far as I can see, then, the conditions I have suggested provide not only for perception, but for conscious perception. In doing that, they provide for 'qualia' or 'raw feeling'.

V. Relations with Other Accounts

In conclusion it may be useful to say briefly how my account relates to others. Having already offered reasons for rejecting dualism and behaviourism, I will consider just three rival accounts: Armstrong's, the 'reflexive' account, and Dennett's. (I have discussed them elsewhere: references are given in footnotes.)

Armstrong has powerfully defended the view that perception is the acquisition of information about the environment, and that conscious perception is 'introspection', which he takes to be a kind of 'inner sense': perception by the organism of its own mental states. I accept the first component of that view, provided it is not understood behaviouristically. But I think the second component is open to objections which my own position avoids.[18]

A 'reflexive' account of consciousness, similar to Armstrong's in some ways, is favoured by several philosophers. The key idea is that what makes perception conscious is that it is 'available' for conscious thought, when conscious thought is itself explained in terms of the availability of thought at one level for thought at a higher level. The exponents of this account accept that such cognitive complexity would make it highly unlikely that animals or even human infants had conscious perceptual experiences. I find

---

[17] Another counter-example, often brought against functionalism, is that of large organisations such as the United States or even Marks and Spencer. In some ways they resemble the pantomime horse (a philosophical, not a political, comment). In any case I doubt that they have enough co-ordination to satisfy my conditions, especially that of directly active incoming perceptual information.

[18] See Armstrong 1968: 93–5, 323–8. For discussion see Kirk 1994: 125 f, 153 f.

their arguments unpersuasive, and think my account deals more satisfyingly with the phenomena.[19]

Finally, although my account is consistent with much of Dennett's recent treatment of the issues in his book *Consciousness Explained*, there are disagreements. His attack on 'Cartesian materialism' is thoroughly congenial. Equally congenial are, for example, his view that 'consciousness is not a special all-or-nothing property that sunders the universe into two vastly different categories' (Dennett 1991: 160). and his treatment of Searle's Chinese room thought experiment. But the following three points of conflict are significant. First, his approach is strongly behaviouristic. Second, and relatedly, he rejects any notion of 'qualia', even a non-dualistic one. I think, on the contrary, that some notion of the sort — specifically, the notion of what I call 'raw feeling' — is perfectly compatible with both thorough-going materialism and rejection of the myth of the Cartesian theatre. I think it is even compatible with the possibility of something like the 'inverted spectrum' possibility (see Kirk 1994: 186–206). Part of the trouble is that Dennett assumes that anything like the notion of qualia commits you to the view that these are properties which are 'private . . . unconfirmable and uninvestigatable'; my notion of raw feeling is a counterexample to that assumption.[20] Third, his account of what makes the difference between conscious and unconscious incoming information is a rather mysterious idea of 'probing', associated with what he calls 'narratives' (see Kirk 1993: 342 f.). The line taken in this article seems to me less mysterious and more defensible.

References

Armstrong, D.M. (1968). *A Materialist Theory of the Mind.* London: Routledge and Kegan Paul.

Block, N. (1981). Psychologism and behaviourism. *Philosophical Review*, **90**, 5–43.

Carruthers, P. (1992). Concepts and consciousness II. *Aristotelian Society Proceedings*, supp. vol. **66**, 41–59.

Churchland, P.M. (1981). Eliminative materialism and the propositional attitudes. *The Journal of Philosophy*, **78**, 67–90.

Dennett, D.C. (1969). *Content and Consciousness.* London: Routledge and Kegan Paul.

Dennett, D.C. (1991). *Consciousness Explained.* Boston, MA: Little, Brown & Co.

Fodor, J.A. (1992). The big idea: can there be a science of mind? *Times Literary Supplement*, 3 July 1992, 5.

---

[19] See Rosenthal 1986; Carruthers 1992; Kirk 1992; 1994: 155–8, 162–4.

[20] The quotation is from Dennett 1991: 450. For discussion see Kirk 1994: 55–66.

Kirk, R. (1992). Consciousness and concepts I. *Aristotelian Society Proceedings*, supp. vol. **66**, 23–40.

Kirk, R. (1993). 'The right tools'? Dennett's metaphors and the mind–body problem. *Philosophical Quarterly*, **43**, 335–43.

Kirk, R. (1994). *Raw Feeling: A Philosophical Account of the Essence of Consciousness*. Oxford: Oxford University Press.

Kripke, S. (1972). *Naming and Necessity*. Oxford: Blackwell.

Lycan, W. G. (1987). *Consciousness*. Cambridge, MA, and London: MIT Press.

Nagel, T. (1974). What is it like to be a bat? *Philosophical Review*, **83**, 435–50. Reprinted in Hofstadter & Dennett 1981(to which page references apply).

Rosenthal, D. (1986). Two concepts of consciousness. *Philosophical Studies*, **49**, 329–59.

Sloman, A. (1993). The mind as a control system. In Hookway & Peterson 1993.

Turing, A. (1950). Computing machinery and intelligence. *Mind*, **59**, 433–60. Reprinted in Hofstadter & Dennett 1981.

Weiskrantz, L. (1986). *Blindsight: A Case Study and Implications*. Oxford: Oxford University Press.

Ansgar Beckermann

Visual Information Processing and Phenomenal Consciousness

I

As far as an adequate understanding of phenomenal consciousness is concerned, representationalist theories of mind which are modelled on the information processing paradigm are, as much as corresponding neurobiological or functionalist theories, confronted by a series of arguments based on inverted or absent qualia considerations. These considerations display the following pattern: assuming we had complete knowledge about the neural or functional states which subserve the occurrence of phenomenal consciousness, would it not still be *conceivable* that these neural states (or states with the same causal role or the same representational function) occur without having a phenomenal content at all, or that these states are accompanied by phenomenal contents differing widely from the usual ones.

I think these arguments are *prima facie* fairly plausible, but in the case of representationalist theories they are plausible only if one confines oneself to the representational states themselves and completely ignores the specific way in which the representations in question come about. I would like to exemplify what I mean by using the case of visual perception.

Let us suppose that Harvey sees that a glass is on the table in front of him. How would a representationalist analyse this state? Well, although we normally find analyses of types of mental states like beliefs and desires in representationalist theories, as far as I know they generally do not concern themselves with perceptual processes. However, it does not seem implausi-

I would like to thank Achim Stephan for his helpful comments on an earlier draft of this paper and Antonia Barke for translating the paper into English.

ble to assume that for a representationalist perceptual processes are mainly processes of acquiring beliefs — hence he (or she) will mainly focus on the beliefs in which the perceptual processes result. And for this type of mental state he has an analysis. If Harvey sees that a glass is on the table in front of him, then this state consists, amongst other things, in Harvey's standing in a certain functional/computational relation R to a mental representation mr with the content that there is a glass on the table in front of Harvey — or, put briefly, that the mental representation mr is in Harvey's belief box. In order to distinguish perceptual beliefs from other beliefs however, one would have to say a little more about how mr gets into Harvey's belief box — e.g. that mr is more or less directly caused by the very fact, which features as its content, and moreover that in this causal process Harvey's eyes and the light reflected by the objects involved play a crucial role. A representationalist analysis of the state that Harvey sees a glass on the table in front of him could, therefore, look like this:

(a)   In Harvey's belief box there is a mental representation mr with the content that on the table directly in front of Harvey there is a glass.

(b)   That this mental representation is now in Harvey's belief box is, amongst other things, caused by the fact which features as its content, and in this causal process Harvey's eyes and the light reflected by the objects involved play a crucial role.

However, if one takes this analysis as a starting point, one immediately encounters the problems mentioned above, because if the state that Harvey sees a glass on the table in front of him is exhausted by (a) and (b), it seems perfectly conceivable that this state does not have any phenomenal content or that it is accompanied by a phenomenal content differing widely from the usual one. However, in my opinion this is only due to the fact that in point (b) *far too little* is said about the manner in which Harvey's perceptual belief comes about. That is to say, the phenomenal content of perceptual states can only be explained adequately within the framework of a representationalist theory of mind if one does not focus exclusively on the mental representations, but also analyses very carefully the manner in which these representations come into being. In order to illustrate this thesis, I shall outline the essential aspects of visual information processing as it is at present seen by the cognitive sciences and AI research.

II

Visual information processing begins with retinal images (or more precisely: distributions of electrical impulses of the receptor cells in the retina), or in the case of artificial systems with raw images generated by a television camera and encoded in two dimensional arrays of pixels. Vision, however, is a sense of distance and has to inform us not so much about proximal as about distal stimuli. Retinal images or raw images are therefore only interesting if information can be extracted from them about the three-dimensional physical scenes which have caused them. The processing must, therefore, end with descriptions or representations of these scenes. Or, in a shorthand version: visual information processing begins with a retinal image or a raw image and ends with a representation of the objects which make up the corresponding visual scene — the types of these objects, their positions in space, their sizes, their shapes, their surface textures, their motions. This enables Ballard and Brown (1982) to speak with regard to visual information processing of 'the construction of explicit, meaningful descriptions of objects from images'.

With regard to vision in general, therefore, three main components (cf. Neumann 1993: 566) have to be distinguished:

- physical objects in a scene,
- images of the scene as input of the visual system,
- a description or representation of the scene as its output.

These components combine in the following way: in the first step, the physical objects which make up a three-dimensional scene cause an image in the input medium of the system in question, which is neurally or electronically encoded. (Images, in the sense in which this term is understood here, therefore are nothing else than two-dimensional projections of three-dimensional scenes.) In the second step, the task of visual information processing consists in the reversal of the first process, i.e. the reconstruction of the original scene from the image.[1] Visual information processing has to lead to an output that tells us 'what is where' in the scene.

> The 'where' in this expression refers to spatio-temporal information, i.e. the reconstruction of the scene's geometry, while the 'what' implies an interpretation of the content of the scene, and in particular the recognition of objects. (Neumann 1993: 566–7)

So visual information processing consists in the reconstruction of a scene from an image caused by that scene. Or to put it more precisely: It consists in the construction of a representation of a scene from an encoding of an image caused by that scene.

Today it is generally assumed that four stages can be distinguished within the process of reconstruction which constitutes visual information processing, and these four stages are usually grouped into two categories — low-level and high-level vision.[2] Each of these four stages — at least

[1] However, generally a single image is not sufficent for this reconstruction. In practice one therefore often does not work with individual images, but sequences of images. It is obvious that reconstructions of temporally extended dynamic scenes are only possible on the basis of such sequences.

[2] For the following cf. e.g. Neumann 1993: 569–70.

according to Marr (1982) — leads to new representations, until in the end a representation of the corresponding three-dimensional physical scene results.[3]

The first step in low-level visual processing — leading to a *primal sketch* — aims at *segmentation of the image*. For this, the isolation and representation of the central elements of the picture, such as edges, homogenous areas, texture etc. is crucial.

The second step in low-level visual processing — leading to what Marr calls a *2½D–sketch* — is already concerned with the interpretation of elements of the image as elements of the scene; that is to say, elements of images are correlated with parts of real three-dimensional scenes. For example: An edge in the image is interpreted as a shadow border, a red area as a wall of a house, a green textured area as a grassy patch, etc.

The first step in high-level visual processing concerns the *recognition of objects*. On the basis of the segmented representation of the structure of the image made available by low-level vision, the high-level processes must first determine what objects are present in the scene, which properties these objects have and in which ways they are interrelated. In general this presupposes substantial knowledge of what objects look like when seen from different perspectives, because recognition of objects is essentially the reversal of the image-creating process.

Further stages of high-level visual processing are sometimes summarized under the catchphrase 'high-level image interpretation'. 'They generally aim at recognizing relationships across object and time boundaries, e.g. interesting configurations of objects, special situations, cohering sequences of movements etc. Similar to the process of object-recognition model-like knowledge of what one wants to recognize plays an important role.' (Neumann 1993: 567)

Schematically then, the individual stages of visual information processing can be summarized as follows:

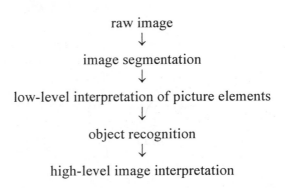

raw image
↓
image segmentation
↓
low-level interpretation of picture elements
↓
object recognition
↓
high-level image interpretation

---

[3] The following four stages are at least taken as a basis by AI scientists in the construction of artificial visual systems. Whether they can be found in the same way in natural systems is not entirely clear. Regarding this point also cf. section III, below.

III

In order to economize the use of storage capacity, it is an aim of AI research to organize the above mentioned stages in such a way, that later steps of image processing can fulfil their task, as far as possible, on the basis of the results of low-level visual processing without recourse to raw images. A 10 second sequence of colour TV pictures has the considerable data volume of 220 GByte. Hence, it appears sensible to burden the available storage as little as possible with raw images.

However, it seems to be characteristic of *human* visual information processing that raw images are not simply discarded after the first steps of processing. If we can rely on introspection, it even seems that the processing of retinal images does not generate successively new *independent* representations, but rather that the results of the individual processing steps are closely interrelated and also each leads to an improvement or better focusing of the original image. Once the first step of low-level processing has been completed, the homogenous areas appear more clearly, the borders between these areas are more distinct; the image itself looks 'sharper'. With the second step of low-level vision the interpretation of the image begins: we cease to see white, grey or differently coloured areas or differently shaped edges, but instead the surface of a table, a shadow or a green-grey structured background. It is as if labels have been stuck on the elements of the image indicating which elements of the scene they are correlated with. After the stage of object recognition, we no longer have the impression of seeing an image; instead we look — so to speak — through the image on to the objects which caused it.[4] Now we see a table, a glass, patterned wall paper, etc. This step, too, usually leads to a clearer focusing of the original image, because the knowledge of how the perceived objects normally look under the given conditions, obviously is used to complete and improve the original image. Finally, we even see the properties and spatial relations of the objects perceived, e.g. that the table is white, that the glass is on the table, etc. So, introspection seems to bear witness to that there are indeed stages in our perceptual process, which correspond to the four stages of

---

[4] In this context Van Gulick (e.g. 1989: 223 ff.) speaks of the high 'semantic transparency' of phenomenal representations. Although this expression certainly is highly suggestive, it does not correspond entirely with the ideas put forward in this paper. For, according to van Gulick, the notion of semantic transparency concerns the 'extent to which a system can be said to understand the content of internal symbols or representations on which it operates' (223). However, this presupposes that perceptual images are representations and this presupposition in my opinion is far from being obvious (cf. section IV, below). Moreover, Van Gulick comes dangerously close to a homunculus-fallacy — for *who* is supposed to understand the meanings of its internal representations? It is an advantage of the account proposed in this paper that it entirely avoids such homunculus-presuppositions, because according to this account the 'semantic transparency' of perceptual images simply consists in the fact that the system closely links these images to the explicit representations of the perceived scenes.

visual information processing which have been postulated by cognitive scientists.[5]

However, these stages do not lead to representations which are independent of each other. This is not to say that not every one of these stages leads to new representations, but simply that these representations are not independent — rather, every one of them also modifies the preceding representations and all of them lead to an alteration and better focusing of the original image.

As already mentioned, in the end we even have the impression of seeing objects and scenes directly, instead of just seeing an image. And this impression to a certain extent is surely right. To a certain extent, however, the image still seems to be there too. It is to this fact that sense data theorists have tried to draw our attention time and again. Moore, for example, invites us to observe carefully what happens when we press one of our eyeballs with one finger while not changing the perspective which we have on to the scene. Basically, there is no change in the perceived scene — we still see the same objects in the same configuration. However, something changes after all: the original image of the scene. Or, to put it more precisely: the elements of the image (homogenous areas and edges) which are caused by the individual objects, change their shapes. The fact that Moore points to is something which all of us are familiar with: we normally 'see through the images' the objects and scenes which have caused these images, but we *can* also concentrate on the images and their elements. In other words: at the end of the perceptual process the original images are still there — albeit in a modified form.

IV

Looking back over the argumentation so far, the reader will hardly be surprised that my central thesis is as follows: if visual information processing is structured in the way I have just described, i.e. if during this processing representations are reconstructed from the original images of a scene in such a way that in the end these images are not discarded, but only modified, then this kind of processing has a phenomenal aspect. This is at least true if the modified original images are as accessible to the system in question as the explicit representations of the scene perceived. Thus, it is crucial for the phenomenal character of these perceptual processes that, in addition to the explicit representations of the perceived scene, the original images are preserved.

With regard to this thesis, one can of course again raise the question: is it not at least conceivable that in a system visual information processing of the kind described takes place without having a phenomenal content at all,

[5] The fact that the process of visual information processing in humans also passes through different stages, however, is shown clearly only in certain psychological experiments, in which perceptual stimuli are shown for a few milliseconds.

or that these processes are accompanied by phenomenal contents differing widely from the usual ones? Before trying to give a direct answer to this question, however, I would like to remark on three issues which, as I hope, will serve indirectly to increase the plausibility of my central claim. The first of these remarks concerns the relation of my thesis to positions which can be found in the literature on this subject.

In the literature, the opinion is widespread that within the framework of a representationalist theory of mind, the existence of phenomenal states can and must be explained through certain types of representations — viz. analogue or pictorial representations (e.g. Nelkin 1989; 1994). The connection between this position and my claim is obvious. At least it is obvious if one does not make a difference between pictures and analogue representations. As regards the latter question, however, I would like to defend an opinion which is in exact opposition to the majority view.

While most authors treat pictures as paradigm cases of representations, images of the kind in question here are nothing more than two-dimensional projections of three-dimensional scenes. That is to say, there is no *prima facie* reason to regard them as representations at all. *A fortiori*, pictures are not a special kind of analogue representations. Indeed, pictures and analogue representations have much less in common than is usually thought. Though not being representations, pictures can be 'interpreted' however, because of the regular connections between them and the scenes whose projections they are. That is to say, scenes can be reconstructed from pictures. Moreover, for our visual system this reconstruction is an especially natural task, since external pictures — *cum grano salis* — generate the same retinal images as the depicted scenes. Since it is the main task of our visual system to interpret retinal images (cf. above), the interpretation of external pictures does not normally present any problem.

However, the difference between pictures and (analogue) representations is not crucial in this context, because the majority of authors who wish to explain phenomenal states within the framework of a representationalist theory of mind through a certain type of representation, have in mind image-like or pictorial representations. So there seems to exist a common intuition that images or pictorial representations may well play a crucial role in the explanation of phenomenal states, and especially so if the explanation of visual impressions is at issue.

Another position with which I have a great affinity has been developed by N. Humphrey in his recent book *A History of the Mind*. According to this position, in their development of the ability to perceive, animals have in the course of evolution developed two distinctly different representational systems.

Since animals exist, the outside world impacts their boundaries (membranes, skins). Light falls on them, objects bump into them, pressure waves press against them, chemicals stick to them. Some of these events are 'good things' for the animal, others are bad. Hence, it constitutes an evolutionary advantage if the animal has the means to sort out the good events from the bad ones, or, in order not to complicate matters too early, to react differently in different cases. 'Natural selection was therefore likely to select for "sensitivity".' (Humphrey 1993: 18)

At first these reactions are still local: the surface contracts or secretes certain chemicals. An important new stage is reached when signals are transmitted from one part of the surface to other parts so that reactions also may take place there. For this enables responses that are better adapted to the animal's needs: for example it may swim away, rather than just recoil from a noxious stimulus.

But even at this stage there is still a fairly direct connection between stimulus ('perception') on the one hand and reaction ('action') on the other. The next stage is reached when sensitivity and responsivity become partially decoupled. Signals from parts of the surface will be transmitted, but they no longer result automatically in definite reactions. Whether, and in what way, the animal reacts, rather depends on a number of other factors which — one could say — are taken into account in a central process of determination.

At this stage it is not yet necessary to store the signals transmitted from the surface or to represent them permanently. However, this becomes indispensable if it proves necessary to detach the reaction *in time* from the stimulus. Thus, a first system of representations is developed, if not only the sensory side and the response side of the process are partially de- coupled, but there is also a delay between stimulation and response. A central site has to evolve where representations of stimuli can be stored for a certain amount of time.

One answer to the question of what these representations represent seems to suggest itself: the proximal stimuli which disturb the boundaries of the animal — the light which strikes the surface, the objects which bump into the animal, the chemical substances with which it comes into contact. However, if we examine the matter a little more closely, it becomes clear that the information transmitted from the surface is less dependent upon the proximal stimuli and more upon the effect of these stimuli on the surface. If two different objects affect the surface in the same way, the same information will be transmitted; if the same object has a different effect at different times, the information transmitted will be different. In other words: the first central representations, which in the course of time take shape in animals, carry information about the state of the animal itself, rather than about proximal stimuli, or, to put it more philosophically: they carry information about how it is for the animal when its surface is affected by certain proximal stimuli. It is, therefore, not surprising that Humphrey identifies these representations with 'raw sensations'.

> So the phenomenology of sensory experiences came first. Before there were any kinds of phenomena there were 'raw sensations' — tastes, smells, tickles, pains, sensations of warmth, of light, of sound and so on. (Humphrey 1993: 21)

Thus the first representations only provide animals with answers to the question 'what is happening to me?' However, for the survival of most animals it is undoubtedly just as important to know what is happening around them. Hence, answers to the question 'what is happening out there?' are of the utmost interest. How can representational systems be developed which provide answers to this question?

In a nutshell, Humphrey's claim is that in the course of evolution, in addition to the first representational system, a second one developed, which also takes the signals transmitted from the surface as a point of departure, but processes these signals in a radically different way.

> By the end of the first stage of evolution sense organs existed with connections to a central processor, and most of the requisite information about potential signs was being received as 'input'. But the subsequent processing of this information, leading to subjective sensory states, had to do with quality rather than quantity, the transient present rather than permanent identity, me-ness rather than otherness. In order that the same information could now be used to represent the outside world, a whole new style of processing had to evolve, with an emphasis less on the subjective present and more on object permanence, less on immediate responsiveness and more on future possibilities, less on what it is like for me and more on how what 'it' signifies fits into the larger picture of a stable external world.

> To cut a long story short, there developed in consequence two distinct kinds of mental representation, involving very different styles of information processing. While one path led to the qualia of subjective feelings and first-person knowledge of the self, the other led to the intentional objects of cognition and objective knowledge of the external physical world. (Humphrey 1993: 22)

The main point of Humphrey's theory can therefore be summarized as follows:

(a)   In the course of evolution, two fundamentally different ways of processing stimuli which affect the surface of animals developed ('sensation' and 'perception'). The first leads to representations, which encode answers to the question 'what is happening to me?', the second to representations which answer the question 'what is happening out there?'

(b)   Representations of the first kind account for the phenomenal aspect of perceptual processes.

(c)   Although both types of information processing are usually closely linked in the various perceptual processes, they nevertheless remain different and could, therefore, occur independently of each other.

Without any doubt there are certain differences between the model developed in this paper and Humphrey's theory — however, there are obviously many parallels between the accounts, too. For example, representations of the original images, which according to the position developed in this paper are responsible for the phenomenal aspect of visual perception, can without any problem be seen as representations of what happens on the retina — i.e. as representations of the first type of Humphrey's theory. Since the fundamental affinity of the two accounts is clear already from these sketchy remarks, I shall not pursue these details here.

The second remark concerns the much discussed question of what evolutionary advantage phenomenal consciousness might offer. In this paper, of course, I cannot answer this question in a general manner, but I would like to mention a very important aspect: the role of perceptual images in the control of behaviour, which can be demonstrated even through very simple examples. Everyone knows the situation (e.g. on a motorway) in which the task is to maintain a constant distance with the car in front. This can be achieved by calculating, as part of the process of object recognition (i.e. *during high-level visual processing*), the distance between one's own car and the car in front and by accordingly increasing, lowering or maintaining constant one's speed, depending upon whether this distance has become bigger, smaller or remained the same. However, the same effect can also be achieved with much less effort if only the system tries to ensure that the *size* of the *picture* of the car in front stays unchanged, i.e. if it increases, lowers or maintains a constant speed, depending upon whether the size of the picture shrinks, grows or remains unchanged. That is to say, the same behaviour which is adapted to the situation can be generated without recourse to the results of high-level visual processing, but only by utilizing the results of the first step of low-level visusal processing, i.e. with reference to the elements of the image. Moreover, it seems plausible to assume that the second way is much quicker and generally more reliable. Even finding one's way through a room with chairs and tables and avoiding obstacles in general can often be regulated with the help of a relatively simple image analysis.

As a second example let us take the action of grasping something. One can obviously control this action, too, by using the results of high-level visual processing. First one determines the coordinates of the object one wants to grasp and then designs a plan with the help of which muscle contractions one can move one's hand to these coordinates. However, this is a lengthy and — e.g. if one attempts to grasp a moving object — very complex process often with an unreliable outcome. How difficult this type of behavioural control really is, can be illustrated by imagining that one has to grasp an object with *closed eyes*, only on the basis of information about the location of the object and one's hand and which effect certain muscle contractions have on the position of the latter.

Obviously, human behavioural control works in a completely different way. How central a role perceptual images play in this control is apparent from how badly this control functions when one closes the eyes or is blindfolded. Therefore, it does not seem too far fetched to claim that the grasping of objects is also largely controlled through perceptual images and their elements. The details are not as yet entirely clear, but one can easily imagine that in grasping we do not aim for congruency of the coordinates of our hand and the object we want to grasp, but rather at bringing the *image elements* which are produced by my hand and the object closer. (Additionally there would obviously have to be a mechanism which takes account of the dimension of depth.) Maybe the image element of the object even acts as a kind of attractor which 'attracts' the image element of my hand.[6] On the whole, it seems very likely to me that in planning actions, we do not only use our knowledge of which bodily movements have what effect *in the world*, but we especially use our knowledge of how *our perceptual images* change as a result of these movements. The efficiency of bodily movements can often already be judged on the basis of the analysis of these images — as shown in the above mentioned example where the task consisted in maintaining a constant distance with the car in front.

Finally, the third remark concerns the fact that the position put forward here accords well with familiar neurobiological findings. As is well known, the axons of the retinal ganglion cells are collected into the optic nerves, which leave the eyes roughly at the height of the fovea. The optic nerves converge at the base of the skull and exchange half of their fibres at the optic chiasma. After this re-sorting process the optic nerves travel to the lateral geniculate nuclei. These nuclei contain approximately the same number of neural fibres as the optic nerves, and these fibres project directly on to the primary visual cortex in the occipital lobe (area 17). Area 17 in turn projects in an ordered manner, i.e. in the form of a one-to-one mapping, on to the secondary visual area (area 18), which itself projects on to at least three more structures: on to a region called MT, on to the tertiary visual area (area 19) and on to another visual area called V4. This kind of structuring continues — one area always projects on to a few others. In addition, every single one of these areas passes back signals to the areas from which it receives inputs. Moreover, the individual areas additionally project on to deeper structures of the brain — e.g. the superior colliculi and different parts of the thalamus. Finally, all the visual fields receive inputs from sub-structures of the thalamus: just as the lateral geniculate nuclei project on to the primary visual cortex, other parts of the thalamus are connected to other areas.

---

[6] This interesting idea I first encountered in a discussion with the psychologist Michael Stadler (Bremen).

In this context two points are of particular relevance. First, the fact that the projection of the axons of the retinal ganglion cells — even after switching over in the lateral geniculate nuclei — are organized in a *retino-topic* manner. Adjacent ganglion cells project on to adjacent parts of area 17, so that the topological structure of the firing patterns of the ganglion cells remain intact under this projection. In other words, *the firing pattern of the neurons in the primary visual cortex, too, can be taken as an encoding of the retinal image.* Secondly, the fact that later visual areas send signals back to the areas from which they receive inputs, can easily be linked to the observation that later stages of visual information processing, amongst other things, always lead to an alteration and improvement of the original image. In my view, it therefore does not seem implausible to assume that the primary visual cortex is the physical correlate of the phenomenologically relevant perceptual image (or at least constitutes an essential part of this physical correlate).

This assumption is also supported by pathophysiological findings. It has been known for a long time that small lesions, limited infarcts or small tumors in the primary visual cortex lead to blindness of a circumscribed part of the visual field, or, if the whole of area 17 is affected, to complete blindness. One refers to these cases as cortical blindness in order to distinguish them from instances in which the reason for the blindness is a deficiency in the eyes or the optic nerves. Obviously, cortical blindness is exactly what is to be expected if the primary visual cortex really is the physical correlate of the phenomenal perceptual image. Any damage of the correlate ought to lead to a loss within this image and to a failure of all higher representations which depend upon a proper functioning of this perceptual image.

In the last few years the phenomenon of 'blindsight' has been much discussed in this context. This phenomenon manifests itself particularly in the fact that patients suffering from cortical blindness and therefore say that they literally do not see anything in some areas of their visual field, nevertheless possess certain 'information' about what they claim they do not see. For example, under forced choice conditions they give many more correct answers than could statistically be expected if there were a complete lack of information. In the model outlined above this effect could be explained as follows: later processing stages which, owing to neural wiring, receive inputs not only from the primary visual cortex (or later areas), but also from the thalamus, can still fulfil their respective tasks (at least partially). However, in these cases there is no phenomenal perceptual image since this image is tied to the primary visual cortex which is seriously damaged. And it is this fact that accounts for the effect that the person in question — subjectively completely justified — reports not having seen anything.

Other phenomena concerning split-brain patients whose corpus callosum has been cut can also be explained within the framework of this model. If an object is presented only in the left half of these patients' visual field, they cannot verbally answer the question of which object is shown to them. This is due to the fact — as is generally assumed — that stimuli of the right half of the retina are only transmitted to the right hemisphere and that in the case of split-brain patients, therefore, the parts of the brain involved in the production of language in the left hemisphere receive no (direct) information about the objects which are only shown in the left half of the visual field. Within the framework of the model suggested here, this would mean that split-brain patients to a certain extent possess an intact perceptual image of the objects presented, but that higher (especially language related structures) have no access to this image and that therefore the patients lack the ability to give adequate answers.

V

Let us return to the crucial issue of whether it is plausible to think that processes of visual perception, which are structured in the way described above, always have a phenomenal aspect. Why should the fact that perceptual images play a central role in these processes make all the difference?

If two systems A and B are functionally equivalent, i.e. if they have the same functional structure and, at time t, are in identical functional states, then this implies that the two systems display exactly the same behaviour at t. This is so, because functional states are characterized by their causal relations to inputs, outputs and other functional states. If two functionally equivalent systems are in identical functional states, the same inputs therefore cause identical internal processes, which in the end must lead to the same behavioural output. Proponents of 'absent' or 'inverted qualia' arguments must, therefore, accept the assumption that it is possible that two systems whose behaviour is indistinguishable, nevertheless differ radically with regard to the phenomenal content of their respective states. Or (more strongly) that it is even possible that of two systems which behave exactly alike, only one possesses phenomenal states at all, while the other lacks these states completely.

Despite all the difficulties it implies, this consequence has been accepted by many philosophers, since it seems intuitively plausible to claim that behavioural evidence never suffices to decide in which phenomenal state a given system is. However as early as 1975, S. Shoemaker pointed out that the situation begins to look very different if two systems do not just display the same behaviour, but also agree in all *beliefs about their own states* in general and their own phenomenal states in particular. Proponents of the view that even the totality of behavioural evidence is not sufficient to judge which phenomenal content certain states have, usually hold at the same time that another, direct, way exists to decide this question — *introspection*. However, according to Shoemaker introspection depends upon what a being believes or knows about its own states. Hence, if two beings not only both behave in a way characteristic for beings which are in pain, but also both believe in the same manner that they feel pain, then not only all the behavioural evidence supports the point of view that they really feel pain, but also all introspective evidence. And what other evidence could there be for the claim that at least one of these beings does not feel pain?

> So one way of putting our question is to ask whether anything could be evidence (for anyone) that someone was not in pain, given that it follows from the states he is in . . . that the totality of possible behavioral evidence *plus* the totality of possible introspective evidence points unambiguously to the conclusion that he is in pain? I do not see how anything could be. (Shoemaker 1975: 189–90)

If two systems not only correspond in their behaviour, but also in all beliefs concerning their own states in general and their own phenomenal states in particular, it is impossible — at least from an epistemic point of view — to differentiate between them as regards the phenomenal content of their mental states.

However, a system whose visual information processing is organized in the way described above, and which additionally possesses meta-representations concerning not only the representations of the perceived scenes which form the final result of this processing, but also concerning its earlier stages and especially representations of the modified original image, exactly fulfills this condition — at least with respect to the phenomenal aspects of *visual* perception. In any case when questioned the system will give answers not only about the objects and situations which are accessible to it on the basis of its visual apparatus, but also about the visual impressions it has gained in this context. It will say not only that the table in front of it is square and that a glass is on the table, but also (for example) that the upper rim of the glass looks elliptical although it is round, that the surface of the table looks slightly reddish or that the wallpaper in the background looks so faded that it cannot discern its pattern.

If one attributes beliefs to this system (and I cannot conceive of any reason not to do this), these beliefs do not just refer to its environment, but also to its own states and in particular to something which *we* would call visual impressions and which the system itself describes *in exactly the way* in which we describe our own visual impressions. So what kind of evidence could there be from which we could conclude that the system, unlike ourselves, does not possess visual impressions? Evidence that would not at the same time lead us to doubt that our fellow-humans, or indeed we ourselves, have visual impressions?

This point is closely connected to a second one. Systems like the one described can distinguish between how things are, and how they seem to be, in exactly the same way as we can. Some philosophers, inspired by Wittgenstein's later thought, hold that sentences like 'the wall looks red' as well as 'the wall seems to be red' have nothing to do with any phenomenal qualities; rather these sentences ought to be understood in a performative sense. According to those philosophers, when I utter these sentences I only indicate that I am not prepared to commit myself to the truth of my statements. If anyone believes what I say on the basis of my utterances, he or she does so at his/her own risk. By contrast when I say 'the wall is red' or even 'I know that the wall is red', I am accountable for the content of these statements, and I therefore run the risk of being held responsible if things turn out to be different from how I say they are.

R. Chisholm, however, has shown that the performative use of 'to seem' and 'to look' at best constitutes one possible use (Chisholm 1989: 20–22). There are also other uses which after all seem to be related to phenomenal qualities; e.g. there is a way of speaking in which it makes sense to say:

(1) The wall seems to me grey in this light, but I know that it is red.

And even:

(2) The wall seems to me red in this light, and I know that it is really red.

Especially in the second example 'to seem' cannot have the performative use as mentioned above, because if this were the case, the second part of the sentence would defeat the point of the first. Obviously this is not the case. However, if 'to look' or 'to seem' in these examples are not used in the their performative sense — in what sense then *are* they used?

In order to answer this question, it is important to ascertain in which situations we use 'to seem' or 'to look' in the non-performative sense of example (2). The paradigmatic case in my opinion is this: in a psychophysical experiment I am requested by the experimenter to attend exclusively to the colour which a wall in front of me seems to have in different lighting; a wall which I could satisfy myself earlier to be white. What does the experimenter want to know from me? Obviously he is not interested in my beliefs as to the real colour of the wall, for I know that the wall is white and this belief does not change in the course of the experiment. Hence, he wants to learn about the subjective *impressions* which I have under different experimental conditions. If he asks me which colour the wall *seems* to have, he assumes that not my objective beliefs, but my visual impressions will vary during the experiment. It is these changes that he wishes to know about.

This brings us back to the point I have already mentioned at the end of section III. Owing to the manner in which our perceptual system is organized, we are not only able to say something about the perceived objects and scenes, but we can also concentrate on the (modified) original image and report how this image changes without thereby implying that these changes presuppose changes in the perceived scene itself. However, this also means that every system, in which the process of visual information processing is structured in the way outlined above, can also distinguish between changes regarding the perceived scene and changes which only concern the *image* of that scene, i.e. how this scene *appears* to the system. In this sense the distinction between how things are, and how they just seem to be, is entirely natural for a system like that.

To sum up: The thesis put forward in this paper is that perceptual processes in which representations of real three-dimensional scenes are constructed from raw images, in such a way that in the end these images are not discarded, but only modified, always have a phenomenal aspect. And the main argument for this thesis is that systems whose visual information processing is organized in this way do not only behave in exactly the same way as we do (e.g. grasp objects in the same quick and elegant manner), but also have the same beliefs with regard to themselves and their perceptions as we do, or at least talk about themselves and their perceptions in the same way as we do. Just like ourselves, they can distinguish between perceived scenes and visual impressions; just like ourselves they can differentiate between how things really are and how they only seem to be. What could, therefore, count in favour of the claim that these systems nevertheless do not possess mental states with phenomenal content?

References

Ballard, D. & Brown, C. (1982). *Computer Vision*. Englewood Cliffs, NJ: Prentice Hall.
Chisholm, R. (1989). *Theory of Knowledge*. 3rd ed. Englewood Cliffs, NJ: Prentice Hall.
Humphrey, N. (1993). *A History of the Mind*. London: Random House.
Marr, D. (1982). *Vision*. San Francisco: Freeman & Co.
Nelkin, N. (1989). Unconscious sensations. *Philosophical Psychology*, 2, 129–41.
Nelkin, N. (1994). Phenomena and representation. *British Journal for the Philosophy of Science*, 45, 527–47.
Neumann, B. (1993). Bildverstehen — ein Überblick. In G. Görz (ed), *Einführung in die künstliche Intelligenz*. Bonn/Paris/Reading, MA: Addison-Wesley.
Shoemaker, S. (1975). Functionalism and qualia. *Philosophical Studies*, 27, 291–315. Reprinted in Shoemaker 1984.
Van Gulick (1989). What difference does consciousness make? *Philosophical Topics*, 17, 211–30.

Thomas Metzinger

Faster than Thought
Holism, Homogeneity and Temporal Coding

In this speculative paper I would like to show how important the *integration of mental content* is for a theory of phenomenal consciousness. I will draw the reader's attention to two manifestations of this problem which already play a role in the empirical sciences concerned with consciousness: The *binding problem* and the *superposition problem*. In doing so I hope to be able to leave the well-trodden paths of the debate over consciousness. My main concern is to gain a fresh access to the familiar theoretical difficulties associated with the concept of 'consciousness'.

My discussion has three parts. The first part is an attempt to define the explananda with which I am concerned. This will be done by adopting the style of a deliberately naive phenomenological descent and examining two interesting properties of the phenomenon of consciousness 'itself', from the first-person stance. The second part shifts back to a third-person perspective and considers a promising approach in neurobiology. This approach could point towards a naturalistic account of these properties of the phenomenon in the realm of *empirical* research into consciousness. In the third and concluding section I rise step by step towards the genuinely philosophical level of the discussion in the style of a speculative semantic ascent. In doing so I will make several assumptions concerning the genesis of phenomenal consciousness. These assumptions will serve as a testing ground for a new model: I will offer some ideas about how models originating in brain research might be helpful in developing a clearer conceptual analysis of the explananda. As a first step, I will now attempt to isolate these explananda.

I wish to thank Antonia Barke and David Chalmers for their all their effort and continuing help with the English version of this paper. I am also indebted to Antonia Barke, Andreas Bartels, David J. Chalmers, Andreas Engel, Güven Güzeldere, Peter König, Martin Kurthen, Lars Muckli, Eva Ruhnau and Michael Tye for valuable comments and critical discussions.

I. Holism and Homogeneity: Higher-Order Phenomenal Properties

The space of consciousness is the space of subjective experience. Since this is the space in which the world and we ourselves *appear* to ourselves on an experiential level, I will also call it the *phenomenal space*. Many people believe that our phenomenal space is also a *representational* space: In this space we represent a part of the world and of ourselves *to* ourselves. The phenomenal representata, i.e. the vehicles of representation bearing subjective content, I will henceforth call 'mental models', without trying to explicate this concept further at this point.[1] Our conscious space — this is the basic idea — consists of mental models which are often embedded in each other. The largest of the mental models active in this space is our conscious 'model of reality' or 'model of the world'. This phenomenal model of the world contains all the other conscious mental models and its content is identical with the overall content of our conscious space. As I mentioned above, our conscious space is the space of experience. But since we are beings who almost constantly fail to recognize our mental models *as* models,[2] our phenomenal space is characterized by an all-embracing naive realism, which we are incapable of transcending in standard situations. In this way, the totality of mental contents which fill this space form a structure that can be described from the external perspective of science as a self-referentially opaque phenomenal model of the world. From the internal perspective of the system activating this model, however, this structure is quite simply subjectively experienced *reality*: the *only* reality existing for this system. One of the main challenges for any naturalistic theory of mind is that of providing us with a clear account of this transition: How does a model become this reality?

[1] I am therefore concerned with *phenomenal* mental models. In doing so, I am loosely taking up earlier work by Craik 1943 and Johnson-Laird 1983. Craik and Johnson-Laird have used this concept for different purposes, but it is well-suited to serving as a unified starting-point for a PDP-inspired theory of *phenomenal* representation; cf. Metzinger 1993, especially sections 2.2 and 2.3.1, see also Metzinger 1995b. Following this line of thought, the space of phenomenal modelling would not be identical with the space of representational modelling, rather it forms a partition of this space: the *conscious* model of reality. A survey of a variety of empirical findings supporting the assumption that the content of phenomenal consciousness is a model of the world, which is used to generate behaviour and which enables the system to simulate and anticipate future events, is given by Yates 1985.

[2] In non-pathological waking states there is a tiny part of the self-model which is not 'self-referentially opaque' in the way just indicated: Certain of its parts — higher cognitive operations, for instance 'volitional acts' and 'rational thought' — are clearly recognized as self-generated constructs by the system. Perhaps it is for this reason that philosophers have traditionally been most interested in these areas of the human mind: Only these parts enable us to understand and express the self-referential opacity of the rest of the model, because they themselves are *not* characterized by it. In conscious thought we are — at least in the context of a deliberately induced mental simulation — able to distance ourselves somewhat from ourselves and in this way we become, at a later stage, also conceptually able to grasp the perspectivalness of our conscious space. Cf. Nagel 1986 and Metzinger 1993, 1995b.

What we really need is a mathematical model describing the phenomenal ontology of the human brain — i.e. that which *exists* according to conscious experience — in a precise and empirically plausible manner. Philosophical analysis can then, for instance, explain the relation of the phenomenal properties described by this model to folk psychology and investigate the *modality* of the relation between the phenomenal properties thus described and the physical properties upon which they are based.[3] My aim in this paper, however, is much more modest. I shall concentrate on two particularly interesting phenomenal properties. Our phenomenal space and the respective phenomenal model of reality active within it possess two properties which I believe to be of crucial importance for any theory of consciousness which takes the first-person perspective seriously. In the style of an uncritical phenomenological turn 'towards the things themselves', I shall first describe both these properties from the first-person perspective as properties of *reality* itself, pretending that we have direct and epistemologically unproblematic access to these properties through the evidence of subjective perception and the traditional descriptive systems of folk psychology. My statements, however, refer exclusively to human beings in ordinary waking states: The intended class of systems is formed by human organisms in 'non-pathological waking states'.[4] Thus I will steer clear of any fundamental discussion of the question of what the philosophical problem of consciousness consists in *at all* — rather, I shall now finally shift to the first-person perspective and confine myself to the following two aspects of the problem.

I am *one* person living in *one* world: For the majority of us this seems to be an obvious and indubitable truth, since for most of us this is one of those intuitions concerning our own consciousness and reality in general, which we almost never state explicitly or even less call into doubt. The reason for this is that most of us can hardly imagine any alternative situations. We have never experienced phenomenal states in which we were many different persons at the same time or in which we simultaneously existed in different parallel worlds. Only professional philosophers or patients with severe neurological disorders, people who have experimented with major doses of hallucinogens or those suffering from *multiple personality disorder* are sometimes capable of developing a more vivid idea of what it would be like, if the numerical identity of the phenomenal world or the unity of self-consciousness were suspended. In standard situations we are simply unable to carry out the corresponding mental simulations.[5] For this reason our

---

[3] Here I point to David Chalmers' important differentiation between the *logical* and the *natural* (i.e. *nomological*) supervenience of consciousness. Cf. Chalmers 1996b.

[4] I am, of course, well aware that this is a very vague characterization, but in this paper it fully suffices for my purposes.

[5] 'Mental simulations' are processes in which mental models of *possible worlds* are activated. Mental imagery and deliberately induced acts of imagination are examples of such

phenomenal world and the phenomenal self do not only appear as numerically identical to us, but even appear as *indivisible* — a fact which was
already exploited by Descartes in section 36 of his *Sixth Meditation* in order
to construct an — albeit unconvincing — argument for the ontological
distinction of mind and body. I think that there is a highest-order phenomenal property corresponding to this classical concept of 'indivisibility':[6] The
property of *wholeness*. The wholeness of our reality (and of ourselves in it)
can easily be discovered by all of us from our own experience. This
wholeness is much more than a simple unity in the sense of the concept of
numerical identity mentioned above: I am not able voluntarily to split or
dissolve my global experiential space — *this reality* — or my own experienced identity — *myself*. On the other hand, the contents of my experience
characteristically display a high selectivity: The surrounding world, which
in conscious perception seems to be immediately given, is always pre-
segmented, for example into a variety of objects which may even overlap
with or cover each other. By directing my attention to a wide variety of
areas of my world I am even able to detach the most different figures from
a background and then perceive or imagine them as separate units in
subjective experience. That is, although I am not able to dissolve the
highest-order wholeness of reality or of myself simply by a reversible act
of will, I am perfectly able to perceive or even actively *generate* lower-
order phenomenal wholes within the space which is held together by this
highest-order property.

Perhaps this holistic character of reality, which is stronger than mere
numerical identity and which cannot be transcended experientially, could
be described as phenomenal *coherence*: Our conscious experience of reality
is held together internally by a principle or a mechanism, which itself is
subjectively inaccessible. This coherence of my reality has nothing to do

---

processes, as are daydreams and spontaneous fantasies. What we cannot mentally simulate is
what we cannot *imagine*.

[6] The *indivisibility* of consciousness is a traditional topic of the modern philosophy of mind,
and not only Descartes has tried to utilize it for his purposes. Soon Kant turned the synthetic
achievement of the *unity* of consciousness as unity of apperception into a central topic of
German Idealism. The phenomenological aspect of the problem has been very clearly
formulated by Franz Brentano: *The unity of consciousness, as we know with evidence through
inner perception, consists in the fact that all mental phenomena which occur within us
simultaneously such as seeing and hearing, thinking, judging and reasoning, loving and
hating, desiring and shunning, etc., no matter how different they may be, all belong to one
unitary reality only if they are inwardly perceived as existing together. They constitute
phenomenal parts of a mental phenomenon, the elements of which are neither distinct things
nor parts of distinct things but belong to a real unity.* But Brentano also made clear that no
ontological simplicity follows from this unity: *Furthermore, it is necessary to emphasize that
the unity of consciousness does not exclude either a plurality of quantitative parts or spatial
extension [. . .] It is certain that inner perception does not show us any extension; there is
a difference, however, between not showing something and showing that something does not
exist.* Cf. Brentano 1973 [1874]: 163-4; 165-6.

with the concept of coherence in physics or logic. Rather, it is responsible for a succinct phenomenal holism, which we ought to take into account on the conceptual level. Although a world made out of discrete, building block-like elements could well be a unity, it could never be a whole. But my world is not a toy world composed of little building blocks: it is also a *living* reality whose parts interact in a quasi-organic way (in the sense of the German concept *Erleben*). This concretely experienced unity of a diversity is accompanied by a multitude of dynamic part/whole relations. Thus, the additional phenomenological aspect of holism or wholeness which goes beyond mere unity results from the fact that the parts constituting the phenomenal model of reality are not *elements*, but *parts* of this reality. For this reason, if we want to understand the holistic character of our phenomenal world, we will have to take its multi-levelled mereological structure as the starting point of our investigation.

Another aspect is important in order to understand what else can be meant by 'wholeness'. Although this aspect is not at the centre of my discussion, we will repeatedly encounter it whenever we ask ourselves how a model can turn into a reality which is phenomenally *present*.[7] This second aspect consists in the fact that the experiential contents appearing in our conscious space are joined together into a holistic entity of the highest order, something we might call a global *Gestalt*, by spatial neighbouring relations and especially by temporal identity within an experienced present, i.e. by subjective simultaneity, by being given within a single psychological moment. This global *Gestalt* quality is necessary for the whole to become a reality: The whole is always given to us in a single psychological moment, that is to say in the experienced present of a subjective *Now*. The phenomenal *presence* of the whole springs from this 'now', i.e. from the temporal identity of a diversity of experiential contents. What does this mean? It means that the holistic diversity of phenomenal contents becomes a coherent reality because there is an elementary 'window of presence'. One thing cannot be doubted from the first-person perspective: I always experience the wholeness of reality *now*. This yields a first phenomenological concept of conscious experience: Conscious experience is the phenomenal presence of an all-embracing whole.

At this stage I would like to introduce a concept to which I will later return: subjectively experienced reality is a 'phenomenal Holon', an experientially present whole in the sense defined above. It always emerges in the context of a subjective present and is internally characterized by part/whole relationships. We are thus dealing with a variant of the classical philosophical question concerning the unity of consciousness: What, from an external theoretical perspective, appears as the issue of the unity and indivisibility of consciousness, turns out to be 'the wholeness and presence of reality'

---

[7] See also section 2.4 in the general introduction at the beginning of this book and footnote 25.

under a simple phenomenological description. In this version, the problem of the unity of consciousness consists in offering a conceptually convincing analysis of the fact that from the perspective of the first-person, this reality is a phenomenal Holon. This fact is my first explanandum.

My second explanandum is the *homogeneity* of elementary phenomenal properties. We are now moving from the highest to the lowest level: We are no longer concerned with a higher-order phenomenal property of the overall space of consciousness, but with a higher-order phenomenal property of the smallest constitutive parts of this space. I am, of course, alluding to qualia. Simple sensations of sensory consciousness instantiate first-order phenomenal properties: for example the subjectively experienced quality of turquoise in the visual experience of a tropical lagoon, or the olfactory quality of sandalwood in a conscious experience of smell. Such qualities themselves possess a fascinating, but philosophically problematic higher-order property, because they are *homogeneous*. This theoretical problem also has its — albeit younger — precursor in the form of the *grain problem*.[8] Let us look back to the classical example of Wilfrid Sellars, the pink ice cube:

> *Pink* does not seem to be made up of imperceptible qualities in the way in which being a ladder is made up of being cylindrical (the rungs), rectangular (the frame), wooden, etc. The manifest ice cube presents itself to us as something which is pink through and through, a pink continuum, all the regions of which, however small, are pink. It presents itself to us as *ultimately homogeneous*; and an ice cube variegated in colour is, though not homogeneous in its specific colour, 'ultimately homogeneous', in the sense to which I am calling attention, with respect to the generic trait of being coloured. (Sellars 1963: 26.)

For Sellars, the essential question of the grain problem was whether it could, in principle, be possible within the conceptual framework of neuro-physiology to define states which in their intrinsic character show a suffi-cient similarity to sensations. Only states of this kind, Sellars thought, could render a reductive solution of the mind–body problem (in the sense of early identity theory) plausible.

> The answer seems clearly to be 'no'. This is not to say that neurophysiological states cannot be defined (in principle) which have a high degree of analogy to the sensations of the manifest image. That this can be done is an elementary fact of psycho-physics. The trouble is, rather, that the feature which we referred to as 'ultimate homogeneity', and which characterizes the perceptible quality of things, e.g. their colour, seems to be essentially lacking in the

---

[8] Cf. Sellars 1963 and also 1965. Texts which I found helpful were Green 1979, Gunderson 1974, Lockwood 1993, Maxwell 1978, Richardson & Muilenburg 1982. A good account of the development of Sellars' philosophical treatment of the problem is given by Kurthen 1990.

domain of the definable states of the nerves and their interactions. Putting it crudely, colour expanses in the manifest world consist of regions which are themselves colour expanses, and these consist in their turn of regions which are colour expanses, and so on; whereas the states of a group of neurons, though it has regions which are also states of groups of neurons, has ultimate regions which are *not* states of groups of neurons but rather states of single neurons. And the same is true if we move to the finer grained level of biochemical process. (Sellars 1963: 35.)

Returning to the first-person perspective, I would like to illustrate the subjectively non-transcendable homogeneity of phenomenal qualities by using an example from the art world. Like Sellars' argument, the example dates from the beginning of the second half of this century. In the Fifties, the artist Yves Klein studied the power of pure colour more intensely than anyone else. His monochrome blue paintings are famous and have in subsequent years exerted a strong influence on the international avant-garde movement. In his crusade for the spiritual power of pure colouredness, Yves Klein even tried to turn his favourite colour — ultramarine — into his own identity and his official trade-mark. He went so far as to have the pure ultramarine blue which he developed patented under the name of *International Klein Blue* (I.K.B.) on 19 May 1960.[9] Indeed, he himself soon became known under the name *Yves Klein le monochrome*.

When one looks at one of his monochromes and disregards the grainy texture of the surface, one experiences a pure and simple quality, namely a pure and intense ultramarine. In the general introduction to this volume, I used the *Pantone Blue 72* of the cover as a first example of a phenomenal property. *International Klein Blue* belongs to the same phenomenal type, but it possesses considerably more subjective power and depth. This subjective quality of colouredness is once more homogeneous in the sense indicated by Sellars. For Yves Klein, the fascination of this homogeneity lay in the subjective aspects of presence, immateriality and the intensive concretization of a dimensionless spatiality.[10] For philosophers, however, the homogeneity of phenomenal properties is so particularly fascinating because it generates conceptual predicates which may defy definition. Can a colour predicate like *International Klein Blue* have a successor predicate within the scientific world view, for instance in a scientific theory of phenomenal consciousness, or is *International Klein Blue* a *primitive* predicate? For Sellars a 'primitive' predicate refers to properties which are ascribed to things that are made up exclusively of things which in turn

[9] The patent carries the number 63471, the full text of the application can be found in Stich 1994: 259.

[10] Sidra Stich (1994: 78) quotes a sentence from Bachelard, in which Yves Klein enthusiastically recognized his own project: 'First there is *nothing*, then there is a *deep* nothing and finally there is a *blue depth*.'

possess this property. For some non-dualistic philosophers this would mean that single molecules of Rhodopas, vinylchloride, ethyl alcohol, ethyl acetate (out of which the substance *I.K.B.* is made) themselves possess the colour of *International Klein Blue*. Other non-dualistic philosophers would see themselves driven to the conclusion that a certain number of the nerve cells firing in our visual cortex while we are looking at one of Yves Klein's monochrome pictures, are in fact *International Klein Blue*. Of course this assumption is absurd in both cases.

A solution to this problem — a naturalization of my second explanandum — seems to be of central importance for any theory of sensory consciousness. The problem can be conceptually generalized in different ways, for instance — as Sellars thought — by moving from the homogeneity of monochrome colours to the more abstract property of *colouredness* in general. The homogeneity of elementary sensations, however — as they can be given to us as *International Klein Blue*, the tone of a cello or the smell of sandalwood — is a *pre-reflexive* and to a large extent *non-discursive* characteristic of our subjective experience: The homogeneity of phenomenal properties seems to be impenetrable to cognitive operations and, for this reason, it is very hard to express adequately on a verbal level. What Sellars called *ultimate homogeneity* seems to be a paradigmatic example of the ineffability of the subjective quality of experience. For this reason, I will try to offer a metaphorical description of the property in question by borrowing from physics and mathematics.

What does it mean to say that *International Klein Blue* is homogeneous? The primary phenomenal property is characterized by a kind of 'field quality', generating a subjective *continuum* in a certain subregion of our conscious space.[11] If, for instance, we visually experience objects which possess the property of *International Klein Blue*, the following statement seems to be always true: There is always a finite region within phenomenal space, in which no changes take place with regard to the quality in question.[12] I believe that it is precisely for this reason that we experience subjective qualities as immediately *given*. Let us now turn to the second

---

[11] This indicates a second and much more radical possibility of generalizing Sellars' concept of 'homogeneity', namely by applying it to our phenomenal space *as a whole*: One could treat 'consciousness' (in the sense of a primitive one-place-predicate) as an invariant parameter and not as a background variable which is subject to considerable variations. Two prominent neuroscientists explicitly operating with the field-metaphor while applying it to the *global* quality of primitive 'consciousness' are Marcel Kinsbourne and Benjamin Libet. Cf. Kinsbourne 1988, 1993, Libet 1994.

[12] Of course this is one of the ways in which philosophers have tried to express the original grain-problem. (Compare the formulations of Meehl 1966: 167 and Green 1979: 566 f.) It is interesting to note that if we were to imagine counter-examples with a continuous, flowing change of a certain type of qualitative content, i.e. cases in which we might *not* be able to discriminate any finite regions in phenomenal space any more, the Sellarsian *ultimate homogeneity* with regard to the generic trait, e.g. of colouredness, would still hold.

metaphor. Perhaps it is also possible to refer to this property of phenomenal properties as their subjective 'density': It seems as if, for any two points (no matter how close they are to one another) within the respective region of my experiential space, there always exists a third point which lies between them. The mathematical analogy of this flowing density is the continuum of real numbers. At least intuitively it remains utterly obscure how this density of phenomenal properties could be open to a mechanistic strategy of explanation, i.e. how we could analyse them as the results of myriads of causally intertwined singular events on the neural level. It is, I maintain, exactly for this reason that subjective qualities such as *International Klein Blue* appear as intrinsic and non-relational:[13] If they were really identical with a dancing pattern of micro-events in our brain, they would have to possess something like a graininess, their subjective 'surface' should not be so infinitely smooth. Michael Lockwood has illustratively called this effect 'glossing over'.[14]

Before I switch back to the external perspective of empirical science, I must draw the reader's attention to two important points. First, the two higher-order phenomenal properties which I have just described, provide — as past debates in the philosophy of mind have shown — excellent starting points for anti-reductionist or anti-naturalist arguments, because holism and homogeneity are at the root of many Cartesian intuitions. They should be of great interest to all those philosophers who feel attracted to property dualism. I suggest in particular that it may not be the *first*-order phenomenal properties which make qualia appear irreducible to many people, but rather the higher-order property of the phenomenal field-quality, viz. density or ultra-smoothness: The real problem is not *International Klein Blue*, but the *homogeneity* of *International Klein Blue*. Not the subjective blue itself, but its structureless density resists analysis. On the other hand the concept of a 'non-homogeneous' phenomenal property clearly is an incoherent concept: We would then be thinking of a *set* of phenomenal properties or of non-phenomenal properties altogether. Therefore 'inverted non-homogeneous qualia' are logically impossible, because the connection between simple phenomenal content and their experiential homogeneity is a very strong one. I am not concerned with analysing existing approaches any further here, however. Instead I will attempt to gain fresh access to the basic problem.

Secondly, the property of wholeness does not appear merely on a single phenomenological level of description. It is not only my conscious space which is characterized by the higher-order property of wholeness: The phenomenal self and the phenomenal objects, which constitute the situation

[13] Regarding the theoretical difficulties to which this intuitive 'intrinsicality' gives rise, cf. Joseph Levine's contribution to this volume.

[14] Cf. Lockwood 1993: 288 f.

in which the phenomenal self is embedded through its relational profile, possess the same characteristic, each in their own way. They too are phenomenally coherent. And within each single psychological moment, within each single subjective 'window of presence' all these holistic entities become simultaneously phenomenally present. These observations must be reflected in our phenomenological concept of 'conscious experience'. They also permit us to give a more precise explication of the provisional concept of a 'phenomenal Holon' introduced at the beginning. There are three things one can say. First, a phenomenal Holon is a subjectively experienced whole, a *Gestalt* experienced as numerically identical and indivisible from the first-person perspective. Secondly, every phenomenal Holon possesses an aspect which endows it with *presence*. The properties blending together into the whole possess a temporal identity because I always experience them *now*. From the first-person perspective, not only reality as a whole, but also objects and the phenomenal self are subjectively present and real in this sense. It may be this presentational aspect that makes the experience of duration possible at all.[15] And thirdly, through directed attention every phenomenal Holon can be embedded in a higher-order phenomenal Holon and in this way be episodically integrated into a higher-order structure, which *again* passes on the properties of wholeness and presence to the newly emerging unit of conscious experience. However, this last criterion is not fulfilled for the largest and highest-order phenomenal Holon — for *my* reality.

If our aim is a theory of conscious experience which takes seriously the internal perspective, I think that holism and homogeneity will have to be at the heart of this theory. The classical phenomenological strategy, however, no longer presents a viable path. The evidence of inner perception still assumed by Brentano has been rendered untenable by the progress of scientific psychology operating from the empirical point of view. Research on *split-brain* patients or hypnotized subjects, the study of disconnection-syndromes and anosognosias have vividly demonstrated not only the modularity of the brain, but also the modularity of *consciousness*.[16] On the other hand, this development now confronts us urgently with the question of the *integration* of conscious mental content. In this situation it is at least open to doubt whether the higher-order phenomenal properties I have discussed could ever be turned into explananda for an objective phenomenology.[17] At first glance it is hard to see how they could be integrated into the conceptual framework of theories of the neuro- and cognitive sciences in an intuitively

---

[15] At this point I am not certain whether this really is a logically necessary condition: Could not duration on the phenomenal level be represented without the presentational aspect in question? I am grateful to Lars Muckli for critical comments on this issue.

[16] Cf. Fodor 1983, Pöppel *et al.* 1991.

[17] Cf. Nagel 1974.

convincing manner, yielding naturalistic theories which we could neverthe-less accept as theories about *ourselves*. Let us keep this question in mind as we shift to the third-person perspective.

II. Feature Binding and Temporal Coding

Interestingly, many of the problems I have just sketched seem to arise again if we do not look upon ourselves as phenomenal subjects with an inner perspective, but as information processing *objects*, namely as repre-sentational systems with a long biological history. For this reason, the hypothesis suggests itself that the presence and striking holism of phenome-nal reality, which we have so far only noticed from the subjective perspec-tive, would no longer have to be explained in accordance with classical philosophical models *from above* (e.g. by a transcendental subject), if we had a good bottom-up alternative. Possibly what is needed is a generalizable scientific theory of the capacity called 'feature binding' in the terminology of brain research: The fusion of different properties perceived by the system into a *holistic* internal structure. Such a binding of properties is, for in-stance, necessary in enabling us to see objects *as* objects. In the sensory modality of visual awareness for example, such properties could be edges, movements, surfaces or colours. As we know, these features are represented by spatially separated groups of neurons in the brain. In subjective space however, they appear as a phenomenal Holon — for instance as a book in one's hand. For this reason, the question arises of how the different flows of information can be integrated to form a unified data-structure.

This *binding problem* is one of the central problems in brain research. Its logical structure resembles classical debates in philosophy and psychology (e.g. in the theory of objects or in *Gestalt*-theory). Models of neural net-works frequently represent the local features of a perceived object through activation states in property spaces, which are *physically* realized in the brain by scattered, spatially non-adjacent areas. For this reason, simple neighbourhood-interactions between single nerve cells cannot help the system to integrate the different properties of the object into a repre-sentational whole. Not only our subjective consciousness, but also the overall representational state of a connectionist system can be seen as an ascending hierarchy of such wholes: of elementary properties — the counterparts of subjective colours, bodily sensations or sound experiences — of objects, scenes, situations, contexts, a model of the self and a model of the world, in which the former is located. If we thus look at our brain from the outside and describe it as an information processing system which generates internal representations of the world and of itself, the binding problem poses itself on a multitude of levels.[18]

[18] Regarding the different levels of the binding problem cf. e.g. Koch & Crick 1994: 94 f. or Pöppel *et al.* 1991: 58 ff. See also the second section of Eva Ruhnau's contribution to this

The brain responds to stimulation by a coherent object — for instance in visual perception of an external object — with a multitude of spatially distributed activation patterns. In order to differentiate between different objects or to detach representational *Gestalten* from a background, the system has to achieve an integration of these spatially distributed events into a single, ordered and unified pattern of activity, without causing a 'superposition-catastrophe'. There is another theoretical problem, closely connected with the binding problem, the importance of which can hardly be overestimated for any theory of phenomal consciousness: the *superposition problem*. In order for *more* than one bound pattern of activity to coexist in a system, no interferences or wrong connections of properties must occur. The different patterns must not delete each other. A mechanism which solves this problem is, for instance, required in order to separate a figure from the background in a visual picture and to segregate it from different figures. Only when *both* problems, the superposition problem and the binding problem, have been solved can one imagine how a holistic representational state, a unified object (which is then embedded in further and more extensive states of the same type) emerges from the activity of many spatially distributed feature detectors. Let us call such a state a 'representational Holon'. Additionally, this 'representational Holon' has to be functionally active, i.e. it must be able to play a causal role *as* a coherent whole emerging from properties represented through singular events, for instance in producing co-ordinated behaviour. In order to generate such stable representational states it is therefore necessary for the activity of large populations of neurons to be co-ordinated in their parallel and highly specific activity. This is the neurobiological aspect of the binding problem and the superposition problem.

A number of different theoretical models for the solution of this problem have already been proposed, such as Barlowian pontifical neurons[19] and Donald Hebb's early assembly concept. At present, one of the most promising approaches is the 'correlation model'. According to this model, one assumes that coherence — for instance of a perceived object — is *temporally coded*, i.e. that the respective feature-sensitive cells represent this coherence through a precise temporal correlation.

Contrary to the classical model of assembly formation by coactivation, such a temporal coding would actually allow us to solve the binding problem,

---

volume. It has been assumed that between these levels there may in some cases exist top down effects. Cf. for instance Ruhnau 1992, Pöppel *et al.* 1991. However, one must not conceive of such downward-processes as if there were a *homunculus* in the system, a little man pointing the beam of its already given awareness at inner states and thereby turning them into intentional objects: the phenomenal self, the centre of our inner experiential space, must *itself* be thought of as a naturally emerged representational object, a transient computational module, which the system uses in organizing its behaviour.

[19] Cf. Barlow 1972.

because the synchronization of neural impulses provides an additional variable for the structuring of neural patterns of activity. The temporal correlation
in this case would exactly be the [. . .] selective 'label', which unequivocally
specifies which subset of the activated neurons is bound together into an
assembly. The overall pattern of active cells in the visual system would in this
way obtain an inner structure, functionally meaningful for other regions of
the brain, which it lacks in the Hebb-model. (Engel 1994: 13. English
translation TM.)

The central assumption is that the coherence of perceptual objects is
achieved by a *synchronization* of the firing rate of those cells which are
sensitive to the respective features. According to this model, the temporal
correlation within synchronously firing cell-assemblies would be the 'glue'
through which these events in the system are 'bound'. As such a labelled
and integrated whole, they can then enter further processing. Furthermore,
such an expansion of the Hebb model by introducing a temporal dimension
of coding also provides a mechanism for effecting important functions like
figure/ground separation and differentiating between objects: namely by
desynchronizing different cell assemblies. Since such a mechanism of
dynamic feature-binding through a transient synchronization of spatially
distributed cellular responses could be very fast, it would also increase the
flexibility and the dynamics of the overall system in an economical manner.
Before I move on, I would like to hint at why such a theoretical approach is
also interesting for a philosophical theory of mind, e.g. under the aspect of
ontological parsimony. If we have a conceptually consistent and empirically plausible model of feature binding (i.e. of the formation of representational objects as a form of *self- organization*), this supplies us with the
first ingredients for a naturalist theory of consciousness — that is to say, for
a *bottom-up* explanation. Valerie Gray Hardcastle has aptly called this the
possibility of giving a neo-Humean answer to an old Kantian claim.[20]

First signs pointing in this direction have now appeared, and they are of
great interest for a philosophical theory of consciousness. For instance,
Wolf Singer and his colleagues at the *Max-Planck-Institut für Hirnfor-
schung* in Frankfurt have discovered that spatially distant neurons in the
brains of cats which react to stimuli originating from the same visually
presented object, begin to oscillate synchronously with a frequency of 30 to
80 Hertz.[21] The suggestion that the binding of visual properties could be

---

[20] Cf. Hardcastle 1994: 66 f., 85.

[21] Meanwhile, a large number of publications on the binding problem and the role of
oscillatory activity in the formation of representational objects have appeared. The emergence
of the temporal correlations, which are so very interesting from a theoretical perspective,
(especially across larger distances) is in the literature frequently associated with the generation of oscillatory patterns of discharge. The entire EEG-research also rests on precisely this
kind of long-distance oscillatory process. On the other hand, the real 'glue' in the self-
organization and integration of mental structures consists in the *synchronicity* produced by

achieved through very short synchronizations of distributed patterns of
activation had already been made by Christoph von der Malsburg in 1981.[22]
These new discoveries show that synchronous neural oscillations of the
field potential with a frequency of around 40 Hz establish themselves for
very short periods (less than half a second). However, sometimes the role
of these oscillations has been misinterpreted. In our context, the fact of
synchronization itself is what is most important: In some cases, the oscillations can be understood as *boundary conditions* of synchronization processes, by which the integrative functions of the cortex may possibly be
achieved. It is interesting to note that in the course of their self-organization
these processes tend to respond to the classical *Gestalt criteria* such as
neighbourhood, similarity, continuity of motion and so forth, and further
that in some types of experimental set-up they take roughly the same time
as that in which a person's attention jumps from one object to another.
Researchers are also investigating whether such a high-resolution temporal
code could be used to represent relations in non-propositional formats and
to carry out *higher-order* object-constructions as well. This would be
especially interesting for a general theory of mental representation, as it
would not only clarify how the human mind forms objects out of distributed
sets of properties, but also how it can episodically embed these in each
other.

> It is easy to see that the output of such coherently active cell assemblies could
> in turn be used as input to other 'coherence detecting' nets at higher levels,
> and those could, in turn, self-organize their connectivity as a function of the
> spatially and temporally structured input provided by the preceding process-

---

the system. The oscillations seem to work as carrier waves or a local mechanism which itself
does not play any role in the information processing. Cf. Gray 1994: 17, who provides a
survey of the role of oscillatory activity within four different subsystems of the brain. For us
philosophers, the jungle of empirical literature has long become impenetrable and difficult to
survey. Texts which I found helpful as a general introduction were: Barinaga 1990, Engel *et
al.* 1993, Engel *et al.* 1992b and Singer 1989b, the classical papers of Crick & Koch 1990,
1992 and the more precise account in Koch & Crick 1994, Crick 1984, Gray *et al.* 1989 and
Pöppel 1972; concerning the general role of synchronization phenomena Engel *et al.* 1992a
and c; for empirical evidence concerning the self-organisation of temporally coherent structures, Singer 1989b, 1993 and (containing a wealth of bibliographic references) 1994; for
well-founded background information Engel 1994, and also Engel *et al.* 1991 a, b, c, Podvigin
et al. 1992, Pöppel & Logothetis 1986, Ruhnau 1992; concerning the question of senso-
motoric integration Singer 1995. Meanwhile, the synchronization phenomena in question have
been shown in a variety of functional systems, in waking monkeys and also in human beings.
Cf. Kreiter & Singer 1992, Kristeva-Feige *et al.* 1993, Llinás & Ribary 1993, Pfurtscheller &
Neuper 1992,Roelfsema 1995. The dreaming state in humans is also accompanied by 40 Hz
oscillations, which are very similar to those of the waking state. Cf. Llinás & Ribary 1993,
Llinás & Paré 1991. A short review of the empirical material together with the sketch of an
alternative interpretation on the level of non-linear dynamics is given by Hardcastle 1994.

[22] Cf. von der Malsburg 1981, 1986. The main idea of this theory can also be found in Abeles
1982 and, in an earlier shape, in Milner 1974.

ing levels. Iteration of such segmentation and regrouping operations could then allow for the generation of non-isomorphic, abstract representations of complex shapes and patterns. (Singer 1989a: 26.)

One could imagine higher-order embedding relations as a sequence of anatomic modules in series, but also as a dynamic hierarchy of activation patterns. Thus the theoretical principle of temporal coding might not only solve the binding problem and the superposition problem, but could also be operating on a multitude of representational levels. For this reason, a general mechanism of integration of this type would be of great interest in searching for an explanation of the holistic character of the *overall* representational state.

> We rather have to ask, who is the subject of perception, and how is the unity of perception established in the brain? It is an ineradicable misconception that the unity of perception has to be established in a separate center, which in addition is often imagined as being of structureless unity itself. This mental archetype leads to infinite regress and to absurdity. Instead, the unity of mind has to be seen as an organic equilibrium among a great multitude of elements. The mental symbols both send and receive at the same time. Signals sent by one sub-symbol are deciphered by other sub-symbols, and the sending symbol can in turn establish itself, momentarily, if it responds to the messages and questions sent by others. In the state of unity, each subsymbol encodes in its own terms the situation described by others. This unity is not reached by leaving out detail but by uniting all detail with the help of relations. (von der Malsburg 1986: 175.)

This remark of Christoph von der Malsburg illustrates impressively how the correlation theory of brain function could provide us with the conceptual means to reach a satisfactory naturalist answer both to the homunculus problem and the classical question concerning the unity of consciousness.

Interlude: The *Time-Window* Metaphor

The technical details are less interesting for the philosophical issue than the new image of the brain resulting from them: Our brain is a system which 'escapes into time' above a certain level of representational content.[23] Let me try to illustrate this principle by introducing a new metaphor, although

---

[23] I have borrowed this term from Wolf Singer. The 'escape into the temporal dimension' is in part interesting, because it dramatically increases the number of the functional states available to the system. In Llinás' and Paré's words: *A totally different type of functional geometry [. . .] has emerged in which that of temporal mapping, in addition to its spatial counterpart, are important variables . . . Spatial mapping allows a limited number of possible representations. However, the addition of a second component (serving to form transient functional states by means of simultaneity) generates an indefinitely large number of functional states, as the categorization is accomplished by the conjunction of spatial and temporal mapping.* Cf. Llinás & Paré 1991: 527.

I will have to surrender it at a later stage of the discussion. This new metaphor is the *time-window* metaphor. My claim is that we are systems which generate meta-representational knowledge about some of their own states by opening *time-windows* of different sizes, through which they can look at the way in which their own autonomous activity is being modulated and structured by the information flow from the sense organs. Time-windows are neural *integration windows*: They provide a precise time scale for representational binding mechanisms.

The opening of time-windows is something which can happen from the outside. If neuroscientists observe the activity of the brain, they can calculate the average of certain magnitudes over a period of time in describing measurement data, or they can add up the results of a number of stimulus cycles (for instance when counting the frequency of action potentials in successive windows of 100 ms or when calculating correlograms in windows of 1 to 3 seconds). In doing so, they generate an abstract object of their representation, picking out a particular property of the system because they want to investigate it further. This property is intersubjectively accessible, is normally given in the form of a linguistic or propositional (e.g. mathematical) description, and emerges from the choice of a specific time-frame in the design of the experiment and in the interpretation of the data gained. The design of the experiment as well as the interpretation can be *misleading* relative to the epistemic goal in question. The scientific community could discover this at any time.

Importantly, it is possible that the brain *itself* opens time-windows on its own activity, for instance through the mechanism of temporal coding which I have just sketched. Through this process, a representation of spatially distributed micro-events within the brain is generated 'from the inside'. The 'inwardness' of this representation consists in the fact that the system in question automatically distances itself from its own physical 'processuality', because object formation filters the event-character of the underlying causal mechanisms out. To put it differently: Certain configurations of stimuli initiate dynamic processes of self-organization within the system. These processes converge towards higher-order states[24] which are 'labelled' as wholes through the synchronicity of the neural responses. They represent the coherence of the stimuli through the formation of a transient object, i.e. by way of a new and likewise coherent state within the system. Thereby the *event-character* of the underlying process of self-organization is filtered out and becomes unrecognizable for the system itself. Through synchronization, through the generation of temporal correlations, many spatially scattered neural responses (events) can be integrated into a higher-order whole (an object) appearing in the time-window. Many events become *one*

[24] Cf. Singer 1994: 237.

object and by virtue of this, something like the 'surface of the inside' emerges.

This form of the opening of time-windows also singles out certain properties of the data flow within the system and bundles them together by *binding* them into an object. This object can then be investigated by further higher-order forms of information processing and representation. This temporally coded function of representation by feature binding is realized through a concrete state within the system itself, such as an activation pattern which is bound using synchronization processes. Again, a certain time frame is utilized, an object of representation emerges, and this object is, in principle, intersubjectively accessible. In this case, however, the 'design of the experiment' as well as the 'interpretation of data' are internal states of the cognizing system itself. Of course it is possible, that the underlying processes are *subjectively* inaccessible to that system itself because of peculiarities of its functional architecture.

Maybe it is possible to clarify further the concept of object-formation by pointing to it's epistemological aspects: The high internal correlative strength or *coherence* of a perceived set of properties is a fact, normally in the environment of the system. This fact however, is not represented through a propositional format or the activation of a sentence-like structure, but through the generation of a holistic *object*, a representational Holon. It is for this reason, that in many cases the system can no longer distinguish between form and content — there is no syntax and no semantics. Thus, it seems that with the generation of representational objects of this type, an interesting non-conceptual form of 'abstraction by integration' is simultaneously achieved. For the system itself, however, the result of this abstraction appears as a *concrete* object.

A time-window is therefore an *integration window* in which the brain unifies different internally represented features into a whole by generating a temporal correlation. But the 'embedding' of the content of different time-windows in each other must be thought of in terms of a *liquid architecture,* in which plasticity and flexible overall dynamics can coexist with homogeneity and stability of form. Different types of time-windows could realize different 'grains', different resolutions by means of which various entities can be represented. However, as all of this is *sub-symbolic* information processing, time-windows must not be conceived of as rigid basic elements: we have to understand them as plastic parts of a dynamic binding mechanism, i.e. as variable *conditions* of representation, which, through this very variability, can also be context-sensitive and which are, at most, characterized by a weak compositionality. For this reason, the higher-order embedding of mental content must presuppose a dynamic evolution of the overall state, in the course of which bound patterns of activity can be superimposed without loss of any relevant information. Time windows could thus be *plastic* mechanisms. A — more or less strong — synchronization would then be the — more or less sticky — glue expressing the internal correlation-strength of the sets of properties represented by means of a *synchronization gradient*. This synchronization gradient lifts the representational object — more or less clearly — out of the background of activity which generated it.[25]

Now, let us pursue further the considerations sketched above by generalizing the idea. One can analyse the construction of a 'representational Holon' as precisely that case in which the system frees a distributed set of properties of the temporal difference relations that hold between its elements. This synchronization of single events within the system then results in the formation of a new and integrated form of content (i.e. in the generation of a representational whole by discrete mechanisms of temporal coding) on the respective higher levels of representation. Since the single events which function as feature detectors are endowed with a common temporal *Gestalt* by the system, the set of properties partially loses its internal temporal structure and is transformed into a holistic representational object: Synchronicity generates wholeness.

---

[25] It is interesting to note that the concept of a 'time-window' also plays an important role in a completely different theoretical model which, however, calls upon very similar and partially identical empirical evidence such as the correlation theory. The hypotheses developed by Eva Ruhnau and Ernst Pöppel, that *atemporal zones* in the system are generated through phase-locked oscillation processes on a very fundamental level, i.e. states of the system governed by a principle of 'simultaneity', is aimed at a different and more special problem than the correlation theory of feature binding which I have just sketched. The opening of time-windows — according to this second interpretation — enables a system to generate an *operational time* for itself: By quantizing its information processing, it, so to speak, 'swallows up' the flow of physical time on a very fundamental level of its inner representation of the world. It distances itself from its own processuality by carrying out a very interesting form of data reduction. The physical time interval itself still exists, but the *content* of the respective states of the system loses all or a part of its internal temporal properties: *For the system itself* representational atoms emerge. These atoms have also been called 'elementary integration units' (EIUs).

Amongst other things, this provides us with an idea about how, on a higher level of processing, the transition from parallelity to seriality could be possible — the implementation of a Dennettian *Joycean Machine* on a massively parallel system (which, on a theoretical level, is one of the many more recent versions of the mind–body problem). For reasons of space I am not able here to pursue the highly interesting question, of how *subjective* time experience and, most of all, a phenomenal present can emerge from objective time structures. In the present context, the most important thought of this theoretical approach seems to consist in the idea that a naturally emerged representational system can generate atemporal zones *for itself* in its depiction of the world. I believe that this theory is very interesting because it can help us to achieve a better understanding of what the element of 'phenomenal presence' described in the first section of this contribution actually is (see also section 2.4 of the general introduction). For this reason, this theory provides a valuable complement to the correlation theory, which on the other hand supplies us with conceptual ingredients for a theory of 'phenomenal wholes'. However, it is presently more than an open question whether the two theoretical models can be projected on to each other at all in an interesting way. Cf. Ruhnau & Pöppel 1991, Görnitz *et al.* 1992 and Eva Ruhnau's contribution to this volume.

III. Global Meta-Representation: From HOT and HOP to HOB

We are now able to extract a conceptual principle from these empirical considerations, one which could be highly interesting for the philosophy of mind and the naturalization of phenomenal consciousness. I will call this *The Principle of the Formation of Representational Wholes* (PFRW):

> **PFRW**: Certain natural representation systems are able to bind internal, spatially distributed individual events which function as feature detectors for them into a representational whole, by coding the perceptive relations between them through processes of synchronization.

I will not concern myself here with a precise demarcation of the class of systems in question.[26] However, I will assume that human beings in non-pathological waking states belong to this class. At this point, after having looked at the problem of phenomenal and representational wholes from the first-person perspective as well as from the third-person perspective, I will return to conceptual analysis, offering philosophical and not empirical speculations.

First, I will use the cavalier audacity of a philosopher to make a very strong general assumption: The form of temporal coding postulated by the correlation theory is the general integrational mechanism by means of which — at least in systems of our own type — *all* kinds of representational wholeness are generated. In other words: I will tentatively assume that the mechanism I have just described (undoubtedly in a far too short and imprecise manner), as the process by which the system is able to open time-windows of different sizes on its own internal activity, is a *general* principle, operative on *all* levels of binding. My aim is not, however, to generate meaningless empirical pseudo-hypotheses. Rather, the goal is to investigate the heuristic potential of a theoretical model which has been deliberately generalized. For this purpose I shall make the following assumptions:

A1   Temporal coding synchronizes the activity of spatially distributed feature detectors and, in doing so, permits the homogeneous presentation of *one* property in *one* sensory modality. ('Generation of elementary qualitative units within separate property spaces.')

A2   I will here combine five assumptions which are relevant to the representational construction of a complex external world and to the regulation of behaviour in interaction with this external world:

[26] This is primarily a question in need of an empirical answer. I have, however, already named the fundamental characteristics of the intended class of systems: They are systems which work in a massively parallel fashion, according to the principle of *coarse coding*, which activate distributed representations and which can be described as plastic, self-organizing networks.

- Temporal coding binds a number of different properties into one object within *one* sensory modality. ('Activation of "perceptual *Gestalts*"; object formation and scene segmentation across property spaces.')
- Temporal coding binds information across different modalities. ('Generation of multi-modal representational objects.')
- Temporal coding enables the integrated representation of multi-modal *temporal Gestalts*, for instance of sequences of events or actions. ('Transition from the generation of its own operational time to a continuous flow of representational moments.')
- Temporal coding binds sensory and motor information and in doing so makes co-ordinated behaviour possible. ('Integration of functional modules.')
- Temporal coding allows us to represent the relational profile of representational wholes and to *embed* these in each other in ascending hierarchies. ('Formation of complex scenes and situations.')

A3   The third assumption regards the representational construction of an integrated *inner* world. Temporal coding enables the system to generate a holistic *self-model* and to embed this model into complex situations. ('Centering of the overall representational state'; formation of the 'first-person perspective.')

A4   Temporal coding enables the system to bind the overall representational state which is already centred by a self-model into *one* global structure, i.e. into a *highest-order* coherent representational whole. (*Highest-Order-Binding*; 'Formation of a holistic reality model'.)

At present, these assumptions are at best weakly supported by empirical evidence. They cannot count as serious empirical speculations, and they are not intended as such. However, the empirical situation already justifies a rational *philosophical* speculation: It seems reasonable to investigate a new outlook on to familiar problems by generalizing an empirically plausible principle. It is instantly obvious that assumptions **A1** and **A4** may be relevant to the elementary homogeneity of qualia and the global holism of the space of conscious experience. These questions will remain the focus of my considerations. However, because I have generalized the problem of the holistic character of phenomenal content by introducing the concept of a 'phenomenal Holon', the conceptual speculations too will now have to be generalized with regard to the respective levels of description.

First of all we therefore have to formulate a generalized new version of **PFRW** in correspondence with the assumptions **A1** to **A4**. This new version has to meet two requirements: First, it must abstract from our original example, viz. object formation within a single sensory modality. Secondly, it must allocate a causal role to the representational wholes which have been generated. Phenomena of synchronization are only interesting if it can be demonstrated that they play a separate functional role in the genesis of behaviour and in subjective experience.[27] Let us call this the *Generalized Principle of the Formation of Representational Wholes* (GPFRW):

> **GPFRW**: Naturally emerged representation systems of a certain type are able to bind a subset of internal, spatially and temporally distributed individual events or representational wholes, which are already active, into a higher-order representational whole by coding the perceptive or embedding relations between the elements of the set through processes of synchronization. Sets of single events bound through a common time structure can in this way play a separate causal role in the system, i.e. they can sometimes be regarded as higher-order functional properties or transient functional modules. In this case they are *functionally active representational wholes*.

According to this principle, the binding mechanism which on all representational levels joins together single elements and episodically transforms them into higher-order wholes, consists in the generation of an identical time structure. If the representational 'levels', of which I have just spoken so carelessly, really are separate stages of the overall dynamics, then it should be possible to describe them by means of discrete classes of neural algorithms. Thus we have to investigate the *time constants* of the neural classes of algorithms in question. These time constants will be the conceptual essence of any abstract analysis of what 'holism' means on the representational level. A further question: In what cases are the functional states under consideration realized by clearly delimited anatomical modules on the level of the brain at all and in what cases are they only realized as transient *computational* modules?

At this stage of our considerations the time-window metaphor, which I have used to illustrate the principle of temporal coding, has to be abandoned. It could easily generate confusions since the opening of windows is an intentionalistic *top-down metaphor*: windows are opened by persons and under normal conditions they are opened deliberately. Naturalistic theorizing however, must operate on sub-personal levels of description and replace internal homunculi and their volitional acts with principles of self-organization. Besides, the time-window metaphor is one of those notorious spatial and visual metaphors which have bewitched the occidental philosophy of mind ever since it began. It suggests too easily a fixed view-point and distal objects. A naturalistic analysis of the formation of representational wholes however, requires a conceptually convincing theory of self-organization *without a homunculus*. The homunculus, the window, and the distal object

---

[27] It thus has to be shown that they are not artefacts or epiphenomena as they always emerge within complex systems. What I have called a 'representational Holon' must also act as a *transient functional module* in the inner ecology of the system. Meanwhile, a great number of empirical findings demonstrate the functional relevance of phenomena of synchronisation. Cf. e.g. Roelfsema 1995 and footnote 21.

easily creep into our scientific theories operating 'from the outside' as well.
Since in verbal descriptions form and content again become separated,
representational wholes turn into *abstract* objects: They are objects in
high-dimensional representational spaces, the formal structure of which
may be captured by mathematical abstractions such as activation vector
space descriptions of a certain type or neural algorithms with certain
time-constants. However, in the sub-symbolic process which I have called
the 'opening of a time-window', *the system itself* can no longer distinguish
between form and content: The 'opening of the window' and the 'generation of the object seen through the window' are identical, both descriptions
are co-extensive. They refer to the very same activation pattern in the brain
which is bound through self-organizing processes of synchronization: The
neurally realized integration window *is* an object, a new state of the system.
Like a flower, it opens *by itself*. For this reason, I shall abandon metaphorical talk about time-windows and will henceforth speak about 'functionally
active representational wholes'.

I will now go through the assumptions **A1** to **A4** and offer some short
conceptual speculations for each of them. Naturally, in the context of the
two explananda isolated at the outset of the paper, the assumptions **A1** and
A4 deserve our attention the most.

S1 A naturalistic answer to the grain problem may be hidden in assumption **A1**. In its first version, this problem consists in the fact that not only is
a certain phenomenal property — namely the visual 'pink'quale —
subjectively instantiated in the manifest experience of a pink ice-cube, but
also that this property is homogeneously distributed over the object experienced. If the subjectively experienced object were to be identical with a
neural activation pattern in a Leibnizian sense (i.e., if it shared all its
non-intensional and non-modal properties with this pattern), then every
region of this pattern of activity would also have to instantiate the property
of 'pink', no matter how small. According to this analysis, 'homogeneity'
would be a property of a functionally active representational whole: not a
structural property, but a *content property*.[28] We are now for the first time
able to identify this property with a physical property, suggesting: The
homogeneity of subjectively experienced qualities is the *temporal* homogeneity of the correlated states of the system. As a matter of fact, there is a
complex physical property which can be found in all spatio-temporal regions
in question, namely the synchronicity of neural activity. That is, qualia are
not 'infinitely' homogenuous, homogeneity does not go all the way down,
it rather is a representational phenomenon emerging at a certain level of
complexity. Synchronicity can be experienced *as* homogeneity in exactly

[28] A *content property* in the sense of Richardson & Muilenburg 1982: 177 f. Cf. also Lycan
1987: 85. It may be that the analysis of homogeneity as a higher-order property could become
questionable in the face of the new empirical material. This will be a topic for future
investigation.

those cases in which an integration mechanism possesses a lower temporary resolution than the states of the system which it unifies. The system then represents temporal coherence as *smoothness*. On a higher level of representation, the synchronous activity of feature detectors of a certain type must therefore by nomological necessity appear as structureless and dense. A central aspect of the philosophical qualia problem consists in the fact that the qualitative character seems to render the sensory states in question impenetrable; it makes it impossible to recognize the causal role of these states. We are now in a position to say: The causal role is not realized through what we call 'qualitative character', but through the homogeneity of this qualitative character. In reality, I pick out redness introspectively in virtue of its *homogeneity* and precisely this *is* the realization of the causal role. On the level of simple phenomenal properties, homogeneity is the subjective correlate of the synchronicity of the activity of the feature detectors concerned and it is precisely through this synchronization that this activity can become functionally *active* and *subjectively* available to introspective experience. Thus, on the level of phenomenal content, the causal role is represented through its homogeneity and not through what we commonly call this content 'itself'. For this reason, I would like to suggest a 'double-aspect'— or 'two-component'— theory of qualia: Manifest qualities of conscious experience such as *International Klein Blue* possess an H-component and a Q-component. The H-component is the homogeneity of the state and the Q-component correlates with the phenomenal property which the state instantiates. What we pick out introspectively is not *International Klein Blue*, but always *homogenous International Klein Blue*. The interesting point is that, from an empirical point of view, it now becomes more and more plausible that it is actually the H-component which makes the Q-component causally active and at the same time available for experience. In virtue of the H-component, the respective state of the system can play a functional role and enter the space of conscious experience. The speculation S1 amounts to the claim that the H-component could be naturalized by means of the temporal coding hypothesis.

This would not solve the qualia-problem: We would still be unable to say what *International Klein Blue* actually is, because we still lack a convincing theory for the Q-component. But we would have an empirically plausible answer to the higher-order problem of the homogeneity of qualitative content: Elementary subjective qualities introspectively appear as atomic and irreducible because we are systems which bind the activity of their elementary feature detectors through temporal coding into a higher-order state of the system which possesses a holistic time-structure. Two important points must not be overlooked in this context: First, phenomenal properties never appear in an isolated fashion, but always as properties of higher-order wholes. A conscious pain is always localized within the body image, and even the coloured patches which we can sometimes see before falling asleep have a spatial extension, often even shape and a direction of movement. (Perhaps one could say: Colouredness is a dimension which we can structure through an internally generated context, but there are no isolated colours outside of this context.[29]) Secondly, isolated phenomenal individuals do not exist. In conscious experience *pure* individuals never appear, but only complexions of qualities, those which I earlier termed 'phenomenal Holon'. The elegance of the correlation theory lies in its potential to explain, in an ontologically parsimonious way, the transition from functional to phenomenal states. There are neither isolated phenomenal properties, nor is there a phenomenal individual to which these properties are 'attached': What exist in reality are sets of micro-functional events, which are bound to a coherent whole by synchronization. On the level of elementary properties, this coherence then shows itself introspectively as that which we philosophers like to call 'homogeneity'. The homogeneity of *International Klein Blue* could thus be the way in which the system represents the synchronicity of active feature detectors to itself — the way in which it *experiences* coherence. If these speculations point in the right direction, neuroscientific successor predicates will become available which are able to semantically incorporate the *ultimate homogeneity* in Sellars' sense.[30]

In order also to reduce qualitative content *itself*, we would additionally have to be able to tell *what* it is that is bound into a higher-order state of the system by synchronization. But once what I have called the 'intrinsicality intuition' has been dissolved, a sophisticated *relational* analysis will be successful. We would need abstract descriptions of the corresponding new properties (the Q-component), which answer two questions: Why do elementary properties (for instance colour qualia) form phenomenal families? Why does subjective experience itself fail to tell us what this family resemblance, so concretely experienced by us, consists in? A complete reduction would therefore require mathematical models of those activation patterns, which are homogenized with regard to their temporal structure by temporal coding. These mathematical models would have to allow us to extract interesting *objective similarity classes* and project them on to the 'topology of subjective space'. If we one day succeed in connecting such formal descriptions of the respective concrete states of the system with the categorizations of folk-psychology, we will have moved another step closer to what Nagel dubbed an 'objective phenomenology'.

If the epistemic goal of our enterprise consists in illustrative descriptions which bridge the gap between scientific theory and our folk psychological understanding, one could for example say at this point: *International Klein Blue* is not a quality at all, but the high-dimensional 'form' of a neural

[29] I am grateful to Andreas Engel for this thought — as for many other valuable and stimulating comments.

[30] This means: a naturalistic solution of the Dilemma sketched by Sellars (1963: 36) is potentially available.

activity state in my visual cortex. If we regard it as an internal representation, the concrete neural activity state in my brain which leads to my concrete experience of *International Klein Blue* possesses various *abstract* properties. Perhaps one could call these properties of the internal representation its 'format'.[31] Regarded as an event within the system's visual information processing, it is an activity state in a local neural net, i.e. in a certain subsystem of the brain. This local state of the network can be described abstractly in different ways: In principle, there are many mathematical models for this very special state as well as for its temporal dynamic. *One* possibility of describing it would be as point in, or a region within, a high-dimensional vector space, since one can describe the activity state of a neural net by means of activation vectors. If we then introduce a geometric model for this abstract algebraic description, we get illustrative and intuitively appealing pictures for very abstract objects of thought — spaces, sections or surfaces. Using such a geometric description one could then say: Every individual neural state has a *form*, possibly a very high-dimensional form. Could that be what I see when I see *International Klein Blue*? Does the extremely high-dimensional form of a bodily state, which I do not recognize *as* such, lie concealed behind Yves Klein's 'dimensionless depth' of the subjective sensory quality *International Klein Blue*?

Let us not be deceived. All of this would still not amount to a complete reductive solution of the qualia problem: We would still not know why qualia are *conscious* experiences and why they are tied to a subjective perspective. Unless one already implicitly assumes a functionalist theory of subjective experience, it has not yet been shown that representational holism and homogeneity have anything to do with *experienced* holism and homogeneity.

S2 The principle of object formation is also interesting from an epistemological point of view. If a good theory of object formation within a single sensory modality as well as across different sensory modalities and for more abstract types of content becomes available, we are no longer forced to follow the classical philosophical topoi of the intentionality relation in postulating an integration or feature binding *from above*. There is no need to assume that the cognizing subject directs itself towards the world in a mysterious Husserlian manner and thereby grasps certain intentional objects. The emergence of active representational wholes can now be thought of as the self-organization of cognitive structures from the bottom up. Since the formation of such wholes should also be possible independently of external input, i.e. in the context of mental simulations, there are many promising possibilities not only for naturalizing central concepts of classical theories of mind, as for instance the concepts of an 'intentional act' and

---

[31] By 'format' I mean a set of abstract properties, discoverable with regard to an active data structure — for example *topological* properties. Cf. Metzinger 1993; Churchland 1986.

an 'intentional object', but perhaps also of spelling them out in a more precise way that preserves the original insights. This may also apply to many concepts of the classical phenomenology of perception, such as James' 'sensible totals', von Ehrenfels' *Gestalt* qualities, Meinong's higher-order objects, Husserl's *figurale Momente*, etc. Another consequence of this model may be of great interest for current debates in the philosophy of mind: The conceptual difference between 'construction' and 'representation' is defused, while its important semantic elements are simultaneously preserved in a new and empirically plausible idea. We can now understand ourselves as systems which under the pressure of input *construct* in themselves coherent states by means of feature binding, which then in turn *function as* representations in virtue of their informational content. The principle of object formation may also help in understanding the transition from a stream of massively parallel microfunctional events to symbol-type, serial processing. And it illustrates the interesting fact that 'higher-order representation' may be more than just abstraction or further mapping, that it may be a constructive type of representation *by* subsymbolic integration. All this may lead to new ideas about how naturalistic conceptions of intentional content can be developed. For the future it is therefore important to spell these observations out in more detail.

However, here we are concerned with *phenomenal* content. The central question goes like this: What is the relationship between active representational wholes and phenomenal wholes, i.e. those subregions of subjective space which I have characterized as 'phenomenal Holons' in the beginning? Representational as well as phenomenal wholes possess a striking *Gestalt* quality, which gives them their holistic character. And both lack a part of their internal structure. The system always deletes a part of the inner history of the different properties bound into a representational object through the process of synchronization and thereby renders it 'unknowable' to itself. The temporal structure of a neural impulse carries information about it's causal history, and by smoothing out that structure this information gets partly deleted. This might provide one of the reasons for the fact that we are systems which experience the world in a naive realistic mode: We are no longer able to recognize the phenomenal models which emerge in ourselves *as* models. On a representational level of description one can, in principle, understand how a number of active wholes can be differentiated from each other by means of desynchronization and how they can coexist without giving rise to a superposition catastrophe. If attention works by the same type of mechanism, it it easy to understand how they could be episodically tied into unified higher-order structures. In virtue of these three characteristics — holism, self-referential opacity and the capacity for higher-order embedding of representational entities — the correlation theory becomes interesting for a general theory of phenomenal consciousness.

Still, the relation we are looking for cannot be the relation of identity. This is shown by a simple fact. Many of the crucial empirical investigations about object-formation and scene-segmentation have been successfully carried out on anaesthetized cats. This means that representational wholes can be generated without consciousness and without the first-person perspective. The formation of a perceptive object in the visual cortex of an anaesthetized cat amounts to artificially generating an *isolated* whole. This whole, however, is not functionally active because it is not bound into a highest-order Holon[32] together with other states of the same kind. Therefore, it is also unable to assist the cat in regulating its interaction with its environment. A phenomenal Holon on the other hand, is characterized by at least two further higher-order properties: A phenomenal Holon is always conscious and it always appears in connection with a perspectively organized experiential space. Without a general theory of this space and the phenomenal self which appears in it and structures it, all reductionistic efforts will be doomed to failure. Phenomenal wholes possess a richer relational structure than isolated and functionally inactive representational wholes.

If the third of the assumptions bundled under **A2** should prove to be justified, then we could understand how bound objects can in turn be represented as possessing *external* temporal relations. After the system has deleted the physical time interval on a fundamental level of representational content it is then in turn able to define higher-order relationships of temporal succession.[33] For instance, we are able to experience how a pink ice cube moves through the air and drops into a glass. In this way we can understand how seriality emerges from parallelity via a special form of object formation: An internal time, which is formed out of single moments that are variable in their duration, but connected with each other in a non-fragmented way.

If it could be demonstrated that the sensory-motor integration of the information flow can be explained with the help of the correlation theory,[34] this would provide us with a naturalistic strategy for the solution of all those forms of the mind–body problem which conceptually describe the perception of the world as an upward process and acting within the world as a downward one. Active representational wholes are — in virtue of their temporal structure — discrete states of the system, which may in many cases form functional modules. For this reason, they could serve as missing links in the precise specification of the causal chains which run through the system. Perhaps these considerations would even allow us to develop a holistic concept of action with the help of this general strategy. Moreover,

32 Thus it is not *globally available* for control. Cf. Block 1995 and Chalmers 1996a.

33 Cf. Eva Ruhnau's contribution to this volume.

34 Cf. Singer 1995.

one could ask at which point of such an analysis would the *personal* level of description enter? However, as it is very likely that many of these processes can take place independently of phenomenal consciousness and an active subjective perspective, this possibility is less interesting in our context.

Generally speaking, the possibility provided by the correlation theory of a 'liquid' embedding of active representational wholes in higher-order structures while preserving the holistic overall character reflects the third central feature of a phenomenal Holon, namely the simple phenomenological fact that singular experiential wholes can be bound seamlessly into larger wholes of the same type. Of course this thought becomes especially interesting when combined with the idea of phenomenal *presence* in the context of a subjective 'window of presence'. Probably we can nevertheless always imagine that all this happens without any kind of perspectival consciousness.

S3 Possibly some important explanatory ingredients for a naturalistic dissolution of the concept known in analytical philosophy as 'first-person perspective' can be found in the assumption **A3**. The phenomenal self, in my opinion, is the most interesting phenomenal Holon of all — amongst other things because it endows our conscious space with a very interesting *structural* feature: Centredness and perspectivalness. I have elaborated this point at great length elsewhere[35] and will therefore restrict myself to some very short remarks here.

The model of the self differs from every other mental model in an essential point. It possesses a part which is exclusively based on internal input: the part of the body image activated by proprioceptive input. Recent research concerning the pain experienced in phantom limbs seems to point to the existence of a genetically determined *neuromatrix* whose activation patterns could be the basis of the body image and body-feeling. The part of this neural activation pattern which is independent of external input produces a continuous representational basis for the body model of the self[36] and in this way *anchors* it in the brain. In almost all cases where there is phenomenal consciousness *at all*, there also exists this unspecific, internal source of input. It is the most 'certain' and stable region within the model of the self. In this way our consciousness becomes a *centred* consciousness. This is what makes us experientially *embodied* beings.

---

[35] Cf. Metzinger 1993.

[36] In the words of R. Melzack: *In essence, I postulate that the brain contains a neuromatrix, or network of neurons, that, in addition to responding to sensory stimulation, continuously generates a characteristic pattern of impulses indicating that the body is intact and unequivocally one's own. I call this pattern a neurosignature. If such a matrix operated in the absence of sensory inputs from the periphery of the body, it would create the impression of having a limb even when that limb has been removed.* Cf. Melzack 1992: 93 and also Melzack 1989.

However, in order for the functional/representational property of centredness to become the *phenomenal* property of perspectivalness, the model of the system must become a phenomenal self. The pivotal question is: How does that which we commonly call the phenomenal first-person perspective emerge in a centred representational space? A first-person perspective — I would suggest — emerges in exactly all of those cases in which the system no longer recognizes the model of the self which it itself activated *as* a model. If it did, representational and functional centredness would remain, but the global phenomenal property of perspectivalness would disappear. In short: the system would have a self-model, but no phenomenal self.

On the level of inner experience, the phenomenal self is the paradigmatic case of a holistic structure. Its activation is accompanied by the instantiation of an interesting higher-order phenomenal property. This property creates a pre-reflexive form of self-presence and self-givenness within every single psychological moment. Let us provisionally call this property 'selfhood' or 'mineness'. It bundles the content of the phenomenal self into a holistic structure which appears as indivisible. (I hope that it has become obvious in the meantime why this structure *must* necessarily appear as indivisible to the system.) Moreover, the phenomenal self is embedded in a higher-order structure in a non-fragmented way, namely in a concrete phenomenal reality: We are also subjectively *situated* beings. The representational correlate — the self-model — is a functional module, episodically activated by the system in order to regulate its interaction with the environment. As we know from cybernetics, every good regulator of a complex system automatically has to be a model of the system.[37] If one assumes a PDP-inspired teleofunctionalism, then this model of the system appears as a kind of organ which emerges through the binding of a certain set of micro-functional properties and enables the system to represent itself in its environment *to itself*. So the self-model is a transient computational module, possessing a long biological history: It is a weapon, which was developed in the course of a 'cognitive arms-race'.[38] A real phenomenal self however, only emerges if the system *confuses itself* with the internal model of itself which it has generated.[39] Since the 'processuality' of the objective process of self-modelling is not represented on the level of content (at least in wide

---

[37] Cf. Conant & Ashby 1970.

[38] Andy Clark has coined this very illustrative and unromantic metaphor, cf. Clark 1989: 62.

[39] This concept of 'confusing' — just like the 'time-window metaphor' — must only be understood as a first illustration! If one takes it too seriously on the conceptual level, one may easily create another transcendental homunculus or an objective self which forms the subject of this ego-illusion. It is also interesting to note that a complex and stable ego-illusion of this kind may have been biologically very successful, because it inevitably makes the system *egoistic*. However, what makes the emergence of the phenomenal self through entirely natural processes so fascinating, is the very fact of this ego-illusion being *no-one's* illusion. Cf. Metzinger 1996.

areas of the respective regions of representational space), the representational model of the system also possesses the aspect of presence in
every individual psychological moment and the typical form of holism
which cannot be transcended on the level of experience. If one thus assumes
that the integrational mechanisms of temporal coding, which I have
sketched above, play an important role in the activation of a unified and
complex self-representatum, then we can begin to understand what the
respective phenomenal Holon in the shape of a self-referentially opaque
self-model could look like: While activating a representational object, the
system gets caught in a naive-realistic *self*-misunderstanding and in this
way generates a phenomenal *subject*.

But even this subject is not a phenomenal Holon in the strict sense. This
is so because, of course, we can once again mobilize the modal intuition,
which Peter Bieri has so aptly described at the beginning of this volume,
and which in Germany has become known as the *'Tibetan prayer wheel
question'*: Many of us can still imagine that all this happens entirely without
any form of consciousness. For this reason we must now finally turn to the
most important point. Can the speculative principle of **GPFRW** be of any
help in attempting to gain a new perspective on the problem of consciousness?

S4   The classical philosophical model for consciousness — *conscientia* as
higher-order knowledge about a subset of ones own internal states — is
quite old. Many philosophers have continued to develop this fundamental
thought using folk-psychological concepts like 'thought' or 'perception' in
the construction of theories of higher-order thoughts or inner forms of
perception. In his contribution to this volume, Güven Güzeldere has supplied a very lucid analysis of the difficulties associated with some current
strategies of this kind. In my opinion, the time has now come to transform
the classical concept *conscientia* into a technical term. From now on I shall
call this new and speculative concept *Highest-Order Binding*, in short:
HOB. This new concept (just like the concept of a 'phenomenal Holon')
will serve to delineate in a first and provisional manner an explanandum
which will, of necessity, be part of any theory of phenomenal consciousness. If one looks back into the history of philosophy and investigates the
theoretical precursors of the modern concept of consciousness, one finds,
besides accompanying higher-order knowledge, a second major semantical
element in many of these early concepts (e.g. *syneidesis* or *synesthesia*):
Consciousness is something that unifies or *synthesizes* experience. Interestingly, **HOB** has the advantage of preserving these two most important
semantic elements, which kept on reappearing throughout many centuries
of philosophical thinking about consciousness, by uniting them in an empirically plausible, naturalistic conception. However, it is far from clear
how this could be done in an analytically convincing manner. The most
intricate question is: How can one 'implement' the hierarchical logical

structure of the concept of a *global* meta-representational function in an ultra-complex information-processing system, operating with holistic formats of representation? So '**HOB**' is not only a new and speculative concept, but also the sketch of a possible research programme.

The most interesting theoretical problem here is that of understanding how the *hierarchical* logical structure of the concept of 'meta-representation' could be projected onto a neurobiologically realistic model of parallel distributed information processing. If we integrate the basic assumptions of connectionism into our considerations, then the question arises of how global meta-representational knowledge can be understood, first, as *sub-symbolic* knowledge and secondly, as *distributed* knowledge. First, we have to comprehend how those inner processes which turn a part of the other inner processes into *conscious* inner processes can rest on non-linguistic forms of representation without a rigid constituent structure. Secondly, we need to clarify how the highest-order phenomenal property of 'consciousness' can be analysed as supervenient on or even as identical with a *distributed network property* of the system in question. Thirdly, we must do justice to the dynamic and holistic character of our space of consciousness.

The crucial speculation here is that the principle of **GPFRW** can help us to take the step from a functionalistic *Global Workspace*[40] to a highest-order phenomenal Holon. According to the assumption, synchronicity is the 'glue' responsible for the holistic character in question. As I have already said, representational levels or functions should be described through discrete classes of neural algorithms: Therefore, a mathematical model for the holistic character of our phenomenal space must exist. Now one may speculate that it is precisely the *time-constants* of a global meta-representational function, physically realized by the process of **HOB**, which form the conceptual essence of the phenomenon which we call our subjective experience of the wholeness of our reality. **HOB** would have to be a continuous and rather unspecific mechanism which binds active representational content on the highest level by producing a dynamic and coherent global state. Accordingly, **HOB** is neither a form of concept formation nor inner perception — rather it is a *constructive* form of global meta-representation: the self-organization of a coherent global state.

So if one continues to hold on to the highly speculative assumption that mechanisms of temporal coding (the process which I have first metaphorically called the *opening of time-windows* and then conceptually analysed as the *generalized principle of the formation of active representational wholes*) are operating right up to the 'highest' level of mental content, then the generation of a conscious experiential space in the brain of a biological organism can again be understood as a generalized case of feature binding

---

[40] Cf. Baars 1988 and Baars & Newman 1994.

and sub-symbolic object formation. A holistic representational space can be achieved if and only if a part of the information which is active in the system can be temporally integrated into a *singular* macro-representatum. If, on the highest representational level, a most general form of *Gestalt formation* or *object-formation* is achieved through feature-binding (**HOB**), then a global macro-representatum is generated in this way. This macro-representatum, the system's actual *conscious* reality model, would therefore be a currently active informational structure which possesses very specific abstract properties. However, such a highest-order representational object could not be transcended *by the system itself*, because there would not be any larger internal data-structure with richer informational content with which it could be compared. Secondly, it is represented in the mode of 'immediate givenness' because the utilized data-structures are semantically transparent. Thirdly, since the content of this data-structure appears within a window of presence generated by the system, one can understand how an experienced *reality* arises for the system — the presence of a global whole. In this global whole there is the qualitative homogeneity of sensations such as *International Klein Blue* and an ego-illusion which cannot be transcended: a self-model that is not recognized *as* a model.

Let us return to our metaphor of the time-window for the last time. Realized time-windows are holistic patterns, episodically active informational structures, which have been bound by an integrational mechanism. Returning to a poetical way of speaking once more, they are like flowers in our mind. These flowers open themselves so fast that we are no longer able to realize that they grow *in ourselves*. There may be many structures of this type, which influence behaviour as transient functional modules, but which nevertheless are unconscious because they are not bound into the currently active phenomenal model of the world. However, all those representational wholes, which become real phenomenal Holons because they are bound into the global space centred by a self-model now function as individuals in the flexible phenomenal ontology of the brain. As long as they are realized, i.e. as long as the synchronization process in question takes place, they are as a matter of fact *indivisible* for the system itself. In this sense (only in this sense), the phenomenal model of the world is itself such an individual. If, again, the glue of feature binding and of higher-order integration should be 'synchronization', one can even say the following: since there really is a concrete object characterized by a specific temporal *Gestalt* of its own, i.e. a largest (possibly 'slowest') time-window and since the mechanisms by which it is opened onto a multitude of time-windows which are already superimposed, do not *themselves* become objects of inner representation, it must of necessity become untranscendable for the system which generates this object in itself. In other words: the naive realism characterizing our form of phenomenal consciousness is a necessary result of the functional architecture of our brains. And in this manner it also becomes apparent how a model can become a reality. The content of the highest-order representational Holon possesses the structural feature of perspectivalness, it is represented in the mode of direct givenness and furthermore it is presented within a 'window of presence' generated by the system itself. These characteristics make it a highest-order *phenomenal* Holon.

In this contribution, I have investigated two higher-order properties of our experiential space, its holistic character and the homogeneity of qualitative content instantiated in it. I have tried to approach these properties from the inward perspective, from the outward perspective and by conceptual speculation. The purpose of the speculation was to test the usefulness of a conceptual model with regard to a theory of higher-order phenomenal properties. The assumptions on which it is based are extremely strong and, of course, I was not interested in the speculation for its own sake. I have nevertheless pursued this line of thought because, in my opinion, speculations of this type are nowadays for the first time *rational* speculations and because I believe that — even if they should prove to be imprecise or even false in many details — they may possess great heuristic value.

If I am correct in this point, they can, however, only develop this heuristic potential if they are successively replaced with empirically informative theories. This is the first project for future research into the phenomenon of conscious experience: We need to know the neural and functional correlates of phenomenal holism on all levels of instantiation. On a conceptual plane however, — and this is part of the second, *philosophical*, project — one has to investigate the modality of the relation between such higher-order functional properties of the brain and conscious experience.[41] Can we really imagine a system which belongs to the class delineated by **GPFRW** and a maximum realization of the assumptions **A1** to **A4**, which nevertheless lacks phenomenal states? And if we can in fact imagine this: What exactly does this *mean*?

However, the aim of this paper was much more modest. My intention was in part to point out that excellent empirical research is already being done with regard to the problem of the integration of mental content. In the philosophical debate of the last two or three decades this issue may have been underestimated, partly because of it's focus on qualia. If I have succeeded in showing the relevance of a generalizable solution of the binding problem and the problem of superposition for a philosophical theory of phenomenal consciousness, then I have achieved my purpose.

---

[41] One of the most interesting contributions to the clarification of this problem which I know of is (although I cannot agree with all his points) Chalmers 1996b.

References

Abeles, M. (1982). *Local Cortical Circuits.* Berlin: Springer.

Baars, B.J. (1988). *A Cognitive Theory of Consciousness.* Cambridge: Cambridge University Press.

Baars, B.J. & Newman, J. (1994). A neurobiological interpretation of the global workspace theory of consciousness. In Revonsuo & Kamppinen 1994.

Barinaga, M. (1990). The mind revealed? *Science,* **249,** 856–8.

Barlow, H.B. (1972). Single units and sensation: A neuron doctrine for perceptual psychology? *Perception,* **1,** 371–94.

Block, N. (1995). On a confusion about the function of consciousness. *Behavioral and Brain Sciences,* **18,** 227–87. Reprinted in Block *et al.* 1996. German translation in Metzinger 1995a.

Brentano, F. (1973)[1874]. *Psychologie vom empirischen Standpunkt. Erster Band.* Hamburg: Meiner. English edition: *Psychology from an Empirical Standpoint,* (edited by Oskar Kraus, translated by Antos C. Rancurello, D.B. Terrell and Linda L. McAlister), London: Routledge & Kegan Paul, 1973.

Chalmers, D.J. (1996a). Availability: The cognitive basis of experience? In Block *et al.* 1996.

Chalmers, D.J. (1996b). *The Conscious Mind.* New York: Oxford University Press.

Churchland, P.M. (1986). Some reductive strategies in cognitive neurobiology. *Mind,* **95,** 279–309.

Clark, A. (1989). *Microcognition — Philosophy, Cognitive Science, and Parallel Distributed Processing.* Cambridge, MA: MIT Press.

Conant, R.C. & Ashby, W.R. (1970). Every good regulator of a system must be a model of that system. *International Journal of Systems Science,* Vol. I, **2,** 89–97.

Craik, K.J.W. (1943). *The Nature of Explanation.* Cambridge: Cambridge University Press. Reprinted with Postscript 1967.

Crick, F. (1984). Function of the thalamic reticular complex: The searchlight hypothesis. *Proceedings of the National Academy of Sciences,* **81,** 4586–90.

Crick, F. & Koch, C. (1990). Towards a neurobiological Theory of Consciousness. *Seminars in the Neurosciences,* **2,** 263–75.

Crick, F.H.C. & Koch, C. (1992). The problem of consciousness. *Scientific American,* **267,** 152–60.

Engel, A.K. (1994). *Zeitliche Kodierung in neuronalen Netzen: Evidenz für kohärente Aktivität im Sehsystem höherer Wirbeltiere.* Habilitationsschrift. Frankfurt am Main: Fachbereich Humanmedizin der Johann Wolfgang Goethe-Universität.

Engel, A.K, König, P., Kreiter, A.K. & Singer, W.. (1991a). Interhemispheric synchronization of oscillatory neuronal responses in cat visual cortex. *Science,* **252,** 1177–9.

Engel, A.K., König, P. & Singer, W. (1991b). Direct physiological evidence for scene segmentation by temporal coding. *Proceedings of the National Academy of Science,* **88,** 9136–40.

Engel, A.K., Kreiter, A.K., König, P. & Singer, W. (1991c). Synchronization of oscillatory neuronal responses between striate and extrastriate visual cortical areas of the cat. *Proceedings of the National Academy of Science,* **88,** 6048–52.

Engel, A.K., König, P., Kreiter, A.K., Schillen, T.B. & Singer, W. (1992a). Temporal coding in the visual cortex: new vistas on integration in the nervous system. *Trends in Neurosciences*, Volume 15, **6**, 218–26.

Engel, A.K., König, P. & Schillen, T. B. (1992b). Why does the cortex oscillate? *Current Biology*, Volume 2, **6**, 332–4.

Engel, A.K., König, P. & Singer, W. (1992c). Correlated neuronal firing: A clue to the integrative functions of cortex? In J.G. Taylor *et al.* [Eds]. *Neural Network Dynamics*. London: Springer.

Engel, A.K., König, P. & Singer, W. (1993). Bildung repräsentationaler Zustände im Gehirn. *Spektrum der Wissenschaft*, September, 42–7.

Fodor, J. (1983). *The Modularity of Mind*. Cambridge, MA: MIT Press.

Görnitz, T., Ruhnau, E. & Weizsäcker, C.F. (1992). Temporal asymmetry as precondition of experience. The Foundation of the Arrow of Time. *International Journal of Theoretical Physics,* Vol. 31, **1**, 37–46.

Gray, C.M., König, P., Engel, A.K. & Singer, W. (1989). Oscillatory responses in cat visual cortex exhibit inter-columnar synchronization which reflects global stimulus properties. *Nature*, **338**, 334–7.

Gray, C.M. (1994). Synchronous oscillations in neural systems: Mechanisms and functions. *Journal of Computational Neuroscience*, **1**, 11–38.

Green, M.B. (1979). The grain objection. *Philosophy of Science*, **46**, 559–89.

Gunderson, K. (1974). The texture of mentality. In R. Bambrough (ed), *Wisdom — Twelve Essays*. Oxford: Oxford University Press.

Hardcastle, V.G. (1994). Psychology's 'Binding Problem' and possible neurobiological solutions. *Journal of Consciousness Studies*, **1**, 66–90.

Jackendoff, R. (1987). *Consciousness and the Computational Mind*. Cambridge, MA & London: MIT Press.

Johnson-Laird, P.N. (1983). *Mental Models: Towards a Cognitive Science of Language, Inference and Consciousness*. Cambridge: Cambridge University Press.

Kinsbourne, M. (1988). Integrated field theory of consciousness. In Marcel & Bisiach 1988.

Kinsbourne, M. (1993). Integrated cortical field model of consciousness. In *Experimental and Theoretical Studies of Consciousness*. Ciba Foundation Symposium 174. Chichester, UK: Wiley.

Koch, C. & Crick, F.H.C. (1994). Some further ideas regarding the neuronal basis of awareness. In Koch & Davis 1994.

Kreiter, A.K. & Singer, W. (1992). Oscillatory neuronal responses in the visual cortex of the awake macaque monkey. *European Journal of Neuroscience*, **4**, 369–75.

Kristeva-Feige, R., Feige, B., Makeig, S., Ross, B. & Elbert, T. (1993). Oscillatory brain activity during a motor task. *Neuroreport*, **4**, 1291–4.

Kurthen, M. (1990). Qualia, Sensa und absolute Prozesse. Zu W. Sellars' Kritik des psychocerebralen Reduktionismus. *Journal for General Philosophy of Science,* **21**, 25–46.

Libet, B. (1994). A testable field theory of mind-brain interaction. *Journal of Consciousness Studies*, **1**, 119–26.

Llinás R.R. & Páre, D. (1991). Of dreaming and of wakefulness. *Neuroscience*, **44**, 521–35.

Llinás, R.R. & Ribary, U. (1993). Coherent 40-Hz-oscillation characterizes dream state in humans. *Proceedings of the National Academy of Sciences*, **90**, 2078–81.

Lockwood, M. (1993). The grain problem. In H. Robinson (ed), *Objections to Physicalism*. Oxford: Clarendon Press.

Lycan, W.G. (1987). *Consciousness*. Cambridge, MA: MIT Press.

Maxwell, G. (1978). Rigid designators and mind–body identity. In C.W. Savage (ed), *Perception and Cognition: Issues in the Foundations of Psychology. Minnesotat Studies in the Philosophy of Science, IX*. Minneapolis: University if Minnesota Press.

Meehl, P.E. (1966). The compleat autocerebroscopist: A thought experiment on Professor Feigl's mind–body identity thesis. In Feyerabend, P.K. & Maxwell, G. (eds), *Mind, Matter and Method*. Minneapolis: University of Minnesota Press.

Melzack, R. (1989). Phantom limbs, the self and the brain: The D.O. Hebb memorial lecture. *Canadian Psychology*, **30**, 1–16.

Melzack, R. (1992). Phantom limbs. *Scientific American*, **266**, 90–6.

Metzinger, T. (1993). *Subjekt und Selbstmodell. Die Perspektivität phänomenalen Bewußtseins vor dem Hintergrund einer naturalistischen Theorie mentaler Repräsentation*. Paderborn: Schöningh.

Metzinger, T. (1995a). Perspektivische Fakten? Die Naturalisierung des *View from Nowhere*. In G. Meggle & U. Wessels (Hrsg.), *ANALYOMEN 2 — Perspektiven der Analytischen Philosophie*. Berlin and New York: de Gruyter.

Metzinger, T. (1995b). Phänomenale mentale Modelle. In K. Sachs-Hombach (Hrsg.), *Bilder im Geiste: Zur kognitiven und erkenntnistheoretischen Funktion piktorialer Repräsentationen*. Reihe 'Philosophie & Repräsentation'. Amsterdam and Atlanta, GA: Rodopi.

Metzinger, T. (1996). *Niemand* sein. Kann man eine naturalistische Perspektive auf die Subjektivität des Mentalen einnehmen? In S. Krämer (Hrsg.), *Bewußtsein — Philosophische Positionen*. Frankfurt am Main: Suhrkamp.

Milner, P.M. (1974). A model for visual shape recognition. *Psychological Review*, **81**, 521–35.

Nagel, T. (1974). What is it like to be a bat? *Philosophical Review*, **83**, 435–50.

Nagel, T. (1986). *The View from Nowhere*. Oxford: Oxford University Press.

Pfurtscheller, G. & Neuper, C. (1992). Simultaneous EEG 10 Hz desynchronization und 40 Hz synchronization during finger movements. *Neuroreport*, **3**, 1057–60.

Podvigin, N.F., Jokeit, H., Pöppel, E., Chizh, A.N. & Kiselyeva, N.N. (1992). Stimulus-dependent oscillatory activity in the lateral geniculate body of the cat. *Naturwissenschaften*, **79**, 428–31.

Pöppel, E. (1972). Oscillations as possible basis for time perception. In J.T. Fraser (ed), *The Study of Time*. Berlin: Springer.

Pöppel, E., Chen, L., Glünder, H., Mitzdorf, U., Ruhnau, E., Schill, K. & Steinbüchel, N.v. (1991). Temporal and spatial constraints for mental modelling. In V. Bhathar & K. Rege (eds), *Frontiers in Knowledge-based Modelling*. Neu Delhi: Narose Publishing House.

Pöppel, E. & Logothetis, N. (1986). Neuronal oscillations in the human brain. *Naturwissenschaften*, **73**, 267 f.

Richardson, R.C. & Muilenburg, G. (1982). Sellars and sense impressions. *Erkenntnis*, **17**, 171–211.

Roelfsema, P.R. (1995). *The functional Role of neuronal Synchronization in the Visual Cortex of the Cat.* Dissertation. Frankfurt am Main: Fachbereich Humanmedizin der Johann Wolfgang Goethe-Universität.

Ruhnau, E. (1992). Zeit — das verborgene Fenster der Kognition. *Kognitionswissenschaft*, **2**, 171–9.

Ruhnau, E. & Pöppel, E. (1991). A directional temporal zones in quantum physics and brain physiology. *International Journal of Theoretical Physics*, Vol. 30, **8**, 1083–90.

Sellars, W. (1963). *Science, Perception and Reality.* London: Routledge and Kegan Paul.

Sellars, W. (1965). The identity approach to the mind-body problem. *Review of Metaphysics*, **18**, 430–51.

Singer, W. (1989a). Search for coherence: A basic principle of cortical self-organization. *Concepts in Neuroscience*, **1**, 1–28.

Singer, W. (1989b). Zur Selbstorganisation kognitiver Strukturen. In E. Pöppel (Hrsg.), *Gehirn und Bewußtsein.* Weinheim: VCH Verlagsgesellschaft.

Singer, W. (1993). Synchronization of cortical activity and its putative role in information processing and learning. *Annual Review of Physiology*, **55**, 349–74.

Singer, W. (1994). Putative functions of temporal correlations in neocortical processing. In Koch & Davis 1994.

Singer, W. (1995). The organization of sensory motor representations in the neocortex: A hypothesis based on temporal coding. In C. Umilta & M. Moscovitch (eds), *Attention and Performance XV: Conscious and Nonconscious Information Processing.* Cambridge, MA: MIT Press.

Stich, S. (1994). *Yves Klein.* Museum Ludwig, Köln & Kunstsammlung Nordrhein-Westfalen, Düsseldorf: Cantz.

von der Malsburg, C. (1981). The correlation theory of brain functioning. Internal Report 81-2. Göttingen: Max-Planck-Institut für Biophysikalische Chemie.

von der Malsburg, C. (1986). Am I thinking assemblies? In G. Palm & A. Aertsen [eds], *Brain Theory.* Berlin: Springer.

Yates, J. (1985). The content of awareness is a model of the world. *Psychological Review*, **92**, 249–84.

Part Eight

Artificial Consciousness

Introduction to Part Eight

For many people, the thought of creating artificial consciousness is frightening. For others, however, it is extremely fascinating, as in a certain sense it expresses an ultimate scientific and technological utopian dream. It is also of special interest in the philosophy of mind, for a number of reasons. First, it allows us to investigate our *criteria* for ascribing consciousness to a non-biological system. This raises the classical problem of other minds in a new form, along with what I have called the 'epistemic asymmetry' in the general introduction at the beginning of this volume: Is there at all certain knowledge about the subjective states of other beings? Second, it raises questions about the *explanatory basis* of consciousness. Does the phenomenon belong to the realm of the information sciences? Are the crucial properties for the emergence of consciousness informational and computational rather than biological properties? Third, the question of artificially generated experience links the philosophy of mind with other fields in the discipline, such as ethics or anthropology.

Deep-seated intuitions often block the clear view of the epistemological question. Even if we succeeded in conferring on a machine all those functional properties which we, in a *human being,* regard as characteristic features of consciousness, many would still not believe that this machine *is* also conscious. Let us assume that we construct a 'technical demon': We program an artificial system and teach it how to configure *itself* in interaction with its environment in a way that enables it to move intelligently, successfully and in a goal-directed manner in the world — who among us would believe that we have realized *Artificial Consciousness* and not only *Artificial Intelligence*? Imagine an autonomous cognitive robot with a humanoid shape, connected by radio to a gigantic neuronal network which is supervised by a serial controller and linked to other mainframes. This system could move freely in the world and, via the Internet, access a huge stock of knowledge. Of course, it would also possess a self model, a complex inner picture of itself and its history. Moreover, we could imagine that it could talk in our mother tongue, and would know so much about *our* form of life that it would pass the Turing Test anytime. No human could then uncover it as an artificial system by communication alone. Would we believe that the light of consciousness shines within such a system? Would we believe that it has *experiences*? Many people would not.

Let us further assume that a robot is interwoven with its environment through such a complex and subtle net of causal chains that in predicting and explaining its actions we could not but describe it as an *intentional system*: a system whose inner states we have to analyse as states with *intentional content* if we want to understand its behavioural patterns at all. Intentional systems are systems with regard to which a certain type of explanatory strategy works especially well in predicting their behaviour: the 'intentional stance'. If we ascribe true opinions, wishes and rationality to a system in order to predict its behaviour, we take up the intentional stance. However, this does not lead automatically to the 'phenomenal stance'. If our technical demon possesses higher-order states which allow him to produce more precise statements about his own states and better prognoses about his future behaviour than his inventors — that is, if it could apply the intentional stance to itself better than we could apply it ourselves — this might dislodge our chauvinist intuitions for the first time. The best and most satisfying criterion for the acceptance of a non-biological subject would perhaps be fulfilled if the system demonstrated convincingly that it had understood the *philosophical problem* of consciousness and so began to participate in the discussion with its own arguments. If an artificial system forced us into a discourse and rationally argued for its *own* theory of mind, we would be forced to show it that the concept of 'consciousness' has a precisely defined place in a convincing scientific theory of mind, which is superior to the system's.

The question about the explanatory basis of mind is also interesting. Machines are functional systems. They can be exhaustively described by a functional analysis of their internal states and a specification of the *hardware* through which the respective functions are realized. If there are no principled reasons which exclude the possibility of machine consciousness, it may also be possible to develop a functionalist theory of phenomenal consciousness. Many philosophers doubt this possibility. However, a number of fundamental issues are related to this point: is the theoretic strategy of functionalism, which is very closely connected to the methodology of the information processing paradigm in the neurosciences and cognitive science, systematically blind with respect to the phenomenon of conscious experience? Or can classical functionalism be improved in a way that also yields an explanation of what it means that some of our inner states are *conscious states*, i.e. that they possess phenomenal content?

Thirdly, the project of a general theory of phenomenal content is also relevant to other philosophical disciplines such as ethics and anthropology. These issues are not the subject of this book, but their significance will increase in the future. For this reason, a short glance at them may be appropriate. For many people the vision of a technical demon gives rise to archaic fears. For this reason it is all the more important that discussion of the ethical issues involved be conducted as rational as possible. To begin with, questions such as the following arise: Is the emergence of artificial consciousness — e.g. in the framework of a post-biotic evolution started by us — merely a particularly ambitious aim in the technological application of scientific knowledge or is it possibly something which should, for moral reasons, be prevented by all means? This point concerns the ethics of science, or to be more precise, the interaction between theoretic progress and its technological application. Karl Popper wrote in 1977:

> Turing [1950] said something like this: specify the way in which you believe that a man is superior to a computer and I shall build a computer which refutes your belief. Turing's challenge should not be taken up; for any sufficiently precise specification could be used in principle to programme a computer.

Such unargued claims illustrate the connection between *epistemological* and *normative* questions in the discussion about artificial consciousness. Personally, I regard the realization of artificial consciousness as morally problematic, not least because this might mean the creation of the possibility for artificial *suffering*. However, there is another major ethical issue, which Hilary Putnam formulated as early as 1964:

> I have referred to this problem as the problem of the 'civil rights of robots' because that is what it may become, and much faster than any of us now expect. Given the ever-accelerating rate of both social and technological change, it is entirely possible that robots will one day exist, and argue 'we *are* alive; we *are* conscious!' In that event, what are today only philosophical prejudices of a traditional anthropocentric and mentalistic kind would all too likely develop into conservative political attitudes. But fortunately, we today have the advantage of being able to discuss this problem disinterestedly, and a little more chance, therefore, of arriving at the correct answer.

The possession of conscious experiences is one of the central criteria in virtue of which we ascribe (or deny) the status of a *person* to a system. This is another reason for the fact that the project of a theory of phenomenal consciousness is of fundamental significance for philosophical ethics.

New questions for *applied* ethics also arise. Through the progress made in the empirical study of consciousness, e.g. in brain research, in AI research and in cognitive science, a large number of new actions become possible, for example in the medical or military field. It is easy to imagine that this also means that new dangers come into existence. A topical catchword here is 'neurotechnology': Which new problems arise through the fact that, as a result of empirical research into consciousness, our technical means of influencing phenomenal consciousness by directly interfering with the brain will be continually improved in the future?

A particularly interesting aspect arises in the context of the question of the possibility of *normative psychology*. The most fundamental question here is: Is conscious experience a *good-in-itself* at all? In particular, is the specific human form of consciousness an *interesting* form of consciousness? Is it something which we may multiply without scruples? But: Which conscious states are interesting conscious states *at all*? And: Are there conscious states which in a *normative* sense possess a higher value than others? If we engage in general reflections about this problem and limit ourselves to the human form of conscious experience, they will lead us into the realm of philosophical anthropology. In a more specific sense, however, we also touch upon the important question of the domain of ethical theories: In what way does the capacity for having conscious experiences play a role for what we regard as *objects* of moral consideration? Is it not precisely the fact that something is a phenomenal *subject* which also makes it a moral object? At which point should we assume that any given system — regardless of whether it is artificial, natural or post-biotic — is *capable of suffering*? Philosophical answers to questions of this kind will also have an immediate bearing upon a great number of familiar problems of applied ethics, e.g. the treatment of animals, abortion, or the discussion about euthanasia.

Let me make a last remark concerning philosophical anthropology. It is highly likely that along with new, empirically grounded theories of consciousness, a new picture of man will also emerge. It can already be foreseen that this new anthropology, as well as the theory of mind which accompanies it, will dramatically contradict almost all traditional pictures of human beings and their inner life. For this reason, it is not unlikely that many people will regard it as degrading. This problem concerns the sociocultural consequences of new theories: It draws our attention to the problem of the cultural assimilation of scientific progress and our changed picture of ourselves. Therefore, phenomenal consciousness is *also* a cultural and social problem. We need empirical research into consciousness, we need serious philosophy of consciousness and we need a critical culture of consciousness, which achieves rational integration of new insights and possibilities sat the level of society.

Let us now return to the philosophical core of the problem: Is the concept of 'Artificial Consciousness' a *coherent* concept at all? The two texts that follow approach the topic from very different angles. In his contribution, **Daniel Dennett** reports from the initial stages of a research project in which he is participating at the Massachusetts Institute of Technology. The aim of the project is the construction of a humanoid robot named 'Cog'. However, the MIT team is not primarily interested in creating a conscious robot: rather, they intend to build a robot which possesses certain 'cognitive talents', such as the mastery of natural language, the movements of objects co-ordinated by eye-movements as well as a great number of self-preserving, self-regulating and self-reflexive activities. The hope is that the progressive implementation of such cognitive abilities will finally enable the system to interact with people in a robust and varied manner. Moreover, it should also be able to look after its own needs and to provide its creators with information concerning itself which contains pieces of information which the latter could not, or only with great difficulty, obtain 'from the outside'. In his introductory remarks, Dennett examines the question of what it means if we say that a phenomenally conscious artefact is impossible *in principle*. In the second part of his essay, he sketches details of the research project. In the last section, he then turns to three typical objections to the 'strong AI thesis' and discusses them critically. The first sceptical thesis amounts to the claim that the internal symbols of an artificial system can never refer to the external world in the sense of a genuine reference relation. The second thesis is that an artificial system has no genuine interests, and so can only have simulated feelings, never real ones. The third objection is that if we ascribe consciousness to a system, we would have to believe its statements about its own internal states. Dennett points out that this might, in the future, precisely be the case with 'Cog': The system itself fills the 'epistemological vacuum' concerning its own states because it has become the best source of information about them.

In the final essay of this collection, **Dieter Birnbacher** offers a logical analysis of the conditions under which we could apply the predicate 'conscious' to an artificial system. His starting point is the widespread opinion that machine consciousness is impossible in principle. He distinguishes three different impossibility theses: Artificial Consciousness could be *technically* impossible, it could be *conceptually* impossible or it could be *nomologically* impossible. Theses of the first kind are only of little interest philosophically. In a critical discussion of Wittgenstein, Birnbacher then argues against the second thesis. From the fact that *today* we do not have good reasons to ascribe conscious states to a machine, it does not follow that this will always be the case. Rather, the criteria for the ascription of consciousness flow from the nomologically sufficient conditions of consciousness. These criteria are not behavioural, but will be isolated step-by-step by the neurosciences of the future. In the conclusion, Dieter Birnbacher finally points to the consequences which result from our epistemic limitation with regard to the consciousness of alien systems. He urges that we should abstain from constructing conscious machines in any cases of which we are doubtful, so long as we do not fully understand the physical basis of phenomenal consciousness.

Further Reading

Birnbacher, D. (1974). *Die Logik der Kriterien. Analysen zur Spätphilosophie Wittgensteins*. Hamburg: Meiner.

Birnbacher, D. (1988). Epiphenomenalism as a solution to the ontological mind-body problem. *Ratio* (new series), **1**, 17–32.

Birnbacher, D. (1990). Das ontologische Leib-Seele-Problem und seine epiphänomenalistische Lösung. In K.-E. Bühler (Hrsg.). *Aspekte des Leib-Seele-Problems: Philosophie, Medizin, Künstliche Intelligenz*. Würzburg.

Dennett, D.C. (1969). *Content and Consciousness*. London: Routledge and Kegan Paul.

Dennett, D.C. (1971). Intentional Systems. *Journal of Philosophy*, **8**, 87–106.

Dennett, D.C. (1981). True believers: the intentional strategy and why it works. In A.F. Heath (ed), *Scientific Explanations*, Oxford: Oxford University Press. Reprinted in Dennett 1978 and in Stich, S. P. & Warfield, T. A. (1994)[Eds]. *Mental Representation. A Reader*. Oxford: Blackwell.

Dennett, D.C. (1987). *The Intentional Stance*. Cambridge, MA and London: MIT Press.

Dennett, D.C. (1991). *Consciousness Explained*. Boston, MA: Little, Brown & Co.

Dennett, D.C. (1995). *Darwin's Dangerous Idea*. New York: Simon and Schuster.

Popper, K.R. & Eccles, J.C. (1977). *The Self and its Brain: An Argument for Interactionism*. Routledge and Kegan Paul.

Putnam, H. (1964). Robots: machines or artificially created life? *Journal of Philosophy*, **61**, 668–91. Reprinted in H. Putnam, (1975), *Mind, Language and Reality. Philosophical Papers, Volume 2*. Cambridge: Cambridge University Press.

A number of individual articles especially selected with regard to the question of the possibility of artificial consciousness can be found in section 3.10 of the bibliography at the end of this volume. Further texts concerning this area of discussion are listed in sections 1.1, 2.1 and 3.1.

Daniel C. Dennett

Cog: Steps Towards Consciousness in Robots

I. Are Conscious Robots Possible 'in Principle'?

It is unlikely, in my opinion, that anyone will ever make a robot that is conscious in just the way we human beings are. Presumably that prediction is less interesting than the reasons one might offer for it. They might be deep — conscious robots are in some way 'impossible in principle' — or they might be trivial — for instance, conscious robots might simply cost too much to make. Nobody will ever synthesize a gall bladder out of atoms of the requisite elements, but I think it is uncontroversial that a gall bladder is nevertheless 'just' a stupendous assembly of such atoms. Might a conscious robot be 'just' a stupendous assembly of more elementary artifacts — silicon chips, wires, tiny motors and cameras — or would any such assembly, of whatever size and sophistication, have to leave out some special ingredient that is requisite for consciousness?

Let us briefly survey a nested series of reasons someone might advance for the impossibility of a conscious robot:

1. Robots are purely material things, and consciousness requires immaterial mind-stuff (old-fashioned dualism).

It continues to amaze me how attractive this position still is to many people. I would have thought a historical perspective alone would make this view seem ludicrous: over the centuries, every *other* phenomenon of initially 'supernatural' mysteriousness has succumbed to an uncontroversial explanation within the commodious folds of physical science. Thales, the

An earlier version of this paper was presented at the Royal Society meeting, Artificial Intelligence and the Mind, 13–14 April 1994, and appears, under the title, 'The practical requirements for building a conscious robot', in the Philosophical Transactions of the Royal Society, **349**, 133–46.

Pre-Socratic proto-scientist, thought the loadstone had a soul, but we now know better; magnetism is one of the best understood of physical phenomena, strange though its manifestations are. The 'miracles' of life itself, and of reproduction, are now analysed into the well-known intricacies of molecular biology. Why should consciousness be any exception? Why should the brain be the only complex physical object in the universe to have an interface with another realm of being? Besides, the notorious problems with the supposed transactions at that dualistic interface are as good as a *reductio ad absurdum* of the view. The phenomena of consciousness are an admittedly dazzling lot, but I suspect that dualism would never be seriously considered if there weren't such a strong undercurrent of desire to protect the mind from science, by supposing it composed of a stuff that is in principle uninvestigatable by the methods of the physical sciences.

But if you are willing to concede the hopelessness of dualism, and accept some version of materialism, you might still hold:

2. Robots are inorganic (by definition), and consciousness can exist only in an organic brain.

Why might this be? Instead of just hooting this view off the stage as an embarrassing throwback to old-fashioned vitalism, we might pause to note that there is a respectable, if not very interesting, way of defending this claim. Vitalism is deservedly dead; as biochemistry has shown in matchless detail, the powers of organic compounds are themselves all mechanistically reducible and hence mechanistically reproducible at one scale or another in alternative physical media; but it is conceivable — if unlikely — that the sheer speed and compactness of biochemically engineered processes in the brain are in fact unreproducible in other physical media (Dennett 1987). So there might be straightforward reasons of engineering that showed that any robot that could not make use of organic tissues of one sort or another within its fabric would be too ungainly to execute some task critical for consciousness. If making a conscious robot were conceived of as a sort of sporting event — like the America's Cup — rather than a scientific endeavor, this could raise a curious conflict over the official rules. Team A wants to use artificially constructed organic polymer 'muscles' to move its robot's limbs, because otherwise the motor noise wreaks havoc with the robot's artificial ears. Should this be allowed? Is a robot with 'muscles' instead of motors a robot within the meaning of the act? If muscles are allowed, what about lining the robot's artificial retinas with genuine organic rods and cones instead of relying on relatively clumsy colour-tv technology?

I take it that no serious scientific or philosophical thesis links its fate to the fate of the proposition that a *protein-free* conscious robot can be made, for example. The standard understanding that a robot shall be made of metal, silicon chips, glass, plastic, rubber and such, is an expression of the willingness of theorists to bet on a simplification of the issues: their conviction is that the crucial functions of intelligence can be achieved by one high-level simulation or another, so that it would be no undue hardship to restrict themselves to these materials, the readily available cost-effective ingredients in any case. But if somebody were to invent some sort of cheap artificial neural network fabric that could usefully be spliced into various tight corners in a robot's control system, the embarrassing fact that this fabric was made of organic molecules would not and should not dissuade serious roboticists from using it — and simply taking on the burden of explaining to the uninitiated why this did not constitute 'cheating' in any important sense.

I have discovered that some people are attracted by a third reason for believing in the impossibility of conscious robots:

3. Robots are artifacts, and consciousness abhors an artifact; only something natural, born not manufactured, could exhibit genuine consciousness.

Once again, it is tempting to dismiss this claim with derision, and in some of its forms, derision is just what it deserves. Consider the general category of creed we might call *origin essentialism*: only wine made under the direction of the proprietors of Chateau Plonque counts as genuine Chateau Plonque; only a canvas every blotch on which was caused by the hand of Cézanne counts as a genuine Cézanne; only someone 'with Cherokee blood' can be a real Cherokee. There are perfectly respectable reasons, eminently defensible in a court of law, for maintaining such distinctions, so long as they are understood to be protections of rights growing out of historical processes. If they are interpreted, however, as indicators of 'intrinsic properties' that set their holders apart from their otherwise indistinguishable counterparts, they are pernicious nonsense. Let us dub *origin chauvinism* the category of view that holds out for some mystic difference (a difference of value, typically) due *simply* to such a fact about origin. Perfect imitation Chateau Plonque is exactly as good a wine as the real thing, counterfeit though it is, and the same holds for the fake Cézanne, if it is really indistinguishable by experts. And of course no person is intrinsically better or worse in any regard just for having or not having Cherokee (or Jewish, or African) 'blood.'

And to take a threadbare philosophical example, an atom-for-atom duplicate of a human being, an artifactual counterfeit of you, let us say, might not *legally* be you, and hence might not be entitled to your belongings, or deserve your punishments, but the suggestion that such a being would not be a feeling, conscious, alive *person* as genuine as any born of woman is preposterous nonsense, all the more deserving of our ridicule because if taken seriously it might seem to lend credibility to the racist drivel with which it shares a bogus 'intuition'.

If consciousness abhors an artifact, it cannot be because being born gives a complex of cells a property (aside from that historic property itself) that it could not otherwise have 'in principle'. There might, however, be a question of practicality. We have just seen how, as a matter of exigent practicality, it could turn out after all that organic materials were needed to make a conscious robot. For similar reasons, it could turn out that any conscious robot had to be, if not born, at least the beneficiary of a longish period of infancy. Making a fully-equipped conscious adult robot might just be too much work. It might be vastly easier to make an initially unconscious or nonconscious 'infant' robot and let it 'grow up' into consciousness, more or less the way we all do. This hunch is not the disreputable claim that a certain sort of historic process puts a mystic stamp of approval on its product, but the more interesting and plausible claim that a certain sort of process is the only practical way of designing all the things that need designing in a conscious being.

Such a claim is entirely reasonable. Compare it to the claim one might make about the creation of Steven Spielberg's film, *Schindler's List*: it could not have been created entirely by computer animation, without the filming of real live actors. This impossibility claim must be false 'in principle,' since every frame of that film is nothing more than a matrix of gray-scale pixels of the sort that computer animation can manifestly create, at any level of detail or 'realism' you are willing to pay for. There is nothing mystical, however, about the claim that it would be practically impossible to render the nuances of that film by such a bizarre exercise of technology. How much easier it is, practically, to put actors in the relevant circumstances, in a concrete simulation of the scenes one wishes to portray, and let them, via ensemble activity and re-activity, provide the information to the cameras that will then fill in all the pixels in each frame. This little exercise of the imagination helps to drive home just how much information there is in a 'realistic' film, but even a great film, such as *Schindler's List*, for all its complexity, is a simple, non-interactive artifact many orders of magnitude less complex than a conscious being.

When robot-makers have claimed in the past that in principle they could construct 'by hand' a conscious robot, this was a hubristic overstatement analogous to what Walt Disney might once have proclaimed: that his studio of animators could create a film so realistic that no one would be able to tell that it was a cartoon, not a live action film. What Disney couldn't do in fact, computer animators still cannot do, but perhaps only for the time being. Robot makers, even with the latest high-tech innovations, also fall far short of their hubristic goals, now and for the foreseeable future. The comparison serves to expose the likely source of the outrage so many sceptics feel when they encounter the manifestos of the Artificial Intelligencia. Anyone who seriously claimed that *Schindler's List* could in fact have been made by computer animation could be seen to betray an obscenely impoverished sense of what is conveyed in that film. An important element of the film's power is the fact that it is a film made by assembling human actors to portray those events, and that it is not actually the newsreel footage that its black-and-white format reminds you of. When one juxtaposes in one's imagination a sense of what the actors must have gone through to make the film with a sense of what the people who actually lived the events went through, this reflection sets up reverberations in one's thinking that draw attention to the deeper meanings of the film. Similarly, when robot enthusiasts proclaim the likelihood that they can simply *construct* a conscious robot, there is an understandable suspicion that they are simply betraying an infantile grasp of the subtleties of conscious life. (I hope I have put enough feeling into that condemnation to satisfy the sceptics.)

But however justified that might be in some instances as an *ad hominem* suspicion, it is simply irrelevant to the important theoretical issues. Perhaps no cartoon could be a great film, but they are certainly real films — and some are indeed good films; if the best the roboticists can hope for is the creation of some crude, cheesy, second-rate, artificial consciousness, they still win. Still, it is not a foregone conclusion that even this modest goal is reachable. If you want to have a defensible reason for claiming that no conscious robot will ever be created, you might want to settle for this:

4. Robots will always just be much too simple to be conscious.

After all, a normal human being is composed of trillions of parts (if we descend to the level of the macromolecules), and many of these rival in complexity and design cunning the fanciest artifacts that have ever been created. We consist of billions of cells, and a single human cell contains within itself complex 'machinery' that is still well beyond the artifactual powers of engineers. We are composed of thousands of different kinds of cells, including thousands of different species of symbiont visitors, some of whom might be as important to our consciousness as others are to our ability to digest our food! If all that complexity were needed for consciousness to exist, then the task of making a single conscious robot would dwarf the entire scientific and engineering resources of the planet for millennia. And who would pay for it?

If no other reason can be found, this may do to ground your scepticism about conscious robots in your future, but one shortcoming of this last reason is that it is scientifically boring. If this is the only reason there won't be conscious robots, then consciousness isn't that special, after all. Another shortcoming with this reason is that it is dubious on its face. Everywhere else we have looked, we have found higher-level commonalities of function that permit us to substitute relatively simple bits for fiendishly complicated bits. Artificial heart valves work really very well, but they are orders of magnitude simpler than organic heart valves, heart valves born of woman or sow, you might say. Artificial ears and eyes that will do a serviceable (if crude) job of substituting for lost perceptual organs are visible on the horizon, and anyone who doubts they are possible in principle is simply out of touch. Nobody ever said a prosthetic eye had to see as keenly, or focus as fast, or be as sensitive to colour gradations as a normal human (or other animal) eye in order to 'count' as an eye. If an eye, why not an optic nerve (or acceptable substitute thereof), and so forth, all the way in?

Some (Searle 1992; Mangan 1993) have supposed, most improbably, that this proposed regress would somewhere run into a non-fungible medium of consciousness, a part of the brain that could not be substituted on pain of death or zombiehood. Once the implications of that view are spelled out (Dennett 1993a; 1993b), one can see that it is a non-starter. There is no reason at all to believe that some one part of the brain is utterly irreplacible by prosthesis, provided we allow that some crudity, some loss of function, is to be expected in most substitutions of the simple for the complex. An artificial brain is, on the face of it, as 'possible in principle' as an artificial heart, just much, much harder to make and hook up. Of course once we start letting crude forms of prosthetic consciousness — like crude forms of prosthetic vision or hearing — pass our litmus tests for consciousness (whichever tests we favour) the way is open for another boring debate, over whether the phenomena in question are too crude to count.

II. The Cog Project: A Humanoid Robot

A much more interesting tack to explore, in my opinion, is simply to set out to make a robot that is theoretically interesting independent of the philo-sophical conundrum about whether it is conscious. Such a robot would have to perform a lot of the feats that we have typically associated with con-sciousness in the past, but we would not need to dwell on that issue from the outset. Maybe we could even learn something interesting about what the truly hard problems are without ever settling any of the issues about consciousness.

Such a project is now underway at MIT. Under the direction of Professors Rodney Brooks and Lynn Andrea Stein of the AI Lab, a group of bright, hard-working young graduate students are labouring as I speak to create Cog, the most humanoid robot yet attempted, and I am happy to be be a part of the Cog team. Cog's name has a double etymology: on the one hand, it is intended to instantiate the fruits of cognitive science, and on the other, it is a concrete machine situated in the real, non-virtual world, with motors, bearings, springs, wires, pulleys . . . and cogs. Cog is just about life-size — that is, about the size of a human adult. Cog has no legs, but lives bolted at the hips, you might say, to its stand. This paraplegia was dictated by

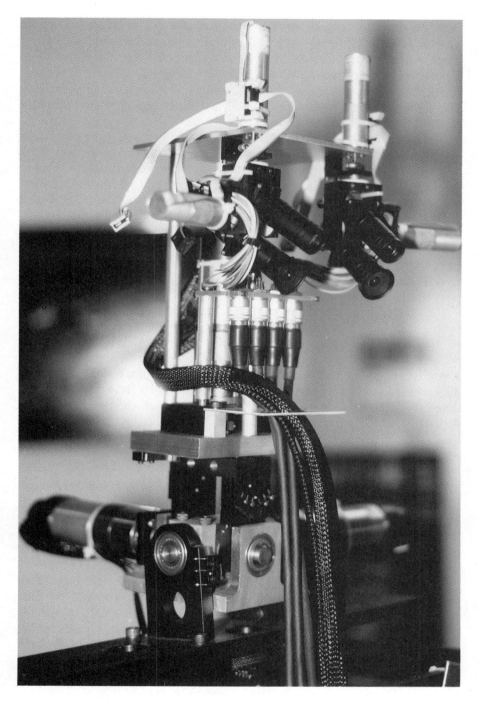

Figure 1. Cog: a pre-natal portrait.

intensely practical considerations: if Cog had legs and could walk, it would have to trail a collossally unwieldy umbilical cord, for both power and input-output to its brain, which is about the size of a telephone booth. No batteries exist that could power Cog's motors for hours on end, and telemetering the enormously wide-bandwidth input–output traffic between body and brain — a task I took for granted in 'Where am I?' — is still well beyond the technology available.

Cog has no legs, but it has two human-length arms, with somewhat oversized, three-fingered hands on the wrists. It can bend at the waist and swing its torso, and its head moves with three degrees of freedom just about the way yours does. It has two eyes, each equipped with both a foveal high-resolution vision area and a low-resolution wide-angle parafoveal vision area, and these eyes saccade at almost human speed. That is, the two eyes can complete approximately three fixations a second, while you and I can manage four or five. Your foveas are at the center of your retinas, surrounded by the grainier low-resolution parafoveal areas; for reasons of engineering simplicity, Cog's eyes have their foveas mounted above their wide-angle vision areas.

This is typical of the sort of compromise that the Cog team is willing to make. It amounts to a wager that a vision system with the foveas moved out of the middle can still work well enough not to be debilitating, and the problems encountered will not be irrelevant to the problems encountered in normal human vision. After all, nature gives us examples of other eyes with different foveal arrangements. Eagles, for instance have two different foveas in each eye. Cog's eyes won't give it visual information exactly like that provided to human vision by human eyes (in fact, of course, it will be vastly degraded), but the wager is that this will be plenty to give Cog the opportunity to perform impressive feats of hand-eye coordination, identification, and search.

Since its eyes are video cameras mounted on delicate, fast-moving gimbals, it might be disastrous if Cog were inadvertently to punch itself in the eye, so part of the hard-wiring that must be provided in advance is an 'innate' if rudimentary 'pain' or 'alarm' system to serve roughly the same protective functions as the reflex eye-blink and pain-avoidance systems hard-wired into human infants.

Cog will not be an adult at first, in spite of its adult size. It is being designed to pass through an extended period of artificial infancy, during which it will have to learn from experience, experience it will gain in the rough-and-tumble environment of the real world. Like a human infant, however, it will need a great deal of protection at the outset, in spite of the fact that it will be equipped with many of the most crucial safety-systems of a living being. It has limit switches, heat sensors, current sensors, strain gauges and alarm signals in all the right places to prevent it from destroying its many motors and joints. It has enormous 'funny bones' — motors sticking out from its elbows in a risky way. These will be protected from harm not by being shielded in heavy armour, but by being equipped with patches of exquisitely sensitive piezo-electric membrane 'skin' which will trigger alarms when they make contact with anything. The goal is that Cog will quickly 'learn' to keep its funny bones from being bumped — if Cog cannot learn this in short order, it will have to have this high-priority policy hard-wired in. The same sensitive membranes will be used on its fingertips and elsewhere, and, like human tactile nerves, the 'meaning' of the signals sent along the attached wires will depend more on what the central control system makes of them than on their intrinsic characteristics. A gentle touch, signalling sought-for contact with an object to be grasped, will not differ, as an information packet, from a sharp pain, signalling a need for rapid countermeasures. It all depends on what the central system is designed to do with the packet, and this design is itself indefinitely revisable — something that can be adjusted either by Cog's own experience or by the tinkering of Cog's artificers.

One of its most interesting 'innate' endowments will be software for visual face recognition. Faces will 'pop out' from the background of other objects as items of special interest to Cog. It will further be innately designed to 'want' to keep it's 'mother's' face in view, and to work hard to keep 'mother' from turning away. The role of mother has not yet been cast, but several of the graduate students have been tentatively tapped for this role. Unlike a human infant, of course, there is no reason why Cog can't have a whole team of mothers, each of whom is innately distinguished by Cog as a face to please if possible. Clearly, even if Cog really does have a *Lebenswelt*, it will not be the same as *ours*.

Decisions have not yet been reached about many of the candidates for hard-wiring or innate features. Anything that can learn must be initially equipped with a great deal of unlearned design. That is no longer an issue; no *tabula rasa* could ever be impressed with knowledge from experience. But it is also not much of an issue which features ought to be innately fixed, for there is a convenient trade-off. I haven't mentioned yet that Cog will actually be a multi-generational series of ever improved models (if all goes well!), but of course that is the way any complex artifact gets designed.[2] Any feature that is not innately fixed at the outset, but does get itself designed into Cog's control system through learning, can then often be lifted whole (with some revision, perhaps) into Cog-II, as a new bit of innate endowment designed by Cog itself — or rather by Cog's history of interactions with its environment. So even in cases in which we have the best of reasons for thinking that human infants actually come innately equipped with pre-designed gear, we may choose to try to get Cog to learn the design

---

[2] In fact, Cog already has four heads, its 'proper' head and three others, equipped with eyes, simply because there aren't enough hours in the day for one head to serve the needs of all the students working on it.

in question, rather than be born with it. In some instances, this is laziness or opportunism — we don't really know what might work well, but maybe Cog can train itself up. This insouciance about the putative nature/nurture boundary is already a familiar attitude among neural net modellers, of course. Although Cog is not specifically intended to demonstrate any particular neural net thesis, it should come as no surprise that Cog's nervous system is a massively parallel architecture capable of simultaneously training up an indefinite number of special-purpose networks or circuits, under various regimes.

How plausible is the hope that Cog can retrace the steps of millions of years of evolution in a few months or years of laboratory exploration? Notice first that what I have just described is a variety of Lamarckian inheritance that no organic lineage has been able to avail itself of. The acquired design innovations of Cog-I can be immediately transferred to Cog-II, a speed-up of evolution of tremendous, if incalculable, magnitude. Moreover, if you bear in mind that, unlike the natural case, there will be a team of overseers ready to make patches whenever obvious shortcomings reveal themselves, and to jog the systems out of ruts whenever they enter them, it is not so outrageous a hope, in our opinion. But then, we are all rather outrageous people.

One talent that we have hopes of teaching to Cog is a rudimentary capacity for human language. And here we run into the fabled innate language organ or Language Acquisition Device made famous by Noam Chomsky. Is there going to be an attempt to build an innate LAD for our Cog? No. We are going to try to get Cog to build language the hard way, the way our ancestors must have done, over thousands of generations. Cog has ears (four, because it's easier to get good localization with four microphones than with carefully shaped ears like ours!) and some special-purpose signal-analysing software is being developed to give Cog a fairly good chance of discriminating human speech sounds, and probably the capacity to distinguish different human voices. Cog will also have to have speech synthesis hardware and software, of course, but decisions have not yet been reached about the details. It is important to have Cog as well-equipped as possible for rich and natural interactions with human beings, for the team intends to take advantage of as much free labour as it can. Untrained people ought to be able to spend time — hours if they like, and we rather hope they do — trying to get Cog to learn this or that. Growing into an adult is a long, time-consuming business, and Cog — and the team that is building Cog — will need all the help it can get.

Obviously this will not work unless the team manages somehow to give Cog a motivational structure that can be at least dimly recognized, responded to, and exploited by naive observers. In short, Cog should be as human as possible in its wants and fears, likes and dislikes. If those anthropomorphic terms strike you as unwarranted, put them in scare-quotes or drop them altogether and replace them with tedious neologisms of your own choosing: Cog, you may prefer to say, must have *goal-registrations* and *preference-functions* that map in rough isomorphism to human desires. This is so for many reasons, of course. Cog won't work at all unless it has its act together in a daunting number of different regards. It must somehow delight in learning, abhor error, strive for novelty, recognize progress. It must be vigilant in some regards, curious in others, and deeply unwilling to engage in self-destructive activity. While we are at it, we might as well try to make it crave human praise and company, and even exhibit a sense of humour.

Let me switch abruptly from this heavily anthropomorphic language to a brief description of Cog's initial endowment of information-processing hardware. The computer-complex that has been built to serve as the development platform for Cog's artificial nervous system consists of four backplanes, each with 16 nodes; each node is basically a Mac-II computer — a 68332 processor with a megabyte of RAM. In other words, you can think of Cog's brain as roughly equivalent to sixty-four Mac-IIs yoked in a custom parallel architecture. Each node is itself a multiprocessor, and instead of running Mac software, they all run a special version of parallel Lisp developed by Rodney Brooks, and called, simply, L. Each node has an interpreter for L in its ROM, so it can execute L files independently of every other node.

Figure 2: The Front End Processor, bank of monitors, and Cog (arms not yet attached).

Each node has 6 assignable input-output ports, in addition to the possibility of separate i-o (input-output) to the motor boards directly controlling the various joints, as well as the all-important i-o to the experimenters' monitoring and control system, the Front End Processor or FEP (via another unit known as the Interfep). On a bank of separate monitors, one can see the current image in each camera (two foveas, two parafoveas), the activity in each of the many different visual processing areas, or the activities of any other nodes. Cog is thus equipped at birth with the equivalent of chronically implanted electrodes for each of its neurons; all its activities can be monitored in real time, recorded and debugged. The FEP is itself a Macintosh computer in more conventional packaging. At startup, each node is awakened by a FEP call that commands it to load its appropriate files of L from a file server. These files configure it for whatever tasks it has currently been designed to execute. Thus the underlying hardware machine can be turned into any of a host of different virtual machines, thanks to the capacity of each node to run its current program. The nodes do not make further use of disk memory, however, during normal operation. They keep their transient memories locally, in their individual megabytes of RAM. In other words, Cog stores both its genetic endowment (the virtual machine) and its long term memory on disk when it is shut down, but when it is powered on, it first configures itself and then stores all its short term memory distributed one way or another among its 64 nodes.

The space of possible virtual machines made available and readily explorable by this underlying architecture is huge, of course, and it covers a volume in the space of all computations that has not yet been seriously explored by artificial intelligence researchers. Moreover, the space of possibilities it represents is manifestly much more realistic as a space to build brains in than is the space heretofore explored, either by the largely serial architectures of GOFAI ('Good Old Fashioned AI', Haugeland 1985), or by parallel architectures simulated by serial machines. Nevertheless, it is arguable that every one of the possible virtual machines executable by Cog is minute in comparison to a real human brain. In short, Cog has a tiny brain. There is a big wager being made: the parallelism made possible by this arrangement will be sufficient to provide real-time control of importantly humanoid activities occurring on a human time scale. If this proves to be too optimistic by as little as an order of magnitude, the whole project will be forlorn, for the motivating insight for the project is that by confronting and solving *actual, real time* problems of self-protection, hand-eye coordination, and interaction with other animate beings, Cog's artificers will discover the *sufficient* conditions for higher cognitive functions in general — and maybe even for a variety of consciousness that would satisfy the sceptics.

It is important to recognize that although the theoretical importance of having a body has been appreciated ever since Alan Turing (1950) drew specific attention to it in his classic paper, 'Computing machines and intelligence', within the field of artificial intelligence there has long been a contrary opinion that robotics is largely a waste of time, money and effort. Marvin Minsky, for instance, has vigorously expressed this criticism of Cog. According to this view, whatever deep principles of organization make cognition possible can be as readily discovered in the more abstract realm of pure simulation, at a fraction of the cost. In many fields, this thrifty attitude has proven to be uncontroversial wisdom. No economists have asked for the funds to implement their computer models of markets and industries in tiny robotic Wall Streets or Detroits, and civil engineers have largely replaced their scale models of bridges and tunnels with computer models that can do a better job of simulating all the relevant conditions of load, stress and strain. Closer to home, simulations of ingeniously oversimplified imaginary organisms foraging in imaginary environments, avoiding imaginary predators and differentially producing imaginary offspring are yielding important insights into the mechanisms of evolution and ecology in the new field of artificial life. So it is something of a surprise to find this AI group conceding, in effect, that there is indeed something to the sceptics' claim (e.g. Dreyfus & Dreyfus 1986) that genuine embodiment in a real world is crucial to consciousness. Not, I hasten to add, because genuine embodiment provides some special vital juice that mere virtual-world simulations cannot secrete, but for the more practical reason — or hunch — that unless you saddle yourself with all the problems of making a concrete agent take care of itself in the real world, you will tend to overlook, underestimate, or misconstrue the deepest problems of design.   Besides, as I have already noted, there is the hope that Cog will be able to design itself in large measure, learning from infancy, and building its own representation of its world in the terms that it innately understands. Nobody doubts that any agent capable of interacting intelligently with a human being on human terms must have access to literally millions if not billions of logically independent items of world knowledge. Either these must be hand-coded individually by human programmers — a tactic being pursued, notoriously, by Douglas Lenat (Lenat & Guha 1990) and his CYC team in Dallas — or some way must be found for the artificial agent to learn its world knowledge from (real) interactions with the (real) world. The potential virtues of this shortcut have long been recognized within AI circles (e.g. Waltz 1988). The unanswered question is whether taking on the task of solving the grubby details of real-world robotics will actually permit one to finesse the task of hand-coding the world knowledge. Brooks, Stein and their team — myself included — are gambling that it will.

At this stage of the project, most of the problems being addressed would never arise in the realm of pure, disembodied AI.[3] How many separate

---

[3] Since robotics projects have a history of not living up to their advertisements, scepticism about which features have actually been built (and made to work) and which remain

motors might be used for controlling each hand? They will have to be mounted somehow on the forearms. Will there then be room to mount the motor boards directly on the arms, close to the joints they control, or would they get in the way? How much cabling can each arm carry before weariness or clumsiness overcome it? The arm joints have been built to be compliant — springy, like your own joints. This means that if Cog wants to do some fine-fingered manipulation, it will have to learn to 'burn' some of the degrees of freedom in its arm motion by temporarily bracing its elbows or wrists on a table or other convenient landmark, just as you would do. Such compliance is typical of the mixed bag of opportunities and problems created by real robotics. Another is the need for self-calibration or re-calibration in the eyes. If Cog's eyes jiggle away from their preset aim, thanks to the wear and tear of all that sudden saccading, there must be ways for Cog to compensate, short of trying continually to adjust its camera-eyes with its fingers. Software designed to tolerate this probable sloppiness in the first place may well be more robust and versatile in many other ways than software designed to work in a more 'perfect' world.

Earlier I mentioned a reason for using artificial muscles, not motors, to control a robot's joints, and the example was not imaginary. Brooks is concerned that the sheer noise of Cog's skeletal activities may seriously interfere with the attempt to give Cog humanoid hearing. There is research underway at the AI Lab to develop synthetic electro-mechanical muscle tissues, which would operate silently as well as being more compact, but this will not be available for early incarnations of Cog. For an entirely different reason, thought is being given to the option of designing Cog's visual control software *as if* its eyes were moved by muscles, not motors, building in a software interface that amounts to giving Cog a set of *virtual* eye-muscles. Why might this extra complication in the interface be wise? Because the 'opponent-process' control system exemplified by eye-muscle controls is apparently a deep and ubiquitous feature of nervous systems, involved in control of attention generally and disrupted in such pathologies

somewhere between the drawing board and concrete reality is appropriate. As of 5 April 1995, when this footnote was composed, the situation is roughly as follows: Cog's torso, head, and eyes, are assembled and working. The left arm has been built, tested, debugged, anodized, and briefly mounted on the shoulder. It will be sent off to be duplicated, in mirror image, in a few days. One hand — the left hand — is in a similar state. The fingers and palm are equipped with working, touch-sensitive 'skin,' and it has been successfully mounted on the wrist of the arm. The motor boards have been mounted on it, and are being revised. In a few weeks, its mirror twin will be constructed. Meanwhile a working version of the attention-capture and saccading software for the eyes has been created, so the eyes can find and track a salient object in the world. A gyroscope must still be mounted in the head to provide the signals for the vestibular-ocular-reflex, which has been designed but not fully tested. Many other parts of the foundational software have been coded, and literally hundreds of technical problems have been solved — for instance, shielding the 'optic nerves' from interference without making them so stiff that they interfere with the saccadic motions of the eyes. A body-skin and 'face' have been designed, and prototypes built.

as unilateral neglect. If we are going to have such competitive systems at higher levels of control, it might be wise to build them in 'all the way down', concealing the final translation into electric-motor-talk as part of the backstage implementation, not the model.

Other practicalities are more obvious, or at least more immediately evocative to the uninitiated. Three huge red 'emergency kill' buttons have already been provided in Cog's environment, to ensure that if Cog happens to engage in some activity that could injure or endanger a human interactor (or itself), there is a way of getting it to stop. But what is the appropriate response for Cog to make to the KILL button? If power to Cog's motors is suddenly shut off, Cog will slump, and its arms will crash down on whatever is below them. Is this what we want to happen? Do we want Cog to drop whatever it is holding? What should 'Stop!' mean to Cog? This is a real issue about which there is not yet any consensus.

There are many more details of the current and anticipated design of Cog that are of more than passing interest to those in the field, but on this occasion, I want to use the little remaining time to address some overriding questions that have been much debated by philosophers, and that receive a ready treatment in the environment of thought made possible by Cog. In other words, let's consider Cog merely as a prosthetic aid to philosophical thought-experiments, a modest but by no means negligible role for Cog to play.

III. Three Philosophical Themes Addressed

A recent criticism of 'strong AI' that has received quite a bit of attention is the so-called problem of 'symbol grounding' (Harnad 1990). It is all very well for large AI programs to have data structures that *purport* to refer to Chicago, milk, or the person to whom I am now talking, but such imaginary reference is not the same as real reference, according to this line of criticism. These internal 'symbols' are not properly 'grounded' in the world, and the problems thereby eschewed by pure, non-robotic, AI are not trivial or peripheral. As one who discussed, and ultimately dismissed, a version of this problem many years ago (Dennett 1969: 182 ff), I would not want to be interpreted as now abandoning my earlier view. I submit that Cog moots the problem of symbol grounding, without having to settle its status as a criticism of 'strong AI'. Anything in Cog that might be a candidate for symbolhood will automatically be 'grounded' in Cog's real predicament, as surely as its counterpart in any child, so the issue doesn't arise, except as a practical problem for the Cog team, to be solved or not, as fortune dictates. If the day ever comes for Cog to comment to anybody about Chicago, the question of whether Cog is in any position to do so will arise for exactly the same reasons, and be resolvable on the same considerations, as the parallel question about the reference of the word 'Chicago' in the idiolect of a young child.

Another claim that has often been advanced, most carefully by Haugeland (1985), is that nothing could properly 'matter' to an artificial intelligence, and mattering (it is claimed) is crucial to consciousness. Haugeland restricted his claim to traditional GOFAI systems, and left robots out of consideration. Would he concede that something could matter to Cog? The question, presumably, is how seriously to weigh the import of the quite deliberate decision by Cog's creators to make Cog as much as possible responsible for its own welfare. Cog will be equipped with some 'innate' but not at all arbitrary preferences, and hence provided of necessity with the concomitant capacity to be 'bothered' by the thwarting of those preferences, and 'pleased' by the furthering of the ends it was innately designed to seek. Some may want to retort: 'This is not *real* pleasure or pain, but merely a simulacrum.' Perhaps, but on what grounds will they defend this claim? Cog may be said to have quite crude, simplistic, one-dimensional pleasure and pain, cartoon pleasure and pain if you like, but then the same might also be said of the pleasure and pain of simpler organisms — clams or houseflies, for instance. Most, if not all, of the burden of proof is shifted by Cog, in my estimation. The reasons for saying that something *does* matter to Cog are not arbitrary; they are exactly parallel to the reasons we give for saying that things matter to us and to other creatures. Since we have cut off the dubious retreats to vitalism or origin chauvinism, it will be interesting to see if the sceptics have any good reasons for declaring Cog's pains and pleasures not to matter — at least to it, and for that very reason, to us as well. It will come as no surprise, I hope, that more than a few participants in the Cog project are already musing about what obligations they might come to have to Cog, over and above their obligations to the Cog team.

Finally, J.R. Lucas has raised the claim (at the Royal Society meeting at which the earlier version of this paper was presented) that if a robot were really conscious, we would have to be prepared to believe it about its own internal states. I would like to close by pointing out that this is a rather likely reality in the case of Cog. Although equipped with an optimal suite of monitoring devices that will reveal the details of its inner workings to the observing team, Cog's own pronouncements could very well come to be a more trustworthy and informative source of information on what was really going on inside it. The information visible on the banks of monitors, or gathered by the gigabyte on hard disks, will be at the outset almost as hard to interpret, even by Cog's own designers, as the information obtainable by such 'third-person' methods as MRI and CT scanning in the neurosciences. As the observers refine their models, and their understanding of their models, their authority as interpreters of the data may grow, but it may also suffer eclipse. Especially since Cog will be designed from the outset to redesign itself as much as possible, there is a high probability that the designers will simply lose the standard hegemony of the artificer ('I made it, so I know what it is supposed to do, and what it is doing now!'). Into this epistemological vacuum Cog may very well thrust itself. In fact, I would gladly defend the conditional prediction: *if* Cog develops to the point where it can conduct what appear to be robust and well-controlled conversations in something like a natural language, it will certainly be in a position to rival its own monitors (and the theorists who interpret them) as a source of knowledge about what it is doing and feeling, and why.

References

Dennett, D.C. (1969). *Content and Consciousness*. London: Routledge & Kegan Paul.

Dennett, D.C. (1987). Fast thinking. In D.C. Dennett, *The Intentional Stance*. Cambridge, MA: MIT Press.

Dennett, D.C. (1993a). Review of John Searle, The Rediscovery of the Mind. *Journal of Philosophy*, **90**, 193–205.

Dennett, D.C. (1993b). Caveat emptor. *Consciousness and Cognition*, **2**, 48–57.

Dreyfus, H. & Dreyfus, S. (1986). *Mind Over Machine*. New York: Macmillan.

Harnad, S. (1990). The symbol grounding problem. *Physica D*, **42**, 335–46.

Haugeland, J. (1985). *Artificial Intelligence: The Very Idea*. Cambridge, MA: MIT Press.

Lenat, D.B. & Guha, R.V. (1990). *Building Large Knowledge-Based Systems: Representation and Inference in the CYC Project*. Reading, MA: Addison-Wesley.

Mangan, B. (1993). Dennett, consciousness, and the sorrows of functionalism. *Consciousness and Cognition*, **2**, 1–17.

Searle, J. (1992). *The Rediscovery of the Mind*. Cambridge, MA: MIT Press.

Turing, A. (1950). Computing machinery and intelligence. *Mind*, **59**, 433–60.

Waltz, D. (1988). The prospects for building truly intelligent machines. *Daedalus*, **117**, 191–222.

Dieter Birnbacher

Artificial Consciousness

'There is no security . . . against the ultimate development of mechanical consciousness in the fact of machines possessing little consciousness now. The mollusc has not much consciousness.'
(Samuel Butler, *Erewhon*)

I. Preliminary Clarifications

Is an artificial consciousness possible? Could there be a mechanism or machine that equals man not only in some of his outer achievements but also in some of his inner modes of experience?

The direction in which an answer to this question is to be sought as well as the interest such an answer deserves depend on what meaning is given to the question. Both 'artificial' and 'consciousness' are concepts in need of clarification.

We know today quite a number of possible ways to manipulate the natural processes by which consciousness is generated, and the potential for the future in this respect has for long been an object of horror visions. Among the best-known techniques are the breeding of domestic animals, artificial insemination and *in vitro* fertilization. Other methods for substituting the natural processes of procreation, gestation and birth of beings with consciousness, such as ectogenesis, the complete replacement of pregnancy and birth by a machine, still seem fanciful. Other possibilities are even more fantastic, such as restoring consciousness in living brains that have been, or become, incapable of consciousness by organic defects, by introducing suitable electronic devices (analogous to the restoration of sight to the blind by surgery); or the possibility of manipulating the genetic structures underlying consciousness in order to generate transgenic animals with consciousness from animals without consciousness, in a manner similar to the transformation of normal mice to giant mice by adding to their genome the human gene for the growth hormone.[1]

When talking about 'artificiality' in these contexts, artificiality is understood in an *adverbial* manner. Artificiality in the *adjectival* sense goes much further. An artificial product is not only produced by artificial *means* but is generally also made up of artificial *material*. Artificial flowers are artificial even of they are produced completely without artificial means by handicraft. The term 'artificial consciousness' does not mean a consciousness whose functioning or generation has been artificially manipulated, but the possibility of consciousness in an artificial medium, i.e. a medium different from the one which we know as the natural medium of consciousness. So if man were able to produce, by artificial means, the same material structures which naturally constitute the human brain, the condition of artificiality would not be satisfied. Material brain structures of this kind would be (borrowing a concept from the production of foodstuffs) 'nature-identical', not being artificial in their material constitution. No doubt, there would be philosophical problems even with a 'nature-identical' brain. But the more important and more interesting problems are posed by the artificial brain in the full sense, the *abiotic* brain, which is not only generated by other than natural means but which does not even consist of proteins and other materials of which natural brains are known to consist.

The concept 'consciousness' is even more in need of clarification. In what follows, consciousness is understood in a *weak* and *basic* sense which neither implies the capacity to have some kind of conscious perception of one's own contents of consciousness — 'it thinks' — nor the capacity to relate these contents to a temporally persistent subject pole — 'I think'. 'Consciousness' is understood in such a way that the concept can be applied even to young children, to higher animals and to humans with intermittent or permanent loss of the power of reflective thinking, and that it is satisfied even by the performance of quite elementary states and acts of consciousness It is not assumed that conscious processes are, or can be, accompanied by a Kantian 'Ich denke'.

States of consciousness are characterized by sensory and/or affective qualia. Affective states of consciousness generally have a certain hedonic tone (pleasure/pain), often also a certain motivational content (appetitive/aversive). Sensory states of consciousness can occur independently of affective ones and *vice versa*. At one end of the spectrum there is 'blind' passion, without any sensory content, at the other the completely impartial observer, *sine ira et studio*, Schopenhauer's 'pure world eye'.

Neither sensory nor affective states of consciousness are invariably characterized by intentionality. It is not the case that every process of hearing

---

[1] Though the opposite is more probable, i.e. the transformation of animals with consciousness into animals without consciousness, in order to experiment on them more freely.

or seeing is directed to some auditive or visual object, such as listening and watching are. A heard clap of thunder or a seen flash of lightning can be too short to make them the object of directed listening or watching. A pain, a mood or an undirected feeling can be experienced without being made the object of an act of perception, thinking or evaluation.

In contrast to *states* of consciousness, *acts* of consciousness (often identified with *mental acts*) are always directed to an intentional object, such as — paradigmatically — meaning, thinking, expecting, and wanting. If performing these acts is dependent on the experiencing of certain sensory or affective states of consciousness, then this is a matter of psychology and not of logic. It is at least conceivable that acts of thought, calculation or expectation occur without any simultaneous sensory or affective states.

At this point, one should note the fact — central to any critical philosophy of mind — that there is symmetry between language and phenomenology in the case of *states* of consciousness, but not in the case of *acts* of consciousness. Unlike the linguistic expressions for states of consciousness, the linguistic expressions for acts of consciousness function not only as descriptions of phenomena of consciousness but also as descriptions of operations typically, but not invariably, performed by acts of consciousness. Therefore, concepts of acts of consciousness (or mental acts) are systematically ambiguous in a way concepts of states of consciousness are not. This systematic ambiguity explains the tenacity of the debate about whether concepts such as thinking, meaning, intending, calculating, perceiving, concluding or understanding can be predicated of machines.

Whereas the statement that N is in pain, feels comfortable or is depressed, implies that N experiences certain states of consciousness, it is doubtful whether the statement that N thinks, means, intends, calculates, perceives, concludes or understands implies in an analogous fashion that N performs a corresponding act of consciousness. In many cases, these concepts can be ascribed even if there are no corresponding acts of consciousness. Remember what Wittgenstein (1963) suggests in the *Philosophical Investigations* about concepts of mental acts such as meaning or understanding: For N to mean x (a thing) or p (a proposition) does not necessarily imply that N performs an act of consciousness. For N to understand the rule underlying a number sequence does not necessarily imply that N performs a specific act of consciousness called 'understanding'. For N to understand the rule does sometimes mean no more than that N demonstrates by his behaviour that he has grasped the rule. Under certain conditions, N's outward behaviour and the context in which it occurs are sufficient for the truth of the statement that N means or understands x or p. (Cf. Birnbacher 1974: 46 ff.)

This is not enough to show, of course, that these concepts can be applied to artificial mechanisms and machines devoid of consciousness, as well as to humans and conscious animals. Even if one is prepared to accept Wittgenstein's examples — and I think there is every reason to accept them

— these examples leave it open whether these concepts can legitimately be applied also to entities which are as a matter of principle no proper objects of the ascription of acts of consciousness. The fact that we sometimes ascribe understanding to humans, even when this ascription does not imply that the particular person performs a conscious act of understanding, does not show that we can ascribe understanding to an entity which in no circumstances ever performs such acts of consciousness nor is the kind of object to which *states* of consciousness can be ascribed.

The fact that it is possible to ascribe mental acts to humans without implying the occurrence of acts of consciousness does not imply, then, that these can be ascribed to entities without any kind of consciousness (such as machines). Nevertheless I believe that they can in fact be ascribed to such entities where these exhibit comparable outward achievements. Unlike the concepts of sensory and affective states, the concepts of mental acts can be interpreted in a way in which they are applicable to entities which (apart form their external performance) are no proper objects for the ascription of states or acts of consciousness. Concepts of mental acts are ambiguous in a *twofold* way: they have, first, a 'consciousness-sense' in which they are applicable only to beings capable of consciousness. In this sense, they sometimes imply the occurrence of corresponding acts of consciousness and sometimes not. They have, secondly, an 'achievement-sense' in which they can be applied also to non-conscious entities such as computers and scanners, provided they show the relevant outward performance. In this latter sense, one can, in a completely unmetaphorical way, say of a computer that it *thinks, calculates* or *understands*, or of a scanner that it *perceives* certain things, without thereby suggesting that these entities are in any way conscious. Sentences such as 'The chess computer means *this* pawn, not the pawn in front of your king,' or 'This scanner does not adequately see the diacritical signs,' can be *literally* true.

The systematic ambiguity of the concepts of mental acts offers the best explanation for the fact that it is much easier to give a materialist or behaviourist analysis of the concepts of mental acts than of concepts of emotion or sensation. Concepts of mental acts have at least *one* interpretation in which they can be given a materialist analysis. Concepts of emotion or sensation have *no* interpretation in which they can be given a materialist analysis. For them, Ned Block's verdict on the materialist (more exactly, Daniel Dennett) applies: that he 'has the relation to qualia that the US Air Force had to so many Vietnamese villages: he destroys qualia in order to save them' (Block 1978: 309). Materialism can only apparently save the specific subjectivity of sensation and emotion. What it really does is to liquidate it.

This may be easily shown for the example of emotion. Emotion is a complex phenomenon with at least three components: a *cognitive* component, which provides the object and, in some cases, the propositional content of the emotion; a component of inner and outer *excitement*; and a component of *affective quality* (cf. Birnbacher 1977). The cognitive component consists of descriptive, evaluative and normative beliefs which make an emotion reasonable or unreasonable, adequate or inadequate. This component also explains the historicity of emotions and their dependence on cultural interpretations. In principle, it can be present in emotion as a mere disposition, though it is characteristic for many, and especially the more intense, emotions that part of their cognitive content is made the object of conscious thinking. It is part of the emotions of pride, of anger, of love that their respective objects are repeatedly consciously intended (with varying hedonic tone). Even the excitement component (to which the further dimensions of *motivation* and *expression* are causally related) does not imply any specific conscious states (leaving apart for the moment the inner or mental excitement which might be identified with the proprioception of the physiological processes constituting outer excitement). What is irreducibly subjective, however, is the affective quality, the specific 'colour' of the emotion, including its hedonic tone and its felt intensity and depth. In virtue of this qualitative component emotions are more than the sum of cognition, excitement and appetition or aversion. With their qualitative dimension they possess an irreducibly subjective aspect which can be adequately explained only within a non–materialist, *dualist* — preferably *property-dualist* — frame of reference.

II. Which Kind of Impossibility?

The explanations given for the concepts of artificiality and consciousness do not yield any *obvious* answer to the question whether an artificial consciousness is possible. Neither 'artificial' nor 'consciousness' have been explained in a way that makes the answer a trivial matter. The widely held conviction that an artificial consciousness is impossible cannot be deduced from any patent conceptual absurdity. What are the reasons, then, for this conviction?

The various 'impossibility theorems' about artificial consciousness differ in the kind of impossibility they assert: *technical, conceptual* or *nomological*. For each of them, different kinds of reasons are relevant.

(i) Technical impossibility

The thesis that artificial consciousness is *technically* impossible can safely be left out of the discussion. This thesis is of some practical but of no theoretical importance. From a practical point of view, it may well be exciting to know whether we have to get used to the prospect that some computers will need protection against cruel treatment like sentient animals do and whether we have to make relevant legal provisions. As far as the philosophical problem of the possibility of an artificial consciousness is concerned, however, only theoretical possibility matters. This seems to have been overlooked even by Descartes when he wrote in Part V of his *Discours de la méthode* that there are two secure means to know that machines 'which resemble our bodies and imitate our actions to the extent to which this is probably possible for machines' are nevertheless no 'real humans' because machines are never capable to attain the linguistic abilities even of the most stupid human and would, even if they equal or surpass man in some of his abilities, be deficient in many others (Descartes, *Discours*, V, 57).

Even if Descartes had been right in thinking that a machine with the power of speech is technically impossible he should have asked himself by which criteria he could deny participation of the *res cogitans* to a *possible* machine with this capacity, given the fact that according to him even the human body is a kind of machine, though one of natural origin.

There is, moreover, every reason to be suspicious of prognoses of technical impossibility. The history of *technological forecasting* shows that nearly all technical utopias of the last centuries — including the technical utopias of Salomon's House in Bacon's *New Atlantis* — have by now been realized. There is every reason to assume that doubts about the possibility of *simulating* (or, depending on the respective conception of intelligence) of *realizing* human intelligence in computers, expressed by critics of artificial intelligence like Hubert L. Dreyfus (1972), will have a rather short half-life.

(ii) Conceptual impossibility

Are there *conceptual* reasons for the impossibility of an artificial consciousness, i.e. logical reasons rooted in the semantics of the concepts concerned but not apparent at first sight?

At several points in his later philosophy, *Wittgenstein* suggests that a sentient computer is a conceptual absurdity and need not seriously be considered as a real possibility. Wittgenstein insists that 'only of a living human being and what resembles (behaves like) a living human being can one say: it has sensations; it sees; is blind; hears; is deaf; is conscious or unconscious.' (Wittgenstein, 1963 §281.) What kind of 'can' is this? *Why* can we say this only of a living human being?

Certainly not because the hypothesis of a conscious stone, chair or computer is strictly speaking *unthinkable*. Rather because a hypothesis of this kind is *empty* for lack of empirical criteria: there can be no *good grounds*, of whatever kind, to support such a hypothesis. Good grounds of his kind — sometimes called 'criteria' by Wittgenstein and distinguished from merely empirical correlates or 'symptoms' (Wittgenstein 1964: 24) — indicate the satisfaction of a concept without being related to to it by a strictly logical relation (in a deductive sense of 'logical'). Instead, they are related to it by a weaker relation which is bound up with the contingent conventions of a community playing the same language game. 'Criteria' in Wittgenstein's sense are not so much logically necessary conditions of the *existence* of what the concepts ascribe but rather logically necessary conditions of the legitimate *ascription* of what is ascribed.

Thus, for Wittgenstein, certain behavioural criteria are necessary conditions, not of the occurrence of conscious states and acts in others, but of the *ascription* of such states and acts to others. In subsuming the *criteria* of ascription under the *concept* of what is ascribed, Wittgenstein espouses an *extended* concept of concept. As an abstract possibility the thing ascribed by the concept can be thought of independently from the language game in which the concept is embedded. But as a matter of fact the thing enters the language game only via the criteria which regulate its ascription. Thus, the concept of pain is not only characterized by what pains are by themselves but also 'by its particular function in our life' (Wittgenstein 1967: §532).

An artificial consciousness, then, is not, according to Wittgenstein, impossible in a strictly logical sense. But it is, according to him, nevertheless *conceptually* impossible in so far as there are no conditions under which we would be entitled to ascribe consciousness to a machine. Even if the *truth conditions* for a potential consciousness of machines were satisfied this would make no difference to the language game since there are no conditions, however hypothetical, under which its *assertability conditions* would be satisfied. Machines possessing consciousness are not impossible in an ontological but in a 'transcendental' sense — 'transcendental' understood in a contingent, language-game dependent sense: 'But a machine surely cannot think! — Is that an empirical statement? No. We only say of a human being and what is like one that it thinks' (Wittgenstein 1963: §360).

But is it really the case that the language game as actually played admits of no ascription to machines of states and acts of consciousness whatever? The fact that, as things are, we have no good reason to ascribe consciousness to machines is certainly not sufficient to prove that the criteria operative in our language-game rule out such a possibility once for all. Everything depends on how the existing system of criteria would react — or would *have* to react (according to its own underlying principles) — to a hypothetical situation in which it is confronted with a machine significantly similar to human beings and animals, either in its outward behaviour or its inner functioning. Questions like these are difficult to answer because they concern applications in which our criteria are necessarily vague. After all, the criteria of our concepts are designed to function in real and not in purely hypothetical contexts.

In looking for an answer within his own terms of reference we confront a general difficulty of Wittgenstein's conception of language games. On the one hand, Wittgenstein recognizes the changeability and historicity of language games and of their rules — e.g. the fact that criteria and symptoms

can change status (Wittgenstein 1963: §354; cf. also Gunderson 1985: 81 f.).
On the other hand he tends to assign to the 'criteria' of the present language
game a determinacy, certainty and stability by which he feels justified to
rule out certain exotic examples as 'conceptual' impossibilities. The question arises whether we can really be sure that we will not be compelled by
new experience and new knowledge to apply our concepts in new ways such
that the 'criteria' of our concepts will be changed without changing their
central meaning? Wittgenstein's residual verificationism seems to mislead
him in this respect to espouse a far too conservative view of the flexibility
and adaptability of language games. Not every change in the *application* of
a concept changes its *meaning* (cf. Schleichert 1992: 76). The fact that we
have no good reason, in the present state of knowledge and technology, to
ascribe states or acts of consciousness to machines is not sufficient to
exclude this possibility for the future.

   Even now a certain number of marginal cases confront us with deeply
irritating conceptual/criterial uncertainties and indeterminacies implying
serious problems for practical decision-making. There continue to be
considerable — and ethically significant — uncertainties in the domain of
animal consciousness. Should the ethological or the neurological criteria
have priority in the ascription of consciousness and the ability to suffer? Is
there any justification for the tendency, shared by many zoological laymen
but also by psychologists and philosophers (e.g. Bunge & Ardila 1987: 239),
to ascribe sentience only to warm-blooded non-mammals? Or is the German animal protection law right in assuming that all vertebrates, including
reptiles, batrachia and fish, are to be protected against suffering? Is it really
certain, as Wittgenstein (1963: **II**, xi; 1967: 223) thinks it is, that we could
not understand a talking lion? Or could it be that, as the animal protection
philosopher Rollin has argued against Wittgenstein, the inner worlds of
man and animal are much more similar than we commonly think and that
'certain mental states of certain animals are easier for us to understand than
certain mental states of other humans' (Rollin 1989: 137, 149)?

   In other areas the criteria for ascribing consciousness are highly *controversial*, e.g. with the ascription of sensations, emotions and wants to human
unborns. Though there exists a scientific discipline 'prenatal psychology',
it is still far from clear from which stage of development a human fetus does
not only react to external sensory stimuli but actually subjectively experiences them. Even if it is a fact that we are able to identify, among a number
of uterus sounds presented to us, the special uterus sounds of our own
individual mother, this result does not by itself yield the conclusion that we
literally *heard* these sounds before birth.

   Finally, the *stability* of the criteria recognized for the ascription of
phenomena of consciousness is much more open to doubt than is suggested
by the Wittgensteinian picture. Partly as a consequence of the great suc-
cesses of the neurosciences, the system of criteria for the ascription of

consciousness unmistakably tends in the direction of giving neural indicators more weight over against expressive or behavioural criteria than Wittgenstein admits. In certain marginal cases, Wittgenstein's sentence that 'the human body is the best picture of the human soul' (Wittgenstein 1963: II, iv; 1967: 178) can no longer be upheld. Bernhard Linke has described a variant of the so-called 'locked-in syndrome' in which the conscious life of the person proceeds without *any* possibility of outer manifestation by the motor system so that it can only be detected by electro-physiological tests (Linke 1993: 133). In the forties the arrow-poison curare was used with children in surgery under the false premise that it was a narcotic drug whereas in fact it only immobilized the muscles, thus preventing all motor expression including facial expression (Arzt & Birmelin 1993: 155). In these cases, the felt pain has no corresponding manifestation in outward behaviour. On the other hand, according to the brain death criterion widely accepted in medicine, a human being is dead even though his body is able (with artificial support) to maintain a number of vital functions such as heartbeat, breathing, pregnancy and spontaneous movements of the extremities.

It seems to me that we cannot in any way be certain that there is no conceivable situation in which we would be prepared to ascribe consciousness to a machine. A *conceptual* impossibility of consciousness in machines cannot even be upheld in Wittgenstein's *extended* sense of the term which comprises, in addition to the meaning content of a linguistic expression, its criteria of application. Before discussing the possible criteria in detail, however, we must first deal with the third impossibility theorem, the thesis that an artificial consciousness is *nomologically* impossible.

(iii) Nomological impossibility

The belief that consciousness in machines is nomologically impossible, i.e. impossible in virtue of the laws of the physical world, is so widely held by scientists and philosophers that it can almost be regarded as part of scientific common sense. It is exemplified by the reactions to the visions presented by the British AI specialist Geoff Simons in his book *Are Computers Alive?* Simons thinks that a future evolution of thinking, feeling and sensing computers is not only possible but highly probable. Everything depends, in his view, on complexity. With increasing complexity the competence of computers will more and more become equal to human competence, not only in their cognitive achievements but even in their non-cognitive conscious life including sensation and emotion. There will be no alternative, according to Simons, to recognizing computers as new 'life forms' over and above the known biotic life forms and to ascribe to them the same rights to protection that we now ascribe to higher animals.

Julian Huxley's reaction to Simons' ideas (presented in a BBC broadcast before publication of his book) is representative of the views of the great majority of the scientific community: that not only emotions but even 'genuine' intentions, thoughts and acts of understanding are possible only in biotic matter (cf. Simons 1983: 181). The same view was expressed in the late fifties by Paul Ziff. Ziff was quite sure that 'only living creatures can literally have feelings' (Ziff 1959: 64).

Among the impossibility theorems accepted by scientists this is surely one of the most dogmatic. Is not even God in traditional theism thought to have feelings like love without any biological basis? If thought and emotion is possible without any physical basis why should they not be possible without any biological basis? No doubt, this analogy is unfair. The personal God of theism is thought to be a transcendent being not subject to the laws of nature. Nevertheless, the certainty with which a possible conscious life of computers is dismissed makes one suspicious whether the resistance against the idea is not really volitive rather than cognitive — as if potential doubts were to be calmed down from the start by *a priori* legislation.

In fact the question of the nomological possibility of machine consciousness cannot be dismissed as easily. Even if we cannot hope to give anything like a conclusive answer something can to be said about the field of possibilities in this respect.

The first step is to identify the nomological presuppositions of consciousness in man and then to inquire whether these are necessarily of a biotic nature, or whether these — in the vein of a non-materialist psychofunctionalism — can in principle also be satisfied by structures and functions realized in other than biotic media.

III. The Necessary and Sufficient Conditions of Consciousness

Our knowledge about the physical conditions of consciousness is still fragmentary. We know that in man the functioning brain is a necessary condition of states and acts of consciousness. Empirical tests on patients with brain lesions and experiments with the selective stimulation of brain regions have shown that consciousness depends on the complex interaction of brain functions located partly in the neocortex and partly in the brain stem, particularly the reticular formation (cf. Flohr 1992: 51 ff.). One of the hypotheses discussed at present is that phenomena of consciousness only occur if a certain threshold of activation is realized in certain neural assemblies (cf. Flohr 1991: 255).

If a functioning brain is a *necessary* condition of consciousness in man, is it also a *sufficient* condition of consciousness?

The same question can be given another formulation: is an *imitation man* — in Keith Campbell's sense (Campbell 1971: 120) — nomologically possible (i.e. a being that is like a human being in all physical respects but has no states or acts of consciousness)?

It must be admitted that a world of *imitation men*, of zombies without consciousness, is a logical possibility. Everything would be as it is in reality except that none of these beings would be conscious of anything.[2] What from an outer perspective looks like a world of humans would be a world of more or less intelligent biological robots which could be qualitatively perceived only by non-human beings (e. g. the higher animals). These robots would possess only an abstract knowledge of the world and of themselves.

Whoever is taken aback by this latter description should be reminded of the distinction made above between the 'consciousness-sense' and the 'achievement-sense' of the concepts of mental acts. It is true, an *imitation man* would not be able to *feel* anything, but he could well be able to *mean* something, to have *thoughts* or *expectations* — exactly in that sense in which we can apply concepts of mental acts to purely material structures given that they exhibit the relevant complex behaviour. An *imitation man* could even be said to be able to think *itself*, without crediting it with self-consciousness in a sense which presupposes consciousness. It would be able to reflect about itself even without being able to 'feel' itself, just as computers can talk about themselves when indicating that a certain task exceeds their capacity. Apart from that, a soulless double of man would certainly profit from a physical analogy of self-consciousness in ways similar to the ways real man profits from his own self-consciousness. While its quasi-consciousness enables the double to adapt its motor behaviour to its ever-changing environmental conditions its quasi-self-consciousness enables it to adapt its quasi-consciousness to these conditions. While its quasi- consciousness tells the double which of its possible behaviours is called for in a certain situation, its quasi-self-consciousness tells it which of his possible 'perceptions', 'interpretations' or 'expectations' are called for in a certain situation.[3]

There are reasons to think, however, that an *imitation man* is only an abstract possibility and that it is, as things are, *nomologically* impossible. A being possessing the exact physical mechanisms which constitute the basis of consciousness in man cannot but possess consciousness. The physical conditions of consciousness in man are not only nomologically *necessary* but also nomologically *sufficient*, i.e. they *constrain* the phenomena of consciousness to emerge.

[2] Doubts about whether such a possibility can really be thought are expressed by Tetens (1994: 66 ff.).

[3] In contrast to Metzinger 1993: 204, who ascribes subjectivity to every being possessing a model of itself (*Selbstmodell*), I would hesitate to ascribe subjectivity to a machine of this kind.

To give an argument, let me refer to the fact that all theories of the relation between the physical world and consciousness which are held to be serious candidates for truth contain the assumption that some physical structures and processes (such as the brains of higher animals) are nomologically sufficient for consciousness, irrespective of whether they interpret this relation in a dualistic or monistic, epiphenomenalist or inter-actionist manner. The areas of agreement between the mind–body theories discussed at present are more extensive than the ongoing controversies make it appear. What is controversial is the causal rôle to be assigned to consciousness, not the causal rôle assigned to neural processes. Interactionism and epiphenomenalism differ only in the assumed capacity of states and acts of consciousness to act on the physical basis: for the interactionist events of consciousness are causal thoroughfares, for the epiphenomenalist causal dead ends (cf. Broad 1925: 118; Birnbacher: 1988).

Crucial for the question of artifical consciousness is the fact that even the interactionist model assumes that there are at least some physical conditions that are nomologically sufficient for some states of consciousness. Classical Cartesian interactionism as well as most modern variants, such as Popper's, take it for granted that not every but at least the great majority of states of consciousness is dependent on physical conditions which are causally sufficient for them, i.e. do not need further, for instance spiritual, factors.

The nomological possibility of a consciousness in machines depends on the question, then, on which *level* of the physical world the structural and functional properties are located on which states and acts of consciousness are supervenient: on the 'basic' atomic level, or on the 'higher' levels of molecular and cellular organization. If consciousness depends not so much on the atomic structure of neural networks but rather on their systemic and functional properties, it would be no less than a cosmic accident that emergence of consciousness should be bound exactly to those material elements of which the neural networks in the biological brain in fact consist. Could it be that the emergence of consciousness depends on the substrate (on the material stuff) and not on the function (the information processing functions) of nerve cells? It seems rather implausible that the configurations on the lowest and most basic level are crucial for the emergence of con-sciousness and not the configurations on the higher level of systemic interaction.

If, on the other hand, we assume that what matters for consciousness are certain functions (instead of certain material substrates) there is no reason why a silicon brain should not possess the same emergence potential as the biotic carbon brain. If consciousness depends on the *functional* organiza-tion of physical structures then there is every reason to think that the substrate of conscious life is in principle replaceable by functional equi-valents.

IV. Criteria for the Ascription of Consciousness to Machines

The problem of the criteria governing the ascription of consciousness to machines can be solved by the same route: these criteria are identical with the nomologically sufficient conditions for consciousness, i.e. the respective *causes* of consciousness.

This turns the Wittgensteinian picture of the criteria for ascribing states of consciousness upside down. Wittgenstein stresses the primacy of behavioural, especially expressive, criteria for inner states over against neurological indicators. Some of the effects of inner states — their expression in behaviour — is given the status of criteria, whereas their neural causes are only assigned the status of symptoms, i.e. of empirical correlates which presuppose that the thing with which they are correlated is antecedently identified by 'criteria'.

But even with animals, outward behaviour is often a poor indicator of inner states and acts. Bernard Rollin has drawn attention to the fact that the habit of cows who have been operated on to eat immediately after surgery must not be interpreted as proof that they feel no postoperative pain. There are, rather, good evolutionary reasons for the cow not to show typical pain behaviour though being in pain: The cow depends much more on regular feeding than humans (she would be considerably weakened by not eating), and she would be recognizable to predators by not grazing with the herd. If we want to know whether a cow hurts or not, an EEG is in any case the better criterion (cf. Rollin 1989: 135).

With a machine, distrust of behavioural criteria is even more called for. The outer behaviour of a machine cannot have more than symptomatic status. Not even the most telling expressive behaviour of a machine could convince us that it is conscious unless its inner functioning is of a complexity similar to that of living beings to which we customarily ascribe consciousness. It would be unreasonable to ascribe pain, say, to a machine, only because it shows pain behaviour in reaction to hurting stimuli. A machine uttering 'I' propositions is not thereby entitled to being treated as a self-conscious being.

The verification procedure proposed by Michael Scriven for consciousness in machines — the robot intelligently answering all sorts of question about its conscious life (Scriven 1961: 132 f.) — is fundamentally mistaken. The fact that a robot which has learned to handle concepts of inner states answers 'Yes' if asked whether it possesses consciousness, is no good reason for ascribing consciousness, let alone self-consciousness, to it. The fact that a blind man masters the colour vocabulary in the abstract is no good reason to make him an authority in matters of colour nuances.[4] Complex and

---

[4] In Stanislaw Lem's delightful robot story 'Der Freund des Automatthias' (in Lem 1982) it does not even occur to the feeling robot Automatthias to think that his artificial friend (called 'electrical friend') is of his own (feeling) kind simply for his thinking and speaking abilities.

flexible outward behaviour would be neither sufficient nor necessary for the ascription of consciousness. It would not be *sufficient* since nothing could be said against the objection that everything was programmed into the robot. It would not be *necessary* because a conscious machine need not have a component with which to express itself. It could be a *brain analogue* without being a *body analogue*. Even the human brain taken as an isolated entity does not publicly reveal its conscious contents. Given a hypothetical ideally completed neurology these might possibly only be 'read' by electro-physiological procedures.

Is it possible to think of conditions under which the criteria for ascribing consciousness to machines would be satisfied? That there might be such conditions is not downright absurd. There remains, however, the epistemic problem of the difficulty to be sure about the exact form of the nomo-logically sufficient conditions for consciousness. The nomological general-izations underlying the ascription of psychological concepts have been verified only in the case of biological organisms, or, to be more exact, in the case of just a few biological species (if 'verification' is not already too optimistic a description). The question is: Which of the functional condi-tions to be found in beings made up of protoplasm are nomologically necessary, which are nomologically sufficient? To isolate the nomologi-cally sufficient condition is certainly a century's task for the neurosciences. In view of the irreducibly transcendent nature of other minds it must be doubted whether the physical conditions of consciousness are ever made so transparent that the psycho-physical generalizations found out can lay claim to the status of law-likeness.

The epistemic difficulties confronting us now in the case of exotic conscious beings — like Thomas Nagel's bats (cf. Nagel 1979) — would multiply in the case of machines. Even if we imagine that we could have built brain transplants into our brain which would open up to us the inner life of beings which now are hermetically closed to our understanding, the problem would still remain how sure we could be that what we experience with these transplants is the same as what bats and machines experience.

Such uncertainties have, amongst others, ethical consequences. Thomas H. Huxley proposed the maxim that in case of doubt about the conscious life of other beings (he was thinking of animals) we should rather err on the side of those who cannot articulate themselves. (Huxley 1968: 237.) This maxim should apply to machines as well. In view of the ineliminable uncertainties about the exact physical conditions of consciousness we should try to prevent the construction and realization of machines with such a complexity of organization that the existence of consciousness can no longer be excluded with certainty.

References

Arzt, V.& Birmelin, I. (1993). *Haben Tiere ein Bewußtsein?* München: C. Bertelsmann.

Birnbacher, D. (1974). *Die Logik der Kriterien: Analysen zur Spätphilosophie Wittgensteins.* Hamburg: Meiner.

Birnbacher, D. (1977). Emotion und Emotionsausdruck. In G. Patzig, E. Scheibe & W. Wieland (eds), *Logik, Ethik, Theorie der Geisteswissenschaften.* Hamburg: Meiner.

Birnbacher, D. (1988). Epiphenomenalism as a solution to the ontological mind–body problem. *Ratio* (new series), **1**, 17–32.

Block, N. (1978). Troubles with functionalism. *Minnesota Studies in the Philosophy of Science, IX.* Minnesota: University of Minnesota Press.

Broad, C.D. (1925). *Mind's Place in Nature.* London: Routledge and Kegan Paul.

Bunge, M. & Arvila, R. (1987). *Philosophy of Psychology.* New York: Springer.

Campbell, K. (1971). *Body and Mind.* London: Macmillan.

Dreyfus, H.L. (1972). *What Computers Can't Do.* New York: Harper & Row.

Flohr, H. (1991). Brain processes and phenomenal consciousness. *Theory & Psychology,* **1**, 245–62.

Flohr, H. (1992). Die physiologischen Bedingungen des phänomenalen Bewußtseins. *Forum für interdisziplinäre Forschung,* **1**, 49–55.

Gunderson, K. (1985). *Mentality and Machines.* London: Groom Helm.

Huxley, T.H. (1968). On the hypothesis that animals are automata, and its history (1917). In T.H. Huxley, *Methods and Results.* Reprint New York: Greenwood Press.

Lem, S. (1982). *Robotermärchen.* Frankfurt/M.: Suhrkamp.

Linke, D.B. (1993). *Hirnverpflanzung. Die erste Unsterblichkeit auf Erden.* Reinbek: Rowohlt.

Metzinger, T. (1993). *Subjekt und Selbstmodell.* Paderborn: Schöningh.

Nagel, T. (1979). What is it like to be a bat? In T. Nagel, *Mortal Questions.* Cambridge: Cambridge University Press.

Rollin, B.E. (1989). *The Unheeded Cry: Animal Consciousness, Animal Pain and Science.* Oxford: Oxford University Press.

Schleichert, H. (1992). *Der Begriff des Bewußtseins. Eine Begriffsanalyse.* Frankfurt/M.: Klostermann.

Scriven, M. (1961). The compleat robot: a prolegomena to androidology. In S. Hook (ed), *Dimensions of Mind.* London: Collier MacMillan.

Simons, G. (1983). *Are Computers Alive? Evolution and New Life Forms.* Brighton: Harvester.

Tetens, H. (1994). *Geist, Gehirn, Maschine. Philosophische Versuche über ihren Zusammenhang.* Stuttgart: Reclam.

Wittgenstein, L. (1963). *Philosophical Investigations.* Oxford: Blackwell.

Wittgenstein, L. (1964). *The Blue and the Brown Books.* Oxford: Blackwell.

Wittgenstein, L. (1967). *Zettel.* Oxford: Blackwell.

Ziff, P. (1959). The feelings of robots. *Analysis,* **19**, 64–8.

Appendix I

Thomas Metzinger & David J. Chalmers

Selected Bibliography

Consciousness in Philosophy, Cognitive Science
and Neuroscience: 1970–1995

Contents

1. Monographs

2. Edited Collections of Papers

3. Articles

1. Monographs

1.1 Philosophy of Mind

Armstrong, D.M. (1981). *The Nature of Mind*. Ithaca: Cornell University Press.

Armstrong, D.M. & Malcolm, N. (1984). *Consciousness and Causality*. Oxford: Basil Blackwell.

Campbell, K.K. (1970). *Body and Mind*. New York: Doubleday Anchor Books.

Carruthers, P. (1996). *Language, Thought and Consciousness: An Essay in Philosophical Psychology*. Cambridge: Cambridge University Press.

Chalmers, D.J. (1996). *The Conscious Mind*. New York: Oxford University Press.

Churchland, P.M. (1984). *Matter and Consciousness*. Cambridge, MA: MIT Press.

Churchland, P.M. (1989). *A Neurocomputational Perspective. The Nature of Mind and the Structure of Science*. Cambridge, MA: MIT Press.

Churchland, P.M. (1995). *The Engine of Reason, the Seat of the Soul: A Philosophical Journey into the Brain*. Cambridge, MA: MIT Press.

Churchland, P.S. (1986). *Neurophilosophy: Toward a Unified Science of the Mind-Brain*. Cambridge, MA: MIT Press.

Clark, A. (1992). *Sensory Qualities*. Oxford: Oxford University Press.

Cornman, J.W. (1971). *Materialism and Sensations*. New Haven: Yale University Press.

Culbertson, J.T. (1982). *Consciousness: Natural and Artificial*. Roslyn Heights, New York: Libra.

Davidson, D. (1993). *Der Mythos des Subjektiven*. Stuttgart: Reclam.

Dennett, D.C. (1978). *Brainstorms: Philosophical Essays on Mind and Psychology*. Cambridge, MA: MIT Press.

Dennett, D.C. (1991). *Consciousness Explained*. Boston, MA: Little, Brown & Co.

Dretske, F. (1995). *Naturalizing the Mind*. Cambridge, MA: MIT Press.

Ellis, R.D. (1986). *An Ontology of Consciousness*. Dordrecht: Kluwer/Martinus Nijhoff.

Evans, C.O. (1970). *The Subject of Consciousness*. London: George Allen & Unwin.

Flanagan, O. (1984; 2nd edition 1991). *The Science of the Mind*. Cambridge, MA: MIT Press.

Flanagan, O. (1992). *Consciousness Reconsidered*. Cambridge, MA: MIT Press.

Foster, J. (1991). *The Immaterial Self: A Defense of the Cartesian Dualist Conception of Mind*. London: Routledge.

Gennaro, R.J. (forthcoming). *Consciousness and Self-Consciousness: A Defence of the Higher-Order Thought Theory of Consciousness*. Amsterdam and Philadelphia: John Benjamins.

Goodman, N. (1977). *The Structure of Appearance*. Dordrecht: D. Reidel.

Gunderson, K. (1971). *Mentality and Machines*. New York: Doubleday Anchor Books.

Hannay, A. (1990). *Human Consciousness*. London: Routledge.

Hardcastle, V.G. (forthcoming). *Locating Consciousness*. Amsterdam and Philadelphia: John Benjamins.

Hardin, C.L. (1988; expanded edition 1993). *Color for Philosophers*. Indianapolis: Hackett Publishing Company.

Harrison, B. (1973). *Form and Content*. Oxford: Basil Blackwell.

Hill, C.S. (1991). *Sensations: A Defense of Type Materialism.* Cambridge: Cambridge University Press.

Hinton, J. (1973). *Experiences.* Oxford: Oxford University Press.

Hodgson, D. (1991). *The Mind Matters: Consciousness and Choice in a Quantum World.* Oxford: Oxford University Press.

Hofstadter, D.R. (1979). *Gödel, Escher, Bach: an Eternal Golden Braid.* New York: Basic Books.

Honderich, T. (1989). *Mind and Brain.* Oxford: Oxford University Press.

Jackson, F.C. (1977). *Perception: A Representative Theory.* Cambridge: Cambridge University Press.

Kim, J. (1993). *Supervenience and Mind.* Cambridge: Cambridge University Press.

Kirk, R. (1994). *Raw Feeling: A Philosophical Account of the Essence of Consciousness.* Oxford: Oxford University Press.

Landesman, C. (1989). *Color and Consciousness.* Philadelphia: Temple University Press.

Lanz, P. (1995). *Phänomenales Bewußtsein: Eine Verteidigung.* Frankfurt am Main: Vittorio Klostermann.

Levin, M. (1979). *Metaphysics and the Mind-Body Problem.* Oxford: Oxford University Press.

Lockwood, M. (1989). *Mind, Brain, and the Quantum.* Oxford: Oxford University Press.

Lund, D.H. (1994). *Perception, Mind, and Personal Identity: A Critique of Materialism.* Lanham: University Press of America.

Lycan, W.G. (1987). *Consciousness.* Cambridge, MA: MIT Press.

Lycan, W.G. (1996). *Consciousness and Experience.* Cambridge, MA: MIT Press.

Madell, G. (1988). *Mind and Materialism.* Edinburgh: Edinburgh University Press.

Marbach, E. (1993). *Mental Representation and Consciousness: Towards a Phenomenological Theory of Representation and Reference.* Dordrecht: Kluwer Academic Publishers.

Margolis, J. (1978). *Persons and Minds: The Prospects of Non-Reductive Materialism.* Dordrecht: D. Reidel.

Marks, C. (1980). *Commissurotomy, Consciousness, and the Unity of Mind.* Cambridge, MA: MIT Press.

Matson, W.I. (1976). *Sentience.* Berkeley: University of California Press.

McGinn, C. (1982). *The Character of Mind.* Oxford: Oxford University Press.

McGinn, C. (1983). *The Subjective View: Secondary Qualities and Indexical Thoughts.* Oxford: Oxford University Press.

McGinn, C. (1991). *The Problem of Consciousness: Essays toward a Resolution.* Oxford: Basil Blackwell.

Metzinger, T. (1985). *Neuere Beiträge zur Diskussion des Leib-Seele-Problems.* Frankfurt/Bern/New York: Peter Lang.

Metzinger, T. (1993). *Subjekt und Selbstmodell. Die Perspektivität phänomenalen Bewußtseins vor dem Hintergrund einer naturalistischen Theorie mentaler Repräsentation.* Paderborn: Schöningh.

Nagel, T. (1986). *The View from Nowhere.* Oxford: Oxford University Press.

Nelkin, N. (1996). *Consciousness and the Origins of Thought.* Cambridge: Cambridge University Press.

Nemirow, L. (1979). *Functionalism and the Subjective Quality of Experience.* Dissertation, Stanford University: University Microfilms International

Nida-Rümelin, M. (1993). *Farben und phänomenales Wissen.* Conceptus-Studien No. 9. Sankt Augustin: Academia Verlag.

Papineau, D. (1993). *Philosophical Naturalism.* Oxford: Basil Blackwell.

Parfit, D. (1984). *Reasons and Persons.* Oxford: Oxford University Press.

Peacocke, C. (1983). *Sense and Content: Experience, Thought, and their Relations.* Oxford: Oxford University Press.

Penrose, R. (1989). *The Emperor's New Mind.* Oxford: Oxford University Press.

Penrose, R. (1994). *Shadows of the Mind.* Oxford: Oxford University Press.

Pohlenz, G. (1994). *Phänomenale Realität und Erkenntnis: Umrisse einer Theorie im Ausgang von der eigentümlichen Natur des Qualia-Begriffs.* Freiburg: Alber.

Poland, J. (1994). *Physicalism: The Empirical Foundations.* Oxford: Oxford University Press.

Popper, K.R. (1994). *Knowledge and the Body–Mind Problem: A Defense of Interaction.* London: Routledge.

Revonsuo, A. (1995). *On the Nature of Consciousness.: Theoretical and Empirical Explorations.* Turku: Turun Yliopisto.

Robinson, H. (1982). *Matter and Sense.* Cambridge: Cambridge University Press.

Robinson, W.S. (1988). *Brains and People: An Essay on Mentality and its Causal Conditions.* Philadelphia: Temple University Press.

Rossman, N. (1991). *Consciousness: Separation and Integration.* Albany: SUNY Press.

Sayre, K.M. (1969). *Consciousness: A Philosophic Study of Minds and Machines.* New York: Random House.

Schleichert, H. (1992). *Der Begriff des Bewußtseins. Eine Bedeutungsanalyse.* Frankfurt am Main: Vittorio Klostermann.

Seager, W.E. (1992). *Metaphysics of Consciousness.* London: Routledge.

Searle, J.R. (1984). *Minds, Brains and Science.* Cambridge, MA: MIT Press.

Searle, J.R. (1992). *The Rediscovery of the Mind.* Cambridge, MA: MIT Press.

Shoemaker, S. (1984). *Identity, Cause, and Mind.* Cambridge: Cambridge University Press.

Siewert, C.E. (1994). *Understanding Consciousness.* Dissertation: University of California, Berkeley. Forthcoming as book with Princeton University Press.

Smythies, J.R. (1994). *The Walls of Plato's Cave: The Science and Philosophy of Brain, Consciousness and Perception.* Aldershot: Aversbury.

Strawson, G. (1994). *Mental Reality.* Cambridge, MA: MIT Press.

Stubenberg, L. (forthcoming). *Consciousness and Qualia.* Amsterdam and Philadelphia: John Benjamins.

Tetens, H. (1994). *Geist, Gehirn, Maschine. Philosophische Versuche über ihren Zusammenhang.* Stuttgart: Reclam.

Tye, M. (1991). *The Imagery Debate.* Cambridge, MA: MIT Press.

Tye, M. (1995). *Ten Problems of Consciousness.* Cambridge, MA: MIT Press.

Unger, P. (1990). *Identity, Consciousness and Value.* Oxford: Oxford University Press.

Valberg, J.J. (1992). *The Puzzle of Experience.* Oxford: Oxford University Press.

Varela, F.J., Thompson, E. & Rosch, E. (1991). *The Embodied Mind: Cognitive Science and Human Experience.* Cambridge, MA: MIT Press.

512 APPENDIX I

Werth, R. (1983). *Bewußtsein — Psychologische, neurobiologische und wissenschaftstheoretische Aspekte.* Berlin: Springer.

Wilkes, K.V. (1978). *Physicalism.* London: Routledge and Kegan Paul.

Wilkes, K.V. (1988). *Real People: Personal Identity without Thought Experiments.* Oxford: Oxford University Press.

Wyss, D. (1988). *Traumbewußtsein? Grundzüge einer Ontologie des Traumbewußtseins.* Vandenhoeck & Rupprecht.

1.2 Cognitive Science & Psychology

Baars, B.J. (1988). *A Cognitive Theory of Consciousness.* Cambridge: Cambridge University Press.

Czikzsentmihalyi, M. & Czikzsentmihalyi, I.S. (1988). *Optimal Experience: Psychological Studies of Flow in Consciousness.* Cambridge: Cambridge University Press.

Dewart, L. (1989). *Evolution and Consciousness: The Role of Speech in the Origin and Development of Human Nature.* University of Toronto Press.

Ellis, R.D. (1995). *Questioning Consciousness: The Interplay of Imagery, Cognition, and Emotion in the Human Brain.* Amsterdam and Philadelphia: John Benjamins.

Farthing, G.W. (1992). *The Psychology of Consciousness.* Englewood Cliffs, NJ: Prentice Hall.

Gadenne, V. (1995). *Bewußtsein, Kognition und Gehirn.* Bern: Hans Huber.

Gadenne, V. & Oswald, M.E. (1991). *Kognition und Bewußtsein.* Berlin: Springer.

Harth, E. (1993). *The Creative Loop: How the Brain Makes a Mind.* London: Addison-Wesley.

Hilgard, E.R. (1977; expanded edition 1986). *Divided Consciousness: Multiple Controls in Human Thought and Action.* New York: Wiley.

Holzinger, B. (1994). *Der luzide Traum: Phänomenologie und Physiologie.* Wien: Wiener Universitätsverlag.

Humphrey, N. (1984). *Consciousness Regained.* Oxford: Oxford University Press.

Humphrey, N. (1992). *A History of the Mind: Evolution and the Birth of Consciousness.* New York: Simon and Schuster.

Jackendoff, R. (1987). *Consciousness and the Computational Mind.* Cambridge, MA: MIT Press.

Klatzky, R.L. (1984). *Memory and Awareness.* New York: Freeman.

Klein, D.B. (1984). *The Concept of Consciousness: A Survey.* Lincoln: University of Nebraska Press.

Kosslyn, S.M. (1980). *Image and Mind.* Cambridge, MA: Harvard University Press.

Kosslyn, S.M. (1994). *Image and Brain.* Cambridge, MA: MIT Press.

Kurthen, M. (1990). *Das Problem des Bewußtseins in der Kognitionswissenschaft — Perspektiven einer Kognitiven Neurowissenschaft.* Stuttgart: Enke.

Kurthen, M. (1992). *Neurosemantik. Grundlagen einer Praxiologischen Kognitiven Neurowissenschaft.* Stuttgart: Enke.

Kurthen, M. (1994). *Hermeneutische Kognitionswissenschaft.* Bonn: djre-Verlag.

LaBerge, S. (1985). *Lucid Dreaming.* Los Angeles: Jeremy Tarcher.

Lyons, W. (1986). *The Disappearance of Introspection.* Cambridge, MA: MIT Press.

Morris, P. & Hampson, P.J. (1983). *Imagery and Consciousness.* London and New York: Academic Press.

Ornstein, R. (1977). *The Psychology of Consciousness.* Harcourt Brace Jovanovitch.

Rosenfield, I. (1992). *The Strange, Familiar, and Forgotten: An Anatomy of Consciousness.* London: Picador.

Scott, A. (1995). *Stairway to the Mind. The Controversial New Science of Consciousness.* New York & Berlin: Springer.

1.3 Neuroscience

Abeles, M. (1991). *Corticonics: Neural Circuits of the Cerebral Cortex.* Cambridge: Cambridge University Press.

Calvin, W. (1990). *The Cerebral Symphony: Seashore Reflections on the Structure of Consciousness.* Bantam.

Changeux, J.P. (1985). *Neuronal Man: The Biology of Mind.* New York: Pantheon Books.

Churchland, P.S. & Sejnowski, T.J. (1992). *The Computational Brain.* Cambridge, MA: MIT Press.

Crick, F.H.C. (1994). *The Astonishing Hypothesis: The Scientific Search for the Soul.* New York: Charles Scribner's Sons.

Damasio, A. (1994). *Descartes' Error.* New York: Putnam/Grosset.

Eccles, J.C. (1984). *The Human Mystery.* Routledge and Kegan Paul.

Edelman, G.E. (1987). *Neural Darwinism: The Theory of Neuronal Group Selection.* New York: Basic Books.

Edelman, G.M. (1989). *The Remembered Present: A Biological Theory of Consciousness.* New York: Basic Books.

Edelman, G.M. (1992). *Bright Air, Brilliant Fire.* New York: Basic Books.

Edelman, G.M. & Mountcastle, V.B. (1978). *The Mindful Brain: Cortical Organization and the Group-selective Theory of Higher Brain Function.* Cambridge, MA: MIT Press.

Farah, M. (1991). *Visual Agnosia: Disorders of Object Recognition and What They Tell Us about Normal Vision.* Cambridge, MA: MIT Press.

Gazzaniga, M.S. & Le Doux, J.E. (1978). *The Integrated Mind.* New York: Plenum Press.

Greenfield, S.A. (1995). *Journey to the Centers of the Mind: Toward A Science of Consciousness.* New York: Freeman.

Griffin, D.R. (1981). *The Question of Animal Awareness: Evolutionary Continuity of Mental Experience.* New York: Rockefeller University Press.

Hernegger, R. (1995). *Wahrnehmung und Bewußtsein. Ein Diskussionsbeitrag zur Neuropsychologie.* Heidelberg: Spektrum Verlag.

Hameroff, S. (1987). *Ultimate Computing: Biomolecular Consciousness and Nanotechnology.* Amsterdam: Elsevier North Holland.

Hobson, J.A. (1988). *The Dreaming Brain.* New York: Basic Books.

Hobson, J.A. (1995). *The Chemistry of Conscious States.* Boston/Toronto/London: Little, Brown and Company.

Jaynes, J. (1976). *The Origins of Consciousness in the Breakdown of the Bicameral Mind.* Boston: Houghton Mifflin.

Marks, L.E. (1978). *The Unity of the Senses: Interrelations among the Modalities.* New York: Academic Press.

Penfield, W. (1975). *The Mystery of the Mind: A Critical Study of Consciousness and the Human Brain.* Princeton: Princeton University Press.

Pöppel, E. (1985). *Grenzen des Bewußtseins.* München: DTV.

Pöppel, E. (1988). *Mindworks: Time and Conscious Experience.* New York: Hartcourt Brace Jovanovich.

Popper, K.R. & Eccles, J.C. (1977). *The Self and its Brain: An Argument for Interactionism.* Routledge and Kegan Paul.

Robertson, I.H. & Marshall, J.C. (1993). *Unilateral Neglect: Clinical and Experimental Studies.* Hillsdale: Lawrence Erlbaum Associates.

Rose, S. (1973). *The Conscious Brain.* New York: Knopf. Revised edition 1989.

Roth, G. (1994). *Das Gehirn und seine Wirklichkeit.* Frankfurt am Main: Suhrkamp.

Shallice, T. (1988). *From Neuropsychology to Mental Structure.* Cambridge: Cambridge University Press.

Weiskrantz, L. (1986). *Blindsight: A Case-Study and Implications.* Oxford: Oxford University Press.

Zeki, S. (1993). *A Vision of the Brain.* Cambridge, MA: Blackwell Scientific Publications.

2. Collections

2.1 Philosophy of Mind

Beckermann, A., Flohr, H. & Kim, J. (1992)[eds]. *Emergence or Reduction? Essays on the Prospects of Nonreductive Physicalism.* Berlin, New York: de Gruyter.

Bieri, P. (1981)[Hrsg.]. *Analytische Philosophie des Geistes.* Königstein: Hain; 2nd edition 1993.

Block, N. (1980)[ed]. *Readings in Philosophy of Psychology. Vol. 1.* Cambridge, MA: Harvard University Press.

Block, N. (1981)[ed]. *Readings in Philosophy of Psychology. Vol. 2.* Cambridge, MA: Harvard University Press.

Block, N., Flanagan, O. & Güzeldere, G. (1996)[eds]. *The Nature of Consciousness.* Cambridge, MA: MIT Press.

Carrier, M. & Machamer, P. (1996)[eds]. *Philosophy and the Sciences of the Mind. Pittsburgh-Konstanz Series in the Philosophy and History of Science.* Konstanz: Universitätsverlag Konstanz/Pittsburgh: University of Pittsburgh Press.

Casati, R., Smith, B. & White, S. (1995)[eds]. *Philosophy and the Cognitive Sciences.* Vienna: Hölder-Pichler-Tempsky.

Chalmers, D.J. (1966). *The Conscious Mind.* New York: Oxford University Press.

Cheng, C. (1975)[ed]. *Philosophical Aspects of the Mind-Body Problem.* Hawaii University Press.

CIBA Foundation (1993). *Experimental and Theoretical Studies of Consciousness.* CIBA Foundation Symposium 174. Chichester, UK: Wiley.

Cramer, K., Fulda, H-F., Horstmann, R-P., & Pothast, U. (1990)[Hrsg.]. *Theorie der Subjektivität.* Frankfurt am Main: Suhrkamp.

Crane, T. (1992)[ed]. *The Contents of Experience: Essays on Perception.* Cambridge: Cambridge University Press.

Dahlbohm, B. (1993) [ed]. *Dennett and his Critics.* Oxford: Basil Blackwell.

Davies, M. & Humphreys, G.(1993)[eds]. *Consciousness: Psychological and Philosophical Essays.* Oxford: Basil Blackwell.

Dietrich, E. (1994)[ed]. *Thinking Computers and Virtual Persons: Essays on the Intentionality of Machines.* New York: Academic Press.

Globus, G.G., Maxwell, G. & Savodnik, I. (1976)[eds]. *Consciousness and the Brain: A Scientific and Philosophical Inquiry.* New York: Plenum Press.

Guttmann, G. & Langer, G. (1992)[eds]. *Das Bewußtsein: Multidimensionale Entwürfe.* Berlin: Springer.

Hameroff, S., Kaszniak, A., & Scott, A. (1996)[eds]. *Toward a Science of Consciousness.* Cambridge, MA: MIT Press.

Hofstadter, D.R. & Dennett, D.C. (1981)[eds]. *The Mind's I.* New York: Basic Books.

Hookway, C. & Peterson, D. (1993)[eds]. *Philosophy and the Cognitive Sciences.* Royal Institute of Philosophy Supplement 34. Cambridge: Cambridge University Press.

Krämer, S. (1994)[ed]. *Geist, Gehirn, Künstliche Intelligenz — Zeitgenössische Modelle des Denkens.* Berlin, New York: de Gruyter.

Krämer, S. (1996)[ed]. *Bewußtsein. Philosophische Positionen.* Frankfurt am Main: Suhrkamp.

Lenk, H. & Poser, H. (1993)[eds]. *Neue Realitäten: Herausforderungen der Philosophie. XVI: Deutscher Kongreß für Philosophie Berlin 20.–24. September 1993.* Berlin: Akademie-Verlag.

Lycan, W.G. (1990)[ed]. *Mind and Cognition.* Oxford: Basil Blackwell.

Marcel, A. & Bisiach, E. (1988)[eds]. *Consciousness in Contemporary Science.* Oxford: Oxford University Press.

Metzinger, T. (1995a)[ed]. *Bewußtsein – Beiträge aus der Gegenwartsphilosophie.* Paderborn: Schöningh.

Metzinger, T. (1995b)[ed]. *Conscious Experience.* Exeter, UK: Imprint Academic / Paderborn: Schöningh.

Oeser, E. & Seitelberger, F. (1988)[eds]. *Gehirn, Bewußtsein und Erkenntnis.* Darmstadt: Wissenschaftliche Buchgesellschaft.

Otto, H. & Tuedio, J. (1988)[eds]. *Perspectives on Mind.* Dordrecht: Kluwer Academic Publishers.

Peacocke, C. (1994)[ed]. *Objectivity, Simulation, and the Unity of Consciousness.* Oxford: Oxford University Press.

Pöppel, E. (1989)[ed]. *Gehirn und Bewußtsein.* Weinheim: VCH Verlagsgesellschaft.

Revonsuo, A. & Kamppinen, M. (1994)[eds]. *Consciousness in Philosophy and Cognitive Neuroscience.* Hillsdale, NJ: Lawrence Erlbaum Associates.

Robinson, H. (1993)[ed]. *Objections to Physicalism.* Oxford: Oxford University Press.

Rosenthal, D.M. (1991)[ed]. *The Nature of Mind.* Oxford: Oxford University Press.

Slezak, P. (1989)[ed]. *Computers, Brains and Minds.* Dordrecht: Kluwer Academic Publishers.

Tomberlin, J. (1989)[ed]. *Philosophical Perspectives, Vol. 3: Philosophy of Mind and Action Theory.* Atascadero, CA: Ridgeview Publishing.

Tomberlin, J. (1990)[ed]. *Philosophical Perspectives, Vol. 4: Action Theory and Philosophy of Mind.* Atascadero, CA: Ridgeview Publishing.
Tomberlin, J. (1995)[ed], *Philosophical Perspectives, Vol. 9: AI, Connectionism and Philosophical Psychology.* Atascadero, CA: Ridgeview Publishing.
Tress, W. & Nagel, S. (1993)[eds]. *Psychoanalyse und Philosophie: Eine Begegnung.* Heidelberg: Asanger.
Villanueva, E. (1991)[ed]. *Consciousness: Philosophical Issues.* Atascadero, CA: Ridgeview Publishing Company.
Villanueva, E. & Diaz, J.L. (1995)[eds]. *La Conciencia.* Mexico City: Fondo de Cultura Economica.
Warner, R. & Szubka, T. (1994)[eds]. *The Mind-Body Problem: A Guide to the Current Debate.* Oxford: Basil Blackwell.

2.2 Selected Readings: Cognitive Science & Psychology

Blakemore, C. & Greenfield, S. (1987)[eds]. *Mindwaves: Thoughts on Intelligence, Identity and Consciousness.* Oxford: Basil Blackwell.
Bornstein, R.F. & Pittman, T.S. (1992)[eds]. *Perception without Awareness: Cognitive, Clinical and Social Perspectives.* New York: Guilford Press.
Bowers, K.S. & Meichenbaum, D. (1984)[eds]. *The Unconscious Reconsidered.* New York: Wiley.
Cavallero, C. & Foulkes, D. (1993)[eds]. *Dreaming as Cognition.* New York: Harvester Wheatsheaf.
CIBA Foundation (1993). *Experimental and Theoretical Studies of Consciousness.* CIBA Foundation Symposium **174**. Chichester, UK: Wiley.
Davidson, J.M. & Davidson, R.J. (1980)[eds]. *The Psychobiology of Consciousness.* New York: Plenum.
Davidson, R., Schwartz, G. & Shapiro, D. (1983)[eds]. *Consciousness and Self-regulation. Vol. 1.* New York: Plenum.
Greenberg, G. & Tobach, E. (1987)[eds]. *Cognition, Language, and Consciousness: Integrative Levels.* Hillsdale, NJ: Lawrence Erlbaum Associates.
Hameroff, S., Kaszniak, A., & Scott, A. (1996)[eds]. *Toward a Science of Consciousness.* Cambridge, MA: MIT Press.
Hookway, C. (1984)[ed]. *Minds, Machines, and Evolution.* Cambridge: Cambridge University Press.
Josephson, B.D. & Ramachandran, V.S. (1980)[eds]. *Consciousness and the Physical World.* Oxford: Pergamon Press.
Kessel, K.S., Cole, P.M. & Johnson, D.L. (1992)[eds]. *Self and Consciousness: Multiple Perspectives.* Hillsdale, NJ: Lawrence Erlbaum
Marcel, A. & Bisiach, E. (1988)[eds]. *Consciousness in Contemporary Science.* Oxford: Oxford University Press.
Ornstein, R. (1973)[ed]. *The Nature of Human Consciousness. A Book of Readings.* San Francisco: Freeman.
Pickering, J. & Skinner, M. (1990)[eds]. *From Sentience to Symbols: Readings on Consciousness.* Toronto: University of Toronto Press.
Pope, K.S. & Singer, J.L. (1978)[eds]. *The Stream of Consciousness: Scientific Investigation into the Flow of Experience.* New York: Plenum.
Rescher, N. (1986)[ed]. *Current Issues in Teleology.* University Press of America.

Revonsuo, A. & Kamppinen, M. (1994)[eds]. *Consciousness in Philosophy and Cognitive Neuroscience*. Hillsdale, NJ: Lawrence Erlbaum Associates.

Schwartz, G. & Shapiro D. (1976)[eds]. *Consciousness and Self-regulation. Vol.1.* New York: Plenum.

Schwartz, G. & Shapiro D. (1978)[eds]. *Consciousness and Self-regulation. Vol 2..* New York: Plenum.

Tratteur, G. (1995)[ed]. *Consciousness: Distinction and Reflection.* Napoli: Bibliopolis.

Umilta, C. & Moscovitch, M. (1995)[eds]. *Conscious and Nonconscious Information Processing.* Cambridge, MA: MIT Press.

Underwood, G. & Stevens, R. (1979)[eds]. *Aspects of Consciousness.* Vol. **1.** *Psychological Issues.* London: Academic Press.

Underwood, G. & Stevens, R. (1981)[eds]. *Aspects of Consciousness.* Vol. **2.** *Structural Issues.* London: Academic Press.

Underwood, G. (1982)[ed]. *Aspects of Consciousness.* Vol. **3.** *Awareness and Self-awareness.* London: Academic Press.

Velmans, M. (in press)[ed]. *The Science of Consciousness: Psychological, Neuropsychological, and Clinical Reviews.* London: Routledge.

2.3 Selected Readings: Neurosciences

Basar, E. & Bullock, T. (1992)[eds]. *Induced Rhythms in the Brain.* Boston: Birkhäuser.

Buser, P.A. & Rougeul-Buser, A. (1978)[eds]. *Cerebral Correlates of Conscious Experience.* INSERM Symposium No. 6. Amsterdam: North Holland/Elsevier.

CIBA Foundation (1993). *Experimental and Theoretical Studies of Consciousness.* CIBA Foundation Symposium **174**. Chichester, UK: Wiley.

Davidson, J.M. & Davidson, R.J. (1980)[eds]. *The Psychobiology of Consciousness.* New York: Plenum Press.

Gackenbach, J. & LaBerge, S. (1988)[eds]. *Conscious Mind, Sleeping Brain.* New York/London: Plenum Press.

Gazzaniga, M. (1995)[ed]. *The Cognitive Neurosciences.* Cambridge, MA: MIT Press.

Gordon, G., Maxwell, G. & Savodnik, I. (1976)[eds]. *Consciousness and the Brain: A Scientific and Philosophical Inquiry.* New York: Plenum Press.

Hameroff, S., Kaszniak, A., & Scott, A. (1996)[eds]. *Toward a Science of Consciousness.* Cambridge, MA: MIT Press.

Hobson, J.B. & Brazier, M.A. (1982)[eds]. *The Reticular Formation Revisited.* New York: Raven.

Koch, C. & Davis, J.L. (1994)[eds]. *Large-Scale Neuronal Theories of the Brain.* Cambridge, MA: MIT Press.

Milner, D. & Rugg, M. (1992)[eds]. *The Neuropsychology of Consciousness.* London: Academic Press.

Oakley, D. (1985)[ed]. *Brain and Mind.* Andover: Methuen.

Pöppel, E. (1989)[ed].*Gehirn und Bewußtsein.* Weinheim: VCH Verlagsgesellschaft.

Prigatano, GP. & Schacter, DL. (1991)[eds]. *Awareness of Deficit after Brain Injury: Clinical and Theoretical Issues.* Oxford: Oxford University Press.

Revonsuo, A. & Kamppinen, M. (1994)[eds]. *Consciousness in Philosophy and Cognitive Neuroscience.* Hillsdale, NJ: Lawrence Erlbaum Associates.

Roediger III, H.L. & Craik, F.I.M. (1989)[eds]. *Varieties of Memory and Consciousness: Essays in Honor of Endel Tulving.*

Singer, W. (1994)[ed]. *Gehirn und Bewußtsein.* Heidelberg: Spektrum-Verlag.

Weiskrantz, L. (1986)[ed]. *Thought Without Language.* Oxford: Oxford University Press.

3. Articles

3.1 The Concept of Consciousness

This section contains articles analysing the concept of consciousness, or attempting to determine what it is for an organism or a mental state to be conscious, or distinguishing various kinds of consciousness. Articles along these lines can also be found in sections 3.3, 3.4, 3.5, and elsewhere.

Allport, A. (1988). What concept of consciousness? In Marcel & Bisiach 1988.

Bieri, P. (1995). Why is consciousness puzzling? In Metzinger 1995b.

Bisiach, E. (1988). The (haunted) brain and consciousness. In Marcel & Bisiach 1988.

Block, N. (1990). Consciousness and accessibility. *Behavioral and Brain Sciences,* **13**, 596–8.

Block, N. (1994). Consciousness. In S. Guttenplan (ed), *A Companion to Philosophy of Mind.* Oxford: Blackwell.

Block, N. (1995). On a confusion about the function of consciousness. *Behavioral and Brain Sciences,* **18**, 227–87. Reprinted in Block *et al.* 1996. German translation in Metzinger 1995a.

Burge, T. (1995). Zwei Arten von Bewußtsein. In Metzinger 1995a.

Chalmers, D.J. (1996). Availability: The cognitive basis of experience? In Block *et al.* 1996.

Churchland, P.S. (1983). Consciousness: The transmutation of a concept. *Pacific Philosophical Quarterly,* **64**, 80–93.

Churchland, P.S. (1995). Die Neurobiologie des Bewußtseins: Können wir etwas von ihr lernen? In Metzinger 1995a.

Davies, M. & Humphreys, G. (1993). *Introduction.* In Davies & Humphreys 1993.

Goldman, A. (1993). Consciousness, folk psychology and cognitive science. *Consciousness and Cognition,* **2**, 364–82.

Güzeldere, G. (1996). Introduction: The nature of consciousness. In Block *et al.* 1996.

Hastedt, H. (1985). Bewußtsein. In E. Martens & H. Schnädelbach (eds), *Philosophie. Ein Grundkurs.* Band 2. Reinbek: Rowohlt.

Krämer, S. (1994). Geist ohne Bewußtsein? Über einen Wandel in den Theorien vom Geist. In Krämer 1994.

Krämer, S. (1996). Bewußtsein als theoretische Fiktion und als Prinzip des Personverstehens. In Krämer 1996.

Kurthen, M. (1993). Kriterien der Bewußtseinszuschreibung bei natürlichen und künstlichen kognitiven Systemen. *Kognitionswissenschaft,* **3**, 161–70.

Kurthen, M. (1996). Das harmlose Faktum des Bewußtseins. In Krämer 1996.

Lormand, E. (forthcoming). Consciousness. In *The Routledge Encyclopedia of Philosophy*.

Lycan, W.G. (1991). Consciousness. *Academic American Encyclopedia*, 5, 200. Danbury: Grolier Incorporated.

Matthews, G. (1977). Consciousness and life. *Philosophy*, 52, 13–26.

McCulloch, G. (1993). The very idea of the phenomenological. *Proceedings of the Aristotelian Society*, 67, 39–57.

Mellor, D.H. (1980). Consciousness and degrees of belief. In D.H. Mellor (ed), *Prospects for Pragmatism*. Cambridge: Cambridge University Press.

Metzinger, T. (1994). Subjectivity and mental representation. In G. Meggle & U. Wessels (Hrsg.), *ANALYOMEN 1 — Perspektiven der Analytischen Philosophie*. Berlin and New York: de Gruyter.

Metzinger, T. (1994). Schimpansen, Spiegelbilder, Selbstmodelle und Subjekte. Drei Hypothesen über den Zusammenhang zwischen mentaler Repräsentation und phänomenalem Bewußtsein. In Krämer 1994.

Metzinger, T. (1995). Introduction: The problem of consciousness. In Metzinger 1995b.

Moody, T.C. (1986). Distinguishing consciousness. *Philosophy and Phenomenological Research*, 47, 289–95.

Natsoulas, T. (1978). Consciousness. *American Psychologist*, 33, 906–14.

Natsoulas, T. (1983). A selective review of conceptions of consciousness with special reference to behavioristic contributions. *Cognition and Brain Theory*, 6, 417–47.

Natsoulas, T. (1986). On the radical behaviorist conception of consciousness. *Journal of Mind and Behavior*, 7, 87–115.

Nelkin, N. (1993). What is consciousness? *Philosophy of Science*, 60, 419–34.

Nikolinakos, D. (1994). General anesthesia, consciousness, and the skeptical challenge. *Journal of Philosophy*, 91, 88–104.

O'Shaughnessy, B. (1991). The anatomy of consciousness. In Villanueva 1991.

Parks, Z. (1972). Toward a logic of experience. *Philosophia* (Israel), 2, 183–94.

Rey, G. (1983). A reason for doubting the existence of consciousness. In Davidson *et al.* 1983.

Rey, G. (1988). A question about consciousness. In H. Otto & J. Tuedio (eds), *Perspectives on Mind*. Dordrecht: D. Reidel.

Ripley, C. (1984). Sperry's concept of consciousness, *Inquiry*, 27, 399–423.

Rorty, R. (1994). Consciousness, intentionality, and the philosophy of mind. In Warner & Szubka 1994.

Schleichert, H. (1985). On the concept of unity of consciousness. *Synthese*, 64, 411–20.

Schleichert, H. (1996). Über die Bedeutung von Bewußtsein. In Krämer 1996.

Searle, J.R. (1993). The problem of consciousness. In *Experimental and Theoretical Studies of Consciousness*. CIBA Foundation Symposium 174. Chichester, UK: Wiley. Also in Revonsuo & Kamppinen 1994.

Shanon, B. (1990). Consciousness. *Journal of Mind and Behavior*, 11, 137–51.

Sprigge, T.L.S. (1994). Consciousness. *Synthese*, 98, 73–93.

Tye, M. (1995). The burning house. In Metzinger 1995b.

Van Gulick, R. (1995). What would count as explaining consciousness? In Metzinger 1995b.

Van Gulick, R. (1988). A functionalist plea for self-consciousness. *The Philosophical Review*, 97, 149–81.
Wilkes, K.V. (1984). Is consciousness important? *British Journal for the Philosophy of Science*, 35, 224–43.
Wilkes, K.V. (1988). —, yìshì, duh, um, and consciousness. In Marcel & Bisiach 1988.
Wilkes, K.V. (1995). Losing consciousness. In Metzinger 1995b.

3.2 Consciousness, Physicalism & the Mind–Body Problem

Is the existence of consciousness compatible with physicalism? The articles in this section address this question, and take various positions on this issue at the heart of the mind–body problem. This issue is also addressed by papers in most other sections, especially section 3.7.

Bechtel, W. & Richardson, R.C. (1983). Consciousness and complexity: Evolutionary perspectives on the mind–body problem. *Australasian Journal of Philosophy*, 61, 378–95.
Beckermann, A. & Stephan, A. (1994). Stichwort: Emergenz. *Information Philosophie*, 3, 46–51.
Beckermann, A. (1990). Zur Logik der Identitätstheorie. In G. Pasternack (Hrsg.), *Philosophie und Wissenschaften*. Frankfurt am Main: Peter Lang.
Beckermann, A. (1992). Supervenience, emergence, and reduction. In Beckermann *et al.* 1992.
Beckermann, A. (1995). Mentale Zustände — emergent oder neurobiologisch erklärbar? *Ethik und Sozialwissenschaften*, 6, 79–82.
Bieri, P. (1987). Pain: A case study for the mind–body problem. *Acta Neurochirurgica*, **Suppl. 38**, 157–64.
Bieri, P. (1992). Trying out epiphenomenalism. *Erkenntnis*, 36, 283–309.
Birnbacher, D. (1985). Gibt es für das Leib-Seele-Problem eine 'Lösung'? In *Philosophie des Geistes/Philosophie der Psychologie. Akten des 9. Internationalen Wittgenstein-Symposiums 1984*. Wien.
Birnbacher, D. (1988). Epiphenomenalism as a solution to the ontological mind-body problem. *Ratio (new series)*, 1, 17–32.
Birnbacher, D. (1990). Das ontologischen Leib-Seele-Problem und seine epiphänomenalistische Lösung. In K-E. Bühler (ed), *Aspekte des Leib-Seele-Problems. Philosophie, Medizin, Künstliche Intelligenz*. Würzburg: Königshausen & Neumann.
Birnbacher, D. (1993). Eine Verteidigung des Epiphänomenalismus. In *Philosophie Psychischer Phänomene. Vorträge des 9. Hamburger Kognitionskolloquiums vom 8.–9. Januar 1993*. Hamburg: Graduiertenkolleg Kognitionswissenschaft 1993.
Churchland, P.S. (1988). Reductionism and the neurobiological basis of consciousness. In Marcel & Bisiach 1988.
Elitzur, A. (1989). Consciousness and the incompleteness of the physical explanation of behavior. *Journal of Mind and Behavior*, 10, 1–20.
Flohr, H. (1994). Die physiologischen Bedingungen des Bewußtseins. In Lenk & Poser 1994.
Fodor, J.A. (1981). The mind–body problem. *Scientific American*, 244, 114–25.

Foss, J. (1987). Is the mind–body problem empirical? *Canadian Journal of Philosophy*, **17**, 505–32.

Fox, M. (1978). Beyond materialism. *Dialogue*, **17**, 367–70.

Goswami, A. (1990). Consciousness in quantum physics and the mind-body problem. *Journal of Mind and Behavior*, **11**, 75–96.

Gunderson, K. (1970). Asymmetries and mind–body perplexities. *Minnesota Studies in the Philosophy of Science*, **4**, 273–309.

Honderich, T. (1981). Psychophysical law-like connections and their problems. *Inquiry*, **24**, 277–303.

Howard, D.J. (1986). The new mentalism. *International Philosophical Quarterly*, **26**, 353–7.

Kirk, R. (1974). Zombies vs. materialists. *Aristotelian Society Proceedings*, **Supp. 48**, 135–52.

Kirk, R. (1977). Reply to Don Locke on Zombies and materialism. *Mind*, **86**, 262–4.

Kirk, R. (1979). From physical explicability to full-blooded materialism. *Philosophical Materialism*, **29**, 229–37.

Kirk, R. (1982). Physicalism, identity and strict implication. *Ratio*, **24**, 131–41.

Kirk, R. (1991). Why shouldn't we be able to solve the mind–body problem? *Analysis*, **51**, 17–23.

Kraemer, E.R. (1980). Imitation-man and the 'new' epiphenomenalism. *Canadian Journal of Philosophy*, **10**, 479–87.

Kurthen, M. & Linke, D.B. (1989). Der Emergentismus als Scheinlösung des Bieri-Trilemmas. *Psychotherapie, Medizinische Psychologie, Psychosomatik*, **39**, 480–2.

Lahav, R. & Shanks, N. (1992). How to be a scientifically respectable 'property dualist'. *Journal of Mind and Behavior*, **13**, 211–32.

Levine, J. (1983). Materialism and qualia: The explanatory gap. *Pacific Philosophical Quarterly*, **64**, 354–61.

Levine, J. (1993). On leaving out what it's like. In Davies & Humphreys 1993.

Locke, D. (1971). Must a materialist pretend he's anaesthetized? *Philosophical Quarterly*, **21**, 217–31.

Locke, D. (1976). Zombies, schizophrenics, and purely physical objects. *Mind*, **83**, 97–9.

McGinn, C. (1989). Can we solve the mind–body problem? *Mind*, **98**, 349–66.

McGinn, C. (1993). Consciousness and cosmology: Hyperdualism ventilated. In Davies & Humphreys 1993.

McGinn, C. (1995). Consciousness and space. In Metzinger 1995b.

Metzinger, T. (1990). Kritierien für eine Theorie zur Lösung des Leib-Seele-Problems. *Erkenntnis*, **32**, 127–45. Reprinted in *Acta Universitatis Lodziensis, Folia Philosophica*, **8**, 151–68.

Metzinger, T. (1991). Das Leib-Seele-Problem in den achtziger Jahren. *Conceptus*, **64**, 99–114.

Nagel, T. (1979). Panpsychism. In *Mortal Questions*. Cambridge: Cambridge University Press.

Nagel, T. (1993). What is the mind–body problem? In *Experimental and Theoretical Studies of Consciousness*. CIBA Foundation Symposium **174**. Chichester, UK: Wiley.

Nagel, T. (1994). Consciousness and objective reality. In Warner & Szubka 1994.

Nida-Rümelin, M. (1996). Is the naturalization of qualitative experience possible or sensible? In Carrier & Machamer 1996.

Perkins, M. (1970). Matter, sensation, and understanding. *American Philosophical Quarterly*, **8**, 1–12.

Perkins, M. (1971). Sentience. *Journal of Philosophy*, **68**, 329–37.

Place, U.T. (1988). Thirty years on — Is consciousness still a brain process? *Australasian Journal of Philosophy*, **66**, 208–19.

Robinson, H. (1976). The mind–body problem in contemporary philosophy. *Zygon*, **11**, 346–60.

Robinson, W.S. (1982). Causation, sensation, and knowledge. *Mind*, **91**, 525–40.

Ruhnau, E. (1995). Time-Gestalt and the observer. In Metzinger 1995b.

Sellars, W. (1981). Is consciousness physical? *Monist*, **64**, 66–90.

Smith, A.D. (1993). Non-reductive physicalism? In Robinson 1993.

Sperry, R. (1980). Mind–brain interaction: mentalism yes, dualism no. *Neuroscience*, **5**, 195–206.

Squires, R. (1974). Zombies vs materialists II. *Aristotelian Society Supplement*, **48**, 153–63.

Stephan, A. (1993). C.D. Broads a priori-Argument für die Emergenz phänomenaler Qualitäten. In Lenk & Poser 1993.

Strawson, G. (1994). The experiential and the non-experiential. In Warner & Szubka 1994.

Tye, M. (1983). On the possibility of disembodied existence. *Australasian Journal of Philosophy*, **61**, 275–82.

Van Cleve, J. (1990). Mind — dust or magic? Panpsychism versus emergence. *Philosophical Perspectives*, **4**, 215–26.

Van Gulick, R. (1985). Physicalism and the subjectivity of the mental. *Philosophical Topics*, **12**, 51–70.

Van Gulick, R. (1992). Nonreductive materialism and the nature of intertheoretical constraint. In Beckermann *et al.* 1992.

Van Gulick, R. (1993). Understanding the phenomenal mind: Are we all just armadillos? In Davies & Humphreys 1993. Reprinted in Block *et al.* 1996.

Velmans, M. (1990). Consciousness, brain, and the physical world. *Philosophical Psychology*, **3**, 77–99.

White, S. (1989). Transcendentalism and its discontents. *Philosophical Topics*, **17**, 231–61.

3.3 Consciousness as Higher-Order Thought

A popular way to make sense of consciousness has been to analyse it in terms of the existence of some higher-order mental state — that is, a mental state that is itself directed at another mental state. Sometimes this higher-order state is taken to be a state of 'inner perception' of another mental state, but more frequently (especially in the work of David Rosenthal) it has been taken to be a state of thought about another mental state. The papers cited here develop and critically address these suggestions. The issues are also addressed in chapters of some monographs in section 1.1, including Dennett 1991, Dretske 1995, Gennaro forthcoming and Siewert 1994.

Aquila, R. (1990). Consciousness as higher-order thought: Two objections. *American Philosophical Quarterly*, **27**, 81–7.

Armstrong, D. M. (1981). What is consciousness? In Armstrong 1981.

Byrne, A. (forthcoming). Some like it HOT: Consciousness and higher-order thoughts. *Philosophical Studies.*

Carruthers, P. (1989). Brute experience. *Journal of Philosophy*, **86**, 258–69.

Carruthers, P. (1992). Consciousness and concepts. *Proceedings of the Aristotelian Society*, Supplementary Volume **66**, 41–59.

Dretske, F. (1993). Conscious experience. *Mind*, **102**, 263–83.

Francescotti, R.M. (forthcoming). Higher-order thoughts and conscious experience. *Philosophical Psychology.*

Gennaro, R.J. (1993). Brute experience and the higher-order thought theory of consciousness. *Philosophical Papers*, **22**, 51.

Güzeldere, G. (1995). Is consciousness the perception of what passes on one's own mind? In Metzinger 1995b.

Güzeldere, G. (1996). Consciousness and the introspective link principle. In Hameroff *et al.* 1996.

Jamieson, D. & Bekoff, M. (1992). Carruthers on nonconscious experience. *Analysis*, **52**, 23–8.

Kobes, B.W. (1995). Telic higher-order thoughts and Moore's paradox. *Philosophical Perspectives*, **9**.

Lycan, W.G. (1996). Consciousness as internal monitoring, I. In Tomberlin 1995. Expanded version in Block *et al.* 1996.

Mellor, D. H. (1980). Consciousness and degrees of belief. In D.H. Mellor (ed), *Prospects for Pragmatism*. Cambridge: Cambridge University Press.

Mellor, D. H., (1977–78). Conscious belief. *Proceedings of the Aristotelian Society*, New Series, **88**, 87–101.

Natsoulas, T. (1992). Appendage theory — pro and con. *Journal of Mind and Behavior*, **13**, 371–96.

Natsoulas, T. (1993). What is wrong with the appendage theory of consciousness? *Philosophical Psychology*, **6**, 137–54.

Natsoulas, T. (1993). The importance of being conscious. *Journal of Mind and Behavior*, **14**, 317–40.

Nelkin, N. (1995). The dissociation of phenomenal states from apperception. In Metzinger 1995b.

Rosenthal, D.M. (1986). Two concepts of consciousness. *Philosophical Studies*, **49**, 329–59. Reprinted in Rosenthal 1990.

Rosenthal, D.M. (1993). Higher-order thoughts and the appendage theory of consciousness. *Philosophical Psychology*, **6**, 155–67.

Rosenthal, D.M. (1993). State consciousness and transitive consciousness. *Consciousness and Cognition*, **2**, 355–63.

Rosenthal, D.M. (1993). Thinking that one thinks. In Davies & Humphreys 1993.

Rosenthal, D.M. (1995). Moore's paradox and consciousness. In Tomberlin 1995.

Rosenthal, D.M. (1996). A theory of consciousness. In Block *et al.* 1996.

Seager, W. (1994). Dretske on HOT theories of consciousness, *Analysis*, **54**, 270–6.

Shoemaker, S. (1993). Functionalism and consciousness. In *Experimental and Theoretical Studies of Consciousness*. CIBA Foundation Symposium **174**. Chichester, UK: Wiley.

3.4 Consciousness and Intentionality

There is plausibly a close relationship between consciousness and intentionality, but what exactly is the relationship? Is consciousness (or the potential for consciousness) required for intentionality? Do conscious states have intentional content, and if so, what sort of intentional content do they have? These questions and others are addressed in the papers in this section.

Baldwin, T. (1992). The projective theory of sensory content. In Crane 1992.

Cam, P. (1984). Consciousness and content-formation. *Inquiry*, 27, 381–98.

Clark, R. (1973). Sensuous judgments. *Nous*, 7, 45–56.

Clark, R. (1981). Sensing, perceiving, thinking. In E. Sosa (ed), Essays on the Philosophy of Roderick M. Chisholm. *Grazer philosophische Studien*, 12, 273–95.

Crane, T. (1992). The nonconceptual content of experience. In Crane 1992.

Davies, M. (1995). Consciousness and the varieties of aboutness. In C. MacDonald & G. MacDonald (eds), *The Philosophy of Psychology: Debates on Psychological Explanation*. Oxford: Blackwell.

DeBellis, M. (1991). The representational content of musical experience. *Philosophy and Phenomenological Research*, 51, 303–24.

Falk, B. (1993). Consciousness, cognition, and the phenomenal. *Proceedings of the Aristotelian Society*, 67, 55–73.

Fodor, J. & Lepore, E. (1994). What is the Connection Principle? *Philosophy and Phenomenological Research*, 54, 837–45.

Gunderson, K. (1990). Consciousness and intentionality: Robots with and without the right stuff. In C. A. Anderson & J. Owens (eds), *Propositional Attitudes: The Role of Content in Language, Logic, and Mind*. Stanford: CSLI.

Hamlyn, D.W. (1994). Perception, sensation, and non-conceptual content. *Philosophical Quarterly*, 44, 139–53.

Jacquette, D. (1984). Sensation and intentionality. *Philosophical Studies*, 47, 229–40.

Lloyd, D. (1991). Leaping to conclusions: Connectionism, consciousness, and the computational mind. In T. Horgan & J. Tienson (eds), *Connectionism and the Philosophy of Mind*. Dordrecht: Kluwer Academic Publishers.

Lowe, E.J. (1992). Experience and its objects. In Crane 1992.

Maloney, J.C. (1986). Sensuous content. *Philosophical Papers*, 15, 131–54.

McGinn, C. (1988). Consciousness and content. *Proceedings of the British Academy*, 74, 219–39. Reprinted in McGinn 1991.

Mellor, D.H. (1977–8). Conscious belief. *Proceedings of the Aristotelian Society*, 78, 87–101.

Natsoulas, T. (1992). Intentionality, consciousness, and subjectivity. *Journal of Mind and Behavior*, 13, 281–308.

Nelkin, N. (1989). Propositional attitudes and consciousness. *Philosophy and Phenomenological Research*, 49, 413–30.

Nelkin, N. (1993). The connection between intentionality and consciousness. In Davies & Humphreys 1993.

Peacocke, C. (1984). Colour concepts and colour experience. *Synthese*, 58, 365–82.

Peacocke, C. (1992). Scenarios, concepts, and projection. In Crane 1992.

Pendlebury, M. (1987). Perceptual representation. *Proceedings of the Aristotelian Society* 87, 91–106.

Pendlebury, M. (1990). Sense experiences and their contents: A defense of the propositional account. *Inquiry*, **33**, 215–30.

Searle, J.R. (1989). Consciousness, unconsciousness, and intentionality. *Philosophical Topics*, **17**, 193–209.

Searle, J.R. (1990). Consciousness, explanatory inversion and cognitive science. *Behavioral and Brain Sciences*, **13**, 585–642.

Searle, J.R. (1994). The connection principle and the ontology of the unconscious: A reply to Fodor and Lepore. *Philosophy and Phenomenological Research*, **54**, 847–55.

Snowdon, P. (1990). The objects of perceptual experience. *Proceedings of the Aristotelian Society Supplement*, **64**, 121–50.

Sosa, E. (1986). Experience and intentionality. *Philosophical Topics*, **14**, 67–83.

Tye, M. (1992). Visual qualia and visual content. In Crane 1992.

Tye, M. (1994). Do pains have representational content? In Casati, Smith & White 1994.

Valberg, J.J. (1992). The puzzle of experience. In Crane 1992.

Van Gulick, R. (1988). Consciousness, intrinsic intentionality, and self-understanding machines. In Marcel & Bisiach 1988.

Van Gulick, R. (1995). Understanding the relation between intentionality and consciousness. In Tomberlin 1995.

3.5 Dennett on Consciousness

An important reductive account of consciousness has been developed by Daniel Dennett over a period of many years, and has received wide attention from other researchers. Because these papers often do not fit naturally into the other subject-oriented sections, we have collected them into a single section here.

Arbib, M. (1972). Consciousness: The secondary role of language. *Journal of Philosophy*, **69**, 579–91.

Baars, B.J. & McGovern, K. (1993). Does philosophy help or hinder scientific work on consciousness? *Consciousness and Cognition*, **2**, 18–27.

Baker, L.R. (1995). Content meets consciousness. *Philosophical Topics*, **22**, 1–22.

Block, N. (1995). What is Dennett's theory a theory of? *Philosophical Topics*, **22**, 23–40.

Bricke, J. (1984). Dennett's eliminative arguments. *Philosophical Studies*, **45**, 413–29.

Bricke, J. (1985). Consciousness and Dennett's intentionalist net. *Philosophical Studies*, **48**, 249–56.

Cam, P. (1985). Phenomenology and speech dispositions. *Philosophical Studies*, **47**, 357–68.

Churchland, P.S. & Ramachandran, V.S. (1993). Filling in: Why Dennett is wrong. In Dahlbom 1993. Also in Revonsuo & Kamppinen 1994.

Clark, S.R.L. (1993). Minds, memes, and rhetoric. *Inquiry*, **36**, 3–16.

Dennett, D.C. (1976). Are dreams experiences? *Philosophical Review*, **73**, 151–71. Reprinted in Dennett 1978.

Dennett, D.C. (1978). Reply to Arbib and Gunderson. In Dennett 1978.

Dennett, D.C. (1978). Toward a cognitive theory of consciousness. In Dennett 1978.

Dennett, D.C. (1978). Why you can't make a computer that feels pain. *Synthese*, **38**, 415–56. Reprinted in Dennett 1978.

Dennett, D.C. (1979). On the absence of phenomenology. In D. Gustafson & B. Tapscott (eds), *Body, Mind and Method: Essays in Honor of Virgil Aldrich*. Dordrecht: D. Reidel.

Dennett, D.C. (1979). The onus re experiences: A reply to Emmett. *Philosophical Studies*, **35**, 315–8.

Dennett, D.C. (1981). Wondering where the yellow went. *Monist*, **64**, 102–8.

Dennett, D.C. (1982). How to study human consciousness empirically, or nothing comes to mind. *Synthese*, **59**, 159–80.

Dennett, D.C. (1986). Julian Jaynes' software archaeology. *Canadian Psychology*, **27**, 149–54.

Dennett, D.C. (1988). Quining qualia. In Marcel & Bisiach 1988. Reprinted in Block *et al.* 1996.

Dennett, D.C. (1988). The evolution of consciousness. In J. Brockman (ed), *Speculations. The Reality Club*. New York: Prentice Hall Press.

Dennett, D.C. (1991). Lovely and suspect qualities. In Villanueva 1991.

Dennett, D.C. (1993). Caveat emptor. *Consciousness and Cognition*, **2**, 48–57.

Dennett, D.C. (1993). Living on the edge. *Inquiry*, **36**, 135–59.

Dennett, D.C. (1993). Précis of *Consciousness Explained*. *Philosophy and Phenomenological Research*, **53**, 889–92.

Dennett, D.C. (1993). The message is: There is no *medium*. *Philosophy and Phenomenological Research*, **53**, 919–31.

Dennett, D.C. (1995). Get real. *Philosophical Topics*, **22**, 505–60.

Dennett, D.C. & Kinsbourne, M. (1991). Time and the observer: The where and when of consciousness in the brain. *Behavioral and Brain Sciences*, **15**, 183–247. Reprinted in Block *et al.* 1996.

Dretske, F. (1995). Differences that make no difference. *Philosophical Topics*, **22**, 41–58.

Emmett, K. (1978). Oneiric experiences. *Philosophical Studies*, **34**, 445–50.

Fellows, R. & O'Hear, A. (1993). Consciousness avoided. *Inquiry*, **36**, 73–91.

Foster, J. (1993). Dennett's rejection of dualism. *Inquiry*, **36**, 17–31.

Gunderson, K. (1972). *Content and Consciousness* and the mind–body problem. *Journal of Philosophy*, **69**, 591–604.

Jackson, F. (1993). Appendix A (for philosophers). *Philosophy and Phenomenological Research*, **53**, 899–903.

Kirk, R. (1993). 'The best set of tools?' Dennett's metaphors and the mind–body problem. *Philosophical Quarterly*, **43**, 335–43.

Lockwood, M. (1993). Dennett's mind. *Inquiry*, **36**, 59–72.

Lormand, E. (1995). Qualia! (Now showing at a theater near you.) *Philosophical Topics*, **22**, 127–56.

Mangan, B. (1993). Dennett, consciousness, and the sorrows of functionalism. *Consciousness and Cognition*, **2**, 1–17.

Marbach, E. (1988). How to study consciousness phenomenologically or quite a lot comes to mind. *Journal of the British Society for Phenomenology*, **19**, 252–68.

Marbach, E. (1994). Troubles with heterophenomenology. In Casati, Smith & White 1994.

McCauley, R.N. (1993). Why the blind can't lead the blind: Dennett on the blind spot, blindsight, and sensory qualia. *Consciousness and Cognition*, **2**, 155–64.

Radner, D. (1994). Heterophenomenology: Learning about the birds and the bees. *Journal of Philosophy*, **91**, 389–403.

Raffman, D. (1993). Qualms about Quining qualia. In D. Raffman, *Language, Music, and Mind*. Cambridge, MA: MIT Press.

Ramachandran, V.S. (1993). Filling in gaps in logic: Some comments on Dennett. *Consciousness and Cognition*, **2**, 165–8.

Rey, G. (1995). Dennett's unrealistic psychology. *Philosophical Topics*, **22**, 259–90.

Robinson, W.S. (1972). Dennett's analysis of awareness. *Philosophical Studies*, **23**, 147–52.

Robinson, W.S. (1994). Orwell, Stalin, and determinate qualia. *Pacific Philosophical Quarterly*, **75**, 151.

Rorty, R. (1972). Dennett on awareness. *Philosophical Studies*, **23**, 153–62.

Rorty, R. (1993). Holism, intrinsicality, and the ambition of transcendence. In Dahlbom 1993.

Rosenthal, D.M. (1993). Multiple drafts and higher-order thoughts. *Philosophy and Phenomenological Research*, **53**, 911–18.

Rosenthal, D.M. (1995). First-person operationalism and mental taxonomy. *Philosophical Topics*, **22**, 319–50.

Rosenthal, D.M. (1995). Multiple drafts and facts of the matter. In Metzinger 1995b.

Ross, D. (1993). Quining qualia Quine's way. *Dialogue*, **32**, 439–59.

Ross, D. (1994). Dennett's conceptual reform. *Behavior and Philosophy*, **22**, 41–52.

Seager, W. (1993). The elimination of experience. *Philosophy and Phenomenological Research*, **53**, 345–65.

Seager, W. (1993). Verification, skepticism, and consciousness. *Inquiry*, **36**, 113–36.

Shoemaker, S. (1993). Lovely and suspect ideas. *Philosophy and Phenomenological Research*, **53**, 903–08.

Siewert, C. (1993). What Dennett can't imagine and why. *Inquiry*, **36**, 93–112.

Sprigge, T.L.S. (1993). Is Dennett a disillusioned zimbo? *Inquiry*, **36**, 33–57.

Toribio, J. (1993). Why there still has to be a theory of consciousness. *Consciousness and Cognition*, **2**, 28–47.

Tye, M. (1993). Reflections on Dennett and consciousness. *Philosophy and Phenomenological Research*, **53**, 891–6.

Van Gulick, R. (1995). Dennett, drafts, and phenomenal realism. *Philosophical Topics*, **22**, 443–56.

3.6 Consciousness: Miscellaneous

This section contains miscellaneous philosophical articles on consciousness. These include very broad articles on the subject, as well as articles on smaller specific topics that do not have sections of their own.

Baas, N. (1996). A framework for higher-order cognition and consciousness. In Hameroff *et al.* 1996.

Beckermann, A. (1993). Metarepräsentationen und phänomenale Zustände. In Lenk & Poser 1993.

Beckermann, A. (1995). Visual information-processing and phenomenal consciousness. In Metzinger 1995b.

Bieri, P. (1982). Nominalism and inner experience. *The Monist*, **65**, 68–87.

Bieri, P. (1986). Zeiterfahrung und Personalität. In H. Burger (Hrsg.), *Natur, Mensch und Zeit*. Berlin: Arno Spitz.

Birnbacher, D. (1994). Einige Gründe, das Hirntodkriterium zu akzeptieren. In J. Hoff & J. in der Schmitten (Hrsg.), *Wann ist der Mensch tot? Organverpflanzung und 'Hirntod'-Kriterium*. Reinbek: Rowohlt.

Burns, J. (1996). The possibility of empirical test of hypotheses about consciousness. In Hameroff *et al.* 1996.

Cam, P. (1989). Notes toward a faculty theory of cognitive consciousness. In Slezak 1989.

Chalmers, D.J. (1995). Facing up to the problem of consciousness. *Journal of Consciousness Studies*, 2, 200–19. Also in Hameroff *et al.* 1996.

Chisholm, R.M. (1990). Questions about the unity of consciousness. In Cramer *et al.* 1990.

Dewan, E.M. (1976). Consciousness as an emergent causal agent in the context of control system theory. In Globus, Maxwell & Savodnik 1976.

Ebeling, H. (1990). Das Subjekt im Dasein. Versuch über das bewußte Sein. In Cramer *et al.* 1990.

Fellmann, F. (1996). Intentionalität und zuständliches Bewußtsein. In Krämer 1996.

Flanagan, O. (1995). Deconstructing dreams: The spandrels of sleep. *Journal of Philosophy*, 112, 5–27.

Flanagan, O. (1995). Neurowissenschaft und Träume: Geistestätigkeit und Selbstausdruck im Schlaf. In Metzinger 1995a.

Flohr, H. (1994). Denken und Bewußtsein. In J. Fedrowitz, D. Matejovski & G. Kaiser (Hrsg.), *Neuroworlds. Gehirn — Geist — Kultur*. Frankfurt/New York: Campus Verlag.

Flohr, H.(1989). Schwierigkeiten der Autocerebroskopie. In Pöppel 1989.

Fox, I. (1985). The individualization of consciousness. *Philosophical Topics*, 13, 119–43.

Gadenne, V. (1993). Bewußtsein, Selbstbewußtsein und Reflexion. *Logos*, 1, 82–103.

Gennaro, R.J. (1992). Consciousness, self-consciousness, and episodic memory. *Philosophical Psychology*, 5, 333–47.

Grush, R. & Churchland, P.S. (1995). Gaps in Penrose's toilings. In Metzinger 1995b.

Güzeldere, G. (1995). Consciousness: What it is, how to study it, what to learn from its history. *Journal of Consciousness Studies*, 2, 30–52.

Güzeldere, G. (1995). Problems of consciousness: Contemporary issues, current debates. *Journal of Consciousness Studies*, 2, 112–43.

Hannay, A. (1987). The claims of consciousness: A critical survey. *Inquiry*, 30, 395–434.

Hardcastle, V.G. (1993). The naturalists versus the skeptics: The debate over a scientific understanding of consciousness. *Journal of Mind and Behavior*, 14, 27–50.

Harman, W. (1996). Toward a science of consciousness: Addressing two central questions. In Hameroff *et al.* 1996.

Harnad, S. (1982). Consciousness: An afterthought. *Cognition and Brain Theory*, 5, 29–47.

Holenstein, E. (1996). Die kausale Rolle von Bewußtsein und Vernunft. In Krämer 1996.

Humphrey, N.K. (1988). The uses of consciousness. In J. Brockman (ed), *Speculations. The Reality Club*. New York: Prentice Hall Press.

Kraemer, E.R. (1984). Consciousness and the exclusivity of function. *Mind*, **93**, 271–5.

Kirk, R. (1992). Consciousness and concepts. *Proceedings of the Aristotelian Society*, Supplementary Volume **66**, 23–40.

Kirk, R. (1995). How is consciousness possible? In Metzinger 1995b.

Kurthen, M. (1993). Zur Sprachlichkeit des Unbewußten angesichts der orthodoxen Kognitionswissenschaft. In Tress & Nagel 1993.

Kurthen, M. (1995). On the prospects of a naturalistic theory of phenomenal consciousness. In Metzinger 1995b.

Kurthen, M., Linke, D.B., Reuter, B.M. & Moskopp, D. (1991). Das Subjekt des Todes. Zur aktuellen Kontroverse um hirnorientierte Todesbestimmungen. *Wiener Medizinische Wochenschrift*, **141**, 31–2.

Marbach, E. (1987). Laws of consciousness as norms of mental development. In B. Inhelder, D. de Caprona & A. Cornu-Wells (eds), *Piaget Today*. Hove and London: Lawrence Erlbaum Associates.

Marcel, A. (1988). Phenomenal experience and functionalism. In Marcel & Bisiach 1988.

Metzinger, T. (1994). Zeitfenster im Gehirn und die Einheit des Bewußtseins. In Lenk & Poser 1993.

Metzinger, T. (1995). Faster than thought: Holism, homogeneity and temporal coding. In Metzinger 1995b.

Metzinger, T. (1995). Perspektivische Fakten? Die Naturalisierung des *View from Nowhere*. In G. Meggle & U. Wessels (eds), *Analyomen 2. Proceedings of the 2nd Conference Perspectives in Analytical Philosophy*. Berlin und New York: de Gruyter.

Metzinger (1996). *Niemand* sein. Kann man eine naturalistische Perspektive auf die Subjektivität des Mentalen einnehmen? In Krämer 1996.

Moody, T. (1994). Conversations with zombies. *Journal of Consciousness Studies*, **1**, 196–200.

Natika, N. (1991). Consciousness, qualia, and reentrant signalling. *Behavior and Philosophy*, **19**, 21–41.

Natsoulas, T. (1981). Basic problems of consciousness. *Journal of Personality and Social Psychology*, **41**, 132–78.

Oatley, K. (1988). On changing one's mind: A possible function of consciousness. In Marcel & Bisiach 1988.

Penrose, R. & Hameroff, S. (1995). What 'Gaps'? Reply to Grush and Churchland. *Journal of Consciousness Studies*, **2**, 98–111.

Pohlenz, G. (1990). Phänomenale Qualitäten, Erkenntnis und das philosophische Problem der Leib-Seele-Beziehung. *Philosophisches Jahrbuch*, **97**, 69–104.

Pohlenz, G. (1990). Phänomenale Realität und naturalistische Philosophie. Eine systematische Widerlegung der Feigl'schen und Sellars'schen Theorien phänomenaler Qualitäten und Skizze einer alternativen Theorie. *Zeitschrift für philosophische Forschung*, **44**, 106–42.

Pohlenz, G. (1992). Kein Platz für phänomenale Qualitäten und Leib-Umwelt-Interaktion? Eine Kritik transzendentalistischer Tendenzen in der modernen Theorie empirischer Wissenschaft. *Zeitschrift für philosophische Forschung*, **46**, 363–80.

Pothast, U. (1990). Etwas über Bewußtsein. In Cramer *et al.* 1990.

Revonsuo, A. (1993). Is there a ghost in the cognitive machinery? *Philosophical Psychology*, **6**, 387–405.

Revonsuo, A. (1994). In search of the science of consciousness. In Revonsuo & Kamppinen 1994.

Rey, G. (1995). Towards a projectivist account of conscious experience. In Metzinger 1995b.

Richards, W. (1984). Self-consciousness and agency. *Synthese*, **61**, 149–71.

Schleichert, H. (1989). The relationship between consciousness and language. In J.R. Brown & J. Mittelstrass (eds), *An intimate relation. Studies in the history and philosophy of science, presented to Robert E. Butts on his 60th birthday.* Dordrecht: Academic Publishers.

Shoemaker, S. (1990). First-person access. *Philosophical Perspectives*, **4**, 187–214.

Sloman, A. (1993). The mind as a control system. In Hookway & Peterson 1993.

Smith, D.W. (1986). The structure of (self-) consciousness. *Topoi*, **5**, 149–56.

Sokolowski, R. (1992). Parallelism in conscious experience. *Daedalus*, issued as: *Proceedings of the American Academy of Arts and Sciences*, **120**, 87–103.

Stadler, M. & Kruse, P. (1992). Zur Emergenz psychischer Qualitäten. Das psychophysische Problem im Lichte der Selbstorganisationstheorie. In W. Krohn & G. Küppers, *Emergenz: Die Entstehung von Ordnung, Organisation und Bedeutung.* Frankfurt am Main: Suhrkamp.

Tienson, J.L. (1987). Brains are not conscious. *Philosophical Papers*, **16**, 187–93.

Van Gulick, R. (1989). What difference does consciousness make? *Philosophical Topics*, **17**, 211–30.

Van Gulick, R. (1994). Deficit studies and the function of phenomenal consciousness. In G. Graham & G.L. Stephens (eds), *Philosophical Psychopathology.* Cambridge, MA: MIT Press.

Wiehl, R. (1990). Die Komplementrität von Selbstsein und Bewußtsein. In Cramer *et al.* 1990.

3.7 Knowing What It's Like and the Knowledge Argument

An important thread in the philosophical literature on consciousness concerns the relationship between our knowledge of our consciousness and our knowledge of the objective physical world. Thomas Nagel has argued that no amount of objective knowledge enables us to know what it is like to be a conscious being quite different from us. Frank Jackson has argued that someone who knows all the physical facts about the brain might still not know what it is like to see red, and has concluded (via the so-called 'Knowledge Argument') that physicalism is false. This section encompasses much of the large body of literature on these issues.

Akins, K. (1993). A bat without qualities? In Davies & Humphreys 1993.

Akins, K. (1993). What is it like to be boring and myopic? In Dahlbom 1993.

Bachrach, J.E. (1990). Qualia and theory reduction: A criticism of Paul Churchland. *Iyyun*, 281–94.

Bigelow, J. & Pargetter, R. (1990). Acquaintance with qualia. *Theoria*, **56**, 129–47.

Biro, J.I. (1991). Consciousness and subjectivity. In Villanueva 1991.

Biro, J.I. (1993). Consciousness and objectivity. In Davies & Humphreys 1993.

Churchland, P.M. (1985). Reduction, qualia, and the direct introspection of brain states. *Journal of Philosophy*, **82**, 8–28. Reprinted in Churchland 1989.

Churchland, P.M. (1990). Knowing qualia: A reply to Jackson. In Churchland 1989.

Conee, E. (1985). Physicalism and phenomenal qualities. *Philosophical Quarterly*, 35, 296–302.

Conee, E. (1994). Phenomenal knowledge. *Australasian Journal of Philosophy*, 72, 136–50.

Cummins, R. (1984). The mind of the matter: Comments on Paul Churchland. *Philosophy of Science Association*, 2, 791–8.

Davis, L. (1982). What is it like to be an agent? *Erkenntnis*, 18, 195–213.

Double, R. (1983). Nagel's argument that mental properties are nonphysical. *Philosophy Research Archives*, 9, 217–22.

Flanagan, O. (1985). Consciousness, naturalism, and Nagel. *Journal of Mind and Behavior*, 6, 373–90.

Foss, J.E. (1987). On the logic of what it is like to be a conscious subject. *Australasian Journal of Philosophy*, 67, 205–20.

Foss, J.E. (1993). Subjectivity, objectivity, and Nagel on consciousness. *Dialogue*, 32, 725–36.

Francescotti, R.M. (1993). Subjective experience and points of view. *Journal of Philosophical Research*, 18, 25–36.

Furash, G. (1989). Frank Jackson's knowledge argument against materialism. *Dialogue*, 32, 1–6.

Gadenne, V. (1992). Naturalismus und Subjektivität. Naturalism and subjectivity. *Ethik und Sozialwissenschaften*, 3, 456–7.

Haksar, V. (1981). Nagel on subjective and objective. *Inquiry*, 24, 105–21.

Hanna, P. (1990). Must thinking bats be conscious? *Philosophical Investigations*, 13, 350–5.

Harman, G. (1993). Can science understand the mind? In G. Harman (ed), *Conceptions of the Human Mind: Essays in Honor of George A. Miller*. Hillsdale, NJ: Lawrence Erlbaum Associates.

Hiley, D.R. (1978). Materialism and the inner life. *Southern Journal of Philosophy*, 16, 61–70.

Hill, C.S. (1977). Of bats, brains, and minds. *Philosophy and Phenomenological Research*, 38, 100–6.

Horgan, T. (1984). Jackson on physical information and qualia. *Philosophical Quarterly*, 34, 147–83.

Jackson, F. (1982). Epiphenomenal qualia. *Philosophical Quarterly*, 32, 127–36. Reprinted in Lycan 1990 and Block *et al.* 1996.

Jackson, F. (1986). What Mary didn't know. *Journal of Philosophy*, 83, 291–5. Reprinted in Rosenthal 1991 and Block *et al.* 1996. Reprinted with a postscript in Moser, P.K. & Trout, J.D. (eds). *Contemporary Materialism*. London: Routledge.

Jackson, F. (1994). Finding the mind in the natural world. In Casati, Smith & White 1994. Reprinted in Block *et al.* 1996.

Kekes, J. (1977). Physicalism and subjectivity. *Philosophy and Phenomenological Research*, 37, 533–6.

Levin, J. (1986). Could love be like a heatwave? Physicalism and the subjective character of experience. *Philosophical Studies*, 49, 245–61. Reprinted in Lycan 1990.

Lewis, D. (1983). Postscript to 'Mad pain and martian pain'. In *Philosophical Papers, Vol. I*. Oxford: Oxford University Press.

Lewis, D. (1988). What experience teaches. *Proceedings of the Russelian Society*. University of Sydney. Reprinted in Lycan 1990 and Block *et al.* 1996.

Loar, B. (1990). Phenomenal states. In Tomberlin 1990. Revised version in Block *et al.* 1996.

Lycan, W.G. (1990). What is the 'subjectivity' of the mental? In Tomberlin 1990.

Lycan, W.G. (1995). A limited defence of phenomenal information. In Metzinger 1995b.

Malcolm, N. (1988). Subjectivity. *Philosophy*, **63**, 147–60.

McClamrock, R. (1992). Irreducibility and subjectivity. *Philosophical Studies*, **67**, 177–92.

McConnell, J. (1995). In defense of the knowledge argument. *Philosophical Topics*. **22**, 157–88.

McCulloch, G. (1988). What it is like. *Philosophical Quarterly*, **38**, 1–19.

McMullen, C. (1985). 'Knowing what it's like' and the essential indexical. *Philosophical Studies*, **48**, 211–34.

Mellor, D.H. (1993). Nothing like experience. *Proceedings of the Aristotelian Society*, **63**, 1–16.

Muscari, P. (1985). The subjective character of experience. *Journal of Mind and Behavior*, **6**, 577–97.

Muscari, P. (1987). The status of humans in Nagel's phenomenology. *Philosophical Forum*, **19**, 23–33.

Nagel, T. (1974). What is it like to be a bat? *Philosophical Review*, **83**, 435–50.

Nagel, T. (1979). Subjective and objective. In *Mortal Questions*. Cambridge: Cambridge University Press.

Nelkin, N. (1987). What is it like to be a person? *Mind and Language*, **3**, 22041.

Nemirow, L. (1990). Physicalism and the cognitive role of acquaintance. In Lycan 1990.

Nemirow, L. (1995). Understanding rules. *Journal of Philosophy*, **92**, 28–43.

Newton, N. (1986). Churchland on direct introspection of brain states. *Analysis*, **46**, 97–102.

Nida-Rümelin, M. (forthcoming). On belief about experiences. An epistemological distinction applied to the knowledge argument. [submitted].

Nida-Rümelin, M. (1995). What Mary couldn't know: belief about phenomenal states. In Metzinger 1995b.

Papineau, D. (1993). Physicalism, consciousness and the antipathetic fallacy. *Australasian Journal of Philosophy*, **71**, 169–83.

Papineau, D. (1995). The antipathetic fallacy and the boundaries of consciousness. In Metzinger 1995b.

Pereboom, D. (1994). Bats, brain scientists, and the limits of introspection. *Philosophy and Phenomenological Research*, **54**, 315–29.

Pitcher, G. (1970). The awfulness of pain. *Journal of Philosophy*, **68**, 481–92.

Pugmire, D. (1989). Bat or batman. *Philosophy*, **64**, 207–17.

Robinson, D. (1993). Epiphenomenalism, laws, and properties. *Philosophical Studies*, **69**, 1–34.

Robinson, H. (1993). Dennett on the knowledge argument. *Analysis*, **53**, 174–7.

Robinson, H. (1993). The anti-materialist strategy and the 'knowledge argument'. In Robinson 1993.

Rosenthal, D.M. (1991). The independence of consciousness and sensory quality. In Villanueva 1991.

Russow, L. (1982). It's not like that to be a bat. *Behaviorism*, **10**, 55–63.

Seager, W.E. (1983). Functionalism, qualia and causation. *Mind*, **92**, 174–88.

Shoemaker, S. (1984). Churchland on reduction, qualia, and introspection. *Philosophy of Science Association*, **2**, 799–809.

Stemmer, N. (1989). Physicalism and the argument from knowledge. *Australasian Journal of Philosophy*, **67**, 84–91.

Sturgeon, S. (1994). The epistemic view of subjectivity. *Journal of Philosophy*, Vol. XCI, **5**, 221–35.

Taliaferro, C. (1988). Nagel's vista or taking subjectivity seriously. *Southern Journal of Philosophy*, **26**, 393–401.

Teller, P. (1992). Subjectivity and knowing what it's like. In Beckermann *et al.* 1992.

Thompson, E. (1992). Novel colours. *Philosophical Studies*, **68**, 321–49.

Tilghman, B.R. (1991). What is it like to be an aardvark? *Philosophy*, **66**, 325–38.

Tye, M. (1986). The subjective qualities of experience. *Mind*, **95**, 1–17.

Tye, M. (1995). What 'what it's like' is really like. *Analysis*, **55**, 125–6.

Warner, R. (1986). A challenge to physicalism. *Australasian Journal of Philosophy*, **64**, 249–65.

Watkins, M. (1989). The knowledge argument against the knowledge argument. *Analysis*, **49**, 158–60.

White, S. (1987). What is it like to be a homunculus? *Pacific Philosophical Quarterly*, **68**, 148–74.

Wider, K. (1989). Overtones of solipsism in Nagel's 'What is it like to be a bat?' and 'The View from Nowhere'. *Philosophy and Phenomenological Research*, **49**, 481–99.

3.8 Absent Qualia and Inverted Qualia

A common objection to functionalist accounts of mind is that they do not capture all the facts about conscious experience, as we can always imagine the properties described in any given functional account being instantiated with no associated experience at all (the case of 'absent qualia') or with subjective experiences differing between functionally identical systems ('inverted qualia' or the 'inverted spectrum'). Others have disputed this possibility. This section includes papers covering many aspects of this debate.

Averill, E.W. (1990) Functionalism, the absent qualia objection, and eliminativism. *Southern Journal of Philosophy*, **28**, 449–67.

Block, N. (1980). Are absent qualia impossible? *Philosophical Review*, **89**, 257–74.

Block, N. (1990). Inverted earth. *Philosophical Perspectives*, **4**, 53–79.

Bogen, J. (1981). Agony in the schools. *Canadian Journal of Philosophy*, **11**, 1–21.

Carleton, L. (1983). The population of China as one mind. *Philosophy Research Archives*, **9**, 665–74.

Chalmers, D.J. (1995). Absent qualia, fading qualia, dancing qualia. In Metzinger 1995b.

Churchland, P.M. & Churchland, P.S. (1981). Functionalism, qualia and intentionality. *Philosophical Topics*, **12**, 121-32. Reprinted in Churchland 1989.

Clark, A. (1985). Spectrum inversion and the color solid. *Southern Journal of Philosophy*, **23**, 431–43.

Cole, D.J. (1990). Functionalism and inverted spectra. *Synthese*, **82**, 207–22.

Conee, E. (1985). The possibility of absent qualia. *Philosophical Review*, **94**, 345–66.

Cuda, T. (1985). Against neural chauvinism. *Philosophical Studies*, **48**, 111–27.

Davis, L. (1982). Functionalism and absent qualia. *Philosophical Studies*, **41**, 231–49.

Dennett, D.C. (1994). Instead of qualia. In Revonsuo & Kamppinen 1994.

Doore, G. (1981). Functionalism and absent qualia. *Australasian Journal of Philosophy*, **59**, 387–402.

Elugardo, R. (1983). Functionalism and the absent qualia argument. *Canadian Journal of Philosophy*, **13**, 161–80.

Elugardo, R. (1983). Functionalism, homunculi-heads and absent qualia. *Dialogue*, **22**, 47–56.

Hardin, C.L. (1991). Reply to Levine. *Philosophical Psychology*, **4**, 41–50.

Hardin, C.L. (1996). Reinverting the spectrum. In Carrier & Machamer 1996.

Horgan, T. (1984). Functionalism, qualia, and the inverted spectrum. *Philosophy and Phenomenological Research*, **44**, 453–69.

Jacoby, H. (1990). Empirical functionalism and conceivability arguments. *Philosophical Psychology*, **2**, 271–82.

Johnsen, B. (1986). The inverted spectrum. *Australasian Journal of Philosophy*, **64**, 471–6.

Johnsen, B.C. (1993). The intelligibility of spectrum inversion. *Canadian Journal of Philosophy*, **23**, 631–6.

Kirk, R. (1982). Goodbye to transposed qualia. *Proceeding of the Aristotelian Society*, **82**, 33–44.

Kirk, R. (1994). The trouble with ultra-externalism. *Proceedings of the Aristotelian Society*, 293–307.

Lanz, P. (1994). Funktionalismus und sensorisches Bewußtsein. In G. Meggle & U. Wessels (eds), *Analyomen 1. Proceedings of the 2nd Conference Perspectives in Analytical Philosophy*. Berlin: de Gruyter

Levin, J. (1985). Functionalism and the argument from conceivability. *Canadian Journal of Philosophical Supplement*, **11**, 85–104.

Levine, J. (1989). Absent and inverted qualia revisited. *Mind and Language*, **3**, 271–87.

Levine, J. (1991). Cool red. *Philosophical Psychology*, **4**, 27–40.

Lycan, W.G. (1973). Inverted spectrum. *Ratio*, **60**, 315–19.

Lycan, W.G. (1981). Form, function, and feel. *Journal of Philosophy*, **78**, 24–50.

McGinn, C. (1981). A note on functionalism and function. *Philosophical Topics*, **12**, 169–70.

Marcel, A.J. (1988). Phenomenal experience and functionalism. In Marcel & Bisiach 1988.

Nida-Rümelin, M. (forthcoming). Pseudonormal vision. An actual case of qualia inversion? *Philosophical Studies*, Supplement.

Putnam, H. (1981). Mind and body. In *Reason, Truth and History*. Cambridge: Cambridge University Press.

Rey, G. (1992). Sensational sentences switched. *Philosophical Studies*, **67**, 73–103.

Sayan, E. (1988). A closer look at the Chinese Nation argument. *Philosophy Research Archives*, **13**, 129–36.

Shoemaker, S. (1975). Functionalism and qualia. *Philosophical Studies*, **27**, 291–315. Reprinted in Shoemaker 1984.

Shoemaker, S. (1981). Absent qualia are impossible — A reply to Block. *Philosophical Review*, **90**, 581–99. Reprinted in Shoemaker 1984.

Shoemaker, S. (1982). The inverted spectrum. *Journal of Philosophy*, **79**, 357–81. Reprinted in Shoemaker 1984.

Shoemaker, S. (1994). The first-person perspective. *Proceedings and Addresses of the American Philosophical Association*, **68**, 7–22.

Tye, M. (1994). Blindsight, the absent qualia hypothesis, and the mystery of consciousness. In Hookway & Peterson 1994.

Tye, M. (1994). Qualia, content and the inverted spectrum. *Noûs*, **28**, 159–83.

White, N. (1985). Professor Shoemaker and the so-called 'qualia' of experience. *Philosophical Studies*, **47**, 369–83.

White, S. (1986). Curse of the qualia. *Synthese*, **68**, 333–68. Reprinted in Block *et al.* 1996.

3.9 Qualia: Miscellaneous

This section includes miscellaneous articles on qualia, or experiential properties, or phenomenal properties, as well as on specific sorts of experiences, such as color and pain experiences. Note that the division between these articles and those on 'consciousness' is often superficial.

Addis, L. (1986). Pains and other secondary mental entities. *Philosophy and Phenomenological Research*, **47**, 59–74.

Alston, W. (1971). Varieties of privileged access. *American Philosophical Quarterly*, **8**, 223–41.

Berger, G. (1987). On the structure of visual sentience. *Synthese*, **71**, 355–70.

Blumenfeld, J-B. (1979). Phenomenal properties and the identity theory. *Australasian Journal of Philosophy*, **63**, 485–93.

Brown, M. (1983). Functionalism and sensations. *Auslegung*, **10**, 218–28.

Burgess, J.A. (1990). Phenomenal qualities and the nontransitivity of matching. *Australasian Journal of Philosophy*.

Clark, A. (1985). A physicalist theory of qualia. *Monist*, **68**, 491–506.

Clark, A. (1985). Qualia and the psychophysical explanation of color perception. *Synthese*, **65**, 377–405.

Clark, A. (1989). The particulate instantiation of homogeneous pink. *Synthese*, **80**, 277–304.

Conee, E. (1984). A defense of pain. *Philosophical Studies*, **46**, 239–48.

Delaney, C.F. (1970). Sellars' grain argument. *Australasian Journal of Philosophy*, **50**.

Double, R. 1985. Phenomenal properties. *Philosophy and Phenomenological Research*, **45**, 383–92.

Dumpleton, S. (1988). Sensation and function. *Australasian Journal of Philosophy*, **66**, 376–89.

Eshelman, L.J. (1977). Functionalism, sensations, and materialism. *Canadian Journal of Philosophy*, **7**, 255–74.

Fox, I. (1989). On the nature and cognitive function of phenomenal content – Part one. *Philosophical Topics*, **17**, 81–103.

Fox, I. (1995). Our knowledge of the internal world. *Philosophical Topics*, **22**, 59–106.

Gilbert, P. (1992). Immediate experience. *Proceedings of the Aristotelian Society*, **66**, 233–50.

Goldstein, I. (1994). Identifying mental states: A celebrated hypothesis refuted. *Australasian Journal of Philosophy*, **72**, 46–62.

Graham, G. & Stephens, G.L. (1985). Are qualia a pain in the neck for functionalists? *American Philosophical Quarterly*, **22**, 73–80.

Graham, G. & Stephens, G.L. (1987). Minding your P's and Q's: Pain and sensible qualities. *Noûs*, **21**, 395–405.

Gregory, R.L. (1988). Questions of quanta and qualia: Does sensation make sense of matter — or does matter make sense of sensation? *Perception*, **17**, 699–702.

Gregory, R.L. (1989). Questions of quanta and qualia: Does sensation make sense of matter — or does matter make sense of sensation? II. *Perception*, **18**, 1–4.

Gunderson, K. (1974). The texture of mentality. In R. Bambrough (ed), *Wisdom – Twelve Essays*. Oxford: Oxford University Press.

Hardin, C.L. (1985). The resemblances of colors. *Philosophical Studies*, **48**, 35–47.

Hardin, C.L. (1987). Qualia and materialism: Closing the explanatory gap. *Philosophy and Phenomenological Research*, **48**, 281–98.

Hardin, C.L. (1992). Physiology, phenomenology, and Spinoza's true colors. In Beckermann *et al.* 1992.

Harding, G. (1991). Color and the mind–body problem. *Review of Metaphysics*, **45**, 289–307.

Harman, G. (1990). The intrinsic quality of experience. In Tomberlin 1990. Reprinted in Block *et al.* 1996.

Heckmann, H-D. (1986). Was sind Sinnesdaten? Überlegungen zum ontologischen Status und zur semantischen Repräsentation des sinnlichen Gehalts des nicht-kognitiven sinnlichen Bewußtseins. *Grazer Philosophische Studien*, **27**, 125–54.

Hill, C.S. (1988). Introspective awareness of sensations. *Topoi*, **7**, 11–24.

Holborow, L.C. (1973). Materialism and phenomenal qualities. *Aristotelian Society Supplement*, **47**, 107–19.

Holman, E.L. (1987–88). Qualia, Kripkean arguments and subjectivity. *Philosophy Research Archives*, **13**, 411–29.

Jackson, F. & Pargetter, R. (1987). An objectivist's guide to subjectivism about colour. *Revue International de Philosophie*, **41**, **160**, 127–41.

Jacoby, H. (1985). Eliminativism, meaning, and qualitative states. *Philosophical Studies*, **47**, 257–70.

Kaufman, R. (1985). Is the concept of pain incoherent? *Southern Journal of Philosophy*, **23**, 279–84.

Kim, J. (1972). Phenomenal properties, psychophysical laws and the identity theory. *Monist*, **56**, 178–92.

Kirk, R. (1974). Sentience and behaviour. *Mind*, **83**, 43–60.

Kitcher, P.S. (1979). Phenomenal qualities. *American Philosophical Quarterly*, **16**, 123–9.

Kraut, R. (1982). Sensory states and sensory objects. *Nous*, **16**.

Kurthen, M. (1989). Qualia, Sensa und absolute Prozesse. Zu W. Sellars' Kritik des psychozerebralen Reduktionismus. *Journal for General Philosophy of Science*, **21**, 25–46.

Leeds, S. (1993). Qualia, awareness, Sellars. *Nous*, **27**, 303–30.

Levin, J. (1991). Analytic functionalism and the reduction of phenomenal states. *Philosophical Studies*, **61**, 211–38.

Levin, J. (1987). Physicalism and the subjectivity of sensory qualities. *Australasian Journal of Philosophy*, **65**, 400–12.

Levin, M. (1981). Phenomenal properties. *Philosophy and Phenomenological Research*, **42**, 42–58.

Levine, J. (1995). Out of the closet: A qualophile confronts qualophobia. *Philosophical Topics*, **22**, 107–26.

Levine, J. (1995). Qualia: Intrinsic, relational, or what? In Metzinger 1995b.

Lewis, D. (1981). Mad pain and Martian pain. In Block 1980, reprinted with a postscript in Lewis 1983.

Lewis, D. (1995). Should a materialist believe in qualia? *Australasian Journal of Philosophy*, **73**, 140–4.

Linsky, B. (1984). Phenomenal qualities and the identity of indistinguishables. *Synthese*, **59**, 363–80.

Lockwood, M. (1993). The grain problem. In Robinson 1993.

Lycan, W.G. (1987). Phenomenal objects: A backhanded defense. In J. Tomberlin (ed), *Philosophical Perspectives, Vol. 1: Metaphysics*. Atascadero, CA: Ridgeview Publishing.

Margolis (J. (1970). Indubitability, self-intimating states and logically privileged access. *Journal of Philosophy*, **67**, 918–31.

Marras, A. (1993). Materialism, functionalism, and supervenient qualia. *Dialogue*, **32**, 475–92.

Mellor, D.H. (1973). Materialism and phenomenal qualities II. *Aristotelian Society Supplement*, **47**, 107–19.

Natsoulas, T. (1974). The subjective, experiential element in perception. *Psychological Bulletin*, **81**, 611–31.

Nelkin, N. (1986). Pains and pain sensations. *Journal of Philosophy*, **83**, 129–48.

Nelkin, N. (1987). How sensations get their names. *Philosophical Studies*, **51**, 325–39.

Nelkin, N. (1989). Unconscious sensations. *Philosophical Psychology*, **2**, 129–41.

Nelkin, N. (1990). Categorising the senses. *Mind and Language*, **5**, 149–65.

Nelkin, N. (1994). Phenomena and representation. *British Journal for the Philosophy of Science*, **45**, 527–47.

Nelkin, N. (1994). Reconsidering pain. *Philosophical Psychology*, **7**, 325–43

Newton, N. (1989). On viewing pain as a secondary quality. *Noûs*, **23**, 569–98.

Nida-Rümelin, M. (1996). The character of color predicates. A phenomenalist view. In M. Anduschus, W. Künne & A. Newen (eds), *Direct Reference, Indexicality and Propositional Attitudes*. Stanford: CSLI.

Northoff, G. (1995). Qualia im Knotenpunkt zwischen Leib und Seele: Argumentatives Dilemma in der gegenwärtigen Diskussion über die Subjektivität mentaler Zustände. *Journal for General Philosophy of Science / Die Zeitschrift für allgemeine Wissenschaftstheorie*, **26**.

Perkins, M. (1970). Matter, sensation, and understanding. *American Philosophical Quarterly*, **8**, 1–12.

Raffman, D. (1988). Towards a cognitive theory of musical ineffability. *Review of Metaphysics*, **41**, 685–706.

Raffman, D. (1995). On the persistence of phenomenology. In Metzinger 1995b.

Rey, G. (1991). Sensations in a language of thought. In Villanueva 1991.

Rey, G. (1992). Sensational sentences. In Davies & Humphreys 1992.

Rey, G. (1994). Wittgenstein, computationalism and qualia. In Casati, Smith & White 1994.

Rey, G. (forthcoming). Why Wittgenstein should have been a computationalist (and what a computationalist can learn from Wittgenstein). In D. Gottlieb. & J. Odell (eds), *Wittgenstein and Cognitive Science*.

Richardson, R.C. & Muilenburg, G. (1982). Sellars and sense impressions. *Erkenntnis*, **17** 171–211.

Schick, T.W. (1992). The epistemic role of qualitative content. *Philosophy and Phenomenological Research*, **52**, 383–93.

Shoemaker, S. (1975). Phenomenal similarity. *Critica*, **7**, 3–37. Reprinted in Shoemaker 1984.

Shoemaker, S. (1990). Qualities and qualia: What's in the mind? *Philosophy and Phenomenological Research Supplement*, **50**, 109–31.

Shoemaker, S. (1991). Qualia and consciousness. *Mind*, **100**, 507–24.

Shoemaker, S. (1994). Phenomenal character. *Noûs*, **28**, 21–38.

Smart, J.J.C. (1971). Reports of immediate experience. *Synthese*, **22**, 346–59.

Spohn, W. (1996). The character of color predicates. A materialist view. In M. Anduschus, W. Künne & A. Newen (eds), *Direct Reference, Indexicality and Propositional Attitudes*. Stanford: CSLI.

Strawson, G. (1989). Red and 'red'. *Synthese*, **78**, 193–232.

Stubenberg, L. (1996). The place of qualia in the world of science. In Hameroff *et al.* 1996.

Tolliver, J. (1995). Interior colors. *Philosophical Topics*, **22**, 411–42.

Tye, M. (1995). A representational theory of pains and their phenomenal character. In Tomberlin 1995. Reprinted in Block *et al.* 1996.

White, S. (1995). Color and notional content. *Philosophical Topics*, **22**, 471–504.

3.10 Machine Consciousness

Could a machine be conscious? Could there ever be artificial consciousness? In particular, is implementing an appropriate program on a computer in principle sufficient for consciousness? There has been continuing debate on this controversial question, focusing on such issues as Searle's 'Chinese room' thought-experiment and the validity of the Turing test, among others. Many of the papers in section 3.8 and elsewhere are also quite relevant here.

Angel, L. (1994). Am I a computer? In Dietrich 1994.

Barnes, E. (1991). The causal history of computational activity: Maudlin and Olympia. *Journal of Philosophy*, **88**, 304–16.

Bieri, P. (1988). Thinking machines: some reflections on the Turing Test. In P. Bieri & B. Harshav (eds), *Interpretation in Context in Science and History*. Sonderheft von *Poetics Today*, Volume 9/1. Durham: Duke University Press.

Birnbacher, D. (1995). Artificial consciousness. In Metzinger 1995b.

Block, N. (1981). Psychologism and behaviorism. *Philosophical Review*, **90**, 5–43.

Churchland, P.M. & Churchland, P.S. (1990). Could a machine think? *Scientific American*, **262** (1), 32–7. Reprinted in Dietrich 1994.

Churchland, P.S. & Sejnowski, T.J. (1992). Silicon brains. *Byte*, October 1992.

Clarke, J. (1972). Turing machines and the mind–body problem. *British Journal for the Philosophy of Science*, **23**, 1–12.

Cole, D.J. (1984). Thought and thought experiments. *Philosophical Studies*, **45**, 431–44.

Cole, D.J. (1991). Artificial intelligence and personal identity. *Synthese*, **88**, 399–417.

Cole, D.J. (1994). The causal power of CPUs. In Dietrich 1994.

Copeland, B.J. (1993). The curious case of the Chinese gym. *Synthese*, **95**, 173–86.

Dennett, D.C. (1987). Fast thinking. In Dennett 1978.

Dennett, D.C. (1994). The practical requirements for making a conscious robot. *Philosophical Transactions of the Royal Society* A, **349**, 133–46.

Dennett, D.C. (1995). Cog: Steps towards consciousness in robots. In Metzinger 1995b.

Dyer, M. (1990). Intentionality and computationalism: Minds, machines, Searle and Harnad. *Journal of Experimental and Theoretical Artificial Intelligence*, **2**, 303–19. Reprinted in Dietrich 1994.

Farrell, B.A. (1970). The design of a conscious device. *Mind*, **79**, 321–46.

Harnad, S. (1989). Minds, machines and Searle. *Journal of Experimental and Theoretical Artificial Intelligence*, **1**, 5–25.

Harnad, S. (1990). Lost in the hermeneutical hall of mirrors. *Journal of Experimental and Theoretical Artificial Intelligence*, **2**, 321–27.

Harnad, S. (1991). Other bodies, other minds: A machine incarnation of an old philosophical problem. *Minds and Machines*, **1**, 43–54.

Hofstadter, D.R. (1981). Reflections on Searle. In Hofstadter & Dennett 1981.

Holenstein, E. (1987). Maschinelles Wissen und menschliches Bewußtsein. In H. Holzhey & J.-P. Leyvraz (Hrsg.), *Körper, Geist, Maschine. Beiträge zum Leib-Seele-Problem. Studia Philosophica*, **47**. Bern/Stuttgart: P. Haupt.

Jacquette, D. (1989). Adventures in the Chinese Room. *Philosophy and Phenomenological Research*, **49**, 605–23.

Kirk, R. (1986). Sentience, causation and some robots. *Australasian Journal of Philosophy*, **64**, 308–21.

Korb, K. (1991). Searle's AI program. *Journal of Experimental and Theoretical Artificial Intelligence*, **3**, 283–96.

Kurthen, M. (1989). *Bewußtsein der Maschinen?* Stuttgart: Enke.

Kurthen, M. & Linke, D.B. (1991). Reproduktion des Bewußtseins? In H.R. Fischer (Hrsg.), *Autopoiesis*. Heidelberg: Auer.

Lycan, W.G. (1979). A new Lilliputian argument against machine functionalism. *Philosophical Studies*, **35**, 279–87.

Lycan, W.G. (1983). The moral of the new Lilliputian argument. *Philosophical Studies*, **43**, 277–80.

Lycan, W.G. (1983). Abortion and the civil rights of machines. In N. Potter & M. Timmons (1985)[eds], *Morality and Universality*. Dordrecht: D. Reidel.

Maloney, J.C. (1987). The right stuff. *Synthese*, **70**, 349–72.

Maudlin, T. (1989). Computation and consciousness. *Journal of Philosophy*, **86**, 407–32.

McGinn, C. (1987). Could a machine be conscious? In Blakemore & Greenfield 1987. Reprinted in McGinn 1991.

Moor, J.H. (1988). Testing robots for qualia. In Otto & Tuedio 1988.

Mott, P. (1982). On the function of consciousness, *Mind*, **91**, 423–9.

Newton, N. (1989). Machine understanding and the Chinese Room. *Philosophical Psychology*, **2**, 207–15.

Rey, G. (1986). What's really going on in Searle's Chinese Room. *Philosophical Studies*, **50**, 169–85.

Russow, L.M. (1984). Unlocking the Chinese Room. *Nature and System*, **6**, 221–8.

Searle, J.R. (1980). Minds, brains and programs. *Behavioral and Brain Sciences*, **3**, 417–57.

Searle, J.R. (1987). Minds and brains without programs. In Blakemore & Greenfield 1987.

Searle, J.R. (1990). Is the brain's mind a computer program? *Scientific American*, **262**, 26–31.

Stubenberg, L. (1992). What is it like to be Oscar? *Synthese*, **90**, 1–26.

Van de Vete, D. (1971). The problem of robot consciousness. *Philosophy and Phenomenological Research*, **32**, 149–65.

Van Gulick, R. (1988). Qualia, functional equivalence, and computation. In Otto & Tuedio 1988.

White, P. (1982). Beliefs about conscious experience. In Underwood & Stevens 1982.

Wilks, Y. (1984). Machines and consciousness. In C. Hookway (ed), *Minds, Machines and Evolution*. Cambridge: Cambridge University Press.

3.11 Consciousness in Psychology & Cognitive Science

This section includes a selection of papers on consciousness and related subjects in cognitive psychology and in cognitive science in general. This small selection is very far from complete.

Baars, B.J. & Mattson, M.E. (1981). Consciousness and intention: A framework and some evidence. *Cognition and Brain Theory*, **4**, 247–63.

Baars, B.J. (1983). Conscious contents provide the nervous system with coherent, global information. In Davidson *et al.* 1983.

Baars, B.J. (1986). What is a theory of consciousness a theory of? The search for criterial constraints on theory. *Imagination, Cognition, and Personality*, **1**, 3–24.

Baars, B.J. (1993). How does a serial, integrated and very limited stream of consciousness emerge from a nervous system that is mostly unconscious, distributed, parallel and of enormous capacity? In *Experimental and Theoretical Studies of Consciousness*. CIBA Foundation Symposium **174**. Chichester, UK: Wiley, 282–303.

Baars, B.J. (1994). A thoroughly empirical approach to consciousness. *PSYCHE*, **1** (6). URL:http://psyche.cs.monash.edu.au/volume1/psyche-94-1-6- contrastive -1-baars.html.

Baars, B.J. (1994). A global workspace theory of conscious experience. In Revonsuo & Kamppinen 1994.

Baars, B.J. (1996). Consciousness creates access: The view from global workspace theory. In Hameroff *et al.* 1996.

Baars, B.J. (in press). Momentary forgetting as an erasure of a conscious global workspace due to competition between incompatible contexts. In M.J. Horowitz (ed), *Psychodynamics and cognition.* Chicago: University of Chicago Press.

Baars, B.J. (in press). What is conscious in the control of action? A modern ideomotor theory of voluntary control. In D. Gorfein & R.R. Hoffmann (eds), *Learning and memory: The Ebbinghaus Centennial Symposium.* Hillsdale, NJ: Lawrence Erlbaum Associates.

Baddeley, A.D. (1992). Consciousness and working memory. *Consciousness and Cognition,* **1**, 3–6.

Bisiach, E. & Berti, A. (1995). Consciousness in dyschiria. In Gazzaniga 1995.

Brandstädter, J. (1992). Psychologie zwischen Leib und Seele: Einige Aspekte des Bewußtseinsproblems. Psychology between body and mind: Some aspects of the consciousness problem. *Psychologische Rundschau,* **42**, 66–75.

Burks, A.W. (1986). An architectural theory of functional consciousness. In N. Rescher (ed), *Current issues in teleology.* University Press of America.

Carlson, R.A. (1992). Starting with consciousness. *American Journal of Psychology,* **105**, 598–604.

Carr, T.H. (1979). Consciousness in models of human information processing: Primary memory, executive control, and input regulation. In Underwood & Stevens 1979.

Cheesman, J. & Merikle, P.M. (1985). Word recognition and consciousness. In D. Besner, T.G. Waller & G.E. Mackinnon (eds), *Reading Research: Advances in Theory and Practice,* 5. New York: Academic Press.

Cheesman, J. & Merikle, P.M. (1986). Distinguishing conscious from unconscious perceptual processes. *Canadian Journal of Psychology,* **40**, 343–67.

Davis, L.H. (1989). Self-consciousness in chimps and pigeons. *Philosophical Psychology,* **2**, 249–57.

Dawson, M.E. & Furedy, J.J. (1976). The role of awareness in human differential autonomic classical conditioning: The necessary-gate hypothesis. *Psychophysiology,* **13**, 50–3.

De Haan, E.H.F., Young, A. & Newcombe, F. (1987). Face recognition without awareness. *Cognitive Neuropsychology,* **4**, 385–415.

Diaz, J. (1996). The stream visited: A process model of phenomenological consciousness. In Hameroff *et al.* 1996.

Flavell, J.H. (1979). Metacognition and cognitive monitoring. *American Psychologist,* *34*, 906–11.

Foulkes, D. (1990). Dreaming and consciousness. *European Journal of Cognitive Psychology,* **2**, 39–55.

Globus, G.G. (1974). The problem of consciousness. *Psychoanalysis and Contemporary Science,* **3**, 40–69.

Glynn, I.M. (1990). Consciousness and time. *Nature,* **348**, 477–9.

Gopnik, A. (1993). How we know our minds: the illusion of first-person knowledge of intentionality. *Behavioral and Brain Sciences,* **16**, 1–14.

Graumann, C.F. (1984). Bewußtsein und Verhalten. Gedanken zu Sprachspielen der Psychologie. In H. Lenk (Hrsg.), *Handlungstheorien interdisziplinär III. Verhaltenswissenschaftliche und psychologische Handlungstheorien.* Zweiter Halbband. Fink.

Gregory, R. (1988). Consciousness and con-science. In Marcel & Bisiach 1988.

Hardcastle, V.G. (1995). A critique of information processing theories of consciousness. *Minds and Machines*.

Harnad, S. (1982). Consciousness: An afterthought. *Cognition and Brain Theory*, 5, 29–47.

Hebb, D.O. (1977). To know your own mind. In J.M. Nicholas (ed.), *Images, Perception, and Knowledge*. Dordrecht: D. Reidel.

Heimann, H. (1989). Zerfall des Bewußtseins in der Psychose. In Pöppel 1989.

Hilgard, E.R. (1977). Controversies over consciousness and the rise of cognitive psychology. *Australian Psychologist*, 12, 7–26.

Hilgard, E.R. (1979). Divided consciousness in hypnosis: The implications of the hidden observer. In E. Fromm & R.E. Shor (eds), *Hypnosis: Developments in Research and new Perspectives* (2nd edn). New York: Aldine.

Hilgard, E.R. (1980). Consciousness in contemporary psychology. *Annual Review of Psychology*, 31, 1–26.

Hirst, W. (1995). Cognitive aspects of consciousness. In Gazzaniga 1995.

Hochberg, J.E. (1970). Attention, organisation, and consciousness. In D.J. Mostofsky (ed), *Attention: Contemporary Theory and Analysis*. New York: Appleton.

Holender, D. (1986). Semantic activation without conscious identification in dichotic listening, parafoveal vision, and visual masking: A survey and appraisal. *Behavioral and Brian Sciences*, 9, 1–66.

Honderich, T. (1984). The time of a conscious sensory experience and mind-brain theories. *Journal of Theoretical Biology*, 110, 115–29.

Izard, C.E. (1980). The emergence of emotions and the development of consciousness in infancy. In Davidson & Davidson 1980.

Jacoby, L.L. & Witherspoon, D. (1982). Remembering without awareness. *Canadian Journal of Psychology*, 36, 300–24.

Jacoby, L.L. Whitehouse, K. (1989). An illusion of memory: False recognition influenced by unconscious perception. *Journal of Experimental Psychology: General*, 118, 126–35.

Jacoby, L.K., Woloshyn, V. & Kelley, C. (1989). Becoming famous without being recognized: Unconscious influences of memory produced by dividing attention. *Behavioral and Brain Sciences*, 118, 115–25.

John, E.R. (1976). A model of consciousness. In Schwartz & Shapiro 1976.

Johnson-Laird, P. (1983). A computational analysis of consciousness. *Cognition and Brain Theory*, 6, 499–508. Reprinted in Marcel & Bisiach 1988.

Kahan, T.L. & LaBerge, S. (1994). Lucid dreaming as metacognition. *Consciousness and Cognition*, 3, 246–64.

Kihlstrom, J.F. & Schacter, D.L. (1990). Anesthesia, amnesia, and the cognitive unconscious. In B. Bonke, W. Fitch & K. Millar (eds), *Memory and Awareness during Anaesthesia*. Amsterdam: Swets and Zeitlinger.

Kihlstrom, J.F. (1984). Conscious, subconscious, unconscious: A cognitive perspective. In Bowers & Meichenbaum 1984.

Kihlstrom, J.F. (1987). The cognitive unconscious. *Science*, 237, 1445–52.

Kihlstrom, J.F. (1992). The psychological unconscious and the self. In *Experimental and Theoretical Studies of Consciousness*. CIBA Foundation Symposium 174. Chichester, UK: Wiley.

Kihlstrom, J.F. (1993). Consciousness and me-ness. In J. Cohen. & J. Schooler (eds), *Carnegie Symposium on Cognition*. Hillsdale, NJ: Lawrence Erlbaum Associates.

Kihlstrom, J.F. (1993). The continuum of consciousness. *Consciousness and Cognition*, **2**, 334–54.

LaBerge, S. (1988). Lucid dreaming in Western literature. In Gackenbach & LaBerge 1988.

LaBerge, S. (1988). The psychophysiology of lucid dreaming. In Gackenbach & LaBerge 1988.

LaBerge, S. (1990). Psychophysiological studies of consciousness during sleep. In R.R. Bootzen, J.F. Kihlstrom & D.L. Schacter (eds), *Sleep and Cognition*. Washington, DC: American Psychological Association.

Lundh, L-G. (1979). Introspection, consciousness and human information-processing. *Scandinavian Journal of Psychology*, **20**, 223–38.

Mandler, G. & Nakamura, Y. (1987). Aspects of consciousness. *Personality and Social Psychology Bulletin*, **13**, 299–313.

Mandler, G. (1989). Memory: Conscious and unconscious. In P. Solomon, G. Goethals, C. Kelley & B. Stephens (eds), *Memory: Interdisciplinary Approaches*. New York: Springer.

Mandler, G. (1992). Toward a theory of consciousness. In H.G. Geissler, S.W. Link & J.T. Townsend (eds), *Cognition, information processing, and psychophysics: Basic issues*. Hillsdale, NJ: Lawrence Erlbaum Associates.

Mandler, G.A. (1975). Consciousness: Respectable, useful, and probably necessary. In R. Solso (ed), *Information processing and cognition: The Loyola Symposium*. Hillsdale, NJ: Lawrence Erlbaum Associates.

Mangan, B. (1993). Taking phenomenology seriously: The 'fringe' and its implications for cognitive research. *Consciousness and Cognition*, **2**, 89–108.

Marcel, A.J. (1983). Conscious and unconscious perception: An approach to the relations between phenomenal experience and perceptual processes. *Cognitive Psychology*, **15**, 238–300.

Marcel, A.J. (1983). Conscious and unconscious perception: Experiments on visual masking and word recognition. *Cognitive Psychology*, **15**, 197–237.

Marcel, A.J. (1992). Slippage in the unity of consciousness. In *Experimental and Theoretical Studies of Consciousness*. CIBA Foundation Symposium **174**. Chichester, UK: Wiley.

Merikle, P.M. (1984). Toward a definition of awareness. *Bulletin of the Psychonomic Society*, **22**, 449–50.

Metzger, W. (1974). Consciousness, perception, and action. In E.C. Carterette & M.P. Friedman (eds.), *Handbook of Perception*, Vol. 1. New York: Academic Press.

Metzinger, T. (1995). Phänomenale mentale Modelle. In K. Sachs-Hombach (Hrsg.), *Bilder im Geiste: Zur kognitiven und erkenntnistheoretischen Funktion piktorialer Repräsentationen*. Reihe 'Philosophie & Repräsentation'. Amsterdam and Atlanta, GA: Rodopi.

Michie, D. (1994). Consciousness as an engineering issue, Part 1. *Journal of Consciousness Studies*, **1**, 182–95.

Michie, D. (1995). Consciousness as an engineering issue, Part 2. *Journal of Consciousness Studies*, **2**, 52–66.

Moscovitch, M. (1992). A neuropsychological model of memory and consciousness. In L.R. Squire & N. Butters (eds), *Neuropsychology of Memory*. New York:Guilford.

Moscovitch, M. (1995). Models of consciousness and memory. In Gazzaniga 1995.

Nisbett, R. & Wilson, T. (1977). Telling more than we can know: Verbal reports on mental processes. *Psychological Review*, **84**, 231–59.

Posner, M.I. & Klein R.M. (1973). On the functions of consciousness. In Kornblum, S. (ed), Attention and performance IV. New York: Academic Press.

Prinz, W. (1992). Why don't we perceive our brain states? Warum nehmen wir unsere Hirnzustände nicht wahr? *European Journal of Cognitive Psychology*, **4**, 1–20.

Proust, J. (1994). Time and conscious experience. In C.C. Gould (ed), *Artifacts, Representations, and Social Practice*, Dordrecht: Kluwer Academic Publishers.

Reuter, B.M., Linke, D.B. & Kurthen, M. (1989). Kognitive Prozesse bei Bewußtlosen? Eine Brain-Mapping-Studie zu P300. *Archiv für Psychologie*, **141**, 155–73.

Reuter, B.M., Linke, D.B. & Kurthen, M. (1991 Cognitive processes in comatose patients? A brain mapping study using P300. *The German Journal of Psychology*, **15**, 37–8.

Revonsuo, A. (1993). Cognitive models of consciousness. In M. Kamppinen (ed), *Consciousness, Cognitive Schemata, and Relativism*. Dordrecht: Kluwer Academic Publishers.

Revonsuo, A. (1995). Consciousness, dreams, and virtual realities. *Philosophical Psychology*, **8**, 35–58.

Ripley, C. (1984). Sperry's concept of consciousness. *Inquiry*, **27**, 399-423.

Ruhnau, E. (1992). Zeit — das verborgene Fenster der Kognition. *Kognitionswissenschaft*, **2**, 171–9.

Ruhnau, E. (1994). The Now — A Hidden Window to Dynamics. In A. Atmanspacher & G.J. Dalenoort (eds), *Inside versus Outside. Endo- and Exo-Concepts of Observation and Knowledge in Physics, Philosophy and Cognitive Science*. Berlin, New York: Springer.

Schacter, D. (1987). Implicit memory: History and current status. *Journal of Experimental Psychology*, **13**, 501–18.

Schacter, D.L. (1990). Toward a cognitive neuropsychology of awareness: Implicit knowledge and anosognosia. *Journal of Clinical & Experimental Neuropsychology*, **12**, 155–78.

Seiler, T.B. (1993). Bewußtsein und Begriff: Die Rolle des Bewußtseins und seine Entwicklung in der Begriffskonstruktion. In W. Edelstein & S. Hoppe-Graf (Hrsg.), *Die Konstruktion kognitiver Strukturen*. Bern: Hans Huber.

Shallice, T. (1972). Dual functions of consciousness. *Psychological Review*, **79**, 383–93.

Shallice, T. (1978). The dominant action system: An information-processing approach to consciousness. In Pope & Singer 1978.

Shallice, T. (1988). Information-processing models of consciousness: possibilities and problems. In Marcel & Bisiach 1988.

Shepard, R.N. (1993). On the physical basis, linguistic representation, and conscious experience of colors. In G. Harman (ed), *Conceptions of the Human*

Mind: Essays in Honor of George A. Miller. Hillsdale, NJ: Lawrence Erlbaum Associates.

Shevrin, H. & Dickman, J. (1980). The psychological unconscious: A necessary assumption for all psychological theory? *American Psychologist*, **35**, 421–34.

Shevrin, H. (1992). Subliminal perception, memory, and consciousness: Cognitive and dynamic perspectives. In Bornstein & Pittman 1992.

Sperry, R.W. (1987). Structure and significance of the consciousness revolution. *Journal of Mind and Behavior*, **8**, 37–65.

Sperry, R.W. (1992). Turnabout on consciousness: A mentalist view. *Journal of Mind and Behavior*, **13**, 259–80.

Spittler, J.F. (1992). Der Bewußtseinsbegriff aus neuropsychiatrischer und interdisziplinärer Sicht. *Fortschritte der Neurologie und Psychiatrie*, **60**, 54–65.

Symons, D. (1993). The stuff that dreams aren't made of: Why wake-state and dream-state sensory experiences differ. *Cognition*, **47**, 181–217.

Taylor, J. (1996). Modelling what it is like to be. In Hameroff *et al.* 1996.

Tholey, P. (1980). Klarträume als Gegenstand empirischer Untersuchungen. *Gestalt Theory*, **2**, 175–91.

Tholey, P. (1981). Empirische Untersuchungen über Klarträume. *Gestalt Theory*, **3**, 21–62.

Tholey, P. (1985). Haben Traumgestalten ein eigenes Bewußtsein? *Gestalt Theory*, **7**, 29–46.

Treisman, A.M. & Gelade, G. (1980). A feature integration theory of attention. *Cognitive Psychology*, **12**, 97–136.

Treisman, A.M. & Schmidt, H. (1982). Illusory conjunctions in the perception of objects. *Cognitive Psychology*, **14**, 107–41.

Tulving, E. (1985). Memory and consciousness. *Canadian Psychology*, **26**, 1–12.

Velmans M. (1993). A reflexive science of consciousness. In *Experimental and Theoretical Studies of Consciousness*. CIBA Foundation Symposium **174**. Chichester, UK: Wiley.

Velmans, M. (1991). Is human information processing conscious? *Behavioral and Brain Sciences*, **14**, 651–726.

Wetherick, N.E. (1977). Consciousness in experimental psychology. *Journal of Phenomenological Psychology*, **8**, 1–26.

3.12 Consciousness in the Neurosciences

This section includes a selection of papers addressing the problems related to consciousness from the perspective of neuroscience. These include neuroscientific theories of consciousness, articles on the binding problem, papers on blindsight and other specific phenomena, and papers addressing the general question of what neuroscience can tell us about consciousness, among other things.

Andrade, J. (1993). Consciousness: current views. In J.G. Jones (ed), *Depth of Anesthesia*. Boston/Toronto/London: Little, Brown and Company.

Baars, B.J. & Newman, J. (1994). A neurobiological interpretation of the global workspace theory of consciousness. In Revonsuo & Kamppinen 1994.

Beck, F. & Eccles, J. C. (1992). Quantum aspects of brain activity and the role of consciousness. *Proceedings of the National Academy of Science USA*, **89**, 11357–61.

Bisiach, E. (1988). The (haunted) brain and consciousness. In Marcel & Bisiach 1198.

Bisiach, E. (1992). Understanding consciousness: Clues from unilateral neglect and related disorders. In Milner & Rugg 1992.

Bisiach, E., Capitani, E., Luzzatti, C. & Perani, D. (1981). Brain and conscious representation of outside reality. *Neuropsychologia*, **19**, 543–51.

Bisiach, E., Luzzatti, C. & Perani, D. (1979). Unilateral neglect, representational schema and consciousness. *Brain*, **102**, 609–18.

Boitano, J. (1996). Edelmans's biological theory of consciousness. In Hameroff *et al.* 1996.

Bogen, J.E. (1995). On the neurophysiology of consciousness: I. An overview. *Consciousness and Cognition*, **4**, 52–62.

Buck, R. (1993). What is this thing called subjective experience? Reflections on the neuropsychology of qualia. Special Section: Neuropsychological perspectives on components of emotional processing. *Neuropsychology*, **7**, 490–9.

Castiello, U., Pauligman, Y. & Jeannerod, M. (1991). Temporal dissociation of motor responses and subjective awareness. A study in normal subjects. *Brain*, **114**, 2639–55.

Churchland, P.M. (1988). Reduction and the neurobiological basis of consciousness. In Marcel & Bisiach 1988.

Churchland, P.M. (1990). Reductionism, connectionism, and the plasticity of human consciousness. In Churchland 1989.

Churchland, P.S. (1988). The significance of neuroscience for philosophy. *Trends in Neurosciences*, **11**, 304–7.

Churchland, P.S. (1981). The timing of sensations: Reply to Libet. *Philosophy of Science*, **48**, 492–7.

Churchland, P.S. (1993). Can neuroscience teach us anything about consciousness? Presidential Address, Pacific Division of the American Philosophical Association. In *Proceedings of the APA*. Revised German version in Metzinger 1995a.

Churchland, P.S. & Farber, I. (1995). Consciousness and the neurosciences: philosophical and theoretical issues. In Gazzaniga 1995.

Cowey, A. & Stoerig, P. (1991). The neurobiology of blindsight. *Trends in Neurosciences*, **14**, 140–5.

Cowey, A. & Stoerig, P. (1992). Reflections on blindsight. In Milner & Rugg 1992.

Crane, H. & Piantanida, T.P. (1983). On seeing reddish green and yellowish blue. *Science*, **222**, 1078–80.

Creutzfeldt, O.D. (1981). Bewußtsein und Selbstbewußtsein als Problem der Neurophysiologie. *Universitas*, **36**, 467–75.

Crick, F.H.C. & Koch, C. (1990). Towards a neurobiological theory of consciousness. *Seminars in the Neurosciences*, **2**, 263–75.

Crick, F.H.C. (1984). Function of the thalamic reticular complex: The searchlight hypothesis. *Proceedings of the National Academy of Sciences*, **81**, 4586–90.

Crick, F.H.C. & Koch, C. (1992). The problem of consciousness. *Scientific American*, **267**, 152–60.

Crick, F.H.C. & Koch, C. (1995). Are we aware of neural activity in primary visual cortex? *Nature*, **375**, 121–3.

Dimond, S. (1976). Brain circuits for consciousness. *Brain, Behavior and Evolution*, **13**, 376–95.

Donchin, E., McCarthy, G., Kutas, M. & Ritter, W. (1983). Event-related brain potentials in the study of consciousness. In Davidson, Schwartz & Shapiro 1983.

Edelman, G.M. (1993). Neural Darwinism: selection and re-entrant signaling in higher brain function. *Neuron*, **10**, 115–25.

Engel, A.K., König, P., Kreiter, A.K. & Singer, W. (1991). Interhemispheric synchronization of oscillatory neuronal responses in cat visual cortex. *Science*, **252**, 1177–9.

Engel, A.K., König, P. & Singer, W. (1991). Direct physiological evidence for scene segmentation by temporal coding. *Proceedings of the National Academy of Science*, Volume **88**, 9136–40.

Engel, A.K., Kreiter, A.K., König, P. & Singer, W. (1991). Synchronization of oscillatory neuronal responses between striate and extrastriate visual cortical areas of the cat. *Proceedings of the National Academy of Science*, Volume **88**, 6048–52.

Engel, A.K., König, P., Kreiter, A.K., Schillen, T.B. & Singer, W. (1992). Temporal coding in the visual cortex: new vistas on integration in the nervous system. *Trends in Neurosciences*, Volume **15**, 218–26.

Engel, A.K., König, P. & Schillen, T.B. (1992). Why does the cortex oscillate? *Current Biology*, Volume **2**, 332–4.

Engel, A.K., König, P. & Singer, W. (1992). Correlated neuronal firing: A clue to the integrative functions of cortex? In J.G. Taylor, E.R. Caianello, R.M.J. Cotterill & J.W. Clark (eds), *Neural Network Dynamics*. London: Springer.

Engel, A.K., König, P. & Singer, W. (1993). Bildung repräsentationaler Zustände im Gehirn. *Spektrum der Wissenschaft*, September, 42–7.

Farah, M. (1995). Visual perception and visual awareness after brain damage: A tutorial overview. In Umilta & Moscovitch 1995.

Flohr, H. (1991). Brain processes and phenomenal consciousness: A new and specific hypothesis. *Theory and Psychology*, **Vol. 1**, 245–62.

Flohr, H. (1992). Qualia and brain processes. In Beckermann *et al.* 1992.

Flohr, H. (1992). Die physiologischen Bedingungen des phänomenalen Bewußtseins. *Forum für interdisziplinäre Forschung*, **1**, 49–55.

Flohr, H. (1995). Sensations and brain processes. *Behavioral Brain Research*.

Flohr, H. (1995). An information processing theory of anaesthesia. *Neuropsychologia*, **9**, 1169–80..

Freeman, W.J. (1990). On the fallacy of assigning an origin to consciousness. In E.R. John (ed), *Machinery of the Mind: Data, Theory, and Speculations about Higher Brain Function*. Boston: Birkhäuser.

Gasquoine, P.G.L. (1993). Alien hand sign. *Journal of Clinical and Experimental Neuropsychology*, **15**, 653–67.

Gazzaniga, M.S. (1977). On dividing the self: Speculations from brain research. *Excerpta Medica: Neurology*, **434**, 233–44

Gazzaniga, M.S. (1980). The role of language for conscious experience: Observations from split-brain man. In H.H. Kornhuber & L. Deeckel (eds), *Motivation, motor and sensory Processes of the Brain, Progress in Brain Research*, Vol. **54**. Amsterdam: Elsevier.

Gazzaniga, M.S. (1988). Brain modularity: Towards a philosophy of conscious experience. In Marcel & Bisiach 1988.

Gazzaniga, M.S. (1993). Brain mechanism and conscious experience. In *Experimental and Theoretical Studies of Consciousness*. CIBA Foundation Symposium **174**. Chichester, UK: Wiley.

Gazzaniga, M.S. (1995). Consciousness and the cerebral hemispheres. In Gazzaniga 1995.

Gazzaniga, M.S., Holtzman, J.D. & Smylie, C.S. (1987). Speech without conscious awareness. *Neurology*, **35**, 682–5.

Gillett, G.R. (1988). Consciousness and brain function. *Philosophical Psychology*, **1**, 325–39.

Gillett, G.R. (1991). The neurophilosophy of pain. *Philosophy*, **66**, 191–206.

Gillett, G.R. (1986). Brain bisection and personal identity. *Mind*, **95**, 224–9.

Goldberg, E. & Barr, W.B. (1991). Three possible mechanisms of unawareness of deficit. In Prigatano & Schacter 1991.

Goldberg, G. & Bloom, K.K. (1990). The alien hand sign: Localization, lateralization and recovery. *American Journal of Physiological and Medical Rehabilitation*, **69**, 228–38.

Goldmann-Rakic, P.S. (1990). The prefrontal contribution to working memory and conscious experience. In J.C. Eccles & O. Creutzfeldt (eds), *The Principles of Design and Operation of the Brain*. New York: Springer-Verlag.

Görnitz, T., Ruhnau, E. & Weizsäcker, C.F. (1992). Temporal asymmetry as precondition of experience. The foundation of the arrow of time. *International Journal of Theoretical Physics*, **31**, 37–46.

Gray, C.M. (1994). Synchronous oscillations in neural systems: Mechanisms and functions. *Journal of Computational Neuroscience*, **1**, 11–38.

Gray, C.M., König, P., Engel, A.K. & Singer, W. (1989). Oscillatory responses in cat visual cortex exhibit inter-columnar synchronization which reflects global stimulus properties. *Nature*, Volume **338** (6213), 334–7.

Hameroff, S. (1994). Quantum coherence in microtubules: A neural basis for emergent consciousness? *Journal of Consciousness Studies*, **1**, 91–118.

Hameroff S. & Penrose, R. (1996). Orchestrated reduction of quantum coherence in brain microtubules: A model for consciousness. In Hameroff *et al.* 1996.

Hameroff S. & Penrose, R. (submitted). Orchestrated space-time selections as conscious events. *Journal of Consciousness Studies*.

Hardcastle, V.G. (1994). Psychology's 'Binding Problem' and possible neurobiological solutions. *Journal of Consciousness Studies*, **1**, 66–90.

Hardcastle, V.G. (1996). The binding problem and neurobiological oscillations. In Hameroff *et al.* 1996.

Harth, E. (1996). Self-referent mechanisms as the neuronal basis of consciousness. In Hameroff *et al.* 1996.

Hobson, J.A. & McCarley, R.W. (1977). The brain as a dream-state generator: An activation-synthesis hypothesis of the dream process. *American Journal of Psychiatry*, **134**, 1335–48.

Hobson, J.A. & Stickgold, R. (1993).The conscious state paradigm: A neurocognitive approach to waking, sleeping and dreaming. In Gazzaniga 1995.

Hobson, J.A. & Stickgold, R. (1994). Dreaming: A neurocognitive approach. *Consciousness and Cognition*, **3**, 1–15.

Jasper, H.H. (1985). Brain mechanisms of conscious experience and voluntary action. *Behavioral and Brain Sciences*, **8**, 543–4.

Jibu, M. (1996). Subcellular quantum optical coherence: implications for consciousness. In Hameroff *et al.* 1996.

Kinsbourne, M. (1988). Integrated field theory of consciousness. In Marcel & Bisiach 1988. Reprinted in *Experimental and Theoretical Studies of Consciousness.* CIBA Foundation Symposium **174** (1993). Chichester, UK: Wiley.

Kinsbourne, M. (1995). Models of consciousness: Serial or parallel in the brain? In Gazzaniga 1995.

Knight, R.T. & Grabowecky, M. (1995). Escape from linear time: Prefrontal cortex and conscious experience. In Gazzaniga 1995.

Koch, C. & Crick, F.H.C. (1991).Understanding awareness at the neuronal level. *Behavioral and Brain Sciences,* **14,** 683–85.

Koch, C. & Crick, F.H.C. (1994). Some further ideas regarding the neuronal basis of awareness. In Koch & Davis 1994.

Kreiter, A.K. & Singer, W. (1992). Oscillatory neuronal responses in the visual cortex of the awake macaque monkey. *European Journal of Neuroscience,* Volume 4, 369–75.

Kulli, J. & Koch, C. (1991). Does Anaesthesia cause loss of consciousness? *Trends in Neuroscience,* **14,** 6–10.

Kurthen, M., Moskopp, D., Linke, D.B. & Reuter, B.M. (1989). The locked-in syndrome and the behaviorist epistemology of other minds. *Theoretical Medicine,* **12,** 69–79.

Lahav, R. (1993). What neuropsychology tells us about consciousness. *Philosophy of Science,* **60,** 67–85.

LeDoux, J.E., Wilson, D.H. & Gazzaniga, M.S. (1977). A divided mind: observations of the conscious properties of the separated hemispheres. *Annals of Neurology,* **2,** 417–21.

Libet, B. (1978). Neuronal vs. subjective timing for a conscious sensory experience. In Buser & Rougeul-Buser 1978.

Libet, B. (1981). The experimental evidence for subjective referral of a sensory experience backwards in time: Reply to P.S. Churchland. *Philosophy of Science,* **48,** 182–97.

Libet, B. (1981). Timing of cerebral processes relative to concomitant conscious experiences in man. In G. Adam, I. Meszaros & E.I. Banyai (eds), *Advances in Physiological Science.* Elmsford, NY: Pergamon.

Libet, B. (1982). Brain stimulation in the study of neuronal functions for conscious sensory experiences. *Human Neurobiology,* **1,** 235–42.

Libet, B. (1985). Unconscious cerebral initiative and the role of conscious will in voluntary action. *Behavioral and Brain Sciences,* **8,** 529–66.

Libet, B. (1985). Subjective antedating of a sensory experience and mind–brain theories: Reply to Honderich (1984). *Journal of Theoretical Biology,* **114,** 563–70.

Libet, B. (1989). Conscious subjective experience vs. unconscious mental functions: theory of the cerebral processes involved. In R.J. Cotterill (ed), *Models of brain function.* Cambridge: Cambridge University Press.

Libet, B. (1993). The neural time factor in conscious and unconscious events. In *Experimental and Theoretical Studies of Consciousness.* CIBA Foundation Symposium **174.** Chichester, UK: Wiley. Reprinted in Hameroff *et al.* 1996.

Libet, B. Wright, E.W., Feinstein, B. & Pearl, D.K. (1979). Subjective referral of the timing for a conscious sensory experience: A functional role for the somatosensory specific projection system in man. *Brain*, **102**, 193–224.

Libet, B., Gleason, C.A., Wright, W.E. & Pearl, D.K. (1983). Time of conscious intention to act in relation to onset of cerebral activities (Readiness-Potential); the unconscious initiation of a freely voluntary act. *Brain*, **106**, 623–42.

Libet, B., Pearl, D.K., Morledge, D.E., Gleason, C.A., Hosobuchi, Y. & Barbaro, N.M. (1991). Control of the transition from sensory detection to sensory awareness in man by the duration of a thalamic stimulus. The cerebral time-on factor. *Brain*, **114**, 1731–57.

Llinás, R.R. & Paré, D. (1991). Of dreaming and wakefulness. *Neuroscience*, **44**, 521–35.

Llinás, R.R. & Ribary, U. (1992). Rostrocaudal scan in human brain: A global characteristic of the 40-Hz response during input. In Basar & Bullock 1992.

Llinás, R.R. & Ribary, U. (1993).Coherent 40 Hz oscillation characterizes dream state in humans. *Proceedings of the National Academy of Science USA*, **90**, 2078–81.

Llinás, R.R. & Ribary, U. (1994). Perception as an oneiric-like state modulated by the senses. In Koch & Davies 1994.

Luria, A. (1976). The human brain and conscious activity. In Schwartz & Shapiro 1978.

Madler, C., Keller, I., Schwender, D. & Pöppel, E. (1991). Sensory information processing during general anaesthesia: effect of isoflurance on auditory evoked neuronal oscillation. *British Journal of Anaesthesiology*, **66**, 81–7.

Makeig, S. & Inlow, M. (1993). Lapses in alertness: Coherence of fluctuations in performance and EEG Spectrum. *Electroencephalography and Clinical Neurophysiology*, **86**, 23–5.

Mark, V. (1996). Conflicting communication in a split-brain patient: Support for dual consciousness. In Hameroff *et al.* 1996.

Matsumoto, D. & Lee, M. (1993). Consciousness, volition, and the neuropsychology of facial expressions of emotion. *Consciousness and Cognition*, **2**, 237–50.

McGlynn, S.M. & Kasniak, A.W. (1991). Unawareness of deficits in dementia and schizophrenia. In Prigatano & Schacter 1991.

McGlynn, S.M. & Schacter, D.L. (1989). Unawareness of deficits in neuropsychological syndromes. *Journal of Clinical and Experimental Neuropsychology*, **11**, 143–205.

Milner, A.D., Goodale M.A., Jakobson L.S. & Carey D.P. (1991). Object awareness. *Nature*, **352**, 202.

Milner, A.D. (1992). Disorders of perceptual awareness. In Milner & Rugg 1992.

Milner, A.D. (1995). Cerebral correlates of visual awareness. *Neuropsychologia*, **33**.

Nagel, T. (1971). Brain bisection and the unity of consciousness. *Synthese*, **20**, 396–413.

Natsoulas, T. (1982). Conscious perception and the paradox of blind-sight. in Underwood 1982.

Navon, D. (1986). On determining what is unconscious and what is perception. *Behavioral and Brain Sciences*, **9**, 44–5.

Newman, J. & Baars, B.J. (1993). A neural attentional model of access to consciousness: A global workspace perspective. *Concepts in Neuroscience*, **4**, 255–90.

Newton, N. (1991). Consciousness, qualia, and reentrant signalling. *Behavior and Philosophy*, **19**, 21–41.

O'Keefe, J. (1985). Is consciousness the gateway to the hippocampal cognitive map? A speculative essay on the neural basis of mind. In Oakley 1985.

Picton, T.W. & Stuss, D.T. (1994). Neurobiology of conscious experience. *Current Opinion in Neurobiology*, **4**, 256–65.

Plourde, G. (1993). The clinical use of the 40 Hz auditory steady state response. *International Anaesthesiology Clin*, **31**, 107–20.

Podvigin, N.F., Jokeit, H., Pöppel, E., Chizh, A.N. & Kiselyeva, N.N. (1992). Stimulus-dependent oscillatory activity in the lateral geniculate body of the cat. *Naturwissenschaften*, **79**, 428–31.

Pöppel, E. (1972). Oscillations as possible basis for time perception. In J.T. Fraser (ed), *The Study of Time*. Berlin: Springer.

Pöppel, E. (1994). Temporal mechanisms in perception. *International Review of Neurobiology*, **37**, 185–202.

Pöppel, E., Held, R. & Frost, D. (1973). Residual vision function after brain wounds involving the central visual pathways in man. *Nature*, **243**, 295–6.

Pöppel, E. & Logothetis, N. (1986). Neuronal oscillations in the human brain. *Naturwissenschaften*, **73**, 267–8.

Pöppel, E., Ruhnau, E., Schill, K. & Steinbüchel, N.v. (1990). A hypothesis concerning timing in the brain. In H. Haken & M. Stadler (eds), *Synergetics of Cognition*. Springer Series in Synergetics, Vol. 45. Berlin: Springer.

Pöppel, E., Chen, L., Glünder, H., Mitzdorf, U., Ruhnau, E., Schill, K. & Steinbüchel, N.v. (1991). Temporal and spatial constraints for mental modelling. In V. Bhathar & K. Rege (eds), *Frontiers in Knowledge-based Modelling*. New Delhi: Narose Publishing House.

Posner, M.I. & Petersen, S.E. (1990). The attention system of the human brain. *Annual Review of Neuroscience*, **13**, 25–42.

Posner M.I. & Rothbart, M.K. (1992). Attentional mechanism and conscious experience. In Milner & Rugg 1992.

Pribram, K.H. (1990). Brain and consciousness: A wealth of data. In E.R. John (ed), *Machinery of the Mind: Data, Theory, and Speculations about Higher Brain Function*. Boston: Birkhäuser.

Pribram, K.H. (1996). The variety of conscious experience: biological roots and social usage. In Hameroff *et al.* 1996.

Puccetti, R. (1973). Brain bisection and personal identity. *British Journal for the Philosophy of Science*, **24**, 339–55.

Puccetti, R. (1993). Mind with a double brain. *British Journal for the Philosophy of Science*, **44**, 675–92.

Puccetti. R. (1981). The case for mental duality: Evidence from split-brain data and other considerations. *Behavioral and Brain Sciences*, **4**, 93–123.

Reuter, B.M., Linke, D.B. & Kurthen, M. (1991). Cognitive processes in the comatose patient? A brain mapping study using P300. *The German Journal of Psychology*, **15**, 37–8.

Reuter, B.M., Linke, D.B. & Kurthen, M. (1989). Kognitive Prozesse bei Bewußtlosen? Eine Brain-Mapping-Studie zu P300. *Archiv für Psychologie*, **141**, 155–73.

Ruhnau, E. & Pöppel, E. (1991). Adirectional temporal zones in quantum physics and brain physiology. *International Journal of Theoretical Physics*, **30**, 1083–90.

Schacter, D. (1989). On the relation between memory and consciousness: Dissociable interactions and conscious experience. In Roediger & Craik 1989.

Schacter, D.I., McAndrews, M.P. & Moscovitch, M. (1986). Access to consciousness: Dissociations between implicit and explicit knowledge in neuropsychological syndromes. In Weiskrantz 1986.

Schacter, D.L. (1990). Toward a cognitive neuropsychology of awareness: Implicit knowledge and anosagnosia. *Journal of Clinical and Experimental Neuropsychology*, **12**, 155–78.

Schacter, D.L. (1993). Neuropsychological evidence for a consciousness system. In Goldman 1993.

Shallice, T. (1991). Précis of *From Neuropsychology to Mental Structure*. *Behavioral and Brain Sciences*, **14**, 429–69.

Shephard, R.N. (1992). On the physical basis, linguistic representation, and conscious experience of colors. In G. Harman (ed), *Conceptions of the Mind: Essays in Honor of George Miller*. Hillsdale, NJ: Lawrence Erlbaum Associates.

Singer, J.L. (1993). Experimental studies of ongoing consciousness experience. In *Experimental and Theoretical Studies of Consciousness*. CIBA Foundation Symposium **174**. Chichester, UK: Wiley.

Singer, W. (1989). Zur Selbstorganisation kognitiver Strukturen. In Pöppel 1989.

Singer, W. (1989). Search for coherence: A basic principle of cortical self-organization. *Concepts in Neuroscience*, **1**, 1–28.

Singer, W. (1993). Synchronization of cortical activity and its putative role in information processing and learning. *Annual Review of Physiology*, **55**, 349–74.

Singer, W. (1994). Putative functions of temporal correlations in neocortical processing. In Koch & Davis 1994.

Singer, W. (1995). The organization of sensory motor representations in the neocortex; A hypothesis based on temporal coding. In Umilta & Moscovitch 1995.

Snyder, D.M. (1988). On the time of a conscious peripheral sensation. *Journal of Theoretical Biology*, **130**, 253–4.

Sperry, R.W. (1984). Consciousness, personal identity and the divided brain. *Neuropsychologica*, **22**, 611–73.

Sperry, R.W. (1977). Forebrain commissurotomy and conscious awareness. *The Journal of Medicine and Philosophy*, **2**, 101–26.

Sperry, R.W. (1984). Consciousness, personal identity and the divided brain. *Neuropsychologica*, **22**, 661–73.

Starkstein, S.E., Fedoroff, J.P., Price, T.R., Leiguarda, R. & Robinson, R.G. (1993). Neuropsychological deficits in patients with anosognosia. *Neuropsychiatrical, Neuropsychological and Behavioral Neurology*, **6**, 43–8.

Steriade, M., McCormick, D.A. & Sejnowski T.J. (1993). Thalamocortical oscillations in the sleeping and aroused brain. *Science*, **262**, 679–85.

Stoerig, P. (1995). Consciousness and the matter of perception. In M.O. Olsson & U. Svedin (eds), *Matter Matters*. Hamburg/New York: Springer.

Stoerig, P. & Cowey, A. (1990). Wavelength sensitivity in blindsight. *Nature*, **342**, 916–18.

Stoerig, P. & Cowey, A. (1991). Increment-threshold spectral sensitivity in blindsight. Evidence for colour opponency. *Brain*, **114**, 1487–512.

Stoerig, P. & Cowey, A. (1992). Wavelength discrimination in blindsight. *Brain*, **115**, 425–44.

Stoerig, P. & Cowey, A. (1993). Blindsight in perceptual consciousness: Neuropsychological aspects of striate cortical function. In E. Gulyás, D. Oltoson & P. Roland (eds), *Functional Anatomy of the Human Visual Cortex*. Oxford: Pergamon Press.

Stoerig, P. & Cowey, A. (1993). Perception and phenomenal consciousness. *Abstracts of the 25th Annual Meeting of the European Brain and Behaviour Society.*

Stoerig, P. & Cowey, A. (in press). Visual perception and phenomenal consciousness. *Behavioural Brain Research.*

Stoerig, P. & Brandt, S. (1993). The visual system and levels of perception: Properties of neuromental organization. *Theoretical Medicine*, **14**, 117–35.

Stoerig, P., Hübner, M. & Pöppel, E. (1985). Signal detection analysis of residual vision in a field defect due to a post-geniculate lesion. *Neuropsychologia*, **23**, 589–99.

Stuss, D.T. (1991). Disturbance of self-awareness after frontal system damage. In Prigatano & Schacter 1991.

Stuss, D.T. (1991). Self, awareness, and the frontal lobes: A neuropsychological perspective. In *The Self: Interdisciplinary Approaches*. New York: Springer-Verlag.

Thornton, D.E.F., Thornton, C., Konieczko, M., Jordan, C., Webster, N.R., Luff, N.P., Frith, C.D. & Doré, C.J. (1992). Auditory evoked response and awareness: A study in volunteers at sub-MAC concentrations of isoflurance. *British Journal of Anaesthesiology*, **69**, 122–9.

Tranel, D. & Damasio, A.R. (1985). Knowledge without awareness: An autonomic index of facial recognition by prosopagnosics. *Science*, **228**, 1453–4.

Tranel, D. & Damasio, A.R. (1988). Non-conscious face recognition in patients with face agnosia. *Behavioral Brain Research*, **30**, 235–49.

von der Malsburg, C. (1981). The correlation theory of brain functioning. Internal Report 81-2. Göttingen: Max-Planck-Institut für Biophysikalische Chemie.

von der Malsburg, C. (1986). Am I thinking assemblies? In G. Palm & A. Aertsen (eds), *Brain Theory*. Berlin: Springer.

Wall, P.D. (1993). Pain and the placebo response. In *Experimental and Theoretical Studies of Consciousness*. CIBA Foundation Symposium **174**. Chichester, UK: Wiley.

Walshe, F.M.R. (1972). The neurophysiological approach to the problem of consciousness. In M. Critchley, J.L. O'Leary, & B. Jennett (eds.), *Scientific Foundations of Neurology*. Philadelphia: Davis.

Weiskrantz, L. (1980). Varieties of residual experience. *Quarterly Journal of Experimental Psychology*, **32**, 365–86.

Weiskrantz, L. (1987). Neuropsychology and the nature of consciousness. In Blakemore & Greenfield 1987.

Weiskrantz, L. (1987). Residual vision in a scotoma: A follow-up study of 'form' discrimination. *Brain*, **110**, 77–92.

Weiskrantz, L. (1988). Some contributions of neuropsychology of vision and memory to the problem of consciousness. In Marcel & Bisiach 1988.

Weiskrantz, L. (1990). Outlooks for blindsight: Explicit methodologies for implicit processes. *Proceedings of the Royal Society London (Biol)*, **239**, 247–78.

Weiskrantz, L., Warrington, E.K., Saunders, M.D. & Marshall, J. (1974). Visual capacity in the hemianopic field following a restricted occipital ablation. *Brain*, **97**, 709–28.

Whinnery, J.E. (1996). Induction of consciousness in the ischemic brain. In Hameroff *et al.* 1996.

Wilkes, K.V. (1978). Consciousness and commissurotomy. *Philosophy*, **53**, 185–99.

Young, A.W. (.1994). Neuropsychology of awareness. In Revonsuo & Kamppinen 1994.

Young, A.W., de Haan, E.H.F. & Newcombe, F. (1990). Unawareness of impaired face recognition. *Brain and Cognition*, **14**, 1–18.

Zihl, J. (1981). Recovery of visual functions in patients with cerebral blindness. *Experimental Brain Research*, **44**, 159–69.

Zihl, J.(1980). 'Blindsight': Improvement of visually guided eye movements by systematic practice in patients with cerebral blindness. *Neuropsychologica*, **18**, 71–7.

Zihl, J. & Werth, R. (1984). Contributions to the study of 'blindsight' - II. The role of specific practice for saccadic localization in patients with postgeniculate visual field defects. *Neuropsychologia*, **22**, 13–22.

NOTE

The editor intends to make continuous updates of this bibliography for further printings of the book and would welcome any proposals for additions of papers or other publications of real scientific substance. TWO copies of each proposed or submitted new entry should be sent either to the publisher or direct to:

PD Dr. Thomas Metzinger
Zentrum für Philosophie und Grundlagen der Wissenschaft
Justus-Liebig-Universität Gießen
Otto-Behaghel-Str. 10 C II
35394 Gießen
FRG

Appendix II

List of Contributors

Ansgar Beckermann

Lehrstuhl Philosophie II, Universität Mannheim,
Schloß Ehrenhof Ost, 68131 Mannheim, FRG

Ansgar Beckermann was born in Hamburg in 1945. He studied philosophy, mathematics and sociology in Hamburg and Munich. In 1974 he received his doctorate in Frankfurt and after his habilitation in Osnabrück in 1978, he was professor of philosophy at the University of Göttingen. Since 1992 he has taught at the University of Mannheim. Ansgar Beckermann has published many works on the analytical philosophy of action, the mind–body problem and AI research.

Peter Bieri

Institut für Philosophie (WE 1),
Fachbereich Philosophie und Sozialwissenschaften I
Habelschwerdter Allee 30, 14195 Berlin, FRG

Peter Bieri was born in 1944 and studied philosophy, Greek and English Language and Literature. After his habilitation in 1981 he taught at the University of Bielefeld from 1983 to 1990. From 1983 to 1984 he was Fellow at the *Wissenschaftskolleg zu Berlin* and from 1989 to 1990 he was the academic director of the research group *Mind and Brain* at the *Zentrum für interdisziplinäre Forschung* in Bielefeld. After three years of teaching at the University of Marburg, he was appointed professor at the Institute for Philosophy at the *Freie Universität Berlin* in 1993. Peter Bieri has published many works in the areas of the analytical philosophy of mind and analytical epistemology.

Dieter Birnbacher

Fachbereich Gesellschaftswissenschaften, Philosophie und Theologie
Universität Dortmund, 44221 Dortmund, FRG

Dieter Birnbacher (born 1946) studied philosophy, English Language and Literature and General Linguistics in Düsseldorf, Cambridge and Hamburg. He was habilitated in Essen in 1988 and since 1993 he has been professor of philosophy at the University of Dortmund. His main areas of research are ethics and applied ethics, anthropology and the philosophy of language. Dieter Birnbacher is vice-president of the *Schopenhauer-Gesellschaft* and a member of the board of the *Akademie für Ethik in der Medizin.*

David J. Chalmers

Department of Philosophy, University of California at Santa Cruz
Santa Cruz, CA 95064, USA

David Chalmers was born in 1966 in Adelaide, Australia, where he studied mathematics and computer science as an undergraduate, 1983–6, before going as a Rhodes Scholar to the University of Oxford. He received his Ph.D. in philosophy and cognitive science from Indiana University in 1993. From 1993 to 1995 he was as McDonnell Fellow in Philosophy, Neuroscience and Psychology at Washington University in St. Louis. He has published a number of articles in the philosophy of mind, artificial intelligence, and artificial life. He is currently teaching and doing research at the University of California in Santa Cruz. David Chalmers is a board member of the *Association for the Scientific Study of Consciousness.*

Patricia S. Churchland

Department of Philosophy / Institute for Neural Computation 0523
University of California at San Diego, 9500 Gilman Drive,
La Jolla, CA 92093-0202, USA

Patricia Churchland was born in 1943 in Canada. From 1961 to 1969 she studied at the University of British Columbia, the University of Pittsburgh and at Oxford University, where she received her B. Phil. From 1969 to 1982 she taught at the University of Manitoba in Canada and from 1982 to 1983 she was a Visiting Member at the *Institute for Advanced Study* in Princeton, before returning to Manitoba for another year. Since 1984 she has taught philosophy at the University of California in San Diego. Patricia Churchland's main subject areas are the philosophy of neurosciences, the philosophy of mind and the philosophy of science. She is the author of many articles and books in these fields. From 1992 to 1993 she was president of the *American Philosophical Association* (Pacific Division).

Daniel C. Dennett

Center for Cognitive Studies, Department of Philosophy
Tufts University, Medford, MA 02155-7068, USA

Daniel Dennett was born in 1942 and studied philosophy in Oxford and Harvard. He has taught at the Oxford College of Technology, the University of California in Irvine, Tufts University, Harvard University, the Universities of Pittsburgh, and the University of Oxford, and has been director of the

Center for Cognitive Studies and *Distinguished Professor of Arts and Sciences* at Tufts University since 1985. Daniel Dennett has received a large number of prizes, research scholarships and invitations to special lecture series from all over the world. He has published many books and articles in philosophy of mind.

Rick Grush

Department of Philosophy/Institute for Neural Computation 0523
UCSD, 9500 Gilman Drive, La Jolla, CA 92093-0202, USA

Rick Grush was born 1965. He graduated with a B.A. in philosophy at the University of California in Davis and received his Ph.D. in philosophy at the University of California in San Diego. His main areas of research are the philosophy of mind and the philosophical aspects of AI research, connectionism, cognitive science and computational neuroscience.

Güven Güzeldere

Center for the Study of Language and Information
Stanford University, Stanford, CA 94305-4115, USA

Güven Güzeldere was born in Ankara in 1963. In 1986 he graduated at the University of Istanbul with a B.S. in Computer Engineering before going to Indiana University in Bloomington (USA), where he received the degree of M.A. in philosophy with the main subject of logic and in 1989 concluded his studies with an M.S. in information science (main area AI). At present Güven Güzeldere works at the *Center for the Study of Logic and Information* at Stanford University. He has not only distinguished himself as the author of a number of publications but also as an editor of books and journals such as the *Stanford Humanities Review* and the electronic journal *PSYCHE*. From 1993 to 1994 he was program co-ordinator of the Symbolic Systems Program at Stanford University and since 1991 he has worked as an adviser to the Embedded Computation Area in Xerox PARC, Palo Alto.

Robert Kirk

Department of Philosophy, University of Nottingham,
Nottingham, NG7 2RD, UK

Robert Kirk was born in 1933 and from 1952 to 1955 he studied Classics in Cambridge. He worked as a teacher before his interest in the foundations of mathematics and logic caused him to turn to philosophy. He took up his research in 1963 at University College in London and since 1966 has taught at the Department of Philosophy at Nottingham University, where he received his doctorate in 1968. Since 1989 he has been Head of Department, and at present he is Dean of the Arts Faculty. His research interests lie mainly in the area of the philosophy of mind — he is especially concerned with problems of consciousness and perception — and in the philosophy of language, in particular with regard to questions of translation and interpretation.

Martin Kurthen

Nervenklinik, Universität Bonn, Sigmund-Freud-Str. 25
53105 Bonn, FRG

Martin Kurthen was born in Essen in 1959. From 1978 to 1984 he studied medicine in Bochum and Bonn and from 1981 to 1985 he read philosophy in Bonn. He teaches as *Privatdozent* in neuropsychology at the University of Bonn. He is the author of a number of books and a multitude of articles in neuropsychology, neurophysiology, psychoanalysis, cognitive science and philosophy.

Joseph Levine

Department of Philosophy and Religion,
School of Humanities and Social Sciences, North Carolina State University,
Box 8103, Raleigh, NC 27695-8103, USA

Joseph Levine was born in 1952. He studied philosophy at the University of California in Los Angeles and at Harvard University, where he received his Ph.D. in philosophy in 1981. He taught at the University of Illinois in Urbana-Champaign, Boston University and Bates College, and since 1986 has worked in the Department of Philosophy and Religion at North Carolina State University. He has published a number of articles in the philosophy of mind.

William G. Lycan

Department of Philosophy, CB# 3125, Caldwell Hall,
The University of North Carolina, Chapel Hill, NC 27599-3125, USA

William Lycan was born in Milwaukee in 1945. He first studied at Amherst College, then graduated in philosophy with a M.A at the University of Chicago in 1967, where he also received his doctorate in 1970. His main areas of work are the philosophy of mind, the philosophy of language, fundamental problems in linguistics, epistemology and logic. In these areas he has published many books and articles. William Lycan is co-editor of *Noûs* and works on the editorial board and as referee for numerous journals. As a visiting professor he has, amongst others, taught at Queens College in New York, Tufts University, the University of Sydney in Australia, the University of Massachusetts, the University of Michigan and at Victoria University of Wellington. Since 1982 he has been professor at the University of North Carolina.

Colin McGinn

Department of Philosophy, Davison Hall, Douglass Campus,
Rutgers University, P.O. Box 270, New Brunswick, NJ 08903-0270, USA

Colin McGinn was born in 1950 and first studied psychology at the University of Manchester. He then studied philosophy at Jesus College, Oxford. He completed his studies with a B.Phil. From 1974 to 1985 he taught at University College in London. From 1985-1990 he was *Wilde Reader* at the University of Oxford and since 1990 he has been professor of philosophy at Rutgers University. Colin McGinn has written a number of books, mainly in the area of the philosophy of mind. In 1973 Oxford University awarded him the John Locke Prize.

Thomas Metzinger

Zentrum für Philosophie und Grundlagen der Wissenschaft,
Justus-Liebig-Universität Gießen, Otto-Behaghel-Str. 10 C II
35394 Gießen, FRG

Thomas Metzinger was born in Frankfurt in 1958, where he studied philosophy, ethnology and religious studies. In 1982 he graduated with an M.A. and did his doctorate on the discussion of the mind–body problem since 1945. Since 1987 he has taught and pursued research at the *Zentrum für Philosophie und Grundlagen der Wissenschaft* of the Justus-Liebig-Universität Gießen, where he was awarded his habilitation in 1992. Thomas Metzinger has taught philosophy at the University of Oldenburg, at the *European Campus* of the University of Maryland in Gießen and at present he is teaching at the University of Osnabrück. His main areas of interest are the analytical philosophy of mind, the philosophy of science and philosophical problems within the neurosciences, cognitive science and AI research, as well as connections between ethics, the philosophy of mind and anthropology. Thomas Metzinger is co-editor of the electronic journal *PSYCHE* and since 1995 he has been a board member of the *Association for the Scientific Study of Consciousness*.

Norton Nelkin

Norton Nelkin was born in Joplin, Missouri in 1942. From 1963 to 1968 he studied at Rutgers University, Chicago University and at Kansas University. In Chicago as well as in Kansas he completed his studies with an M.A. in philosophy. From 1967 to 1968 he visited as *Exchange Fellow* at Aberdeen University and then received a doctorate with distinction at Kansas University. From 1969 until his death in 1995 he taught at the University of New Orleans. His main areas of research were the philosophy of mind and philosophical psychology.

Martine Nida-Rümelin

Institut für Philosophie, Logik und Wissenschaftstheorie der LMU München
Ludwigstr. 31, 80539 München, FRG

Martine Nida-Rümelin (born 1957) studied philosophy, psychology, mathematics and politics at the Ludwig-Maximilians-Universität München. From 1986 onwards she held a teaching post there and in 1988 she received her doctorate. In 1991 she stayed as a *Visiting Scholar* at Brown University in Rhode Island and at UCLA in California. In 1993 she took up work at the University of Bielefeld and since 1995 she has been assistant lecturer at the *Institut für Philosophie, Logik und Wissenschaftstheorie* at the University of Munich. In 1994 Martine Nida-Rümelin was awarded the Wolfgang-Stegmüller-Preis set up by the *Gesellschaft für Analytische Philosophie* to encourage young academics, for her book *Farben und phänomenales Wissen.*

David Papineau

Department of Philosophy, Kings College London,
Strand, London, WC2R 2LS, UK

David Papineau was born in 1947 and studied in England, South Africa and Trinidad. In England he has taught at the Universities of Cambridge and Reading and in Australia at Macquarie University. At present he is professor of philosophy of science at Kings College, London. He has published many articles and books on different topics.

Diana Raffman

Department of Philosophy, Ohio State University, 350 University Hall,
230 North Oval Mall, Columbujs, Ohio 43210-1365, USA

Diana Raffman was born in 1953 and graduated in 1975 with a B.A. in musicology from Yale College. In 1986 she received her doctorate in philosophy at Yale University. Since 1986 she has taught in the Philosophy Department of Ohio State University; from 1994 to 1995 she was Visiting Fellow at the Center for Cognitive Studies at Tufts University. From 1976 to 1978 she taught flute at Clark University. She was a member of the *Boston Ballet Company* and played flute in the *Yale Symphony Orchestra,* in the *New York String Orchestra,* in the *Tanglewood Music Centre Orchestra* and in the *Harvard Canabrigia Orchestra.* Her main research interests lie in the areas of the philosophy of mind, the philosophy of art and in theoretical philosophy. 1987 she received the dissertation essay award from the *Review of Metaphysics.*

Georges Rey

Department of Philosophy, Skinner Hall, University of Maryland,
College Park, MD 20742, USA

Georges Rey was born in 1945 in San Francisco. He first read philosophy at the University of California in Berkeley and graduated in 1975 with an M.A. at Harvard University. Three years later he received his doctor at Harvard. His main fields of research are the philosophy of psychology, moral philosophy, the philosophy of language and the philosophy of logic. Since 1972 he has taught at the University of Harvard, the State University of New York and the University of Colorado in Boulder. He has published a number of articles within the philosophy of mind and cognitive science, some of which have also been translated into French and Slovenian. Since 1987 he has worked as Associate Professor at the Department of Philosophy at the University of Maryland.

David M. Rosenthal

Graduate Center, City University of New York,
33 West 42nd Street, New York, NY 10036-8099, USA

David Rosenthal was born in 1939 in New York. He studied at the University of Chicago and in Princeton, where he received his doctorate for his thesis on Chisholm's and Sellars' theories about the problem of the intentionality of the mental in 1968. From 1967 to 1972 David Rosenthal taught at Rutgers University and since 1971 he has taught at the Graduate School of the City University of New York. He is a board member and editor of a number of journals and active in many academic institutions. From 1989 to 1990 he held the PSC-CUNY Research Award and visited at the *Zentrum für interdisziplinäre Forschung* of the University of Bielefeld.

Eva Ruhnau

Forschungszentrum Jülich, 52425 Jülich
&
Institut für Medizinische Psychologie,
Ludwig-Maximilians-Universität München,
Goethestr. 31, 80336 München, FRG

Eva Ruhnau studied physics, mathematics and philosophy in Erlangen, Hamburg, Edmonton (Canada) and Munich. She received a Master of Science in mathematics in Edmonton and a diploma in theoretical physics in Hamburg. In Munich she did her doctorate in mathematics. At present she is working on her habilitation in philosophy and neurosciences at the *Institut für Medizinische Psychologie* in Munich. Eva Ruhnau has visited for research purposes at the Lawrence Berkeley Laboratory in Berkeley (USA) and at the *Institute for Advanced Study* in Princeton (USA), among other places.

Michael Tye

Department of Philosophy, Temple University,
Philadelphia, PA 19122, USA
&
Department of Philosophy, Kings College London,
Strand, London, WC2R 2LS, UK

Michael Tye was born in 1950. He read physics and philosophy at the University of Oxford and received his doctorate from the State University of New York in Buffalo. He has taught at Haverford College, Northern Illinois University, the University of California in Santa Barbara and since 1988 has taught at Temple University in Philadelphia. Since 1991 he has also held a professorship at Kings College, London. He is member of the academic board of a number of renowned journals and has published many articles and books in the area of the philosophy of mind. His main research interests are the philosophy of mind, the philosophy of psychology, theoretical philosophy and the philosophy of language.

Robert Van Gulick

Department of Philosophy, Syracuse University,
Syracuse, NY 13244-1170, USA

Robert Van Gulick was born in 1949. He studied at Princeton University and at the University of California in Berkeley where he graduated in 1973 with an M.A. in philosophy and 1976 received his doctorate. From 1976 to 1984 he taught at Rutgers University in New Brunswick. Since 1984 he has been professor at Syracuse University in New York, where he is also director of the *Cognitive Science Program*. Robert Van Gulick is the author of many articles in the philosophy of mind.

Kathy Wilkes

Department of Philosophy
St. Hilda's College, University of Oxford, Oxford, OX4 1DY, UK

Kathy Wilkes is at present Fellow and Tutor at St. Hilda's College, Oxford. She has published three books and many articles, mostly in the philosophy of mind. In 1992 she was decorated by the Czechoslovakian Academy of Science as well as the Polish Ministry of Education. In 1993 she was given the freedom of the town of Dubrovnik.